D1083006

D. H. LAWRENCE:

A COMPOSITE BIOGRAPHY

Man is a thought-adventurer.
Man is more,
he is a life-adventurer.
Which means he is
a thought-adventurer,
an emotion-adventurer,
and a discoverer of himself
and of the outer universe.
A discoverer.
—*Kangaroo*

D. H. LAWRENCE:

A COMPOSITE BIOGRAPHY

Portrait of Lawrence by Millicent Beveridge (March, 1921). This reproduction has been taken from the photograph of the portrait sent by Lawrence to Catherine Carswell, and inscribed by him for her. (See *Letters*, p. 520.) From the photograph in the possession of George L. Lazarus.

D. H. LAWRENCE:

A COMPOSITE BIOGRAPHY

Gathered, arranged, and edited

by Edward Nehls

Volume Two, 1919–1925

THE UNIVERSITY OF WISCONSIN PRESS

Published 1958
The University of Wisconsin Press
Box 1379, Madison, Wisconsin 53701

Printings 1958, 1977

Printed in the United States of America
ISBN 0-299-81502-1; LC 57-9817

The letters in this volume are published with the permission of the
Viking Press, holders of publication rights in all letters of
D. H. Lawrence. All inquiries about reprinting of the
letters in other publications should be referred to Viking.

TO RICHARD ALDINGTON

FOREWORD

Edward Nehls's three-volume biography is compositely and objectively built of quotations from D. H. Lawrence, and from others concerning him, with no direct opinions added by the compiling editor. However, choice of excerpts is more or less indicative of opinion, and in at least this part of an exhaustive and valuable work, which is all I have had time to read before contributing a few prefatory paragraphs to the second volume, I could not at first help one misgiving: perhaps Frieda Lawrence's basic dignity in her husband's as well as her own life, and her creative influence on his work, are understressed or not understood. Among the books which have become a small library on Lawrence, the men's are not so spitefully telling as the women's; but they, too, like the women's, incline to overlook the power, sometimes explosive but mainly steadying, with which she measured, admired, and guided her husband and his writing: a maturer, more grounded power than the young, tenderly devoted influence of Jessie Chambers had been on the living and writing of *Sons and Lovers*.

However, I have often wondered since the issue of my *Journey With Genius*—and am glad of this chance to say so—if I may have overdone a wish not to use hindsight ahead of its time and if I failed to enter early enough in the book, for casual readers, my later realization of the fact that, sick though Lawrence was, he had never given me any evidence of his illness by complaint in words or faltering in spirit but only by bursts and acts of temper. Perhaps I have not appreciated how fairly

Mr. Nehls keeps the order and proportioning of record, round wife as well as husband, and gives a true chronological transcript.

In this volume I have relived the time when I watched Lawrence write *The Plumed Serpent*, extolling the noble savage in print while he dreaded or disliked him in person. Two years later he could still state, in regard to the book which I still consider his least discerning or important: "My Quetzalcoatl novel lies nearer my heart than any other work of mine," and a month after that he could write, "We had an Indian and his wife to do for us, till last week; then we sent them away. Savages are a burden." Fear had given place to irritation. And the growing irritation was not only with savages. "I feel so weary of *people*—people, people, people," he wrote, and again, "The world gives me the gruesomes, the more I see of it. That is, the world of people," or "I don't feel so easy in my skin."

The truth of the matter was that people of any sort anywhere could depress him almost to a pitch of madness because he was sick and unknowingly blamed them for the way he felt. It was as simple as that. Under it all and from the start he was oppressed by the wooden voodoo of caste and yet as bound and impressed by a sense of its sanctity as Jane Austen was, or Thackeray or Meredith or almost any recorder of human doings. At the same time, his lifelong struggle was to prove that somehow, somewhere the natural peasant, though not necessarily The Noble Savage, is truly and powerfully the aristocrat,—and to bluster away his own physical and social shyness and the almost painful purity of philandering's sternest foe by verbal precocity as to the physical acts, like a small boy leading his playmates, his followers, his potential cult. And in somewhat the same way he never really wanted to outgrow a small boy's delicious faithful terror of the dark.

Finally, despite often hysterical sharpness against people, he loved them well enough to want to lead them out of desolation. And toward the natural world he remained one of the tenderest lovers of all time. In particular he loved the beauty of New Mexico with magic ardor. On his small ranch near Taos his life nearly came true. But his illness felled him in Europe and he could not flee again.

In Mr. Nehls's concluding volume, I anticipate further aptly assembled evidence of Lawrence's essential devotions, as well as of his suffering the fate of the average man, helplessness against ego, against mankind, and against death.

WITTER BYNNER

Santa Fe, New Mexico, June 21, 1957

PREFACE

The three volumes constituting this present composite biography of D. H. Lawrence were conceived as a single unit several years ago, and brought to their present stage of completion by plans worked out in advance by the Director and Editorial Staff of the University of Wisconsin Press and myself. The principles laid down in the preface to the first volume, therefore, have remained constant, and I have little choice but to repeat them here.

I have continued to be guided by the single desire to collect and preserve as much trustworthy material concerning D. H. Lawrence as I could locate, and to give each contribution its full significance by proper placement in a context. The work is intended to be both autobiography and biography, a blend of Lawrence's life as he himself and others saw it.

I have furnished the full text of all unpublished letters to which I have had access, but have not thought it necessary to employ an irksome editorial apparatus to flag up occasional lapses in punctuation and spelling.

To enable the reader to identify Lawrence's own voice, I have employed a distinguishing type face. And to keep the chronology of the Lawrence story clearly before the reader, I have supplied the dates of all letters whenever possible, but standardized the addresses from which they were written. The dates plus the pertinent passages from the letters have thus been arranged to give the effect of a journal; but in "Notes and Sources" I have supplied the name of the addressee and the form of the address given in the original letter, as well as the source from which the excerpt was taken.

Again I have been obliged to cut full-length memoirs, but have in each case tried to include as much as I could, and within the necessary limitations to choose those passages which seemed especially relevant to any consideration of Lawrence the artist and the man, which provided source material for his writing, which explicitly amplified or contradicted another memoir. Whenever possible, I have submitted my own tentative selections from book-length memoirs to the authors concerned. I have used material from the late Mrs. Frieda Lawrence Ravagli only when she alone could tell the story; whenever a third person is on record, I have chosen to use the outsider's point of view. I have often been obliged to break the reminiscences into short sections in order that the over-all chronology might be preserved. But I have never deliberately omitted ill-tempered or damaging portraits of Lawrence. I have sincerely tried to include all valid reminiscences, whether they fitted my own preconceived notions of Lawrence or not.

By the use of ellipsis points I have tried to indicate that a cut has been made in a Lawrence letter or a published memoir, and in my "Notes and Sources," to be precise in supplying the exact pages on which the material was originally printed.

To facilitate reference, I have placed the pertinent biographical data for the memoir-writers in an appendix, "The Lawrence Circle." On occasion, I have supplied more detailed biographical data in "Notes and Sources," following initial source identifications.

I have provided the reader with two bibliographies: one, a list of the sources used in the compilation of this volume; the other, a list of the major first editions of Lawrence.

I have tried to be alert to errors in the memoirs when I found them, and to supply corrections when I could. But the reader must make his own allowances for differences in observations, lapses in memory, variations in spellings. When the memoirs have been published in both the United States and England, I have given the American source whenever the American copyright is still valid; in certain instances when an English source has been cited, I have done so either because the English is the only source, or because the American copyright is no longer in force. All material published for the first time is so indicated. Subject to the demands of space, I have tried to the best of my ability to identify various people the memoir-writers mention in passing, but only those not readily found in standard works of reference. Because it is unlikely that the reader would have available to him the periodicals and newspapers in which Lawrence's short stories, articles, and poems first appeared, I have usually cited the titles of collections in which they were published.

Again I have been allowed to print here almost everything I asked for. The exceptions are two. I had hoped to reprint a series of extracts from the full-length memoirs of the late Mr. Knud Merrild, originally published in his *Poet and Two Painters,* but have failed in my attempts to obtain the necessary copyright clearance. I must also record regretfully my inability to print a certain few of Lawrence's letters to the late Miss Mollie L. Skinner.

For me, it has been a great personal disappointment to be unable to submit the MS of this second volume, as I did that of the first, to the late Mrs. Frieda Lawrence Ravagli, if not for her approval, then at least for her amusement. Her encouragement was a source of great support to me, but my last letter to her, as always full of plans and questions, lies unanswered.

E. N.

Urbana, Illinois
Summer, 1957

ACKNOWLEDGMENTS

I

I wish to thank the following publishers for permission to make use of the materials from the books indicated. Detailed acknowledgment is made in the bibliographical citations accompanying the text.

Jonathan Cape, Ltd., for permission to quote from *Peter Warlock: A Memoir of Philip Heseltine*, by Cecil Gray; and *Reminiscences of D. H. Lawrence*, by John Middleton Murry.

Chatto and Windus, Ltd., for permission to quote from *Looking Back*, by Norman Douglas.

Collins, Sons & Co., Ltd., for permission to quote from *More Than I Should*, by Faith Compton Mackenzie.

The John Day Company, Inc., for permission to quote from *Journey with Genius*, by Witter Bynner.

Dodd, Mead and Company, Inc., for permission to quote from *The West Wind of Love*, by Compton Mackenzie.

Faber and Faber, Ltd., for permission to quote from *The Night Is Long*, by Sarah Gertrude Millin.

William Heinemann, Ltd., for permission to quote from *The Red Knight*, by Francis Brett Young; and for permission to make use of hitherto unpublished letters of D. H. Lawrence.

Alfred A. Knopf, Inc., for permission to quote from D. H. Lawrence's Introduction to *Memoirs of the Foreign Legion*, by Maurice Magnus; and *The Letters of Katherine Mansfield* and *The Letters of Katherine Mansfield to John Middleton Murry, 1913–1922*, edited by John Middleton Murry.

J. B. Lippincott Company, for permission to quote from *Lawrence and Brett: A Friendship*, by Dorothy Brett.

McDonald and Company, for permission to quote from *Life Interests*, by Douglas Goldring.

Julian Messner, Inc., for permission to quote from *Between Two Worlds: An Autobiography*, by John Middleton Murry.

Secker and Warburg, Ltd., for permission to quote from *The Savage Pilgrimage: A Narrative of D. H. Lawrence*, by Catherine Carswell.

The University of New Mexico Press, for permission to quote from *The Frieda Lawrence Collection of D. H. Lawrence Manuscripts: A Descriptive Bibliography*, by E. W. Tedlock, Jr.

The University of Texas, for permission to quote from *D. H. Lawrence: Reminiscences and Correspondence*, by Earl and Achsah Brewster.

The Viking Press, Inc., for permission to quote from *"Not I, But the Wind . . . ,"* by Frieda Lawrence Ravagli. Copyright 1934 by Frieda Lawrence. Reprinted by permission of The Viking Press, Inc., New York; from *Ending in Earnest: A Literary Log*, by Rebecca West; and for permission to make use of hitherto unpublished letters of D. H. Lawrence.

II

For permission to reprint, in whole or in part, contributions to periodical publications, I wish to thank the following:

John Bull, for permission to quote from "A Book the Police Should Ban," by W. Charles Pilley.

Meanjin: A Literary Quarterly, for permission to quote from "Lawrence in Australia," by Katharine Susannah Prichard; and "D. H. Lawrence and *The Boy in the Bush*," by Mollie Skinner.

The New York Times Book Review, for permission to quote from "With D. H. Lawrence in Sicily," by Henry James Forman.

The Pine Cone, for permission to quote from "Lawrence in Mexico . . . ," by Edward Weston; and "Lawrence the Wayfarer," by Jeanne d'Orge.

Poetry Magazine, for permission to quote from "D. H. Lawrence," by Harriet Monroe.

Southerly, for permission to quote from "D. H. Lawrence in Australia—Some Unpublished Correspondence," by H. E. L. Priday; and "Correspondence: D. H. Lawrence," by Mollie Skinner.

Southwest Review, for permission to quote from "D. H. Lawrence in Mexico," by Bud Villiers [Willard Johnson].

III

For permission to use the works indicated, I wish to thank the following literary agents and executors.

Pearn, Pollinger and Higham, Ltd., for permission to quote from the Preface to the Severn Edition of *The Red Knight*, by Francis Brett Young.

Laurence Pollinger, literary executor for the Estate of D. H. Lawrence, for permission to print hitherto unpublished letters and hitherto unidentified material by D. H. Lawrence.

A. P. Watt & Son, literary agents for the executor of Cecil Gray, for permission to quote from *Peter Warlock*.

IV

As in Volume I, my debt continues to the following: the late Mrs. Frieda Lawrence Ravagli; Mr. Laurence Pollinger, literary executor of the D. H. Lawrence estate; the Viking Press; Mr. Richard Aldington; Professor Harry T. Moore and his publisher, Farrar, Straus, and Young; and many others mentioned in the Acknowledgments of Volume I.

For both hospitality and generous assistance, I am indebted to Miss Eleanor Farjeon, Mrs. May E. Gawler, Mr. Laurence Pollinger, Mrs. Rosalind Popham, Mrs. Joanna Ramsey, Mr. Bertram Rota, and Mr. Eric Whelpton of London; Mr. George L. Lazarus of Chesham Bois, Bucks.; Mrs. F. A. Minchin and Mrs. Violet Stevens of Sonning, Reading, Berks.; and Miss Rebecca West of Ibstone, Nr. High Wycombe, Bucks.

For patiently and courteously answering my many questions by correspondence, I am indebted to these people of England: Mrs. Barbara Barr, Mr. John Carswell, Mr. Frederick Carter, Mrs. G. H. Cotterell, Miss Nancy Cunard, Mr. David Garnett, Mr. Douglas Goldring, Lady Compton Mackenzie, Sir Compton Mackenzie, the late Mr. John Middleton Murry, Mrs. Rose Isserlis Odle, and Miss Joyce Weiner.

To these of Australia: Mrs. Clare M. A. Burt, Mr. C. B. Christesen, Mr. F. W. L. Esch, Mrs. W. V. Farraher, Mr. Arthur Dennis Forrester, Mrs. Phyllis Harrison, Mr. P. G. V. Jenkins, Miss Phyllis Mander Jones, Mr. William McLean, Mrs. Katharine Susannah Prichard, Mr. H. E. L. Priday, Mrs. Marjorie Rees, the late Miss Mollie L. Skinner, and Mrs. Beatrice E. Southwell.

To these of Mexico: Mrs. Anne E. Conway, Dr. Manuel Gamio, Mr. Roy MacNicol, Dr. Luis Quintanilla, Sr. Eduardo Rendón, and Mr. George E. Rickards.

To these of the United States: Mr. Carleton Beals, Mr. Albert Boni, the Hon. Dorothy E. Brett, Miss Naomi Burton, Mr. Witter Bynner, Mrs. Carl Cherry, Mr. John Collier, Mr. Kyle S. Crichton, Mr. Andrew Dasburg, Mrs. Ida Rauh Eastman, Mr. Majl Ewing, Mr. Henry James Forman, Mrs. Carolyn Harrow, Mr. W. Willard Johnson, Mr. Jan Juta, Mr. Frederic W. Leighton, Mr. Maurice Lesemann, Mrs. Mabel Dodge Luhan, Mrs. Jessica North MacDonald, Dr. Edward D. McDonald, Mr. Robert Mountsier, Miss Ann Peyton, Mrs. Harwood Picard, Dean H. H. Ransom, Mr. F. W. Roberts, Mr. Gilbert Seldes, Mrs. Remington Stone, Mr. E. W. Tedlock, Jr., Miss Geraldine Udell, Professor Ruth Wallerstein, and Mr. Edward Weston.

And to these of various countries: Mr. Earl H. Brewster of India; Sgr. Francesco Cacópardo of Sicily; Mr. Kai Gótzsche and Mrs. Else Merrild of Denmark; Professor R. G. Howarth, Mrs. Sarah Gertrude Millin, and Mrs. Jessica Brett Young of South Africa; and Captain Percy Grenville Holms, O.B.E., of Ireland.

In addition to others mentioned, I wish to thank the following for enabling me to copy and use hitherto unpublished Lawrence letters: Mrs. G. H. Cotterell, Mr. Kyle S. Crichton, Mrs. Rosalind Popham, Dr. Luis Quintanilla, Mrs. Violet Stevens, Mrs. Remington Stone, and Mr. Edward Weston.

To all individuals and publishing firms who have allowed me to reprint here selections from their printed works, and to those many friends of Lawrence who have written original memoirs for use in this book, I extend my thanks. It has been impossible for me to acknowledge by name all of those to whom I am indebted for assistance, but to them as well I offer my gratitude.

CONTENTS

LIST OF ILLUSTRATIONS

D. H. LAWRENCE:

A COMPOSITE BIOGRAPHY

CHAPTER ONE

1919–1922: Italy, Capri, Sicily, Austria

Lovely, lovely Sicily, the dawnplace, Europe's dawn, with Odysseus pushing his ship out of the shadows into the blue. Whatever had died for me, Sicily had then not died: dawn-lovely Sicily, and the Ionian Sea.

—Introduction to Memoirs of the Foreign Legion, p. 41

I

Rosalind Thornycroft Popham

t was about autumn 1919 that Lawrence decided to go to Italy, and as I was also thinking of doing so, he helped me considerably in making preliminary arrangements. My father, Sir Hamo Thornycroft,[1] had written to an artist's model, Orazio Cervi,[2] who had worked for him and for other English artists many years ago, and who had retired on his savings to Italy and built himself a large house in his native village in the Abruzzi mountains. He asked if I could come and stay with him. This sounded delightful, but Lawrence warily suggested that it might not be suitable for young children. And so it was decided that he and Frieda should go on ahead and report on Orazio's house in Picinisco.

Meanwhile preparations went on, and, having warned me that the journey would be long and cold (European railways were still disorganized from the war), Lawrence made two little sheepskin overcoats for two of my little girls. He always took a big part in domestic work, infusing into it an especial relish, and illuminating with a superrational quality the most menial thing, all of which was a complete revolution in thought for such a person as myself.

Because of the light they throw on the final, Abruzzi section of *The Lost Girl*, the following letters from Orazio Cervi to my father and me may be of interest:

Picinisco the 24th of October 1919

Dear Sir

I have had so much pleasure on riceiving a letter from you that I find difficult to discribe in writing and now I will say that my little house will be at your onours disposal for any length of time you should riquire it. I thing it would suit your good daughter and friends as to the position but I must say with great shame that it is not well furnished. Knowing so well how the Inglish Houses are furnished but some things may be borrowed from some relations and some may be bought. I regreat very much to say that 12 monts agow I lost my good wife and since then I have been terribly miserable. and now my friends are advicing me to take another wife. but my childrin have all rebelled agaist it. my son is in London and so one of my daughters. there is no one living with me exept a cat and a dog. and so I may probably take my friends advise and take an other wife. in spite of my childrens objections if it be I take her in about six week's time. that would be good for the comfort of the Ladies you would be sending me. I must beg of you to let me know about when they would arrive if they should decide to come in thise parts my place is 45 miles from Naples the nearist railway station is Cassino St. Germano which is 30 miles from Naples and 15 from me, for 10 miles they can get on a motor post and the rest on a private cariage of course I should gow to meet them at the station if we make an appointment two days before the time they would get there because if they send a telegram to Picinisco it will take thre or four hours before I get it myself. Cassino station is 80 miles from Rome and 30 from Naples all trains stop there if the Ladies do *not speack* Italian at all they should give the train guard this little piece of paper which I inclose in this letter which tells him to call the Ladies when the train is nearing the station. I must know weather ther come from Naples or from Rome this is all I say in this letter. and now I wait for full instructions from you. great pleasure I have to see thre new inijials aded to your good name and if I have the good fortune to see you here I shall always feel very proute that Sir W. Hamo Thornycroft has leaved in this poor abitation of mine. . . .

With many respects I remain Sir yours obediently

Orazio Cervi

On a separate scrap of paper, Signor Cervi had written the following:

per favore avvertiteci quando siamo per giungere alle Stazione di Cassino siamo straniere

Picinisco/17 November 1919

Dear Madam,

with great pleasure I have received your letter and I quite understand all you tell me. I am very glad that Mr Lawrense will come first so we may arrange things for your confort better together with him than I can alone and if he should not find this place suitable enough for you I would take him to some other place and see if he would like to leave there better   it may be well to give you a little description of this place so you may be able to judge whether it would suit you or not so I together with Mr Lawrense may look for an other place. This House is about 500 yards distand from the cariage Road and a river has to be crossed by a wooden bridge the foot roads are not very good in the winder time it rains a goodill in the winder and we gett even some snow some time. The climet is much milder near Naples. here it be nice to live in the spring and somer time but you will be better able to judge for yourself when you come. as for the milk you can get cows milk just now but after cristmass you can get plenty of goats milk. You may like bring a few tins of dried milk in case of an accident.

I am so grateful to your good Father for the kind words said to you of me. him and his three sisters have been my best friends all the time I have lived in England, and now I will do my very best to repay that kindness I have received from him. I hope madam you will get this letter before Mr Lawrense starts from England you should tell him to let me know in good time when he takes the train to Cassino so I may gow to meet him there we must arrange how we should reconise each other I must have at least three days warning so I may be there before him. now Madam I wish only to tell you if you would bring a little Tea service with you for your own use it would be convenient as it is not very easy to get good things from here.

I hope madam you will be able to understand my bad writing a little as I have forgotten a gooddill how to write in Inglish.

My shortist and most correct address you should put

Orazio Cervi
Picinisco Serre. Caserta Italy

and when you are in Italy and want to communicate with me you should put only Picinisco Serre—Caserta not Italy

I am yours madam
obedient servant

Orazio Cervi

Although Lawrence certainly read the first letter from Signor Cervi to my father, he could not at that time have seen the one to me nor the second letter to my father:

Picinisco/21 November 1919

Dear Sir Hamo
I did receive a letter from Mrs Baynes she wished to know whether she could get fresh milk. I replyed that any quantity of goats milk can be got after christmas but just now only cows milk can be got and I also gave a little description of what sort of place this is to live in and it would be well to tell you some thing about it too. this place is rather cold during the winter months and often wet. it is very nice in the summer. but that is all over the world. the air here is certeinly always good. She said in her letter that her friend Mr. Lawrence is coming to my place first. and that is well because Mr Lawrence will be able to judge for himself and for her whether the place will suit them or not and so we may look together for a better place in case my house should not suit him as for the food the meat can be obteined in any

7

quantity and it is good. You can get beef, veal, and sheeps meat the bread is difficult to get the best way is to buy the wheat and make home made bread of course everything is dear. The fish is not to be got at any price except on rare occasions good many other inconvenienses I might discribe but as Mr. Lawrence is coming alone parheps there will be time anough to decide what is to be done. as for any revolution there is no danger in this part. Naples and Rome some times the people try to make demonstrations but they are soon suppressed. I say no more at presend but I shall always be very pleased to answer any question you may ask me.

I am Sir

Yours very obediently
Orazio Cervi [3]

5, Acacia Road/St. Johns Wood/London, N.W. 8 [4]/Wednesday [12 November 1919]

⟨[I leave Charing Cross
    8.0 a.m. Friday
[To Rosalind Thornycroft Popham]

I am going by train on Friday morning. That actual ship didn't come off—but I could definitely have another in ten more days. However, I hear there is a big strike in Genoa harbour, ships can't leave, passengers can't find hotels—best get on by land. My luggage I am sending to Rome by Gondrand Frères: I shall only have what I can carry. I shall take a ticket to Turin— . . . swindle one on the exchange—which is today 50–52 Lira for £1.—enormous. Tomorrow I shall try to buy Italian money at the Banca Italiana. I think I shall stay in Turin—perhaps with some people,[5] until I hear from Frieda.[6] Charing Cross to Turin is about 22 hours only, all being well. I have no letters from Frieda—hear that the passenger train service is completely suspended in Germany. It must start again. From Turin I may go to Florence, & wait for F. there—then to Rome—then to Picinisco. What did you find for Grazio's [7] address? I shall write him from Italy. If you think of starting very soon, wire me tomorrow, and I could look after you at Turin or Rome: otherwise I shall write you immediately I have an address. Your luggage you can send direct from Pangbourne to Gondrand—46 Gt. Tower St. E.C. 3. But write him first. Will you take Ivy? [8] Nasty about that cheque & Nellie.[9] Can one trust anybody? Did you send the books? If you didn't, have you still got that big children's book—the Dulac? If you have, post it for me to Mrs. Dunlop, 63 Worple Road, Wimbledon, S.W. 19. Dunlop [10] is the consul, and he has done a lot of inquiring for me—I feel I owe his children something—they love fairy tales. You can have those books of mine—or the proceeds—to pay for

Dulac. I can't afford to buy anything.[11] Watch the Italian exchange, & buy before it goes down. *It can't be much higher. A good bank should give you 51 Lira—but ask them first. Your father or Godwin* [12] *might do that for you.* —*It is perfectly easy getting the visas at the Italian & French Consulates, but go pretty early in the morning—Italian at 10.0—French next—8/- each. You can get them both in one morning. Push forward in the Italian, ask the clerk if you can go inside the barrier to fill up the inquiry form.*[13] *Ivy would have to go personally. You want an extra photograph for each visa.*

Au revoir,
D.H.L.[14]

Train/17 November 1919

[To Rosalind Thornycroft Popham]

❨ I must say, trains in France & Italy are the dead limit. I got to Paris about 6.30 p.m. Friday evening [14 November]—taxi to Gare de Lyon— left Gare de Lyon 9.30 p.m.—arrive Modane (frontier) about 1.30 p.m. next day—Turin 8.0. p.m. (Saturday). The trains simply sit still half the time. I left Turin this morning at 8.30—am now still sitting in a motionless train, beside a lovely sunset sea, & it is 5.30. From Genoa for 50 miles it is all sea, the sea almost touching the rails, & most beautiful, blazing sun & blue sky & Italy quite herself. Only you do as you like here—if you don't want the train to go, you just stand with the door open, & they graciously wait for you. —I shall stop the night in Spezia, go to Florence in the morning.

If you come by train, get a sleeper from Paris to Rome—wagon-lit— never mind the expense. I believe then the night boat is best, & the 2.0 train out of Paris (Gare de Lyon). Make Cooks tell you. But have a sleeper, & you'll be perfectly all right.

If you come day boat, they tell me the 10.0 train Victoria Newhaven Dieppe is best—longer on sea, shorter on land. I had a lovely crossing. This (the Dieppe) train gets to Paris about 6.0 p.m., but usually is an hour late; so it is 7.0 or more. Then a taxi quick to Gare de Lyon. You can come second class perfectly happily from London to Paris—but after that, have a sleeping car. Make Cooks tell you very definitely if the 2.0 p.m. train out of Paris is better than the 9.35 p.m.—if so, about the night boat.

It is all perfectly easy—only slow slow—slow. No bother at frontiers— only rather a crush. Change a little French money on boat in 1st Class saloon—get ready to disembark as boat draws near, and move to the passport gangway on the boat—near the lower deck (1st class) cabins, in front. Seize the first porter, give him all your luggage, let him take it to the Douane, & let him get you 3 seats. Always seize a porter the moment you get anywhere & make him do everything for you. They are very trustworthy & sensible! —The Customs is a very slight business—so is passports— only the crowd—which is not so bad on the trains, however.

At Modane, every confusion. But an English Tommy will tell you everything. Leave the children in their carriage—don't open your bags for Italian customs—they'll just chalk them. Take three or four bags in the train with you—porters will cope with them. Also take some nice food—my train had no restaurant car from Paris to Turin.

—As I say, at Modane seize a porter—tell him 1st Class or 2nd Class to Rome or wherever it is—he does the rest, you merely go in front of the bench & see them chalked. There are plenty of nice porters—In Italy shout "facchino."

Italy is nice—very nice indeed—lovely lovely sun & sea.

I'll tell you when I have an address.

The sea is going dark—the sky is still a brilliant red line.

D.H.L.[15]

❰ I stayed two nights [at Turin] on the way with rich English people [16] . . . O.B.M. or O.B. something—parvenu, etc.—great luxury—rather nice people, really—but my stomach, my stomach, it has a bad habit of turning a complete somersault when it finds itself in the wrong element, like a dolphin in the air. The old Knight and I had a sincere half-mocking argument, he for security and bank-balance and power, and I for naked liberty. In the end he rested safe on his bank-balance, I in my nakedness; we hated each other—but with respect. But c'est lui qui mourra. He is going to die— moi, non. He knows that, the impotent old wolf, so he is ready in one half to murder me. I don't want to murder him—merely leave him to his death.[17]

Norman Douglas

I knew [Lawrence] before his marriage, in *White Peacock* days, and still hope that a certain photograph of him taken at that time may be reproduced somewhere. It was a charming likeness, with an ethereal expression in those youthful features. Then he came to see me with his newly-married wife; I cooked, in her honour, a German luncheon.

He sometimes turned up at the *English Review* office with stories like "The Prussian Officer" written in that impeccable handwriting of his. They had to be cut down for magazine purposes; they were too redundant; and I was charged with the odious task of performing the operation. Would Lawrence never learn to be more succinct, and to hold himself in hand a little? No; he never would and he never did; diffuseness is a fault of much of his work. In *Women in Love*, for example, we find pages and pages of drivel. Those endless and pointless conversations! That dreary waste of words! To give your reader a sample of the chatter of third-rate people is justifiable; ten consecutive pages of such stuff is realism gone crazy.

Lawrence never divined that conversations and dialogues are precious contrivances, to be built up *con amore;* that they should suggest a clue to character and carry forward the movement instead of retarding it; that they should be sparkling oases, not deserts of tiresome small-talk. Reading these flatulent passages, one wonders by what process his brain came to conceive them; one wonders, next, how he could bring himself to write them down, and next, how, having written them, he could bear to see them in print. He must have known they were rubbish. His state of health, maybe, engendered an imperious need of unburdening himself of every idle thought which flitted through his head.

I suppose he was not much concerned with the form of his novels. They were explorations into himself. That is why, for us, they are explorations into Lawrence. There is *Kangaroo:* well, that intrusion of a Cornish element is an artistic outrage. Yet he could not help infecting Australian surroundings with this exotic taint; *c'était plus fort que lui;* and if it injures the story it certainly reveals some secrets of Lawrence's own psychology. The same applies to *The Trespasser*—the tale, a well-motivated one, of a husband entangled with another woman, who is harassed to such a point by his legitimate wife and family that, instead of pounding them all into a jelly, he hangs himself. Self-exploration! There was in Lawrence a masochistic strain, a strain of Christ, prophet and sufferer. Both of them were in disharmony with their environment; both took every opportunity of saying so, although in Jesus—if he ever existed—we find less hysteria than in Lawrence, whose Messianic utterances are delivered in shrill tones, and often in so paradoxical a language that he becomes a mere screamer, peevish and frothy. And even as Jesus performed the menial task of washing his disciples' feet, so Lawrence was never happier than when scrubbing floors or peeling potatoes: how frequently in his books are the men portrayed as doing the work of women or of servants!

Aaron's Rod lays bare another aspect of his character, namely, his love of scoring off people to whom he is under an obligation. The book teems with examples of this trait; I alone could give five of them,[18] although not a quarter of the persons described are known to me. Here is one. The distinguished old gentleman introduced in the twelfth chapter as "Sir William"[19] had never met Lawrence; he had been induced by some third party to offer him hospitality. He is now dead, and those who are dispassionately interested in such problems will do well to compare Lawrence's fictitious account of "Sir William" and his household with the following extract of a letter dated 27 February 1925, giving me "Sir William's" own comments on this proceeding:

. . . Some years ago, during the War, a friend wrote me that Lawrence was on his way to Turin, where at that time it was difficult to get accommodation; would I put him up? In due time one evening when, with a party of guests, I had just sat down to dinner, a visitor was announced. I went to the door—it was a cold wet evening—and there was a homespun-clad figure, carrying some sort of travelling bag. I received him hospitably, sent him upstairs to a bedroom to wash; he joined us at the dinner table and remained until the following day. I had a good deal of conversation with him but, as the sequel showed, without creating a favourable impression, although at the time we appeared to be on terms of friendship and sympathy. He sent me a couple of his books, *Twilight in Italy*, which is a very good book, although I do not see why he named it thus, and *Sons and Lovers*, which has some remarkably effective chapters, but on the whole, left as it were a bad taste in my mouth. So when I noticed a new book by Lawrence in one of the magazines, *Aaron's Rod*, I decided to try another sample of his art and had it sent to me. To my astonishment I found in it, though with disguised names of places and persons, a description of his visit to my house. The scene was laid in Novara, but the particulars tallied perfectly with the circumstances of his arrival, the features of my entrance gate, lodge and grounds being faithfully reproduced.

He also described the conversations at the dinner table and afterwards, all of which, according to him, were on a despicably low intellectual level. He also portrays myself and my wife, and I grieve to say that we did not impress him at all favourably, as I appear in his pages as a kind of physically decrepit and vulgarly ostentatious plutocrat. My wife thought proper to compare to Queen Victoria, which, however gratifying to my loyal British sentiments, was unflattering in the sense that he was evidently not alluding to the admirable qualities which Queen Victoria possessed in such abundant measure, but rather to her physical shortcomings. He also referred to the staircase, to the blue silk hangings of his bedroom (and to the unpardonable circumstance that his breakfast was served with the refinement of a decent household) in disparaging terms. He had felt like throwing these indications of an effete civilization out of the window!

Now, I have no objection to make to his chronicling his impressions with sincerity, but I can never pardon him for the fact that the considerable number of pages which he devoted to us, as well as the whole of the book, were so insufferably dull. If he had at least made me out an amusing jackanapes I would not have minded it, but, that I should have been the source of inspiration of such shockingly wearisome tirades, somewhat humiliates me. It is true that in one passage he acknowledges that I had been exceedingly hospitable to an utter stranger, but that is his only concession to what the Italians call "creanza." . . .

A student of Lawrence's psychology will not gloss over this trait of character—it is too persistive and too pronounced; he will not condemn, but endeavour to understand. It has given me food for thought, and my reading of the matter is this: everybody, in his heart of hearts, dislikes being under the necessity of accepting help, financial or otherwise, however willingly bestowed. It is a form of patronage. We object to being patronized; it makes us resentful. Now most of us have learnt to dominate or mask this feeling of resentment; we accept help when it is required, and then utter due expressions of gratitude. This gratefulness is an indirect reaction, a social conventionality and a modern one (the Homeric Greeks never thanked the giver of a gift; they thanked the gods, whose instrument he was, or their luck). Secondary reactions were irksome to Lawrence. In accepting aid he had placed himself in a position of inferiority and subjection; the account must be evened. This is the primary reaction: resentfulness. In this particular, and not only in this, Lawrence might be compared to a sensitive plate. He recorded instantaneously. He could not control the impulse to be long-winded in *Women in Love*, nor to be spiteful towards "Sir William" and those other protectors whom he chastises for their kindness to him. I know that state of mind. Like Lawrence, I have often felt inclined to curse people for being in a position to help me. Unlike him, I never let the cat out of the bag. Yet many of those who knew him best will prefer a simpler and less charitable explanation. They will say that his caricature of "Sir William's" household was inspired by sheer envy and cattishness. Lawrence was certainly one of the most envy-bitten mortals I have known. He was envious of other men's social rank, of their reputations and natural gifts, their health, and chiefly of their bank-balances; even the relative affluence of his own family was a grievance to him. "Sir William" was rich beyond the dreams of avarice.

For the rest, the prevalent conception of Lawrence as a misanthrope

13

is wrong. He was a man of naturally blithe disposition, full of childlike curiosity. The core of his mind was unsophisticated. He touched upon the common things of earth with tenderness and grace, like some butterfly poised over a flower—poised lightly, I mean, with fickle *insouciance* (for his books contain strange errors of observation). This, once more, was the direct reaction, the poet's reaction; the instantaneous record. No intervening medium, no mirage, hovered between Lawrence and what his eyes beheld. These things lay before him clear-cut, in their primordial candour, devoid of any veil of suggestion or association. It was his charm. There was something elemental in him, something of the *Erdgeist*.

His genius was pictorial and contemplative, impatient of causes save where the issue was plain to an infant's understanding, as in the matter of that pamphlet on Pornography and Obscenity [20]—a noble pronouncement. Lawrence was no Bohemian; he was a provincial, an inspired provincial with marked puritan leanings. He had a shuddering horror of Casanova's Memoirs; [21] he was furious with a friend for keeping two mistresses instead of one, and even with Florentine boys for showing an inch or so of bare flesh above the knee—"I don't like it! I don't like it! Why can't they wear trousers?"; [22] my own improprieties of speech he ascribed to some perverse kink of nature, whereas they were merely an indication of good health. Had he been concerned for his own peace of mind he should have left the department of exact thinking to take care of itself and devoted his energies to that of feeling, for he insisted on discovering ever fresh riddles in the Universe, and these riddles annoyed him. He could flounder in philosophy as few have yet floundered; in his descriptive writings are phrases which none save Lawrence could have struck out. His life was restless, ever moving from place to place. His work moves restlessly from subject to subject, and sometimes, as in certain of his tales, with an enviable flair, an enviable freshness, an enviable mastery.

It is true that, being inwardly consumed and tormented, he never clarified his outlook. Lawrence had neither poise nor reserve. Nor had he a trace of humour. He had courage. He knew what would be the consequence if a notorious book of his should ever be published: a howl of execration. He went ahead. I think the writings of Lawrence have done good; his influence was needed by a large class of our fellow-creatures. He has done good negatively, as a warning to thinkers and on occasion to writers; positively, because his work is in the nature of a beneficent, tabu-shattering bomb. An American friend tells me that Lawrence's romances have been of incalculable service to genteel society out there. The same applies to genteel society in England. Scholars and men of the world will not find much inspiration in these novels. Lawrence opened a little window for the bourgeoisie. That is his life-work.[23]

((On a dark, wet, wintry evening in November, 1919, I arrived in Florence, having just got back to Italy for the first time since 1914. My wife was in Germany, gone to see her mother, also for the first time since that fatal year 1914. We were poor; who was going to bother to publish me and to pay for my writings, in 1918 and 1919? I landed in Italy with nine pounds in my pocket and about twelve pounds lying in the bank in London. Nothing more. My wife, I hoped, would arrive in Florence with two or three pounds remaining. We should have to go very softly, if we were to house ourselves in Italy for the winter. But after the desperate weariness of the war, one could not bother.

So I had written to N—— D——[24] to get me a cheap room somewhere in Florence, and to leave a note at Cook's. I deposited my bit of luggage at the station, and walked to Cook's in the Via Tornabuoni. Florence was strange to me: seemed grim and dark and rather awful on the cold November evening. There was a note from D——, who has never left me in the lurch. I went down the Lung 'Arno to the address he gave.

I had just passed the end of the Ponte Vecchio, and was watching the first lights of evening and the last light of day on the swollen river as I walked, when I heard D——'s voice:

"Isn't that Lawrence? Why of course it is, of course it is, beard and all! Well, how are you, eh? You got my note? Well now, my dear boy, you just go on to the Cavelotti—straight ahead, straight ahead—you've got the number. There's a room for you there. We shall be there in half an hour. Oh, let me introduce you to M——" [25]

I had unconsciously seen the two men approaching, D—— tall and portly, the other man rather short and strutting. They were both buttoned up in their overcoats, and both had rather curly little hats. But D—— was decidedly shabby and a gentleman, with his wicked red face and tufted eyebrows. The other man was almost smart, all in grey, and he looked at first sight like an actor-manager, common. There was a touch of down-on-his-luck about him too. He looked at me, buttoned up in my old thick overcoat, and with my beard bushy and raggy because of my horror of entering a strange barber's shop, and he greeted me in a rather fastidious voice, and a little patronizingly. I forgot to say I was carrying a small hand-bag. But I realized at once that I ought, in this little grey-sparrow man's

15

eyes—he stuck his front out tubbily, like a bird, and his legs seemed to perch behind him, as a bird's do—I ought to be in a cab. But I wasn't. He eyed me in that shrewd and rather impertinent way of the world of actor-managers: cosmopolitan, knocking shabbily round the world.

He looked a man of about forty, spruce and youngish in his deportment, very pink-faced, and very clean, very natty, very alert, like a sparrow painted to resemble a tom-tit. He was just the kind of man I had never met: little smart man of the shabby world, very much on the spot, don't you know.

. . . .

He knew all the short cuts of Florence. Afterwards I found that he knew all the short cuts in all the big towns of Europe.

I went on to the Cavelotti and waited in an awful plush and gilt drawing-room, and was given at last a cup of weird muddy brown slush called tea, and a bit of weird brown mush called jam on some bits of bread. Then I was taken to my room. It was far off, on the third floor of the big, ancient, deserted Florentine house. There I had a big and lonely, stone-comfortless room looking on to the river. Fortunately it was not very cold inside, and I didn't care. The adventure of being back in Florence again after the years of war made one indifferent.[26]

[Pension Balestra/5 Piazza] Mentana, Florence/Monday [24 November 1919, Postmark: 24 November 1919]

⟨ Dear Hilda [Brown Cotterell],

Here I sit in my room over the river Arno, and wait for Mrs. Lawrence.

I had a wire from her—she is arranging her passport and will come down through Switzerland. Italy is very nice, sunny and gay still, with good red wine.

I have friends here in Florence, so amuse myself. When Mrs. Lawrence comes we shall stay a few days more here, then go down to Rome. I wonder how you all are.

Kindest greetings
D. H. Lawrence [27]

5, Piazza Mentana/Florence/Friday/28 November [1919]

⟨ Dear Rosalind [Thornycroft Popham]

I have your little note—see that you will come early in January.

Frieda will come next Wednesday—Dec. 3rd. We stay here till about
Dec. 9th—then to Rome for 5 or 6 days: and then to Picinisco, at least to
see what it is like. I want ultimately to have a house in Sicily for a more or
less permanent place. But Picinisco can be a base.

You will probably go to a pension in Naples for the winter, you say.
Most places are expensive: Rome is enormous. Cooks will book you an
hotel for a night: but you must have a room booked, or you'll be on the
street, in Rome.

This is a very good & cheap pension. It comes to about 85 francs a week,
including everything, save wine. 10 francs a day pension, about 10 francs a
week heat & light—then washing. The food is good & plenty. It is as cheap
a place as any in Italy. If you feel like trying this, let me know about your
rooms & requirements. I got 50 Lira for £1. So that 100 francs is just
£2. You might perhaps have your meals in your room, with the children,
for about 300 francs a week, all included: probably for 250 francs. The
rooms are large, overlook the Arno—and central heating. Everything is a
bit haphazard and untidy, but pleasant, kind, easy going. Signorina Pia
speaks English well. Of course you would have 2 rooms, with a connecting
door. But you'd have to wire to me, because we're going away. I think you
might like Florence for a couple of months—there is an English Institute,
everything English you need for a start.

I feel one must coast round before settling on any permanent place.

You could no doubt have a day nurse here.

                                                              D.H.L.

[P.S.] You might possibly arrive here before we leave—fun it would be.
I feel one must go south—but carefully, because of money. Florence is a
good town, the cheapest in Italy probably. I would really advise you to
try it.

If you wire: say rooms, date of arrival, length of stay, nurse, etc.

You change at Pisa: which is not quite 3 hours from here. The through
train leaves Paris on Tuesdays, Thursdays, & Saturdays, at 2.0 p.m. arr.
Modane (frontier) at 2.0 a.m.—leave Modane 4.10 a.m., arr. Pisa 3.15 p.m.
In Pisa you must wait, unfortunately, till 8.30 p.m. arrive Florence 11.5
p.m. If you like, I will meet you in Pisa, if we are still in Florence. We
could have a meal, look at the Cathedral, & so to Florence.

I don't see why you should stay in Paris—what's wrong with the night
crossing? The children can sleep in the train.

Trains may alter for Dec. 1st—Cooks will know. You would have to
say on your wire "meet me Pisa."

[P.P.S.] Of course, if you come here, you can see Italy stage by stage, on your way down. Venice isn't very far. If you wire, say if you will bring nurse—& for how long here. No doubt you could come at once.[28]

Rome/Saturday [13 December 1919, Postmark: 13 December 1919]

[To Hilda Brown Cotterell]

⟨ This is the great St. Peter's Cathedral. Mrs. Lawrence and I don't care for Rome very much. We are going on—the permanent address

Picinisco
Prov. di Caserta–Italy

Mrs. Lawrence will send you a little thing from Picinisco. Hope it will come for Christmas.

Best wishes
D. H. Lawrence [29]

16 December 1919   Picinisco

⟨ Rome being vile, we came on here. It is a bit staggeringly primitive. You cross a great stony river bed, then an icy river on a plank, then climb un-footable paths, while the ass struggles behind with your luggage. The house contains a rather cavelike kitchen downstairs—the other rooms are a wine-press and a wine-storing place and corn bin: upstairs are three bedrooms, and a semi-barn for maize-cobs: beds and bare floor. There is one teaspoon —one saucer—two cups—one plate—two glasses—the whole supply of crockery. Everything must be cooked gipsy-fashion in the chimney over a wood fire. The chickens wander in, the ass is tied to the doorpost and makes his droppings on the doorstep, and brays his head off. The natives are "in costume"—brigands with skin sandals and white-swathed strapped legs, women in sort of Swiss bodices and white shirts [30] with full, full sleeves— very handsome—speaking a perfectly unintelligible dialect and no Italian. The village 2 miles away, a sheer scramble—no road whatever—the market at Atina, 5 miles away—perfectly wonderful to look at, costume and colour —there you buy your week's provisions. We went yesterday. There is milk —also bread when you get it—also meat—no wine hardly—and no woman in the house, we must cook over the gipsy fire and eat our food on our knees in the black kitchen on the settle before the fire.

Withal, the sun shines hot and lovely, but the nights freeze: the mountains round are snowy and very beautiful.

Orazio is a queer creature—so nice, but slow and tentative. I shall have to dart round. We are having a little fireplace in an upstairs room—shall buy grass mats and plates and cups, etc.—and settle in for a bit. But if the weather turns bad, I think we must move on. At the moment a terrible commotion, bagpipes under the window, and a wild howling kind of ballad, utterly unintelligible—Christmas serenade. It happens every day now, till Christmas.

. . . .

If the weather turns bad, I think we really must go on, to Naples or Capri. Poor Orazio! [31]

20 December 1919   Picinisco

⟨ Picinisco is too cold—on Monday [22 December 1919] we are going to Naples and the Island of Capri: the address c/o Compton Mackenzie, Esq., Casa Solitaria, Isola Capri, Naples. Mackenzie is a novelist—Capri will be warm.[32]

9 January 1920   Palazzo Ferraro, Capri

⟨ We fled here. We got on the ship—a little iron tub of a steamer—takes 4 hours to Capri. Of course the sea rose—we got to Capri, where there is no landing stage, in the darkness about 8.0 at night, after 5 hours' wallowing: the sea so high, that when a boat came to take us off it almost hopped on to our deck, and then fell back into an abysmal gulf of darkness, amid yells unparalleled almost even in Italy. In terror, half swamped, it turned for shore, leaving us rolling with a lot of spewing Italians. We had to put back to mainland, and roll at anchor in the shelter of Sorrento till morning, when once more we pushed across to Capri, as the magnificent red dawn came up over the Mediterranean—and like sacks we were hurled into the curvetting boats.

However, here we are, high in this old palace, with two great rooms, three balconies, and a kitchen above, and an enormous flat roof, one of the most wonderful places in the world: Ischia, Naples, Vesuvius slowly smoking to the north—the wide sea to the west, the great rock of our Monte Solaro in front—rocks and the gulf of Salerno south. *Below us, all the tiny jungle of Capri town—it is about as big as Eastwood, just from the church to Princess Street—oh, less than that, very tight and tiny. Below is the piazza, the little square, where all the island life throbs—across the little gulf of the street by the end balcony is the comical whitewashed cathedral.*

The island here is about 1½ miles wide, we're on the very neck-steep round ridge of the hill. Altogether Capri is about 4 miles by 2 miles: but really almost mountainous, sheer precipices above us even here. There are heaps of cosmopolitan dwellers—English, American, Russian by the dozen, Dutch, German, Dane—everybody on this tiny spot. Compton Mackenzie has a nice villa here and does the semi-romantic—but I like him, he's a good sort: also we found Mary Cannan, who was Barrie's wife: also Brett Young, a novelist with wife: and lots of other people if we cared to know them. But I prefer the Italians.[33]

Francis Brett Young

The Black Diamond was finished at Anacapri in the winter of 1920, in a cold little house called *Rosaio* [34] which we rented, furnished, for 7s. 6d. per week, where Compton Mackenzie had written part of *Sinister Street*, and where Respighi had scored *Boutique Fantasque*. Mackenzie taking pity on us lent us his warm seaside cottage at the Marina Piccola, warning us that there was another cold novelist, D. H. Lawrence, in the offing. Lawrence soon announced his arrival with a visiting-card slipped under our front door at *Rosaio*. On the card was written: "We called today, wondering if you were going down to the Piccola Marina or staying here—and if we could have one or other of the houses. Leave word for me at Morgano's café will you? D.H.L." As the seaside cottage was not ours, we couldn't let him have either, but he soon established himself in an apartment belonging to an aged priest, above Morgano's café.[35]

Lady (Faith) Compton Mackenzie

While I was in London Monty [36] was in Capri writing *Rich Relatives*, having an attack of sciatica on an average once in ten days, and seeing a lot of D. H. Lawrence. While Lawrence was writing of Monty, "He seems quite rich and does himself well and walks a sort of aesthetic figure . . . in a pale blue suit to match his eyes, and a large woman's brown velour hat to match his hair" [37] (oh, Hilhouse!),[38] Monty was writing to me of Lawrence what extremely good company he was. "He's really excellent." They shouted "Sally in our Alley" and "Barbara Allen," while J. E. Brooks [39] pounded the accompaniments on the Erard grand. In almost every letter there is some affectionate allusion to Lawrence and Frieda his wife. He records that Lawrence gave him a bottle of Benedictine on his birthday, which evidently pleased him very much.

From Mrs. Carswell's *Savage Pilgrimage* we read that Lawrence "had come to like Compton Mackenzie, but not his island, nor his influence." [40] He was sick of "this cat Cranford of Capri." [41] But, however sick of Capri we get, we return again, and Lawrence was no exception. It is a fascinating cat, even for puritans.[42]

25 January 1920   Palazzo Ferraro, Capri

❨ *Well—as it happens, the weather is wondrous fine—brilliant, hot sun, brilliant, beautiful. I watched him go down red into the sea. How quickly he hurries round the edge of the horizon, as if he had an appointment away below. A lovely red evening. . . . Compton Mackenzie lives away below. He is amusing and nice. He talks also of the South Seas: and of my going: but alas, a sort of réclamé trip, written up and voiced abroad and even filmed. Alas, I could not be filmed. I should feel, like a savage, that they had stolen my "medicine."* [43]

Lady (Faith) Compton Mackenzie

A voyage to the South Seas had been in the air for some time; there was talk of taking a cinema outfit, and D. H. Lawrence was to be one of the party. An advertisement in *The Times* for a secretary who was prepared for any kind of adventure brought in a number of replies which made good reading. But a totally unexpected turn of the wheel was effected by another advertisement in *The Times*, which was seen by Martin Secker and brought to Monty's attention with friendly craft, for he did not at all want him to wander away into the Pacific, and possibly never come back.

Two small members of the Channel Islands group, Herm and Jethou, had been occupied for many years by Prince Blücher, who was German by birth. When war broke out he was evicted as an alien, though he was an old man and well known to be a passionate Anglophile. Herm had been garrisoned by a handful of soldiers during the war, and now, in 1920, the crown was ready to lease it and Jethou for £1,000 a year.

Monty now needed little persuasion to abandon the South Seas trip, which was already threatening to ruin every one concerned in the project. To lease Herm, even for £1,000, and live there seemed by comparison a wise measure of economy, and he immediately applied for the islands before he had seen them. The Crown accepted his offer at the end of August, and the next week-end he and Martin Secker went down to inspect. There was no doubt about it—Herm was the perfect retreat for a man who wanted to get away from everything and work in peace. Besides, there was a capital farm which could be run for profit, and probably in time the island would pay its way.

Jethou had not been visited. It was tiny and derelict, but it was a nice shape and had two attendant islets, Crevichon and Fauconnaire. There was music in their names, and they would be pleasant for picnics. The expedition had been a rapturous success; even the boat journey from Weymouth to Guernsey and back had not been without charm, and the travellers returned full of infectious enthusiasm. The South Seas melted into oblivion and Herm would be occupied in the autumn.[44] The only member of the hypothetical party who did go to the South Seas was D. H. Lawrence, and whatever flicker of desire for the Pacific still remained was damped by his postcard from Raratonga [20 August 1922]:

"If you are thinking of coming out here, *don't*. The people are brown and soft."[45]

27 January 1920   Amalfi

《 We have come a trip to the mainland tired of the post strike and the railway strike and no letters and no work possible. Amalfi is marvellous . . . . It is blazing sun, so hot we are sunburned—we came eight miles by steamer, eight miles on foot, and twelve miles in carriage. The coast is full of flowers—crocuses, violets, narcissi, and purple anemones, wild everywhere—and peach and almond in full flower—and beans and peas in flower and potatoes being dug . . . . The strike has ended today.[46]

Katherine Mansfield

[Letters to John Middleton Murry, from Mentone, France]
7? February 1920
I want to mention something else. Lawrence sent me a letter today. He spat in my face and threw filth at me and said: "I loathe you. You revolt me stewing in your consumption. . . . The Italians were quite right to have nothing to do with you" and a great deal more. Now I do beseech you, if you are my man, to stop defending him after that and never to crack him up in the paper.[47] *Be proud!* In the same letter he said his final opinion of you was that you were a "dirty little worm." Well, *be proud.* Don't forgive him for that please.[48]

10 February 1920
I wrote to Lawrence: "I detest you for having dragged this disgusting reptile across all that has been." When I got his letter I *saw* a reptile, *felt* a reptile—and the desire to hit him was so dreadful that I knew if ever I met him I must go away *at once.* I could not be in the same room or house, he is somehow filthy. I never had such a feeling about a human being. Oh, when I read your reply do you know I *kissed* it. I was lying on my face—dressed in nothing but a lace cap. Mlle. Burger had gone off in the middle of doing my back and I was alone for a minute. *As* I read it, *as* I kissed it, I had the queer, the *queer* feeling as though somehow one was caught in some wave of tradition that passes round and round the earth—as though hundreds and hundreds of years ago, a woman lying like I was, being massaged by some one, had been handed a letter from her lover who swore to smite his enemy and she kissed it and laid it against her cheek. That's NOT nonsense. But you must hit him when you see him. There's nothing else to do.[49]

11 February 1920
Heard from Mary Cannan this morning: she is at Capri and had heard from L. that I was a "very sick woman" and you a "great swell." I thereupon wrote her an intimate letter and just put her right about US and just told her what you really were like and what your loyalty to L. had been and so on. I just felt I must do this.[50]

25? March 1920

Love, you are too lenient. Is it much to ask you to be yourself and to condemn what you don't approve of? . . . Will you one day forget and forgive Lawrence—smile—give him your hand? Oh, that I should dare to write that. Forgive me. But, my own, do, I beseech you, keep clear of bad people till I return. Be fastidious. HURT bad people rather than be hurt by them.[51]

5 February 1920   *Palazzo Ferraro, Capri*

❨ *We went a little excursion on the mainland last week, down the Amalfi coast. I tell you it is lovely there—much lovelier than Capri. I am very sick of Capri: it is a stewpot of semi-literary cats—I like Compton Mackenzie as a man—but not as an influence. I can't stand his island. I shall have to risk expense and everything, and clear out: to Sicily, I think.*[52]

Sir Compton Mackenzie

Daniel Rayner's [53] inquiry to which John alluded in his letter to Athene had come on a postcard from a private hotel in Bloomsbury:

You told me just before the war that we ought to come to Italy. Can you find rooms for Hildegarde and me in Citrano? D.R.

The Rayners arrived two days after David and Prudence left. Hildegarde looked exactly the same as she had looked in August 1914, even to the floppy dress of some light material which she was wearing then and apparently was still wearing now. She was not fuller blown nor less buxom. Her teeth were as dazzlingly white, her smile as wide and genial, her guttural talkativeness as rollicking. Rayner himself had grown a reddish beard and the pallor of his face had taken on a kind of translucency during the weary years of the war.

But weary was not the epithet for Rayner's time during the war. It had been for him a period of continuous mental torment. Even before the war he had been to a large extent at odds with circumstance. In the first place he had sprung from the people, preserving the Midland accent of his upbringing among the ribbon-and-lace makers of Warwickshire and his education at a council school. Neither should have been a handicap at the University of Birmingham, but that English respect even for the synthetic gentility that is painfully manufactured by third-rate public-schools pretending to the authentic tradition of the historical factories of the English gentleman implanted in him early a resentment against the reminders, sometimes real but often imaginary, of his humble origin. The natural result was that conscious of his own genius he became aggressive and self-assertive. During his time as a student at Birmingham he had met the German wife of a prominent doctor in the city, and the two of them fell in love, brought together by their discomfort in and hatred of English provincial life: she a foreigner of good family married to the wrong man, he a clever young man with a scholarship being educated, as was believed by the smug bourgeois, above his station. They had eloped, and in due course had been married. Rayner's poems and novels published before the war had brought his genius immediate recognition from most of what mattered in contemporary opinion, and the onset of war revived all the worst horrors of existence for the outraged egotism of genius. To him the war presented itself as an outrageous intrusion and interference. His wife, herself in the galling position of a German woman among the enemies of her race, fed Rayner's bitterness. There were one or two silly pieces of self-assertiveness which brought them into trouble with local authority. Blinds were left up in lighted windows. The roof of a cottage they had been lent on the Welsh coast was painted with black and red cubes, which alarmed the coastguards and led to the Rayners being expelled from South Wales. On top of that the Home Office had prosecuted a novel of his for obscenity, committing thereby one of those insufferable acts of bureaucratic oppression of which the wretched dullards of that institution have too often been guilty.

John wished that Rayner had taken it into his head to come to Citrano in the autumn of 1917, when he could have fed his own mood of disillusionment. In his present eupeptic mood made up of relief at the end of the war, of exhilaration at the prospect of being united again to Athene by next autumn, and of the reassurance about his own ability to entertain the post-war world, he feared he might exasperate Rayner's discontent.

However, greatly to his pleasure, Hildegarde told him that Rayner had let her know on the very night of their arrival that in John he believed he had found somebody with whom he could feel perfect sympathy and who seemed likely to feel an equal sympathy with him.

"I have never known R-r-rayner so happy as he is now since the war," she proclaimed enthusiastically.

In spite of his own eupeptic outlook at the moment, John was not feeling any undue confidence in the ability of western man to extricate himself from the morass in which he was already struggling before the war, itself a desperate and convulsive effort to do so.

"But there's not going to be another war," Rayner declared one day as he and John were walking back to the Allegra down a walled valley. And then snatching John's stick from him he struck the wall. "*I* won't have another war," he proclaimed shrilly.[54]

John was not sure whether Rayner was displaying incipient messianic megalomania or whether he was by a violent figure of speech identifying himself with the common secret resolve in the heart of the average man. He decided at the time to accept the latter explanation, and agreed that, however deep western man was plunged in the morass, a convulsive effort like war was certainly not the right method to free himself.

"To what do you attribute the sickness of western man, Rayner? I incline more and more to say it is the gradual abandonment of the practical teaching of the Christian faith, which incidentally is leading me toward an inevitable belief in Christ as the only complete expression of God. And I think this abandonment has been rapidly accelerated by the development of machinery."

"Wait a minute," said Rayner, "let's begin with the first. I don't accept the practical teaching of the Christian faith, because the Christian faith has failed to sustain its practical teaching. I've exhausted the Christian faith. I've tried it. I was even a local preacher when I was young. It's an impotent faith. It saps. Why should I accept as God a man whose teaching I know to be wrong, and whose magic I know to be either his own trickery or the trickery of his disciples?"

"In the first place I don't accept your statement that the teaching is wrong. As for your accusation of trickery, argument can never settle that, and, anyway, once convinced that Christ was the complete expression of God's love I should not be worrying my head about miracles. You say you were a local preacher. That leaves me unimpressed. As a local preacher you merely voiced your own interpretation of the already inadequate interpretation of whatever Little Bethel or Ebenezer you followed. You observed that the professing Christians in your neighbourhood were miserable examples of a creed's influence, and you turned against the creed itself. You are like the people who claim to have lost their faith in God because He allowed the war, which is to accept determinism as the motive force of the universe. But let's put aside the discussion of the Christian faith and take my second point. Is machinery to man's advantage?"

"I have no grudge against machinery if it's used as man's slave instead of his master."

"Don't you think that the comparatively swifter evolution of the machine may have outstripped man's capacity to evolve within the same lapse of time a mind adapted to deal with the transformation of values which machinery has effected?"

"Man went off the track long before machinery was developed," Rayner replied contemptuously. "Man went off the track when he started to think here," he tapped his forehead, "instead of here," he pointed to the generative centre. "I want to find people who think here," he declared passionately, and somewhat to the surprise of passing country-folk stood still in the middle of the alley with his long white index finger directed like a signpost toward the fly of his trousers. "And I'm going to find them," he declared, as they walked on. "I may find them in the South Pacific. I may find them in Mexico. They're not to be found any longer in Europe. I believe they vanished with the old religion of Etruria. I believe those damned Romans destroyed them in Europe." [55]

"Aren't you restating in your own terms the Genesis story of the fall of man?" John suggested. "And anyway your solution won't touch the problem created by machinery. The subtlest phallological process won't help that."

"If men go back to thinking as I intend they shall think, that will settle machinery," Rayner insisted.

"Yes, if man could go back on his own development much would be settled, but I don't believe he can," John argued. "The invention of steam may have been a disaster. For that matter so may the invention of printing . . . ."

"For that matter then the plough may have been a disaster," Rayner broke in.

"The Golden Age," said John meditatively. "Darwin made such a conception sound absurd, but orthodox Darwinianism has been so badly shaken during the last twenty-five years that perhaps there *was* a Golden Age when man was in perfect harmony with the natural order. That Golden Age is a constant feature of all religious folk-lore. It responds to some atavistic memory in all of us. It was your mention of the plough which set me off on that. What I fear is that the evolution of man may be directed now toward the achievement, on an infinitely vaster and more elaborate scale, of what has been achieved by bees and ants and termites. Individual man may be doomed, and this rapid acceleration of mechanical progress may be the sign of that doom. That is why I dread this default from Christianity. By strictly following the teaching of Christ individuals can exist without detriment to the existence of other individuals. Christianity is mocked at by lunatic egoists like Nietzsche as a

27

religion of slaves, and certainly it throve among the oppressed classes. Yet without Christianity what would have emerged from the collapse of the Roman Empire? Isn't it because Christianity has become to a large extent a convenience for the privileged to maintain their privilege that you distrust it?"

"What do *you* know about privilege?" Rayner asked scornfully. "You can know nothing about privilege so long as you are a part of it. If you had had my beginnings you could begin to talk about privilege."

"Do you regret your beginnings?"

"That's a damned silly question. Nobody can regret what he is. All I'm telling you is to shut your mouth about privilege because unless you are one of the unprivileged you can't know a damned thing about it."

"Imagination . . ." John began.

"Imagination rubbish! That kind of imagination an old man has when he sticks a paper cap on his crown and thinks he's a child again. It doesn't take in real children, does it?"

"No, but . . ."

"No, but my eye! Nor will your imagination take you far with the unprivileged," Rayner snapped.

"All right, have it your own way, but in that case think what an advantage you have as a creative artist over somebody like myself dragging round with him the impedimenta of a public-school and university education. You question my imagination. I shall question yours if you can't appreciate that. I am denied, if you like, the ability to project myself into the point of view of the unprivileged. You are denied the ability to project yourself in the other direction. Who loses more? You or I? I do, every time."

"You have an easier life, though."

"Do you want an easier life? I doubt it. You rejoice, and rightly, in the washing of your own shirts. It is an expression of the independence you cherish. The war interfered to an intolerable extent with that independence, but the war is over. You gained a great deal more by not taking an active part than I did by doing so. But we've come down to talking about ourselves, which was not what I intended when I asked you for your diagnosis of the sickness of western man."

Day and night for nearly a month John and Rayner talked, and then early on a June morning Rayner came to the tower when John was still in bed and announced that he and Hildegarde were leaving Citrano that morning.

"I'm choked here," he announced. "These small bright people get on my nerves. It's like watching a butterfly on the inside of a greenhouse fluttering up and down with the glass between him and the sun."

A week later John received a postcard from Monte Cassino: *This place is rotten with the past.* A year later came a postcard from Rarotonga: *If you are thinking of coming here, don't. These soft brown people are disappointing.*

So, like an angry red star, Rayner sank below the horizon. Was he a prophet of woe? Had he, rising from the myriads who by the trend of the time were doomed to be the first victims of man's own ingenuity, been sent to warn them against the mechanical progress which would destroy them? Was he a portent, a phenomenon, or merely a freak? Were the circumstances of modern life exasperating to egomania the consciousness of his own vital personality? These maddened egoes were becoming more and more frequent. It was Nietzsche all over again. Byron's jealousy had stopped short of Shakespeare. The jealousy of Rayner and Nietzsche extended to Jesus Christ. Perhaps Rayner could not be called mad yet, but he seemed moving toward madness. Yet in this muddled world might not what was held madness be the only true sanity?

Yet what salvation was offered to the spirit of man by Rayner's gospel? It could not even save his own soul from the terror of the road along which humanity was hurrying. To fling away sterile cerebration and substitute for it the fecundity and warmth of feeling? Back to the land . . . back to the noble savage . . . back to simplicity . . . nudism . . . negro sculpture . . . primitive rhythms . . . atonal music . . . a mess made of the Divine order, and a revolt from it to human disorder in a vain attempt to escape from the results of mechanization.[56]

19–21 February 1920   Monte Cassino

⟨ *We twisted up and up the wild hillside, past the old castle of the town, past the last villa, between trees and rocks. We saw no one. The whole hill belongs to the monastery.*[57] *At last at twilight we turned the corner of the oak wood and saw the monastery like a huge square fortress-palace of the sixteenth century crowning the near distance. Yes, and there was M—— just stepping through the huge old gateway and hastening down the slope to where the carriage must stop. He was bareheaded, and walking with his perky, busy little stride, seemed very much at home in the place. He looked up to me with a tender, intimate look as I got down from the carriage. Then he took my hand.*

29

"So very glad to see you," he said. "I'm so pleased you've come."

.   .   .   .

We were seated, in the sunny afternoon, on the wild hilltop high above
the world. Across the stretch of pale, dry, standing thistles that peopled
the waste ground, and beyond the rocks was the ruined convent. Rocks
rose behind us, the summit. Away on the left were the woods which hid
us from the great monastery. This was the mountain top, the last foothold
of the old world. Below we could see the plain, the straight white road,
straight as a thought, and the more flexible black railway with the railway
station. There swarmed the ferrovieri like ants. There was democracy, in-
dustrialism, socialism, the red flag of the communists and the red, white
and green tricolor of the fascisti. That was another world. And how bitter,
how barren a world! Barren like the black cinder-track of the railway, with
its two steel lines.

And here above, sitting with the little stretch of pale, dry thistles around
us, our back to a warm rock, we were in the Middle Ages. Both worlds
were agony to me. But here, on the mountain top, was worst: The past, the
poignancy of the not-quite-dead past.

"I think one's got to go through with the life down there—get somewhere beyond it. One can't go back," I said to him.[58]

21 February 1920   Palazzo Ferraro, Capri

❨ Returned from Monte Cassino.[59]

25 February 1920   Palazzo Ferraro, Capri

❨ It is as hot as June here—all the butterflies fluttering among the flowers
. . . . To-morrow I am going by sea to Sicily—from Naples. If I find a
house we shall go over.[60]

Francis Brett Young

The arrival of Lawrence enormously enlivened our Capri life, but his
presence was a double-edged blessing, for it soon became apparent that,
much as we enjoyed and were stimulated by his company, Capri was

rather too small for three novelists at once. Lawrence, who had been shocked by the suppression of *The Rainbow*, had no intention at the moment of writing anything more. "After all," he said, "what do our dirty little books matter anyway?" It was equally certain that if he couldn't write nobody else on the Island would be allowed to. So Jessica [61] and I jumped at the opportunity of accompanying him to Sicily in search of a house. Sicily, his friend Magnus had told him, had been waiting for him ever since the days of Theocritus. It certainly had. After a series of adventures of the kind which always seemed to beset Lawrence's progress, we eventually deposited him in a house called *Fontana Vecchia* in Taormina, with a wide view embracing the snows of Etna and the local cemetery. In this house he spent several happy years of his tempestuous life. It was during our long walks together in the Sicilian spring that I first made the acquaintance of Norman-Saracen architecture and many examples of Sicilian Baroque; and I think the style must have influenced me in the writing of *The Red Knight*: so great a contrast in its ornament to the simplicity of *The Black Diamond*. It is certainly written more elaborately than any of my earlier books and I can only attribute this change to the Sicilian adventure in Lawrence's stimulating company. [62]

4 March 1920　　　　　　　　　　　Villa Fontana Vecchia, Taormina

❲ I have found such a charming house here in a big garden—Frieda arrives Saturday, I hope. . . .

Fontana Vecchia means old fountain—the name of the house. [63]

Francesco Cacópardo

When D. H. Lawrence and Frieda rented our villa near Taormina, I was away in Manchester, England, working as a professional chef, so my family handled the original transaction. However, I have many recollections of Lawrence from the time I met him after my return.

As I remember him, Lawrence was primarily a simple man, with a quiet manner, but occasionally releasing a fiery temper in the way often ascribed to red-haired people. He was tall and slender of build and had a short, dark-red beard. In the summer he often wore a light, short, red-striped Eton jacket and a big straw hat. He enjoyed picking his own fruit fresh from the trees in the morning—oranges and *nespoli*—and was particularly attracted to "the lovely mimosa" and the eucalyptus trees in the garden. He would often lie and read under the eucalyptus. I recall Frieda as being a stout woman, about the same height as Lawrence, and having a pleasant face.

The situation of Villa Fontana Vecchia—Old Fountain, it is called— is picturesque and appealing in its tranquillity, free from any abrupt noise except the tinkle of goat bells and now and then the playing of a Sicilian flute along the path. It rests on a terraced slope overlooking a wide, green valley lined with citrus groves and vineyards. From the sun-porch one looks down the valley to a magnificent, solitary beach, and sees Homer's Rock of the Sirens rising from the water in the curve of the Cape of St. Andrea, and in effect, it is a cloud home.

Lawrence occupied the second and third floors, which form a unit to themselves and have their own ground-level entrance, while my family retained the first floor. Except for the addition of modern plumbing in the kitchen and bathrooms, the apartment stands now just as Lawrence left it. The main living room is quite large with a fireplace and big, gothic-style windows. Before Lawrence moved in, these windows were hung with full, dark-red curtains. Almost the first thing he did was to remove them, exclaiming, "You build these beautiful windows and then hang curtains that keep the sun from coming in!" They have never been rehung.

My mother often laughed about the time Lawrence came down to ask for goat's milk soon after he arrived. He had a habit of squinting his eyes until they were almost closed when trying to remember something, and on this day he tried to learn the phrase *May I have some goat's milk?* So now he closed his eyes, strained his face, and asked, "*Si posso avere latte di capro?*" giving the goat a masculine gender.

In those days the town had no central water supply, and cistern water supplied our household needs; but our drinking water came from a spring about 100 yards away. Lawrence often went to fetch it himself, fresh and cool, in a big terra cotta jug. Sometimes these trips took several hours, for he would loiter along the way and then relax on the little wall surrounding the reservoir, watching the other people come and go. He walked a great deal—up into the mountains when the Sicilian wildflowers were in bloom, and down into the valley to visit the olive press. There he spent most of the day, watching the long process from beginning to end and taking his lunch with the workers.

When the Lawrences learned that my mother baked her own bread each week, they were eager to see just how it was done. They went into the wheat fields to see the grain separated in the age-old manner of tossing it into the air and letting the wind take away the waste. They saw it ground and then baked in the large, primitive oven in our kitchen, and asked that we bake a little loaf for them, which we always did after that.

Lawrence had a preference for seeing people at breakfast and at no other time of the day if it could be avoided. An amusing incident occurred one morning: The Mayor of Taormina came to call on him out of respect for a celebrated English writer. When he arrived, Lawrence was in the middle of a quarrel with Frieda, which ended with his hurling a dish of fried potatoes at her. He hardly heard a word the Mayor said, and the Mayor left in confusion, convinced that he had been the cause of the whole incident.[64]

Lawrence was the first writer to stay in the villa, but since then it has been rented almost exclusively to writers and musicians.[65] Perhaps he left it a kind of artistic legacy. Before leaving, he gave me a large, red silk handkerchief as a little *omaggio* which I still keep, although it is now in tatters. With my brother, Carmelo, he left an overcoat, which is also still in his possession.

When Lawrence discovered that I planned to leave Taormina and resume my previous work in Manchester, he could not understand why I wished to forsake the Mediterranean climate and beauty of Sicily for life in England.

"How can you prefer Manchester to this happy, smiling land?" he asked.

A short time later, however, he forsook it himself and went away to Ceylon, Australia, and the New World. He wrote me one or two letters from Mexico, which I appreciated because they showed that he had not forgotten Taormina. I have regretted many times since then that I destroyed these letters after reading them, but I am afraid I did not realize how famous he was to become.[66]

15 March 1920   *Villa Fontana Vecchia, Taormina*

❲ *Here we are, in Sicily. We've got a nice big house, with fine rooms and a handy kitchen, set in a big garden, mostly vegetables, green with almond trees, on a steep slope at some distance above the sea—looking east. To the left, the coast of Calabria, and the Straits of Messina. It is beautiful, and green, green, and full of flowers. . . .*

I must say I like this place. There are a good many English people, but fewer than Capri, and not so all-overish—and one needn't know them. It seems so peaceful and still and the earth is sappy, and I like the strong Saracen element in the people here. They are thin and dark and queer. It isn't quite like Europe. It is where Europe ends, finally. Beyond is Asia and Africa. One realizes, somehow, how non-European, how Asiatic Greece was—tinged with Phoenician.[67]

31 March 1920   Villa Fontana Vecchia, Taormina

⟨ Here it is very beautiful. Yes, we are north of the village, outside. We don't see Etna. Beautiful flowers are out. There is a tiny blue iris as high as your finger which blooms in the grass and lasts a day. It is one of the most morgen-schön flowers I have ever seen. The world's morning—that and the wild cyclamen thrill me with this sense. Then there are the pink gladioli, and pink snapdragons, and orchids—old man and bee and bird's nest. . . .

I look up at Monte Venere and think I will set off. Why don't I? But the dawn is so lovely from this house. I open my eye at 5.0, and say Coming; at 5.30, and say yellow; at 6.0, and say pink and smoke blue; at 6.15, and see a lovely orange flare and then the liquid sunlight winking straight in my eye. Then I know it's time to get up. So I dodge the sunlight with a corner of the blanket, and consider the problem of the universe: this I count my sweetest luxury, to consider the problem of the universe while I dodge the dawned sun behind a corner of the sheet; so warm, so first-kiss warm.[68]

⟨ In early April [1920] I went with my wife to Syracuse for a few days: lovely, lovely days, with the purple anemones blowing in the Sicilian fields, and Adonis-blood red on the little ledges, and the corn rising strong and green in the magical, malarial places, and Etna flowing now to the north-ward, still with her crown of snow. The lovely, lovely journey from Catania to Syracuse, in spring, winding round the blueness of that sea, where the tall pink asphodel was dying, and the yellow asphodel like a lily showing her silk. . . .

We came back, and the world was lovely: our own house above the almond trees, and the sea in the cove below. Calabria glimmering like a changing opal away to the left, across the blue, bright straits, and all the *great blueness of the lovely dawn-sea in front, where the sun rose with a splendour like trumpets every morning, and me rejoicing like a madness in this dawn, day-dawn, life-dawn, the dawn which is Greece, which is me.*[69]

Frieda Lawrence Ravagli

Later Magnus appeared at our Fontana Vecchia at Taormina, having fled from Montecassino. He came almost taking for granted that we would be responsible for him, that it was our duty to keep him. This disturbed Lawrence.

"Is it my duty to look after this man?" he asked me.

To me it was no problem. Had I been fond of Magnus, had he had any meaning, or purpose—but no, he seemed only antisocial, a poor devil without any pride, and he didn't seem to matter anyhow. With the money Lawrence had lent him, he stayed at the best hotel in Taormina, to my great resentment, we who could not afford to stay even in a second-rate hotel. I felt he made a fool of Lawrence, and afterwards, when we went to Malta, crossing second class from Palermo, whom should I discover gaily swanking and talking to an English Navy officer but Magnus on the first-class deck! The cheek of the man! He had written to Lawrence: "I am sweating blood till I am out of Italy." I know his sort, people always sweating blood and always going to shoot themselves. But Magnus, anyhow, did commit suicide at the end. It was a shock, but there was nothing else for him to do. It seemed to me he had put his money on the wrong horse. He thought the splendour of life lay in drinking champagne, having brocade dressing gowns, and that kind of thing. But Lawrence felt deeply disturbed by Magnus and did feel a responsibility for him.[70]

7 May 1920   Villa Fontana Vecchia, Taormina

❨ *It is very dry here—all the roses out, and drying up, all the grass cut, the earth brown. There is a lot of land, peasant land, to this house. I have just been down in the valley by the cisterns, in a lemon grove that smells very sweet, getting summer nespoli. Nespoli look like apricots, and taste a bit like them—but they're pear-shaped. They're a sort of medlar. . . . The sea is pale and shimmery today, the prickly pears are in yellow blossom.*

I've actually finished my new novel, The Lost Girl: not morally lost, I assure you. That bee in my bonnet which you mention, and which I presume means sex, buzzes not over-loud.[71]

12 May 1920   Villa Fontana Vecchia, Taormina

❨ Mary Cannan has a studio here—nice—for 3 more months. She is dying to go to Malta—the boat runs from Syracuse. But she can't go alone. So she wants us to go if she pays our ship fare—it's only 8 hours crossing. It might be amusing, for 4 or 5 days. But Malta isn't wildly attractive, and I am doubtful if I want to spend the money.[72]

24 May 1920   Valetta, Malta

❨ We came here for two days—kept here for eight by the Sicilian steamer strike.

    Land of plenty, land of comfort—Britain, wheresoever found.

    Bacon and eggs for breakfast.

    But a horrible island—to me: stone, and bath-brick dust. All the world might come here to sharpen its knives.[73]

Douglas Goldring

Coincidentally, with the founding of the "People's Theatre Society," [74] I had persuaded an enterprising publisher, C. W. Daniel, to start a series of revolutionary plays, under my general editorship, the title of the series being "Plays for a People's Theatre." It grew out of my own pamphlet play, *The Fight for Freedom,* which I had submitted to him for publication. This I had provided with a preface detailing my scheme for an "all-red" theatre of the kind that was beginning to spring up in various parts of Europe. The opportunity came of, at least, getting *Touch and Go* into print. No other publisher would then look at it, and it has only quite recently been re-issued, among Lawrence's collected works.[75] Daniel accepted *Touch and Go* at my instigation, and I believe paid an advance which, however small, must have been welcome. It was not really a suitable play for the series, because . . . Lawrence detested "propaganda" and, though I did not realise it at the time, was completely out of sympathy with my earnest and rather naive political preoccupations. Nevertheless, it was a great pity, from every point of view, that the series was not launched under the cloak of Lawrence's literary prestige. As it happened, Mr. Daniel not unnaturally published the plays in the order in which he received them, so that Lawrence's came second. This annoyed him until my explanatory letter, which had been delayed in the post, arrived, with the rain, to soothe his "social nerves."

I have lost many of Lawrence's letters to me, owing to my rolling-stone existence, but the few I have found are sufficient to indicate that —unlike most of his friends, disciples and fetch-and-carry men—I escaped anything like a quarrel with him.

Palazzo Ferraro,/Capri,/Naples./3 January 1920.
Dear Goldring,

We have struggled our way down Italy, perpetually on the move, and no sort of rest. That's why I haven't written before. I suppose we shall sit here for a time.

There, if I'd known, I wouldn't have let Macdermott [76] have that option— but it doesn't much matter, and if necessary, could no doubt be bought back from him for his £15.

I heard from Scott and Seltzer [77]—they sent me £50 for the novel [78]—but I doubt if they'll publish it. Probably Secker will do it in England.[79]

Italy is frightfully expensive, particularly travelling. I daren't shift again —and Berne is far off. One lives on the financial verge as ever—but so be it. I expect *Touch and Go* will soon be out. Could you give Daniel my address here, and let me know when he is sending out publishers' copies. I might write to one or two people, and make the reviewers act, anyhow.

I am glad Chapman & Hall are going to do you. Yes, I am pleased if you inscribe to me.[80] Why the devil did the reviewers ignore your play? Could you send me a copy? I might get the *Times* to come in, at this late hour.

My wife loved Baden—really better than Italy. The Italians have a grudge against us now.[81] Perhaps in May we shall go to Germany. Let us all meet there and have a good time. We often speak of you. I don't want to come back to England, anyhow.

I do hope Mrs. Goldring gets out of that pamphlet shop: it's horrible.[82] A thousand greetings from us both.

D. H. Lawrence

Fontana Vecchia,/*Taormina,*/Messina, Sicily./March 9, 1920.
Dear Goldring,

I have just got yours of February 28th. We have taken a house here for a year. Note address.

About the Fight,[83] Barbusse [84] will put his party-umbrella over it all right. If you'd had a Barbusse preface at first, it would have been luck. But best not to be too political.

37

Yes, do squeeze *Touch and Go* out of McDermott—tell him he can have his £15 back. I am so curious to know what they do with Mrs. Holroyd at Altrincham: [85] should like to see B., with her big nose as Mrs. H.[86] She's got the silent quality.

I like Irene Rooke so much—or did when I met her—also Rosmer.[87]

I doubt if England will ever be Clarté'd.[88]

Everything feels unsure here—but at last, after seven months drought, it rains a little. That will soothe the social nerves.

Send me word.

D. H. Lawrence

Osborne Hotel,/50 Strada Mezzodi,/Valetta,/Malta./May 26, 1920
Dear Goldring,

Ages since I heard from you—the post is simply abominable. I think they just *burn* the conglomerated mail when the strikes have done with it. But I got *The Black Curtain* which we read and which is interesting. But ugh, how I hate the War—even a suggestion of it.

We came to Malta for a few days—a strike held us up—no steamers. Thank God we go back to Taormina to-morrow. But oh Lord, I'm glad to return to Sicily.

I got copies of *Touch and Go* just before we came here. It has a nice appearance—book. How *is* your People's Theatre? Hope it goes. Is there any news of it? A man here showed me MS. of various plays—good ones, really—translations.

Love's Tragedy—by Knut Hamsun, 4 act, a famous thing, unknown in England.

To the Stars—Leonid Andreyeff, 4 act—weird.

The Snake Charmer—very comic—2 act—German.

Julius Bierbaum.

Lady Sofia—George von Omptede—4 act—comedy.

The White Fan—Hugo von Hoffmansthal—1 act—poetic.

Do you think anything could be done with these? Magnus—the man who has the MSS.—wants to publish the things if possible—sell them outright to a publisher. But he retains the acting rights.

Let me know how everything is. You may of course be gone to Germany or the ends of the earth—or you may be producing plays like billy-o. I'm going back to Taormina to work. How is Mrs. Goldring?—feeding herself, for a change?

Yrs.,
D. H. Lawrence

The "Magnus" referred to is the Maurice Magnus who wrote the *Memoirs of the Foreign Legion*. I had already been put in touch with him by Norman Douglas and had received the MS. of his *Memoirs*, which I tried in vain to get a publisher to print. We corresponded frequently, although we never met. This I regret, notwithstanding Law-

rence's ferocious but superb description of the man, in his introduction
to the *Memoirs*. I wish I could find the other letters which Lawrence
wrote to me from Malta, as they threw further sidelights on Magnus.
Perhaps they are still mouldering in an old suitcase, left behind in somebody's cellar and forgotten.

In July 1920 I sent Lawrence a copy of my *Reputations*, which Chapman and Hall had issued. This contained an essay called "The Later
Work of D. H. Lawrence," which appeared first in *Art and Letters*. Lawrence liked this book—he had not liked either my play or the novel called
The Black Curtain, which I dedicated to him—and, in a letter dated
July 20, 1920, from Taormina, part of which is printed on pages [514–15]
in *The Letters of D. H. Lawrence*, edited by Aldous Huxley, he observes: "I had your *Reputations* this morning: find it very witty and
amusing. God, it is time those stuffed geese were carved: the old stagers,
and semi-old stagers. In the end, I suppose, I shall have you hacking
at me, for an old bird." I must have told him that my circumstances were
improving a bit, for he adds later: "So glad you are getting rich. Good!
I do hope you are taking it out of the mouth of the Murrys and Walpoles
of this world. I am creeping on in my own measured way, cook and the
captain bold, etc. But even we have a little bit more than usual." [89]

Douglas Goldring (and Maurice Magnus)

I had known Norman Douglas in the *English Review* days and was
delighted to see him again in 1920 when I was conducting a pioneer
party of Lunn tourists to Florence, Rome and Naples. My flock looked
after themselves in Florence and I was thus able to spend an unforgettable week in his company. In some way or another, perhaps because
of my connexion with the New York publisher, Thomas Seltzer, I had got
into communication with Douglas's friend, Maurice Magnus. This unfortunate figure has found his niche in literature as a result of the battle
over his memory which broke out after his death, between D. H. Lawrence and Douglas.[90] Magnus sent me a number of MSS. which I tried,
unsuccessfully, to place for him, with Douglas's encouragement, in London and New York. Finally, just before he ended his life, although he
had made Norman Douglas his literary executor, he made over the
rights of one of his books, *Memoirs of the Foreign Legion*, to D. H.
Lawrence who was then staying in Malta. Poor Magnus was almost
everything that Lawrence disliked and disapproved of. He was a de-

cayed "gentleman," incapable of earning his living, always in debt, always borrowing money, and homo-sexual into the bargain. Lawrence on the other hand had all the financial self-respect and scrupulous honesty in money matters which are among the basic virtues of the thrifty working-class. If he had £2 a week he could live on it with ease, and save. Magnus, on the other hand, was the kind of man who, if he was given £2 would spend it at once on a good dinner and then starve. He had borrowed a considerable sum of money from a Maltese friend of Lawrence's.[91] Lawrence therefore determined to secure the publication of the Foreign Legion MS., in order to get this debt repaid. After Stanley Unwin,[92] to whom I had offered it, finally turned it down it was published by Martin Secker, prefaced by a long, brilliant and merciless account of the author by D. H. Lawrence. In a letter to Curtis Brown, printed in *The Letters of D. H. Lawrence,* Lawrence records the circumstances. "Magnus," he wrote, "was a man I knew in Italy. He committed suicide [November, 1920] in Malta, after borrowing money from a nice and not rich Maltese whom I knew. Magnus left several MSS. of not much value: one about his experiences in the Foreign Legion. In order to get some money back for Michael Borg, the Maltese, I wrote a long memoir of Magnus to go before the Legion book."[93] The dispute with Douglas was on two main points. In the first place Douglas, as literary executor, had, with my active help, taken an infinity of trouble, though without success, to get the MSS. of Magnus printed and published, and therefore should, at least, have been consulted. Secondly, Douglas, who probably knew and understood Magnus much better than Lawrence, thought that Lawrence's bitter portrait of his friend was grossly unfair. He replied to it in a pamphlet which in its way is as brilliant as Lawrence's memoir.[94] As I never personally met Magnus I am not in a position to judge whether Lawrence's depreciation, or Douglas's appreciation, was nearer the truth. It was in any case a duel between masters of their craft. The fact that his personality produced such a memorable literary combat is my reason for quoting the letters from Magnus which follow.

Notabile P.O.,/Malta./June 25th, 1920.

Dear Mr. Goldring,

D. H. Lawrence writes me you liked the Legion. I am very glad. Mr. Unwin writes him it isn't going to pay—"American edition—buy sheets for English editions." That of course I will *not* do. Done that before and it forms a chapter in my memoirs (not yet printed). Most subtle way of receiving money and not receiving it! If Mr. Unwin wants the British copyright—O.K.—if not I have asked him to return MSS. The American rights are 'spoken for' and a copy of the entire manuscript in U.S.A. at this moment.

I am sending you under separate cover by registered post 'Love's Tragedy,' by Knut Hamsun. I saw this first in the Moscow Art Theatre years ago. Wonderfully produced—and was much impressed—applied for the English and American stage and book rights from Hamsun and got them translated. The original title is 'The Gamble of Life,' in Moscow they called it 'Love's Tragedy.' Alice Kauser, dramatic agent in U.S.A. had the play for some time, but did not do anything with it—no wonder—after I saw the shocking state of the American stage last year.

Also I am sending you 'To the Stars,' by Leonid Andreyeff. This is probably too literary and subtle for the Anglo-Saxon theatre-going public. It is very readable. Have all the rights. I should be delighted if you could do anything with either—if not for stage then for publication.

The little one-act play 'Twilight' was written by an amateur—I touched it up. It is very charming. The man who wrote it is the son of a Governor (ancient régime) in the heart of Russia, who owned and lived in Turgenieff's house there, which he kept as Turgenieff had left it.

If you do anything with 'Love's Tragedy' I should want to go over it once more before going to press.

Many thanks for your interest,
Faithfully yours,
Maurice Magnus.

The Legion book is to be called 'Dregs; a Foreign Legion Experience,' by an American.

Notabile P.O.,/Malta./August 10th, 1920.

Dear Mr. Goldring,

The manuscript and book came yesterday. I commenced reading 'The Fight for Freedom' and didn't lay down the book until I had finished. It is one of the strongest plays I have read in modern literature—in fact, one of the strongest plays I have ever read. The characters are splendidly defined—there isn't a vague person in it and the dialogue is a masterpiece. The dramatic technique shows the actor—you must have had good theatre training. As to the subject it is the one vital thing at present—and I think you express the ideas of thousands, no, of the majority not only in England, but *everywhere*, where I have been within the last few years: Italy, America, France, Germany, here, Greece, etc.

Our battle will be largely against the Margarets [95] who just complicate things—they are not one thing nor the other—they are just in the way.

I'd like to read 'The Fortune.' [96] Will you send me that?

Of course I must seem impertinent to write you so frankly and very likely you were not asking for criticism, but were just nice in sending me one of your books. I thank you for the great pleasure your play gave me.

Did you ever read 'Tizer,' [97] a play Mitchell Kennerley N.Y. published some years ago?

Did you ever read 'Fate' by Louis Couperus? Both the play and the novel will interest you, I think. In each the authors are striking out from the terrible rut of the Victorian influence and facing us with very actual problems. I grasp your hand.

Magnus.

1 Strada S. Pietro,/Notabile,/Malta./Sept. 2nd, 1920.

Dear Mr. Goldring,

Thank you very much for your kind letter. I fear you will find America worse than England. But try. Fifteen years ago the drama and literature there gave great promise: on my recent trip I found that the good germs had been smothered by a luxuriance of weeds.

I am just retiring from any further effort to do anything but write the stuff I want to, and live cheap in a decent climate. I have reduced my necessities to a minimum.

It is good of you to recommend my stuff to Alec Waugh [98] and I shall send him the final part by next post. Too late today. The agents—alas—my experiences have been so painful. The best have usually succeeded in doing one-fifth of what I did from a thousand miles distance, both in N.Y. and in London. Ask Waugh to show you the MS. I shall send—if you care to see it. Don't forget to send me 'The Fortune,' *please*.

Never mind the attitude of the B.P.[99] and you are doing big things—and that is the main issue. People never do like to hear the truth, and especially in England those who tell it, or do something beautiful, end in exile or prison. However, there are exceptions where England has appreciated her sons of the muses *via* the Continent. That may be your fate. I am glad you are being translated.

[Last page missing]

Notabile,/Malta./October 31st, 1920.

Dear Mr. Goldring,

'The Solvent' [100] is very clever and a wonderful propaganda book—dreadfully inhuman. I think the only human person is Margaret, and one doesn't see too much of her. You don't mind my saying this—I hope—since it is not all yours. In 'The Fight for Freedom' and 'The Fortune' you are so infinitely human and so very real to life—without any frills—so absolutely sincere—depicting strength and weakness as it comes that somehow I don't recognise you in 'The Solvent,' except here and there. Will you do me a favour? X, the publisher, accepted two of my Andreyeff translations. I wrote and agreed to his terms, asking [him] because I am simply up against it, to give me an advance and to send contract. A postcard, dated September 1 arrived saying my letter was received and will be attended to in a day or two. No other communication has reached me although a month ago I wrote and said so. Probably you will be able to find out the mystery of this. I should be most grateful.

I am sitting here on this rocky islet gazing at the deep blue sea . . . yes, and that is all . . . one mail a week . . . and the rest you can imagine.

Fraternally yours,
Maurice Magnus.

I should like to believe that Magnus's references to my play *The Fight for Freedom*, and to *The Solvent*, were genuine criticisms, not merely the flattery doled out by a struggling writer to one from whom he expects reciprocal benefits. Unfortunately, I am not capable of this amount of self-deception. The central incident in the play and the whole theme of *The Solvent* were not so much suggested as forced upon me by one who, at that period of my life, exerted a dominating influence. By instinct, I disliked both. Most writers resent being told, by amateurs, what to put in their books. Both plots are curiously old-fashioned, almost Victorian, while the whole idea of *The Solvent* was based upon the fallacy that "money" and "gold" are synonymous. I hated being forced to write this novel in collaboration—which meant, of course, that I had to do the "actual writing"—and was relieved when it failed. *The Fight for Freedom* is in a different category, as the characters, the dialogue, and the message —it was what Lawrence called a "pamphlet play"—are, for better or worse, my own. Had it been translated from German or Hungarian, instead of being translated into those languages, it might have made a hit in advanced circles and secured, at least, a Sunday production.

In search of further references to Magnus I have come across a bundle of old letters from Norman Douglas, written from Florence at various dates between November 1921 and April 1922. In them he refers to the fact that he was Magnus's literary executor, and asks me to rout out the MSS. which Magnus sent to me. Some of these, including a volume of Russian Memoirs, I must have forwarded to America and never recovered; others I was able to find and forward to Douglas, in spite of the fact that the people in one of the London houses of which I was an occasional occupant had a tiresome habit of destroying stray papers while "tidying up"!

.   .   .   .

As far as I am aware the *Memoirs of the Foreign Legion*, with Lawrence's introduction, was the only one of poor Magnus's literary remains which ever saw the light.[101]

1 June 1920   *Villa Fontana Vecchia, Taormina*

⟨ *We went to Malta, and it was so hot I feel quite stunned. I shouldn't wonder if my skin went black and my eyes went yellow, like a negro's. The south is so different from the north. I believe morality is a purely climatic thing.*

The bougainvillia creeper is bright magenta, on the terrace here, and through the magenta the sea is dim blue and magical, summer-white. Nearly all the strangers have gone from Taormina, we are alone with the natives, who lie about the streets with a sort of hopeless indifference. Here the past is so much stronger than the present, that one seems remote like the immortals, looking back at the world from their other world. A great indifference comes over me—I feel the present isn't real.

The corn is already cut, under the olive orchards on the steep, sloping terraces, and the ground is all pale yellow beneath the almonds and the vines. It is strange how it is September among the earth's little planets, the last poppy falling, the last chicory flower withered, stubble and yellow grass and pale, autumn-dry earth: while the vines are green and powerful with spring sap, and the almond trees, with ripe almonds, are summer, and the olives are timeless. Where are we then?

We love our Fontana Vecchia, where we sit on our ledge and look far out, through the green, to the coast of Greece. Why should one travel— why should one fret? Why not enjoy the beautiful indifference. Earnest-ness seems such bad taste, with this coast in view.

But Frieda is a bit scared of the almighty sun. She hankers after Germany, after the Schwarzwald—fir-trees, and dewy grass. She makes plans that we shall go north to Baden in August, for a couple of months. But I don't know. It costs so much, to travel, and is such a horrible experience now-adays, particularly in Italy.[102]

Rosalind Thornycroft Popham

The Lawrences' experience having proved Picinisco impossible, I did not go there, but settled in Florence in January 1920 at the Villa Canovaia, San Gervasio, which is on the first bluff of hill as one goes up from Florence to Fiesole and looks across to the city. It is an ancient villa which before the war had belonged to a German count, and which was furnished very beautifully in the late 14th century style. In half of it lived the peasant family Giuseppe and Maria and their small children. In the arcaded courtyard were lemon and orange trees, and in the gar-den cypresses, cactuses, roses, vines, wistaria, and lizards, tortoises, night-ingales, cicalas, and fireflies.

From Taormina Lawrence wrote a letter dated 15 March 1920, describ-ing the Fontana Vecchia.[103] And in June, and again in July, others fol-lowed.[104]

Fontana Vecchia/Taormina, Sicily/2 June [1920]

❨ My dear Ros. [Rosalind Thornycroft Popham],

We went away to Malta, & were away nearly a fortnight: it isn't very far from here—sail from Syracuse. It was rather wonderful: but so hot, that we were quite stunned & dazed, and haven't quite got over it yet. And therefore I think we shall sit still for some time now: not move this month. Where are you going, in the mountains?—near Florence?—Vallombrosa way? Where do you want to go, for the sea for Bridget [105] for winter? Why not come here? I can find you a house, & Taormina is simply perfect in the winter.

We too love our house—it is so cool and high and beautiful. I was thankful to get back from Malta. Frieda wants to go to Germany in the early autumn. But why go so far. We might meet her mother on the Lago Maggiore which is nearer—& then see you. We will make sure of a meeting in autumn, and you decide on your coming here for winter, & I'll find you a house now—not to fix you, that is, but just have it in one's eye.

If we come up north, I'd like to go to Venice for a little time. It's the one town I've not seen, that I'd like to see.

There'll be nothing to do here now but to aestivate—sort of summer sleep. But I want to get some work done, earn some money.

.   .   .   .

You've been quite at home, all your family with you. Wish we were having a tea-party together.

How much does it cost you to live in San Gervasio? I find we spend more than in Hermitage.

When Frieda has recovered a bit, she will write: at present she is sun-dazed.

Are the three young graces all well?

D.H.L.[106]

[Fontana Vecchia, Postmark: Taormina] 11 June 1920

[To Hilda Brown Cotterell]

❨ Very pleased to have your letter. We went to Malta, and found it when we came back. Malta isn't very far—about eight hours crossing over the sea from Syracuse, a smooth passage, but so hot, we gasped.

It is cooler here now. All the corn is cut practically, and they are making threshing floors to tread it out with the asses. We watch them from our terraces. The garden is drying up—but there are marrows and beans still— and little tomatoes. It is good to have such long sunny days. Sometimes we bathe in the sea. But we often think of Hermitage, with all its flowers and woods. We shall come back one day. Mrs. Lawrence sends her love.

D.H.L.[107]

20 July 1920   Villa Fontana Vecchia, Taormina

❨ We are still here: I live in pyjamas, barefoot, all day: lovely hot days of bright sun and sea, but a cool wind through the straits. We do our own work—I prefer it, can't stand people about: so when the floors must be washed (gently washed merely) or when I must put my suit of pyjamas in the tub, behold me in puris naturalibus, performing the menial labours of the day. It is very nice to shed so much.

.   .   .   .

Frieda wants to go to Germany. It is still inhospitable to foreigners (so they say). Therefore she goes alone. And I shall move about Italy, seeing one person and another. Suppose we shall be back here in early October or Sept.: leave in about two weeks' time.

I finished a novel, The Lost Girl. Secker's got it, and is enthusiastic about it. "I am quite sure of your future." What Jehovah is this squeaking? [108]

Fontana Vecchia/Taormina/22 July [1920]

❨ Dear R. [Rosalind Thornycroft Popham]

Your letter this morning—sorry you won't come here—could have found you a house, very nice.

Mary Cannan (Mrs. Gilbert Cannan, once Mrs. J. M. Barrie) is coming to Florence today—she's been here 5 months—came from Capri with us. She is staying at the Pension Lucchesi, on the Lung Arno della Zecca. You might see her, if you feel like it, & hear all news of Taormina. On 1st Aug. she is going to Vallombrosa—Hotel Panorama. I give her this letter to post in Florence.

F. thinks of going to Germany second week in August. Where will you be, in the mts.? I might come & see you—I shall come north, I think, but *shan't go out of Italy. Give me your address at once—& I might meet you about end August.*

Give me also address of those rooms in Venice, and tell me how much they cost. I might wait in Venice for F.'s return, in Sept.—both come on here again end of Sept.

It isn't at all unbearably hot here, in the house.

Perceval [109] is here for 1 month.

Write at once, post is so slow.

D.H.L.[110]

Fontana Vecchia/Taormina/Sicily/30 July 1920

{[Dear Hilda [Brown Cotterell],

The holiday is come, and we think of last year and Pangbourne,[111] and hope that this year you'll have a good time. We are just going away also: first to some friends in the mountains near Rome—then Mrs. Lawrence is going to Germany again to see her mother. I shall go with her as far as Milan—and from Milan to Baden is only about twenty hours. We rather dread the journey from here to Milan 36 hours direct. But thank heaven the weather is cooler. It has been hot blazing sun for week after week, day after day, and so hot lately it was too much. I have lived for weeks in a pair of pyjamas, and nothing else—barefoot; and even then too hot. Now thank heaven clouds have come from the north, welcome and lovely. It has rained a tiny spattering today. Everywhere is burnt dry, the trees have shed nearly all their leaves. It is autumn. Only the vines are green. The grapes are just about ripe, hanging purple under the broad leaves.

Vegetables are all gone—except melanciani—egg plant, purple things. But there are tomatoes in abundance—twopence a pound, fresh from the gardens. And the second lot of figs and peaches just coming. We had a nice lot of apricots—quite cheap for once. Potatoes are twice as dear as apricots, and about the same price as peaches. But Italy is very expensive nowadays for ordinary things, worse than England.

We often wonder about you, and the cottage, and the garden. Are there many greengages?—will there be apples?—how are the potatoes and marrows and the good beans? Is there a black pig in the sty? What news of Hermitage? Does your Dad still trudge across to Oare and your mother ride on Polly Wernham's bicycle? And is Mrs. Allan better?—remember us to her.

I send you a pound for your holiday. Put your name on the back, and

47

anybody will cash the cheque for you: Mr. Boshier or Mrs. Lowe. It is for you to spend exactly as you please, on as much nonsense as you like.

Have we told you that Peggy has a baby sister?—born about a month ago.[112] There's an addition to this family.

Send a line and tell us how you are and address it to me

> presso Signor Juta [113]
> San Filippo
> Anticoli–Corrado
> Prov. di Roma
> Italy

Mind you write decently, or heaven knows what the Italian postman will say to me.

Mrs. Lawrence sends love.

D. H. Lawrence

A lovely moonlight night tonight, with a moon bright on the sea, and a few moving dark clouds—shadows. So nice to see clouds and their darknesses.

I'll bet you never got that scholarship, you careless young baggage. Peg of course has got one—sharp-shins that she is. They say no news is good news: but not about scholarships.

Kindly say what the flower garden looked like this year—if any of my efforts came to anything and if your Dad was any less scornful than usual.

D.H.L.[114]

2 August 1920   Villa Fontana Vecchia, Taormina

⟨ Leave for Anticoli.[115]

Rosalind Thornycroft Popham

In August when it got very hot, I went up into the Apennines, and one day heard that all the windows of the Villa Canovaia had been blown out by an explosion at a nearby ammunition dump in the Campo di Marte. As the Count had still not returned from Germany, and no repairs could be done, the house agent arranged for me to spend the winter at a villa in Fiesole.[116]

San Filippo/Anticoli–Corrado/10 August [1920]

⟨ My dear Ros. [Rosalind Thornycroft Popham]
    Had your letter yesterday—glad to hear. We move north on Thursday
[12 August 1920]—get to Milan about 17th. I'm meeting two friends, man
& wife, from London. They will be in Italy about 3 weeks. I think we shall
walk round Como—perhaps go to Venice. Many thanks for address.
We might come to Florence. Is Canovaia empty? Might we stay a week
there?
    I'm not sure about coming to Rifredo. But certainly we'll be with you
in Canovaia in October. We can linger with you before going down to
Sicily. I look forward to that.
    Here is very nice—the Abruzzi—hills & trees, cool after Sicily.
    Send me a line c/o Thomas Cook & Son, Milano. If we went to Flor-
ence, the Whittleys [117] & I, it would be about Sept 1st. When are you
coming back?
    I feel all unstuck, as if I might drift off anywhere.

rivederci
D.H.L.[118]

Rosalind Thornycroft Popham

    While still in Sicily, Lawrence had hoped to come to Florence, and
said he would like to take on the Canovaia in spite of the lack of windows. Eventually he did come, and he stayed there two or three weeks
before going on to Venice where later Frieda joined him en route from
Germany. While he was there he wrote "The Evangelistic Beasts," the
tortoise poems, "The Pomegranate," "The Peach," and "The Figs." [119]
Sometimes he came to Fiesole where I was now living, climbing by a
steep track up through the olives and along under the remains of Fiesole's
Etruscan walls, and arriving rather jauntily, carrying something peculiar
and humorous—a salamander or a little baby duck as a pet for the children. Or he came and cooked the Sunday dinner—an English Sunday
dinner with roast beef and batter pudding. And there were tea parties
with friends up from Florence, and evenings when we sat on the terrace
high above the lights of the city, having our supper of mortadella and
marsala. It was here several other poems were suggested—"Cypresses,"

for example. I remember very well meeting with the Turkey Cock, the swart grape, and the sorb apple,[120] and how Lawrence spoke of these things as we were walking among the farms and country lanes above Fiesole.[121]

Ponte della Maravegie 1061/Venezia/Thursday [7? October 1920]

[To Rosalind Thornycroft Popham]

(Had your letter yesterday. So you didn't go to Canovaia after all. I can't imagine the Villa Ada,[122] but it sounds all right.

I expect Frieda this evening "if her passport is ready." And I'm sick of mouching about in Venice, & a gondola merely makes me bilious. I hope we can leave by the 14th & be back in Taormina by the 16th.

I do no work, am out all day, either alone or with Juta & the others. The Lido is deserted, and, in the open part, quite lovely now, with tall clouds advancing over the sea, and many burnt sails. I take my lunch and sit and watch from the sand hills, & bathe. Sometimes we all go in gondola a long way over the lagoons, past Malamocca.

I hear from Mary [Cannan?]. She loves Monaco, & says it is heaven after Italy. There seems more & more bolshy scare here—not in Venice, but in the Romagna. I suppose we shall just have to be wise & wary, that's all.

Insole & Mrs. Hansard & her husband [123] are coming to Florence. I'll give them your address, you might like Mrs. H. She is a Juta, from South Africa, wrote a novel called The Tavern. I believe Insole would like to see Canovaia, to have it in spring if possible.

We had our first touch of autumn chill yesterday: but brilliant sun.

Wonder where we'll meet next.

D.H.L.[124]

Venice/12 October [1920, Postmark: 1920]

[To Hilda Brown Cotterell]

(Dear Hilda,

Mrs. Lawrence is back from Germany. We are leaving on Sunday for Rome. Write us a line there, and tell all the news.

Love to you from us both

D. H. Lawrence [125]

20 October 1920   Villa Fontana Vecchia, Taormina

◖ Returned to Taormina.[126]

16 November 1920   Villa Fontana Vecchia, Taormina

◖ It rains with such persistency and stupidity here that one loses all one's initiative and remains cut off.

.   .   .   .

Everywhere seems very far off. Sicily at the moment feels like a land inside an aquarium—all water—and people like crabs and black-grey shrimps creeping on the bottom. Don't like it. Don't think Christmas would be any good here either. We shall be coming north in the spring—have promised to go to Germany—perhaps do a book on Venice as John Lane [127] asked me—perhaps Sardinia—who knows? [128]

30 November 1920   Villa Fontana Vecchia, Taormina

◖ Here we sit in Sicily & it has done nothing but rain masses of rain since we are back. But today a rainbow and tramontana wind & blue sea, & Calabria such a blue morning-jewel I could weep. The colour of Italy is blue, after all. Strange how rare red is. But orange underglow in the soil & rocks here.

The little rose cyclamens are almost over: the little white & yellow narcissus are out among the rocks, scenting the air, and smelling like the world's morning, so far back. Oranges are nearly ripe, yellow and many— and we've already roasted the autumn kids: soon it will be Christmas.[129]

Katherine Mansfield

[Letter to John Middleton Murry, from Villa Isola Bella, Menton, France]
? December 1920
I made these notes. Read them, will you?
The Lost Girl

It's important. It ought not to be allowed to pass.

The Times [130] gave no inkling of what it was—never even hinted at its dark secret.

Lawrence denies his humanity. He denies the powers of the Imagination. He denies Life—I mean *human* life. His hero and heroine are non-human. They are animals on the prowl. They do not feel: they scarcely speak. There is not one memorable *word*. They submit to the physical response and for the rest go veiled—blind—*faceless*—*mindless*. This is the doctrine of mindlessness.

He says his heroine is extraordinary, and rails against the ordinary. Isn't that significant? But look at her. Take her youth—her thriving on the horse-play with the doctors. They might be beasts butting each other—no more. Take the scene where the hero throws her in the kitchen, possesses her, and she returns singing to the washing-up. It's a *disgrace*. Take the rotten rubbishy scene of the woman in labour asking the Italian into her bedroom. All false. All a pack of lies!

Take the nature-study at the end. It's no more than the grazing-place for Alvina and her sire. What was the "green hellebore" to her? Of course, there is a great deal of racy, bright, competent writing in the early part— the "shop" part. But it doesn't take a writer to tell all that.

The whole is false—*ashes*. The preposterous Indian troupe of four young men is—a fake. But how on earth he can keep it up is the problem. No, it's not. He has "given way." Why stop then? Oh, don't forget where Alvina feels *"a trill in her bowels"* and discovers herself with child. A TRILL—what does that mean? And why is it so peculiarly offensive from a man? Because it is *not on this plane* that the emotions of others are conveyed to our imagination. It's a kind of sinning against art.

Earth closets, too. Do they exist *quâ* earth closets? No. I might describe the queer noises coming from one when old Grandpa X was there—very strange cries and moans—and how the women who were washing stopped and shook their heads and pitied him and even the children didn't laugh. Yes, I can imagine that. But that's not the same as to build an earth-closet because the former one was so exposed. No.

Am I prejudiced? Be careful. I feel privately as though Lawrence had possessed an animal and fallen under a curse. But I can't say that. All I know is, This is bad and ought not to be allowed. I feel a horror of it— a shrinking. But that's not criticism. But here is life where one has blasphemed against the spirit of reverence.[131]

1 January 1921   Villa Fontana Vecchia, Taormina

❨ . . . meditate trip to Sardinia . . . .[132]

3 January 1921   Villa Fontana Vecchia, Taormina

❨ Going to Palermo for Sardinia (?) in the morning.[133]

❨ Ah, the lovely morning! Away behind us the sun was just coming above the sea's horizon, and the sky all golden, all a joyous, fire-heated gold, and the sea was glassy bright, the wind gone still, the waves sunk into long, low undulations, the foam of the wake was pale ice-blue in the yellow air. Sweet, sweet wide morning on the sea, with the sun coming, swimming up, and a tall sailing barque, with her flat fore-ladder sails delicately across the light, and a far-far steamer on the electric, vivid morning horizon.

The lovely dawn: the lovely pure, wide morning in the mid-sea, so golden-aired and delighted, with the sealike sequins shaking, and the sky far, far, far above, unfathomably clear. How glad to be on a ship! What a golden hour for the heart of man! Ah, if one could sail for ever, on a small, quiet, lonely ship, from land to land and isle to isle, and saunter through the spaces of this lovely world, always through the spaces of this lovely world. Sweet it would be sometimes to come to the opaque earth, to block oneself against the stiff land, to annul the vibration of one's flight against the inertia of our terra firma! but life itself would be in the flight, the tremble of space. Ah, the trembling of never-ended space, as one moves in flight! Space, and the frail vibration of space, the glad lonely wringing of the heart. Not to be clogged to the land any more. Not to be any more like a donkey with a log on its leg, fastened to weary earth that has no answer now. But to be off.

To find three masculine, world-lost souls, and, world-lost, saunter and saunter on along with them, across the dithering space, as long as life lasts! Why come to anchor? There is nothing to anchor for. Land has no answer to the soul any more. It has gone inert. Give me a little ship, kind gods, and three world-lost comrades. Hear me! And let me wander aimless across this vivid outer world, the world empty of man, where space flies happily.

.   .   .   .

The crowd is across the road, under the trees near the sea. On this side stroll occasional pedestrians. And I see my first [Sardinian] peasant in costume. He is an elderly, upright, handsome man, beautiful in the black-and-white costume. He wears the full-sleeved white shirt and the close black bodice of thick, native frieze, cut low.. From this sticks out a short kilt or frill, of the same black frieze, a band of which goes between the legs, between the full loose drawers of coarse linen. The drawers are banded below the knee into tight black frieze gaiters. On his head he has the long black stocking-cap, hanging down behind. How handsome he is, and so beautifully male! He walks with his hands loose behind his back, slowly, upright, and aloof. The lovely unapproachableness, indomitable. And the flash of the black and white, the slow stride of the full white drawers, the black gaiters and black cuirass with the bolero, then the great white sleeves and white breast again, and once more the black cap—what marvellous massing of the contrast, marvellous, and superb, as on a magpie.—How beautiful maleness is, if it finds its right expression.—And how perfectly ridiculous it is made in modern clothes.

There is another peasant too, a young one with a swift eye and hard cheek and hard, dangerous thighs. He has folded his stocking-cap, so that it comes forward to his brow like a Phrygian cap. He wears close knee-breeches and close sleeved waistcoat of thick brownish stuff that looks like leather. Over the waistcoat a sort of cuirass of black, rusty sheepskin, the curly wool outside. So he strides, talking to a comrade. How fascinating it is, after the soft Italians, to see these limbs in their close knee-breeches, so definite, so manly, with the old fierceness in them still. One realises, with horror, that the race of men is almost extinct in Europe. Only Christ-like heroes and woman-worshipping Don Juans, and rabid equality-mongrels. The old, hardy, indomitable male is gone. His fierce singleness is quenched. The last sparks are dying out in Sardinia and Spain. Nothing left but the herd-proletariat and the herd-equality mongrelism, and the wistful, poisonous, self-sacrificial, cultured soul. How detestable.

But that curious, flashing, black-and-white costume! I seem to have known it before: to have worn it even: to have dreamed it. To have dreamed it: to have had actual contact with it. It belongs in some way to something in me—to my past, perhaps. I don't know. But the uneasy sense of blood-familiarity haunts me. I know I have known it before. It is something of the same uneasiness I feel before Mount Eryx: but without the awe this time.

.   .   .   .

[We] found ourselves in the vegetable market [of Cagliari]. . . . *Peasant women, sometimes barefoot, sat in their tight little bodices and voluminous, coloured skirts behind the piles of vegetables, and never have I seen a lovelier show. The intense deep green of spinach seemed to predominate, and out of that came the monuments of curd-white and black-purple cauliflowers: but marvellous cauliflowers, like a flower show, the purple ones intense as great bunches of violets. From this green, white, and purple massing struck out the vivid rose-scarlet and blue-crimson of radishes, large radishes like little turnips in piles. Then the long, slim, grey-purple buds of artichokes, and dangling clusters of dates, and piles of sugar-dusty white figs, and sombre looking black figs, and bright burnt figs: basketfuls and basketfuls of figs. A few baskets of almonds, and many huge walnuts. Basket-pans of native raisins. Scarlet peppers like trumpets: magnificent fennels, so white and big and succulent: baskets of new potatoes: scaly kohlrabi: wild asparagus in bunches, yellow-budding sparacelli: big, clean-fleshed carrots: feathery salads with white hearts: long, brown-purple onions, and then, of course, pyramids of big oranges, pyramids of pale apples, and baskets of brilliant shiny mandarini, the little tangerine oranges with their green-black leaves. The green and vivid-coloured world of fruit-gleams I have never seen in such splendour as under the market roof at Cagliari: so raw and gorgeous.*[134]

14 January 1921   Villa Fontana Vecchia, Taormina

⟨ Came back from Sardinia last night.[135]

20 January 1921   Villa Fontana Vecchia, Taormina

⟨ We made a dash to Sardinia—liked the island very much—but it isn't a place to live in. No point in living there. A stray corner of Italy, rather difficult materially to live in.

I have said I will keep this house on another year. But I really don't believe I shall come back for another winter. The south is so lifeless. There's ten times more "go" in Tuscany.

If I knew how to, I'd really join myself to the revolutionary socialists now. I think the time has come for a real struggle. That's the only thing I care for: the death struggle. I don't care for politics. But I know there must and should be a deadly revolution very soon, and I would take part in it if I knew how.[136]

Douglas Goldring

Early in 1921 Lawrence conceived the idea of appointing me, in an honorary capacity, his official London representative. I suppose the reason for this was partly the success of my efforts on his behalf in America, partly the fact that there was no one else among his friends with a similar knowledge of publishing whom he felt he could trust. I did not grudge either the time or the energy required to undertake the job, but on reflection—and after some conversation with Kot and Barbara Low—I felt I ought not to take on such a big responsibility. The tide was turning now in Lawrence's favour and his literary affairs needed the expert handling of a professional agent. I accordingly advised him to go to Curtis Brown (since he had left J. B. Pinker on friendly terms) and in his letter written from Taormina on April 4, 1921—quoted in the *Letters* on page [519]—he acknowledges the force of my arguments and takes my advice. Lawrence, as Kot had already warned me and as I was fully prepared to believe, was a dangerous man to work for and any hint that he was being helped made him see red. Nevertheless he was by no means the snobbish cad which Mrs. Carswell unwittingly makes him out to be in her book *The Savage Pilgrimage*. Writing of those, other than herself, who were trying to be useful to Lawrence, in 1916, she observes: "I did not fit well with them, and there was something in their relations with him that saddened me. If he needed them, then he did, and it was his affair. But I got the feeling that he did not think much of them, and was using them for what he needed, not so much willingly as *malgré lui*." [137] This was before I met Lawrence, so I do not know at whom these shafts are aimed, unless one of them was Philip Heseltine. It was one of Lawrence's weaknesses to give people the impression that he "did not think much of" friends who happened not to be present. I remember that he gave me this impression about Mrs. Carswell, of whose "clinging" disposition he complained, but I quickly saw through it as a harmless foible. [138]

16 March 1921   Villa Fontana Vecchia, Taormina

《 Frieda is in Rome, doing her passport. . . . Meanwhile I sit in Fontana Vecchia, and feel the house very empty without F. Don't like it at all. . . .

I am having my portrait painted; hope that today will be the last sitting, as I am tired. I look quite a sweet young man . . . . The weather is once more sunny and beautiful, the sea so blue, and the flowers falling from the creeper.

I have no news as yet from F. from Rome, but hope she is managing everything easily. I am all right in Taormina: people invite me to tea and dinner all the time. But I don't want to go very badly. I am correcting the MS. of my diary of a Trip to Sardinia . . . .[139]

4 April 1921   Villa Fontana Vecchia, Taormina

⟨ I'll send you also a photograph of a portrait a Scotch woman—Millicent Beveridge [140]—painted of me. . . .

Frieda is in Baden-Baden. Her mother was very ill, so she went—about a month ago. I am leaving Taormina on Saturday—Palermo—Rome— then perhaps a walking tour in Sardinia: [141] then I don't know: to Germany probably. Suppose we shall come back here in autumn.[142]

Achsah Barlow Brewster

It was a bright May [143] morning [1921] in Capri when I first saw [Lawrence]. He did not seem the tormented soul, tortured beyond endurance—as he had been described to us—when suddenly he came lilting along through the poppies under the olives on the upper terrace of Quattro Venti, the sun shining on his warm brown hair, making his beard flicker in red flames on his long chin. His eyes were of a blue to match the sea and sky, wide apart and set low under the dome of his forehead. Debonair and gay he moved with lithe precision, subtly directed as a panther, his feet alive in his shoes. His delicate hands were instinct with sensibility—falling into repose simply as does a cat. Peace rested on his quiet hands. The nose was blunted and from certain angles together with his great brow suggested the statues of Socrates. His mouth was curiously unmodelled like those the Greeks assigned to Pan and the satyrs. A trick of drooping the head pensively; his gentle expression; the dignity of his pose; the way the beard grew from his delicate, high cheek-bones; the fall of his hair over the forehead; all these made him look like the Christ figure on many a carved crucifix. Again he seemed like Whistler's portrait of Carlyle. In the Paris Salon I have seen a carved

wooden head, painted, with blue eyes and red beard, labelled "the bol-
shevik." It might have been done for Lawrence. For me these images
merge and shift; but there is left always a brightness of flaming beard
and blue eyes, a shine of some fire glowing within. His voice was individual; low, with a reed timbre, flexible, full of variation. He had a silent
little laugh when he would just open his mouth and swallow it down.
Again he had a short snort of indignation, but mostly a low mirth-
provoking laugh. Well, there he stood, laugh and all, debonair and gay,
out in the poppies under the olives. Springtime seemed much more springtime because he was there.

He had been passing through the Roman Campagna and was full of
its loveliness. When we said that we had lived out there on a hill under
Anticoli Corrado, at a place called San Filippo,[144] his blue eyes beamed
as he exclaimed that he had lived there, also in that very garden where
the great fountain spurted up through the ilex trees.

He was on his way from Taormina. We mentioned that there we had
gone on our honeymoon, living a Theocritan idyll in a spot called Fontana Vecchia. Lawrence ran his long fingers through the mass of hair
twisting a lock, announcing that this was the very place where he was
making his home at the time. We must know if the carob tree by the fountain (where in his poem [145] the snake crawled) was as large and shady
as ever.

Didn't he like to have PACE carved on the threshold? Peace, he rejoined,
carved in molten black lava, red-hot peace! He went down the path, this
man of red-hot peace, who had found the same remote corners that we
had found, probably for the same reasons—more beauty, solitude, reality, simplicity.

Again in the afternoon Lawrence came swinging up the garden path.
We were alone, and he told us that he was writing *Aaron's Rod*, and began outlining the story.. It seemed more beautiful as he narrated it in
his low sonorous voice with the quiet gesture of his hands, than it ever
could written in a book. Suddenly he stopped, after Aaron had left his
wife and home and broken with his past, gravely asking what he should
do with him now.

We ventured that only two possible courses were left to a man in
his straits—either to go to Monte Cassino and repent, or else to go through
the whole cycle of experience.

He gave a quiet chuckle of surprise and added that those were the
very possibilities he had seen, that first he had intended sending him to

Monte Cassino, but found instead that Aaron had to go to destruction to find his way through from the lowest depths.

The next morning he came for a walk. In the evening he returned for dinner and stayed for hours. It was cold. The fire burned red in that small stove called a "Porcellino," beside which he sat on the green-tiled floor, his hands clasped around his knees, telling us the news and gossip of Taormina. We could see each person he mentioned, so perfect was his mimicry—our first experience of him as an impersonator.

We were seized with the desire to go on tours of exploration. Lawrence was fired with enthusiasm and maintained that what we needed was a "lugger." Then we should start and go—up, down, around, inside and outside of every piece of land on this terrestrial globe. We should put geography into practice. Many happy hours we lingered, planning to lugger around the world. We should stop just wherever and whenever we pleased and the seas were to behave accordingly. We seemed to need only the tiniest crew, in fact maybe we could manage it by ourselves, if we could do what was required by the captain. It looked as though Lawrence would be the captain! Often we think lingeringly of that phantom lugger that never materialized.

Earl [146] and I were projecting a Buddhistic pilgrimage in the autumn. When the next day he left Capri, Lawrence promised to see us again before we departed for Ceylon.[147]

Earl H. Brewster

Lawrence had been described to me as an "agonized soul"! I had thought of him as haggard, brooding, and sensual. Our first meeting was in Capri. How different he was from what I had imagined! How different from his own drawings of himself! [148] These he made appear physically stronger. Instead I saw a tall delicate man. His face was pale; his hands long, narrow, capable; his eyes clear-seeing and blue; his brown hair and red beard glowing like flames from the intensity of his life; his voice was flexible, generally of medium pitch, with often a curious, plaintive note, sometimes in excitement rising high in key. He always appeared to be carelessly dressed, but it was only that apparent carelessness which arises from a fastidious nature.

That morning of which I am writing he wore a short jacket of pale homespun. He brought with him some quality of the outdoor world, from the shrubs and flowers. The sweetness of sun-dried leaves and grass seemed never to leave him. My first impression was that he looked like a man who lived devoted to the study of such life—a botanist. Immediately I felt that he was sensitive beyond others, that he knew intuitively the life of those about him, and wished to establish with them a sincere relationship. There was no condescension in his manner, his conviviality was quiet and dignified, his attitude seemed to arise from the respect which he had for the vital being one might be. Never was there the slightest sign in him of the self-conscious author.

On that first meeting we went with others to the Piccola Marina to bathe. It was a typical May [April] day in southern Italy, with sun, sirocco and haze. We lay on the rocks, but Lawrence did not bathe, declaring that he did not enjoy it. He was to be in Capri only a few days.

The following morning he joined me for a walk from our house, Torre dei Quattro Venti, to the Molino, beyond Anacapri, a distance of two or three miles. It was the first occasion we were alone together. He must have known of my pre-occupation with Buddhist philosophy and its solution of the problem of suffering, for immediately upon our departure from the house he turned to me, and said:

"You don't look the intellectual type: you were not meant to be governed by the centre between your eyebrows. We should *not* pass beyond suffering: but you can find the power to endure, and equilibrium and a kind of bliss, if you will turn to the deepest life within yourself. Can't you rest in the actuality of your own being? Look deep into the centre—to your solar plexus."

Vaguely I knew of the Hindu theory of the "chakras," but years passed before I felt the significance of what he said to me then. Nevertheless he inspired me to tell him my intimate experiences.

He spoke of his desire for an environment where his contact with people would be more vital.

That evening before our roaring fire he was full of wit and humorous anecdotes. He was against idealism, also against what he called the attempt to overcome the tiger, whose being in us is real, he maintained, and not to be suppressed or sublimated.

.   .   .   .

I was planning to leave in the autumn with my wife and child [149] for Ceylon, to continue the study of Buddhism. Lawrence talked much of the difficulty of entering into the thoughts and feelings of another race.[150]

60

Rebecca West

One spring day . . . I was lunching in Florence with Reggie Turner [151] and Norman Douglas. Reggie Turner has been described by Max Beerbohm [152] as Artemus in his paper on wits in *And Even Now,* and there is no need to add a line save to commemorate a supremely imaginative act of charity. When Oscar Wilde came out of prison, Reggie Turner sent him one of the most expensive and completely useless fitted dressing-cases that Bond Street has ever achieved. There is need to tell over again the tale of Norman Douglas's accomplishments, because the mind finds them so incredible that it has a disposition to forget them. Besides being a master of English prose, he is one of the finest classical scholars in Europe, a great linguist (he can even speak and write Russian), a pianist, a composer, a caricaturist, a botanist, and a landscape gardener —all to the highest degree of accomplishment. By one of those ironies which forbids us to believe that Nature is neutral, even when one has been forced to give up one's faith that she is kindly, Reggie Turner, in whose heart is innocence, wears the winking face of a devil off a quattrocento choir stall; and Norman Douglas, whose heart, so far as innocence is concerned, is as the Gobi desert, looks as one who has never seen Dr. Cadman [153] would imagine him to look. There are what one has been led to believe are the stigmata of moral earnestness: the penetrating eyes under level brows, compressed lips, head set sturdily between the shoulders, as if here reason were firmly rooted in the moral law, and hair white as if the scalp itself had renounced all such vanity as colour. And indeed there is here some of the quality suggested. There is in him an austere loyalty to an interpretation of life that might, if need pushed him to it, not baulk at renunciation. Less than paganism is his religion. Things are what they are. If the landscape seems to form a pattern and the figure of a god emerge, then that does but prove that a god is but a landscape seeming to form a pattern. That being so, all things are equal and unrelated, perpetually dissolvent back to their point of least significance. Believing this he will not forswear his belief. That day at lunch his conversation perpetually made and unmade the world till late in the afternoon; and then, though there would have seemed to an observer no reason why we should ever move, we were entertaining each other so well, we rose to our feet. Lawrence was coming in by some slow train that crawled up from Rome laden with poor folks that could not pay for speed, and would by now be installed in his hotel. To each of us, different though we were in type, it appeared of paramount importance that we should go and pay him our respects at the first possible moment.

He was staying in a poorish hotel overlooking what seems to me, since I am one of those who are so enamoured of Rome that they will not submit themselves to the magic of Florence, to be a trench of drab and turbid water wholly undeserving of the romantic prestige we have given the Arno. Make no mistake, it was the hotel that overlooked the Arno, not Lawrence. His room was one of the cheaper ones at the back. His sense of guilt which scourged him perpetually, which was the motive-power of his genius, since it made him inquire what sin it was which he and all mankind have on their conscience, forbade him either enjoying comfort or having the money to pay for it, lest he should weaken. So it was a small, mean room in which he sat tapping away at a typewriter. Norman Douglas burst out in a great laugh as we went in and asked if he were already writing an article about the present state of Florence; and Lawrence answered seriously that he was.[154] This was faintly embarrassing, because on the doorstep Douglas had described how on arriving in a town Lawrence used to go straight from the railway station to his hotel and immediately sit down and hammer out articles about the place, vehemently and exhaustively describing the temperament of the people. This seemed obviously a silly thing to do, and here he was doing it. Douglas's laughter rang out louder than ever, and malicious as a satyr's.

But we forgot all that when Lawrence set his work aside and laid himself out to be a good host to us. He was one of the most polite people I have ever met, in both naïve and subtle ways. The other two knew him well, but I had never seen him before. He made friends as a child might do, by shyly handing me funny little boxes he had brought from some strange place he had recently visited; and he made friends too as if he were a wise old philosopher at the end of his days, by taking notice of one's personality, showing that he recognized its quality and giving it his blessing. Also there was a promise that a shy wild thing might well give and exact from its fellows, that he would live if one would let him live. Presently he settled down to give, in a curious hollow voice, like the soft hoot of an owl, an account of the journey he had made, up from Sicily to Capri, from Capri to Rome, from Rome to Florence. There seemed no reason why he should have made these journeys, which were all as uncomfortable as cheap travelling is in Italy, nor did there seem any reason why he was presently going to Baden-Baden. Yet, if every word he said disclosed less and less reason for this journeying, it also disclosed a very definite purpose. These were the journeys that the mystics of a certain type have always found necessary. The Russian saint goes to the head of his family and says good-bye and takes his stick and walks out with no objective but the truth. The Indian fakir draws lines with his bare feet across the dust of his peninsula which describe a diagram, meaningless to the uninitiated, but significant of holiness. Lawrence travelled, it seemed, to get a certain Apocalyptic vision of mankind that he registered again and again and again, always rising to a pitch of ecstatic agony. Norman Douglas, Reggie Turner, and I, none of whom would have moved from one place to another except in the greatest comfort procurable and with a definite purpose, or have endured a disagreeable experience twice if we could possibly help it, sat in a row on the bed and nodded. We knew that what he was doing was right. We nodded and were entranced.

The next day Norman Douglas and I went a walk with Lawrence far out into the country, past the Certosa. It was a joy for me to leave the city, for I cannot abide trams and Florence is congested with them. Impossible to pass through the streets without feeling that one is being dogged by a moaning tram one had betrayed in one's reckless youth; and it had been raining so hard that there had for long been no opportunity to walk in the country. Now there had been a day's sunshine, and the whole world was new. Irises thrust out of the wet earth like weapons suddenly brought into action. The cypresses, instead of being lank funereal plumes commemorating a foundered landscape, were exclamation marks drawn in Chinese ink, crying out at the beauty of the reborn countryside. About the grassy borders of the road there was much fine enamel work in little flowers and weeds as one has seen it on the swards of Botticelli. Of the renascent quality of the day Lawrence became an embodiment. He was made in the angelic colours. His skin, though he had lived so much in the Southern countries, was very white, his eyes were light, his hair and beard were a pale luminous red. His body was very thin, and because of the flimsiness of his build it seemed as if a groove ran down the centre of his chest and his spine, so that his shoulder blades stood out in a pair of almost wing-like projections. He moved quickly and joyously. One could imagine him as a forerunner, speeding faster than spring can go from bud to bud on the bushes, to tell the world of the season that was coming to save it from winter. Beside him Norman Douglas lumbered along stockily. Because he knew what emperor had built this road and set that city on a hill, and how the Etruscans had been like minded in their buildings before him, he made one feel that there have been so many springs that in effect there is no spring, but that that is of no great moment. Bending over a filemot-coloured flower that he had not seen since he found it on Mount Olympus, his face grew nearly as tender as a mother bending over her child. When a child tumbled at his feet from the terrace of an olive orchard, his face became neither more nor less tender than before. They moved in unison of pace along the road, these two, and chatted. They were on good terms then, Ormuzd and Ahriman.[155]

We stopped for lunch at a place that was called the Bridge of Something: an inn that looked across a green meadow to a whitish river. We ate at a table on which a trellis of wisteria painted a shadow far more substantial than the blue mist that was its substance. The two men talked for long of a poor waif,[156] a bastard sprig of royalty, that had recently killed himself after a life divided between conflicting passions for monastic life, unlawful pleasures, and financial fraud. He had sought refuge at the monastery of Monte Cassino, that nursery of European culture, where St. Thomas Aquinas himself was educated; but soon was obliged to flee down one side of the sugar loaf mountain while the carabinieri climbed up the other with a warrant for his arrest on charges connected with the Italian law of credit. Then he had gone to Malta, and played more fantasies on the theme of debt, till his invention was exhausted. This was the man whose recollections of service in the French Foreign Legion were published with a preface by Lawrence which provoked Norman Douglas to a savage retort that stands high among the dog fights of literary men. But then they were joined in amity while they talked of him with that grave and brotherly pitifulness that men who have found it difficult to accommodate themselves to their fellow men feel for those who have found it impossible. They broke off, I remember, to look at some lads who made their way across the meadow and began to strip by the river bank. "The water will be icy," said Douglas, "it won't be warm till the snow goes off the mountains." He began to chuckle at the thought of the shock that was coming to the boys who had been tempted by the first hot day. Lawrence let his breath hiss out through his teeth at the thought of their agony; but he seemed to find pleasure in it, as he would in any intense feeling.

Presently we rose, and went on our way. Norman Douglas took the landlord's hand and wrung it heartily, saying a fervid good-bye. Lawrence exclaimed, "Douglas, how can you shake hands with these people!" He meant by this that the antipathy between the Northern and the

Southern peoples was so great that there could be no sincere attempt at friendship with them. Douglas answered with a grin, "Oh, it takes something off the bill next time." He did not mean that. It was simply the first way that came to hand of saying that he would not get excited about these fine points, that in his universe every phenomenon was of equal value. We walked away. After a minute or two I looked back through the olive trees and saw the landlord standing where we had left him, sending after us a hard black Italian stare. "Do you know, Douglas," said Lawrence suddenly, though he had not looked back, "I can't help thinking that the man understood English." "Oh no," I said falsely, "I'm sure he didn't." But Douglas, laughing more deeply than ever, said, "I got that too." We all walked along without speaking, ill at ease, though Douglas kept his eyes crinkled as if he were still laughing. Ormuzd and Ahriman alike did not want unnecessary explosions of the forces they well knew to be latent in their universe.

Later Lawrence began to talk of the Sicilian peasants and how full of hatred and malice he had found them. There was a great tale about some old crones who had come up at twilight to his house in Taormina with some jars of honey they had wanted him to buy, and had crouched down on his terrace while he tested their goods with malignity in their eyes, in their squatting bodies. They had meant to cheat him, for it was last year's honey and ill preserved. He detected the fraud in an instant, with his sturdy wisdom about household matters, and bade them be gone. Silently they rose and filed out through his olive trees with their jars on their shoulders, with increased malignity in their eyes and in their prowling bodies, because they had not been able to cheat him. "Such hatred!" he cried in effect. "Such black loathing." Again I felt embarrassed, as I did when we discovered him pounding out articles on the momentary state of Florence with nothing more to go on than a glimpse of it. Surely he was now being almost too flatly silly, even a little mad? Of course peasants try to cheat one over honey or anything else, in Italy or anywhere else, and very natural it is, considering how meagrely the earth gives up its fruits. But as for hatred and black loathing, surely this is persecution mania? I was a little unhappy about it, which was a pity, for that made an unsatisfactory ending to what was to be my last meeting with Lawrence, though mercifully not my last contact with him. For a few months ago I received a letter from him thanking me for some little tribute I had paid him during the trouble about his pictures in London.[157] This letter showed the utmost humility in him to take notice of such a small courtesy; and it showed more than that. With marvellous sensitiveness he had deduced from a phrase or two in my article that I was troubled by a certain problem, and he said words that in their affectionate encouragement and exquisite appositeness could not have been bettered if we had spent the ten years that had intervened since our meeting in the closest friendship.

The point about Lawrence's work that I have been unable to explain save by resorting to my personal acquaintance with him is this: that it was founded on the same basis as those of his mental movements which then seemed to me ridiculous, and which, now that I have had more experience, I see as proceeding in a straight line to the distant goal of wisdom. He was tapping out an article on the state of Florence at that moment without knowing enough about it to make his views of real value. Is that the way I looked at it? Then I was naïve. I know now that he was writing about the state of his own soul at that moment, which, since our self-consciousness is incomplete, and since in consequence our vocabulary also is incomplete, he could only render in symbolic terms; and the city of Florence was as good a symbol as any other. If he was foolish in taking the material universe and making allegations about it that were true only of the universe within his own soul, then Rimbaud was a great fool also. Or to go further back, so too was Dante, who made a new Heaven and Hell and Purgatory as a symbol for the geography within his own breast, and so too was St. Augustine, when in *The City of God* he writes an attack on the pagan world, which is unjust so long as it is regarded as an account of events on the material plane, but which is beyond price as an account of the conflict in his soul between that which tended to death and that which tended to life. Lawrence was in fact no different from any other great artist who has felt the urgency to describe the unseen so keenly that he has rifled the seen of its vocabulary and diverted it to that purpose; and it took courage to do that in a land swamped with naturalism as England was when Lawrence began to write.

When he cried out at Douglas for shaking hands with the innkeeper because the North and South were enemies, and when he saw the old crones who had come to cheat him out of an odd lira or two over the honey as maenads too venomous even to be flamboyant, I thought he was seeing lurid colours that were in his eyes and not in the universe he looked on. Now I think he was doing justice to the seriousness of life, and had been rewarded with a deeper insight into its nature than most of us have.[158]

? May? 1921   Ludwig-Wilhelmstift, Baden-Baden

❲ I am finishing Aaron. And you won't like it at all. Instead of bringing him nearer to heaven, in leaps and bounds, he's misbehaving and putting ten fingers to his nose at everything. Damn heaven. Damn holiness. Damn Nirvana. Damn it all.

.   .   .   .

Weather-report. My wife and I are in a little inn about 3 miles from Baden—among the hills, just on the edge of the Black Forest—the deep, deep green meadows, with bell flowers and big daisies, and the old black and white village scattered amongst, and amongst trees; the reddish castle ruin sticking above, out of green maple and beeches: the opening walnut-trees beside the loop of the road: the great woods on the final hills, many-pointed fir-woods, and edges of flaming beech: the hills just steeply ceasing, and the wide Rhine-plain beyond, seen from the window, with a loop of river: the nice little northern, barefoot children playing, playing so child-like, not Italian adult-infant; the yellow oxen in the long wagons of grass: everybody nice but rather spent, rather life-empty: and all so different from before the war: and so different from Taormina. . . .[159]

? July 1921   Villa Alpensee, Thumersbach, Zell-am-See, Austria

❲ I am not sure how long we stay here. The weather is hot again—Florence would be intolerable. Yet I want to go south.[160]

3 August 1921   Villa Alpensee, Thumersbach, Zell-am-See, Austria

❲ You know we are with Frieda's younger sister, Johanna,[161] her husband, son and daughter. The villa is on the edge of the lake, we bathe and boat and go excursions into the mountains. The snow isn't far. And the Schreibershofens are really very nice with us. And yet, I feel I can't breathe. Everything is free and perfectly easy. And still I feel I can't breathe. Perhaps it is one can't live with people any more—en ménage. Anyhow, there it is. Frieda loves it and is quite bitter that I say I want to go away. But there it is—I do.

There is a very nice flat [162] we can have in Florence, for not very much.

*Only this terrific heat—when is it going to end? But, anyhow, I shall leave
here about 12th August. If it keeps so hot I shall stay somewhere near
Meran for a while, and perhaps look round and see if I might like to live
there. I don't much want to go back to Taormina again. If the weather
breaks, and it rains, I shall go to Florence.*[163]

Villa Alpensee/Thumersbach/Zell-am-See bei Salzburg/Austria/9 August
1921

⟦ Dear Rosalind [Thornycroft Popham]

Your letter from Rifredo here. We have been in the north since April
—in Baden Baden and then here, with Frieda's sister. Very nice here—
lake, snow mountains etc. We shall stay, I suppose, while the heat lasts.

No, I didn't know you had been in Switzerland. . . . But Zurich is
a dreary-souled city. Austria is quite without morale—of that sort. . . .

What are you doing for the winter?—staying in Florence? I suppose we
shall go back to Taormina in October. I will let you know when we go
through Florence—stay then I don't know how long.

No work doing here: impossible to work in this country: no wits left,
all gone loose & scattered. I shan't be sorry to come back to Italy again:
but feel Europe is a bit empty altogether. Only the States are worse, I'm
sure.

We had a friend here . . . from New York. He badly wanted us to
go there for the winter: me lecture. But I got such a strong distaste for
Yankees, seeing him every day, that at the moment wild horses wouldn't
drag me. I suppose I shall go one day—because one chafes so here in Europe,
& that seems the only way out. But it's a pis aller.

We might come to Florence for a month—in September. But not if it's
going to be awfully hot. Here is very pleasant—we have our own boats
& bathing & pony-carriage & all very easy. Too easy. Too pleasant. Austria
is very cheap, reckoning the exchange—and you can get everything with
enough Krone. The krone is now 3,000 to £1. It was before the war about 23.
But here in the country nobody is poor.

.   •   •   •   •   •   •   •   •   •   •   •

What's the news of Joan, Bertie, the children, Eleanor, Alexander, and
everybody? [164] I have heard nothing for such a long time. I intended to go
to England—but didn't want to, when I got near enough. I liked Germany
—we were near Baden Baden, in the Black Forest, in a peasant inn [165]

for 3 months. I loved the forest—the great landscape—so big—and the stillness. It made a big impression on me. Everybody very pleasant.

F. sends greetings.

D.H.L.[166]

? August 1921   Villa Alpensee, Thumersbach, Zell-am-See, Austria

⟨ It has been hot also here—so we bathe twice a day. We have four boats—must row across to Zell for everything. Drove yesterday with the pony to Ferlistur under the glacier—very beautiful, the great sloping white mass.[167] The flowers a bit higher up are really lovely.[168]

Katherine Mansfield

[Letter to the Hon. Dorothy Brett]
29 August 1921

What makes Lawrence a *real* writer is his passion. Without passion one writes in the air or on the sand of the seashore. But L. has got it all wrong, I believe. He is right, I imagine—or how shall I put it . . . ? It's my belief that nothing will save the world but love. But his tortured, satanic demon love I think is all wrong.[169]

1 September 1921   32, Via dei Bardi, Florence

⟨ Everything goes well with us: we like your flat more every day: have all our meals on the terrace, when the wind isn't too strong. I find it lovely and cool . . . .[170]

Catherine Carswell

That summer [1921] we had arranged to leave the boy [171] at home, and to meet the Lawrences either in Tirol or in Italy. At first it was to be the former. By the middle of July they were at Constance on their way to Lake Zell, near Salzburg. Frieda's younger sister Johanna (it was the older sister Else to whom Lawrence had dedicated *The Rainbow*) had taken a house at Tumersbach and was there with her husband and children.

69

But lovely as this was, Lawrence soon wearied to be gone. . . . He did not want to live again at Taormina, but Germany made him home-sick for Italy. We were bringing him various things, including signed passport forms, as their passports were almost expired and they did not know how to have them renewed in either Germany or Italy. Though he sent us all the needful information and was ready to engage a room in the neighbouring peasant hotel, we could feel that he was restless. Also the weather broke at Tumersbach. We therefore made our own plans to walk from Innsbruck independently, and to reach Florence when he should be there in September.

After crossing, mainly on foot, in hot but stormy weather from Innsbruck to Meran we turned up the Brenner again and wandered through the battle-area to Cortina d'Ampezzo, where we got on the train for Venice. We did not stay there long. What with bad weather and bugs —1921 was a great bug year in Italy and Austria—after a day or two we were glad to leave for Florence.

The Lawrences, whom we had advised of our train, were to meet us. But something not anybody's fault went wrong, and Lawrence spent a large part of the morning meeting trains in which we were not. When we did arrive there was nobody about for us, but just as we left the station we caught sight of Frieda hastening away. She had seen the train come in, but somehow had missed us. Such missings are a fatality in my family. Our joyful greeting on the road outside has quite obliterated what followed immediately upon it. I know we appointed to meet later for lunch all four together.

Lawrence and Frieda were in a furnished upper flat on the other side of the Arno, 32, Via dei Bardi, the house that is traditionally pointed out as Romola's. Lawrence had recommended a pension on the other side of the river where he had lived himself; but we found it too grand for us, and going farther on took a room in the Rigatti, a pleasant bell-haunted remnant of the Palazzo Alberti, at which Donald had stayed on a former visit.

Of our daily meetings for the week we were there, our meals together, our walks and our talks, Lawrence wrote to me soon afterwards—"it seems only a moment we saw you—but the sympathy is there."[172] Both these remarks ring true to me to-day. Looking back now the week presents itself as rather less than a moment—a hazy moment at that, and we seem to have said and done nothing in particular, nor to have been particularly happy. Though I never felt more drawn to Lawrence, there was about him something restless, remote and even impatient, which blurred the approach and made me doubt sadly once or twice if my sympathy found any response. I therefore did my best to conceal it. Sometimes I was relieved to get out of his presence.

To use his own phrase, he was now "done with Italy," and with Europe. It might turn out to be only for the time—it did in fact so turn out—but that made it none the less urgent. Even Sicily, which he had so loved, had ceased to hold him, and he was willing to return to it only that he might pack up and be off. He knew that we could not or would not go with him and he was bound to identify us in some degree with what he longed to leave. As companion adventurers we had failed him. But we were still acknowledged friends, more deeply acknowledged perhaps than ever before, as he needed friends, if only to leave behind. Even if we were only pillars of salt we stood for something. Lawrence was like the young son in the fairy tale who would one day come and touch his stony brethren with the far-fetched herb, and turn them once more into brethren of flesh. Meanwhile we were safe in our surroundings, and he was of that threatened frailty of flesh that needs all its wits about it.

Lawrence had loved Italy as much as any English poet ever did, and he got from it more than most. He was grateful till the end of his life for that carelessness of the South which dispelled like an unconscious benison the harsh and petty carefulness of his Northern upbringing. Travelling north would always make him feel ill and resentful. Turning south would always offer ease and healing. "It cures one of caring, and a good thing too!" He felt this at the beginning and returned to it at the end, but, bask as he might now for a time in the essential tolerance of southern Italy, with its classical mentality and its good-humoured physicalness, it could not assuage for ever his northern thirst for "something beyond." He must seek further for that *other* world that is within and behind the real world. The easy and eminently workable Latin compromise with life had gone a little stale, a little rancid in his mouth. It, or something like it, might yet prove to be a practical solution. But there was much to be looked into before this could be accepted.

Lawrence's friends, the Brewsters, who were Buddhists and were shortly leaving Sicily for the East, were urging him to follow them to Ceylon where he could see the working out of Buddhism. At the end of the week he was going to see them off. He was in a restless state of waiting. He knew that he must move soon himself, but was still undecided as to whether the move should be East or West.

As always, there were several stray people who whirled for the time in Lawrence's orbit. I vaguely remember a large American woman who was studying singing, and who had brought with her a stout son of four-teen who carried a cudgel in Fascist fashion, and Lawrence introduced us to at least one of the well-known residents among his acquaintance in Florence. I seem to remember a smallish clean-shaven face that man-aged to be at once red and dried up. Even this picture, as of something both parched and glowing, may be mistaken. A casual introduction will often thus afflict me with blindness and deafness as well as aphasia.

Again I remember a young woman whom I cannot place, and of whom I have only a single recollection. We were all on the roof of the Lawrences' house. A camera is a thing I scarcely ever use, but I had brought a Brownie with me for our walk across the Dolomites, and when I saw Lawrence standing laughing near the parapet I had the sudden desire to take a snapshot of him. I don't think he was more than faintly irritated. Anyhow he went on laughing and did not say anything to stop me. But the young woman thought she divined in Lawrence some serious distaste and tried to prevent the photograph from being taken. At any other time I believe I might have submitted. But feeling certain that Lawrence did not really mind, and longing to have a picture of him in his present light and gay mood, I persisted. I am very glad to have the picture now.[173] It is, I think, a misfortune that by far the most of the photographs and portraits of Lawrence show him as thoughtful—either fiercely or sufferingly so. His usual expression was a kind of sparkling awareness, almost an "I am ready for anything" look which was invigorating to behold.

The Lawrences' flat was second from the top. In the small top floor was Mary Cannan.[174] Once at least we all went to her room for a meal, which was more sumptuous and varied than the meals we shared with the Lawrences. White-haired and with exquisitely pretty features, Mary was always the elegant one of the company. One day when Mary was out, Frieda displayed to me a cupboard full of her enviable clothes. While the rest of us were still content with knitted wool or silk of the common kind, Mary had several handknitted dresses of silk *bouclé*—then the very latest thing from Paris. Passing it appreciatively through her hands, Frieda, who prided herself on a "feeling for textures," assured me with solemn emphasis that it was "enormously expensive." It was perhaps a certain lack of response in me on this occasion that led Frieda to the conclusion that "Catherine had taste but no *feeling* for textures." I ad-mired the *bouclé* frigidly and without desiring to handle it.

I was jealous of Mary. That summer Donald and I had been roughing it—drenched by storms, devoured by bugs, several nights bedless in the mountains—which was all very well *in* the mountains, but now in civilized surroundings, tired out from over-walking, I was obliged to appear on every occasion in a faded garment of flowered cotton which had originally been intended as a garden overall. When it fell to me, as it often seemed to do, to walk behind Lawrence and Mary, Lawrence attired with impressive suitability in natural coloured silk (a sort of Palm Beach suit) and Mary all that was urbane and charming, I almost hated Mary. Frieda had advised me to apply to her for the secret of a particular face-bleaching lotion which she used and, I understood, had received directly from Sarah Bernhardt. This I never did, but I have often wondered about it since. I saw that Lawrence liked to walk with a fashionably dressed woman, and though he could and did make fun of Mary behind her back (as indeed he could and did of any of us) and was sometimes clearly bored before her face, he was fond of her and took a lot of trouble over her, largely because she looked always so nice. She had written a book, still in MS., about all the dogs she had ever had as pets. Lawrence, at her request, went over it most carefully, suggesting alterations and improvements. Remembering my experience with my own novel, I found this distressing.[175]

Though not in the least rich, Lawrence just then, owing to the placing of short stories in the United States through Mountsier, had become distinctly more prosperous than he had been when I last saw him [November, 1919]. This was reflected in his and Frieda's clothes. He would never be a dandy, but he liked to appear in the unmistakable role of *il signore*. I felt we Carswells were failing to keep pace. It was unfortunate, too, for me that I had Anglo-Italian cousins in Florence to whom I introduced Lawrence without good effect. My cousins had the right to consider themselves of the Italian aristocracy. But they showed themselves blind alike to Lawrence's genius and his charm, and he disliked what he saw of them. Like so many well-bred Italians they knew nothing of English literature later than Oscar Wilde, except for modern rumours of Hall Caine, Marie Corelli, and possibly Mr. Galsworthy. As they had been associated with some of the romantic passages of my childhood, this state of matters made me feel absurdly jangled, especially in view of several unlucky contacts which I brought about. I suppose most lives contain similar "pockets," in which a fetish of youth has remained so long undisturbed that the turning out demands a certain resolution.

One specially unlucky incident distressed me out of measure. One of my cousins lived in an old villa, really a little castle, some way out of Florence. This existed in its own world, with some hundreds of peasants living on the estate under the *mezzadria* system. Everything, from the wine and the bread to the restored panelling of the rooms, was home-grown and home-made. Having boasted to Lawrence and Frieda of the beauties of this place, at which Donald and I were going to spend a week-end, I arranged that an invitation should be given. The Lawrences—and, I think, Mary Cannan—were to take the tram from Florence to the near-est hamlet that was some two or three miles from the villa, and a car-riage ordered by my cousins was to bring them out to spend the Sunday and meet Professor Guglielmo Ferrero.[176]

Sunday came, but no Lawrence party arrived, and only at the hour they were expected did I learn that my cousin had forgotten, or had anyhow omitted, to order the carriage which should have been done beforehand in the hamlet as she had not one of her own. In desperation I set out to meet them on foot; but when, after traversing about a mile, I saw no signs of them, I knew it was useless to go on. By the time I reached the village, if—as it appeared—they had failed to find a carriage for them-selves, they would have gone home. It was a frightfully hot day.

On the Monday in Florence we found, as I had feared, that they had come as far as the hamlet by a wearisome tram, had found no further means of transport, and had gone back. Lawrence treated the matter lightly and said it was of no consequence. The worst thing was that my cousin didn't think it of any consequence either. She regarded Lawrence as nothing more than an obscure English bohemian friend of ours. The lapse was a nightmare of abasement to me, all the more that so little was said on either side. So I could not help rejoicing in my cousin's humiliation when, to his undisguised and very vocal rage, she inadvertently introduced the great Ferrero under the name of his father-in-law, Lombroso.

On Lawrence's thirty-seventh birthday [11 September], which fell dur-ing our week, we supped alone with Frieda and him at his flat and were gay in a quiet sort of way. I cannot remember much that was said, except that we discussed the break with Pinker, and I recall much praise of the Italian newspapers at the expense of the English ones. How much better than *The Times* was the *Corriere della Sera!* How much less "base"! When reading the English newspapers in Italy he felt ashamed to be an English-man, and that was a thing he hated. His John Bullishness was able to raise its head again, however, and its voice, in acute disgust of the use to which the shingle on the other side of the arno was put by the Florentine *gio-vinezza*. If anybody should find an inconsistency or a discrepancy between this disgusted Lawrence and the Lawrence who painted certain of his pictures,[177] that person must think again, and think hard.

Another day the Lawrences ate with us at a little downstairs restaurant off the Via dei Calzaioli. I remember only one thing vividly. Shortly before we met for our meal I had been nagging at Donald for what I took to be some small breach of manners on his part with regard to the same cousin who failed to send the carriage for Lawrence. In certain ways, I had argued, the Italians are formal, and in not observing their formalities we give them the opening to despise us and our friends. Smarting under her lack of courtesy to Lawrence, I was annoyed by any possible lapse on our part. So I had been scolding, and Donald at dinner had complained of this, good-naturedly, to Lawrence. "You ought to hit her!" said Lawrence fiercely—"Hit her hard. Don't let her scold and nag. You mustn't allow it, *whatever* it is you have done!" We all laughed and felt refreshed. When, the other day, I recalled this to Donald he had no recollection of it. But I have never forgotten.

I have said that the stout son of the American lady singer carried a cudgel in the Fascist fashion. During that summer of 1921, the Fascist order had not yet been established in Italy, but it was coming on fast and there were constant street fights in Florence. Though I witnessed several rushes of a street crowd, I never saw any actual shooting. Lawrence, however, had, and his descriptions were so lively that I had to think twice before saying just now that I was not present myself. He told us how, on the sound of a shot, the crowded street was an empty one before you could wink. The people, he declared, ran up the fronts of the houses like flies and down into the earth like mice. One moment they were there, strolling slowly and thickly after the manner of a Florentine crowd. The next moment not a soul in sight.[178] When Lawrence had seen anything like this that excited him, he was able by word and voice and gesture to make you share perfectly in his bygone excitement. As in his description of the bull-fight at the opening of *The Plumed Serpent,* he made a point of avoiding all the more familiar forms of exaggeration. But when, especially in talking, a single, carefully selected enlargement was necessary to convey the force of his own emotion to the listener, he chose his point infallibly. I never once heard him exaggerate the wrong point or fail to convey the strict emotional truth by means of the exaggeration he had chosen. He would have made a great descriptive reporter.

Our time of holiday was nearly done, and we wished to go on to Rome before returning to London. Lawrence had seen neither Perugia nor Siena. I had associations with both places, and liked Perugia in particular. Lawrence specially wished to see Siena. So it was arranged that, if possible, we should meet him there on our way back. We talked about how much we should enjoy ourselves. There would just be Frieda and Lawrence and Donald and I.

But somehow I did not believe it would happen, and it did not. We went by ourselves to Perugia, and we heard from Lawrence that on arriving in Siena he had hated it so much that he could not bear to stay on another day. What happened to make Siena so hateful to him I never learned. I agreed, however, with his finding that travelling was "peculiarly disheartening" that year, when the débris of the War was still everywhere, and one was depressed "not so much with inconveniences as by the kind of slow poison one breathes in every new atmosphere." His restlessness, too, I guessed was at a height. He had felt that he must rush away to Capri to see the Brewsters off to Ceylon. This he wrote to us from Siena the day he was to leave, saying he was sorry to miss us but felt sure we should soon be coming to Italy to live. In case that note should not get us, he left another at the Bank in Florence, with a parcel of six stone plates which he begged us to take to England for Ada.[179] My heart felt a bit like this parcel, but we got it triumphantly home and eventually to the Midlands without one of the plates being cracked, which was something. In this puzzling world it is always a comfort to be of some small practical service to those whom one honours most.

It was nearly a week later, on the last day of September, that we, still in Florence, heard again—this time from Sicily. The Brewsters had been seen off, and the Lawrences had reached Taormina on the night of the 29th in a whirlpool of rain—"but so glad to come to rest, I can't tell you —still like this place best—the sea open to the east, to the heart of the east, away from Europe. I had your letter—it seemed only a moment we saw you—but the sympathy is there. You must come here. . . . Love." [180]

From then till after the middle of February 1922, Lawrence stayed on at Taormina. He was still resolved to go to America, but shrank from the directly westward journey. Neither did he see his way financially clear enough to warrant it.[181]

21 September 1921   Siena

⟨[We must leave tonight—must get to Capri to see the Brewsters who are leaving for India.[182]

Achsah Barlow Brewster

[At] the end of September [1921] Lawrence and his wife came to visit us. Our daughter had been making a herbarium. True botanist and lover of flowers, he went over the pages carefully, correcting, enlarging the labels, treating the collection with the dignity due a child of eight, which was fully appreciated by the little girl, who accepted him full-heartedly. She brought out a volume of short stories written and illustrated by herself and read *The Cat's Mother* to him, whereupon he announced that he could do the same thing, launching forth into a long yarn. I remember nothing of it except the amusement and pleasure it left, and that it kept on and on.

One evening his wife, Frieda, induced him to describe a concert in which an aesthetic lady played upon the psaltery.[183] Lawrence rose languidly, arranging imaginary robes that flowed and trailed around him, seating himself gracefully and played with languishing movements long arpeggios upon the psaltery, chanting in an ecstatic voice. Cadences rushed into crescendo and lulled away into rapt silences where he sat with his hands clasped over the imaginary psaltery, his eyes closed in rapture. Full poems were chanted and gracious encores given in this amazing performance.

A canvas of St. Francis preaching to the birds was tacked up on the studio wall. Lawrence stood still and asked fiercely why that miserable-looking fellow had been painted, to which I rejoined that friends said it looked like him, D. H. Lawrence. I agreed that it did. He made a wry face and wanted to know why it was abstract, since people cannot be abstract, and there ensued a discussion on hieratic art.

He burst forth: "You three are just sitting upon rosy clouds. Look out that they don't let you down. At any rate you'll get a good dampening and catch cold."

They left going south to Taormina, their arms full of presents for the *contadina* family at Fontana Vecchia; something for Ciccio and Ciccia, and Ciccia's baby, and Carmelo, and a dress pattern of black-and-white shepherd's plaid for Grazia, the mother.[184] We asked if Grazia saluted him with a kiss as was her custom.

"Aye, that she does," Lawrence answered, holding up the plaid. "I rather fancy her in a full skirt of this with a bright handkerchief over her head." [185]

Earl H. Brewster

That autumn [September, 1921] Lawrence and his wife visited us for several days on their return journey to Taormina. Only a woman as strong and generous as Mrs. Lawrence, with her love for vital experiences and indifferent to the small things, would have suited Lawrence. He was never happy to be long separated from her. Once, many years later, he remarked to me that in view of the marriages most people make he and I indeed should congratulate ourselves.

After their visit I accompanied the Lawrences to Naples, to see them depart on their southern train. It was very cold; and late that night we had to wait long at the railway station, on a dark and dreary platform: we sat huddled up in shawls and rugs like emigrants. I think there was not much conversation, but I am sure that all three of us, in spite of bodily weariness, enjoyed that experience. If the vicissitudes of travel are to be removed, where is the adventure of it? Lawrence, I often noticed in the years to come, seemed to dislike comfort and to relish discomforts as though they belonged to a reality which he preferred. I felt on that dreary platform something passed between the three of us which made us realize our friendship more deeply than before, and gave us the promise of its endurance.

Soon came the first letters from Sicily. We were leaving for Ceylon: Lawrence sent me as a parting gift his *Psychoanalysis and the Unconscious*, which had just been published.[186] Old wine in new bottles indeed—this ancient Hindu conception of the "chakras," interpreted by a modern genius.[187]

28 September 1921   Villa Fontana Vecchia, Taormina

❲ Got here in the dark and rain of last night. But how lovely it is here! I'm sure you've forgotten: the great window of the eastern sky, seaward. I like it much the best of any place in Italy: and adore Fontana Vecchia.

But my heart and my soul are broken, in Europe. It's no use, the threads are broken. I will go east, intending ultimately to go west, as soon as I can get a ship: that is before March. I would come in January for sure, if one could be sure of ships. I had better wait for my tramp steamer, because I should have to go Very Gently, monetarily.

.   .   .   .

I am so glad we came to Capri. Let us pitch our tents side by side in the howling wilderness of these christian countries. Let us go from this Sodom of angels like Lot and Abraham, before the fire falls.[188]

8 October 1921   Villa Fontana Vecchia, Taormina

⟨ My plan is, ultimately, to get a little farm somewhere by myself, in Mexico, New Mexico, Rocky Mountains, or British Columbia. The desire to be away from the body of mankind—to be a bit of a hermit—is paramount. In the old world, even of Buddha, I have no deep hope. But I would like to see it, too, and speak with it.

. . . .

I would much rather approach America from the Pacific than from the Atlantic.[189]

9 October 1921   Villa Fontana Vecchia, Taormina

⟨ After all the shifting about, we are both so glad to be back here, in silence and peace and sunshine. It is lovely weather. The sun rises day after day red and unhidden out of the sea, after the morning star, which is very bright before he comes. I watch the dawn every day from my bed: but when the suns rim makes the first bit of fire, we get up—I love the Ionian sea. It is open like a great blue opening in front of us, so delicate and self-contained. The hibiscus flowers are coming again in the garden. I am so thankful to come south. The north just shatters one inside. Even as far as Naples. But south of Naples—from Amalfi—there is the pristine Mediterranean influence, never to be shattered. Such a lovely morning world: forever morning. I hate going north and I hate snow grinning on the tops of mountains. Jamais plus.

. . . .

Do you have any feeling about Mexico? I have an idea I should like to go there—and have some little place in the country, with a goat and a bit of a garden. But my compass-needle is a shifty devil.[190]

Fontana Vecchia/Taormina/Sicilia/12 October 1921

⟨ Dear [Violet] Monk [Stevens],
     I wanted to write sooner, of course. But we only got back about ten

days ago, and then my cheque-book was empty and I had to write for a new one: which arrived yesterday. Thank you so much for doing the "Gentleman" [191] and sending him off. If you think a pound is right, then I am sure it is. I am sorry I have been so long—but I waited from day to day, as one does.

I wonder what you have called your bungalow. Rome is too big. Call it Capricorn, the Sign of the Goat—or The Triangle, for its three inmates —or call it after a tree, if it's got a nice tree: The Pear Tree, The Fir Tree, The Maple Tree: —or call it Coney Grey if it's got rabbits: or Thorny Croft, if it's got thorns: or Whin Meadows, if it's got gorse like the last: or Maiden Place, if you want to make a joke on yourselves. Do call it Maiden Place.

We are so thankful to be back and settled down a bit: arrived so tired and battered after so many journeys. Another year I simply will not do it.

It is lovely here: brilliant sun all day long, and perfect warm nights with the moon just leaving the sea. It seems like July was, further north. No end to the summer this year. I am hoping really to do some work, but don't feel much like it.

I wish I could send you something for the new house. Only the post is such a curse. I suppose you have got furniture more than enough.

You sound a groggy couple as far as health goes. You want somebody to make you both real cross, twice a day, and the sciatica and the rheumatism would go. But Berkshire is a dozy country. I feel my summer travels didn't do much more than put me in a perfect fury with everything. But then that's the effect most things have on me. The older I get, the angrier I become, generally. And Italy is a country to keep you in a temper from day to day: the people, I mean.

Here they are waiting for the rains, to plough and to sow the seeds and put in potatoes and everything. But luckily it rained a good deal in September, so we have spinach and cabbages and carrots. At the moment it doesn't look as if it would ever rain again. We are eating the last figs and grapes and melons: and the first pomegranates. But the damned goats are all going to have kids, so there's no milk. And there's never any butter, except tinned, from Milan.

Well, I hope it is still summery at Hermitage. This is a lovely time there, when there are chestnuts and the woods are yellow. Do you remember when we went to Evie Burgess' [192] for tea—after finding rather little chestnuts? It seems so much darker and colder, even to think of it. We don't dream of a fire yet: cook on just a handful of charcoal, which you fan with a fan to make it hot: and even that makes the kitchen too warm.

Greet the Lambert.[193] *Tell her she is not to look lamentable over her glasses. Greet also Miss Furlong,[194] who is the only brisk one among you. And don't you hobble about like a witch in gaiters.*

D. H. Lawrence [195]

24 October 1921   Villa Fontana Vecchia, Taormina

Here, of course, it is like a continental Mad Hatter's tea-party. If you'll let it be, it is all tea-party—and you wonder who on earth is going head over heels into the teapot next. On Saturday we were summoned to a gathering of Britons to discuss the erection of an English church here, at the estimated cost of £25,000 sterling—signed Bronte: which means, of course, Alec Nelson-Hood, Duca di Bronte. I didn't go, fearing they might ask me for the £25,000.[196]

Jan Juta

I remember we were sitting on the terrace in the afterglow of the sunset. Below us the almond trees in scented profusion flowed down the slopes of the mountain to the darkening sea—the blue Mediterranean that washes the shores of Sicily; while above us, high under Heaven, floated the icy peak of Mount Etna, the "paradox of smoking snow," with her tall plume of smoke curling a white question mark into the ether. I knew the moment had come to which I had made up my mind—the moment I had rather avoided—when I would broach the subject of painting a portrait of my host. He had rented the lonely farmhouse where we were, not only as a safe retreat from the society of a world which did not usually receive him kindly, but because he knew that to fulfill his own way of life he must live apart and out of the usual pattern. And there among the old world trees and neglected garden terraces set on the outskirts of the town of Taormina, he felt he had found a haven.

I had wanted to paint his portrait ever since we had met. For not only did his appearance interest me, but his individuality so intrigued me that I longed to try to capture in paint the enigma of his character. I had not known him for long, though our friendship had grown very naturally out of a kindly interest on his part, and an inquisitive admiration on mine. I was still an unknown student studying in Rome, and of no importance among the noted friends who had formed a rather closed circle around their "prophet." So I was hesitant to ask this favor of him, though from the first moment of our meeting (January, 1920) I had fallen under the spell of his extraordinary personality, this much criticized, admired, tortured crusader who was David Herbert Lawrence. He affected people like that. They felt either fascinated or repelled; some grew to resent him, others remained forever faithful to the idea he represented to them. And even those who suffered under the whip lash of his tongue were held, often unwillingly, hypnotised by the "other worldliness" the man projected.

By the time we first met, I had read every word he had published thus far, and though we had few friends in common, I had heard the many contradictory opinions about him that circulated through the artistic circles of London and Paris. Some said he was so "queer," so "ill-mannered," a "revolutionary," a "genius with a perverted mind": all the varied ideas trickling from the pens of the critics, who either acclaimed or abused him, to the intellectuals of Bloomsbury. I had listened to them all, fascinated by this complex individual, and I remembered them in a flash as I met him, small, sparse, red-bearded and shy, and faced his hypnotic grey-blue eyes for the first time. He was not what I had expected; for together with the criticisms had come a somewhat garbled story of his life, and I had pictured him in my mind to suit the story. I remembered he was the son of a miner, born somewhere in Nottinghamshire, England, in very humble circumstances; that he had won several scholarships with ease and become a schoolteacher, and then, prompted by a girl he loved, had evolved as the writer who had startled the world of literary criticism by his extraordinary novels and even stranger poems. Then there had come his great romance with the wife of one of his professors, a German lady of breeding, Frieda von Richthofen, the daughter of a one-time governor of Alsace-Lorraine, a "big, gushing blonde," as her critics described her. People said it had all been very dramatic, the courtship and the divorce, for Frieda was much older than Lawrence, had had three children when they met, and was perfectly content in her established, bourgeois world. When suddenly had come along this strange Galahad, this odd determined man with no money, but more important, with a sort of mission, a man with a vision who swept her completely off her well-set feet.

As I looked at him for the first time, he didn't strike me as the sort of man to have done that, but I couldn't estimate his power then, and I had not yet met Frieda. As I talked to him I kept wondering why he meant so many different things to different people. Now I think I understand. At that time I was mainly aware of being in the presence of something I could not define, let us call it a force, something powerful, yet disciplined, nervous and alive as a flame, a piercing, upward-sweeping flame. And yet his voice belied that force; a strange voice he had, and a little laugh, almost a cackle that left me puzzled.

"You must meet my wife," he had said.

And there was Frieda, with a large smile, green-eyed and handsome, a German mother-type full of conscious womanhood.

"Oh, we know about *you*," she said enthusiastically. "Our friends have told us *much*. You will come and see us *soon?*" She emphasized odd words with a full-rounded accent.

And thus it had all begun.

I often went to the Fontana Vecchia—the "old fountain," as their house was called. It suited Lawrence perfectly, for it was simple, almost primitive, set among fruit trees and ancient twisted olives at the end of a narrow pathway, remote and secluded. The garden is perfectly pictured in Lawrence's own words, when describing his departure for Sardinia in the travel book which I illustrated for him. He wrote:

Very dark under the great carob tree as we go down the steps. Dark still the garden. Scent of mimosa, and then of jasmine. The lovely mimosa tree invisible. Dark the stony path. The goat whinnies out of her shed. The broken Roman tomb which lolls right over the garden track does not fall on me as I slip under its massive tilt. Ah, dark garden, dark garden, with your olives and your wine, your medlars and mulberries and many almond trees, your steep terraces ledged high up above the sea, I am leaving you, slinking out.[197]

When he showed me around the garden he said:

"Only people who really like us will ever bother to come here. It's not smart, thank God, not smart enough for all those pretentious, half-baked neurotics."

His devastating criticisms of the people in the town used to anger me, but instinctively I knew he was right—deep down, perfectly right. It is understandable that I was not encouraged to seek him out, conscious as I was of my own inadequacy from his point of view.

Yet when I did go, it was always a wonderful experience, and I gradually grew to understand him better. Everything became an experience with Lawrence. There was always something new, some fresh illumination on a thousand different things, some surprising bit of knowledge for one to think about and absorb, and after talking to him it was as though the shade of a new window onto life had suddenly been raised, and everything outside appeared quite different, for one saw the world and one's own self magnified in terrifying clarity. His mind was always sensitive and aware of life in a way that was unlike any other I have ever met; for realizing that vision is of the mind and not the eye, he had so disciplined his senses that out of his ordered inner-being his vision became prophetic. He had agreed to sit for me, though I was not sure just in what mood I wanted to depict him. But on that spring day of 1920 when we were to begin, I found him in a strange state of mind, nervous and irritable.

"It's no good, Giannino," he said. "I'm so furious I couldn't possibly sit still, and if I tried, I know you would paint me scarlet all over. Let's go for a walk instead, shall we?"

The walks I took with him remain among my most happy memories of our friendship. For then he was at his best, away and at one with the world of nature to which he was so deeply attached. There were few plants he did not recognize, no flower he didn't stoop to examine and appreciate. He would tell me botanically of its structure, describe its habitat, and then would follow an anecdote or a legend connected with it, perhaps from Greece or Egypt; or it might be that he knew its homeopathic values and its uses to the ancients. But always one learnt from his amazing store of knowledge.

That day I felt he was closed in, cut off from any contact, coiled up within himself in anger. I didn't ask what the matter was, for as we walked along the little mountain path that led up behind the town he started to tell me.

"It's Magnus, worrying me again. Now he has the nerve to ask me again for money, when of course he is staying at the best hotel here, spending all the borrowed cash we have given him . . . ."

"You forget I don't know anything about Magnus," I reminded him. "I've only heard you speak of him."

"Well, he is a poor, pathetic little damned soul. *Finito,* I can tell you. And now he throws his 'memoirs' at me and, believe me, I am to write a foreword to them AND get them published for him . . . . Oh, I could kill him, he makes my bowels boil with fury . . . ."

"Why do you have to worry about him? From what I have gathered, you have surely done enough for him."

"I don't know, except that I suppose I am a fool and fall for all his sob stuff, because actually I hate everything he represents . . . ."

I didn't know the story of Magnus until much later, though I met him several times while he was visiting Taormina in that month of May, 1920.

Nor did I fully realize how Lawrence, half willingly it seemed to me, had been victimized by this friend of Norman Douglas. The whole dispute between Lawrence and Douglas on the subject of Magnus is now ancient history. Their literary sword play will stand among the most brilliantly written arguments in contemporary writing, and among the best polemics either of these two famous authors ever produced.

For Lawrence's sake I was to become involved in the Magnus affair more than I ever wished to be, but only one incident connected with it need be recorded. Later Lawrence gave me the famous memoirs to read and criticize, asking me if I could suggest any publisher of my acquaintance who might be interested in producing it. I told him I felt sure no publisher would touch it in its then existing form, but I did mention my interest in some of the writing, particularly the delineation of a certain character who played a leading role in the whole, strange story of the Foreign Legion. Many years later I was a guest in the house of a well-known French authoress, and to my surprise saw a copy of the memoirs lying on the table, though I knew it had eventually been published in an expurgated form, thanks to Lawrence and the famous foreword. I mentioned that I had read the manuscript in its original state, and talked of how impressed I had been by the description of the principal character, remembering every detail of his complex personality.

"Say no more, *mon cher,*" my hostess interrupted, "for now I have the great pleasure of introducing you to him," as Colonel X, tall, grey-haired and distinguished, walked into the room. I need hardly add that I was dumbfounded, never having expected to meet him in the flesh. He seemed quite unlike the character in the book however, and though taken off guard, I naturally never mentioned my acquaintance with the unfortunate author of the memoirs.

Though I tried several times that spring to get Lawrence to pose for me, I managed only a charcoal sketch for the oil portrait I had in mind, either because we were all too busy enjoying Sicily, or because I was too uncertain to force the issue. It was not that he was difficult to paint, but that I could not make up my mind which of the facets of his personality I felt most representative. It was this complexity that baffled so many who, meeting him superficially, so easily misunderstood him. For he was witty, critical, even biting at times, yet underneath it all lay an intense sadness, as though his spirit was longing for release into the light out of the dark shadow that seemed to envelop a part of him. Perhaps it was his illness, perhaps just the weight of his discerning understanding. For there were times when he sat quite still, thinking, or looking with his penetrating eyes into the troubled future, and then he seemed like another being, remote and uplifted. It was this aspect of Lawrence I tried to capture in my charcoal sketch done at Taormina that spring, the Lawrence I saw in my mind's eye as I sat with him on the terrace.

But, reluctantly, I had to leave for Rome without having fulfilled my wish to paint him. In August, 1920, while he was visiting me at Anticoli Corrado, Província di Roma, I made the sketch reproduced in the original Heinemann edition (1932) of the Lawrence *Letters*,[198] but it was another Lawrence I saw then, another aspect I tried to convey.

In early January, 1921, Lawrence and Frieda made their trip to Sardinia. Alan Insole and I met them in Rome on their return, and within the month followed them to Taormina. Lawrence and I had originally planned to visit Sardinia together, so that I might gather the material for my illustrations for *Sea and Sardinia*. As events turned out, I went to Sardinia alone in April; Lawrence had abandoned the plan to go with me, thinking it best I should gather my own impressions of the island alone.

During that brief visit we had much to discuss, considering the various colour printing processes our publisher had suggested. D. H. liked my ideas, and was determined that the projected paintings would get the best possible reproduction in his book. Perhaps it was all the business correspondence involved that troubled him, or possibly a memory of Sardinia that provoked his state of mind, for the island had puzzled and disturbed him. But whatever the cause I saw him again in the mood I had tried to express in my charcoal study, and fearing it might be my last opportunity, in as much as the pattern of life was then so uncertain, I managed to get him to pose for me, and in one sitting painted the portrait I had longed to paint.[199]

There was one other occasion when I saw Lawrence as I had tried to paint him—the man with a vision in his eyes. It was after a tea party given to discuss the raising of funds for the Church in the town, and I had joined the Lawrences for supper at the Fontana Vecchia. All the colony, British and foreign alike, had been invited to the villa of Sir Alexander Nelson-Hood, commonly known as the "Duca." For he had inherited the title of Duca di Bronte, whose ancient castle and domain called "Maniace," set on the rugged slopes of Mount Etna, had been presented together with the title to his ancestor, Lord Nelson, by a Sicily grateful for his many services rendered.[200]

The Duca, aged from long service in the royal household of Queen Alexandra of England, lived in a modernised villa with his sister, Mrs.

Evans, who patterned her every gesture, as well as her coiffure, on the "dear Queen" whose beauty she did not, unfortunately, share.

Everybody came to tea except the much-expected Lawrences. There was the Dutch lady, who lived in a studio and had enjoyed a classical art education, but who was terrified of Lawrence and his ideas on art; the English lady in a large picture hat and flowing "bombazine" dress, who upheld the Church of England in more ways than one, and each Sunday at eleven o'clock noted everyone who did not attend the service; the American painter and his friend, who gave lavish parties in their luxurious house where everyone gossiped and drank far too much; the German photographer, whose doubtful morals caused whispered reports at every street corner because his pictures were only shown to "special" friends; and among the varied group a little lady, Mary Cannan, who had once been the quite famous wife of Sir James Barrie, but whose later romantic attachment to Gilbert Cannan, a rising literary star, had left her somewhat disillusioned, though still attractive and conscious always of her feminine charms. She was the one real friend of the Lawrences at the party, for she had known them from the beginning, and despite flashes of violent jealousy from Frieda, had encouraged and helped D. H. from a sincere admiration for his genius.

We waited anxiously for Lawrence to appear, each in his own way prepared for the unexpected which one usually got from talking to him. But he never came, perhaps wisely; and the Duca, rather hurt by this lack of consideration he felt was his due, retired behind a barrage of Victorian invectives against this "queer-mannered fellow," who was, from his point of view, "just as well out of our picture."

Mrs. Evans was "more than relieved," she told me as she smoothed out her latest piece of embroidery. For this lady spent most of her time trying to interpret in embroidery what she described as "the pink upon the blue," by which one gathered she meant the effect of the pink almond blossoms seen against the sparkling blue of the Mediterranean—a lovely subject, no doubt, but one hardly suited to her medium. She produced numerous pieces of blue satin of different sizes covered with pink silk flowers in haphazard design, stitched in classic precision to produce hideous results, all destined to become cushion covers for unfortunate English friends.

"I can't talk to him at all," she confided to me. "He makes me so uncomfortable! His beard, too, is so very red, isn't it? . . . And his wife reminds me too much of my early visits to the Kaiser's court, and all those gross Germans . . . ."

How we laughed, when later I tactfully described the party to the Lawrences, as we sat looking out onto the sunset sea.

"Be careful, Gianni Schicchi," Lawrence admonished me with a nickname, "they will kill you yet. They are all dead, remember, and they don't want anyone to live, not really live. Be careful, or they will get you, and they are filled with nothing but pretensions and compromise, nothing real, all sawdust in boiled shirts."

I felt he was probably right, for his eye saw right through to the core of people; hence their discomfort, and his disillusion at finding them so often full of the things he despised.

"But don't you give in," he went on, "or ever give up. We've got to be game right to the very end."

This from a man who even then, though I didn't realize it, was gradually dying of tuberculosis—a fighter who was indeed game to his last breath, determined not to yield his body any more than his principles to the attacks of the enemy.

I thought of his unusual type of courage as I watched him moving quietly, rhythmically clearing away the plates and filling our glasses with the *vino rosso* I had brought as a contribution to the feast. For he did everything in a sort of easy rhythm with the orderly neatness of the disciplined artist, from chopping wood to cooking the spaghetti, while in between writing copious letters to his far-flung friends, and rewriting for the third or fourth time his latest novel. Frieda watched him also, watched him doing most of the work, smiling securely, preparing her armour for her next attack on the defenses of this elusive man, her husband. For I soon discovered that even she who loved him, disturbed by his continual fight against the world which he waged in order to stick to his principles, was not prepared to let him thus elude her. He admired the fighting spirit in her, but was confident he could always beat her down. And there were scenes of cold anger and floods of tears which gave rise to the rumour that they were not happy together. It was not true, for they were amazingly happy through every sort of difficulty, welded in a way most people could not understand. But Lawrence's unwillingness to compromise or break faith with the truth of himself roused even his wife to a sort of jealousy. I gradually understood all this as I got to know them better; and as I learnt from him and questioned more, I began to appreciate the rare, pure innocence of his heart which added so much more to the weight of his cross than to his happiness.

For he was aware of his pilgrimage, aware of his aloneness and of the enmity his ideas engendered. And he longed to find the company of a few others who would go along with him, fight with him, believe as he did and live the truth he lived. But he couldn't find them, though he never ceased to search.

I can still hear his cry of almost desperate longing on that very evening, as he gazed out over the sea, straining his eyes as if to catch a glimpse of what he sought beyond the dark coast of Calabria:

"Why, oh why can't we find a little ship and sail away to an island, a Greek island, perhaps, or somewhere remote where we can start afresh and build a new way of life?"

It was the first of many such expressed longings I was to hear from him. But I was one of those who failed him; for though I believed then in his ideal I was not prepared to leave everything and go. One by one most of his friends failed to respond to his appeal to come away from the world with him, and he was left to try to live it alone with Frieda, and die in the effort, a savage messiah with a message no one seemed to want.

And it was at that moment that I knew this was the real Lawrence I had tried to portray. For this was a basic aspect of his whole character, this seeker-after-a-new-way, not the brilliant, sometimes mischievous revolutionary, upsetting the pattern of life in his effort to point the way, but the Lawrence with a vision in his eyes of a world of beauty, where in awful majesty the truth would reign.[201]

John Bull on *Women in Love*
(17 September 1921)

A BOOK THE POLICE SHOULD BAN.

LOATHSOME STUDY OF SEX DEPRAVITY—MISLEADING YOUTH TO UNSPEAKABLE DISASTER.

By W. Charles Pilley, Assistant Editor.

In a general way I have no use for a State censorship of literature. Within broad limits I am all for the freedom of the Press as applied not simply to newspapers, but to the larger realm of fiction. As long as the common restraints of decency are observed, I think the novelist should enjoy the wildest liberty to portray life as he sees it and to limn upon the canvas of the printed page the whole moving drama of human passion. Nevertheless, like other civilised communities we have laws against obscenity which must be rigorously enforced. For this purpose the ordinary law is entirely sufficient if only it is administered sensibly, and without respect of persons. It is not enough to keep a sharp eye upon picture-postcard shops and to terrorise small boys who chalk ribald nonsense on blank walls. When a publisher like Mr. Martin Secker sends out a novel by Mr. D. H. Lawrence which flouts the most elementary canons of decency, the police should be equally alert. It should be remembered, moreover, that Mr. Lawrence is an old offender, and that the edition of his former book, *The Rainbow,* was unceremoniously seized by the police. Undeterred by this experience, Mr. Lawrence has penned another novel, *Women in Love,* which justly merits the fate of its predecessor. I do not claim to be a literary critic, but I know dirt when I smell it and here it is in heaps—festering, putrid heaps which smell to high Heaven.

An Obscene Study.

The title of the novel is misleading, probably of set purpose, for if the author had labelled his literary production more aptly it is doubtful whether Mr. Martin Secker would have taken the risk of publication. I am not going to say that the book is without merit. As a study of certain loathsome forms of mental disease it is thorough and painstaking, and I am not sure that Mr. Lawrence does not deserve some form of special recognition from the Royal College of Physicians. Most of his characters are obviously mad. They do and say the sort of things for which living people are shut up in lunatic asylums. It is not honest animalism that is portrayed. That might pass muster. What Mr. Lawrence has given us is an analytical study of sexual depravity, the more repulsive from the fact that he seems to gloat over its production and to take a positive delight in exhibiting a natural human instinct in its most odious and distorted shape. The female characters of the book are not "women in love"; they are creatures in whom the long repression of the sex instinct has produced the sort of mania that psychologists are familiar with in the pages of Freud and of such English writers as Mr. Havelock Ellis. It is ugly, repellent, vile.

The Borderland of Crime.

In real life we should not be troubled with Mr. Lawrence's characters —they would be safely under lock and key. For instance, there is the idiot who undresses and wallows in wet grass, delighting to have his back scratched with thistles and his skin lacerated with the sharp points of fir cones. Doctors have a name for this sort of thing which at the moment I do not recall. Then there is the female degenerate who half kills her lover in a fit of frenzy and as she strikes the blow feels "a delirium of pleasure" because, as she tells herself, she is "going at last to her consummation of voluptuous ecstasy." We know well enough where this sort of thing leads to in real life. Criminal lawyers know all about it. It is precisely the mania that keeps the gaols full and the hangman busy. But Mr. Lawrence is obsessed with the loathsome thing, and returns to it again and again, tries it the other way round, sets a man at a woman's throat and records his maniacal sensation of "what a perfect voluptuous fulfilment it would be to kill her." The book reeks of these Bedlam horrors. In its pages one can trace a reflection of every perverted instinct that ever vexed the mind of man or tortured the soul of woman. It is an epic of vice. The main episode of the novel deals with the relations of two men, Gerald and Birkin, and is nothing more or less than a shameful glorification of that state of mind which in practice, as every student of crime is aware, leads to conduct which is condemned by the criminal law. The chapter headed "Gladia-torial" is sheer filth from beginning to end, and I pay Mr. Lawrence the compliment of saying that no other novelist than he could have written it. This is the sort of book which in the hands of a boy in his teens might pave the way to unspeakable moral disaster.

The Police Must Act.

If *The Rainbow* was an indecent book this later production is an obscene abomination. The police must act. I have no sympathy with either the publisher or with the author, one of whom knew, and the other ought to have known, the kind of stuff he was trying to foist off on an unsuspecting public. I do not hold the "apron string" theory of youth which assumes that young people can be kept in ignorance of essential facts of life till they reach the adult stage, but I cannot sit idly by and see this neurotic production exposed for sale on the bookstalls as a "novel." It is nothing of the sort. It is a shameless study of sex depravity which in direct proportion to the skill of its literary execution becomes unmentionably vile.[202]

25 October 1921   *Villa Fontana Vecchia, Taormina*

⟨ *I have had Secker very sick, over the John Bull article, and still worse, over a fellow who wants to bring a libel action because he says he's Halli-day. Don't know how it will all end. Snotty little lot of people.*[203]

Philip Heseltine (Peter Warlock)
as told by Cecil Gray

In the autumn of 1921 was published at last the novel of D. H. Lawrence already referred to, *Women in Love,* in which there appeared a malignant and scurrilous caricature of Philip [Heseltine]. This in itself was not a surprise to him, for I had read the book in manuscript shortly after it was finished, as early as 1917, and had acquainted Philip with its contents. He can hardly have been prepared, however, for the extraordinarily venomous character of the libel, and there is no doubt that he was deeply wounded by it. It will be necessary to go into this question also more exhaustively than would otherwise be desirable on account of the indiscretions of another authoress (why must women write books?)—Mrs. Catherine Carswell—who writes as follows in her study of Lawrence entitled *The Savage Pilgrimage:* "Secker had to inform Lawrence that Philip Heseltine, who was no longer friendly towards him, was threatening a libel action, alleging that the Halliday of the novel was a portrait of himself, which in fact it was, though Lawrence modified the character and altered the complexion for the English edition. In law, I believe Heseltine's case was very dubious; but there was already trouble enough about the book, and for peace sake Secker paid him £50 as solatium for injury to feelings and reputation." [204]

As a misunderstanding of facts this is hard to beat. We see clearly from the letters . . . that Philip not only retained a warm admiration for Lawrence as an artist, but also a personal regard for the man, and nothing had happened in the years subsequent to the writing of these letters to alter his feelings. He only ceased to be friendly towards Lawrence on the publication of this offensive lampoon. Secondly, Lawrence did not modify the character and alter the complexion for the English edition until compelled to do so, as a result of the legal proceedings threatened by Philip, in consequence of which the original edition was withdrawn by the publishers,[205] and emendations made in the text. Thirdly, if "his case was dubious," it can only have been so on account of some legal quibble, some technical defect in the law of libel as it exists in this country [England], for there could on the face of it be no clearer case of defamation of character, maliciously perpetrated, than is contained in the passages in question. Lastly, the offensive innuendo contained in Mrs. Carswell's concluding sentence, to the effect that Philip was content to accept £50 as sufficient compensation for injury to feelings and reputation, is absolutely untrue, as the following extracts from letters written by Philip to his solicitors will show.

I should be glad if you would press the claim for damages in respect of the libels in copies already sold as far as ever you can without involving me in great expense or embarking upon an actual case. I can't afford to fight them, but it will be as well to give Mr. Secker and the author the impression that proceedings will certainly be taken if the matter cannot be settled out of court. I leave it to you to decide the proper sum to be claimed as damages. . . . These (alterations) are ridiculously inadequate and make little difference to the libel. But surely the withdrawal of the book from circulation and the submitting of a proof (in Lawrence's handwriting) containing alterations in the personal descriptions,[206] constitutes an admission of the charge of libel on the part of both author and publisher? This seems to me important and I should like to have your opinion as to how much the submitting of this proof implies, legally. If it constitutes an admission of the charge, as I suspect, then we may safely go ahead, not only in claiming damages in respect of copies already sold, but also in threatening further proceedings should the book be reissued even with the suggested alterations. If you look at these corrections you will see that they make no material difference. The circumstances and the situations remain the same.

I am inclined to accept the proposals as regards the alterations—because I fear that further demands for excisions might lead to a case in court which I could not afford—and partly because I am convinced that the second edition will be no less obscene than the first and can therefore be easily suppressed on public grounds. . . . I consider that the libels are not removed by the suggested alterations and cannot be removed except by the omission of the characters altogether. Were the character of the book other than it is, I should press the demand for their omission, since the libel is now clearly admitted by Mr. Secker. But as the second edition will without doubt provide a case for police intervention on general grounds of obscenity (there is almost enough evidence of it in the two chapters submitted in proof) I propose . . . to take such steps as may be necessary to get the book totally suppressed by the police when it next appears. . . . Another reason for not pressing the matter of excisions further is that, if it came to a case, my wife would be an essential witness and I have now finally separated from her.

. . . I purposely left in certain passages which in other circumstances I should have insisted on getting omitted, in order that there should be no dearth of evidence of certain tendencies for which to get the book suppressed by the police. Will you please communicate with Scotland Yard again immediately. Every day's delay is bound to make a difference to the circulation of the book, and I am most anxious that action should be taken in the matter at the earliest possible moment.

Apart from the chapters containing the libels, the second edition does not differ in any way from the first, and if ever a book afforded grounds for prosecution on a charge of morbid obscenity in general and the glorification of homosexuality in particular, this one does.

. . . If Scotland Yard proves dilatory, could you not address a communication to the National Council of Public Morals, urging them to take the matter up and press for police action?

Apart from the exquisitely subtle humour of the last extract (the idea of Philip of all people invoking the activities of the National Council of Public Morals is too rare for laughter—it should be reverently savoured, like the delicate bouquet of a fine old wine) it clearly appears that he was only deterred from bringing an action by lack of funds, the technical impossibility of proving special damage, and his unwillingness to bring his wife into the case. Moreover, so far from being satisfied with the £50 [207] he did not, after receiving it, relax his efforts to have the book suppressed, not merely on personal grounds but as a matter of public interest.

Neither the police nor the National Council took any active steps in the matter; nevertheless part at least of his objective had been attained. The book had been withdrawn and considerably re-written, and his victory was celebrated in a triumphal war-chant which he sent me at the conclusion of the negotiations:

> Come, fill a vial with vintage, *vieux et sec*
>   Fit for the King of Thule's golden *Becher;*
> Get half-seas-over—swamp the blooming deck.
>   Swill swipes, swig swizzle, singing
>   "SUCKS TO SECKER"!

The alterations to which he had assented *faute de mieux,* however, were, as he himself rightly observed, of the most trivial and unimportant kind, consisting chiefly in slight changes of physical description, dark hair being substituted for fair, and so on, but leaving the grossness of the libel fundamentally unimpaired. The caricature, even in the revised version, remains clearly identifiable.

The whole question as to the extent to which an author is entitled to put living persons into a work of fiction is an exceedingly difficult one to decide. Admittedly one cannot expect the novelist to work entirely *in vacuo;* his work is bound to reflect to some degree his personal experience, and the characters he creates, if they are to have any semblance of reality at all, will inevitably possess traits identical with or similar to those of people with whom he has at some time or other come into contact. It is even possible that a straightforward, veracious portrait is comparatively unexceptionable; what one objects to chiefly in Lawrence's innumerable caricatures of his best friends is the spiteful way in which he combines truth and fiction, not merely exaggerating slight defects out of all proportion but also grafting others of his own invention on to the original. A curious and psychologically interesting example of this is to be found in the fact that he represents Philip, in the person of Halliday in the novel, as speaking always in a high-pitched, hysterical squeal or squeak. Actually he had rather a deep and sonorous voice; it was Lawrence himself who in real life perpetually squeaked and squealed in a ridiculous manner, like a eunuch. To ascribe thus one's own ludicrous or revolting peculiarities to one's friends is going a little too far, I think it will be admitted. Again, Lawrence does not merely confine himself to the recording and distorting of incidents which actually took place, but goes out of his way to introduce imaginary ones of inherent plausibility in order to make the conduct of the actors in them seem the more objectionable. Norman Douglas, in his admirable pamphlet *D. H. Lawrence and Maurice Magnus*[,] complains of the way in which Lawrence has recognizably portrayed him in one of his novels and then put into his mouth uncomplimentary and spiteful remarks about his friends, also readily identifiable, which he never made. So with Philip. In Chapter XXVIII of *Women in Love* an incident is recounted in which Halliday (Philip) is represented as reading aloud a private and personal letter which he has received from Birkin (Lawrence himself), to a sniggering bunch of cronies in what is obviously meant to be the Café Royal; whereupon a thinly disguised Katherine Mansfield comes up and snatches the letter from his hand in a transport of heroic indignation, and marches out of the place with it. So plausibly is it told, and so realistic and lifelike are the details, down even to the mock clerical voice in which Halliday reads out the letter—frequently adopted by Philip in satirical vein—that even knowing Lawrence and his methods it never occurred to me to doubt the substantial accuracy of the account until I came across the version of the incident given by Mr. Middleton Murry in his *Reminiscences of D. H. Lawrence;* [208] according to which it appears that it was not a letter that was being read out, but poems from Lawrence's recently published *Amores*. This made me suspicious, because Philip at the time in question still admired Lawrence's work, and I remember well his enthusiasm over this particular volume when it was first published [1916]. I therefore wrote to Mr. Murry and asked him if he could say for certain whether Philip was one of the participants in the scene. He replied that he could not, but referred me to two eyewitnesses, one of whom, Mr. Koteliansky, was able to assure me quite definitely that Philip was not one of the party.[209]

So here we have Lawrence deliberately ascribing to Philip an unworthy act of which he was entirely innocent—or I should say rather what he intends to be regarded as an unworthy act, for, frankly, it does not seem to me personally such a heinous offence to laugh at letters, or even poems, of Lawrence. One had to be singularly humourless, indeed, not to laugh at Lawrence on occasion. Mr. Murry, however, waxes indignant that "his passionate poems should be jeered at by the *canaille*," [210] and there may be others who think so. Well, all I can say is that if there is any *canaille* concerned in the matter, the term is more appropriately to be ascribed to the writer who is capable of such a cowardly and treacherous betrayal, such a stab in the back of a loyal and devoted friend, as the whole of the Halliday episode in *Women in Love*. There is not even the excuse of artistic justification, for the whole episode is dragged in in such a way as to constitute a formal blot on the work as great as that which it confers on Lawrence's reputation as a man. It is painful for me to have to say this, for I knew Lawrence well and cared for him deeply at one time; but in justice to the memory of one for whom I cared more, I have no choice.

It may be thought that all this is trivial, unimportant, unnecessary, but I think that a moment's reflection will show that it is not so. One has only to recall the case of poor Leigh Hunt, a writer of talent and in many ways an admirable man, condemned to go down to posterity in the cruel caricature of him made by Dickens in the person of Harold Skimpole; and since Mrs. Carswell has seen fit to put it on record that Halliday is a portrait of Philip Heseltine it is my obvious duty to point out that the unpleasant person he is represented to be in the pages of Lawrence is a malignant caricature, bearing only the remotest and most deceptive resemblance to actuality. I do not suggest that Lawrence is an artist of the same stature as Dickens, but it is surely none the less true that, despite the flagrant over-estimation of him at the present time [i.e., 1934] which will inevitably bring an equally violent reaction in the opposite direction at no far distant date, he is destined to be regarded as one of the most important writers of his time. The danger, therefore, to which I have alluded, is by no means imaginary.

It is a remarkable fact that Philip should have served as a model for characters created by the two most talented writers of their respective generations in this country: by D. H. Lawrence in *Women in Love* and by Aldous Huxley in *Antic Hay*, which appeared two years later, in 1923.

One of the chief characters in the book, indeed, the young man named Coleman with a blond fan-shaped beard and bright blue eyes, "smiling equivocally and disquietingly as though his mind were full of some nameless and fantastic malice," who enters the Soho restaurant in Chapter IV with a peal of diabolic laughter—this is none other than Philip. More than that, it is true to say that he is the most important, as he is certainly the most vivid and arresting, character in the book, for the slender plot—if plot it can be called—is chiefly woven around the beard of which he was the possessor.

I can even recall quite clearly the occasion on which the central idea for the book presented itself to Huxley. One evening in the summer of 1922, after a Promenade Concert at which Philip and I came across Huxley in company with Eugène Goossens,[211] we all went to Verrey's Café in Regent Street for a drink, and there, in answer to a question asking why he had grown a beard, Philip made a witty and brilliant speech of which the essence is reproduced in the book. His inveterate propensity, moreover, for making outrageous puns and plays on words has undoubtedly suggested to Huxley many of the most entertaining witticisms in his book. "Where the hormones, there moan I," "I long for progeny, I live in hopes. I stope against Stopes," and many similar others, are all in the authentic Philippic tradition.

It is very curious that the same personality should serve as a model to two such talented writers as Lawrence and Huxley for such diametrically opposed creations as Halliday and Coleman. Lawrence depicts a pitifully weak, irresolute, ridiculous, soft, effeminate nonentity; Huxley a virile, sinister, diabolic monster of vice and iniquity, and the contradiction extends down to the smallest details. The explanation, of course, is, as I have already suggested, that they were two entirely different people. Lawrence saw the one, Huxley the other. And it is curiously significant that, deeply though Philip had resented Lawrence's caricature of him, he was positively delighted with that of Huxley; the reason being that, whereas Lawrence's caricature was a caricature of his intrinsic inner self—Philip Heseltine—that of Huxley was a caricature, or rather an enhancement of the fictitious, secondary personality which he had built up for himself and as which he wished to be taken by the world—Peter Warlock. Coleman, in fact, is Peter Warlock raised to the nth power, Peter Warlock as he wished to be; Halliday is Philip Heseltine reduced to a monad of negativity.

At the same time, however, probably without being aware of it, Huxley has drawn a remarkably resembling portrait of the pre-Warlock Philip in the person of the hero or central figure of the novel, Gumbril, the Mild and Melancholy one who, inspired by the example of Coleman, buys himself a false beard, and is thereby straightway transformed into the Complete Man.

Fan-shaped, blond, mounted on gauze and guaranteed undetectable, it arrived from the wig-maker, preciously packed in a stout cardboard box six times too large for it and accompanied by a quarter of a pint of the choicest spirit gum. In the privacy of his bedroom Gumbril uncoffined it, held it out for his own admiration, caressed its silkiness, and finally tried it on, holding it provisionally to his chin, in front of the looking-glass. The effect, he decided immediately, was stunning, was grandiose. From melancholy and all-too-mild he saw himself transformed into a sort of jovial Henry VIII, into a massive Rabelaisian man, broad and powerful and exuberant with vitality and hair—great eater, deep drinker, stout fighter, prodigious lover—Cautiously and with neat, meticulous fingers he adjusted the transformation to his gummed face, pressed it firmly, held it while it stuck fast—One last look at the Complete Man, one final and definitive constatation that the Mild and Melancholy one was, for the time at least, no more; and he was ready in all confidence to set out.

The parallel is revealingly close, for it was in precisely this way that Peter Warlock first came into existence, the only difference being that he grew his beard instead of buying it at Clarkson's. If the reader will turn . . . to the letter written to Colin Taylor [212] from Ireland . . . he will find a quite remarkable adumbration of the experience of Huxley's Gumbril. . . .

July 19th, 1918

. . . .

P.S. The fungus is cultivated for a purely talismanic purpose; as such it works, and this is more important to me than mere appearance. I can't help what I look like, and after all I haven't got such a jaw to boast of! But quite seriously, it does have a certain psychological effect on me; and seeing that now for nearly ten years all my best strength and energy has been used up negatively in keeping out the tide of the world which wants to swamp me and prevent me from doing the only kind of work I can do with any success (and, just now, more than ever, everything is against me, and more than ever I want my whole time and strength for my work)—in view of this fact, it is necessary for me to make use of any little magical energy-saving devices that suggest themselves—and this is one of them.[213]

. . . .

This is what Peter Warlock essentially was—a protection, a façade, a mask, a carapace, a defence erected against a hostile world by a gentle, sensitive nature to whom life had well nigh become unbearable without it. In one of the fragmentary and desultory diaries which he kept from time to time I find the following entry:—"Fourth beard begun; last shave October 23rd, 1921 (nine weeks by Christmas, ten by New Year's Day)"; he was never again without a beard, and from that time the definite ascendancy of Peter Warlock dates, both the man and the musician, the legend and the composer. Up till 1921 Peter Warlock had been merely a convenient pseudonym . . . ; the music written over that signature previous to that date was a pure self-expression of the sensitive, gentle, wistful being revealed in the letters. With the songs written in 1921 and 1922, on the other hand —*Captain Stratton's Fancy, Mr. Belloc's Fancy, Good Ale, Hey troly loly, The Bachelor, Piggesnie,* and so forth—we find ourselves suddenly for the first time in the presence of a wholly different personality—the lusty, roystering[,] swashbuckling, drinking, wenching Peter Warlock of popular legend.

It need hardly be said that this spiritual "change of life" was not as sudden and complete as it might appear to be. The separate constituent elements of this secondary personality had always been there, but hitherto they were more in the nature of the comparatively ordinary contradictions and inconsistencies of character to which everyone is subject. Neither was the change complete; the original Philip Heseltine . . . continued to subsist behind the flamboyant façade of Peter Warlock up to the very end. It is true however that at about this time, 1921, the secondary Warlockian characteristics begin to group, consolidate, and organize themselves into a definite personality which tends henceforward to take the ascendancy over the former. And the psychological explanation of it is clear enough, and has indeed, already been sufficiently indicated. Philip Heseltine, from a worldly point of view, was a failure. Everything he touched went wrong, all his best-laid and most-deserving schemes invariably collapsed; but the moment he put on a mask everything succeeded, not merely in art, but in life as well. Up till the growing of the beard and the appearance of Peter Warlock, he had not been conspicuously successful with women— rather the opposite . . . ; he was too timid, shy and retiring to be successful. And here again there is a quite uncanny resemblance between his experiences and those of Huxley's imaginary Gumbril. Describing a precisely similar *rencontre* Huxley writes[,] "The Mild and Melancholy one would have drifted to the top of the road and watched her, dumbly, disappearing for ever into the Green Park or along the blank pavements of the Bayswater Road; would have watched her for ever disappear and then, if the pubs had happened to be open, would have gone and ordered a glass of port, and sitting at the bar would have savoured, still dumbly, among the other drinkers, the muddy grapes of the Douro, and his own unique loneliness." As it was, caparisoned in his false beard, he made a triumphant conquest. Similarly the Mild and Melancholy Philip, transformed into Peter Warlock, the Complete Man, was masterful and compelling—women could not resist him.

Philip, as opposed to Peter, exhibited the familiar romantic dichotomy in his attitude towards women; they had either to be angels of the Gretchen type, drawing him upwards into the light, or incarnate demons of the *femme fatale, Belle Dame sans Merci* order, dragging him down into the darkness—always the one or the other extreme, never anything intermediate. D. H. Lawrence showed considerable penetration when he wrote about him as follows in his *Letters* [pp. 327–28], where the names are suppressed for good reasons: [214]—"His affection for M—— is a desire for the light because he is in the dark. If he were in the light he would want the dark. He wants M—— for *companionship*, not for the blood connection, the dark, sensuous relation. With P—— he has this second, dark relation, but not the first. . . . Perhaps he is very split, and would always have the two things separate. [. . .] For these people I really believe in two wives. I don't see why there should be monogamy for people who can't have full satisfaction in one person, because they themselves are too split, because they act in themselves separately. Monogamy is for those who are whole and clear, all in one stroke. But for those whose stroke is broken into two different directions, then there should be two fulfilments."

In *Women in Love* he puts it more crudely and offensively, but the implications are the same, "He (Halliday) wants a pure lily, with a baby face, on the one hand, and on the other, he must have the Pussum, just to defile himself with her.—She is the harlot, the actual harlot of adultery to him. And he's got a craving to throw himself into the filth of her. Then he gets up and calls on the name of the lily of purity, the baby-faced girl, and so enjoys himself all round. It's the old story—action and reaction, and nothing between." [215] And at that period, about the time I first met him, and for some years after, he would swing from the one to the other with such a pendulum-like regularity that I came to be able to calculate almost to a day the time when the inevitable reaction would occur. His intimate life was then in a kind of rondo form, in which one persistently recurring and invariable theme alternated with continually new subjects—"A B, A C, A D," and so on. Later, with Peter Warlock, the form became plain sonata form, with two strongly contrasted subjects striving for mastery, or rather mistresshood, first one then the other being in the ascendant; later still he cultivated the contrapuntal forms with marked success and, beginning with two subjects, eventually acquired a remarkable virtuosity in combining a large number of dissimilar themes. But in these days, as I say, it was a rondo which came to an end, roughly, about the same time that Philip came to an end, and Peter began—i.e., about 1921.[216]

26 October 1921   Villa Fontana Vecchia, Taormina

⟨ The Brewsters sailed for Ceylon on Sunday [23 October 1921]—& suddenly the weather broke into gales.[217]

2 November 1921   Villa Fontana Vecchia, Taormina

⟨ I've been in a hell of a temper for three weeks: blank refused to see anybody after the Fisher's [218] last visit: and only the Count Z came and gave me a headache. I begrudged him his tea: and detested him. I've been so disagreeable to old Maria, rooking me, that now she creeps about as if a dagger was at her neck. I've written such very spiteful letters to everybody that now the postman never comes. And I believe even the old capra doesn't have her belated kid for fear I pounce on her. But it is a world of Canaille; absolutely. Canaille, canaglia, Schweinhunderei, stinkpots. Pfui!— pish, pshaw, prrr! They all stink in my nostrils.

That's how I feel in Taormina, let the Ionian sea have fits of blueness if it likes, and Calabria twinkle like seven jewels, and the white trumpet-tree under the balcony perfume six heavens with sweetness. That's how I feel. A curse, a murrain, a pox on this crawling, sniffling, spunkless brood of humanity.

.   .   .   .

There isn't any news, so don't ask for any. I believe Seltzer is bringing out my Sea and Sardinia book just now: and poems called Tortoises. I finished the Unconscious book and sent it to America with a foreword answering some of my darling critics. Called it provisionally Fantasia of the Unconscious. Call it Fantasia to prevent anybody tying themselves into knots trying to "understand" it. Since when I did up a short story,[219] and suddenly wrote a very long story called The Captain's Doll,[220] which I haven't finished yet. But I have just got it high up in the mountains of the Tyrol, and don't quite know how to get it down without breaking its neck. If I hadn't my own stories to amuse myself with I should die, chiefly of spleen.[221]

15 November 1921   Villa Fontana Vecchia, Taormina

⟨ We've got no news except that a woman called Mabel Dodge Sterne [222] writes from Taos, New Mexico, saying we can have a furnished adobe house there, for ourselves, and all we want, if we'll only go. It seems Taos is on a mountain—7,000 feet up—and 23 miles from a railway—and has a tribe of 600 free Indians who she says are interesting, sun-worshippers, rainmakers, and unspoiled. It sounds rather fun. I believe there's a little bunch of American artists there, though. But that might make it easier just to live. Fun it would be if one could get a merchant ship to New Orleans or Galveston, Texas, and miss that awful New York altogether, don't you think? Tell me if you know anything about such a place as Taos.—Of course I haven't settled anything—and we have talked so often of a move, and never made it.—But don't tell anybody else, will you?

.   .   .   .

There are clouds of all sorts of new birds in the garden, suddenly come south. And the storks are passing in the night, whewing softly and murmuring as they go overhead.[223]

11 December 1921   Villa Fontana Vecchia, Taormina

⟨ We had a piece of luck. The professor of English Literature in Edinburgh gave me a prize: a hundred pounds for "The Lost Girl." [224] That is a piece of luck. I hope to have the money next week. A hundred pounds is a nice little sum.

.   .   .   .

A thousand white horses on the hard blue sea and the sailing ships run anxiously with half a wing.[225]

Katherine Mansfield

? January 1922

I should like to have friends, I confess. I do not suppose I ever shall. But there have been moments when I have realised what friendship might be. Rare moments—but never forgotten. I remember once talking it over with Lawrence and he said "We must swear a solemn pact of friendship. Friendship is as binding, as solemn as marriage. We take each other for life, through everything—for ever. But it's not enough to say we will do it. We must *swear*." At the time I was impatient with him. I thought it extravagant—fanatic. But when one considers what this world is like I understand perfectly why L. (especially being L.) made such claims. . . . I think, myself, it is pride which makes friendship most difficult. To submit, to bow down to the other is not easy, but it must be done if one is to really understand the being of the other. Friendship isn't *merging*. One doesn't thereupon become a shadow and one remain a substance. Yes, it is terribly solemn—frightening, even.[226]

2 January 1922   Villa Fontana Vecchia, Taormina

⟨ I had your [Earl H. Brewster's] letter about Kandy. It sounds lovely, the coloured, naked people and the big elephant coming round the corner and the temple throng. I guess you'll love it after awhile. I feel I can't come— that the east is not my destiny. More and more I feel that meditation and the inner life are not my aim, but some sort of action and strenuousness and pain and frustration and struggling through. All the things you don't believe in, I do. And the goal is not that men should become serene as Buddh or as gods, but that the unfleshed gods should become men in battle. God made man is the goal. The gods are uneasy till they can become men. And men have to fight a way for the new incarnation. And the fight and the sorrow and the loss of blood, and even the influenzas and the headache are part of the fight and the fulfilment. Let nobody try to filch from me even my influenza. I've got influenza at the moment, but it only makes me more unbuddhing.

I have decided to go to Taos in New Mexico. There are Indians there, and an old sun magic. And I believe that the clamorous future is in the States. I do not want peace nor beauty nor even freedom from pain. I want to fight and to feel new gods in the flesh.[227]

? January? 1922   Villa Fontana Vecchia, Taormina

⟨ We must find a good ship. Maybe we'll leave next month, but not for sure. . . .

I have had a little influenza, it was very cold, the snow came nearer and nearer down the mountains. Monte Venere was white, also our own Monte Riretto. But right near to us the snow could not reach, the sea said no, and now, thank God, it is warm as summer, the snow has flown away, the sea is blue, and the almonds are busy flowering. Many thousands of birds came down with the cold—goldfinches, blackbirds, redbreasts, red-tails, so gay and coloured, and thank goodness, cartridges are so dear that the Italians can't buy them.[228]

. . . We sit in the salotto, warm and still, with the lamp on the table. Outside, through the door, I see the twilight, the moonlit sea; and the moon through the begonia leaves of our terrace; and all quite still, except from time to time the stove crackles. If I think that we are going away I feel melancholy. But inside I feel sure, that I must go. This is a beautiful end, but better a difficult beginning than only an end.[229]

24 January 1922   Villa Fontana Vecchia, Taormina

⟪ I have once more gone back on my plan. I shrink as yet from the States. Ultimately I shall go there, no doubt. But I want to go east before I go west: go west via the east. I have a friend called Brewster, who went with his wife and child from here last autumn to Kandy, Ceylon. He has got a big old ramshackle bungalow there, and is studying Pali and Buddhism at the Buddhist monastery, and asks me to come. So I shall go there. We had almost booked our passage to America, when suddenly it came over me I must go to Ceylon. I think one must for the moment withdraw from the world, away towards the inner realities that are real: and return, maybe, to the world later, when one is quiet and sure. I am tired of the world, and want the peace like a river: not this whisky and soda, bad whisky, too, of life so-called. I don't believe in Buddhistic inaction and meditation. But I believe the Buddhistic peace is the point to start from—not our strident fretting and squabbling.[230]

Henry James Forman

If Mr. Sumner,[231] who is fond of "suppressing" D. H. Lawrence's books, could meet their author and have half an hour's conversation, he would probably never molest a Lawrence book again for the rest of his life.

For D. H. Lawrence is the mildest of men and one of the pleasantest of companions. With all that, he is perhaps the most serious artist I have ever met.

Last Winter [1921–1922] Lawrence and the writer were neighbors hibernating on the rocks of Taormina. Lawrence occupied a small villa in the rugged hills back of the town, the Fontana Vecchia, approached like many other dwellings in the region only by a mule track. He was gravely ill during the Christmas holidays and the early part of January, with a virulent attack of influenza. Lawrence is frequently ill. He is tall and thin and delicate and his chest is not strong. And though Taormina is said to be a Winter resort, I have seen snow there, and steam heat is paid for at the hotels, though few American visitors have ever been able to isolate it for examination. It is reputedly there, however, and it is certainly paid for.

When during his convalescence, by the kindness of a common friend, I met Lawrence, I was surprised that he ever recovered. I walked up to his villa from the hotel, and the dripping foliage seemed every moment more dank and dripping as I drew nearer to his pink villa. It overhung a valley that with sunshine might have been radiant. But there was no sunshine then. Mrs. Lawrence opened the door and called out:

"Lawrence! Lawrence!" and turned promptly away to her household duties in the kitchen.

Lawrence came down in sandals and with his visitor sat down in the living room, of which the doors and windows stood wide open. The mist of the valley floated in in damp, lazy drifts. I was wearing a Winter overcoat and felt comfortable enough. But Lawrence sat with his thin jacket and sandals, his lips blue with cold, and announced that he was quite over his influenza.

"It is a miracle," I told him, looking at the open doors and windows.

"Ah, I know," he said with a smile that his red beard makes sardonic, "you Americans want a lot of heat in your rooms. I couldn't stand stuffy rooms."

"Call this stuffy?" I murmured.

"No!" he laughed. "But think what it would be if I had steam heat here!"

It began to rain—a rain so wet and hopeless that it seemed almost to rain in the room. Lawrence grew visibly more cheerful as we looked out at the dismal picture.

An almost childlike, whimsical smile lighted his face.

"'Sunny Sicily!" I murmured. He nodded, holding out his hands toward the miserable rain as though it were a crackling fire. That wretched weather was upsetting a generally popular notion that Sicily is always

105

pleasant, forever romantically, idiotically sunny and bright. And to upset preconceived fixed notions of humanity with stark realism is Lawrence's delight. That weather, for the moment, was an ally of his, a prop to the tenets of his art. That is why he chuckled almost as if he were fondling that withering rain.

"What are you doing now?" I asked.

"Oh, I am not working now," he said. "I have just finished a novel.[232] So I am translating some tales of Verga's.[233] Verga has written some very fine things about the Sicilian peasants." Verga's realism is the only thing in modern Italian fiction that makes any appeal to Lawrence. Italian fiction just now is an abysmal slough. But the point is, idleness was impossible for Lawrence.

From then on until late in February when I sailed for Malta and Lawrence and his wife for Ceylon, we met frequently and his companionship was a wonderfully agreeable and revealing experience. Ever since I had read *Sons and Lovers* I had been curious and interested in the personality of the writer who had produced it. Lawrence seldom speaks of his fictions unless he is asked direct questions about them. About *Sons and Lovers* he spoke freely and complained bitterly that he made not one penny out of the American edition.[234]

"Why don't you write more books like that one?" I asked him one day as we were walking down the only street of Taormina, the Corso, on the way to the Post Office.

"That is what nearly everybody asks me." He smiled his peculiar half childlike, half sardonic smile. "But I don't want to write more books like that. I write every book three times," he went on. "By that I don't mean copying and revising as I go along, but literally. After I finish the first draft I put it aside and write another. Then I put the second aside and write a third. The first draft is generally somewhat like *Sons and Lovers*." And he laughed with a rising inflection that is like a little scream —a peculiarity of his.

"Very well," I told him firmly, "then in the next novel write one draft only and see how your sales will mount."

He laughed as though to say that that was the last thing that concerned him.

"I don't want to be rich," he murmured half to himself. "But I do want to be able to do absolutely as I please."

I tried, how unobtrusively soever, to discover why he injects into his novels not sex, but so much of the quality that evidently displeases Mr. Sumner and the soul of Anthony Comstock.[235] To eliminate sex from a

Study in charcoal for the portrait in oils of D. H. Lawrence by Jan Juta. Taormina, Sicily (1920).

Mollie L. Skinner's "Holiday House" at Leithdale, Darlington, W.A., where the Lawrences stayed in May, 1922. Photograph by R. G. Howarth.

Mollie L. Skinner. From a photograph in the possession of Mrs. Marjorie Rees.

novel, the scheme of which requires the treatment of sex, would be as absurd as constantly using the phrase "dry grass" in place of the word hay, or forbidding the use of the word bread because some regions suffer famine. But some of his books undoubtedly seem, consciously or not, to stress the element of sex.

Well, I can only say that in his speech and conversation no priest could be purer or more austere. Always you get the impression of the simple, unaffected artist, with the childlike attachment to his art that one finds only in the great, out of reach of influences, either commercial or clique-ish. With his wife for sole companion, he lives much alone, be it in Tyrol, the Italian Alps, in Taormina, where I saw him, or in Ceylon, where I suppose he now is.[236] Between him and his art as he sees it he allows nothing at all to intervene.

In Taormina he mingled little with the regular inhabitants and less still with the tourists. The English colony, being composed of the best people, very naturally looked down upon him. His books were read there surreptitiously. It was there I read *Women in Love,* and the only copy in the town belonged to the Duca di Bronte, the English collateral descendant of Lord Nelson, who inherits the title of an Italian Duke and the lands thereof, conferred upon the British naval hero more than a hundred years ago. That book, as those who have read it know, contains some of the best writing Lawrence has done. But it undoubtedly does seem to contain a good deal of sex, which even to a sober critic might seem somewhat excessive. Well, there is no doubt that when Lawrence wrote that he believed as always that he was transcribing life. And I thought it conceivable that being frail in body and subject to frequent illness, it may appear to him that life as it might be described in a clinical report or a specialist's case record was the "life" he had the right to put into a novel, just as Dostoyevsky, epileptic, wrote always on his harassed nerves. I told him that there were things in *Women in Love* that perhaps it might have been better to slur, particularly because the novel was, most of it, so fine, so excellent—or so it appeared to me.

"There were others who felt that way," he laughed, and went on with a letter of introduction he was writing for me to some one in Malta.

"And when Hermione 'biffs' her irritating lover in the face,"[237] I told him, "even though it might have happened in real life, it is too preposterous for fiction. Don't you agree?"

He merely laughed again, but his wife spoke up bravely and declared: "That outraged even me."

"Perhaps we are both old fogies," I told her.

We spoke then of his extraordinarily fine book of travel, *The Sea and Sardinia.*

"I never made a single note for that," he said. "I returned home, to Taormina, and had nothing to do. So I wrote the thing in about six weeks or less. Only one draft." [238]

I called his attention to the virtue of one draft for him. I endeavored to learn his views of modern fiction. I expected him, for instance, to be an admirer of Sherwood Anderson's work. But in that I was mistaken. I opened a certain American magazine on his table that contained some pages of our modern vers libre.

"What do you think of that?" I asked him.

"I think it's rubbish," he said, and added with a laugh, "and I am supposed to be able to write this kind of thing myself."

There is no great facility for getting books in Taormina and Lawrence was reading very little and for the most part knew little of the fiction of the time, particularly of American fiction.

We took tea frequently at the tea-room, which is also the circulating library and the general emporium of gossip. But always our talk seemed to run not on books, but on life, on methods in art, on English writers of our acquaintance—H. G. Wells, Gilbert Cannan,[239] Rebecca West, Arnold Bennett, &c. Once, I remember, we took a long walk round the town and sat down upon a ledge of rock in the famous old Graeco-Roman Theatre of Taormina. The burden of our talk was the preponderance of the commercial spirit in the world today and the obstacles against which the artist today labored in those conditions.

"The only thing to do," he declared, "is to keep everlastingly combating it until at last some day things change."

The work of art is to him all important, for that work it is that must bring light into the world. He was looking forward to coming some day to America and living in the Arizona desert—a place of light and bracing vigorous air. I assured him that he could do nothing wiser or better for his health, physical and perhaps even mental. In the meanwhile he was going to India, to Ceylon. The life of the Buddhist monasteries there seemed to have a strange fascination for him.

We had a farewell party at his villa before we all dispersed. The other guests, besides my wife, were a Finnish author [240] and his wife, a writer of sea-tales, who found it difficult to make ends meet. To him Lawrence was all generosity and kindness and, generally, I have never seen a more delightful host. Mrs. Lawrence had loaded the tables with food, cakes and pastry of her own making. And Lawrence's chief concern was that

we should consume all of it. The talk fluctuated vigorously between literature and food. I remember my wife asking him as he stood with a plate
of cakes before her:

"Why do you leave Paul in *Sons and Lovers* so hopeless after his love
affairs with Miriam and Clara—why so stripped of everything?"

"Ah, but he had his courage left," laughed Lawrence—"do have some
of these cakes."

The impression of Lawrence that lingers in the memory is that of the
vividly real personality, the austere artist living so frugally that many
would call it poverty—devoted to the one supreme task, that of transcribing, interpreting life as he sees it.

I remember finding him one day stretched on the sands of Letojani, a
little town where a peasant's fair was being held. The sun that day was
beating down upon us after weeks of rain, and a breeze was blowing
from Africa. He was gazing out over the sapphire expanse of the Ionian
Sea toward Calabria, his eyes filled with the remote speculation of the
dreamer, a speculation far beyond the coast of Calabria. We exchanged
a few words and I passed on to other acquaintances of the beach. But his
image stretched there on the yellow sands haunted me long after I left
Sicily.

"There is a man," I thought, "with the soul of a child, single-minded,
single-hearted, at peace, the type of the true artist." [241]

19 February 1922   Villa Fontana Vecchia, Taormina

❲ We sit waiting to depart—4 trunks—one household trunk, 1 book trunk,
Frieda's and mine, two small valises, a hatbox, and two very small bags:
just like Abraham going to a new land. My heart is trembling now, mostly
with pain—the going away from home and the people and Sicily. But I
will forget it and only think of palms and elephants and monkeys and pea-
cocks. Tomorrow at 10:34 we leave here: eat at Messina, where we must
change, arrive at 8:30 at Palermo, then to the Hotel Panormus where our
friend [242] lives. Thursday to Naples by boat, there at the Hotel Santa Lucia.
Then on the S.S. "Osterley," Orient Line, to Ceylon. The ship goes on to
Australia. You have the address—Ardnaree, Lake View Estate, Kandy,
Ceylon. Think, it is only 14 days from Naples. We can always return
quickly when we've had enough. Perhaps Else [243] is right and we shall return to our Fontana. I don't say no: I don't say anything for certain. Today
I go, tomorrow I return. So things go. [244]

CHAPTER TWO

1922: Ceylon and Australia

How I hated a great deal of my time in Ceylon: never felt so sick in my life. Yet it is now a very precious memory, invaluable. Not wild horses would drag me back. But neither time nor eternity will take away what I have of it: Ceylon and the east.

—Brewster, p. 52.

No wonder Australians love Australia. It is the land that as yet has made no great mistake, humanly. The horrible human mistakes of Europe. And, probably, the even worse human mistakes of America.

—Kangaroo, Chap. XVIII, "Adieu Australia"

28 February 1922   R.M.S. Osterley

❲ We have been gone for two days. We left Naples Sunday evening, 8 o'clock. Monday morning at 8 o'clock we came through the Straits of Messina and then for hours we saw our Etna like a white queen or a white witch there standing in the sky so magic-lovely. She said to me, "You come back here," but I only said, "No," but I wept inside with grief, grief of separation.[1]

7 March 1922   R.M.S. Osterley: Arabian Sea

❲ We stopped three hours in Port Said, and it was quite like the Thousand and One Nights. It was 9 o'clock in the morning, and the ladies of Port Said were all abroad shopping. Little black waddling heaps of black crêpe and two houri eyes between veil and mantle. Comic is the little peg that stands above the nose and keeps veil and head-cloth together. There came a charabanc with twenty black women parcels. Then one of the women threw back her veil and spat at us because we are ugly Christians. But you still see everything—beggars, water carriers, the scribe who sits with his little table, and writes letters, the old one who reads the Koran, the men

113

who smoke their "chibouks" in the open café and on the pavement—and what people! Beautiful Turks, Negroes, Greeks, Levantines, Fellaheen, three Bedouins out of the desert like animals, Arabs, wonderful. We have taken coal on board, and then at midday off again into the Suez Canal, and that is very interesting. The Canal is eighty-eight miles long, and you can only travel five miles an hour. There you sit on this great ship and you feel really on land, slowly travelling on a still land ship. The shores are quite near, you can surely throw an orange at the Arabs that work on the shores. Then you see beautifully, wonderfully, the Sahara Wüste, or desert—which do you say? The waterway goes narrow and alone through red-yellow sands. From time to time Arabs with camels work on the shores and keep on shouting "Hallo, Hallo" when the big ship passes so slowly. In the distance little sharp sand hills so red and pink-gold and sharp and the horizon sharp like a knife edge so clear. Then a few lonely palms, lonely and lost in the strong light, small, like people that have not grown very tall.

Then again only sand, gold-pink and sharp little sand hills, so sharp and defined and clear, not like reality but a dream. Solemn evening came, and we so still, one thought we did not seem to move any more. Seagulls flew about like a sandstorm, and a great black bird of prey alone and cruel, so black between thousands of white screaming, quick flying sea birds. Then we came to the Dead Sea, flat seas that extend very far, and slowly the sun sank behind the desert with marvellous colours, and as the sun had set, then such a sky like a sword burning green and pink. Beautiful it was, I have never seen anything so superhuman. One felt near to the doors of the old Paradise, I do not know how, but something only half human, something of a heaven with grey-browed, overbearing and cruel angels. The palm trees looked so little the angels should be much bigger and every one with a sword. Yes, it is a frontier country.

Next morning we were in the Red Sea. There stands Mount Sinai, red like old dried blood, naked like a knife and so sharp, so unnaturally sharp, like a dagger that has been dipped in blood and has dried long ago and is a bit rusty and is always there like something dreadful between man and his lost Paradise. All is Semitic and cruel, naked, sharp. No tree, no leaf, no life: the murderous will and the iron of the idea and ideal—iron will and ideal. So they stand, these dreadful shores of this Red Sea that is hot like an oven without air. It is a strange exit through this Red Sea—bitter. Behind lie finally Jerusalem, Greece, Rome and Europe, fulfilled and past—a great dreadful dream. It began with Jews and with Jews it ends. You should see Sinai, then you could know it. The ideal has been wicked against men and

Jehovah is father of the ideal and Zeus and Jupiter and Christ are only sons. And God be praised Sinai and the Red Sea are past and consummated.

Yesterday morning we came through the Straits of Bab-el-Mandeb, and again into the open. I am so glad that we came this way. Yesterday we always saw land—Arabia naked and desert but not so red and sharp and like dried blood. Today we see no land but later on we shall pass Cape Socrotra. This ship has gained fifteen hours. We are fifteen hours before time. Perhaps we arrive in Colombo on Sunday evening instead of Monday. It is very warm, but there is always air. The sea is covered with little white sea-horses, but the ship is still and sure. We have not had one single bad moment. All here on board so friendly and so good and comfortable. I work on the translation of Maestro Don Gesualdo and I let my inkpot fall on the deck. The "Osterley" shall wear my black sign for ever. At 11 o'clock in the morning we do not get Bovril any more, but ice cream. The women all wear colourful summer frocks. In the evening we dance. We see now the little flying fish. They are all silver and they fly like butterflies, so wee. There are also little black dolphins that run about like little black pigs.[2]

> Mrs. A. L. Jenkins
> as told by H. E. L. Priday

Although discussion of D. H. Lawrence, his novels and his poems, his personality and his significance as a "prophet" had already spread from London to the Continent of Europe, Australians took but little notice of the English writer during the few months he spent among them. Only in Perth, and that after my return to this country in 1932, have I come across people who treasured clear and personal memories of his stay.

One of these people, Mrs. A. L. Jenkins, a Cottesloe neighbour of mine when I was editing the *Broadcaster*, had travelled with the Lawrences from Naples in 1922, and afterwards corresponded with them. One day she came to me with a bundle of their letters "for me to copy if I wished." I did wish, and there and then made a shorthand note, believing that some day others might be interested, even though the letters cover much the same ground as other, already published correspondence.

Mrs. Jenkins had boarded the Orient liner *Oronsay*[3] in London. In her own words, "on reaching Naples, a thin-faced, bearded man in an old golf jacket came on board with a large blond woman in a long and voluminous skirt—unmistakably the German hausfrau."

The head steward, without mentioning names, brought them along and sat them at Mrs. Jenkins' table. Now Mrs. Jenkins was a great reader of novels, and at this first meal together she happened to be talking of certain books she had brought with her to read at sea. One of those she mentioned was a recently published book, *Sons and Lovers*.[4]

"Oh! That's my husband's book," the large woman immediately exclaimed.

Mrs. Jenkins, née Burt, member of a well known Australian family, was a travelled woman with outspoken and mature views unclouded by sentimentality. She was getting on in years when I knew her, but one was at once captivated by her rich and racily humorous personality. She liked talking, and I am quite sure that D. H. Lawrence liked listening to her. It is evident from their subsequent exchange of letters that both he and his wife enjoyed her company and appreciated the services she was able to do for them in Australia. How much they really liked her is evident from their subsequent invitation to go to Mexico with them.

In the weeks that followed their dining table encounter, the Australian woman spent a great deal of time with the highly-strung novelist and his wife. She told me that although they did not join in the organized deck games and social events, they were friendly and companionable. D. H., alert and active, got round a lot. On Sundays he even turned up on deck for the religious services. Frieda—"a picture of Teuton placidity" as Mrs. Jenkins called her—was content to spend most of her time in a deck-chair, where she was working on a beautiful rug, all colours of the rainbow. Lawrence, when he joined them, asked a tremendous number of questions about Australia, while the two women talked much of Europe and of travel, and Frieda a great deal of Sicily, where Lawrence had just finished *Sea and Sardinia*. She said that he never troubled to read criticism of his work, though she herself read avidly everything that was written about him. She said what a fiendish worker Lawrence was when the mood was on him; and this he himself confirmed, saying that wherever he happened to be, even at the breakfast table, once the spirit moved him he had to stop in the middle of a mouthful and give up from that moment every other plan, to work, work, work, page after page after page, until a book was finished. (He was soon to display his restless energy at Thirroul, when he wrote *Kangaroo*.)

Everything in Lawrence's published correspondence shows up their voyage to Australia as one of the happiest interludes of their lives. Years later, Frieda was to write: "How we enjoyed that trip! Everybody feeling so free and detached, no responsibility for the moment, people going to meet their husbands or wives, people going to Australia full of the wonders that were coming to them, and Lawrence being so interested and feeling so well. How tenderly one loves people on board! They seem to become bosom friends for life." [5]

The Lawrences left the ship at Colombo, "just to have a look at the tropics," while Mrs. Jenkins went on to Fremantle, and thence to her home at Strawberry Hill in the Darling Ranges. This is the point at which her correspondence with the Lawrences starts, for the first mail brought her, in D. H. Lawrence's handwriting, from Ardnaree,[6] Lake View Estate, Kandy, a promised list of all his works published to that date, from *The White Peacock* and *New Poems* to *Sea and Sardinia*— books all published either by Duckworth or by Martin Secker.[7]

Not long afterwards came a postcard:

Kandy/Monday 3 April [1922]
I have just cabled to New York for money—can't stand Ceylon—too hot and sticky—shall come right on—probably by the boat from Colombo April 24th—arrive Freemantle [*sic*] May 4th. What do you say to that? hope you won't just hate it, the quickness—but I think we'll just stay a day or two in Perth, then go on, either south in W.A. or to Sydney. Hope you're well.
D. H. Lawrence
Excuse card—this place makes me irritable.[8]

25 March 1922   *"Ardnaree," Lake View Estate, Kandy, Ceylon*

❨ *We are here and settling down—very hot at first—but one soon takes naturally to it—soon feels in a way at home—sort of root race home. We're in a nice spacious bungalow on the hill above Kandy in a sort of half jungle of a coconut-palm estate—and cocoa—beautiful, and such sweet scents. The Prince of Wales was here on Thursday* [9]*—looks worn out and nervy, poor thing. The Perahera in the evening with a hundred elephants was lovely. But I don't believe I shall ever work here.*[10]

Earl H. Brewster

Frieda and Lawrence arrived in Ceylon [13? March 1922] . . . . I met them at Colombo, where we passed a few pleasant days before going to Kandy. At first Lawrence liked being in Ceylon. "It is good to have gone through the Red Sea, and to be behind Moses," he declared. He wanted at once to begin the study of the Singhalese language.

I had leased an old bungalow surrounded by the broadest verandas.

It was isolated from neighbours in the midst of sixty acres of forest, and stood at the top of the highest hill. In one direction we overlooked the Kandy Lake, in the other the Mahaweliganga, or Great Elephant River. The verdant forests came to our very door. There Frieda and Lawrence came to live with us during their sojourn in Ceylon.

Lawrence began his life with us by saying: "I consider you truly my friends, therefore I shall tell you your faults!" Nor did he fail to do so! Occasionally the "elements of my being" were disturbed by his criticisms, but as I cannot recall what they were I fear I did not profit by them. How easy to forget our faults, even when they are pointed out to us!

The least wasted of times are the walks one has had. I recall the joy of walks with Lawrence through the forests. The world when it was young must have looked like those jungles. In the depths of the forests we visited glowing white temples surrounded by fragrant champa flowers: we crossed the Mahaweliganga in primitive boats; on narrow paths we withdrew respectfully to let the tall dark elephants pass. It was good to watch workmen in the ways of life not dominated by machinery, to touch implements and products moulded by the hand. Monkeys hid in the trees: the brightest birds flitted by our veranda: a trotting bull, so gentle of nature and lovely to look at, grazed near our house, or lay on the front flight of steps as though he would serve for a decorative statue: gorgeous flowers grew on the trees, making some hills as colourful as a New England autumnal wood: radiant day ever succeeded the star-lit night: and never in that clime would we need other than the sun's rays to warm us: yet Lawrence—the worshipper of life—in that abundance and beauty was not content. "My being requires a different physical and psychic environment: the white man is not for this region: it is for the dark-skinned, whose flow of blood consciousness is vitally attuned to these different rays of the sun"—he declared.

Lawrence talked much of racial differences, of those existing in the present, and of those between the present and the past. He attached much importance to actual difference of blood, which he considered affected consciousness—that is, that consciousness and the blood are more closely related than is generally recognized to-day. The elephant especially interested him as the remnant of another age.

If the British activities in Ceylon or India were adversely criticized Lawrence was furious. Such criticism was a privilege reserved for himself! [11]

One day he startled me by saying: "Man himself created the sun and the moon." After a moment I quoted these words of the Buddha: "Verily, I declare to you, my friend, that within this very body, mortal though it be and only a fathom high, but conscious and endowed with mind, is the world, and the waxing thereof, and the waning thereof, and the way that leads to the passing away thereof"! "No, no," responded Lawrence, "I don't mean in your subjective sense." He has written about this in *Fantasia of the Unconscious:* [12] to which book he always referred when I begged him to give more details of the subject treated in *Psychoanalysis and the Unconscious.*

When I urged him to write at greater length on his philosophical and psychological conceptions, he would shake his head and say: "I would contradict myself on every page."

I had gone to Ceylon for the study of Buddhism, and of Pali—the language of its earliest scriptures. For this purpose I passed my mornings in a Buddhist monastery: and other hours were required for the preparation of lessons. Lawrence seemed to disapprove of my devotion to Buddhism: he never again showed as much interest in it as in his last letter from Sicily.[13] But his sympathy for other forms of Hindu thought remained. He seemed to think there had been a prehistoric figure of the seated Buddha, meditating on the lotus at the solar plexus: this was the Buddha, he declared, that interested him. In later years he used often to say of the seated Buddha: "Oh I wish he would *stand up!*"

The climate did not suit Lawrence: he began to grow ill. He proposed our going higher in the mountains; but I thought I could not leave the study of Pali. I did not appreciate then—as I think he did—the significance which our life together possessed. What Lawrence offered had to be *lived;* it was not something merely to be seen intellectually. To talk about it much was to deny it. He wished us to live and work together in a deep and sincere relationship, from which would spring a reality beyond any one of us, informing and enriching us, which he symbolized by the figure of the rainbow. He would say: "I would rather work with you, each doing something with our hands, than to talk together." Often during the years I knew him he declared that he would never write again. He was able to find in the humblest occupation a rhythm and a flow of life which gave him satisfaction.

It was the warmest season Ceylon had had for many years: we were none of us feeling well. Lawrence would not endure it longer. I remember one fateful afternoon we sat on the veranda discussing our future plans. Lawrence and Frieda would sail for Australia: my wife spoke of going to America: I must choose what I would do. I was reluctant to leave Ceylon; and more reluctant still to leave for the West, not having visited India or Burma. "If you *really* want to go to Burma, let Achsah and Harwood make a visit in America while you go to Burma. It is best to do what you very much want to do, and so maybe get it out of your system," advised Lawrence. Then in a teasing humour, picturing me as a Buddhist monk in Burma, he wrote the following:

Apostrophe to a Buddhist Monk

Oh my bald head
Cranium
duck-egg
how thou dost poke up among the spokes of
    my umbrella

Oh my marigold robe
how thou castest up a sickly glare
a bilious blast
a mango-fleshed aura nauseously steaming
a pawpaw effulgence
into my eyes and nostrils.

Oh my wife's brass incense-bowl
bought second-hand from Mrs. Justice Ennis
for 3½ rupees
I am inclined to heap thy coals of
    fire on my own bald and prickly pate
and lick up thy ashes with a repentant tongue
and consider the lily, not the pawpaw
    nor the mango-flesh
and give up the ghost incontinent
in the hope of resurrecting or rather re-incarnating
    as a vendor of fried fish, once more yellow.

In after years, when I asked Lawrence why he had written so little of Ceylon, he replied that because of his illness there he did not trust his impressions. Now I recall only his poem, *Elephant*,[14] as laid in Ceylon.

Lawrence and Frieda went from Ceylon to Australia. Four years passed before I saw him again: during which time he and Frieda travelled from Australia to New Mexico and to Old Mexico, to Europe, back to New

Mexico and to Europe again. My wife, my daughter and I returned to Europe . . . .[15]

30 March 1922   "Ardnaree," Lake View Estate, Kandy, Ceylon

❨ We have been here these last 18 days: the heat in the middle of the day rather overwhelming, but morning and evening delicious: the place beautiful, in its way very, the jungle round the house, palms and noisy, scraping and squeaking tropical creatures: good-looking, more-or-less naked, dark bluey-brown natives. But all a bit extraneous. I feel I don't belong, and never should. I think next week we shall go up higher to Nuwara Eliya.

. . . We were at the Perahera here for the Prince of Wales. It was wonderful, gorgeous and barbaric with all the elephants and flames and devil dances in the night. One realizes how very barbaric the substratum of Buddhism is. I shrewdly suspect that high-flownness of Buddhism altogether exists mostly on paper: and that its denial of the soul makes it always rather barren, even if philosophically, etc., more perfect. In short, after a slight contact, I draw back and don't like it.

The Prince of Wales seemed sad and forlorn. He seemed to be almost the butt of everybody, white and black alike. They all secretly hate him for being a prince, and make a princely butt of him—and he knows it. My sympathy was with him.

. . . I do think, still more now I am out here, that we make a mistake forsaking England and moving out into the periphery of life. After all, Taormina, Ceylon, Africa, America—as far as we go, they are only the negation of what we ourselves stand for and are: and we're rather like Jonahs running away from the place we belong. That is the conclusion that is forced on me. So I am making up my mind to return to England during the course of the summer. I really think that the most living clue of life is in us Englishmen in England, and the great mistake we make is in not uniting together in the strength of this real living clue—religious in the most vital sense—uniting together in England and so carrying the vital spark through. Because as far as we are concerned it is in danger of being quenched. I know now it is a shirking of the issue to look to Buddha or the Hindu or to our working men, for the impulse to carry through. It is in ourselves, or nowhere and this looking to the outer masses is only a betrayal. I think too the Roman Catholic Church, as an institution, granted of course some new adjustments to life, might once more be invaluable for saving Europe: but not as a mere political power.[16]

10 April 1922   "Ardnaree," Lake View Estate, Kandy, Ceylon

(No, the East doesn't get me at all. Its boneless suavity, and the thick, choky feel of tropical forest, and the metallic sense of palms and the horrid noises of the birds and creatures, who hammer and clang and rattle and cackle and explode all the livelong day, and run little machines all the live-long night; [17] and the scents that make me feel sick, the perpetual nauseous overtone of cocoanut and cocoanut fibre and oil, the sort of tropical sweet-ness which to me suggests an undertang of blood, hot blood, and thin sweat: the undertaste of blood and sweat in the nauseous tropical fruits; the nasty faces and yellow robes of the Buddhist monks, the little vulgar dens of the temples: all this makes up Ceylon to me, and all this I cannot bear. Je m'en vais. Me ne vo'. I am going away. Moving on.

. . . .

I wish I could come to America without meeting the awful "cultured" Americans with their limited self-righteous ideals and their mechanical love-motion and their bullying, detestable negative creed of liberty and de-mocracy. I don't believe either in liberty or democracy. I believe in actual, sacred, inspired authority: divine right of natural kings: I believe in the divine right of natural aristocracy, the right, the sacred duty to wield un-disputed authority. Naturally I find myself in diametric opposition to every American—and everybody else, besides Americans—whom I come across. Nevertheless, there it stands. [18]

Kandy, Ceylon [March–April, 1922, Postmark: 1922]

[To Hilda Brown Cotterell]
(Here we are in the heat among the black people, but I think we shall go on to Australia. How are you all. Many greetings from us both
                                                        D. H. Lawrence [19]

11 April 1922   "Ardnaree," Lake View Estate, Kandy, Ceylon

(I've been in Ceylon a month and nearly sweated myself into a shadow. Still it's a wonderful place to see and experience. There seems to be a flaw [flow?] in the atmosphere, and one sees a darkness, and through the darkness the days before the Flood, marshy, with elephants mud-grey and buffaloes rising from the mud, and soft-boned voluptuous sort of people, like plants under water, stirring in myriads.

I think I shall go on to Australia at the end of the month.[20]

Achsah Barlow Brewster

After our arrival in Ceylon, with much searching we had found a home of our own, "Ardnaree." It stood on a hill amidst great groves and jungles, high over the Lake of Kandy. Here Lawrence and Frieda joined us. Pepper-vines and crimson cocoa-pods festooned the drives, jak and bread-fruit trees spread out their green, slender areca palms shot into the air. It was a beautiful spot, with magnificent views from every side of our hill, and the broad verandahs gave each of us a quiet corner of our own. I remember their arrival and Frieda's exclaiming that it was the loveliest spot in the world and Lawrence's saying, "I shall never leave it." That was the first day.

They arrived carrying in their hands the side of a Sicilian cart, painted with scenes from the Palladins. They had admired these painted carts, and a Sicilian friend had taken the opportune moment to give them the broad-side of one as a steamer present. The Saracens looked quite at home on our walls.[21]

One of the first things Lawrence did was to walk around the lake, when he pulled out his watch, which had refused to go, and threw it into the middle of the lake. On his return to the house we were sitting on the north verandah for tiffin, laughing over the episode, when he touched my husband's watch-chain, admiring the design of the curious links of silver-gold, which had been picked up in Kandy. He measured it with his eye and announced that the chain was too long—twice as much as needed, and added: "Let me have the other half." With delicate dexterity he pried open the links. A second fob was found and attached, making the two chains complete. Each of the two put the other half of the same chain into his own pocket.

Generally we sat on the north verandah in the morning. There was early breakfast; then tiffin; then the child went to a little school and Earl studied Pali in a monastery across the lake. Frieda, stretched out on a rattan couch, sewed and embroidered with bright silks. Lawrence sat curled up with a schoolboy's copy-book in his hand, writing away. He was translating Giovanni Verga's short stories from the Sicilian. Across

the pages of the copy-book his hand moved rhythmically, steadily, un-
hesitatingly, leaving a trail of exquisite, small writing as legible as print.
No blots, no scratchings marred its beauty. When the book was finished,
he wrapped and tied it up, sending it off to the publisher.[22] All of this
went on in the family circle. Frieda would come for consultation as to
whether the rabbit's legs should be embroidered in yellow or white. The
pen would be lifted a moment then go on across the page. Sometimes
Lawrence would stop and consult us about the meaning of a word; considering seriously whatever comments were offered. He listened gravely
and intently to everyone.

Each night after the child had been safely tucked into bed, after
Frieda and I had read a chapter of *Swiss Family Robinson* to her, we
shivered as we walked the length of the verandah to the drawing-room.
Perhaps a boa-constrictor, like the one that swallowed the donkey,
would roll up his coils and bounce down upon us. We shut the door very
tight and Lawrence held the lamp down to the crack to see if it were
large enough for a cobra to squeeze through. He was convinced that the
cobra would manage to get in. Then he would read what he had written
through the day.

In the ceiling of each room was a skylight and at night not only could
we hear mortal conflicts over our heads, but could see the wild-cats
through the glass on the roof—five or six of them in combat. In the morning often there would be a trail of blood where a wounded snake had
dragged his length. Sometimes we would hear a shot, and the watchman
would announce the following day that he had killed a Russel's Viper.
There was always a consciousness of teeming life, by day or night. The
little mongoose and striped chipmunks ran up and down the trees; birds
alighted where we sat, counting us one of themselves; crows came flapping greedily to snatch any chance morsel or glittering trinket; the
trotting-bull came up on the verandah when he was thirsty. Lawrence and
the child gave it water in the wash-bowl, holding it while the bull drank.
The birds made a loud metallic clangour. One bird repeated an insistent crescendo eight times until the last cry was deafening. Lawrence
dubbed him the "bell of hell" and forthwith began to sing the verses of
that Salvation Army hymn:

> The bells of hell go ting-a ling-a ling
> For you, but not for me.

This was done with a very personal emphasis and an air of self-
righteousness. He often sang.

At six o'clock the sun gave a plunge into the lake below, with a crimson gleam that immediately sank into night. The blue hills vanished into black silhouettes and the tall areca palms swayed in the wind; the stars came out over the lake which shone below us. "Tom-tom, tom-tom-tom; tom-tom, tom-tom-tom," boomed up from the Temple of the Tooth through the night. We often sat on the steps leading down from the front verandah which faced the west. After its glory had faded Lawrence and Frieda would sing in the dark. For the first time there I heard them sing:

> Joseph was an old man, and an old man was he,
> And Joseph married Mary, the queen of Galilee.

Lawrence enjoyed especially the last verse where Mary retorts to Joseph:

> And *so* you see, Joseph, there *are* cherries for me!

One morning he went to put on his topee (cork-hat), which he had taken off his head the night before, and found a family of rats had made it their home. The teeming life of the place horrified him.

When a dead leaf from the cocoanut palm fell with a crash like a bomb we all jumped in fear. There was an undercurrent of nervous dread lest something awful might happen. On moonlight nights, James the cook, the *appu*, Banda the water boy, and *ayah* assembled on the front verandah after we had gone to bed. They made *puja* to a Buddha painting, then sat cross-legged chanting. Their voices rose and fell in a strange rhythm. Lawrence would say, "Who knows whether they are praying; they may be planning to kill us in cold blood!"

Every day on the table stood a row of six sweets—camel's milk, preserved melon, jaggery-palm sugar, cocoanut sweets invariably, and two other possibilities. The cook dished up wonderful concoctions, rich plum puddings, curries. "How wonderful," said Frieda. So did we all at first, then we began to shake our heads when *appu* passed them solemnly. Lawrence asked in a melancholy voice if it were necessary to have sweets of camel's milk always on the table. Then Frieda brought forth a bottle labelled "liver mixture" and poured out a tablespoonful for each in turn. By the next day Lawrence was heard wishing he could have a bread pudding instead of cocoanut cream with meringue on the top—those dreadful bread puddings he relished. Even with the "liver-mixtures" the climate told on us all, especially on Lawrence, who could scarcely drag about. The season was unusually hot, yet we none of us wished to leave for the higher hills.

Immediately upon his arrival Lawrence had announced that he should tell us all our faults. His horror of repression made him believe that between friends all annoyances should be spoken forth, both to relieve oneself and to clear the situation between them. He tried to put into words what others leave tacit, even in the most trivial matter.

Hastily deciding to go to the village I asked if I were in proper order, to which he answered: "If I were Frieda I should say you look perfectly *beautiful!* but being myself I shall say, you look *decent.*"

A workman was arranging a screen on the verandah where we were seated. He was alert; with sure, graceful movement and fine head; his dark eyes flashing; his features regular; the beard clipped in an elegant line. Lawrence pensively watched him, announcing that he resembled his father—the same clean-cut and exuberant spirit, a true pagan. He added that he had not done justice to his father in *Sons and Lovers* and felt like rewriting it. When children they had accepted the dictum of their mother that their father was a drunkard, therefore was contemptible, but that as Lawrence had grown older he had come to see him in a different light; to see his unquenchable fire and relish for living. Now he blamed his mother for her self-righteousness, her invulnerable Christian virtue within which she was entrenched. She had brought down terrible scenes of vituperation upon their heads from which she might have protected them. She would gather the children in a row and they would sit quaking, waiting for their father to return while she would picture his shortcomings blacker and blacker to their childish horror. At last the father would come in softly, taking off his shoes, hoping to escape unnoticed to bed, but that was never allowed him. She would burst out upon him, reviling him for a drunken sot, a good-for-nothing father. She would turn to the whimpering children and ask them if they were not disgusted with such a father. He would look at the row of frightened children, and say: "Never mind, my duckies, you needna be afraid of me. I'll do ye na harm."

Lawrence could not forgive his mother for having dragged them into those unnecessary scenes. Shaking his head sadly at the memory of that beloved mother, he would add that the righteous woman martyred in her righteousness is a terrible thing and that all self-righteous women ought to be martyred. He sat watching the workman intently; then he reiterated that there was a bit of a gleam about his father, and he wished he had done him more justice.

When a copy of *The Rainbow* appeared on the verandah he snatched it away, saying that the very sight of it was repugnant to him, it had caused him so much suffering. The public had misunderstood him always, even at college; when in his writing a paper he had used the word "stallion," his English professor had taken him aside and said: "My boy, that is a word we do not use." After this reminiscence he hung his head as if in shame for the public who could not face life.

His humanity was outraged at driving in rickshaws. When, frail as he was, he needed to be carried uphill through the heat, he simply could not allow a rickshaw boy to pull him, but got out and walked.

Full of enthusiasm he would come home from the bazaars with bits of bright cotton, plaids, stripes, shot patterns of changeable colours, sandals and beads. We all would fashion them into garments. I can remember standing for hours while Frieda draped a handwoven, gold-bordered Madura saree, Earl insisting it should fall in the lines of a Tanagra figure, and Lawrence finally ripping the whole thing off to demonstrate just how many pleats there should be in the skirt, and where the folds should fall from the shoulders.

Like everyone else in Ceylon he became fascinated by precious stones. The merchants would show us their treasures and tell tales about jewels. Lawrence bought clear, bright, blue sapphires and moonstones.

In honour of the Prince of Wales' visit a great *pera-hera* or religious procession of elephants was arranged. All the available elephants were collected, a hundred or more—tall dark ones with legs like palm-trees and backs like boulders; silver-grey ones speckled over their faces as if they were freckled. Richly caparisoned were they, with velvets and fringes, tassels and tinkling bells. In front of them ran attendants continually spreading out white cloth that the sacred elephants need never tread the earth. Devil dancers, some of them on stilts, performed amazing antics. Drummers and tom-tom players and pipers made strange, pulsating music. We remained until the last sky-rocket sank away into the lake. The pale prince sat in the tower of the Temple of the Tooth reviewing the procession. Every elephant salaaming before him: which scene Lawrence describes in his poem *Elephant*.

Lawrence would sit for hours pondering the new heaven of these eastern skies. He had a vivid star-consciousness, and would lament that people narrowed their view, hardly noticing the stars, not realizing that they were star-doomed.

One day I asserted a belief in the communion of saints. To my surprise Lawrence rejoined that he felt a bond of deep communion with all the great and good ones of all time. Very quietly he added that angels were waiting to help man. An agonized look transformed his face as he added that often he had implored their help, but even the angels had failed him during the war.

A plump young Singhalese would come and relate tales about snakes, especially the "honourable cobra." Lawrence, his bright eyes watching intently to catch whatever his slightly deficient hearing might lose, listened spell-bound to records of snake suicide, their tender concern for the blind, remedies for snake-bites according to the hour of the day and the exact location of the bite and the gesture of the victim, pet cobras in school gardens milk-fed by the children. A tactful word of assent or leading question from Lawrence kept the yarn spinning. Our narrator admired Frieda, who looked to him like pictures of Buddhist saints.[23]

She had lost a brooch given her by Lawrence. It was a hot day, which oppressed Lawrence beyond endurance, so this occurrence caused him to utter a long diatribe against the sin of carelessness; hardly had his burning words been uttered than in a low voice he recanted them all, saying gently that big things alone count and prudence spends itself in pettiness.

During the rainy season the rains came at exactly ten in the morning and four in the afternoon, timed to a minute. We knew how to calculate, except for the first one. We had started out for a walk and were well on our way, when the rain fell, not in gentle drops, but in deluges; one second had drenched us to the bone as though we had been dropped into the sea. Our hair hung like dripping seaweed, our garments clung to us so that we could barely totter, rain poured in cataracts from our cork-hats. We splashed breathlessly to the verandahs. Lawrence stood gaunt and white in the swirl of water. Although it was a tepid bath, and we were glowing with warmth after our climb uphill, still this drenching may have done us no good. As the rainy season continued we felt as mildewed as our garments in the recesses of the rooms where there was waged a continual battle against mould. Lawrence sat disconsolately, his voice reduced to a minor key, reiterating that he felt his "heart's blood oozing away, but literally ebbing out drop by drop." When I added that I had no cosmic consciousness or universal love left, it seemed to raise his spirits! [24] He became quite gay and carefree at the mere thought of having lost such a load.

Lawrence was deeply conscious of our daughter, Harwood, and took an interest in her concerns, which extended even to a doll whose smashed face had been replaced by a home-made affair of a painted silk stocking. This poor substitute was dubbed by Lawrence "Swabina" (dishcloth). This was resented:

"She's little Lucile."

"No, that's Swabina."

"She's Lucile."

"Swabina!"

This anomalous doll drove about in an even more anomalous carriage created by a local carpenter. Lawrence enjoyed the sight of Swabina seated in this white hearse of a chariot that Harwood rumbled around the verandahs, and when it came time to pack he stood staunchly by her demand that she take the perambulator back to Europe with her. For this end he worked hours in the wilting heat, removing the solid wheels and massive handles, packing them around the body of the cart which he filled with her books. A neat arrangement but immovable!—to be inherited by *ayah's* baby!

Before leaving Ceylon, as we had now decided to do shortly, we took many excursions, motoring through the green sea of jungle. A particularly happy trip which Lawrence enjoyed with gusto was the one up to the heights of Nuwara Eliya. We startled a herd of deer crossing our road; the way led first through palms and tropical plants under a hot sun, then tea plantations. When we reached Nuwara Eliya, with its stunted pines, the hoar frost lay thick on the ground. The bazaars of the village enticed us within. Lawrence with one glance discovered the treasure there among the usual tawdry array, and bore off with satisfaction some fine red lacquer candlesticks from Cashmere painted with flowers. He turned them about, inspecting each petal, saying that they were doubly interesting to him because at one time he had saved all the tin boxes and glass bottles that came his way and had decorated them with lacquer-painted flowers.

Another day, breathlessly hot, we set forth to find an isolated tribe of people, said to be descended from kings but now outcasts, who lived in the remote jungles. They wove reed mats with red and black designs of ducks, elephants and other creatures. Following Lawrence's lead in single file along a path barely visible in the rank growth, suddenly we came upon the stinking skins of animals pegged out on the ground to dry in the sweltering sunshine, the skins still bloody and swarming with flies. Lawrence turned hurriedly from the sickening sight. His sensibilities were outraged.

Lawrence visited with us old rock temples where the champak flowers were fragrant on the trees nearby. Earl and I would enter with our hands full of the pale gold and rosy blossoms to make offerings, removing shoes and hats to pay homage to the silent Buddha figures in the caves: coming out, there would be Lawrence standing in his shoes, hat tight on his head, declaring that there was no use, he did not belong there and could not join in.

Lawrence watched the monkeys swinging from the trees, and had a wholesome respect for the size and disposition of the elephants hauling timber on the road.

As the days passed the heat grew worse. Our rattan beds sagged in the middle like hammocks. We all were miserable and Lawrence could scarcely drag about. He had been awarded a prize of one hundred pounds for the best English novel of the season, *The Lost Girl*. Feeling free to move off he sailed for America by way of the South Sea and Australia. We were packing together, they to go further east, we to come west.[25]

17 April 1922   "Ardnaree," Lake View Estate, Kandy, Ceylon

((. . . *Ceylon is too hot. One sweats and sweats, and gets thinner and thinner. I am not staying. We are sailing next Monday, 24th, for West Australia—the address c/o Mrs. Jenkins, Strawberry Hill, Perth, West Australia. It has been lovely to see Ceylon. But I feel the East is not for me. It seems to me the life drains away from one here. The old people here say just the same: they say it is the natives that drain the life out of one, and that's how it seems to me. One could quite easily sink into a kind of apathy, like a lotus on a muddy pond, indifferent to anything. And that apparently is the lure of the east: this peculiar stagnant apathy where one doesn't bother about a thing, but drifts on from minute to minute. I am not at all sure that we shall like Australia either. But it seems to be en route. We shall stay with the Jenkins for a time: if we don't care for that, go on to Sydney. I am taking a ticket to Sydney, as it only costs £6 more. And then after trying Sydney and New South Wales, if I don't like that we shall go across the Pacific to San Francisco, and then I shall have to sit down and earn some money to take the next stride, for I shall be blued. But I don't care. Now I have started, I will go on and on till I am more or less sure. And if I like none of the places I shall come back to Europe with my mind made up, and settle down permanently in England or Italy. So there's the programme.*

.   .   .   .

By the way I detest Buddha, upon a slight contact: affects me like a mud pool that has no bottom to it.—One learns to value what one actually knows and possesses, and to have a wholesome indifference to strange gods. Anyhow these little rat-hole Buddhist temples turn my stomach.[26]

30 April 1922   R.M.S. Orsova to Fremantle

❨ Here we are on a ship again—somewhere in a very big blue choppy sea
with flying fishes sprinting out of the waves like winged drops, and a Catholic Spanish priest playing Chopin at the piano—very well—and the boat
gently rolling.

.   .   .   .

We are going to Australia—Heaven knows why: because it will be cooler,
and the sea is wide. Ceylon steams heat and it isn't so much the heat as the
chemical decomposition of one's blood by the ultra-violet rays of the sun.
Don't know what we'll do in Australia—don't care. The world of idea may
be all alike, but the world of physical feeling is very different—one suffers
getting adjusted—but that is part of the adventure. I think Frieda feels
like me, a bit dazed and indifferent—reckless—I break my heart over England when I am out here. Those natives are back of us—in the living sense
lower than we are. But they're going to swarm over us and suffocate us. We
are, have been for five centuries, the growing tip. Now we're going to fall.
But you don't catch me going back on my whiteness and Englishness and
myself. English in the teeth of all the world, even in the teeth of England.[27]

4 May 1922   Perth, Western Australia

❨ Well, here we are—a raw hole it seems. Got here this morning. Shall
have to wait a fortnight or so for a boat on to Sydney. Doubt if Australia
will see much of me. At the rate I'm going, I ought to be in Taos easily
by August.[28]

Mrs. A. L. Jenkins
as told by H. E. L. Priday

Mrs. Jenkins was there to meet [the Lawrences] when they reached
Fremantle in the *Orsova*, showed them round Perth, fixed them up temporarily in a guest house at Darlington (where they met Nurse Skinner) while they went house-hunting on their own account. And, to satisfy
Lawrence's extreme curiosity about the Australian bush, they arranged

a motor excursion which he vividly described in letters to friends in England since edited for publication by Aldous Huxley.[29]

In Perth, Lawrence made his headquarters or calling place at the Booklovers' Library, where he was happy to find some of his books on sale; he never failed to look in there when in town.[30] But what surprised him most of all in Perth—according to Mrs. Jenkins, who unearthed it for him—was a copy of his banned novel *The Rainbow* in the library of the Mechanics' Institute.[31] This was the last place where Lawrence could have expected to find this novel, which during World War One a Bow Street magistrate had ordered the publishers to destroy as obscene. Its suppression had for a time even frightened them from publishing *Women in Love*, which accounts for its appearance only in 1921, the year before they came to Australia.

Frieda confessed to Mrs. Jenkins that she would like nothing so much as a rest from vagabondage, and a home of her own to keep neat and tidy. But her husband was as unsettled as ever, and within a week or two Mrs. Jenkins received a brief card, pencilled at the Booklovers', which read,

Sat. morning [13 May 1922]/Booklovers/[Postmark: 13 May 1922]
Came into town for an hour—leaving by 12.20. Have decided to go on to Sydney by the Malwa on Thursday [18 May 1922]—no house at Darlington. When shall we see you— What of your black . . . [word undecipherable: *hut? lust?*]?

D. H. Lawrence

On the Wednesday following came another hasty scrawl:

Darlington   Wednesday/[17 May 1922]
Dear Mrs. Jenkins
No cure for depression except to feel downright devil-may-care.
We'll be in tomorrow morning. Mr. Siebenhaar [32] wrote urging us to lunch. I said we would either lunch with him or ask him to lunch with us. Now it occurs to me that you might hate him lunching with us at the Savoy. I'm sure I am only being polite to him. So ring up the Booklovers tomorrow at 9.30 and tell me if I'm to put him off. I can easily invent a story. Then we can have our lunch at the Savoy in moderate peace.
I believe we need not be on board until 3.0 or 3.30: boat leaving at 4.0, according to time-table. I'll call at P. & O. at 9.0 in the morning and make sure. But as I have to get all my luggage down from Perth, and as I suppose I'd better do it myself, please don't think of motoring us. We'll go by train to Fremantle—bags and all.

à demain
D. H. Lawrence

So they met and lunched with Mr. Siebenhaar, who showed them his long and, as it would appear, not so very good poem entitled *Dorothea:* and got down to the ship in time, leaving for Sydney with Mrs. Jenkins to see them off.[33]

May Eva Gawler
as told to Joanna Gawler Ramsey

My meeting with the Lawrences took place in Western Australia when they were en route from Colombo to Sydney in early May 1922. I would never have had the pleasure of meeting them if my great friend Mrs. Jenkins had not been a passenger on the ship with them from Naples to Colombo. She had written to me from Aden, complaining of a deadly dull voyage out. So I was more than surprised when she phoned me on the night of her return, and in awed tones began at once by saying, "Listen, Maisie, the *Lawrences* were on board for part of the voyage, and after I had met them I had a most interesting time. They are due in Fremantle soon, and I want to arrange a drive to The Hills where we'll give them a real Australian picnic lunch—grilled chops on open fire, boiled 'billy' tea, etc."

And so it happened. The weather, I remember, was perfect—a very important factor in picnic parties!

Very late a big touring car drove up to my cottage, and "Jenks," fluttering with excitement, came in to collect and prepare me for meeting The Great Man.

My idea of the appearance of Lawrence was completely shattered when I found standing at the gate a man something between a reddish-bearded, able-bodied seaman and a handy man at the back door! But this was again shattered at once when he came forward and spoke a few words in a low gentle voice. Jenks then led us to the car where Lawrence introduced me to his wife with complete lack of embarrassment. I say this because Mrs. Jenkins had told me that they were not married at the time.[34] Frieda was sitting next to the driver, and I just noticed a rather large "motherly" looking woman who spoke with a strong accent.

During the drive Lawrence sat in the back seat between Jenks and me. Right from the start conversation was easy and gay, and as we drove through the suburbs towards Perth, our lovely capital, Lawrence spoke of the voyage from Naples. Apparently, until the Lawrences found Jenks among the hundreds of passengers, Lawrence was dreading the days of utter boredom and seasickness. And Jenks teased him about all the pills and medicines with which he had dosed himself, while I chipped in and suggested that a "dose of Jenks" was usually a cure-all for anything.

We drove through our famous King's Park, which is a natural stretch of "bush" country overlooking the Swan River and the city of Perth—away to The Hills beyond where our picnic was to take place. We pointed out the wild flowers peculiar to Western Australia and the red gums which form a lovely avenue through the park.

When, from time to time, Lawrence turned to me and asked questions about myself, I then noticed for the first time his eyes: blue, gentle, and wistful. I had been wondering how this rather shabby, slightly coarse, far from spruce and tidy little man could possibly have caused such a flutter, apart from his books. But there—I found it, for he had infinite charm in his make-up, a kind of feminine sympathy. Indeed, as he paid me so much attention, Jenks interrupted, muttering, "I knew I was stupid to introduce Maisie to you, Lawrence, for you haven't addressed one word to me since!" At which Lawrence burst out laughing and said, "A dose of Mrs. Gawler is—well—a tonic."

On arrival up in The Hills, we got out of the car on the side of a slope which looked back, down over the Swan River. And further, about thirty miles in the distance, a tiny ribbon gleamed along the horizon—the Indian Ocean—and the port of Fremantle where the Lawrences had disembarked a day or so before.

While Jenks and I unpacked the picnic basket and the driver collected sticks for an open fire to cook the chops and boil the "billy" for tea, Lawrence lay sprawling just above and seemed to be no longer "with" us. Bringing him back to earth, Jenks pointed out a bungalow in the distance where lived Miss Skinner, whom Lawrence later met.

I think it was during lunch that we discussed travelling. Jenks said that her desire to live in both England and Australia was exactly divided (hence her so frequent journeys abroad), but that instantly she arrived in either place she wished she were in the other. I for my part said I was perfectly content never to leave my garden. And I think it was then that Lawrence tried to explain his wanderings by saying that he intensely longed to visit remote lands and there to live and recreate himself anew. At this I turned on him and said, "You are a restless, dissatisfied-with-yourself wanderer, and you *should* be able to create between the four walls where you were born. In fact," I said, "you are a fool." Lawrence was slightly taken aback, but laughed heartily and replied, "You know, Mrs. Gawler, that's the first time I've been so insulted, and I've a good mind to put that in a book."

Well, he did remember my "insult," for sometime later he wrote to Mrs. Jenkins and sent this message: "Remember me nicely to Mrs. Gawler. Tell her I agree with her; I am a fool." This appeared in print in Huxley's edition of Lawrence's letters.[35]

I saw him only once again. Mrs. Jenkins took us all to tea with a Mrs. Zabel, an intellectual woman who owned the Booklovers' Library in Hay Street, Perth, and was, I believe, of German extraction. Mrs. Jenkins had thought it would be pleasant for Frieda to meet her.

I said good-bye that afternoon, and we hoped to meet again, but we didn't. However, the memory lingers on.

Yes, I met Lawrence, but it was many years ago.

And now I am old.[36]

Phyllis Harrison

Although I now own (I think!) the best bookshop in Western Australia, at the time I met Lawrence I was the junior junior at "The Booklovers"—made the tea, etc. I had the pleasure of making it for him on several occasions, and although I was only fifteen, I was very flattered at the attention he paid me. Our conversation was purely about Western Australia and books, but at that time I did not know what I do now—thirty years later!

He was so charming and unassuming, his pale interesting face and long slender hands made a great impression on me. At that stage I had not read any of his books, but promised him to do so, and he told me to do it by degrees.[37]

15 May 1922   Darlington, Western Australia

⟨ We are here about 16 miles out of Perth—bush all around—marvellous air, marvellous sun and sky—strange, vast empty country—hoary unending "bush" with a pre-primeval ghost in it—apples ripe and good, also pears. And we could have a nice little bungalow—but—but—BUT—well, it's always an anticlimax of buts. I just don't want to stay, that's all. It is so democratic, it feels to me infra dig. In so free a land, it is humiliating to keep house and cook still another mutton-chop.[38]

⟨ I often think of Darlington. . . . Perhaps we shall come back one day. The path down the hollow under the gum trees, to your mother's cottage: and those big ducks. Your mother didn't belong to our broken, fragmentary *generation; with her oriental rugs in that little wooden bungalow, and her big, easy gesture of life. It was too small for her, really.*[39]

Mollie L. Skinner

Brook Cottage,/Darlington, W.A./6th August, 1952
Dear Mr. Howarth,

You came to see me down the precipice track that leads to Brook cottage to ask or to seek something more of D. H. Lawrence. . . . You asked me to write something of the collaboration of the *Boy in the Bush.* . . .[40]

The odd thing is that you seemed to search out the inner person and found it. And so I would like to tell you what I have to tell of Lawrence. It had better go in the shape of a letter, since having been requested quite often to write of him, I have done so, submitted my script, and not had it returned. So copyright raises its head.

You asked how it was he came to Darlington. Well, it happened that a friend called Mrs. Jenkins, "Pussy" to her intimates, a social leader and charming woman, travelled from England on the same boat with the Lawrences. On reaching Fremantle "Pussy" rang me at the Holiday House I was running with my Quaker friend Miss [Ellen] Beakbane at Leithdale, Darlington, and said there was an author D. H. Lawrence with his wife a German Countess who wanted to see Australia. He was a restless nostalgic, arrogant person who would not stay in Perth, so if we had a room vacant she would bring him up.

When they arrived, the maid was out and I had to take them afternoon tea on the verandah. "Pussy" shoved a bag of expensive cakes in my hand but took no more notice of me. There were other ladies I did not know, and two or three men, and I hoped the little one with a red beard was not Lawrence. It turned out that he was.

It was Frieda who had us at her feet at first. She was beautiful, beaming and most fascinating, and it amazed us that she adored the little man and expected everyone else to do so. You must bear in mind that the Sunny West, though twenty-two years a State, was still raw and unhewn. We had little opportunity for reading novels, and most of us had never heard of D. H. Lawrence, only of Lawrence of Arabia.[41] Eustace Cohen, an architect and musician of brilliance, and his young wife, Maudie, were staying with us, so we put the Lawrences at the same table. Maudie told them that Mollie Skinner was a writer too! It makes me blush even now. I only had had a text book on Midwifery, and

Letters of a V.A.D. published; the latter under a nom de plume as I had been a Nursing Sister in the war who would have been cashiered if it were known I had written it.

Maudie gave Lawrence this book to read, and someone gave me Lawrence's *White Peacock* to read. I blinked my eyes—here was *writing*. Writing that came near to my ideal, Katherine Mansfield's writing.

However, we were extremely busy at the time, taking care of our guests, and being Martha I must forget Mary, but Lawrence found Mary.

He followed me to the washtub bringing his white woollen socks to wash himself. In the drawing room I would see him surrounded by adorers—for they found him out. He would sit there in an armchair letting *them* talk, his pale face bored, amused and aloof, his green eyes half-shut. When they went to bed, as we went to ours on the back verandah, we would see him walking off alone up the track in the brilliant moonlight to make acquaintance with the Australian dark gods. He shivered when he told me, declaring they scared him stiff, so empty and void, cruel and vindictive. But how beautiful the paradox, he said, in sunlight with exquisite blossoms growing on harsh prickly brush, or under the gaunt trees, the sensitive tender flowers and delicate fern.

"Why do you go off alone into the bush—we don't like it, you might easily get lost," I said.

"I might—it clutches me with its aged glamour. No one can see it." And then he added "I wonder you don't write of the early days, tell us what drew these early Settlers. Tell us *what kept them here*. Why don't you? I can't for I'm not staying in a place that strains my heart, that I can't fathom—that frightens me."

"I know what you mean, it frightens me too," I said, "But I long to write about it, yet no one would look at a book about the early settlers in this benighted land. Besides I have to earn my bread and butter and there is no other way of doing that for me, except as a nurse."

His scorn, his sorrow, his contempt flung back in the words, "You have been given the Divine Spark!, and would bury it in a napkin."

Now I want to make it clear that upon arriving in Australia after his anguished years defying the War—just over—D. H. Lawrence was in a contrary mood. Not for a moment did he allude to that part of his personality called perverse and often pervert, so I didn't know anything about it. Even Frieda said "I do not know this Law-rence." I wish I could say how she drawled his name, love in every tone of it. "He is so gentle and kind, so—what do you call it?—angelic—since we arrived here. The

mood will pass—you stupid people do not know him as he is, so can-
tankerous, so passionate and disconsolate. I wish he would remain like
this, for I would like to settle down here and have a little farm in the
amethyst atmosphere. Have you noticed the air is the colour of amethyst?"

It made me shake with laughter thinking of the delicate little man
with his frail body harnessing plough horses on a chill winter morning,
while the lovely Frieda lit the fire and cooked his bacon, for we never
saw her as anything else but a Countess, or, as for that, Lawrence with
any background but that of novelist.

Yet day after day he sought me out when I was at leisure, and talked
and talked, though never of himself except to say how miserable it had
made him to have to fight famous authors. He said he had gone round
with the hat to help him finance this visit, telling the others they were
swamping his gift by not recognizing him. He laughed as he told how
Bernard Shaw snubbed him when putting a fiver in the hat—to get rid
of him; how H. G. Wells told him, as he added a few pounds to those
in the hat, that he would do better with his life if he continued teaching, and how Galsworthy turned his back on him.[42] It seems that some
rich woman in Mexico [43] had sent him a big cheque to visit her ranch
and he and Frieda might go on there when the hat money was spilled.
Oh! if I had had a dictaphone to tell what he said in bitter-sweet words
of those contemporaries!

That I forgot his beard, his fragile body and his strange scarlet lips,
it is needless to say, for he told me what to write and how to write it:
early days—settlers making their homes—falling in love with each other.

"But who can I have for a hero?" I asked.

My brother Jack passed by, broken by the war, his handsome legs
dragging; through his spirit he carried his wounded head high.[44] Lawrence seemed to look at him and know him, with his peculiar uncanny
insight. He read him then turned his gaze on me. (Lawrence never spoke
to my brother.)

"You love your brother," he said, "you have always known him. He
came out here to this hoary land when sixteen as a jackaroo, and you
followed him along. Make him your hero."

Perhaps I have wandered from what you want to know, Mr. Howarth.
The Lawrence I knew was so very different to the Lawrence others
knew. I can only find him in two lovely poems, "Kangaroo" and "The
Snake," and maybe in "Fishes." [45] So absurd.

> Fishes, fishes, little fishes,
> Wherefore art thou little fishes?

(*Seated, left to right*) Lawrence, Laura Forrester, Frieda; (*standing*) Mrs. Bill Marchbanks on excursion from "Wyewurk," Thirroul, N.S.W., Australia (Summer, 1922). Photograph by Arthur Denis Forrester.

"Wyewurk," Thirroul, N.S.W., Australia, where the Lawrences lived May–August, 1922. The photograph dates from this period. From a photograph in the possession of Mrs. Beatrice E. Southwell.

"Wyewurk." Photograph by F. W. L. Esch.

(*Left to right*) Frieda, Laura Forrester, and Lawrence at "Wyewurk" (Summer, 1922). Photograph by Arthur Denis Forrester.

Lawrence's MS of "A Britisher has a word with Harriett Monroe," published anonymously as "A Britisher Has a Word with an Editor," in *Palms*, I (No. V, Christmas, 1923), 153–54. From the holograph MS in the possession of Mrs. Idella Purnell Stone.

Typescript of Mrs. Idella Purnell Stone's advertisement "A Year of Christmas," showing Lawrence's revisions. See *Palms*, I (No. V, Christmas, 1923), [160]. From the original typescript in the possession of Mrs. Idella Purnell Stone.

Lawrence several times visited my mother in the little cottage I live in now. She could have lived in a more stylish manner, only that Jack built the cottage for her, next door to the one granted to him as a returned soldier. She wanted to be near the only son she had left to her.

Jack drove the Lawrences to the station when they departed. He said Lawrence put his hands in his pocket to tip him, but thought worse of it. "Ye Gods!" quoth Jack, "what stopped him!"

When we all were saying farewell on our verandah, I said an unaccountable thing which horrified everyone but Lawrence. He gave one of those quick insight flashes of his dreamy eyes and explained. "She means I have bidden her write a book."

What I had said was, "Good-bye, good luck. You have hit me in the solar plexus!"

When it comes to brass tacks why does one say such foolish things and why does one remember them?

I hope this artless letter has something that may interest you. I think what Katharine Susannah Prichard wrote regarding D. H. L. and myself in the tenth birthday number of *Meanjin* will explain something further.[46] She has always been very generous to me, and something more, there is a deep understanding between us apart from politics.

Sincerely yours,

Mollie Skinner [47]

15 May 1922   Darlington, Western Australia

❨ So the new Jews must wander on. Frieda is very disappointed. She had hoped to find a new England or new Germany here, with much space and gayer people.

The land is here, sky high and blue and new as if you'd never taken a breath out of it: and the air is new, new, strong, fresh as silver. And the country is terribly big and empty, still uninhabited. The bush is grey and without end. No noise—quiet—and the white trunks of the gum-trees, all a little burnt: a wood and a prewood, not a jungle: something like a dream, a twilight wood that has not seen the day yet. It needs hundreds of years before it can live. This is the land where the unborn souls, strange and unknown, that will be born in five hundred years, live. A grey, strange spirit, and the people that are here are not really here: only like ducks that swim on the surface of a lake. But the country has a fourth dimension and the white people float like shadows on the surface. And they are not new people: very nervous, neurotic, they don't sleep well, as if they always felt a ghost near. I say, a new country is like sharp wine in which floats like a pearl the soul of an incoming people, till this soul is melted or dissolved. But this is stupid.

Thursday we go on by the P. & O. boat "Malwa" to Adelaide, Melbourne, and Sydney. We stay at Adelaide a day, sleep a night at Melbourne, and arrive at Sydney on the twenty-seventh: nine days from Fremantle. That will be interesting. We have our tickets from Colombo to Sydney. It does please me to go on further. I think from Sydney we may go on to San Francisco, and stay a few weeks at Tahiti. And so round the world.

Oh, mother-in-law, it must be so! It is my destiny, this wandering. But the world is round and will bring us back to Baden.[48]

20 May 1922   R.M.S. Malwa

⟨ Now we are rolling in the Gt. Australian Bight, en route for Sydney. Ceylon was lovely to look at but not to live in. . . . —We stayed two weeks in West Australia—weird place. Don't know how long we shall stay in Sydney—perhaps a month or two—then on into the South Seas, and so to America, to Taos. I've no idea where I shall get the money for the steamer fares, but I don't care. I find on these boats one can travel perfectly second class—nicer than first, simpler—now that there is hardly anybody coming out this way. We are less than thirty passengers second class—nice simple people.—I feel that once I have rolled out of Europe I'll go on rolling. I like it so much. But F. still hankers after "a little 'ome of 'er own." I, no. —But I love straying my own way.—Australia has a marvellous sky and air and blue clarity, and a hoary sort of land beneath it, like a Sleeping Princess on whom the dust of ages has settled. Wonder if she'll ever get up.— I'm not working—don't want to . . . . —As for me, I have started rolling and can't stop yet. Downhill.[49]

Arthur Denis Forrester
as told to F. W. L. Esch

The *Malwa* left England on the Saturday [15 April 1922] following Good Friday and arrived in Sydney exactly six weeks later [27 May 1922]. The Lawrences came aboard the *Malwa* at Fremantle [18 May 1922], and they got off again at Sydney, so we really did not see very much of them during the voyage.

My late wife, Laura, and I were on our way to settle in Australia. I am a hosiery mechanic, and we were being brought out from knitting mills in Nottingham to go to a job in Sydney. I have been in the same job ever since. There was another chap, Bill Marchbanks, and his wife going out to the same job. We travelled together second class, and when we arrived in Sydney we boarded at the same place.

I think the ladies first got friendly with Frieda Lawrence. She was a very friendly person, much less reserved than D. H. As far as I can remember, the friendship began on deck when I lent my field glasses to Frieda to look at a passing ship. That broke the ice, and we used to meet together for chats the way friends do on board ship. When we parted at Sydney, Laura must have given Frieda a forwarding address.

I cannot recall any conversations of particular importance on the *Malwa;* nor when we met the Lawrences again in Sydney and they invited us to "Wyewurk." I do remember that Frieda did most of the talking, while D. H. listened and laughed and seemed to be enjoying himself. Frieda talked mostly about their travels and the amusing experiences they had had. We knew he was a writer, but at that stage we had not read any of his books and he never talked about his work.

As the Lawrences at that time had nowhere definite to stay, we lost sight of them for some time after their arrival in Sydney.[50]

20 May 1922   R.M.S. Malwa

❨ *I am enjoying the face of the earth and letting my Muse, dear hussy, repent her ways. 'Get thee to a nunnery' I said to her. Heaven knows if we shall ever see her face again, unveiled, uncoiffed.*

The earth—& man—is a strange mystery: always rather what you expected, and yet oh, so different. So different. One wonders if all books are just so many parish magazines.—The talk is just on top.

Alas for me and my erotic reputation! Tell them I have sent my Muse into a nunnery while I took a look at the world.[51]

29 May 1922   "Wyewurk," Thirroul, New South Wales, Australia

❨ *[Here] we are safe and sound. Sydney is a great fine town, half like London, half like America. The harbour is wonderful—narrow gateway between two cliffs—then one sails through and is in another little sea, with many bays and gulfs. The big ferry steamers go all the time threading across the blue water, and hundreds of people always travelling.*

But Sydney town costs too much, so we came down into the country. We are about fifty kilometres south of Sydney, on the coast. We have got a lovely little house on the edge of the low cliff just above the Pacific Ocean. —Der grosse oder stille Ozean, says Frieda. But it is by no means still. The heavy waves break with a great roar all the time: and it is so near. We have only our little grassy garden—then the low cliff—and then the great white rollers breaking, and the surf seeming to rush right under our feet as we sit at table. Here it is winter, but not cold. But today the sky is dark, and it makes me think of Cornwall. We have a coal fire going, and are very comfortable. Things go so quietly in Australia. It will not cost much to live here, food is quite cheap. Good meat is only fivepence or sixpence a pound —50 Pfg. ein Pfund.

But it is a queer, grey, sad country—empty, and as if it would never be filled. Miles and miles of bush—forlorn and lost. It all feels like that. Yet Sydney is a huge modern city.

I don't really like it, it is so raw—so crude. The people are so crude in their feelings—and they only want to be up-to-date in the "conveniences"— electric light and tramways and things like that. The aristocracy are the people who own big shops—and there is no respect for anything else. The working people very discontented—always threaten more strikes—always more socialism.

I shall cable to America for money, and sail in July across the Pacific to San Francisco—via Wellington, New Zealand, Raratonga [sic], Tahiti, Honolulu—then to our Taos. And that is the way home—coming back. Next spring we will come to Germany. I've got a Heimweh for Europe: Sicily, England, Germany.[52]

Beatrice E. Southwell

In the year 1922, D. H. Lawrence and Frieda arrived at Thirroul—a mining township on the South Coast of New South Wales, Australia— where they interviewed my sister and brother-in-law, Mr. and Mrs. Alfred Callcott, who were Estate Agents.[53]

They required a furnished cottage, for a few months, that overlooked the Pacific Ocean. As my bungalow "Wyewurk" had recently been vacated by a large family (mentioned in *Kangaroo*), Mrs. Callcott telephoned me at my home in Epping which is some sixty miles from Thirroul to enquire whether I would be willing to have the Lawrences as tenants.

I replied in the affirmative, but said that I would prefer to have the bungalow prepared for them and to replace anything that might be necessary for their comfort.

After inspection the Lawrences were pleased with the solidity of the brick structure and the bright red roof tiles, and decided to take possession, just as it was and while it still retained the atmosphere of the home life of the large family which had just moved out.

The lounge-dining room of "Wyewurk" is 24 feet x 17 feet. The walls are red in colour to the china rail and white above. The ceiling is white also, with dark wooden beams three feet apart. All the woodwork is dark in colour, while an open fireplace suggests winter comfort.

From the large jarrah wood table in this room, on which D. H. Lawrence wrote his Australian classic *Kangaroo*, he could view the vast Pacific Ocean to the horizon with ships and coastal craft passing. The sun seeming to rise from the sea at dawn and the moon casting a silver sheen at night would inspire the soul of an artist, especially as the view could be seen from any of the five windows in this room, all of which faced the sea.

"Wyewurk" contains three bedrooms, kitchen, pantry, bathroom, wide verandah, and garage. Most of the original furniture is still there—six strongly constructed chairs, serving table, and sideboard which, together with the floor, are all built of jarrah wood.

A carpet twelve feet square covered the centre of this floor, and when entering the room after the Lawrences had left, I noticed that the carpet had been taken up but not tacked down again—Frieda had been house cleaning.

There was a food cupboard in the dining room near the entrance to the kitchen which contained a fuel stove, table, draining board and sink, cupboards and china shelves on which were several teapots, jugs, plates, dishes, cups and saucers, etc. which were used by Lawrence and Frieda and were referred to in *Kangaroo*—some may still be there.

Crossing the lawn in front of "Wyewurk" to the edge of the cliff runs a winding path, bordered by coastal growth, that leads down to the beach and the lovely surf referred to by Lawrence and mentioned in a letter written to a friend on June 22nd, 1922.[54]

From the cliff, miles of coast line is seen, and from here, where three beautiful Norfolk Island pine trees now stand so strong and majestic, Lawrence enjoyed the distant view of another headland and more Norfolk Island pines, down Bulli way, and remarked that some day his Soul would return there.

There was a rustic seat in the shade of a native "Bottle Brush shrub" on the lawn. Probably D. H. would have rested there with Frieda, or alone—with thoughts of Australia and the future of this new country and its peoples, also thoughts of the surrounding district, the coal mines, the miners, the iron and steel works of Port Kembla, the latter mentioned in *Kangaroo*, and the city of Wollongong which has since expanded tremendously.

From the back of "Wyewurk" there is a fine view of the famous Bulli Pass Summit from which "lookout" one is charmed with the magnificent panoramic view of the Pacific Ocean, many miles of the coast line, and the township of Thirroul nestling as it were in a basin. ("Thirroul" is the aboriginal name, meaning "In a basin.") Also "Wyewurk" with its red roof can be seen. Lawrence with Frieda may have visited this spot and appreciated the beauty of the scenery near and far.

They were fortunate in locating a temporary home to their satisfaction, of which he writes, "The house is an awfully nice bungalow . . . . Frieda loves it here." [55] And again, "[Here] we don't know a soul: nor want to." [56]

I do not believe that the Callcotts in *Kangaroo* had any connection with the Callcotts living in Thirroul as they do not resemble them in any way, so I assume that the name was used fictitiously.

Few people in Thirroul realized that a famous author had lived in their midst until after Lawrence had left Australia.

For many years afterwards and to the present time admirers of D. H. Lawrence have come to see "Wyewurk," so it was decided by Mrs. Callcott of whom they enquired that she would keep a "Visitors Book."

Within a few months, renovations of "Wyewurk" will be completed and as much as possible will be preserved—just as D. H. Lawrence and Frieda knew it.[57]

Clarice Callcott Farraher

My mother, Mrs. Alfred Callcott, did not know D. H. Lawrence was the author, until she made a visit to "Wyewurk" soon after he left the cottage, and found a number of English magazines. On turning over the pages, she found some missing, and referring to the index, found the name D. H. Lawrence as the writer of the missing pages.

Later, I made a visit to our local doctor (Dr. Crossle) who told me D. H. Lawrence had written a book called *Kangaroo* and had used my mother and father's name—Callcott.

One afternoon, D. H. Lawrence and his wife visited my mother's home and on leaving my mother walked to the gate with them. Frieda admired the garden, and Mother picked a bunch of dahlias for her. The words spoken were the exact words used in *Kangaroo:*

And sure enough, in a few minutes came Harriet's gushing cries of joy and admiration: "Oh, how lovely! how marvellous! but can they really be dahlias? I've never seen such dahlias! they're really too beautiful! But you shouldn't give them me, you shouldn't."

"Why not?" cried Mrs. Callcott in delight.

"So many. And isn't it a pity to cut them?" This, rather wistfully, to the masculine silence of Jack.

"Oh no, they want cutting as they come, or the blooms gets smaller," said Jack, masculine and benevolent.

"And scent!—they have scent!" cried Harriet, sniffing at her velvety bouquet.

"They have a little—not much though. Flowers don't have much scent in Australia," deprecated Mrs. Callcott.

"Oh, I must show them to my husband," cried Harriet, half starting from the fence.[58]

On another occasion, Frieda told my mother that when her husband was writing, she would take him a glass of milk, but he would not speak, just push the glass aside.

I understand that D. H. Lawrence was very reserved; the people he would have come in contact with while at Thirroul have long since moved from the district.

It is known that Dr. Crossle visited him at "Wyewurk," but I do not know if it was a professional visit or otherwise.

Many of the places described in *Kangaroo* at Thirroul were very correct, such as the library and the soldiers' monument.

I am in possession of a visitors' book, which belonged to my mother, in reference to visitors to "Wyewurk" who are interested in D. H. Lawrence. It is dated back to 1934.[59]

Frieda Lawrence Ravagli

We arrived in Sydney harbour—nice it was not knowing a soul.

A young officer on the boat had told me: "The rain on the tin roofs over the trenches always made me think of home." Sydney!

And there they were, the tin roofs of Sydney and the beautiful harbour and the lovely Pacific Coast, the air so new and clean. We stayed a day or two in Sydney, two lonely birds resting a little. And then we took a train with all our trunks and said: "We'll look out of the window and where it looks nice we'll get out." It looked very attractive along the coast but also depressing. We were passing deserted homesteads: both in America and Australia, these human abandoned efforts make one very sad. Then we came to Thirroul, we got out at four and by six o'clock we were settled in a beautiful bungalow right on the sea. Lined with jarra the rooms were, and there were great tanks for rain water and a stretch of grass going right down to the Pacific, melting away into a pale-blue and lucid, delicately tinted sky.

But what a state the bungalow was in! A family of twelve children had stayed there before us: beds and dusty rugs all over the place, torn sailing canvases on the porches, paper all over the garden, the beautiful jarra floors grey with dust and sand, the carpet with no colour at all, just a mess, a sordid mess the whole thing. So we set to and cleaned, cleaned and cleaned as we had done so many times before in our many temporary homes! Floors polished, the carpet taken in the garden and scrubbed, the torn canvases removed. But the paper in the garden was the worst; for days and days we kept gathering paper.

But I was happy: only Lawrence and I in this world. He always made a great big world for me, he gave it me whenever it was possible; whenever there was wonder left, we took it, and revelled in it.

The mornings, those sunrises over the Pacific had all the wonder of newness, of an uncreated world. Lawrence began to write *Kangaroo* and the days slipped by like dreams, but real as dreams are when they come true. The everyday life was so easy, the food brought to the house, especially the fish cart was a thrill: it let down a flap at the back and like pearls and jewels inside the cart lay the shiny fishes, all colours, all shapes, and we had to try them all.

We took long walks along the coast, lonely and remote and unborn. The weather was mild and full of life, we never got tired of the shore, finding shells for hours that the Pacific had rolled gently on to the sand.

Lawrence religiously read the *Sydney Bulletin*.[60] He loved it for all its stories of wild animals and people's living experiences. The only papers Lawrence ever read were the *Corriere della Sera*, in the past, and the *Sydney Bulletin*. I wonder whether this latter has retained the same character it had then; I haven't seen it since that time. It was our only mental food during that time.

I remember being amazed at the generosity of the people at the farms where we got butter, milk, and eggs: you asked for a pound of butter and you were given a big chunk that was nearly two pounds; you asked for two pints of milk and they gave you three; everything was lavish, like the sky and the sea and the land. We had no human contacts all these months: a strange experience: nobody bothered about us, I think.

At the library, strangely enough, in that little library of Thirroul we found several editions of Lawrence's condemned *Rainbow*. We bought a copy—the librarian never knew that it was Lawrence's own book. Australia is like the "Hinterland der Seele."

Like a fantasy seemed the Pacific, pellucid and radiant, melting into the sky, so fresh and new always; then this primal radiance was gone one day and another primeval sea appeared. A storm was throwing the waves high into the air, they rose on the abrupt shore, high as in an enormous window. I could see strange sea-creatures thrown up from the deep: sword-fish and fantastic phenomena of undreamt deep-sea beasts I saw in those waves, frightening and never to be forgotten.[61]

And then driving out of the tidy little town into the bush with the little pony cart. Into golden woods of mimosa we drove, or wattle, as the Australians call it. Mostly red flowers and yellow mimosa, many varieties, red and gold, met the eye, strange fern-trees, delicately leaved. We came to a wide river and followed it. It became a wide waterfall and then it disappeared into the earth. Disappeared and left us gaping. Why should it have disappeared, where had it gone? [62]

Lawrence went on with *Kangaroo* and wove his deep underneath impressions of Australia into this novel. Thirroul itself was a new little bungalow town and the most elegant thing in it was a German gun that glistened steely and out of place there near the Pacific.

I would have liked to stay in Australia and lose myself, as it were, in this unborn country but Lawrence wanted to go to America. Mabel Dodge had written us that Lawrence must come to Taos in New Mexico, that he must know the Pueblo Indians, that the Indians say that the heart of the world beats there in New Mexico.

This gave us a definite aim and we began to get ready for America, in a few weeks.[63]

3 June 1922   *"Wyewurk," Thirroul, New South Wales, Australia*

⟨ I have started a novel and if I can go on with it, I shall stay till I've finished it—till about end of August. But if I can't work I shall come on to America. . . .

.   .   .   .

If I was really going to give up struggling with life, I'd come to Australia. It is a big empty country, with room to be alone.[64]

9 June 1922   "Wyewurk," Thirroul, New South Wales, Australia

❨ Are you angry that we wandered farther away, we wandering Jews? I tell you again, the world is round and brings the rolling stone home again. And I must go on till I find something that gives me peace. Last year I found it at Ebersteinburg. There I finished "Aaron's Rod" and my "Fantasia of the Unconscious." And now "Aaron" has appeared and this month the "Fantasia" will appear in New York. And I, I am in Australia, and suddenly I write again, a mad novel of Australia. That's how it goes. I hope I can finish it by August. . . .

It is nice here. You'd like this house very much: the large room with open fireplace and beautiful windows with red curtains, and large verandas, and the grass and the sea, always big and noisy at our feet. We bathe at midday when the sun is very hot and the shores quite lonely, quite, quite lonely. Only the waves. The village is new and crude. The streets are not built, it is all sand and loam. It's interesting. The people are all very kind and yet strange to me. Postman and newspaper boy come riding on horses and whistle on a policeman's whistle when they have thrown in the letters or newspaper.

. . . .

And heaven and earth so new as if no man had ever breathed in it, no foot ever trodden on it. The great weight of the spirit that lies so heavily on Europe doesn't exist here. You feel a little like a child that has no real cares. It is interesting—a new experience.[65]

13 June 1922   "Wyewurk," Thirroul, New South Wales, Australia

❨ We're in a very nice place: have got a delightful bungalow here about forty miles south of Sydney, right on the shore. We live mostly with the sea —not much with the land—and not at all with the people. I don't present any letters of introduction, we don't know a soul on this side of the continent: which is almost a triumph in itself. For the first time in my life I feel how lovely it is to know nobody in the whole country: and nobody can come to the door, except the tradesmen who bring the bread and meat and so on, and who are very unobtrusive. One nice thing about these countries is that nobody asks questions. I suppose there have been too many questionable people here in the past. But it's nice not to have to start explaining oneself, as one does in Italy.

The people here are awfully nice, casually: thank heaven I need go no further. The township is just a scatter of bungalows, mostly of wood with corrugated iron roofs, and with some quite good shops: "stores." It lies back from the sea. Nobody wants to be too near the sea here: only we are on the brink. About two miles inland there is a great long hill like a wall, facing the sea and running all down the coast. This is dark greyish with gum-trees, and it has little coal-mines worked into it. The men are mostly coal-miners, so I feel quite at home. The township itself—they never say village here—is all haphazard and new, the streets unpaved, the church built of wood. That part is pleasant—the newness. It feels so free. And though it is midwinter, and the shortest day next week, still every day is as sunny as our own summer, and the sun is almost as hot as our June. But the nights are cold.

Australia is a weird, big country. It feels so empty and untrodden. The minute the night begins to go down, even the towns, even Sydney, which is huge, begins to feel unreal, as if it were only a daytime imagination, and in the night it did not exist. That is a queer sensation: as if life here really had never entered in: as if it were just sprinkled over, and the land lay untouched. They are terribly afraid of the Japanese. Practically all Australians, and especially Sydney, feel that once there was a fall in England, so that the powers could not interfere, Japan would at once walk in and occupy the place. They seriously believe this: say it is even the most obvious thing for Japan to do, as a business proposition. Of course Australia would never be able to defend herself. It is queer to find these bogies wherever one goes. But I suppose they may materialize.[66]

Labour is very strong and very stupid. Everything except meat is exorbitantly expensive, many things twice as much as in England. And Australian apples are just as cheap in London as in Australia, and sometimes cheaper. It is all very irritating.

This is the most democratic place I have ever been in. And the more I see of democracy the more I dislike it. It just brings everything down to the mere vulgar level of wages and prices, electric light and water closets, and nothing else. You never knew anything so nothing, nichts, nullus, niente, as the life here. They have good wages, they wear smart boots, and the girls all have silk stockings; they fly around on ponies and in buggies— sort of low one-horse traps—and in motorcars. They are always vaguely and meaninglessly on the go. And it all seems so empty, so nothing, it almost makes you sick. They are healthy, and to my thinking almost imbecile. That's what the life in a new country does to you: it makes you so material, so outward, that your real inner life and your inner self dies out, and you clatter round like so many mechanical animals. It is very like the Wells story—the fantastic stories. I feel if I lived in Australia for ever I should never open my mouth once to say one word that meant anything. Yet they are very trustful and kind and quite competent in their jobs. There's no need to lock your doors, nobody will come and steal. All the outside life is so easy. But there it ends. There's nothing else. The best society in the country are the shopkeepers—nobody is any better than anybody else, and it really is democratic. But it all feels so slovenly, slipshod, rootless, and and empty, it is like a kind of dream. Yet the weird, unawakened country is wonderful and if one could have a dozen people, perhaps, and a big piece of land of one's own—But there, one can't.

There is this for it, that here one doesn't feel the depression and the tension of Europe. Everything is happy-go-lucky, and one couldn't fret about anything if one tried. One just doesn't care. And they are all like that. Au fond they don't care a straw about anything: except just their little egos. Nothing really matters. But they let the little things matter sufficiently to keep the whole show going. In a way it's a relief—a relief from the moral and mental and nervous tension of Europe. But to say the least, it's surprising. I never felt such a foreigner to any people in all my life as I do to these. An absolute foreigner, and I haven't one single thing to say to them.

But I am busy doing a novel: with Australia for the setting: a queer show. It goes fairly quickly, so I hope to have it done by August.[67]

Mrs. A. L. Jenkins
as told by H. E. L. Priday

Mrs. Jenkins had taken it upon herself to re-address Lawrence's correspondence from Perth, which caused him to ask, in a postscript to one of his first letters from Thirroul, "have these letters been an infernal nuisance to you?"

The letter containing the above postscript was dated June 30, 1922. It shows that Lawrence, after only a few weeks in New South Wales, was anxious to be on the move again.

"Wyewurk," Thirroul.   Sth Coast   NSW/30 June 1922
Dear Mrs. Jenkins
Why not come with us on the Tahiti on Aug 10th? Would it be too dear? It costs about £110 I think. It is £60. first & £50 second class to Frisco from Sydney—vice versa—on the Tahiti— £60 & £40 on the Sonoma (American Line). You can easily go second from New York to England. We thought of going 1st to Frisco because it is a long trip. But you see the Pacific Isles—

Raratonga [*sic*] & Tahiti—what fun! Doesn't it tempt you? And even to see Thirroul. Much more fun.

Madame Septcheveux is priceless: Signora Settecapelli: Settecappelli. Those pink legs bowled me over. The corpse of Dorothea wouldn't be so bad, but supposing those pink legs washed up on one's doorstep, years after! And Lady Bareham. Weren't there even seven hairs on the ham?

Frau Drossel . . . was also rather priceless . . . .

Been to Wollongong today: fierce cold wind: blew my hat in the sea, me after it, wave rose, all but washed me away for ever.[68]

How also is the unmarried Mr. Bachelor?

D. H. Lawrence

The address when we *do* get to America is:

c/o Mrs. Mabel Dodge Sterne, *Taos*, New Mexico. U.S.A.

Have those letters been an infernal nuisance to you. I am so sorry. I wrote to the postmaster at Perth to send them direct *here*. They are fools to bother you.

In the Signor Settecapelli referred to it is not hard to find Mr. Siebenhaar, the author of *Dorothea;* and Frau Drossel is just as obviously a fairly well known Australian woman novelist who was then living in Western Australia. . . . (It should be added that one line that might give pain to somebody still living has been omitted from the above letter.) [69]

In the same week in early July that Mrs. Jenkins received Lawrence's warm invitation to join them, she received one in Frieda's big, sprawling childish handwriting also urging her to come.

"Wyewurk"/Thirroul/N.S.W.

Dear Mrs. Jenkins,

We laughed at your letter this morning— Your good spirits haven't quite deserted you yet—or your sense of humour— I have a proposal to make: We leave here on the 10 of Aug. for San Francisco [—] ship "Tahiti"— From here (Sydney) to England via America is *no* dearer than *your* way— So *come with us,* it would be fun, come before the 10th Aug[,] have a look at Sydney and stay with us here—I love it, the sea, the queerness of it all, there are all kinds of things to be done [—] motorbusses [—] though mostly I enjoyed the domestic part after all our wanderings—I seem to *cook* with a zest that is worthy of higher things— It's quite a pretty bungalow—a horrible piano—I wish it were a good one—

In "Taos" New Mexico a rather well known American woman offered us a house. Taos is "the" American artist colony— Lawr has not presented the letter yet to the Bulletin man—[70] He has written his head off—nearly written a novel in a month—

I love Australia—I feel I have "packed all old dull Europe in the old Kit bag["] and thrown it into the sea along with "Dorothea"— Some people called

Throssel [—] *she* a writer called Pritchard [—] wrote to Lawr— No more
to-day [—] I want this to get to you *soon*— Do *come* along—

Yours

Frieda Lawrence

I also had a "tragedy" with my head—*creatures* if you please—must have been
the boat—so *beware*—

.   .   .   .

Mrs. Jenkins, to her sorrow, was unable to join them on their Pacific
trip which D. H. found "almost as lovely as one expects the South Sea
Islands to be," [71] but she kept in touch, hoping to meet them on her
next visit to London.[72]

Katharine Susannah Prichard

My flat in London was perched high over the roof tops and trees of
Chelsea Embankment. After reading *Sons and Lovers* there, soon after it
was published [1913], I felt as if a comet had swung into my ken.

In his [*D. H. Lawrence:*] *Portrait of a Genius, But* . . . Richard Aldington expresses exactly what delighted me in *Sons and Lovers:* its "min-
gling of precise reality with poetic imagination, its truth to ordinary life
and high aspiration, its clear presentation of character and the clash of
deep but completely understood emotions, its vivid writing from beginning to end." [73]

I sought and read everything D. H. Lawrence had written. In *The White
Peacock* and short stories, I did not find quite the sensitive realism and
power which had impressed me so much in *Sons and Lovers*, although his
poetry always captured me. *The Rainbow* and *Women in Love* I read after
my return to Australia, still intrigued by Lawrence's free and easy style
and his use of words: but dissatisfied with the diffuseness, arrogance and
morbid mysticism which had become associated with his work.

Meanwhile I had married and come to live in the Darling Ranges, near
Perth. And it was on the evening of May 21, 1922, that my husband, reading his evening newspaper, remarked casually:

"See there is an English writer, D. H. Lawrence, staying at Miss Skinner's place in Darlington."

"D. H. Lawrence?" I jumped up from the couch on which I was resting.
To know that D. H. Lawrence was in the West, and only a few miles away
over the hills, from our home, was wonderful news. I explained to Jim
that D. H. Lawrence was the most brilliant of modern English writers

and that I would like very much to meet him. Jim promised to drive me over to Darlington next day. But my son was born in the early hours of the morning, and Lawrence had left the West before I was about again.

It was typical of my husband's thought for me, that despite all the joyous commotion of our son's arrival, he should remember that I wanted to meet Lawrence. He telephoned and wrote to Lawrence, asking him to visit us.[74] Lawrence wrote from Sydney to say that he had already fled from the West, in something like a panic, finding Australia a remote and terrifying place. He mentioned a nostalgia for Sicily, which provoked me into replying. This "nostalgia for Sicily" is referred to also in a letter to Mrs. Jenkins, published in Aldous Huxley's *Letters of D. H. Lawrence*,[75] and in Richard Aldington's preface to the new edition of *Kangaroo* (Heinemann [1950, 1955]). Unfortunately I can't find Lawrence's letter to Jim.

When I wrote to Lawrence I enclosed a newspaper cutting about Ric's birth, and told him that I thought my baby had arrived a fortnight sooner than was expected in order to meet him. I said that I felt Lawrence was looking at Australia through his "nostalgia for Sicily," and that he must see Australia as it really is: see the difference between our country and other countries of the world.

His letter from Thirroul was in reply to this:

'Wyewurk',/Thirroul,/South Coast,/N.S.W.,/3 July 1922.
Dear Mrs. Throssell,

Your letter, I suppose, means you are up and about and wearing your little V.C. like a medal at your breast. May he be a rosy cross.—I understand you are prouder of that little newspaper clipping than of all the yards you've had before, for books.

I am sorry, really, that we didn't get your husband's letter before we left W.A. Don't imagine either that I am bolting as fast as all that from Australia. We're not going till August 10th—and three months in one place isn't so bad. For one thing I love Australia: its weird, far-away natural beauty and its remote, almost coal-age pristine quality. Only it's too far for me. I can't reach so awfully far. Further than Egypt. I feel I slither on the edge of a gulf, reaching to grasp its atmosphere and spirit. It eludes me, and always would. It is too far back. It seems to me that generation after generation must people it with ghosts, and catastrophes water it with blood, before it will come alive with a new day of its own. Too far for me: strains my heart, reaching. But I am very glad to have glimpsed it. And I would dearly have liked to see all the things you told me of. We went into the Art Galleries at Adelaide and Melbourne. But nobody has *seen* Australia yet: it can't be done. It isn't visible. Most nearly Puvis de Chavanne's [76] "Winter" at Melbourne—if he weren't so sickeningly affected with his people. But landscape—very Australian—detailed, yet frail and atmospheric. Oh there is a great magic here. But frightens me. (I know Puvis has nothing to do with Australia.)

As for America, I go to it rather with dread, and fully expect to hold my ears and cover my eyes and bolt, as you did. But perhaps not.

Australia seems to me to be a most marvellous country to disappear into. When one has had enough of the world—when one doesn't want to wrestle with another single thing, humanly—then to come to Australia and wrestle with its Sleeping Beauty terrors. No, just to drift away, and live and forget and expire in Australia. To go away. It is a land where one can go out of life, I feel, the life one gets so sick of.

Do you like *Sons and Lovers* so much?—I am sorry, I don't know your books. But *Sons and Lovers* seems a long way back, to me. They've got a copy of *The Rainbow* in the Perth Literary Institute: or had when I was there.

I hope, when I wander disconsolately back to Australia, you will let me see your son, your books, your husband and your farm. Where is Greenmount? exactly? What do you grow on your land?—My wife wants a little farm more than anything else, she says. But how should I sit still so long?

Yours sincerely,
D. H. Lawrence

I thought that it was very generous and friendly of Lawrence to write to me at such length. I sent him the poems of Furnley Maurice,[77] the plays and poems of Louis Esson,[78] and *Songs of Reverie* with music by Henry Tate,[79] to show him how some Australians felt about their country. Also my own *Black Opal*, wishing that it were *Working Bullocks*, which was due for publication by Jonathan Cape, but had not yet arrived.

Lawrence wrote again from Thirroul:

'Wyewurk',/Thirroul,/N.S.W.,/6 August 1922.
Dear Katharine Prichard,

Thank you for the books that came two days ago. I am returning the two that have your name in them, and keeping *Black Opal* and *Eyes of Vigilance*,[80] though I don't know whether you intend me to have them for good. I have read the plays and nearly all the poems. The plays seem to me like life, and the poems are real. But they all make me feel desperately miserable. My, how hopelessly miserable one *can* feel in Australia: *au fond*. It's a dark country, a sad country, underneath—like an abyss. Then, when the sky turns frail and blue again, and the trees against the far-off sky stand out, the glamour, the unget-at-able glamour! A great fascination, but also a dismal grey terror, underneath.

We sail on Thursday—10th: we are keeping *Black Opal* to read on the ship. If ever I come back it will be for good.

I am sending you my last novel, though you won't care for it. If ever you want to send a line: c/o Robert Mountsier, 417 West 118 Street, New York City, is always good. How is the tiny V.C. of your bosom?

D. H. Lawrence.
The immediate address is just *Taos*, New Mexico, U.S.A.

The novel Lawrence sent me was *Aaron's Rod*, which I *did* care for. It is the one of his novels I cared most for, after *Sons and Lovers*. Although there was the magic of his descriptive writing in *The Plumed Serpent,* it was not until he wrote *Lady Chatterley's Lover* that I was thrilled to homage of a masterpiece, as I had been with *Sons and Lovers.*

Kangaroo was a flat disappointment—perhaps because I expected so much from Lawrence's novel written in Australia.

Fantasia of the Unconscious had revealed a philosophy and attitude of life which, to me, were unreal and irresponsible. They seemed the defence of a personality torn by an attempt to reconcile the mysticism of primitive instincts with the intransigence and poetic brilliance of a mind appalled by, and refusing to wrestle with, the problems of our own time. This philosophy and attitude to life were repugnant to me.

I found it particularly irritating in *Kangaroo.* The beauty of Lawrence's descriptive writing, as always, casts a spell. It gives glimpses of Sydney, of the bush in Western Australia, of the South Coast of New South Wales, which are exquisite fragments of word painting. There are shreds and patches of dry-point etching and acrid humor also, in the encounter with workmen in a park beside Macquarie Street, during the lunch hour. And in his interview with the sanitary man. But over and over again, re-reading *Kangaroo* recently, I had to put the book down, infuriated by comments and conclusions drawn from so slight a knowledge of Australian history, character and conditions.

Of course they are typically Lawrentian. But *Kangaroo* was regarded as an authentic picture of Australia and Australians by many English critics. I protest that it is anything but that. It is a reflection of Lawrence in Australia, having little reality where the people of our country, their struggles, aspirations and achievements are concerned.

"Somers felt blind to Australia," Lawrence writes, "and blind to the uncouth Australians. To him they were barbarians. The most loutish Neapolitan loafer was nearer to him in pulse than these British Australians with their aggressive familiarity. He surveyed them from an immense distance, with a kind of horror." [81]

Then follows a discourse on democracy, and the vaguest, wildest conception of what democracy amounts to in Australia.

"Demos was here his own master, undisputed and therefore quite calm about it. No need to get the wind up at all over it; it was a granted condition of Australia, that Demos was his own master." [82]

Lawrence had never heard of the Crimes Act, seemingly, or repressive legislation against the working class in The Transport Workers' Act: the property qualifications of voting for the Legislative Council in State governments, or the economic pressure which forces so many of our people to live in poor and ugly suburbs near the big cities.

"Somers was a true Englishman, with an Englishman's hatred of anarchy, and an Englishman's instinct for authority. So he felt himself at a discount in Australia. In Australia authority was a dead letter." [83]

How fatuous and absurd are yards of Somers' drivel about Australia! The portrait of *Kangaroo* [84] himself camouflages an idealized d'Annunzio or Mussolini, skilfully drawn sur-realist fashion with resemblances to our national animal. There were fascistically inclined elements of the New Guard stirring in Australia, at the time; but Lawrence presents these types, and their opposites in a socialist group, with his own perversity. There is not an ordinarily intelligent and decent Australian among major characters in the book.

Towards the end, Somers could see in the background, Australians who were "really nice, with bright, quick willing eyes." [85] He could exclaim at their "sardonic tolerance . . . the strange Australian power of enduring—enduring suffering or opposition or difficulty—just blank enduring." [86]

He could talk about: "The gentlest country in the world. Really, a high pitch of breeding. Good breeding at a very high pitch, innate, and in its shirt sleeves." [87] He could say, "I love Australia." [88]

"No wonder Australians love Australia. It is the land that as yet has made no great mistake humanly. The horrible human mistakes of Europe. And, probably, the even worse human mistakes of America." [89]

And yet he would go off at a tangent about: "The profound Australian indifference, which is still not really apathy. The disintegration of the social mankind back to its elements. Rudimentary individuals with no desire of communication. Speeches, just noises. A herding together like dumb cattle, a promiscuity like slovenly animals." [90]

I told Lawrence why I was disappointed with *Kangaroo* and why I disliked Richard Lovat Somers.

On a card from the Del Monte Ranch, New Mexico, Lawrence wrote: "No! I thought you were too feminine about *Kangaroo*. You'll probably like *Boy in the Bush* better." [91]

9 July 1922   "Wyewurk," Thirroul, New South Wales, Australia

⟨ *I have nearly finished my novel here—but such a novel! Even the Ulysseans* [92] *will spit at it.*

There is a great fascination in Australia. But for the remains of a fighting conscience, I would stay. One can be so absolutely indifferent to the world one has been previously condemned to. It is rather like falling out of a

picture and finding oneself on the floor, with all the gods and men left behind in the picture. If I stayed here six months I should have to stay forever—there is something so remote and far off and utterly indifferent to our European world, in the very air. I should go a bit further away from Sydney, and go "bush." We don't know one single soul—not a soul comes to the house. And I can't tell you how I like it. I could live like that forever: and drop writing, even a letter: sort of come undone from everything. But my conscience tells me not yet. So we go to the States—to stay as long as we feel like it. But to England I do not want to return.[93]

18 July 1922   "Wyewurk," Thirroul, New South Wales, Australia

❨ I still haven't got the money from Mountsier, so can't finally engage berths. But they are holding Cabin No. 4 for me on the Tahiti. I see the advertisement of her sailing has suddenly changed the date from the 10th to the 16 August. If she sails on the 16th then I don't suppose she arrives in San Francisco till September 10th instead of 4th. I very much want to catch the Tahiti—have done my novel [94] and have nothing further to do here.—I wish the money would come.[95]

Arthur Denis Forrester
as told to F. W. L. Esch

We saw Lawrence next shortly after we had settled in our boarding place in the Sydney suburb of Camperdown. This accommodation had been found for us and the Marchbanks, so that we would be close to the Bonds knitting mills. D. H. knew where we were going, and he came to look us up after he and Frieda had taken the cottage at Thirroul.

I got the impression that they did not know anybody in Sydney, and I think they were quite lonely, Frieda in particular. D. H. of course had his writing. Another reason he came to see us was that his royalties check had not arrived and he was short of cash. Marchbanks had more money than we at the time, and he willingly did what he could to help the Lawrences. It was not a large amount anyhow. Marchbanks went to New Zealand some years later, and I do not know where he is now.

As a result of this contact, D. H. invited the four of us to "Wyewurk" for a week end. My memory is that we went down early in the Australian spring.

Once again I cannot remember any unusual conversations. We just had a good time with a lot of laughing over our experiences. As on the boat, Frieda did most of the talking, and this seemed to satisfy D. H. I had the impression they were very happy together, and that they were enjoying life on the South Coast.

We arrived, I think, on a Saturday morning for lunch, and went home by the evening train on Sunday. D. H. took us for a drive in a hired car on Sunday, and he seemed to get real pleasure from showing us the beauty of the Australian scenery in these parts. We had our lunch at some falls— I think it may have been Fitzroy Falls, which is quite some distance from Thirroul. Anyhow, it was a long and expensive drive.

D. H. was writing something while we were there, because there would be times when he would leave us because he had work to do. We paid a couple of visits to the beach and went for walks along the sand, helping Frieda to collect shells. On both these occasions D. H. stayed behind so that he could do some writing.

That was the last I saw of D. H. and Frieda. We did not go down to "Wyewurk" again. There was no talk of their leaving Australia when we were there, or I cannot recall it. It came as a surprise later when I heard they had left. Then we had the book from New Mexico,[96] and a letter which I have lost. Later still we received another book—an illustrated copy of *Sea and Sardinia*.

I was not surprised when D. H. died suddenly in 1930. He was pallid looking, slender, and, when I saw him, rather delicate. In contrast Frieda was robust, rosey and plump, and when we saw her at "Wyewurk" she had put on a bit of weight. D. H. had not changed. They seemed very happy together, and loved their cottage on the hill overlooking the Pacific. There was no sign of tension between them.[97]

24 July 1922   "Wyewurk," Thirroul, New South Wales, Australia

⟨ We are still in our Wyewurk (I told you it was an Australian humorism Why work?). Australia has a weird and wonderful fascination. . . . The atmosphere is very beautiful, very clear, yet very frail. Though it is winter, it has been perfect weather, (hot sun) save for some cold winds from the mountains—until yesterday when there came a gale of wind and rain from the sea, and it is still blowing and splashing, the sea loud and hoarse, like a northern sea. Usually it booms—like drums and a rattle of kettle-drums. We are waiting to go to Sydney to engage finally our berths on the Tahiti, sailing August 10th. Then September 4th San Francisco, and so to Taos,

New Mexico. I wrote a sort of novel here—short—you won't care for it at all. But this bit of landscape and atmosphere pretty clear. We haven't known a single soul here—which is really a relief. I feel if I lived all my life in Australia I should never know anybody—though they are all very friendly. But one feels one doesn't want to talk to any of them. Though there is a great fascination in the country itself: a sort of lure in the bush. One could pass quite out of the world, over the edge of the beyond. But it is just a bit too soon. That's why I go on to America. If I stayed in Australia I should really go bush. But there is still some fight to fight, I suppose. . . . Having done my novel I am out of work until we sail—but we have only a fortnight longer here. I shall be penniless utterly when I get to Taos: but then I shall only be as usual.[98]

15 August 1922   Wellington, New Zealand

(Here we are at your antipodes—don't want to stop here though—sail this afternoon—are on a nice boat.[99]

Katherine Mansfield

[Letter to S. S. Koteliansky, from Hotel Chateau Belle Vue, Sierre (Valais)]
4 July 1922

Have you read Lawrence's new book [*Aaron's Rod*]? I should like to very much. He is the only writer living whom I really profoundly care for. It seems to me whatever he writes, no matter how much one may "disagree," is important. And after all even what one objects to is a *sign of life* in him. He is a living man. There has been published lately an extremely bad collection of short stories—Georgian Short Stories.[100] And *The Shadow in the Rose Garden* by Lawrence is among them. This story is perhaps one of the weakest he ever wrote. But it is so utterly different from all the rest that one reads it with joy. When he mentions gooseberries these are real red, ripe gooseberries that the gardener is rolling on a tray. When he bites into an apple it is a sharp, sweet, fresh apple from the growing tree. Why has one this longing that people shall be rooted in life? Nearly all people swing in with the tide and out with the tide again like a heavy seaweed. And they seem to take a kind of pride in denying life. But why? I cannot understand.[101]

[Letter to S. S. Koteliansky, from Hotel Chateau Belle Vue, Sierre (Valais)]

17 July 1922

I want to talk to you for hours about—*Aaron's Rod*, for instance. Have you read it? There are certain things in this new book of L.'s that I do not like. But they are not important or really part of it. They are trivial, encrusted, they cling to it as snails to the underside of a leaf. But apart from them there is the leaf, is the tree, firmly planted, deep thrusting, outspreading, growing grandly, alive in every twig. It is a living book; it is warm, it breathes. And it is written by a living man, with *conviction*. Oh, Koteliansky, what a relief it is to turn away from these little pre-digested books written by authors who have nothing to say! It is like walking by the sea at high tide eating a crust of bread and looking over the water. I am so sick of all this modern seeking which ends in seeking. *Seek* by all means, but the text goes on "and ye shall find." And although, of course, there can be no ultimate finding, there is a kind of finding by the way which is enough, is sufficient. But these seekers in the looking glass, these half-female, frightened writers-of-to-day—You know, they remind me of the greenfly in roses—they are a kind of blight.

I do not want to be hard. I hope to God I am not unsympathetic. But it seems to me there comes a time in life when one must realise one is grown up—a man. And when it is no longer decent to go on probing and probing. Life is so short. The world is rich. There are so many adventures possible. Why do we not gather our strength together and LIVE? It all comes to much the same thing. In youth most of us are, for various reasons, slaves. And then, when we are able to throw off our chains, we prefer to keep them. Freedom is dangerous, is frightening.

If only I can be good enough writer to strike a blow for freedom! It is the one axe I want to grind. Be free—and you can afford to give yourself to life! Even to believe in life.

I do not go all the way with Lawrence. His ideas of sex mean nothing to me. But I feel nearer L. than anyone else. All these last months I have thought as he does about many things.[102]

[Letter to S. S. Koteliansky, from Hotel Chateau Belle Vue, Sierre (Valais)]

2 August 1922

It is a pity that Lawrence is driven so far. I am sure that Western Australia will not help. The desire to travel is a great, real temptation. But does it do any good? It seems to me to correspond to the feelings of a sick man who thinks always "if only I can get away from here I shall be better." However—there is nothing to be done. One must go through with it. No one can stop that sick man, either, from moving on and on. His craving is stronger than he. But Lawrence, I am sure, will get well.[103]

[Letter to Sydney Schiff, from 6, Pond Street, Hampstead, London, N.W. 3]

Late August 1922

About Lawrence. Yes, I agree there is much triviality, much that is neither here nor there. And a great waste of energy that ought to be well spent. But I did feel there was growth in *Aaron's Rod*—there was no desire to please or placate the public, I did feel that Lorenzo was profoundly moved. Because of this, perhaps, I forgive him too much his faults.[104]

20 August 1922   *Avatiu Rarotonga in the South Seas*

❲ *Such a lovely island—calling next at Tahiti—it's really almost as lovely as one expects these South Sea Islands to be.*[105]

22 August 1922   *Tahiti*

❲ *Sail on to-morrow afternoon—hot—lovely Island—but town spoilt—don't really want to stay. But having a very good trip.*[106]

❲ *We got pretty tired of the Tahiti, though she was comfortable. But the people uninspiring. We picked up a cinema crowd at Papeete, all of them hating one another like poison, several of them drunk all the trip.*[107]

CHAPTER THREE

1922–1923: New Mexico and Mexico

I think New Mexico was the greatest experience from the outside world that I have ever had. . . . [It] was New Mexico that liberated me from the present era of civilization, the great era of material and mechanical development. Months spent in holy Kandy . . . had not touched the great psyche of materialism and idealism which dominated me. And years, even in the exquisite beauty of Sicily . . . had not shattered the essential Christianity on which my character was established. Australia was a sort of dream or trance, like being under a spell, the self remaining unchanged, so long as the trance did not last too long. . . .

But the moment I saw the brilliant, proud morning shine high up over the deserts of Santa Fé, something stood still in my soul, and I started to attend.

—"New Mexico," in Phoenix, p. 142

Americans must take up life where the Red Indian, the Aztec, the Maya, the Incas left it off. They must pick up the life-thread where the mysterious Red race let it fall.

—"America, Listen to Your Own," in Phoenix, p. 90

5 September 1922   Palace Hotel, San Francisco, Calif.

⟮ We arrived yesterday, the journey good all the way. Now we sit in the
Palace Hotel, the first hotel of San Francisco. It was first a hut with a cor-
rugated iron roof, where the ox-wagons unhitched. Now a big building,
with post and shops in it, like a small town in itself: is expensive, but for a
day or two it doesn't matter.[1] We were twenty-five days at sea and are still
landsick—the floor ought to go up and down, the room ought to tremble
from the engines, the water ought to swish around but doesn't, so one is
landsick. The solid ground almost hurts. We have many ship's friends here,
are still a jolly company.

I think we shall go to Taos Tuesday or Friday: two days by train, a
thousand miles by car. We have such nice letters and telegrams from Mabel
Dodge and Mountsier. Mabel says "From San Francisco you are my guests,
so I send you the railway tickets"—so American![2] Everybody is very nice.
All is comfortable, comfortable, comfortable—I really hate this mechanical
comfort.[3]

8 September 1922   Palace Hotel, San Francisco, Calif.

⟮ Well here I am under the Star-spangled Banner—though perhaps the
Stripes of persecution are more appropriate.[4]

165

San Francisco is sunny & pleasant, though noisy & full of the sound of iron. We leave tonight for Santa Fé. Send me a line, c/o Mrs. Mabel Sterne, Taos, New Mexico . . . .[5]

Mabel Dodge Luhan

Through the months while Lawrence and Frieda hesitated about coming to Taos, I willed him to come. Before I went to sleep at night, I drew myself all in to the core of my being where there is a live, plangent force lying passive—waiting for direction. Becoming entirely that, moving with it, speaking with it, I leaped through space, joining myself to the central core of Lawence, where he was in India, in Australia. Not really speaking to him, but *being* my wish, I became that action that brought him across the sea.

"Come, Lawrence! Come to Taos!" became, in me, Lawrence in Taos. This is not prayer, but command. Only those who have exercised it know its danger. And, as before, when I had tried to bring about my wishes, I had Tony [6] with his powerful influence to help me. I told him we must bring Lawrence to Taos because I knew he could do a great deal to help the pueblo. Tony had helped to bring [John] Collier there and he had seen Collier take up the work in behalf of the Indians, and when I told him that if Lawrence came he would bring power for the Indians by his writing, he, too, used his magic to call him. But with some reluctance—just some reluctance to believe that writing about the Indians would help them. His instinct somewhat opposed it. The Indians believe that utterance is lost and that the closed and unrevealed holds power. But I overruled him and he gave way—and together we called Lawrence; and in the darkness and stillness of the night *became* Lawrence in Taos.

In those days it was a long, difficult trip down to Santa Fe over a narrow, dirt road full of ruts and rocks. We always had to rest at least an hour at noon to recover from the bumps and jolts of the car. So when Tony drove me down to Lamy, twenty miles beyond Santa Fe, to the station, we started in the morning and took all day to meet the early evening train.

We stood waiting in the sweet air, all scented as it was from the charcoal kilns burning piñon-wood. That was always the first impression of New Mexico when one got off the train at Lamy station—the thin, keen air full of a smell of incense.

Lawrence and Frieda came hurrying along the platform, she tall and full-fleshed in a suit of pale pongee, an eager look on her pink face, with green, unfocused eyes, and her half-open mouth with the lower jaw pulled a little sideways. Frieda always had a mouth rather like a gunman.

Lawrence ran with short, quick steps at her side. What did he look like to me that first time I saw him? I hardly know. I had an impression of his slim fragility beside Frieda's solidity, of a red beard that was somehow too old for him, and of a nervous incompetence. He was agitated, fussy, distraught, and giggling with nervous grimaces. Tony and I felt curiously inexpressive and stolid confronting them. Frieda was over-expansive, vociferous, with a kind of forced, false bonhomie, assumed (it felt so to me, at least) to cover her inability to strike just the real right note. As usual when there is a flurry like that, I died inside and became speechless. Tony is never any help at such a moment, and he just stood there. Somehow I herded them into the lunch room of the station, for we had to eat our supper there because it would be too late when we reached Santa Fe.

We got seated in a row at the counter, the atmosphere splitting and crackling all about us from the singular crash of our meeting. There was a vibratory disturbance around our neighborhood like an upheaval in nature. I did not imagine this: it was so. The Lawrences seemed to be intensely conscious of Tony and somehow embarrassed by him. I made out, in the twinkling of an eye, that Frieda immediately saw Tony and me sexually, visualizing our relationship. I experienced her swift, female measurement of him, and how the shock of acceptance made her blink. In that first moment I saw how her encounters passed through her to Lawrence—how he was keyed to her so that he felt things through her and was obliged to receive life through her, vicariously; but that he was irked by her vision; that he was impatient at being held back in the sex scale. He did not want to apprehend us so and it made him very nervous, but she was his medium, he must see through her and she had to see life from the sex center. She endorsed or repudiated experience from that angle. She was the mother of orgasm and of the vast, lively mystery of the flesh. But no more. Frieda was complete, but limited. Lawrence, tied to her, was incomplete and limited. Like a lively lamb tied to a solid stake, he frisked and pulled in an agony, not Promethean so much as Panic.

Can it be possible that it was in that very first instant when we all came together that I sensed Lawrence's plight and that the womb in me roused to reach out to take him? I think so, for I remember thinking: "He is through with that—he needs another kind of force to propel him . . . the spirit. . . ." The womb behind the womb—the significant, extended, and transformed power that succeeds primary sex, that he was ready, long since, to receive from woman. I longed to help him with that—to be used —to be put to his purpose.

Lawrence scurried to the far seat away from us on the other side of

Frieda and she and I sat next each other, with Tony beside me. The meal was an agony—a halt—an unresolved chord, for me, at least, and for Lawrence, I knew. Tony ate his supper with a calm aloofness, unperturbed in the midst of alarm. Frieda continued her noisy, running ejaculations and breathless bursts of emotional laughter. Lawrence hid behind her big body. I scarcely saw him, but we all knew he was there, all right!

As we made our way out into the dark road where the motor waited, he exclaimed:

"Oh! Look how low the stars hang in the southern sky!" It was the first simple, untroubled notice he had taken of anything since they had left the train.

When we reached the automobile, I directed him to the seat beside Tony and took Frieda into the back seat with me, though I wanted it the other way round. But I thought it was easier for Lawrence that way, and that Tony would soothe him down.

As we moved off into the still night, Frieda exclaimed loudly, motioning to Tony's wide back:

"He's wonderful! Do you feel him like a rock to lean on?"

"No—o," I answered, hesitantly, unable to confirm her. Her words passed over to Lawrence with a thump. I saw his shoulders twitch. He did not want Frieda to think Tony was a rock to lean on; he could scarcely avoid understanding her unconscious comparison, or feeling again the old, old lack in himself. We ran smoothly on for a little while, and then, quite suddenly, the car simply stopped in the road.

"Well," said Tony.

He got out and looked under the hood, though I well knew that, no matter what he saw, he would not understand it. He had never learned much about the motor. Only by having the car checked quite often by garage people, we rarely had any difficulty any more, though when he first learned to drive, things were always going wrong. It was extremely unusual for anything to happen as late as 1922, for Tony had been motoring about the country for four years by that time.

We sat there for ages under the stars while Tony tried different ways to make it go again. We didn't talk much. It was peaceful, but it was growing late and I had not engaged rooms anywhere in Santa Fe. The only hotel possible to stay in then had burned down and I had intended to go to a boarding-house I knew about, for the night. As we sat there, quietly, our emotions subsided, our nerves quieted. Suddenly Frieda cut in:

"Get out and see if you can't help him, Lorenzo! Just sitting there! Do get out!"

And Lawrence answered angrily:

"You know I don't know anything about automobiles, Frieda! I *hate* them! Nasty, unintelligent, unreliable things!"

"Oh, you and your hates!" she returned, contemptuously.

A moment of silence broken by a vague picking sound out in the front where Tony pried round inside the machinery. And then Lawrence leaned over from the front seat and said:

"I am a failure. I am a failure as a man in the world of men. . . ."

Tony got into the car and tried it and it moved again.

"I guess there is some snake around here," he said, as we drove on.

I was flustered when we reached Santa Fe. The city was sleeping. We drove to the Riches' house, where I'd hoped to find rooms, but after rousing the house we were told it was full. Lawrence had unloaded their huge bags onto the sidewalk while they waited for me to go in. Frieda had made him do that. When I came out, I found him stamping his foot in a rage and trying to yell quietly in the night at her:

"I won't do it, Frieda! You stop that. . . ."

I interrupted him:

"We can't get in there. But I'll tell you what: Witter Bynner knows you're coming. He's always up. He has room. I know he'd love to have you —and we can go to some other friends here."

They were dubious and upset. But there was nothing else to do and we drove over to Bynner's house. Of course he and Spud Johnson were still up. I was so tired by now, I have forgotten how it seemed; anyway, we left the Lawrences to Bynner and we went and slept somewhere else.

"Do you like him, Tony?" I asked, before we closed our eyes.

"I don't know yet," said Tony, but he made a face.[7]

(*We slept the very first night in New Mexico at Witter Bynner's house in Santa Fé, and Alice Corbin was there.*[8]

Witter Bynner

In 1922 the road from Santa Fe to Taos was formidable—rough, narrow, and through a steep canyon, by no means the easy hour's drive it is today; and Mrs. Sterne, meeting her guests in the capital, had decided to postpone motoring them north until the morrow. She had neglected, however, to arrange lodgings for them. Hotel accommodations were few then; and having found a roof for herself elsewhere, she happened to hit upon me as their host for the night. The adobe house which my secretary, Willard

(Spud) Johnson, shared with me, had not yet grown beyond three rooms; but, persuaded by Mrs. Sterne that the Lawrences would prefer its native roughness to somebody else's more capacious, more modern dwelling, I eagerly assented to the suggestion. Paul Burlin,[9] the painter, had added a kitchen to the original two rooms of the house which I now own but was then renting from him; so it was possible, through use of couches in the living room, for the Lawrences to be given the bedroom—next to the tub and toilet which at that time Spanish-American neighbors used to come and view as curiosities—and for William Penhallow Henderson, with his wife, Alice Corbin, and their fourteen-year-old daughter, Little Alice,[10] as well as Mrs. Sterne and Tony Lujan, the silently impressive Taos Indian who was driving for her, to join us and share a kitchen supper.

Presently the car arrived in my bleak little yard, where I had been assiduously watering downy tufts of green, still ignorant that they were tumbleweed. A red-bearded man started out of the car just as Tony decided to back it a bit, whereupon I heard my first Lawrencian explosion. He had been in Taormina, before continuing eastward round the world, and had bought there a Sicilian peasant-painting: the back panel of a cart vividly decorated with two scenes of medieval jousting.[11] He had carried his trophy, some five feet long and two feet high, from place to place for months, his wife thinking that perhaps he would decide to settle in Taos and that there at last the panel too would rest. It never reached Taos. In my yard the panel and his mind were settled with one savage flash. The board had been under his arm as he was alighting and one end of it, being on the ground when Tony backed, had buckled and split, giving him a shove as it did so. Lawrence's thin shape cleaved air like the Eiffel Tower, his beard flamed, his eyes narrowed into hard turquoise, he dashed the panel to the earth, and his voice, rising in a fierce falsetto, concentrated on the ample woman behind him, "It's your fault, Frieda! You've made me carry that vile thing round the world, but I'm done with it. Take it, Mr. Bynner, keep it, it's yours! Put it out of my sight! Tony, you're a fool!" Mrs. Lawrence maintained a smile toward us; the Indian stirred no eyelash. Mrs. Sterne, pleased with the show, took command of it by introducing us in her pleasant, innocent voice, and Lawrence shook hands with us as affably as though the outburst had not occurred. But despite Frieda's "*jas*" and noddings that she would like to keep the panel even with its crack, nobody's plea could move him to let her have it, though I believe he would have liked to keep it, too. After these many years, Mrs. Lawrence still sees it on occasion in my study and laughs over its connection with our stormy first meeting.

Lawrence's appearance struck me from the outset as that of a bad baby masquerading as a good Mephistopheles. I did not feel in him the beauty which many women have felt. . . . I remember quickly wondering at Santa Fe in 1922 what Lawrence would look like under the beard, which gave somewhat the effect of a mask with the turquoise eyes peering from it. The beard and the hair, too, seemed like covers he was cuddling under —a weasel face hiding under the warm fur of its mother and peeking out. . . . The beard, which he retained through the rest of his life, appeared to me more like a connected part of him than did his mat of hair, with its forward sidelong bang, which looked detachable, like a wig or a cap. In his writings, he forever removed that cap, exposed his cranium and its cerebral contents in all nakedness; but physically the beard clung close over his face as if he wished there the darkness into which his whole nakedness was always striving to return, or to progress. How he would have enjoyed classic proportions and a clean-cut Greek visage instead of the look of a semistarved viking! . . . His own skin was too white, and I do not think he enjoyed it.

.   .   .   .

We had heard the shrillness of the Lawrence voice over the broken wagon board and we heard its variations later that evening in satirical comments on persons and places.

Mrs. Lawrence's presence, meantime, had been easy to take. Her smile from the first had meant, "I'll like you till I find a reason not to and I'll be all of myself whether you like it or not." Her body had German breadth and stature; she was a household Brunhilde; her fine profile was helmeted with spirit; her smile beamed and her voice boomed. In her were none of the physical timidities and reservations which made one questioningly aware of her husband's personality. With her there was no question. On the other hand, she did not intrude her strong presence, did not interrupt with it. It would assent or dissent firmly but with deferent timing. She never had to insist that she was there.

The homing instinct was at that time, probably always, more alive in Mrs. Lawrence than in her husband. He was always seeking a farm, a ranch; but by his own reports it was more because it might be the head-quarters of a group he could head and because it would afford him growing vegetable life around him than because it would house him and his wife and give them a hearthstone. And then he would flee each harbor. For Mrs. Lawrence the search was now different. Flight from the first husband, an uncongenial, pedantic mate, had been the important break, and she did not need all the subsequent little escapes from escape.

On that first night in Santa Fe, after the one outbreak over the Sicilian cart-painting, Lawrence, the excitable fugitive, became Lawrence, the domestic expert. His wife said that when he broke an egg it never drooled and that he never set a dish too near the edge of a table. Deftly he joined the two Alice Hendersons and my awed maid in preparing supper, over which we sat long—quickened with the Lawrences' tale of world voyaging and world figures, with memorable mimicry of some of the latter, including Middleton Murry and Norman Douglas, and with tales from us about our local Spanish-Americans and Indians.

. . . .

When the others had left, the Lawrences, though tired from their journey, sat late into the night; and Johnson and I were drawn and held by their magnetism. Quickly I knew that the reports I had heard as to Mrs. Lawrence being beneath her husband's stature, and something of an incubus, were either malicious or stupidly mistaken. I felt from the first a sense of their good fortune in union: in his having realized his particular need of her and in her having made her warm, wise, earthy womanhood an embracing Eden for this inquisitive, quick-fingering, lean animal of a man—this eager origin of a new species. For all his flares at her, usually over trifles, he knew that she was his mate. Lion-chasers and neurotic women, who tried to disparage Frieda and to attract him by substituting their ambitions and vanities for her fond, amused, understanding, creative patience found presently that a real lion would have been tamer in drawing room or boudoir than this odd simian cat whose interest in them was finally a puzzled, tolerant curiosity. In a way he liked the flattery of their attentions and with almost Frieda's patience indulged their vagaries; but often his purring would stop and a claw would come out. On that first night, despite his extreme good humor and friendliness to all of us, I felt the cat-nature in the man, as well as the monkey-nature, and with a respect for cats I was attracted by it. At least he was no dog, hopping and fawning. He was in a house, moving sleekly; but he would never be properly domesticated.

On September 18, 1922, I wrote Arthur Davison Ficke: [12] "On their way to Mabel Sterne's the other night, the D. H. Lawrences rested in my 'dark bed.'" He must have called it that, "dark," without my yet realizing the respect in his use of the word.

Lawrence's talk that night quickly made clear the fact that Tony's clumsiness in the car had not dulled the Red Indian lure which has been felt by many an Englishman. John Masefield wrote me later: "I envy you your life among the Indians. Even after all these centuries of fire-water, they must be the most interesting of all the peoples now alive."

Lawrence had already indicated his sense of the "Red Indian" spell by the runes of his mimic Indian troupe in *The Lost Girl*. He was now actually present in the neighborhood of his noble savage. Let Tony be clumsy with a car. Motor cars were not Indian business.

In the morning I was up ahead of the alarm clock for once, to make sure that the guests should have a decent breakfast before Mrs. Sterne's arrival to drive them north. Supper dishes were still to be washed in the kitchen. I went quietly around the house to the back door; but Lawrence opened it for me. Every dish had been washed. The table was laid with an ample breakfast. The bed had been neatly made in the room beyond. They had been about to call us. Just then my maid appeared from across the street where she lived; but the Lawrences had finished a complete job. The maid looked ashamed; but the guests were beaming as well as hungry. Frieda said that Lorenzo had done all the cooking. Breakfast proceeded at a hearty pace, giving us another interval of talk before Mrs. Sterne walked in. The night had been the Lawrences' first in an American house. For me it felt like a wholly good omen. It was in reality a mixed omen.[13]

Mabel Dodge Luhan

It was a comfortable, jolly scene at Bynner's in the morning. They were finishing breakfast in his gay kitchen, and everyone seemed to be in good spirits.

.   .   .   .

We made off as soon as we could, for it was a long, tiring drive we had ahead of us. In the car, Lawrence exploded, peevishly:

"These men that leave the world—the struggle and heat of the world—to come and live in pleasant out-of-the-way places—I have little use for them."

"Just what he does himself," I thought. "But he has little use for himself, either. He is a frail cargo that he hauls through life with perpetual distaste."

.   .   .   .

We passed alongside the Rio Grande River in the clear morning sunlight. In the warm valleys between Santa Fe and Taos the apples were ripening and the air was sweet from the juicy apricots. Corn, wheat, and alfalfa filled the fields, and the Mexicans and Indians were singing.

The September day was sunny and still about us all the way home, but when we made our final long climb up the mountain to reach the table-land of Taos Valley and pulled round the curve at the top, we saw the Sacred Mountain over behind Taos looming half-darkened by cloud shadows that hastened over it in great eagle shapes. Wide wings of eagles spread, sinister, over the huddling mountain while its peaks, forming a wide bow, held the last red rays of the sun.

Lawrence caught his breath. Everyone is surprised at that first view of Taos Valley—it is so beautiful. The mountains, eighteen miles away, curve half round it in a crescent, and the desert lies within its dark en-circling grasp. Taos is an oasis, emerald-green beyond the sage-brush, drinking water from the high mountain lakes and streams.

We had just that one long look at Taos in sunlight and shadow . . . , those few moments of sharp light with the eagle clouds in shadow flight across the face of it, when a long, slow flash of lightning zigzagged out of the sky above the mountain and disappeared into it like a snake. And then came, all of a sudden, a terrific explosion of thunder that seemed to fill the whole valley far and near—out of the stillness, out of the windless sky—with a crash so sharp and wild that we could only cower for an instant and cover our ears with our hands.

Tony stopped the car at once, and as he hurried to get out and put up the side-curtains, he threw me a swift, strange look. He was just in time to get us covered, for the rain broke over us in stark sheets, straight down in undivided steel sheets, nipping cold and shutting out all the world around us. It turned almost immediately to hail, battering upon the top of the car like cannon-balls, cracking open on the ground like splitting shells; hail like large stones piled up around the car until the earth was covered with them, and the air was suddenly like a winter night. Crash after crash of thunder, and the lightning zigging now on all sides as though a parent snake had peopled all the world in one immediate cre-ation and filled the universe with serpentine light. East and west and north in turn flashed up out of the rain-darkened land. We saw now Taos, now far Colorado, or the low foot-hills east of Ranchos. Only the south, from where we had come that day, lay open and free of the storm.

In the car, no one spoke till Tony said to Lawrence:

"The white people say that the thunder comes from clouds hitting each other, but the Indians know better," and Lawrence giggled in a high, childish, nervous way.

The storm did not last long, but when it was over, all the crops in Taos

Valley lay on the ground, ruined. There were practically no harvests taken in and the Indians and Mexicans suffered all that year.

It was dark when we reached our hill, a mile out of Taos village. I was shaking and weary, as always after the long, tiring ride. I led the Lawrences into the house and wished I myself were free to leave them and go to bed. But again we had to eat. I had hoped for so long that Lawrence would like our house. It is a strange house, slow grown and with a kind of nobility in its proportions, and with all the past years of my life showing there in Italian and French furniture, pictures from many hands, books from New York, bronzes from Venice, Chinese paintings, and Indian things. And always a fire burning in the fireplaces—"To make life," as Tony says.

Supper was ready. I saw the candles burning on the table in the big, dim dining-room and I led the way down the five round steps from the living-room. I was in a blind retreat behind my face, as always when I get tired from one thing or another: when there is a weight to pull for too long and things don't flow of themselves. After a little while I don't care any more what happens if things don't go of their own accord. Then I am alone, separated, divested of all wishes, indifferent to the whole outside world, forgetful of my high plans and hopes.

I sat them down at the round table, scarcely aware of anything. Blind, departed, nobody home. When I rang the bell to call Albidia, Lawrence giggled as he looked round into the surrounding dimness, from the island of our lighted space, and he said:

"It's like one of those nasty little temples in India!"

I didn't care what he said. I longed to get through—through with the day and away from them to my own room and to sleep—sleep—sleep!

Now this had all been a very inauspicious beginning, hadn't it . . . ? And yet when I saw Lawrence the next morning, none of that mattered. He was as sunny and good as a rested child, and his wide-apart eyes were blue like gentians.

I was rested, too, and we took a good look at each other, neither of us seeming to be doing so. I'm not going to waste any time saying how or why . . . ; you must just take it as a fact when I tell you briefly that, from the first, Lawrence and I knew each other through and through as though we were of one blood. In fact, he told me many times afterwards, both in irritation and in sympathy, that I seemed like his sister. We never knew each other any more than we did at the beginning, for it was complete and immediate in the first hours.[14]

12 September 1922   Taos, New Mexico

❨ We got here yesterday . . . . It is wonderful here—we drove 75 miles across the desert from Santa Fe . . . .
  I am still dazed and vague . . . .[15]

❨ Taos, in its way, is rather thrilling. We have got a very pretty adobe house, with furniture made in the village, and Mexican and Navajo rugs, and some lovely pots. It stands just on the edge of the Indian reservation: a brook behind, with trees: in front, the so-called desert, rather like a moor but covered with whitish-grey sage-brush, flowering yellow now: some 5 miles away the mountains rise. On the north—we face east—Taos mountain, the sacred mt. of the Indians, sits massive on the plain—some 8 miles away. The pueblo is towards the foot of the mt., 3 miles off: a big, adobe pueblo on each side the brook, like two great heaps of earthern boxes, cubes. There the Indians all live together. They are Pueblos—these houses were here before the Conquest—very old: and they grow grain and have cattle, on the lands bordering the brook, which they can irrigate. We drive across these "deserts"—white sage-scrub and dark green piñon scrub on the slopes.[16]

Mabel Dodge Luhan

I had a friend from Buffalo days staying with me: Bessie Wilkinson.[17] One of those prematurely white-haired widows who skim rapidly about the world like swallows, dipping here and there, enjoying themselves, taking life lightly. Lawrence seemed to like her. There was no danger. She did not make Frieda glower, either. Anything that was likely to make Frieda glower, Lawrence avoided. When he was at outs with her, he was thrown off his balance, for she was the root of his existence. He drew life from her so that when anything shook or disturbed that even flow, he was like a cut flower, drying up.

Bessie and I helped them to settle into Tony's house. They liked it very much, and it looked as though we should all have a happy time together.

They were to take their suppers at our house, and when we finished eating that night, Lawrence started telling us about the people on the boat. He was perfectly horrified at the way movie people go on. There had been a great many Hollywood people among the passengers, coming back, evidently, from making an island picture, and apparently Lawrence had observed them to the last!

. . . .

Tony was leaving to go to the Apache fiesta the next day and I begged him to take Lawrence along. Lawrence and Bessie Freeman. I wanted awfully to go, too, but there was not room for Frieda, so I knew I had to stay home with her. Tony didn't want to take Lawrence, but I made him!

He is so good-natured . . . , and I am always *making* him do things that are nice for other people, but that leave him indifferent. You see, I wanted Lawrence to get into the Indian thing *soon*. I counted so much on that. On his understanding, his deep, deep understanding of the mystery and the other-worldness, as he would call it, of Indian life. My need to bring Lawrence and the Indians together was like an impulse of the evolutionary will, apart from me, using me for its own purposes. I could no more help trying to bring this about than I could help staying with Tony. I got tired, bored, indifferent, as with a difficult task; I wished I'd never started it; at such times all I cared for was to rest; but inevitably the same strong compulsion would return after a few hours of quiet.

So Bessie and Tony and Lawrence were to leave for the Apache Reservation, where they would have a dry camp on the side of a hill, opposite the Apache camp, where hundreds of tepees would be set up.

I forget who else was there staying with me at that time, but there were evidently others, for Frieda, in answer to a note from me, speaks of our all going over to her house:

Dear Mabel

I am glad you feel like that. It's true, what you say. I have suffered tortures sometimes when Lawrence talked to people, when they drew him out just to "see his goods" and then jeered at him. I was happy last night. And for all that you will detest Lawrence sometimes and sometimes he talks bosh—but that is so human in him that he isn't "suberbo." It's a joy to me that Tony wants to go with him—but tell Tony that he is frail, he can't stand so very much! Won't you all come here again after your evening meal? I am cleaning and washing.

Love

F.

Yes, I will say if there is anything. I only wish with all my heart we had known you long ago!

She and I had a long talk that day. She was good company when Lawrence was not there, as is the case with nearly all wives. She talked with heartiness and vigor—always with a real, deep, human warmth, albeit sometimes with such obtuseness, such lack of comprehension. So long as one talked of people and their possibilities from the point of view of sex, she was grand. She had a real understanding of that. But one had to be careful all the time—to hide what one knew—to stay back with her.

Any reference to the spirit, or even to consciousness, was antagonistic to her. The groping, suffering, tragic soul of man was so much filthiness to that healthy creature. Offensive. I learned early to keep away from her any sight or sound of unhappiness that was not immediately caused by some mishap of the bed—for really she admitted no other. You see . . . , she was hedged in by her happy flesh, for she had not broken her shell when I knew her. Yet Frieda was very alive to all the simple sights and sounds of the earth. To flowers and birds; to the horses and cows and sheep. She responded to things vigorously with boisterous explosiveness, and with passionate oh's and ah's!

When we first drove them out to the pueblo and they saw it planted there at the foot of the mountain, solid, eternal, and as though its roots were fastened deep in the earth of which it was built, Lawrence was silent and seemingly unaware; but Frieda expressed herself all over the place:

"Oh! It is *wonderful!* How ancient and how perfect! Oh, to think it will probably be spoiled! Oh, Mabel, why don't you *buy* it and keep it like this forever!"

"Oh, Frieda! Don't be vulgar," Lawrence broke in on her delight. "Of course Mabel can't *buy* it. And if it has to go, it will go." [18]

I felt, though, that he was getting it through her, experiencing it, seeing it, and that she was, in a sense, giving it to him. Quite soon afterwards, I think, Frieda and I were alone and again out in the pueblo together, for I remember the cottonwood branches over our heads when these words come back to me. I believe it was while Lawrence was away at the Apache fiesta. I said to her:

"Frieda, it seems to me that Lawrence lives through you. That you have to feel a thing before he can feel it. That you are, somehow, the source of his feeling about things."

"You don't know how right you are," she answered. "He has to get it all from me. Unless I am there, he feels nothing. Nothing. And he gets his books from me," she continued, boastfully. "Nobody knows that. Why, I have done pages of his books for him. In *Sons and Lovers* I actually wrote pages into it. Oh, it was terrible when he was writing that one! I thought it would kill him. That mother . . ."

It was no time at all before Frieda's grievance—her great grievance—appeared on the surface.

"Everyone thinks Lawrence is so wonderful. Well, I am something in myself, too. The Kot thinks I'm not good enough for him!"

"*Who?*" I broke in.

"Kotiliansky. My enemy. He thinks I should just be willing to scrub the floor for Lorenzo. And he would like to separate us. Well, I'd like to see *him* live with Lawrence a month—a week! He might be surprised."

It was right away in these first few days that Frieda and I had together that she told me so much.[19] Afterwards there was nothing between us. This probably added to her old sore feeling of not being appreciated as much as Lawrence was. We started being friends. She was excellent company. She had the gift of immediate intimacy that I had myself, which, compared to ordinary intercourse, is like a live baby beside a talking doll. And there was a quick, spontaneous flow between us. But as soon as Lawrence returned to the scene, he stopped it. He was, in all possible ways, jealous, just as she was. He was annoyed that Frieda and I had become friends, and not only jealous of me, but jealous of her as well. The flow immediately ceased between Frieda and me and started between Lawrence and me. He somehow switched it.

.   .   .   .

I saw that Lawrence and Frieda tried to hold each other in a fixed, unaltered, invariable combination. Each of them immediately checked every permutation that the undomesticated, wandering instinct in the other sought to indulge. Anything that deflected the flow between them, deprived one or the other of his lawful, oh, so lawful! prey, though neither one nor the other was satisfied with what he or she had.[20]

19 September 1922   Taos, New Mexico

❲ We got here last week and since then I have been away motoring for five days into the Apache country to see an Apache dance.[21] It is a weird country, and I feel a great stranger still.

.   .   .   .

I finished Kangaroo and wait for Mountsier to send me the typescript. Then I'll revise it and let Curtis Brown have it.[22]

Mabel Dodge Luhan

Well, when [Lawrence] came back after that few days with Tony and Bessie Wilkinson and found Frieda and I had flowed together in sympathy, he was in a rage. But it must be admitted once and for all that Frieda and I were friends and could have been good friends and had fun together if he had never returned.

That very evening he asked me if I would work on a book with him. He said he wanted to write an American novel that would express the life, the spirit, of America and he wanted to write it around me—my life from the time I left New York to come out to New Mexico; my life, from civilization to the bright, strange world of Taos; my renunciation of the sick old world of art and artists, for the pristine valley and the upland Indian lakes. I was thrilled at the thought of this. To work with him, to give him myself—Tony—Taos—every part of the untold and undefined experience that lay in me like a shining, indigestible jewel that I was unable either to assimilate or to spew out! I had been holding on to it for so long, solitary and aware, but helplessly inexpressive!

Of course it was for this I had called him from across the world—to give him the truth about America: the false, new, external America in the east, and the true, primordial, undiscovered America that was preserved, living, in the Indian blood-stream. I assented with an inward eagerness, but with the usual inexpressive outwardness. I saw him, though, reading my joy, and he gave me a small, happy, sympathetic nod.

. . . .

Lawrence hurried over to our house in the morning ready to begin our work together. As I never dressed early in the morning, but took a sun-bath on the long, flat, dirt roof outside my bedroom, I called to him to come up there. I didn't think to dress for him. I had on moccasins, even if my legs were bare; and I had a voluminous, soft, white cashmere thing like a burnous. He hurried through my bedroom, averting his eyes from the unmade bed as though it were a repulsive sight, though it was not so at all. My room was all white and blue, with whitewashed walls, sunny, bright, and fresh—and there was no dark or equivocal atmosphere in it, or in my blue blankets, or in the white chest of drawers or the little blue chairs. But Lawrence, just passing through it, turned it into a brothel. Yes, he did: that's how powerful he was. We went out into the sun on the long, flat roof. The house seemed to be sailing on a quiet green sea—the desert behind us bordered by the cedar-covered foot-hills, and the alfalfa fields in front, and Taos Mountain north-east of us, looking benevolent that day.

. . . .

We squatted down in the hot earth of the roof, and the sun shone on Lawrence's red beard, making it look like the burning bush. He dropped his chin on his chest in a gloomy silence and I waited for him to say something. The birds were singing all around, and the pigeons, cosy on the roofs of their upraised cottages, were roucouling as they paced amo-rously up and down before each other. Everything was calm and quiet and lovely until Lawrence began to talk.

"I don't know how Frieda's going to feel about this," and he threw an angry look over towards their cottage that lay there, harmlessly enough, like a cat in the sun, with no sign of her about.

"Well, surely she will understand . . ."

"Understand! She can't *understand* anything! It's the German mind. Now, I have always had a sympathy for the Latin mind—for the quick, subtle, Latin spirit that . . . but the north German psyche is inimical to it. The blond conquerors! The soldier soul, strong because it does *not* understand—indelicate and robust!" He ran rapidly on and on. I was immediately on his side. He made a perfect cleavage between the blond, obtuse, and conquering German and ourselves. We were Latin together, subtle, perceptive, and infinitely nimble. And from that mo-ment to this I have been Latin, and Frieda has been Goth.

And also in that spoken sympathy Lawrence drew me to him and would hold me, I believed, forever, for he knew that he and I were the same kind of people. As we were. As we always were.

In that hour, then, we became more intimate, psychically, than I had ever been with anyone else before. It was a complete, stark approxima-tion of spiritual union, a seeing of each other in a luminous vision of reality. And how Lawrence could see!

I won't try to tell you what we said . . . , because I can't remember.

.   .   .   .

But it was in that first long talk together that he repudiated Frieda so strongly, with an intention, apparently, to mark forever in my eyes his desperate and hopeless bondage to one who was the antithesis of him-self and his predilections: the enemy of life—his life—the hateful, de-stroying female.

"You cannot imagine what it is to feel the hand of that woman on you if you are sick," he confided in a fierce, lowered voice. "The heavy, Ger-man hand on the flesh. . . . No one can know . . ."

A great desire to save him, who could not save himself, was surging in me. I *would* save him!

As we got up to go into the house, his eyes shining blue and seeming to be assuaged, he paused an instant and said:

"The burden of consciousness is too great for a woman to carry. She has enough to bear with her ever-recurring menstruation." But I was glad at last for being what I was, for knowing, sensing, feeling all I did, since now it was to have its real, right use at last.

Lawrence went downstairs and I stayed to throw on my dress and my stockings. He was in the big room when I came a few minutes later, and I walked over to his house with him. Being with him keyed one up so that everything was humming and one felt light and happy. We were happy together. We reinforced each other, and made each other feel invulnerable: more solid and more sure. When his querulousness left him, he was such fun! He was without fear and without reproach and needed no longer to carp and criticize.

As we strolled over to Tony's gate and entered his alfalfa field, we saw Frieda, in the distance, hanging clothes on the line.

"She is mad!" chuckled Lawrence, giggling. As we got nearer, she saw us coming and stopped what she was doing. The big, bonny woman, she stood there in her pink cotton dress and faced us with her bare arms akimbo. Lawrence was laughing almost delightedly into his beard and bending down his face to hide. At a distance of two or three hundred yards one could read the mounting rage gathering in her, the astonishment and the self-assurance.

"I guess I'll go back," I murmured, and as he did not press me to go on, I turned and retreated before that figure of wrath. It was not my way to fight in the open—although I certainly would fight!

That long, complete talk on the roof was practically the only time I saw him alone. I had supposed, of course, that he would have his own way about his work at least, but no. I did not see anything more of them that day until evening, but when we met again, they had had it out. There was a tired serenity about both of them when they came over, like pale sunshine on a battlefield. Lawrence looked diminished. He said to me, aside, when he had a chance:

"Frieda thinks we ought to work over in our house."

"With her *there?*" I asked.

How could I talk to Lawrence and tell him my feelings and experiences with *Frieda* in the room? To tell him was one thing—that was like talking to oneself—but one couldn't tell her *anything*. She wouldn't understand and she would make one terribly uncomfortable and self-conscious.

"Well, not in the room—all the time. She has her work to do."

Then and there I saw it was over and I should never have the opportunity to get at him and give him what I thought he needed or have, myself, the chance to unload my accumulation of power.

.   .   .   .

"You *need* something new and different," I cried to him in our corner by the window. "You have done her. She has mothered your books long enough. You need a new mother!"

"She won't let any other woman into my books," he answered, hopelessly.[23]

So that was that.

I rebelled. I said that if I couldn't do it my way, in my house, then I wouldn't do it at all.

"Very well," he acquiesced, without opposition.

But I did try it once in her house. I went over there in the morning and he and I sat in a cold room with the doors open, and Frieda stamped round, sweeping noisily, and singing with a loud defiance. I don't think that anything vital passed between Lawrence and me, for all the dead times are blank in my memory and are not lighted up at all.

The next day he was sick in bed and I was off to Santa Fe with Tony for something or other. Lawrence asked me to try to write out some things for him to work on while I was gone.[24]

.   .   .   .

Frieda's opposition to me released, of course, all my desire for domination. An invisible struggle went on between us for possession of Lorenzo. This accentuated the division in him—for he was already split. Loyal to neither of us, who represented corporeally the separated sides of his nature, he kept us both on tenterhooks by vacillating between us. When he was in a temporary harmony with Frieda, he would, in brilliant vituperative talk, sling mud at the whole inner cosmos, and at Taos, the Indians, the mystic life of the mountain, and the invisible, potent powers of the embodied spirit or at everything, in fact, not apparent, scheduled, and concrete. Then, sometimes, he would go back on the limited scale of obvious, materialistic living and, forgetting Frieda's presence or defying it, would talk just wonderfully, with far-reaching implications, of the power of consciousness, the growth of the soul, its dominion and its triumphs. Talk to me outright, his eyes shining like blue stars.

"I hate all that talk about *soul*," Frieda would rap out viciously, as she sat over her embroidery.

But sometimes he hated us both. I remember one day we were all down in the orchard picking apples and sorting them. It was a still, autumn day, all yellow and crimson. Frieda and I, in a lapse of antagonism, sat on the ground together, with the red apples piled all around us. We were warmed and scented by the sun and the rich earth—and the apples were living tokens of plenitude and peace and rich living; the rich, natural flow of the earth, like the sappy blood in our veins, made us feel gay, indomitable, and fruitful like orchards. We were united for a moment, Frieda and I, in a mutual assurance of self-sufficiency, made certain, as women are sometimes, of our completeness by the sheer force of our bountiful health.

Lawrence dropped out of a tree and caught sight of the two of us; and we were suddenly made one in his eyes. He drooped over us in a funny, wry despair.

"O *implacable* Aphrodite!" he moaned, and hastened again up into the thick branches and out of sight.[25]

22 September 1922　　　　　　　　　　　　　　　　Taos, New Mexico

〖 *It's free enough out here, if freedom means that there isn't anything in life except moving ad lib on foot, horse, or motor-car, across deserts and through canyons. It is just the life outside, and the outside of life. Not really life, in my opinion.*

.　　.　　.　　.　　.　　.　　.　　.　　.　　.　　.　　.

The house is a very smart adobe cottage Mabel Sterne built for our coming; built in native style. It is just one story high, has four rooms and a kitchen, and is furnished with a good deal of "taste" in simple Indian or home-made furniture and Mexican or Navajo rugs: nice. The drawback is, of course, living under the wing of the "padrona." She is generous and nice—but still, I don't feel free. I can't breathe my own air and go my own little way. What you dislike in America seems to me really dislikeable: everybody seems to be trying to enforce his, or her, will, and trying to see how much the other person or persons will let themselves be overcome.[26]

27 September 1922　　　　　　　　　　　　　　　　Taos, New Mexico

〖 *These Indians are soft-spoken, pleasant enough—the young ones come to dance to the drum—very funny and strange. They are Catholics, but still keep the old religion, making the weather and shaping the year: all very secret and important to them. They are naturally secretive, and have their backs set against our form of civilization. Yet it rises against them. In the* pueblo they have mowing machines and threshing machines, and American schools, and the young men no longer care so much for the sacred dances.

And after all, if we have to go ahead, we must ourselves go ahead. We can go back and pick up some threads—but these Indians are up against a dead wall, even more than we are: but a different wall.

Mabel Sterne is very nice to us—though I hate living on somebody else's property and accepting their kindnesses. She very much wants me to write about here. I don't know if I ever shall. Because though it is so open, so big, free, empty, and even aboriginal—still it has a sort of shutting-out quality, obstinate.[27]

29 September 1922   Taos, New Mexico

❨ On Monday we went up a cañon into the Rockies to a deserted gold mine. The aspens are yellow and lovely. We have a pretty busy time, too. I have already learnt to ride one of these Indian ponies, with a Mexican saddle. Like it so much. We gallop off to the pueblo or up to one of the cañons. Frieda is learning too. Last night the young Indians came down to dance in the studio, with two drums: and we all joined in. It is fun: and queer. The Indians are much more remote than Negroes. This week-end is the great dance at the pueblo, and the Apaches and Navajos come in wagons and on horseback, and the Mexicans troop to Taos village. Taos village is a Mexican sort of plaza—piazza—with trees and shops and horses tied up. It lies one mile to the south of us: so four miles from the pueblo. We see little of Taos itself. There are some American artists, sort of colony: but not much in contact. The days are hot sunshine: noon very hot, especially riding home across the open. Night is cold. In winter it snows, because we are 7,000 feet above sea-level. But as yet one thinks of midsummer. We are about 30 miles from the tiny railway station: but we motored 100 miles from the main line.

. . . Perhaps it is necessary for me to try these places, perhaps it is my destiny to know the world. It only excites the outside of me. The inside it leaves more isolated and stoic than ever. That's how it is. It is all a form of running away from oneself and the great problems: all this wild west and the strange Australia. But I try to keep quite clear. One forms not the faintest inward attachment, especially here in America. America lives by a sort of egoistic will, shove and be shoved. Well, one can stand up to that too: but one is quite, quite cold inside. No illusion. I will not shove, and I will not be shoved. Sono io!

In the spring I think I want to come to England. But I feel England has insulted me, and I stomach that feeling badly. Però, son sempre inglese. Remember, if you were here you'd only be hardening your heart and stiffening your neck—it is either that or be walked over, in America.[28]

❨ Never shall I forget the Indian races, when the young men, even the boys, run naked, smeared with white earth and stuck with bits of eagle fluff for the swiftness of the heavens, and the old men brush them with eagle feathers, to give them power. And they run in the strange hurling fashion of the primitive world, hurled forward, not making speed deliberately. And the race is not for victory. It is not a contest. There is no competition. It is a great cumulative effort. The tribe this day is adding up its male energy and exerting it to the utmost—for what? To get power, to get strength: to come, by sheer cumulative, hurling effort of the bodies of men, into contact with the great cosmic source of vitality which gives strength, power, energy to the men who can grasp it, energy for the zeal of attainment.[29]

Mabel Dodge Luhan

At the end of September the Fiesta of San Geronimo was celebrated in the pueblo. . . .

San Geronimo was the Indians' patron saint, handed to them by the Catholic priests several hundred years ago. A wooden image of him dwelt in the church at the pueblo, along with a statue of the Virgin. The Indians regarded these two as their guests, and the church as their house. . . .

In the evening before the race, the Indians always built bonfires of pitch-wood, piled all over the pueblo in hollow squares of split kindlings. In front of the church there was a long avenue of them leading out from the entrance, down through the pueblo and around and back. There was one in front of every house, and some were on the roofs. The priest always came out from town to give them a mass, and when it was over, he drove rapidly away in his buggy, drawn by two black horses. Then the Indians lighted all the fires, and some of the young men stood on each side of the church doors ready with their guns to fire a salute, while the head men of the pueblo lifted the Virgin from the altar and brought her out for her walk. One of them carried her aloft in his arms while four others marched along holding four poles with a white sheet knotted to them to spread over her head.

The fires blazed and the young men fired their guns. A small handful of Mexicans walked with the Indians, piously singing a Catholic tune, but their voices were almost drowned in a sea of shouts and war-whoops and exultant cries. The whole pueblo followed her in her slow progress —men, women, and children. Once a year they took her thus for a walk around the pueblo, down the avenues of fire, and home again; for the irrelevant, pale Virgin had become, by the transforming power of the psyche, the Goddess of the Harvest. It was no mere coincidence that made them celebrate San Geronimo's Day when the wheat was garnered.

The flames of blazing pitch-wood soared high and the wind raced round them. The whole pueblo was given over to a fiery joy and the wonders of the earth.

"What is so powerful as fire?" Tony asked me where we stood together at the church wall. Indians never cease to feel the mystery of it—they never grow used to it so that it becomes for them a matter of course.

Early the next morning they carried the Virgin and San Geronimo to the leafy shrine of yellow cottonwood branches they had erected at the head of the race-track; and at sunrise they started that race that Lawrence has described so well: [30] the race that is not run to win, but to give back power to the earth from whom they have drawn their food. Emerging from the kiva, each one blows a bit of eagle-down to the rising sun to give him eagle power and receive it back again.

The Indians *know* it is all a give and take . . . . They never forget, until they go to school.

Lawrence and I sat together on the top of one of the high structures made of trees and boughs that stand in front of the pueblo houses, carry firewood and hay, and shelter their wagons. The race went on and on. Brown bodies and black hair and the sun shining on them. It is always beyond any telling. Lawrence was really in it—he was able to go into it and participate with them and understand. It dissolved his painful isolation— breaking the barriers around him so that for a while he shared a communal effort and lost himself in the group. Vicariously he too raced and spent himself, offering the sun of his energies to the Great Mother.

It was in him easily to comprehend and readily to sympathize with such an immolation. . . .

When they came to an end of the relayed padding and thumping up and down the track, they broke the pattern and fell into two great groups, singing for a few moments a triumphant harvest song; and then they separated and ran, all variously, down to the river to bathe. Lawrence was out of his spell and released. His eyes shone . . . , he was so happy and free.[31]

4 October 1922   Taos, New Mexico

❴ *What do I find? God knows. Not, not freedom—but freedom is an illusion anyhow . . . . A tension like a stretched bow, which might snap, but probably won't. Something a bit hard to bear. "Stiff-necked and uncircumcised generation"—That inhuman resistance to the Divinity— would be perhaps superhuman and 4th dimensional. But always resistance. Reminds me of the great cries of the Old Testament: "How long will ye harden your hearts against me?" But who is Jehovah in this case, I don't know. An Almighty, however, not a Dove! A Thunderbolt, not a Logos.*[32]

Mabel Dodge Luhan

We were soon leading each other into new ways. Lawrence gave great dissertations upon activity; upon *doing* things. This *doing* business has been one of the principal problems of my whole life. Nothing to do! From childhood until now I've been suffering a great deal of the time from a blank feeling that seems best-expressed in those words, and I have passed countless hours just sitting and staring straight ahead. Now, I don't believe I *ever* saw Lawrence just sit. He was forever doing something. Rather fussily, too. He did a good deal of the housework at home; he always did the baking, and at least half of the cooking and dish-washing. When Frieda and he went off together, he taught her how to do all these things. He taught her how to wash clothes, how to scrub them clean and rinse them in cold water with bluing in it and to hang them in the sun to make them come white; and one of the few things Frieda really liked to do about the house was this washing. She always made quite an affair of it, and it usually put her in a good temper.

Lawrence really had very little sense of leisure. After the housework was done, he usually crept into a hedge or some quiet corner and wrote something, sitting on the ground with his knees drawn up. Midday brought another meal to prepare and to tidy up—and in the afternoons he made up tasks if he had none, odd jobs of carpentering or cleaning, unless he was out somewhere with us.

The only time he appeared to relax at all was at tea-time. He didn't seem to mind chatting then—and he liked his tea. But in the evenings —and we always spent them together in our house or theirs—he either delivered a monologue—a long, passionate harangue or narrative about something that he addressed to himself, his eyes not seeing us, but bent upon his inner picture, usually ending in an argument with Frieda—or else he got us all doing charades or playing some game. He loved charades —and he was so gay and witty when he was playing! He could imitate anything or anybody. His ability to identify himself intuitively with things outside himself was wonderful. We had some boisterous evenings, with Ida [33] and Dasburg and Spud [Johnson] and others, that left us hot and happy and full of ease.

He hated just sitting round and letting things come of themselves. I preferred letting life take its course, and, in talk or in anything else, I was so lazy that I had never attempted to direct it. Only in my relations with people did I ever try and steer things. Lawrence was just the opposite. He was purposeful in impersonal things and left it to the impulse of life in human things. That was where Frieda triumphed. Because he either could not or would not use his will to make things go the way he wanted: she, with less scrupulousness about it, had always had complete control of him. It was, in effect, as though he had no will of his own. I wonder if he had or hadn't! Perhaps he only made a virtue of his passivity and in reality had no choice in the matter.

But everyone needs a bite and a sup occasionally of something more than daily bread. Though Frieda tried to stand with a flaming sword between him and all others, he, subtle, exchanged with me more and more sympathy, but secretly, I think, almost, though not quite, unconsciously. Of course one can never know another person completely, though we came as close to it as is humanly possible, I believe. I can only say for myself for certain that *I* knew when there was passing between us the mysterious effluvium that crosses space and reaches its goal, and that I sought, by nearness to him, to shorten its passage and increase its intensity. When we washed the dishes in the porch outside his kitchen, and our fingers touched in the soap-suds and he exclaimed, with a blue and gold look through the clamor of the magnetic bells: "There is something more important than love!" and I, defiant of definition at the moment, and sure of myself and him—sure that no barriers were able to shut him away from me—questioned: "What?" and he answered, grim: "Fidelity!" —I wondered just how conscious he was then—how passive or how much in control of everything.

189

Sometimes I think that perhaps, far beyond my own conception of the facts, he knew what was what.

Perhaps this is the time to tell you . . . what I think *I* wanted, and not to beat about the bush and cover it up in a maze of words. I wanted to seduce his spirit so that I could make him carry out certain things. I did not want him for myself in the usual way of men with women. I did not want, particularly, to touch him. There was no natural, physical pleasure in contact with him. He was, somehow, too dry, not sensuous enough, and really not attractive to me physically. But I actually awakened in myself, artificially, I suppose, a wish, a willful wish to feel him, and I persuaded my flesh and my nerves that I wanted him. Never approximating any actual touch or union, body to body, with him, that would destroy my illusion of desire, I was able to imagine any amount of passion in myself.

I did this because I knew instinctively that the strongest, surest way to the soul is through the flesh. It was his soul I needed for my purpose, his soul, his will, his creative imagination, and his lighted vision. The only way to obtain the ascendancy over these essential tools was by way of the blood.

.   .   .   .

I wanted Lawrence to understand things for me. To take *my* experience, *my* material, *my* Taos, and to formulate it all into a magnificent creation. That was what I wanted him for.

When this crept gradually into his consciousness I don't know. I certainly tried to hide it. I almost succeeded in fooling myself into thinking I was in love with him and into hiding my real intention from myself. Sometimes he would need to come nearer to me. He was so sensitive that he could get one's emanation and one's vibration by coming near one; and he would pass behind me and stand a moment in the radius of that swinging, swirling circle of force of which each one of us is the core.

.   .   .   .

Very soon, in those first September days, I discovered that Frieda would not let things slide. I mean between them. Their relationship was never allowed to become slack. When, as between all married people, they were going along smoothly, not noticing each other much, when the thing between them tended to slip into unconsciousness and *rest*, Frieda would burst a bombshell at him. She *never* let him forget her. What in the first days must have been the passionate and involuntary attention of love in the splendor of fresh and complete experience had become, when I knew them, the attack and the defense between enemies. To keep the fire burning between them, Frieda would sting him in a tender place— she could attract his attention away from anything or anyone in the world by one of her gibes. She could always get his attention and start him flaming. Friction between them had become necessary, to take the place of the natural heat, and she undertook to keep life burning between them.

At the end of an evening when he had not particularly noticed her, she would begin insulting him. He would almost dance with rage before her where she sat solid and composed, but with a glare in her green eyes, as she puffed her cigarette into his face or—leaving it drooping in the corner of her mouth, a sight he always detested—mouthed some vulgar criticism up at him, one eye closed against the smoke, her head cocked: a perfectly disgusting picture, when she did so!

"Take that dirty cigarette out of your mouth! And stop sticking out that fat belly of yours!" he yelled once, shaking his finger in her face.

"You'd better stop that talk or I'll tell about *your* things," she taunted. All of us there were appalled. This was the end. They had certainly come to the end of hate this time. Frieda gathered her sewing into a bag and nodded good-night to us. He, his head sunk, avoided our eyes. He was ashamed.

"Well!" someone exclaimed.

"But *look*," I whispered in amazement. They had gone round the corner of the house and were passing the long, low window in the moonlight. They were close—close together—arm in arm—in a silent world of their own.

The next day he told me that the bond of hate can be stronger than the bond of love. . . .

.   .   .   .

As I look back, I discover that Tony was away most of the time. I think I did not notice it then, my thoughts were so much with Lawrence. Of course Tony had that threshing-machine and he was always away all day long in the fall, so probably that is why I miss him from these scenes when I go back to them.

But he and I taught Lawrence and Frieda to ride horseback; that much he was with us all. At least, the horses taught them to ride! We merely went along. The first time Lawrence got up on one over there at his house, the horse ran right off down the field, with him bobbing up and down, light as a feather, and humped over the animal's neck the way monkeys ride, in the circus. Tony sat square on his stallion and laughed heartily. By the time Lorenzo had pulled his horse round and run back to us, he was still laughing. Really amused, not malicious. But Lawrence, holding on to his nervous beast, threw half a quick look at Tony and cried furiously:

"That's all right, Tony. Others can laugh, too." I know that at such moments Lawrence took refuge in the thought of the pen, which only then became, for him, mightier than the sword. Ordinarily he kept his writing level, in his mind, with other living acts, like cooking and chopping wood. For him it was just another activity of life. It was not writing, and separate from life. It was the speech or song, for him, of his own voice, and the writing of it never seemed as important to him as the living behind the pen. That is why he was *never* literary—never a writer.

"I'm not laughing," replied Tony, his shoulders still shaking. "It's very nice." He meant he was not being mean—he was just feeling happy. Lawrence caught the idea, but he didn't like to make Tony feel happy because the horse cantered off with him. There was never a moment of sympathy between them after that.

We were soon going on long rides together—Frieda and Lorenzo and I. He was absolutely fearless and he never fell off, no matter what the horse did. Though he was unaccustomed to riding, he took to it naturally and easily, though he always looked uncomfortable on horseback, bent over forward and riding as though the saddle hurt him. He rode with a very free rein. Fast. He couldn't endure to have me go ahead of him across the fields, and I adored to lead him chasing after me if I could get a good start ahead of him. . . . He never let little things pass. Everything was significant and symbolic and became to him fateful in one way or another. Perhaps that is why he made life so thrilling for one. I was used to hearing that I made the house alive and made living exciting around me, but now someone made it intense for *me*. Lawrence raised the pitch. Life became radiant wherever he appeared.[34]

19 October 1922   Taos, New Mexico

⟨ The land I like exceedingly. You'd laugh to see Frieda and me trotting on these Indian ponies across the desert, and scrambling wildly up the slopes among the piñon bushes, accompanied either by an Indian, John Concha, or a Mexican, José. It is great fun. Also we go to hot springs and sit up to our necks in the clear, jumping water.

Of course, humanly, America does to me what I knew it would do: it just bumps me. I say the people charge at you like trucks coming down on you—no awareness. But one tries to dodge aside in time. Bump! bump! go the trucks. And that is human contact. One gets a sore soul, and at time yearns for the understanding mildness of Europe. Only I like the country so much.[35]

25 October 1922   Taos, New Mexico

❨ It is wonderful here, with the aspens yellow on the Rocky Mts., the nights freezing, the days hot, the horses and asses roaming on the whitish, sage-brush desert. My wife and I ride all the afternoon, and love it. But it isn't sympatisch like Australia: more of the will.[36]

Maurice Lesemann

When I opened the door, coming in out of the blue clearness of New Mexico dusk on an October afternoon, a man stood up quickly and turned nervously toward me, looking very dark, very darkly bearded, in the firelight. But when we went in to dinner I saw that he was not so tall as I had thought, and very slight, almost frail, of body, with small shoulders and meagre arms. His head also was not large, not distinguished at all, and rather unshapely, though the reddish beard, thrusting below the chin, made it seem longer. Underneath the brow, which was wrinkled and knotted, the eyes were small and bright blue. They had weary sags beneath them. He sat as if folded in and huddled upon himself, bending over his arms, bending over his red beard. Not that he was quiet and morose—not for a moment—but I realized then, rather suddenly, what an enormous amount of writing Lawrence has done for a man of thirty-seven years, what a monstrous labor it has been, if only labor alone, without any of the desperate questioning it tells of, and the suffering.

We rode out horseback in the morning. The adobe houses of Taos were warm and golden in the sunlight as always, but now the cottonwoods and poplars too were golden for fall, and stood in thin, vibrant screens over the flat roofs and up into the blue. Out toward the Taos Pueblo the Indian fields were reaped and yellow with stubble, and the bushes by the old pueblo wagon road made a smoky mist of lavender and russet. Leaves of the wild plum trailed crimson over them. We passed Indian boys hunting birds with bows and arrows. They hid in the bushes when the ponies came close.

Lawrence was dressed in leather puttees and riding breeches; and a little white woolen coat of Scotch homespun without any collar, a strange garment in this country, with a homely northern look about it, and underneath this, a knitted sweater that a friend had made for him of the very blue to harmonize with his red beard. He was very gay in the crisp clearness of the morning. We talked about America.

This was Lawrence's first visit to America, and he was still in the midst of first impressions. He saw our machine life as an appalling thing, a very terrible thing. It would take the most intense individualism to escape the deep seated American impulse toward uniformity. All that a sensitive person could do now was to live totally to himself. "He must be himself," Lawrence said. "He must keep to *himself* and fight against all that. There is nothing else to do. *Nothing.*"

When he talked, one forgot almost at once that first impression of frailness and weariness. One forgot the heavily knotted brow under the shock and surcharge of his eyes. He spoke gaily and whimsically. His voice was high pitched and thin, soaring high upward for emphasis, and still higher in a kind of amused exultation. Talking of uniformity, he remarked upon the way Americans treat everyone with the utmost familiarity on first acquaintance. It has become a convention with us to presume an exact community of interest. He was amazed at this. "They tell you *all* of their affairs, and then expect *you* to tell them all of yours. They make me furious! And I know that they have the kindest intentions in the world. They mean to be kindly and generous, of course. But I have the feeling of being perpetually insulted!"

He talked of it often, the condition of American life and its possible future. He felt revolution. He felt it somehow in the peculiar mental make up of our people despite their apparent docility. There was a terrible potentiality there, a disposition to join together when aroused, a sense for joining and feeling their strength together. If I took him rightly, it was a sort of child's knowledge of the possession of power. He had an intuitive fear of them and of what they might do if ever they took a notion to overturn things, either little or great. "I feel them dangerous," he said, "dangerous as a race. Far more dangerous than most of the races of Europe."

While we talked the ponies would slacken their pace, gradually, by mutual consent, dropping at last into a slow walk, scarcely placing one foot before another. We passed the Pueblo, rising in terraces into the sun, five terraces rising with golden brown walls against the dark blue peaks of mountains behind them. The Indians were husking corn in the corrals and patios. The streets, usually swept clean as a floor, were littered with rustling husks of corn. Lawrence was always for turning out of the road and off across the fields at a gallop. He pressed his flat white hat tightly to his head and gave the little sorrel free rein, letting her go breakneck over the hardened furrows. Then back through a gap in the underbrush to the road again, the ponies excited after their run, tossing their manes.

"I should like to see the young people gather," he said, "somewhere away from the city, somewhere where living is cheap—in a place like this, for instance; and let them have a farm or a ranch, with horses and a cow, and *not* try to make it pay. Don't let them try to make it pay—like Brook Farm.[37] That was the trouble with Brook Farm. But let them support themselves by their writing, or their painting, or whatever it is." I had been telling him of the large number of young people in America who are intent on creative work in the arts and are up against the kaleidoscopic, emotionally disintegrating life of our commercial centres. He came back again and again to this increasing problem of preserving the individual entity. "They could be *themselves* there," he said, "and they would form a nucleus. Then they would be able gradually to spread their influence and combat the other thing a little. At least they would know they existed. . . .

"At any rate, it would be an interesting experiment."

And with the last words off he would go, urging the little mare into a lope and standing up in the stirrups. He pressed the small white hat tightly to his head and sat far forward in the saddle, leaning over eagerly. He rode eagerly. The white coat flapped behind him in the wind.

This eagerness and exultation were constant in him. One night by the fire he told stories about English people he had known, imitating with absurd nicety their voices and manner, their entire conversation. He described their way of walking, and must needs jump from his chair and pace up and down the floor—yes, all round the room, taking the part first of the Countess and then of the Cabinet Minister—until finally they rose before us—heroic, monumental in caricature. And then Lawrence would remember one thing more, and it so ridiculous that he would have to sit down; and his voice would break and go careering away into a chuckling laugh before he could tell what had overpowered him.

Small trace of humor or whimsy has appeared in his work, although there is an increasing variety of mood in the later novels. The exultation, however, so predominant in the early love poems and in the clear lyricism of *The Trespasser,* still appears—most freely now perhaps in his description, or rather in his deep realization, of flowers and animals, and in his feeling for places, his whole sense of a town or a mountain. But I give you my word that these things do not greatly concern him. He is concerned for the most part with certain human relationships and with certain visions which he has had for the future. He is concerned with finding a philosophy which shall show him a rhythm running through the inconsistent truths of experience. But these other—for which alone many people read him—these come almost unconsidered out of the casual, daily abundance of his mind.

Sometimes, of course, the eagerness and the exultation were more concentrated within him, and there was less of them for the rest of us. Sometimes he was altogether inward, as if there were an actual physical change in him, a periodic withdrawal of his energies deep inside him. At such a time his remarks in criticism of people were very piercing. Very quick, darting out at them and back again. And his voice was a bit aside from us, and a bit wary; sharp, at a moment. And his eyes too were sharp, darting askance. It was almost as if he were at a distance from us in the room, conversing in his high voice at a short but distinct distance, as if he were sitting quite by himself over there beyond the table, under the small shine of the candles.

On such an evening one felt him strangely in the house. Although he talked, and talked gaily and whimsically, yet he himself was present otherwise, in some totally different way. He had an exquisite, almost physical sensitiveness to the personalities about him. Like Cicio in *The Lost Girl,* and others of his most authentic characters—those who are least explained—he became then an enigmatic intuitive being: irritated darkly within by the slightest contacts, feeling them to the point of pain, or stirred with delight in the same mordant fashion, but never ceasing, never relenting. The small blue eyes burned and danced, indestructible. He penetrated the room and its peculiar atmosphere with excruciating understanding.

"If you fall from the tower of a cathedral and your mind says that you shall die, you will *die;* and if your mind is not going to die then, you will *not* die." And I shall always remember his casual remark. For him it is true. His mind must go on without rest, creating beyond itself, thrusting out beyond itself again and again in flashes of vision. One thing, surely, he has done; although Whitman [38] sketched the thought, Lawrence is the first modern to body forth love as one inseparable experience, not as both physical and mental, but as one—one thing; and in that one living substance of love he looks for his solution. He will do more. He will go on, searching for finality and rest. We thought that he would never find rest. And that, at last, was the sense we had of him; it came over us—the sense of a man walking about, or sitting by the fire, or picking apples in the orchard like any other, but inwardly astir with a dark frenzy, his frail body ridden and worn by his daemon.[39]

Andrew Dasburg

It was at the home of Mabel Dodge Luhan that I most often saw Lawrence. Not being a devotee but a mere onlooker little of what he said has lingered on in my mind.

I liked him even when it was quite impossible to agree with some of his extravagant notions. Example—as when he advocated tar and feathers for his hostess and then riding her out of Taos on a rail. (But this was not said in her presence.)

When at peace with himself he was one of the most lovable human beings I have ever known. Gentle as well as radiant with inner happiness and every so often breaking into a low burbling chuckle over the humorous things his thoughts offered him.

No one enjoyed himself more playing charades than he. I still see him in my mind on top of a London bus with raincoat and open umbrella commenting on the vileness of the weather.

He had too much of the evangelist in him for quiet conversation—one had to listen to him—sometimes to violent denunciation or a brilliant dissertation.[40]

John Collier

What follows is a composite of some recollections and impressions of my own, and of remarks in conversation by a neighbor, actually my youngest son, who knew Lawrence as a boy, and who has written nothing concerning Lawrence, nor perhaps ever will.

Lawrence and Frieda, his wife, lived next-door to my wife and our three sons and myself, at the edge of Mabel Luhan's alfalfa field, above the running ditch. So our two families mingled at will. One observation I report: I have heard tales, and heard them then, of violent, even disorderly, quarrels and conflicts between the husband and wife. In our close contact through several months, my wife and sons and I had no evidence of anything of the kind.

I next report my impression that Lawrence essentially was a gentle, kindly and unaggressive individual. Hence, and for other reasons of course, the Taos Indians accepted him and liked him. When they learned of his death years later, they climbed the mountainside, to what had been John Evans' ranch and subsequently became Lawrence's home and workshop, and they painted a large buffalo on his workshop door. (The buffalo, of course, is deep in Indian consciousness; and the buffalo was a tranquil giant, loved and not feared. An 85-year-old Santa Clara Pueblo Indian, a guest of mine at San Francisco, encountering his first buffalo since childhood, wept. The Taos Pueblo cares for a herd of buffalo on its common horse range.)

Myself, I mention, at the time was energetically concerned with practical Indian matters—with the struggle for an Indian "New Deal." I felt no curiosity about the Lawrences, and never discussed with Lawrence anything he had written or experienced. Whether because I belonged to a different universe from his, or because that was his way with people, Lawrence had no resentment toward my inattention and never invited my attention to anything that he himself had written, experienced, or thought.

Somewhat reciprocally, Lawrence took none but a casual interest in the struggle that I and others were engaged in. Many of the artists and writers in New Mexico were fervidly excited about the then existing Indian crisis, as it appeared at the time and as it really was. But not Lawrence. Under somebody's urgence, Lawrence did produce a free verse poem of some 50 lines, expostulating with the American people. It was not good verse and he didn't value it, and I imagine that it was not published or even filed away.

I mention only two particular remembrances. One was a reading aloud by Lawrence to Mabel Luhan and us, through many hours, of Balzac's *Seraphita*. I have never feasted on such a reading of anything by anybody, before or since. The kindly satire and irony of the reading made of this Balzac writing the supreme example of sentimentalism, triumphant and unashamed.

The other recollection is a long meandering at the head of Rio Hondo

Canyon, up the sides of Gold Hill at 10,000 feet. Lawrence was quieter than most children would have been and as sensitively childlike as any child. Neither of us talked, and later, Mabel Luhan mentioned that Lawrence had told her that was the way he liked me best, meandering and not talking.

You invite my estimate as to Lawrence's perception of Indians. I never was a Lawrence scholar, and have not re-read any of his books since years and years ago. The Indians liked Lawrence, and so he must have understood them. My neighbor suggests that Lawrence primarily was a crusader. He was crusading for uninhibited experience, organic and spiritual. He was crusading out of the experience of English middle-class life; and in the Italian people of the hills, somewhat, and in the Pueblo Indians completely, he found nothing to crusade for. They really didn't need him although they liked him well. He added a projection of some deeper chasmic darkness into the Indian, which may have been a perception of something that existed which I had not encountered. As for the conditions which then were assailing the Indians' values—and which assail them now, and most exhaustively in the political crisis of 1956—these were outside of Lawrence's frame of reference, or so he thought them. And yet I mention in conclusion, that it is just the American version and extension of that British middle-class Philistinism which Lawrence hated, which does explain the white man's homicidal behavior toward Indian cultures, in Lawrence's years and now.

Lawrence, in relation to Indians and so much else, died too soon. Had he lived, and come back here to Taos, and gone once more to Mexico, his discernment of Indians might have grown more complete; his self-projection upon Indians might have grown to be more greatly revealing of the anthropological, mystical and human Indian realities.[41]

30 October 1922   Taos, New Mexico

⟪ John Evans [42] got back from Wyoming last night, having motored 1,000,000 [sic] miles since Wednesday—in his new car. He now wants to marry young Alice [Henderson] in 4 weeks time, and take her to the Buffalo grandmother's for January 4th, when my young gentleman comes of age. Whether this speed will be allowed him, remains to be seen.—Alice Corbin here, and leaves tomorrow, full of admiration etc for Mabel, but a little worried in her maternal self, the young Alice being not yet 16.[43]

Mabel Dodge Luhan

I don't remember whether John [Evans] (my son . . . twenty years old) was staying up at the ranch then or not. I had given him this ranch up on Lobo Mountain that I had bought from old Mr. McClure some time back. Lawrence has described it in *St. Mawr.* John and other boys used to go up there and hunt, and he was up and down all the time between there and Taos. He and Alice [Henderson] were engaged then to be married soon, and Alice was staying there with us for a few days along with her mother, Alice Corbin. I had some silver things to give them, and one night when we were all together, I got them out, and my jewel-box, too, and unceremoniously began, saying:

"Well, here they are: spoons, knives, forks. And—"

"But wait—wait!" Lawrence hastened over to where John and Alice and I sat together on the couch. "Let us count them! Lovely silver spoons! Twelve of them—" and he piled them all together. "And then the forks."

He was making a party out of it. I never had the patience to make a nice thing like that myself, but when he played a game, I liked to play it with him.

"Beautiful, heavy silver knives! Twelve of them."

The children were handling the odds and ends in the Chinese box. I gave Alice a few things and then I was through with that game. John was handling the silver things, contemplatively.

"Well, take them away," I began.

"Wait! Let him have his moment," Lawrence said, gently, in a low voice. "This is *his* moment." How kind he was! How entirely understanding! He made me feel unfeeling and unresponsive, as, indeed, I was! I never did know how to feel like a mother to my own son!

I wished he would have a talk with John before he married. *I* did not know what I ought to say to him. I wanted Lorenzo to say it for me —whatever it was that needed to be said.

"Will you, Lorenzo?"

"I'll see. If it comes naturally."

So one night they were in John's log cabin together with the doors closed for an hour; and when they joined us in the big room, John looked quite elated. When Lawrence and Frieda went home, I asked John what he'd said.

"He said a lot. He said for me to be always alone. Always separate. Never to let Alice know my thoughts. To be gentle with her when she was gentle, but if she opposed my will, to beat her. And he said, above all, to be alone. Always."

"Well!" I said.

One day Frieda and I were talking in her sitting-room. She was showing me a piece of lovely pale-blue velveteen she had found in her trunk.

"Look! Won't it make a lovely little jacket?" And she held it around her big bosom.

"Frieda, I feel so fat in these clothes!"

"Lawrence likes fat. He says my stomach is like a big loaf of bread."

"But your legs are long. You have long, thin arms, too. It's different with me. . . ."

Lawrence came in from the back porch.

"Look, Lorenzo! Won't this make me an ador-r-r-able little jacket?" She held the velvet about her. She certainly did look huge in pale-blue velvet. Lawrence was standing behind her. He could not resist throwing me a roguish look of malice, which I could not acknowledge, facing her as I was.

Yet he was loyal, too. I was already writing him long letters. I had so much to say to him and we had no chance to talk. My letters were intimate—I could not have given them to anyone but him, and though I forget now what I wrote, I remember how they felt. They were just for that one, single, separate person, Lorenzo. I know there was a good deal about mothering his books, because our book had lapsed. The interference of Frieda had killed that. I never even saw the chapter he did; I presume she tore it up.[44] Though in the beginning, when she had us coming to her place to work, she told me that the first pages he had done on it were like nothing he had done before.

"There is a kind of vitality and eternal youth in it," she cried.

But, as I was saying, I had started to write him my thoughts, since I could no longer speak them. And as we went out the picket gate into the field one morning, Lawrence said:

"I showed Frieda your letter. Just to make everything square and open."

"Good Lord!" I was shocked to the ground.

He giggled. After that it was hard not to include her in my messages to him.

Lawrence was double in everything. No sooner had he gone close to John in that intimate talk than he hated him for it. The next night, when he was talking or, rather, monologuing about American women and their evil, destructive wills, John, not interested, I suppose, jumped up and went bounding out of the room.

"Young jack-rabbits, all of them," Lorenzo muttered, throwing a dark look after him. "We shall see what we shall see!" And from that time there was no more rapport between *them*, either.[45]

31 October 1922   *Taos, New Mexico*

⟨ Today we have been up to John's ranch—about 20 miles from here. It was so lonely: and rather free, far more so than here. Frieda wants to go and live there. We'll try it first for a week, because it will be colder. But I think we shall do it—and try to make a real life there. It is much more splendid, more real, there, than here.[46]

Mabel Dodge Luhan

Of course [Lawrence] was often gay. I don't want you to think that in those first years he was cross or morose all the time. He was all right so long as things went his way. That is, if nothing happened to slight him. He simply couldn't bear to have anyone question his power, his rightness, or even his appearance. I think his uncertainty about himself, a vague feeling of inferiority, made him touchy. I suppose a *sense* of inferiority comes from some inferiority actually present in one, or one would not have it. Did Lawrence realize, I wonder, that in spite of all his charm, his sensitiveness, and his sympathetic intuition he had a vulgar nose?

He was deeply uncertain about his clothes, like many delicately balanced people, and watchful for looks. He *did* look funny in some kinds of clothes, too. They had to be just right or he looked common. Well, he had a little white homespun coat with no collar that he wore a good deal, and he was most of all lovable in that. Up at the ranch he always wore tan corduroys and a blue shirt that made his beard flaming and his eyes more blue.

He didn't care for men much. Very few, anyway, and never for what we call manly men. He had quite a grudging feeling about cowboys and that kind, and he once wrote an article, or said in a novel, that those strong, silent characters were all inhibited neurotics! [47]

So, really, he was best off when alone, with no one about to poke the hidden wound. He could have got along indefinitely with just the few of us up there on our hill. I was building a protection around him, keeping people away from him as I thought he wished. As I knew he wished, really. But he was perverse. He always suspected one's motives or one's acts. When he found I asked no one to the house, and that no one came, he began to resent it—the very situation I had arranged for *him!* [48]

.   .   .   .

[Our] daily companionship grew to have more and more significance for him. He and Frieda had spent all their married life in little country places with few acquaintances and hardly any friends. They did not know how to live easily and casually with people. I came to know from each of them in turn how they had quarreled, now here, now there. His novels show that. Either he would get jealous and break up the situation or she would grow jealous or, worse, envious. She hated worst of all to feel slighted, left high and dry by Lawrence when he'd soar away from her in a flight she could not follow. One can hardly blame her. He was sorry for her himself at such times, feeling just as he felt the day when we were riding in the desert and, looking back after a fierce, long gallop, we saw Frieda hanging ludicrously, head down, from her saddle. His face was full of compunction as he rode back to extricate her. After that he never rode away from her again; no matter how I tried to make him forget and follow me, I rode away alone.

In every way possible, then, Frieda held him back with her. He told me that what she wanted—the way she liked best to live—was to be off alone somewhere, with him writing his books in the next room while she did her housework in peace.

"Frieda's at her best that way," he said. But sometimes she drove him outside himself with exasperation when she had him to herself.

One morning at nine o'clock I was writing letters in the big room and he came in the door like a current of wind. I was taken aback at seeing him so early, for he hardly ever left his own place before dinner; and when I looked at his face, I couldn't believe my eyes. He was shining, radiant, perfectly transfigured with rage. His eyes had a weird light in them: a high, clear, pale light, so that they looked like two stars. His features were stern. There was really something godlike about him . . . , and he seemed to be immeasurably tall and strong and to tower over me. The real Lawrence stood there at last, burst out from the equivocal chrysalis that showed him, falsely, a dominated and diminished creature.

"I can't stand it over there," were the words that fell from this figure of an archangel. "Frieda has got a woman there sewing! She has your sewing-machine going and there are yards and yards of stuff all over." His irritation was discharging itself into power. The sharp radiance poured over me from his starry eyes. His eyes were flashing messages his reason never knew, I think. He challenged me and claimed me, and, fear forgotten, it was as though all of him was saying to me: "Nothing else matters save this excitement, this flow, this ecstasy."

So we sat together and I became conscious, as often before, that his presence was alterative, that it set up, perhaps involuntarily, changes in whoever came in contact with it. I said:

"I am changing. You are changing me, Lorenzo."

"Perhaps. It is too soon to know. Only a real emotion can change any-one—and I don't know whether your will has given way yet."

"How *can* I give up my will?" I asked, uncomprehendingly.

"Unless you do, you will be destroyed," he answered.

"Never. I have a protection," I told him, lifting my head.

"Oh, you have gone far, but I have gone farther," he said then, as he said in the first days in Taos, "and I know a destruction that passes over your protection. . . ."

Of course I suppose we were a great deal together, though hardly ever alone, for even if Frieda was not there, I think he had promised not to be alone with me. But the communication between us grew deeper all the time and we quickened each other increasingly so that merely being near, even with others there, gave Lawrence more insight and gave me more vitality.

We were living at high pitch, with occasional crashes back to earth when Frieda would recapture him by an irresistible jab and engage him in a fight. At such times he would be severed from me completely—the spell broken—the thread snapped between us—the sympathy no longer flowing back and forth. It was all to make over again! I never got used to his cold, unfriendly face, his repudiating, indifferent look. Never. Any more than I ever got used to the visible signs on Frieda of what took place between them. For when we went to the Hot Springs, I saw the big voluptuous woman standing naked in the dim stone room where we dressed and undressed, and there were often great black and blue bruises on her blond flesh. And sometimes I found her with eyes red and swollen from weeping.

One morning in particular, I remember, I found her in her kitchen, spent and old from too many tears. I asked her what was the matter and she, still undone with misery and discouragement, broke out again into sobs.

"I cannot stand it," she wept. "He tears me to pieces. Last night he was so loving and so tender with me, and this morning he hates me. He hit me—and said he would not be any woman's servant. Sometimes I believe he is mad. . . ."

I knew well that when he revolted away from her, he caromed over to me. That was always the way it went. He vacillated between us and hated each in turn. Every time we went off into the far-away places of consciousness and of the imagination, he did a tail-spin; and whenever, reunited to Frieda, he capitulated to her and sank into the flesh, he beat her up for it afterwards.

And so as the weeks went on, this life of ours grew more extreme and its ups and downs more intense. Seeing him fade away from her too often those days, into what probably seemed to her to be thin, unpalatable, and hostile air, she found her hatred of him grow uncontrollable, so that she could not contain it and had to vent it—even to me, for whom in her heart she felt no real congeniality any more, for I was bad, she thought, for Lawrence. Perhaps she thought of me as bad in myself, apart from any effect I had on him, for she had said to Alice Henderson soon after she first came to Taos:

"What a *person* Mabel is! You can't say she's *good*, of course. She's just *there!*"

"Well, if she doesn't think I'm good, it's likely she thinks I'm bad," I had replied with some assumed defiance. I didn't want anyone to think I was bad. I wasn't bad.

Whenever Frieda and I were left alone now, she began to defame him to me.

"He's done, Mabel. He's finished. He's like glass. Brittle. You don't know what it's like—living with him. Sometimes I think I'll leave him. I could make a real life for myself!"

How terrible this was. He of the warm living flow, whose tenderness was so instant and responsive, he had constantly to watch out that it did not betray him!

I wonder why I swung away from him to her in that moment. I think it was my fatal ability to see any point of view that presented itself. Anyway I was suddenly on her side, seeing him as a rare and specialized creation of nature, something separate and strange and alone except for her. Untempting. I did not want him. Neither did anyone else. Frieda must keep him. He was hers—good luck to her!

"Frieda, you must never leave him. You're the only woman he can live with. Besides, you know, he's not physically attractive to women. I don't think women want to touch him. . . ."

"Of course they don't," she assented, angrily. "He's dry. Well, sometimes I think I'll just get out before it's too late. . . ."

Lawrence came in at the garden door—and my heart ached, for I saw he could feel in the air our antipathy and our abandon; and from that time on they worked together to get away from Taos.

Did she repeat that very night what I had said to her about him? I never knew. But from that day on they were gone, in reality, even though they lingered on for a while in the flesh. They broached departure the next day. They could get a little cottage from the Hawks [49] up on Del Monte Ranch.

"But why? Why?" I questioned in despair. I could not bear to have him go now, when he had lightened life and made it so thrilling.

"Oh! We are better off alone," said Frieda, ambiguously.

"There is destruction here," Lorenzo shot in. "There is a queer menace in the air. Oh, there's a witch's brew on this hill! And the Indians struggle against it—and I will fight it, too. Yes. I value my own little bit of life, and I will fight for it."

I felt perfectly helpless against such an attack. We were friends no more. There was nothing but antagonism between us, scarcely veiled, and Frieda was triumphant and glad.

One day I made a last appeal to them. We were driving all over the valley for a farewell look at the yellow cottonwood trees. The sky was almost black-blue, and the yellow plumes were motionless against it. In Cordovas [Cordova] the white village was peaceful. Great round white clouds boiled up behind it, and the desert was a carpet of yellow between there and Taos. In Seco the alfalfa was piled on top of the corrals, and the earth was pale yellow. The trees were like beaten gold in the sunshine, and the mountains behind Seco were plum-color. Everything was quiet. It was impossible to be unhappy.

"Lawrence, I believe we shall remember this day and wish we could come back to it. We do not know when we are well off."

"It is a miraculous day," assented Frieda.

"Why don't you stay, Frieda?" I begged. "Don't go up to Del Monte. You keep moving and moving and it's always the same. You won't change anything by moving."

"Perhaps that is true, Frieda," Lawrence muttered. "We are always moving on—but we take ourselves along! Shall we try awhile longer?"

"No. I am packed. I have decided to go and we will go. But we'll come down all the time—really we will," she flashed, reassuringly.

But I wanted none of that. I did not care for what I knew would be broken, breathless visits full of errands and practical needs. No. I wanted the flow and the rhythm of daily living. Unless I could have what I wanted, I wouldn't have anything. *My* will be done!

We parted then without good feeling or friendliness. The sympathy was gone. Almost the last thing I remember Lawrence saying to me was:

"You in your fur cap! You are like a great cat—with your green eyes. Well, I snap my fingers at you—like that!"

They were gone. It was the end of the first part . . . .[50]

1 December 1922   Taos, New Mexico

(Just leaving. . . .

I think you will find everything in the house, except a dish and a plate, smashed, and two blankets, the red stripe and the blue stripe, which we borrow to wrap up in. I'll see these come back safely. Then I feel a bit guilty about the big water-tin, accepting the loan of it.

.   .   .   .

So very many thanks for lending us this new house.
Let us hear what is happening. We shall see you soon.[51]

5 December 1922   Del Monte Ranch, Questa, New Mexico

(You see, we have flown again, but not far—only twenty-five kilometres, and here we are in an old log-house with five rooms, very primitive, on this big ranch. Behind, the Rocky Mountains, pines and snow-peaks; around us the hills—pine trees, cedars, greasewood, and a small grey bush of the desert. Below, the desert, great and flat like a shadowy lake, very wide. And in the distance more mountains, with small patches of snow—and the sunsets! Now you see the picture.

The Hawk family live five minutes from here, then no houses for four kilometres. Behind, no house for three hundred kilometres or more. Few people, an empty, very beautiful country.

We have hewn down a great balsam pine and cut it to pieces—like a quarry—the gold wood.

We have for companions two young Danes [Knud Merrild and Kai Gótzsche], painters: [52] they will go into a little three-room cabin nearby. Our nearest neighbour, [William] Hawk, is a young man, thirty years old, has a hundred and fifty half-wild animals, a young wife [Rachel,] is nice, not rich.

You have asked about Mabel Dodge: American, rich, only child, from Buffalo on Lake Erie, bankers, forty-two years old, has had three husbands —one Evans (dead), one Dodge (divorced), and one Maurice Sterne (a Jew, Russian, painter, young, also divorced).[53] Now she has an Indian, Tony, a stout chap. She has lived much in Europe—Paris, Nice, Florence—is a little famous in New York and little loved, very intelligent as a woman, another "culture-carrier," likes to play the patroness, hates the white world and loves the Indian out of hate, is very "generous," wants to be "good" and is very wicked, has a terrible will-to-power, you know—she wants to be a witch and at the same time a Mary of Bethany at Jesus's feet—a big, white crow, a cooing raven of ill-omen, a little buffalo.

. . . .

Basta, we are still "friends" with Mabel. But do not take this snake to our bosom. You know, these people have only money, nothing else but money, and because all the world wants money, all the money, America has become strong, proud and over-powerful.[54]

15 December 1922   Del Monte Ranch, Questa, New Mexico

[. . . Mabel was too near a neighbour. We have come to the Hawks' ranch—next to John Evans' ranch—about 17 miles from Taos: have an old brown log cabin, and are very comfortable. We plan to stay till April . . . .

. . . Thomas Seltzer and his wife are due to arrive in Taos on the 25th —my publisher . . . .

We have quite a good time here: cut down a big tree and with great exertions sawed it and split it up. Ah oh, it burns away so fast in all the fires. I think grudgingly when I see the red embers: all my labour gone into smoke! But it was a sweet balsam pine tree, very bright in the burning. We struggle with pack-rats and pigs and cats. We've got one of Lorraine's little black pups [55] that is now growing up into a young termagant. We go riding: I on a high sorrel thoroughbred [56] that nearly splits me as I split my logs with wedges.—In a 3-room cabin are two young Danes, painters, nice: good *neighbours. And Mountsier is coming next week. Snow is quite deep round us: but no snow on the desert below. The coyotes howl by the gate.*

. . . .

We say we are going to Greenland in the summer. Are we? [57]

30 December 1922   Del Monte Ranch, Questa, New Mexico

❲ *I think of coming to England in the late spring or early summer: perhaps go down to Mexico City and sail from Vera Cruz. The longer I am in America, the less I want to go east, to Chicago, Boston or New York. Don't mind evading them, even if it is a mere evasion. Thomas Seltzer and wife are here: he's a nice tiny man, I think I trust him, really.*

It is good fun on this ranch—quite wild—Rocky Mts.—desert with Rio Grande Canyon away spreading below—great and really beautiful landscape —looking far, far west. We ride off to the Rio Grande to the hot springs, and bathe—and we chop wood and wagon it in, and all that. But there's no inside to the life: all outside. I don't believe there ever will be any inside to American life—they seem so dead—till they are all destroyed.[58]

Thomas Seltzer

. . . In advance, I suppose, one would try to avoid spending a memorable week at the end of 1922 and the beginning of 1923 on Del Monte Ranch with Lawrence and Frieda and two picturesque Danish artists, if one but knew that in a few years one would be relegated thereby to a period distinctly removed from the present. But at the time when we gathered in Lawrence's log house to celebrate New Year's Eve, none of us thought of anything but the enjoyment of the moment in pleasant and far from Philistine company, and each contributed his share to make the modest little party as cheerful as possible. What I was struck by especially was the small but sweet voice of Lawrence. Do you remember his singing some English Christmas carols? I was particularly touched by his rendering of "Good King Quentin." I have heard it sung many a time and was never impressed. Everyone seems to consider it a trifle and so it is. But the way Lawrence sang it, it had a haunting beauty that gripped you. I have often since tried to recapture that beauty and mentally I can do so but not if I try to sing it myself. I have asked others, with good trained voices, to sing it for me in the hope that they would reproduce for me the feel and the tang which it had in Lawrence's perfectly simply [*sic*] and unstrained recital, but always I was completely disappointed.

I mention this because to me it is typical of Lawrence the man as I perceive him. He is known to the world as a great poet and novelist, and as a curiosity, a piquant character, a sort of Don Juan who never practised his theoretical Don Juanism. But except for the fact that he was indeed a great novelist and poet, this conception of him as a man is, I know it for certain, all wrong. It is a fearful distortion. Lawrence was as great a man as he was a writer. In every aspect of life he was natural, without pose and, at bottom, sane. Follow him in the kitchen when he cooks, when he washes and irons his own underwear, when he does chores for Frieda, observe him when he walks with you in the country, when he is in the company of people whom he likes and to a certain extent respects—how natural he is in every movement and yet how distinguished, how satisfying because he is natural; and in his conversation he is almost always inspiring and interesting because of his extraordinary ability to create a flow, a current between himself and the other person. He had extraordinary poise, too. I wonder if you know what I mean? So many people dwell only on his fierce outbreaks. But to me his outbreaks, even if they belonged to the man, were not of the essence of him. The times and his environment are more to blame than himself.[59]

1 January 1923   Del Monte Ranch, Questa, New Mexico

❲ Seltzer is here—with his wife. He is a tiny Jew, but trustworthy, seems to me. . . . Mountsier is due to arrive this very evening. . . . I don't want to write here. I think of going in a few weeks' time down into Mexico— to Mexico City—don't know how long to stay: then to Europe in the summer. But nothing certain. Luckily Women in Love sells well, so I am not so poor.[60]

2 February 1923   Del Monte Ranch, Questa, New Mexico

❲ I got your [John Middleton Murry's] note just now, via Kot, about Katherine.[61] Yes, it is something gone out of our lives. We thought of her,

I can tell you, at Wellington. Did Ottoline ever send on the card to Katherine I posted from there for her? Yes, I always knew a bond in my heart. Feel a fear where the bond is broken now. Feel as if old moorings were breaking all. What is going to happen to us all? Perhaps it is good for Katherine not to have to see the next phase. We will unite up again when I come to England. It has been a savage enough pilgrimage these last four years.[62] Perhaps K. has taken the only way for her. We keep faith —I always feel death only strengthens that, the faith between those who have it.

Still, it makes me afraid. As if worse were coming. I feel like the Sicilians. They always cry for help from their dead. We shall have to cry to ours: we do cry.

I wrote to you [63] to Adelphi Terrace the day after I got your letter, and asked Seltzer to send you Fantasia of the Unconscious. I wanted Katherine to read it.

She'll know, though. The dead don't die. They look on and help.

But in America one feels as if everything would die, and that is terrible.[64]

10 February 1923   Del Monte Ranch, Questa, New Mexico

([Yesterday settled with Mountsier he should no longer be my agent.[65]

10 February 1923   Del Monte Ranch, Questa, New Mexico

([I have made up the complete MS. of Birds, Beasts and Flowers and sent it to Seltzer.[66]

25 February 1923   Del Monte Ranch, Questa, New Mexico

([No, I am not disappointed in America. I said I was coming to Europe this spring. But I don't want to. We leave in a fortnight for Old Mexico. Perhaps I shall come back here. . . .

But I feel about U.S.A., as I vaguely felt a long time ago: that there is a vast unreal, intermediary thing intervening between the real thing which was Europe and the next real thing, which will probably be in America, but which isn't yet, at all. Seems to me a vast death-happening must come first.

211

But probably *it is here, in America (I don't say just U.S.A.), that the quick will keep alive and come through.*[67]

21 March 1923   El Paso, Texas

❨ We cross the frontier into Mexico this morning—already it is hot—such a change from the snow of Del Monte.[68]

24 March 1923   Hotel Monte Carlo, Av. Uruguay 69, Mexico City

❨ Got here last night—quite a journey—tried a big American hotel [69] and didn't like it: this is a nice little place. It is warm—not hot—rains a little— the city pleasant—much more like S. Italy than America—haven't done much yet but wander round. I think we are going to like it.[70]

24? March 1923   Hotel Monte Carlo, Av. Uruguay 69, Mexico City

❨ Had quite a good journey here—Mexico just warm enough and very free and easy, like Naples—to me much pleasanter than U.S.—we shall probably stay at least a few months, though I am not sure—I expect some friends [Witter Bynner and Willard Johnson] down from Santa Fe on Tuesday [27 March 1923]—so good to get a little wine again.[71]

Witter Bynner

Lawrence had heard in Europe high praise of the famous Spanish matadors, Belmonte and Joselito, the latter killed in the ring only three years before; and we were told that the Mexicans, Rodolfo Gaona and Juan Silveti, were performers of comparable skill and prowess. Silveti was to be the star on Sunday.

On Easter morning [1 April 1923],[72] having been to churches Friday and to a sacred movie [73] on Saturday, we were wakened by bells of resurrection and in the afternoon attended the bullfight. It was a first experience for all of us, and we approached it curious but apprehensive.

At the entrance to the arena Lawrence, Johnson, and I, like other males filing through, were frisked for firearms: it had been announced that President Obregón [74] would be present. At the last moment, word spread that he could not attend; but other dignitaries entered the presidential box escorting three or four bright-fluttering women who wore flowered mantillas and high combs.

Since seats cost but half as much in the sun as in the shade, we were sitting in the sun, except that this day, to Lawrence's special pleasure, there was no sun. Our backless bench tier of concrete was within five rows of the ring. Below us, paralleling the wall of the ring was a circling five-foot wooden fence with here and there a gap and before each gap a small barrier, making safety boxes for performers when hard pressed. The crowd, now thickening and seeming less an assemblage than a single mass monster, was already—with its murmurs, growls, and yells—grinding our nerves a little.

"I begin to feel sick," whispered Lawrence. "Look at their faces. The eyes don't seem hard, or the mouths. It's that cruel dent of relish above the nostril."

Opposite us, rose a roar of voices. Somebody's hat had been tossed across the tiers into a group which was scrambling for it. Other hats followed, on our side too. Orange peels began flying. A shoe landed in Lawrence's lap. He sat immobile while someone from behind him seized it and sent it scaling again.

"Shall we leave?" asked Lawrence, his head twitching upward like that of a horse.

Half an orange just missed my bald spot. A second half hit it. Other bare heads were being hit. A kindly Mexican motioned that I should put on my hat. Obeying him, I was spared further pelting. Apparently uncovered heads were permissible targets.

Three bands, one at a time, entered their sections near the President's box and were shouted at for *musica!* When a rousing Mexican march blared out, the vocal din was only accelerated. The crowd had not wanted music so much as a beat for their own noise.

What looked like a folded coat landed in the arena. It seemed a signal. Like water from a broken dam, the mass of men in unreserved seats swelled over the reserved section which in a trice was filled solid. Seatholders who came later were vain claimants.

On the exact moment advertised, a wide gate opened, a square colorful procession strutted with music into the arena toward the President's box to make bows, with waists and trim buttocks held tautly, shoulders back; two groups of fine-stepping *toreros* with bright cloaks above their embroidered boleros and half-length, skin-tight trousers and salmon-

213

colored stockings; then mounted picadors; then *banderilleros* with silver embroidery; then matadors with gold and with red capes, all these men wearing berets over abbreviated pigtails; and finally, in red harness, two dingy teams of three mules each, ready to drag away carcasses. "The right symbol!" muttered Lawrence. "They're all jackasses." The procession, after circling the ring and receiving a round of plaudits, dispersed.

Then, with no warning, no noise, a huge white bull swam into the arena and stood a moment, his tail waving, his head bewildered, apprehending foes. Lawrence's head rose and sank with the bull's. "The bull is beautiful, Lorenzo," said Frieda. The foes were there, the first of them: two stationary horsemen. When the lowered head made clumsily for a horse, the rider warded it off with a lance. The second rider did likewise. And then into the ring came the toreros, to nag him with scarlet mantles. He saw them one at a time. He snorted. He charged a cloak. It was whisked over his head. He curved quickly and charged again, cleaving the air with his horns under a swing of color. Now and then he would corner a torero who, amid jeers and whistlings, would either dodge into one of the safety boxes or vault the *barrera* into the shielded alley way. All of a sudden the bull too had heaved his pawing bulk over the fence. Attendants scurried to cut off a section of the gangway by closing gates. Commotion subsided. "He beat them," Lawrence said as though to himself. "They should let him go." A fluttered cape teased the bull out again into the ring, where he stood still, waving his tail. His belly lifting, falling with his heavy breath, he looked round and lowed; then once more he leaped the fence, this time breaking it. And once more the blocked exit, once more the flashing taunts, the deft weavings and wavings of five toreros; once more his return to the ring, his half-seeing eye, his wasted strength. "They're dastardly!" Lawrence exclaimed.

He turned to us. He had been shifting in his seat and looking sharply at us now and then as if to see what we thought of it all. We could tell that the teasing of the beast, the deliberate baiting and angering had made him as tense as the animal, with whom he was almost identifying himself. "They keep him starved and in the dark," he snapped, "so that when he comes into the ring he's angry but can't see. He's the only one among them with heart or brain. He despises them, but he knows what they are; he knows that he's done for." The toreador jumped the fence to get away from the bull; the bull jumped the fence to get away from the lot of them. "They let the toreador get away. Why don't they let the bull get away?" he exhorted us. "Why don't they respect his intelligence and bow to him instead of to those nincompoops in the box? He's not the brute; they're the brutes. He abhors them and so do I. But he can't get away and I can. Let's get away." He was on his feet. None of us stirred to follow him. He sat down again.

"It sickens me too, Lorenzo," I agreed. "But hadn't we better see at least one round of it through, to know what we're talking about when we say we don't like it? I shan't want to see another bullfight any more than you will."

"Very well," he glared. "But I don't need to see a round through, as you call it. The trouble is that you're as bloodthirsty as the rest of them. You can't resist it. Frieda can't resist it. Spud can't. I could resist it, but I'll give in to you." He sulked back on the bench and looked away from us, away from everything.

But now came a change, a chance for the bull to vent his disgust, if not on a man, then on a decrepit, blindfolded horse. The rider spurred toward him. The picador, with armor under his trousers, urged the shivering mount to expose its belly. The crowd was hushed, expectant, on the edge of its seats. Lawrence was breathing hard and glaring. Suddenly, given a chance not so much by the rider as by the bull, the horse struck with his thin hind legs, fought free and stalked off with an air of doddering valor, only to postpone a next encounter not at the center of the ring where he had had clearance, but close to the barrera, with no room for him to dodge; and though the picador was supposed with his blunt lance to shunt the bull off, the crowd knew better. The bull pawed up earth, slowly bent his head. The lance was futile. The horse reared and floundered. In and up went the horn. While the picador tumbled against the fence and sheepishly found his feet, the bull shoved and gored and ripped; and while the crowd gave a sigh of relief, Lawrence groaned and shook. By the time the toreros had again drawn their prey toward the cloaks and the picador had remounted and forced his steed into motion toward the exit, the horse's bowels were bulging almost to the ground, like vines and gourds. But the bull had not had enough. "Stop it!" cried Lawrence to the bull, jumping out of his seat. But just before the picador reached the gate, horns were lowered again for another snorting plunge, and this time the entire covering of the horse's belly was ripped off. He fell dead, his contents out on the ground, with earth being shoveled over them by attendants. Lawrence had sat down again, dazed and dark with anger and shame. Frieda was watching him. The proud front of the bull—head, neck, chest, leg, hoof—shone crimson in a moment of sun. The crowd was throatily satisfied!

There had been something phallic, Lawrence might have noted, in this fierce penetration, this rape of entrails, this bloody glut. But his nerves exploded. Fortunately people were too intent on the ring to notice him, and only a few of them heard a red-bearded Englishman, risen from his seat, excoriating cowards and madmen. Frieda was as alarmed as Johnson and I, for he was denouncing the crowd in Spanish. But he sickened suddenly, plunged away from us, treading toes, and lurched down the row toward the exit.

"I'll go with him," exclaimed Frieda. "I'd better. There's no knowing. You stay. He'll be worse if you come. You stay. Leave him to me. *Ja!*" And she squeezed her way out.

"Yes, I think we'd better stay," said Johnson, with a drawn face. And we did stay, though we were as revolted by the performance as are most Europeans and Americans. I supposed the audience had more than once seen outraged foreigners bolt away, and learned to ignore them as barbarians. I dreaded what we were still to watch, felt my insides sift like ashes, was sorely tempted to follow the Lawrences. But we did stay.

. . . .

. . . We vowed though, as we filed out, that it was our last bullfight.

In the corridor we came upon a middle-aged Polish professor of psychology, whom we had casually met at the Monte Carlo. He was vacationing from some American university, spoke fair Spanish, and was with a Mexican friend, both of them gesticulating with joy over the events of the afternoon. "Magnificent!" he exclaimed. We bowed, without assenting but without disturbing the ecstasy of chatter between the two. "We are going to Silveti's hotel," the Pole called out. "Why not come with us? My friend knows him well." "Thanks," I answered, "but I must join our own friends. They were shocked and left." "Yes, I saw them," he laughed. "They shouldn't be shocked. They are just new to it. But we'll see you later at the hotel, unless Mr. Johnson will come with us." "Go ahead," I urged. And Spud went.

Lawrence greeted me at the hotel with a hard look of contempt. "So you stayed through all of it. I thought you would. You Americans would run to any street accident to see blood. You are as bad as the dirty Mexicans. You would have held Frieda there in that slaughterhouse. You tried to keep her there."

"No, Lorenzo!" she protested.

"But they wanted you to stay. I know. They not only fooled themselves with their nonsense about 'seeing it through,' they wanted to fool you as well, but you were too fine for them."

"He compliments me," smiled Frieda. "How angry he must be with you!"

At supper, after Johnson's return from the bullfighter's hotel, Lawrence expatiated. "What we saw this afternoon," he snorted, "was the grandeur of Rome, soiling its breeches! You like scatological jokes, Bynner. No wonder you liked this dirt."

"He didn't like it," Spud defended me mildly, "any more than I did."

"You both stayed it through," flamed Lawrence. "The way not to enjoy it was not to stay it through."

The Pole was with his friend at a nearby table and, when they had finished eating, came over to ours and asked if they might join us. But before bringing the Mexican, he touched off the fuse. "It was my sixth bullfight," he gloated. "I was shocked at first, like you, Mrs. Lawrence. I saw that Mr. Lawrence had to take you out. But I've learned now. Didn't you see how happy the bulls were?" He beckoned to the Mexican and continued, "I'd like to have you meet my—"

"No," said Lawrence firmly. "I do not wish to meet your friend, or anyone else in this loathsome country. And I have seen, as well, all that I wish to see of you."

"Ja!" nodded Frieda vigorously.

The Pole was silenced. But as most Mexicans react when bullfights are condemned, the friend was kindled and, more because Lawrence had left the ring than because of this rudeness, he came close and took up the cudgels. "You are English," he challenged in our tongue. "You run after animals, little foxes, tire them out and then let dogs tear them to pieces, while you ride your high horses. We Mexicans face big animals, stronger than we are, and we are not dogs. We face them as men and kill them with our hands. You English hunt little people too and make dogs of your soldiers to tear little people to pieces."

"I abominate fox hunts," sparred Lawrence, in confusion.

But the Mexican did not spare him. "You have judged all Mexico by one bullfight, but I will not judge all England by one Englishman." He bowed to Frieda, turned on his heel and conducted the Pole with him out of the dining room, out of the hotel.

By now Lawrence was seething, and I expected further outbursts against one or all of us. To my surprise the seething settled; and, with no more mention of Poles or Mexicans, we had a pacific session in their

217

room, during which he opened one of those stores of information with which he frequently surprised us. He had been studying somewhere the history of bullfighting and had taken notes, in fact he produced a page of data and he half read, half remembered for us:

"In the sixteenth century the Vatican took a stand against the filthy business, which was going on here even then. Pope Pius V," he glanced at a note, "banned it. So did Sixtus V. But a great protest followed, led by poets," he gave me a look, "and by the whole faculty at Salamanca. With the next Pope," and here a final use of the paper, "yes, Clement VIII, the Church gave in, just as it had to give in to your Penitentes in New Mexico and to letting your Indians add their pagan rites to the Mass. That was different. I like that. I suppose a Church which murdered heretics shouldn't mind the murder of a few bulls." He dropped the sheet of notes into a wastebasket and smiled indulgently when I picked them out again.

.   .   .   .

When *The Plumed Serpent* was issued three years later [1926], Johnson and I discovered the use Lawrence had made of our Mexican experiences together.

It at once became evident that the protagonist, Kate Leslie, was a fusion of himself and Frieda, the hand the hand of Frieda but the voice the voice of Lawrence, that Owen Rhys, her cousin, was I and that Owen's friend, Bud Villiers, was Johnson.[75] My belief then and now is that he had intended our continuing to play rather ignominious American roles throughout the novel but that, having come to know and like us better, he mercifully let us out of it.[76]

11 April 1923   *Hotel Monte Carlo, Av. Uruguay 69, Mexico City*

❨ *We are still here—and I am liking Mexico better—think now of finding a house to live [in] here some months—in the country for preference . . . . We motored out to the pyramids—very fine. This picture is on the way —ourselves, Spud Johnson (Witter Bynner's friend) and the two chauffeurs. We also stayed a few days in Cuernavaca—hot, but very attractive. . . . Mrs. Nuttal[l] [77]—to whom Dr. Lyster gave us a letter—offers us a house of hers in Coyacan [Coyoacán], a suburb here. I'd rather be farther from town. We shall make up our minds next week.—It isn't a bit too hot— but still it takes some getting used to.[78]*

Witter Bynner

To us newcomers Mexico City was still a magnet; and, whatever Lawrence felt about it, he settled back to showing us round. He tried to prevent our buying cheap loot in Frieda's paradise, the *Volador*, the Thieves' Market, or even better stuff in the *Monte de Piedad*, the government pawn-shop. He liked to lean against a low railing over a street corner deeply excavated and to see ancient shadows below him on Aztec pavements and stairways which the digging had exposed. . . .

In some of the government edifices which he showed us, Mexican painters were beginning their now famous frescoes. Through Sr. José Vasconcelos, Minister of Education, the State was giving them, together with room and board and a pittance of pesos, lavish opportunity to whet their talents and beautify the capital. . . .[79]

. . . .

We took occasional short trips to such places as Xochimilco and its canals, where Frieda, like an expanded Cleopatra, lolled on a flower-decked barge and relished the chicken *mole* served us hot from a dug-out drawn alongside, or the ruined monastery, El Desierto de los Leones, in a drizzle as dreary as Lawrence's spirits were that day. On the way to San Juan Teotihuacan, we stopped at another old monastery, San Agustin Acolman, and here he was happy. . . .

. . . .

We climbed the pyramids at Teotihuacan and like other tourists photographed one another on them. . . . In the great quadrangle of Quetzalcoatl, we saw Lawrence stand looking and brooding. The colored stone heads of the feathered snakes in one of the temples were a match for him. The stone serpents and owls held something that he obviously feared. . . .

Perhaps the germ of [*The Plumed Serpent's*] theme came to him then, his half-fascinated, half-frightened impulse to banish from Mexico the gods in human image and replace them with an animal, with this animal of all animals, this "snake of all snakes," this creature part snake and part bird, Mexico's natural god and in many ways his own.

Though I think he was already planning his novel, I doubt if he was yet working on it. But he was by no means idle. In the evenings, after

219

supper at the Monte Carlo, we would have coffee, cordials, and conversation in their room, while Lawrence, reclining on the bed with notebook and pencil, would be busy at essays, sketches, reviews, random writings, which went off in the mails. . . . Here in Mexico we marveled constantly at his ability to be writing and talking at the same moment, but Frieda seemed used to it. He was like a man in a newspaper office, whose copy could come clear, through interruptive confusion. . . .

. . . .

It was at this time that we made our trip to Cuernavaca,[80] where the Lawrences particularly enjoyed a vista down a narrow street at the end of which stood a narrow church flanked by two narrow cypresses. "It's more like Italy," beamed Lawrence. "*Ja*," glowed Frieda, who gave hearty romantic sighs in the Borda Gardens, where the ghosts of the guests, Maximilian and Carlota,[81] still strolled. Lawrence was saddened by evidences of the Zapata [82] uprising and depredation in Morelos: ". . . noble ruined haciendas with ruined avenues approaching their broken splendor," [83] as he later recorded.[84]

Witter Bynner

Ca. 15 April 1923: [85] *Cuernavaca*. I suppose Haniel Long has told you that we are in Mexico with the D. H. Lawrences. I had long been intending a trip here. They came down to Santa Fe from Taos and urged us to accompany them. I had a few misgivings, which have since been borne out. The man himself, and his wife, from a brief earlier meeting, I had liked well enough, but I had never liked the spirit of the man in his books. He had seemed to me a sort of Freudian prig—anything but immoral—and I still find him so. Give me a promiscuous lover any time instead of a promiscuous hater. Promiscuous hate is really a more degraded form of immorality than the other. Fortunately, there are two phases of Lawrence which one may easily and simply enjoy. By nature, and except as he has tampered with himself, he is an impulsive, boyish, gentle soul; and as a writer he is by nature eminently gifted. The trouble with him is that he has let his intellect and his more intemperate inclinations elaborate a code of thought and conduct which permit him all sorts of rather pretentious self-indulgence. I think I should like the man very much indeed if he were a real self instead of a fabricated self. What is left of the reality under the fabrication, together with a rather neat wit, makes him supportable. When his hearty German wife is with him and they take semiseriously their constant petty bickerings, I am amused and at ease. When I am alone with him, I have a hard time not to be bored. A contrast between the stature of this man and that of Meredith shows to what a degree the English novel and the spirit behind it has deteriorated. It has come down from generous genius to a bitter knack.

We are probably due for a few more weeks together. This morning I thought I should have to contrive a pretext for escape; but this afternoon I feel better. The Lawrences' attitude toward Johnson and myself is genial and charming—with always a shadow lurking as to what he will say about us later. So far I have hardly heard him say a decent word about anyone—even those supposed to be his close friends. It is curious to think of literature falling into such clutches.

Today we are in Cuernavaca, the capital of Morelos, a town about the size of Santa Fe. It has beautiful vistas and a rather oppressive magnetism. The peons here baffle me more than people I have met anywhere; seeming simple and amiable, they somehow fail to give one any current of connection—even one who has been prepared by gradual acquaintance among the Pueblos. Lawrence tells me that he has better hope for them than for any of the dark-skinned races; but I more than suspect him of fitting them into a prearranged edifice.[86]

Witter Bynner

. . . [The] second chapter of *The Plumed Serpent* records with extraordinary fidelity the persons and interchange at a tea party given us by Mrs. Zelia Nuttall,[87] an English widow distinguished in Mexico City as archeologist, *grande dame,* and conservative hostess-owner of a historic house in Coyoacán built by Pedro de Alvaro [88] in the time of Cortes.

A wing of this house had been offered him by Mrs. Nuttall. After his arrival in Mexico on March 23, he had written his Danish friend, Knud Merrild on April 11: ". . . I want to find a house. A rich Englishwoman offers us one in Coyoacán, a suburb here. . . . Spit on Taos for me." [89] But he was already gathering spit for Coyoacán. In *The Plumed Serpent* he describes the offered house, the "ponderous" suburban house: "A certain dead, heavy strength and beauty seemed there, unable to pass away, unable to liberate itself and decompose. . . ." [90]

However, I am grateful to him for having pilloried in the novel a stuffy, stubborn British judge whom we met in that house and whom I finally had to let decree, against my own knowledge as a collector of its many colors in China, that jade could be only green. "He trembled with irritation," writes Lawrence of the judge, "like an access of gout." [91]

The novelist tries to scoff at Mrs. Norris, as he calls her in his book, at her life and her ways: "a lonely daughter of culture" with an expression of "tomb-like mockery." But she had a British dignity and authority which beat him down. Reflecting his subjection, he observes: "The world is made up of a mass of people and a few individuals. Mrs. Norris was one of the few individuals. True, she played her social game all the time. But she was an odd number; and all alone, she could give the even numbers a bad time," something he liked well to do himself. Again, she "always put her visitors uncomfortably at their ease, as if they were captives and she the chieftainess who had captured them." [92] In spite of seeing through Mrs. Nuttall's role, he respected it as a role he himself would often have liked to play as successfully, an outworn European role few unimitative Americans would like to play at all. [93]

11 April 1923   Hotel Monte Carlo, Av. Uruguay 69, Mexico City

⟨ *We have been in Mexico about three weeks: are just going to-morrow to Puebla, Tehuccan [Tehuacan], Orizaba, to look at the hotter places, and see if we'd like a house somewhere, for the summer. . . . I intended to come back to Europe in May—shall still possibly do so—but more probably stay here. Witter Bynner, Amer. poet, is with us—and another young Californian [Willard Johnson]. . . . We went to a bull-fight: hated it. It's a queer world.* [94]

Witter Bynner

During our protracted trip from the border to Mexico City [Willard Johnson and I] had seen with wondering interest that armed soldiers rode on top of the cars. Disturbances had been reported in our North American papers; but we had not realized that trains on the main route were liable to attack. Ours had come through with no interference, though we had more than once felt a premonition of bullets piercing the window shades at night. Random shooting would have been easy. Once more, between Mexico City and Puebla, [Lawrence, Frieda, and I] saw armed guards perched on the car tops, like blackbirds on cattle. . . . It was not strikers but rebels or bandits, and the railroad preferred pauses to clashes. One of those pauses had happened to us. We were stalled for hours. Then, as now, passengers' questioning went unanswered; but, with all window shades drawn, they could guess and be patient while the guards atop the cars, I have no doubt, were equally content with delay.

For Frieda and me a different danger was imminent, was close by. Lorenzo, weary of watching travelers and hearing their talk, of reading a novel in Spanish, of chatting or fuming with us and blowing his nose, began to condemn and lacerate. It was the railway service first, the government second, the Mexican race third, the human race fourth. Hour after hour, in a car already hot enough, we scorched under his diatribes. By the ninth hour we were not hearing what he said, not listening, but he was still scolding. Other travelers stared at him and whispered to one another about this foreigner. Finally the train grumbled into motion. Some miles ahead of us government troops and bandits had skirmished with a few casualties on each side. We saw bodies when we passed the spot. But we were safe, except for the glare in Lawrence's eyes. To him the whole episode had been a personal affront. His cold was growing markedly worse.

Puebla appeased us, first the view from the *azotea* of the Hotel Jardin over the city's roofs and tiled domes. . . . There were fine tiles in the kitchen of an old convent. Then there were onyx trifles and Spanish jewelry to be bought, prettier and lower-priced pieces of the latter than we had seen in Mexico City's governmentally run pawnshop. Frieda writes me twenty-six years later: "Puebla I remember, and there were two big pear-shaped pearls I wanted. They were only seven pounds, cheap for what they were but too much for us." Buildings stood about solidly set in ornate Colonial stone. The cathedral had a stronger dignity than its brother in the capital. The mass of twisted lacquer in the Rosario chapel with its cherubs and foliage was the richest of its sort we had seen, though a little too much like a Laocoön statue with muscles and serpents of gold.

Apparently, from later comment, Lawrence was less impressed with the onyx interior of the cathedral and with the Rosario carvings than we were and than we thought he was. Perhaps his view was colored by remembrances of his cold. He notes the "dead interior" of "all Mexican churches, even the gorgeous Puebla cathedral. . . ." [95]

.   .   .   .

After Puebla, we went to Orizaba.[96] It seems to me that our trip was by night and that we arrived there not very well rested and pinched

with an early morning chill. There was at any rate a definite chill in ourselves as soon as we set foot on the platform. Lorenzo, with his cold
worse, with a hard face, and with nervous jerks of his head in this and
that direction, waved porters aside and suddenly walking between them
and us, ejaculated with the now too familiar high pitch of a nervous
seizure: "We are not staying here, Frieda. We are leaving." He inquired
the hour of the next train back. Frieda gave a sigh of relief when we
learned that it was considerably later. She asked him what the matter
was. "Don't you feel it?" he railed. "Don't you feel it through your feet?
It exudes from the platform. The place is evil. I won't go to the town, I
won't go to a hotel, I won't go anywhere. I can stay here at the station
till train time. You can do as you like. The place is evil, the whole air
is evil! The air creeps with it!" And he screamed at the finally intimi-
dated porters to go away.

My patience broke. I tried hard to speak quietly and perhaps did.
"Lorenzo, I am going to see the town. If I like it I am going to spend
the night. There is no reason why I should give in to your whims. . . .
But you're not going to boss me. I'm going to the hotel. If Frieda wants
to come along, you can indulge your nerves here by yourself." I don't
know whether or not my voice shook from the shaking of my ganglion.

He looked extremely and childishly surprised, not as if my standing him
off was a shock, but as if it was an unwarranted attack on him out of
the blue. He was instantly docile and dumb. He followed us into the
vehicle. He sank his beard into his breastbone. He was a deflated prophet.

.   .   .   .

Before we slept, we toured the town and found it not much to our
liking. Perhaps because of our personal vexation, the churches seemed
to us gaunt, the market dirty, the houses not snug, the whole place
uncomfortably different from Cuernavaca and Puebla. It was an indus-
trial place. We saw tired-looking factories. "There was a strike here in
Diaz' [97] time," Lawrence informed us. He had been reading *The Mexican
People: Their Struggle for Freedom,* by L. Gutierrez de Lara and Edg-
cumb Pinchon. "Diaz," he went on, "sent a commission to hear griev-
ances, or to pretend to hear them. What they did do was to summon all
the strikers for a meeting in some building and then lock the place and
set it on fire." I wondered if that was the evil which Lawrence had sensed
oozing up from the station platform. . . .

.   .   .   .

Soon we were at church-filled Cholula, imagining how it had looked when an Aztec temple had stood in the place of every present church. It was here, Lawrence reminded us from recent reading in Prescott, that Spanish Cortes had anticipated the similar cruelty of the Indian Diaz, by assembling a native contingent suspected of disaffection, by blocking them into a building, and by ending doubt with fire.

"It's all of one piece," he protested wearily, "what the Aztecs did, what Cortes did, what Diaz did—the wholesale, endless cruelty. The land itself does it to whoever lives here. The heart has been cut out of the land. That's why hearts had to be cut out of its people. It goes on and on and will always go on. It's a land of death. Look at this dead soil all around us—the dagger-fingered cactus—the half-edged sun! It's all death."

.   .   .   .

After Cholula we paused at a simple, comfortable hostelry in Atlixco . . . .

During our several days at Atlixco Lawrence was as contented as I had seen him anywhere in Mexico. He was amused by remembering the jaunty names lettered on trucks, such as *Ponte Chango, No Besame, Cara Sucia, Yo Sufro Mucho* (Be On Your Monkey-Toes, Don't Kiss Me, Dirty Face, and I Suffer Much). He smiled over a sign he had seen in some restaurant: *Servimos con sonrisa,* accompanied by the English translation, We serve with smile. He led us on long walks through the town and around the countryside. We climbed the spiry shrine-crowned hill against which the town leans and were struck by the dramatic effect it presented with Popocatepetl's huge massive symmetry behind it. We climbed the hill again one day at dawn and stood silent before the very Fujiyama which Hokusai [98] had seen for his wood block, slopes aflame with sun as though with red lava.

"I wonder," mused Lawrence, "if the pyramids looked like that, running with blood." We others were troubled too by the image. The sight was too awesome, the image too remindful of Prescott. But the light soon changed and we relaxed again.

We photographed one another on burros. We read. We were at ease with ourselves and one another. We approved of Mexico. D. H. was at his genial best and, for that reason, so were we. His best was very good. Perhaps he wrote a little then. I think he did. He was enjoying Mme. Calderon de la Barca's book of letters, *Life in Mexico,* and I recall his sharing with us the very Mexican story about her cook, whom she had trained to such culinary skill that diplomatic society was envious. Then the woman and her daughter had suddenly disappeared from the household with no explanation or word of farewell, and every quest for them was vain. One day when, driving in a suburb, Mme. de la Barca saw the pair sitting by the roadside begging, she stopped the carriage to ask what it meant. Hadn't they been comfortable, happy, well treated, well paid? Yes, yes, all that, indeed yes—but "O Jesus, the joy of doing nothing!" "Just the nothing we are doing!" beamed the busy Lawrence, "and, O Jesus, the joy of it!" For once he felt in the Indian no omen of dark doom. He quoted from somewhere else, "*Que hermoso es no hacer nada y luego descanzar!*" ("How delightful it is to do nothing and then rest!") "But I can't continue doing nothing. We must go somewhere and settle. I must write. I want to write, and we've a living to make." There was very little income at that point from his books.[99]

We decided to go back and make our plans with Johnson in Mexico City, where a Spanish troupe was presenting plays by such dramatists as Benavente and Lope de Vega,[100] and where on Sunday a popular Mexican matador was to appear in the bull ring.[101]

"We ought to see both these shows," he advised, "and then go seeking out a place in which to settle and be at work."

"Why not Atlixco?" I wondered. "We like it here." And I meant too that we liked one another in Atlixco.

"No. Though it's small, it's too urban. I want a place with water. Perhaps Mazatlan or Manzanillo on the Pacific. But there are also two lakes, Patzcuaro and Chapala. We'll see. And if there's nothing, we'll sail." [102]

20? April 1923   Orizaba, Mexico

❨ I've had about enough of this country and continent. Think we shall sail at the end of this month to New York and, at the end of May, sail for Europe. That's what I intend to do. I've had enough of this.—We go back to Mexico City tomorrow . . . .[103]

21 April 1923   Hotel Monte Carlo, Av. Uruguay 69, Mexico City

❨ Here we are, circling uneasily round, wondering whether we shall settle for a time, or not. I would like to sit down and write a novel on the American continent (I don't mean about it: I mean while I'm here). But it is hard to break through the wall of the atmosphere.—I didn't really dislike the U.S.A. as much as I expected. And I don't mistrust it half as much as I mistrust the present England, with its false sentimentalism. So I hesitate here.

. . . .

Mexico is interesting—but I feel I haven't got the right hang of it yet.[104]

21 April 1923   Hotel Monte Carlo, Av. Uruguay 69, Mexico City

⟨ I'm still going to look for a place here. Going to see a Dane who has a farm, tomorrow . . . . It's not so easy here. In these states almost every hacienda (farm) is smashed, and you can't live even one mile outside the village or town: you will probably be robbed or murdered by roving bandits and scoundrels who still call themselves revolutionaries.—But I'll try the state of Jalisco.[105]

26 April 1923   Hotel Monte Carlo, Av. Uruguay 69, Mexico City

⟨ I like Mexico, and am still uncertain of my movements. But feel sure I shall be in England before autumn. Only I may stay the summer here, and write a bit. I couldn't do anything in U.S.A. Lunching today with the Minister of Education here—they are good idealists and sensible, the present government—but I feel myself as usual outside the scheme of such things.[106]

Carleton Beals

José Vasconcelos,[107] Minister of Education, invited D. H. Lawrence, Witter Bynner, Roberto Haberman [108] and myself to a luncheon at El Globo. At the last minute Vasconcelos, called to an emergency cabinet meeting, had to postpone the luncheon till the following day.

D. H. Lawrence was then living in a smelly Italian hostelry, the Monte Carlo on Uruguay Street, beside the National Library. He was a thin man, with a body that seemed about to fall into pieces; his face was pasty, expressionless, but his greenish eyes glared from out his pale red beard with curious satyr-like luster. On hearing of the postponement of the luncheon, he flew into a dreadful rage—everything sent him into convulsive loss of self-control, quite un-English, but he was already suffering from incurable consumption. Did anyone, he now demanded, imagine that for one minute he was going to stand on his ear for a two-by-four cabinet minister in a hick country like Mexico? Not on your life. He fumed and frothed and never did show up at the luncheon.

One of his choice remarks was that his books didn't sell in England, only in America. "But the few Englishmen who do read me, at least understand me."

As did most persons—except neurotic females seeking restless freedom—I soon detested him personally, although I could understand many of his difficulties. Several times I took a young newspaper man [109] who idolized him up to the Monte Carlo. On the second visit, just as we were leaving, Lawrence, ignoring the newspaper man, said loudly, "Don't bring him up any more. I've got all I can out of him."

"Don't worry," I replied in a pet. "Nor shall I bring myself up again."

Once, when D. H. came into the hotel room, his wife Freda, a fine handsome woman, one of those Teutonic types that remind me of delicious home-made bread, a woman of great poise, calm and breeding, was talking to a woman friend.

Lawrence began to rail at her over something or other. She paid no attention. Finally, his face purple, he screamed at her: "Why do you sit with your legs apart that way? You're just like all the other dirty sluts."

She completely ignored him and his outburst and went on talking quietly, without a flutter of annoyance. Her passivity merely incensed him the more; he literally frothed at the mouth and flounced out. Undoubtedly, being a very sick man, he was greatly frustrated physically and psychologically by her full, healthy body and poise. I thought Freda, with whom I went one day to look at the cathedral and Diego's [110] frescoes, a grand human being; but Lawrence, for all his genius which I greatly admire, I considered a detestable one.

Lawrence was incapable of doing other than creating a deep love-hate relationship with women, but I have an idea that Freda, in her quiet subterranean way, found means of compensating herself for his numerous spleens and infidelities, putting on the horns, as Mexicans say.

Whatever he did is atoned for, if by nothing else, by his great book *Sons and Lovers*. Other of his works may have more exquisite beauty, but none can compare to it in organization, intensity or masterful simplicity.

Lawrence valiantly tried to get away from English smugness, sextabus and social climbing. He never did. He tried to be a free pagan. But his own mind and body were against him. For years he was a sick man, clinging to the fringe of life, simulating great fury and gusto. And his paganism, far from healthy, even has a prurient quality. It is more like that of a self-conscious child who sticks a toe fearsomely into the edge of a mud puddle, then draws it out hurriedly and weeps to find it covered with slime.

As for Mexico, Lawrence never understood it. At bottom he was terribly afraid of the country, always saw some secret menace in it. He was ever too frightened and neurotic really to examine the things that built up such a great fear in him; he could only dissect his own emotions about them. Hence his *Plumed Serpent* is a remarkably intuitive book, with magnificent descriptions, and a weird insight into many matters that Lawrence sensed rather than understood. The same fear-note and bafflement carried on through his *Mornings in Mexico*. What Lawrence did was to write a big, insoluble, mysterious "X," in a super-tourist fashion, over the Mexican Indian. The novelist is forever rushing past closed doors and conjuring up all sorts of horrible mystery and despair and danger lurking behind them. His neurotic character made it impossible for him to knock and perchance discover, however poverty-stricken the setting, merely a warm hospitality and simple folk facing life's problems as most normal people face them. What Lawrence did was to shoot the skyrockets of his morbid fancy over Mexico, and in the long glimmer of showering sparks he caught remarkable glimpses of the land, glimpses so strange, so fantastic and distorted, yet sometimes so grandiosely true as to make one wonder at the eerie quality of his genius.[111]

Frederic W. Leighton

Twenty-six years have passed, yet some impressions of D. H. Lawrence cling, powerful and vivid. The most vivid memories spring from his temper and his bad manners: the most powerful from the feeling he evoked in me of the tragic destiny of deep insight shackled to violent emotions in a frail body.

His bad manners shocked me, made me wish to apologize for him to somebody, to anybody. Never before or since have I heard a human being, in educated society, repeatedly release such flow of obscene vile abuse on his wife (or on anyone) in the presence of comparative strangers as Lawrence did on Frieda; nor, I must admit, have I heard such apparently uninhibited response. Lawrence was far more eloquent, more varied in his vituperation, but Frieda hardly less emphatic.

Those evenings at the Hotel Monte Carlo, those afternoons on the pretty terrace in Chapala in the spring of 1923 were memorable ones with much conversation, both trivial and important; the words have all fled my memory long ago, a few only of the ideas remain, but there persists sharply today that feeling of wishing to be somewhere else when Lawrence started railing at Frieda.

Anger in the grand manner I recall also. It was that day Lawrence was to lunch with the Minister of Education, José Vasconcelos. As a minor functionary of the Department of Education, and specifically through my immediate superior, Bob Haberman, I had arranged the affair. We gathered in the antechamber of the Minister; Lawrence, Frieda, [Witter Bynner], Spud Johnson, Carleton Beals, and I. We announced our arrival; we waited and we waited. A *mozo* emerged from within, putting his thumb and first finger together in that inimitable, inevitable Mexican bureaucratic gesture, and said "*Un momentito*," one little minute. How I recall those "little minutes" in Mexico that so often stretched into hours! So we waited again. Lawrence was getting decidedly fidgety. Another *mozo* appeared—this one more important—probably a private secretary, and said, "The Minister regrets, but urgent matters of State prevent his receiving you today and will you do him the honor to lunch with him tomorrow?" Lawrence sprang to his feet, blue eyes flashing hot blue fire, "No! I shan't!" he shouted and strode from the room. Though visibly flustered, the rest of us including Frieda replied we'd be happy to accept for the morrow, and the private secretary who didn't know English retreated to inform Mr. Vasconcelos that we'd all accepted for the following day; a luncheon which was duly held at Sylvain's with the Minister at his charming best—but no Lawrence. Lawrence had stuck to his first utterance, "I'll not go! I'll not think of it!" and he had strode back and forth on the third floor inner balcony of the Education building for fully ten minutes before he could be quieted sufficiently to leave. He felt he had been insulted; in him Art, Literature, History, the British Empire, Civilization itself, had been insulted! How anyone's body, to say nothing of a sick, fragile one, could withstand such berserk bursts of passion I did not know.

Thereafter, while Lawrence remained at the Monte Carlo, I was in disgrace; for I had arranged this insulting affair. Of course I was about with [Witter Bynner] and Spud and Frieda, and Frieda was cordial as usual;

but Lawrence, though civil, was distinctly frigid. Then off he went to Chapala. What a strange adventure that was! Nobody we knew had heard much of Chapala in those days, though I had been there the previous autumn and had mentioned it to Lawrence as a good quiet place in which to live and write.[112]

26? April 1923   *Hotel Monte Carlo, Av. Uruguay 69, Mexico City*

❲ *We are still here, still making excursions. We can't make up our minds to go away. Tomorrow I go to Guadalajara and the Chapala Lake. There you have the Pacific breeze again, straight from the Pacific. One doesn't want to come back to Europe. All is stupid, evilly stupid and no end to it. You must be terribly tired of this German tragedy—all without meaning, without direction, idea, or spirit. Only money-greed and impudence. One can't do anything, nothing at all, except get bored and wicked. Here in Mexico there's also Bolshevism and Fascism and revolutions and all the rest of it. But I don't care. I don't listen. And the Indians remain outside. Revolutions come and revolutions go but they remain the same. They haven't the machinery of our consciousness, they are like black water, over which go our dirty motorboats, with stink and noise—the water gets a little dirty but does not really change.*[113]

Witter Bynner

. . . Passage to England loomed again. We lingered at the Monte Carlo through another week while we read *Terry's Guide to Mexico* and debated. Yes, he would give the country one more chance: Chapala. It would have been two chances but for the likelihood of severe heat in Oaxaca. Besides, he had been told that the southern train trip was rough and wearing, perhaps the worst in Mexico, whereas the line to Guadalajara on the way to Chapala was good. Still smarting from experience on other trains, he relinquished Oaxaca that year. He reached it the following year. This time he set us reading Terry's long disquisition on the beauties and attractions of Lake Chapala and its little town of the same name. It was apparently all birds and flowers and friendly villagers. "But Terry's a fool," crackled Lawrence. "He's been a liar about the other places and why should we expect him to be anything else about this one? We'd be lunatics to believe him and all four of us risk it. I'll give the country one more

231

chance. You two stay here with Frieda for May Day [114] and I'll go and investigate. If the place is any good at all, I'll telegraph and we'll share a house and stay awhile. If it isn't, we two'll sail from Vera Cruz and you two can do what you like."

"On one condition," I agreed. "No sharing a house. In one hotel if you wish, or you two in a house and we in a hotel. I can't live in the same house with people. Your hours are different from ours. Besides, you want to work. So do I. And we'll be better off not under one another's feet."

"As you like," said he, vaguely.

So it was settled. He would be on the move again, with only himself to blame, and we for a few days at peace, with the May Day celebration to enjoy as we liked, uncriticized.

We saw him off at the train. Through the window he appeared wistful and forlorn.

"But it was his idea," said I.

"*Ja!*" assented Frieda, looking back along the platform.[115]

3 *May 1923*　　　　　　　　Zaragoza 4, Chapala, Jalisco, Mexico

❲ *Came in this house yesterday—110 pesos a month . . . .*[116]

Captain Percy Grenville Holms, O.B.E.

I first knew D. H. Lawrence when he called on me at Guadalajara, State of Jalisco, Mexico, when I was British Vice-Consul there, to ask if I knew of any suitable house that he could rent on Lake Chapala, and I was able to indicate a bungalow, which he took. Subsequently, my wife and I got to know Lawrence and his wife but only in a casual sort of way.

Even then, Lawrence was a very sick man, pallid, thin and overwrought. He was engaged then in writing *The Plumed Serpent* and deeply absorbed in his work: so much so that he had little time to spare for any social contacts.[117]

3 *May 1923*　　　　　　　　Zaragoza 4, Chapala, Jalisco, Mexico

❲ *Here we are, in our own house—a long house with no upstairs—shut in by trees on two sides.—We live on a wide verandah, flowers round—it is fairly hot—I spend the day in trousers and shirt, barefoot—have a Mexican woman, Isabel, to look after us—very nice. Just outside the gate the big Lake of Chapala—40 miles long, 20 miles wide. We can't see the lake, because the trees shut us in. But we walk out in a wrap to bathe.—There are Camions—Ford omnibuses—to Guadalajara—2 hours. Chapala village is small with a market place with trees and Indians in big hats. Also three hotels, because this is a tiny holiday place for Guadalajara. . . . It may be that even yet I'll have my little hacienda and grow bananas and oranges.*

.   .   .   .

I did have a right bad cold in Puebla, but was better in a few days. Only then, I wanted to go back quickly to Europe. When I feel sick I want to go back. When I feel well I want to stay.[118]

Witter Bynner

4 May 1923: *Guadalajara.* Lawrence, for the most part, is a bad little boy who probably needs to sit for an hour a day in ice-cold water. I really believe that some sort of medical treatment might make him the artist he promised to be in *Sons and Lovers. Aaron's Rod* and *Women in Love,* as far as I've read the latter, seem to me not far removed from the work of Bertha M. Clay [119]—the sort of thing the English lower middle class has always delighted in but which he has now made pretentious with a smear of pseudo science and made semioccasionally rewarding with a paragraph of masterly observation. He is utterly without imagination, humor, or warmth—the qualities of any first-rate creator. The man ought to have been a naturalist. He might then have done less for the titillation of nervous women, but more for the world and his own happiness. Personally he continues very amiable to Spud and me. My fatigue with him results from his unfailing and unfeeling contempt for all things mortal save himself. Secretly I am convinced that it is himself that he despises and makes mankind vicariously suffer for. In Mexico City when for the eleventh time he wavered in his hot resolve to sail to England and for the eleventh time discovered that he hated England also, he set out alone to reconnoiter along Lake Chapala before removing from the capital Frieda and his other luggage. As Frieda prophesied, "When he finds a place by himself, he always likes it." His psychology is simple. He telegraphed his pleasure. Spud and I brought Frieda along to Guadalajara, and then we suddenly swerved off from the Lawrences to be in touch

233

again for a little while with humanity. Mind you, I like Frieda better than ever. A solid, hearty, wise, and delightful woman. The few days we had alone with her in Mexico City were a solace. Her love for Lawrence, probably her worst fault, is genuine and forgivable.

9 May 1923: *Guadalajara.* I'm halfway through *Women in Love,* detesting it and yet granting something of what you say about it. Mrs. is a German brick with plenty of straw to stand the rough usage. The man is much more concerned with hate than with love; but I'm enjoying him at intervals. Really, though, his work seems to me unimportant—till it touches animals. He should have been a naturalist. Hatred can be a worse form of sentimentality than ever love can be. That's what this little generation doesn't see.[120]

11 May 1923   Zaragoza 4, Chapala, Jalisco, Mexico

❨ We've got a house here—very nice—green trees—a Mexican Isabel to look after us—a big lake of Chapala outside—a little village Chapala— but at the same side a little lake-side resort for Guadalajara, which is about 35 miles away.

It isn't too hot. . . .

Don't know how long we shall stay—a month or two. At the moment Witter Bynner is here in the hotel, with Willard Johnson. Very nice.[121]

Willard Johnson

I first met D. H. Lawrence and his wife when they came to the remote and isolated New Mexican village [Santa Fe] where Witter Bynner and I were staying, and finding the hotels crowded, quartered themselves upon us, moving in while I was seeing a Tom Mix show at the movie. We had only a little adobe hut, but we were pleased and flattered to have them. By giving up a bedroom and bunking in the studio, we could always make room for guests. This first informal acquaintance was responsible for another meeting the next spring, when there developed the spontaneous and excited plan for the four of us to go to Mexico together. Lawrence and his wife went on ahead, and Bynner and I joined them in the City of Mexico.

Of the days spent there, some are sharply etched in memory. First, of course, Easter, for which holiday we had hurried south, and which has

(*Left to right*) Willard Johnson, Witter Bynner, and Lawrence standing at rear of Mr. Bynner's home in Santa Fe, N. Mex., before starting to Mexico (March, 1923). From a photograph in the possession of Willard Johnson.

Frieda and Lawrence at the window of their house at Zaragoza 4, Chapala, Jalisco, Mexico (1923). Photograph by Witter Bynner.

Lawrence's home at Zaragoza 4, Chapala, Jalisco, Mexico, shortly before restoration (1954) by its present owner, Mr. Roy MacNicol. The house is now numbered Zaragoza 307. From a photograph in the possession of Mr. MacNicol.

The *Esmeralda* becalmed on Lake Chapala (July, 1923). On the roof (*left to right*), Dr. Purnell, Witter Bynner, Willard Johnson, Idella Purnell Stone, Frieda, and Lawrence. From a photograph in the possession of Willard Johnson.

Witter Bynner (*left*) and Willard Johnson in Chapala (1923). From a photograph in the possession of Willard Johnson.

(*Left to right*) Idella Purnell Stone, Lawrence, Frieda, Willard Johnson, and Dr. Purnell on the occasion of Willard Johnson's twenty-sixth birthday party on the terrace of the Hotel Arzapalo, Chapala (3 June 1923). Photograph by Witter Bynner.

been notably celebrated in *The Plumed Serpent*. That was the day of the bullfight, April 1, and Lawrence and Bynner have said enough on that subject. Then there was the day we discovered Covarrubias in a sort of Greenwich Village café on the Calle de República de Cuba; and the day I went to the hospital followed by a shower of Lawrentian invectives for having drunk too much tequila; [122] and the day Mrs. Lawrence discovered the strawberry shortcake at Sanborn's, and the day the Princess Bibesco [123] arrived. . . . But the other outstanding day was May 1 and Lawrence wasn't there at all.

That was the time we saw the red flag hoisted above the statue of Christ on the Cathedral, the largest Christian edifice on the continent. That was the day Bynner and I accompanied the proletariat to the Cathedral towers and tolled the bells with street-cleaners in honor of the Chicago martyrs for an eight-hour-day [124]—while Mrs. Lawrence, deserted in the Plaza below, saw soldiers arrive and block the tower steps and pined for escorts and lunch. Lawrence had gone to Sayula [Chapala] to make a "preliminary investigation," and we joined him there the next day and began our real summer.[125]

The Lawrences took a house—an el around an old garden, the outer sides even more effectively enclosed in a deep wood which marked the limit of the neighboring estate. It was up from the lake shore a bit on an unfrequented lane and had an enormous tree at its iron gate. The drawing-room was one of those cold, tiled, bare places with a high ceiling and stark chairs. I seem to remember Lawrence sitting in a sort of New England rocker, his feet drawn up onto the seat of the chair and his beard playing hide-and-seek around his knees as he denounced the Obregon government or discussed a Japanese play.[126]

But I remember him again on his hands and knees on the tiled floor, like some strange animal scampering around one corner of a *serape* with a tape-measure. Perhaps that was when Bynner got the idea for his "Studies in Unnatural History" in which he says that he does not know whether Lawrence is "a man wishing to be an animal, or an animal wishing to be a man." [127]

At that time, however, Bynner was similarly occupied on the other side of the *serape* and both of them were making strange notations on a slip of paper and later puttering with water-colors. They had discovered a weaver in a village [Jocotepec] at the end of the lake and were designing their own *serapes* to be made to order.

On such evenings Mrs. Lawrence sat in another New England rocker and knitted—and I merely sat, smoking black cigarettes. Perhaps those were the times when "there was in my eyes the curious basking apathy of a snake asleep," as he said of me in the first version of the *Serpent*.

Mostly, though, we sat on their little *portal* either on warm afternoons over tea, or in the evening when the moonlight made the garden beyond into mysterious shapes which Lawrence, I think, always fancied were bandits. There, also, was a tiled floor, but it was less forbidding than in the drawing-room. And on the wall there always hung a bright *serape* of green and red in which was woven the Mexican eagle standing on a gay cactus and waving a most enchanting snake in its beak.

It was on this cool, shadowy porch that many heated arguments took place between Bynner and Lawrence. And it was here, too, that Lawrence was at his wittiest and best. He would imitate eccentric acquaintances who were "habitués or sons of habitués" of a certain London salon (he was a side-splitting mimic), and sometimes he would read poetry magazines or letters aloud, giving everything the most ludicrous interpretation until we were all roaring with laughter and in the best of humor.

Yet this mood would just as often be interrupted by a violent denunciation or a real tornado of wrath over some insignificant matter or carelessly dropped word.

Other times we walked on the beach of the lake or on the pier when week-end crowds gave a semblance of gayety. We laughed at the fifi-boys —or rather the others did, always with sly digs to the effect that I also was a fifi-boy, which injured my pride tremendously. But my reputation as such became fixed when it was known that I sometimes joined the dancers on the Sunday night side-walks in front of the cafés. Lawrence loved the way the peons interrupted these week-end events by their imperturbable circumambulation of the plaza.

But this is not the story. There we were, Bynner and I at the hotel which fronted the lake; the Lawrences in their tiny villa down the beach. Mornings we all worked, Lawrence generally down towards a little peninsula where tall trees grew near the water. He sat there, back against a tree, eyes often looking over the scene that was to be the background for his novel, and wrote in tiny, fast words in a thick, blue-bound blank book, the tale which he called *Quetzalcoatl*.[128] Here also he read Mexican history and folklore and observed, almost unconsciously, the life that went on about him, and somehow got the spirit of the place.

There were the little boys who sold idols from the lake; the women who washed clothes at the waters' edge and dried them on the sands; there were the lone fishermen, white *calzones* pulled to their hips, bronze legs wading deep in the waters, fine nets catching the hundreds of tiny *charales:* boatmen steering their clumsy, beautiful craft around the peninsula; men and women going to market with baskets of *pitahayas* on their heads; lovers, even, wandering along the windy shore; goatherds; mothers bathing babies; sometimes a group of Mexican boys swimming nude off-shore instead of renting ugly bathing-suits further down by the hotel. . . .

Afternoons we often had tea together or Lawrence and I walked along the mud flats below the village or along the cobbled country road around the Japanese hill—or up the hill itself. We discovered that botany had been a favorite study of both of us at school and took a friendly though more or less ignorant interest in the flora as we walked and talked. Lawrence talked most, of course.

And we swam, too. Bynner generally went in for strenuous water-sports with the gang of boys who always awaited our appearance on the beach. And I dawdled in the water leisurely on the outskirts of the gang or lounged with them in the scalding sun as they tried to pick up English and as we struggled with the vernacular of Mexican Spanish. The Lawrences swam alone below the frequented stretch of beach—he looking, in white trunks, like an ivory "Ocean Christ" by Anatole France.

We lived strangely separate and yet strangely mingled lives. Separate because our inclinations were opposed. Mingled because there was an affectionate interest that bound all of us together and because, being the only English-speaking people in the town, we were dependent upon each other for companionship.

A strange setting for a strange drama. Lawrence and Bynner really liked one another—and yet hated each other, too. Just as Lawrence liked me and I liked him, although he heartily disliked some of my American traits and I some of his English. It was the same sort of thing all around.

Lawrence and Bynner talked about each other blasphemously when they were apart and although they were polite to each other when face to face—even then, in their political arguments or literary discussions, there was the bitterness of completely opposed ideas and a sharp intolerance not only of the absurdities but of the fundamental wrongness of the other's principles and conclusions.

The result, from my point of view, was highly amusing. Here's the way the thing worked out: I became the secretary and confidential companion to both of these writers who were making "copy" as fast as they could out of the situation. All summer long, I was the reservoir for the accumulated wrath of both in saga and song, in invective and confidential confession, in cold-blooded discussion and in hot-blooded reaction.

I don't mean to speak unkindly. They were not exploiting their emotions—it was simply their natural safety-valve they were using.

There they were: Lawrence sitting under a tree at one end of the village writing a novel in which Bynner is made to appear as one of the characters; Bynner sitting, stripped to the waist, on the Japanese hillside at the other end of town, acquiring his vacation tan and relieving his mind of all his ideas about Lawrence! And there was I at a typewriter on a balcony of the hotel overlooking the same lake on which both of them rested their eyes between paragraphs, the lake across which oriental sailboats flew. There was I, copying both manuscripts and chuckling quietly to myself—not at all worried over what both Lawrence and Bynner were writing about me or, indeed, saying, as they buried their hatchets, occasionally, and went off on an excursion together.

"Owen had no soul, only a slow, soft caving-in at the center of him where soul should be," wrote Lawrence—and my fingers flew over the typewriter keys in my bird-like delight over the situation.

"Owen was empty and waiting for circumstances to fill him up," wrote Lawrence, again. "Swept with an American despair of having lived in vain, or of not having *really* lived. Having missed something. Which fearful misgiving would make him rush like mechanical steel filings to a magnet, towards any crowd in the street. And then all his poetry and philosophy gone with the cigarette-end he threw away, he would stand craning his neck in one more frantic effort to *see*—just to see. Whatever it was, he must see it. Or he might miss something. And then, after he'd seen an old ragged woman run over by a motor-car and bleeding on the floor, he'd come back pale at the gills, sick, bewildered, daunted, and yet, yes, glad he'd seen it. It was Life!" [129]

In his turn, Bynner would say:

"Lorenzo is a man without a soul!" And, vehemently, he would analyze this strange creature he had encountered, over our absinthe at a table in the plaza where we were alone late in the evening. "I had not thought that anyone would wilfully choose the dark side of the world, would dig for the bitterest roots."

And I agreed gravely with both of them in silent amazement over their marvelous concurrence on the subject.

That Lawrence was a kind of devil, a spirit of evil, was Bynner's contention in both his prose and in the poems he wrote about him. And these, too, I pounded off on the machine with my "American delight over a new situation":

After wondering a long time, I know now
That you are no man at all. . . .
Only your reddish hair is you
And those narrowing eyes,
Eyes hostile to the flesh of people and to all their motions,
Eyes penetrating their thoughts to the old marrow of the beast,
Eyes wanting a mate and the starlight. . . .

You will always be smouldering against men;
And, after yielding slowly
The nine lives of a domestic cat,
You will be worshipped by the Egyptians. . . .[130]

Then, perhaps the same day, having a beer with Lawrence, or walking with him along the lake, he would make almost exactly the same accusation against Bynner:

"Bynner with his humanitarianism! His all-embracing brotherly love. His Socialism—bah! His kind of love is death. Just death, really, and nothing else.

"Bynner thinks he's a liberal, but isn't. He talks about Socialism but lives on capital. He can't conceive of definitely renouncing the world and his previous life as I have done, and making something new. He's hopelessly wallowing in the old sentimentalities, pampering his whims, catering to his own softness. He's a Playboy of the Western World, playing the rôle of patron of the arts. He's just kidding himself, as you say in America; playing to the public square; taking life as a cocktail before dinner. And that sort of thing is death—just death. One has to take hold of life and do something with it. One can't just go on accepting, turning the other cheek, loving, loving, loving—soft, saccharine, smirking love!"

Exhausted by this effort, he would suddenly realize what an outburst it had been, laugh in his highest pitch and then say gently, almost apologetically, and with an indubitably English inflection, accenting the first instead of the last word:

"Shall we have another glass?"

Always they were spitting fire behind each other's back, with each other's very words in their mouths! Then Bynner, angry with me, would agree with Lawrence that "something ought to be done" about me. Or Mrs. Lawrence and I would confer and pour out our troubles. Or Bynner and Mrs. Lawrence would discuss the outlandishness of a husband as only a bachelor and a married woman can. . . .

Oh, it was quite nice. And through it all, like a chorus to our song, were amicable birthday dinners and pleasant visits from Guadalajara friends and tropical moonlight nights when guitars and wandering singers from across the lake and love-lorn couples made music all night long.

Woven into the pattern of our days were motor-boat trips to this town and that in search of an old church, or a fiesta, or an ancient Indian dance combined with a Spanish miracle-play, or to purchase *serapes* or Toltec idols.

Until it suddenly came to an end with the realization of a dream and its accompanying events. All summer long we had seen and worshipped from afar the great flat-bottomed boats with their immense, fat, bellying sails, which carried on the commerce of the lake region. One day we saw a brand new one, unencumbered with flies or dirt, empty of cargo, rather spacious in a simple twenty-five-foot way. And so we chartered it and its crew and launched out on the wide waters.

Our craft moved when the wind moved, and lay becalmed under myriad stars whole nights. She was poled into quaint old ports where we bought fruit and chickens, eggs and tortillas. She glided magnificently over gentle, choppy waves to islands where mangos and goats' milk replenished our larder—where sometimes a shepherd would kill a kid for our pirate appetites. We cooked most of the food ourselves over a charcoal stove made of an oil can.

Bynner got sick and we shipped him back to port by steamer, but the Lawrences, the crew and I drifted on, slow as the little islands of water-hyacinths from the eastern end of the lake.

There was music on the roof of our one-room boat-house at night, all of us lying on the sloping boards in our night-clothes, Lawrence or myself astraddle the ridge-pole in pajamas, one of the crew posed like a Greek statue at the tiller, half-illumined by a candle or lantern below; maybe Daniel, an Aztec faun, standing beside the mast in silhouette against a rising moon. Then a guitar and Spanish songs. Or no guitar and Lawrence singing English ballads in the nasal falsetto of a country boy lost in the hills. . . .

No wonder we decided to make this the happy ending to Mexico and to return to El Paso before another revolution or another battle between Lawrence and Bynner should shatter our sea-voyage calm. No wonder we wanted this to be our final memory: "the great seething light of the lake, with the terrible blue-ribbed mountains of Mexico beyond." [131]

15 May 1923   Zaragoza 4, Chapala, Jalisco, Mexico

❲ We have taken a house down here for a month or two—like it—a big lake—but it's never so easy living as in Europe—especially Sicily. Yet I don't know if I shall go back—don't know what I shall do—the Lord enlighten me. . . . I'm trying to write a novel—Witter Bynner is still down here. We're rather better off for money. When I get letters from Europe then I never want to go back. When I forget the letters, I do.[132]

Witter Bynner

Early Summer 1923: *Chapala.* My relationships here—with Lawrence and his wife—are much more comfortable than they were. I heartily like Frieda and always shall. Lawrence and I are in pretty thorough disaccord in our views of life, nor are we physically congenial enough to create the real ease which sometimes exists between people with opposite convictions. Without impudence, I am certain that I am more securely grounded in my beliefs than he is in his. Loss of temper, to which he is a chronic victim, is almost always a sign of interior uncertainty, is an attempt to attain equilibrium with wild gestures. Lawrence is a selfish egoist and he assembles all sorts of vehement theories to dispose of his own inner misgivings. On the other hand, he has a flexible mind, is a mass of inconsistencies and, in spite of a mature verbal skill, is probably at a very early stage of his development. He seems to me to have found in life almost nothing that is worth finding and almost everything that is of no value. This may of course be the best possible foundation for a later structure. He is only thirty-six [thirty-seven]. His profundities are marvelously young.[133]

26 May 1923   Zaragoza 4, Chapala, Jalisco, Mexico

❲ I wanted to do a novel. I sort of wanted to do a novel here. I could never begin in Mexico [City]. But I have begun here, in Chapala. It's a big lake 90 miles long, 20 miles across: queer. I hope my novel will go all right. If it does, I ought to finish it—in its first rough form—by end of June. Then seriously I want to come to Europe: via New York: stay there

241

perhaps two weeks: be in London by early August. I really think I shall manage this. It was, I suppose, that undigested novel kept me back till now. But I won't any more say finally that I will do a thing.

I am having the first slight scene of my novel—the beginning of a bull-fight in Mexico City—typed now . . . .

.   .   .   .

It isn't that I am so very keen on leading a remote country life. And I loathe the "playboy" attitude to life. Oh God, there are so many playboys, not only of the western world. And I detest "having a good time." But when I think of England, willy-nilly my gorge rises in a sort of profound mistrust. I suppose there's nothing to do but to come to England and to get it over.

.   .   .   .

A man wanted me to have a banana hacienda with him here in Mexico. I suppose, anyhow, I'd better see England again first. And I feel, perhaps I've no business trying to bury myself in out-of-the-way places.

.   .   .   .

Frieda wants to come to England much more than I do. She has Devonshire on her mind.[134]

31 May 1923   Zaragoza 4, Chapala, Jalisco, Mexico

(You will think we are never coming back to Europe. But it isn't so.

But I always had the idea of writing a novel here in America. In the U.S. I could do nothing. But I think here it will go well. I have already written ten chapters and if the Lord helps me I shall have finished the first full sketch by the end of June. And then we will come home at once.

I must go by way of New York because of business and because it is shorter and cheaper. . . .

Today is Corpus Christi and they have a procession. But there are no lovely birches as in Ebersteinburg two years ago. They only carry little palms into the churches, and palms aren't beautiful like our trees, and this eternal sun is not as joyous as our sun. It is always shining and is a little mechanical.

But Mexico is very interesting: a foreign people. They are mostly pure Indians, dark like the people in Ceylon but much stronger. The men have the strongest backbones in the world, I believe. They are half civilized, half wild. If they only had a new faith they might be a new, young, beautiful people. But as Christians they don't get any further, are melancholy inside, live without hope, are suddenly wicked, and don't like to work. But they are also good, can be gentle and honest, are very quiet, and are not at all greedy for money, and to me that is marvellous, they care so little for possessions, here in America where the whites care for nothing else. But not the peon. He has not this fever to possess that is a real "Weltschmerz" with us.[135]

4 June 1923   Zaragoza 4, Chapala, Jalisco, Mexico

《 I am busy doing a novel: hope it will continue to go well.—Mexico is still much more fun than U.S.A.—much wilder. We have a man to sleep on the verandah with a pistol: and we may not walk outside the village for fear of being robbed or carried off by bandits. And this little village has twenty soldiers to guard it which is all very stupid. We've got a whole stack of servants and semi-servants living at the end of the house: not because we want them, but because they seem to have their holes there, like rabbits—Isabel, Carmen, Maria, Daniele, Pedra and Francisco. Now they're bargaining for eggs—like the devil—at 6 centavos—and we only pay 5.

I think I shall give up this house at the end of the month—and probably go to New York, stay there not more than a fortnight, then go to England. This is what I have promised to do. But whether I shall actually do it, I don't know. I am not very anxious to go back to Europe.

One day you must come to Mexico. It is different from anything I have seen—life has quite a different tempo here.—Bynner & Johnson are still here, in the hotel.—With your revolver, gun & knife you would be just right here: though they are all mostly for show.[136]

Frederic W. Leighton

Some weeks later, when I visited Chapala, Lawrence was quite friendly again. It appeared I had been forgiven, because of my efforts in getting Frieda on to that train [to Guadalajara]. He had then begun *The Plumed Serpent* and was daily entering neat meticulous lines into his copybook.

It was in Chapala I felt that other deeper fire in Lawrence, that hot blue passion turned inward until it touched molten levels below. It was the Lawrence of *Mornings in Mexico*, the Lawrence who at times felt both Huitzilopochtli and Quetzalcoatl in himself, as he lived there on that quiet mountain-circled shore.

I recall walking with him one bright morning along the beach. This was when he propounded his theory—it was no theory to him, it was direct inner apprehension of evident truth—of the races of men who live in mankind, not races with different colors of skin, but races of different capabilities; especially that aristocratic ruling race the members of which appeared from time to time in cottages and palaces, in slums and on farms, in every clime, and of course especially in England, that mystic superhuman near-divine race of aristocrats who were meant to lead and guide the world, who would do so now were its members fully conscious of themselves, who would do so certainly and inevitably in the future. So I recall his talk.

It is hard to disentangle the threads of that conversation, twisted as they are by the rotation of the intervening years. Looking back, however, I remember Lawrence's struggles to emerge from the dull anonymity of a collier's family; looking back, I see in the frailty of his body, the torrential blast of his feelings, the intuitive perception of his mind and spirit, raw material for the forging of this theory. However he came by it, it was what made him the Imperial Englishman in Australia, the confused master-interpreter of sex and woman to America, the petulant mystic who at times rose volcanically to great perceptions.

And who shall say and who can truly evaluate? Does not history reveal, and do we not constantly see, the continual emergence of the great individual from the seething mouldering mass of mediocrity around him? Lawrence, in mystic language and with confused consciousness, was struggling toward an explanation of some very rugged facts in the world of human personality.[137]

Witter Bynner

Late June 1923: *Chapala*. [Lawrence] is one of the uncanniest human beings imaginable. Did I say human? Slowly I am coming to the conclusion that he was misborn as a man, that he is a four-footer of some sort, chafing against human bondage. . . . I usually care very little for his writings; but when he begins on any animal or any bird, I am spellbound. He ought to have been a bird or an animal—or, at least, a naturalist. Think of him again, from that point of view. Think of him waking up in the dawn, without his beautiful claws or feathers and, because of his lack, hating humanity afresh each day. From my point of view, there has seldom been a writer less fitted to discuss human affairs. He struggles and struggles to think as a man, with all those acute animal perceptions, but he cannot. By paying no attention to him, I have won his tolerance for this considerable period, just as I might have won the tolerance of any other self-respecting beast. But he has the contempt for me that he has for all humans. And how can such a man, who could never really care for any human being, treat of human life? He can see it and feel it, but he can never know it.[138]

24 June 1923   Zaragoza 4, Chapala, Jalisco, Mexico

❡ *We are going on Tuesday [26 June 1923] up to Ocotlan on the lake to see if we can rent a little farm there. I am still doubtful if it would be safe. . . . I think probably we should go to New York for a little while to settle business, even if I decided to rent a place: and come back in September, start then before the rains end. It's an uncertain life—and things never behave as they should.*[139]

27 June 1923   Zaragoza 4, Chapala, Jalisco, Mexico

❡ *Came back from trip to Ocotlan & Tizapan—decide to leave Mexico.*[140]

27 June 1923   Zaragoza 4, Chapala, Jalisco, Mexico

❡ *We were away two days travelling on the lake and looking at haciendas. One could easily get a little place. But now they are expecting more revolution, and it is so risky. Besides, why should one work to build a place and make it nice, only to have it destroyed.*

So, for the present at least, I give it up. It's no good. Mankind is too unkind.

We shall leave next Monday [2 July 1923] for Mexico City—and probably shall be in New York by July 15th.[141] *I don't expect to care for the east: don't intend to stay more than a month. Then to England. It is no good, I know I am European, so I may as well go back and try it once more.*

. . . .

. . . If I can't stand Europe we'll come back to Mexico and spit on our hands and stick knives and revolvers in our belts—one really has to—and have a place here. But if Europe is at all possible, much better there. Because the Mexicans are rather American in that, that they would rather pull life down than let it grow up. And I am tired of that. I am tired of sensational, unmanly people. I want men with some honourable manhood in them, not this spiteful babyishness and playboy stupidity and mere greediness of most people. . . . The "world" has no life to offer. Seeing things doesn't amount to much. We have to be a few men with honour and fearlessness, and make a life together. There is nothing else, believe me.[142]

27 June 1923   Zaragoza 4, Chapala, Jalisco, Mexico

❨ The novel is nearly finished—near enough to leave. I must come to New York—and go to England.[143]

2 July 1923   Zaragoza 4, Chapala, Jalisco, Mexico

❨ We are going up to New York next week, and maybe to England.[144]

Witter Bynner

4 July 1923: *Chapala.* Tomorrow [145] we are starting on a three or four day sail in what they call a canoa, a fairly large primitive half-enclosed vessel, like a Chinese junk, with one enormous rounded sail. Until our return, you shall have no word—unless in the meantime you receive a peremptory summons from Mexican bandits! [146]

Idella Purnell Stone

Of course there was a lot of talk by Witter Bynner and Spud Johnson about these two people we were soon to meet; but I recall nothing of it; to me they were just Names. I asked Spud please to tell me, was this the H. D.[147] who contributed so much to *Poetry?* For at that time I confused D. H. L. and H. D. Even warned about the red beard, it was with a sense of shock that I met Mr. Lawrence, so thin, so fragile and nervous-quick, and with such a flaming red beard, and such intense, sparkling, large mischievous blue eyes, which he sometimes narrowed in a catlike manner. His rusty hair was always in disorder, as though it never knew a comb. But otherwise the man seemed neat almost to obsession and frail, as though all his energy went into producing the unruly mop on top and the energetic, stiff beard. Mrs. Lawrence, very large and motherly, seemed placid and soothing and relaxed, but when anything amused her, her laugh was as generous and violent as Bynner's own.

We talked about a recipe for *tepache*. Mrs. Lawrence made some remark which irritated Mr. Lawrence. He turned a mottled red and shouted at her, "Frieda, don't be so stupid! I should slap you for that!" Almost involuntarily I asked, "Should I slap Lawrence?" At which a moment of astoundment filled the patio. And then Bynner whooped and Spud did, and I was saved. After this I remember that Lawrence and Daddy used to go off for long long walks up and down the beach, talking of a thousand things. I recall telling Bynner I had asked D. H. L. to give me some poems for *Palms*.[148] Bynner retorted, "I know you did, and do you know what he said about you? 'Impertinent, stupid little upstart, who does she think she is, to ask ME for poems? I shan't give her any.'" At that time Daddy was doing some canning as a sideline and it occurred to me that Lawrence, being English, might like some of the marmalade. So I filled a five-pound can and sent it to him by camion. To my amazement, by mail only a day or two later, there came a large group of L's poems, from which I was to select anything I liked for *Palms!*[149] And when we saw Lawrence again, he was all smiles and affability and told us how good the marmalade was, with its correct proportion of bitter, so unlike most American marmalades which are only sweet.

I remember Lawrence used to go down to the beach, where the women washed their clothes, and sit under a large tree like a willow writing for hours in long hand in the dime copy books he used for composing. I remember one time he complained bitterly of being annoyed by a goat.

Lawrence always treated Daddy with a real consideration, even affection. I attributed his liking for hour-long strolls along the *playa* with Daddy to two factors: one, that he liked Daddy—everyone does!; two, that he enjoyed all the wonderful observations he could glean for books.

After much brooding over Lawrence and his malevolence (as seen through Bynner's eyes), I wrote a rather long poem about him, in which he was called "the white white slayer with red red beard," and so on. And then, motivated by who knows what impulse, I showed it to him. He liked

it and spent hours of one sunny Chapala morning working over it, polish-
ing it, revising it:

> The fangs of glories he was denied
> Stung like serpents to torture his side.
> He lifted the great sword he was heir to,
> Piercing mountains, cleaving them through.
> He hurled lightning, proclaimed thunder,
> To smite the world and cast it asunder.
> He edged his thunder with obscene red
> And hurtled it forth that the quick might be dead.
>
> And the mountains that were beautiful
> Like slow slugs snake their way
> Over the unrelenting plains
> Into a savage day;
> And the cocks, the donkeys, and one white mule,
> Under the black rain
> Of his sinister magic, shrink with pain
> At the mouthings of a fool.
>
> .   .   .   .
>
> In that light wood
> By the length of the beautiful lake,
> Under the tavachin trees,
> With red beard to his knees,
> A prophet stood.
>
> He lifted his voice to make mountains break,
> He lifted his voice and spake
> The word for the earth to quake.
>
> And the red of the tavachin trees
> Was no redder than his beard
> Against the breeze.
>
> He was one torn and speared
> By demonish ecstasies
> And given to naming them.

> He broke the sacred bud from its stem
> By the soft and holy lake
> And spoke for the earth to quake. . . .

I remember that whenever Bynner was splashing in the lake with fifteen or twenty bootblacks, having a marvelous time, Lawrence on shore would rail against the indiscriminate friendliness; he would say that when one loves everybody, the love has no meaning at all. This used to make me furious; although I was actually half way between his philosophy and Bynner's, Lawrence's attacks on Bynner always seemed to me attacks on his *The New World* [150] and the whole principle of democracy, even of Christianity. I was fascinated by him; and he was no doubt exceedingly amused by me, naive in a fashion not to be understood in these later days! I was also alarmed by him, for I had been surrounded largely by people who tried to be courteous, and he was quite lacking in most of what I regarded as necessary amenities. After the outburst at the tea party, he was never again offensive: however, I always felt that he might be teetering on the brink of another violent eruption. And Bynner, with his poems about Lawrence [151] and Bynner's hatred of much of what he stood for, influenced me to a point of considering him a wicked man, an anti-Christ. Now, in the perspective which the reading of a few of his books and the long years have given me, my feelings have reversed: I think of Bynner—well, not as wicked, but as pagan, and Lawrence I think was a Puritan out of his time. He would have fitted beautifully into the New England of witches, and would have hustled them to ducking-stool and fire.

Lawrence and Bynner and Daddy and Spud had spent hours conferring with one another and going to the water front in a sort of "leave this all to us" attitude which was very masterful indeed. The great day came when Frieda and I were invited to see our new home. It was a rather stripped, rather decrepit canoa—and we wondered why all the men beamed with such pride until they took us to see the toilet they had made of a reed mat swung down across the niche formed by the bow (a petate which ended knee high); and behind it a big wooden box with a hole at the top to fit over a bucket. The men all stood there waiting for our approval. Frieda and I exchanged one look and then burst into the praise which was so clearly expected of us.

We took off amid the applause of the population of Chapala, a large part of which was at the beach.

Everyone went swimming over the side. Blankets were swung down from the beams under the hatch. These made a dressing room for Frieda and me. I was reluctant to go in, since I could not swim, but finally succumbed to urging. By then the rest had come out, dripping, very gay and very happy. I was not happy, for I felt queasy; but everyone said a dip would make me feel better. So down I went, and the moment I accidentally lost hold of the rope ladder I began to drown. On deck all laughed; they thought I was having fun. I thrashed about desperately and finally found the ladder and clung to it, very miserable indeed, while my friends above roared with laughter. The dip did not help my seasickness. That evening passed rather pleasantly, though. Frieda cooked a good, simple supper, and after supper one of the boatmen played my guitar, while we sang. Then three mattresses were spread on the floor by the stern. Frieda and Lawrence occupied the outside mattress, then came Spud and Bynner, then I, with Daddy on the inside. The first four slept with their feet pointing north, and we slept with ours pointing south. No sooner had we all settled down than Lawrence, very quiet and catlike, crept over us all to visit the seat in the bow. Somehow in the dark he kicked over the bucket, and a loud clatter resounded through the boat. Bynner of course could not resist; he never can; he sang out, "We all know what you're up to, Lorenzo." And the dark seemed suddenly to surge with waves of pure hate coming from the affronted dignity of D. H. L. Finally everyone seemed to quiet down, except Bynner, who kept tossing and turning and sighing, and me, still seasick and miserable. About two in the morning rain began to splatter on the roof and to leak in. I asked in a small voice, "Hadn't we better fix the camera so it won't get rained on?" and Bynner agreed, as if pleased to have the night broken by some activity. We fixed the camera, under other packages. Then again we were fairly quiet for a while, until my seasickness became too much for me and I began to fumble for the flashlight. This time Frieda aroused, to know what was wanted: "The flash," I said, and promptly she passed me the flask, full of tequila. "No, I said the flash. The flashlight!" and this time she gave me the right thing. Fortunately I had fewer people to climb over than Lorenzo had had; I managed to reach the toilet without waking everybody and there I was very miserable, retching without relief. Back I went, with a cold sweat on me. And fell asleep, at last!

The next thing I knew my father was excitedly summoning us all to come and see a water snake. I couldn't see why a water snake was of any interest, nor why we had to be awakened so early to see one; there was only a faint gray light under our shelter. But obediently we all went up on top of the hatch. The water snake was a waterspout, a black funnel reaching from the lake to the sky, or rather a chimney, with an elbow in it about half way up. The lake was now gray and angry, a thin rain spattered down, and it was cold. My seasickness was upon me again.

The sail was put up while breakfast was made. The wind blew up rapidly across the lake, and soon we were in danger of shipwreck on the rocky shores just west of Tuxcueca. Now all the men began to pole to keep us off the rocks. Then they saw an Indian who had come down to the desolate shore to watch. By much shouting they made him understand that he was to run for help. Somehow, finally, we reached the wharf and went ashore. Bynner and I sat on the breakwater, while the others set off to buy chickens. And as I revived, Bynner wilted. When the rest came back, they told us that the steamer was soon due. The steamer came, and with relief the others got rid of us. I was thankful that the Y.M.C.A. Taylors [152] were at the Hotel Arzapalo in Chapala and that I could turn Bynner over to Mr. Taylor, for by the time we reached there Bynner was very ill indeed.[153] When the rest came back to Chapala, three or four days later, Bynner was in a Guadalajara hospital; and only I welcomed them back. How unkempt and unshaven and happy they looked! And how filled they were with the delight of their adventure!

One evening when we were sitting in the lobby of the Hotel Arzapalo, Lawrence came in suddenly, looking pale and pursued, and sat by Frieda, saying to her, "Oh, Frieda, protect me from these wretched women!" He almost put his head down in her lap, like a little boy. My feeling about him, after all these years and in light of the things I know now, is that he was sexually immature, upset by misinterpretations of wisdoms, and preoccupied by a desire to understand, with his head, something he could never really understand with his body. Psychologists say that we progress from mother to father worship, then to an incipient form of homosexuality or lesbianism, then to heterosexuality, at last to switch into the "normal" channels. My own feeling about Lawrence is that he never got beyond the first step, and I think he knew it, that that was his deep trouble. I think *Lady Chatterley's Lover* was an attempt to understand a lot which he never would understand.

I remember how he enjoyed baking, lovely crisp loaves of white bread; and he liked to mend things, and sew. He enjoyed designing blankets which the weavers at Jocotepec would make for Bynner or for himself. We seldom went to Chapala without being asked to rejoice over a new blanket.

When the Lawrences left Chapala, Mr. Winfield Scott's [154] daughter, Margaret, and I accompanied them to the station in a boat, round trip paid for by Lawrence. When we got to the station, Frieda unabashedly blew her nose several times with deep emotion into a big, man's handkerchief, saying "I *like* Chapala, I *like* Chapala!" But Lawrence was glad to go.[155]

? July 1923   Texas

❲ It rained all the way in Mexico, but Texas is fierce—hot—queer show—don't feel much elation being here in U.S.[156]

15 July 1923   Hotel de Soto, New Orleans, La.

❲ Back in U.S.A.—regret Mexico—staying here a few days—a dead, steaming sort of place, a bit like Martin Chuzzlewit—dreary going up to New York by boat. The Mississippi is a vast and weary river that looks as if it had never wanted to start flowing. Expect to be in England before September.[157]

15 July 1923   Hotel de Soto, New Orleans, La.

❲ Here we are—got so far on the journey to New York. The moment I am back in these states comes my old feeling of detestation over me again. But I no longer let it trouble me. I just resist them all the time, and shall continue to do so. Only one has to watch that in resisting them one doesn't become hard and empty as they are. I want to keep myself alive inside, for the few people who are still living.

I expect we shall arrive in New York on Wednesday [18 July 1923]. I shall stay long enough to correct all proofs and get my MS. typed—then I suppose we shall go on to Europe. I am not very keen even on going to England. I think what I would like best would be to go back to Mexico. If we were a few people we could make a life in Mexico. Certainly with this world I am at war.

.   .   .   .

New Orleans seems America—but more easy-going—same impudence, however.[158]

20 July 1923   c/o *Thomas Seltzer, 5 West 50th Street, New York City*

⟨ *We got in yesterday—Today are going out to New Jersey to stay in a cottage,*[159] *where I can get proof corrected. . . . I find town wearing.*[160]

Care Seltzer   5 West 50th St.   New York City./26 July 1923.

⟨ Dear Mrs. [A. L.] Jenkins

We got your letter enclosing the one from Elder Walker today. I have meant to write you. We got back six days ago from Old Mexico—we went down there in March & had a house in Chapala, on Lake Chapala. I liked Mexico: find the U.S.A. rather wearing.

We think to come to London in August: then we shall see you. I haven't decided when we shall sail. At the minute we are in the country in New Jersey, & I am busy correcting proofs.

I hope you are feeling better.—I still hear from Mr. Siebenhaar and even had a letter from Miss Skinner, who says she has sent me the MS. of a novel to read: though it hasn't come yet.—I was so sorry her mother died.

I shrink a little from coming back to England. Yet seriously, we intend to come in about three weeks' time. In England my agent's address will always get me:

> Care Curtis Brown
> 6 Henrietta St
> Covent Garden W.C. 2

Greetings & au revoir from us both.

> Yours Sincerely
> D. H. Lawrence [161]

7 August 1923   Union Hill, Dover, New Jersey

⟨ We are still here in America—I find my soul doesn't want to come to Europe, it is like Balaam's ass and can't come any further. I am not coming, but Frieda is. Very likely she will come by the S.S. "Orbita," on the eighteenth, from New York, for Southampton, England. She will be in London on the twenty-fifth, stays there a fortnight, then to Baden. I remain on this side: go to California, Los Angeles, where we have friends [Knud Merrild and Kai Gótzsche], and if it is nice there, Frieda can come there in October.

I don't know why I can't go to England. Such a deadness comes over me, if I only think of it, that I think it is better if I stay here, till my feeling has changed.

I don't like New York—a big, stupid town, without background, without a voice. But here in the country it is green and still. But I like Mexico better. With my heart I'd like to come—also with my feet and eyes. But my soul can't. Farewell. Later on, the ass will be able to come.[162]

7 August 1923   Union Hill, Dover, New Jersey

⟦ *I've been very busy doing proofs here: of Kangaroo, my novel: and Birds, Beasts and Flowers, poems: and Maestro don Gesualdo, the Verga novel. . . .*

Frieda intends to come to England . . . . She will be alone. I ought to come—but I can't. . . . F. wants to see her children. So I think I shall go to the mountains of southern California and perhaps down into Sonora. I don't care at all for these eastern states—and New York just means nothing to me. At the moment this so-called white civilization makes me sicker than ever: I feel nothing but recoil from it. Now I've reached the Atlantic, and see Liberty clenching her fist in the harbour, I only want to go west, to the mountains and desert again. So there I am.[163]

7 August 1923   Union Hill, Dover, New Jersey

⟦ *I think, when Frieda has gone, I shall come to Los Angeles. We [Knud Merrild, Kai Gótzsche, and Lawrence] might like to spend the winter at Palm Springs or among the hills. Or we might go again to Mexico. And I should like to see you [Knud Merrild] and Gótzsche and have a talk about the future. If there was nothing else to do, we might take a donkey and go packing among the mountains. Or we might find some boat, some sailing ship that would take us to the islands: you as sailors, myself as cook: nominal. Frieda, I suppose, will want to join me again at the end of October. Meanwhile we will have made some plan or other.*

Probably I shall be in Los Angeles about the end of this month. Then we'll talk things over.

I care nothing for New York, and don't get much out of New Jersey.

Tell Gótzsche and think of something. I wish we were rich enough to buy a little ship. I feel like that now: like cruising the seas. I am a bit tired of the solid world. But perhaps it is quite nice to do as your engineer friend does, and build an adobe house in the foot-hills.[164]

Bernardine Fritz

I remember the first time I met [Lawrence]. The Seltzers published him in this country. Adela Seltzer was my cousin and, like so many women, she was utterly enslaved. We were at the Algonquin—about eight of us—and Adela, usually so voluble, was barely able to stammer introductions. She sat, entranced, doubtlessly torn between ecstasy at breathing the same air and a sense of unworthiness to do so. I was too young at that time to feel the awe and wonder—if anything I was perhaps just a little smug over being at the same table and seen by so many friends who envied me. He, Lawrence, said practically nothing. Another evening, however, at the Seltzers' home, he was talkative and morose by turns, but compelling and fascinating. It's odd about the aura that certain people achieve. I am sure that if I had known nothing of him, I would, despite his silences, have been deeply impressed.[165]

14 August 1923   Union Hill, Dover, New Jersey

《 It's pleasant here—the trees and hills and stillness. But it is dim to me. Doesn't materialize. The same with New York: like a house of cards set up. I like it best down at the Battery, where the rag-tag lie on the grass. Have met practically nobody: and the same thing, nothing comes through to me from them.

.   .   .   .

It hasn't been hot here—quite pleasant. I wish things were real to me. I see the lake at Chapala, not the hills of Jersey (New). And these people are just as you said of New England—quenched. I mean the natives. As for the trains full of business men—[166]

18 August 1923   Union Hill, Dover, New Jersey

《 I have just got back from seeing Frieda off on the steamer . . . .

.   .   .   .

I ought to have gone to England. I wanted to go. But my inside self wouldn't let me. At the moment I just can't face my own country again. It makes me feel unhappy, like a terrible load.

But I don't care for New York. I feel the people one sees want to jeer at us. They come with a sort of pre-determination to jeer.—But that is literary.

I am going West again—to Los Angeles, & then, if I can get a sailing ship of some sort, out to sea. This New York leaves me with one great desire, to get away from people altogether. That is why I can't go to Europe: because of the many people, the many things I shall have to say, when my soul is mute towards almost everybody.

.   .   .   .

Frieda wanted to see England again: it is four years since we were there. And her mother in Baden Baden. My heart goes like lead when I think of England or Germany.—I am thankful we are no longer poor, so that we can take our way across the world.

Either Frieda will come and join me somewhere west—perhaps in Mexico: or I shall go to her in Europe. . . .

.   .   .   .

[P.S.] I am leaving this Cottage for good on Monday [20 August 1923]—and expect to leave New York on Tuesday.[167]

22 August 1923   Buffalo, New York

❨ I have got so far—am staying in Buffalo till Friday at Mrs. [Elizabeth ("Bessie")] Freeman's. Shall probably stay a day in Chicago, also—perhaps —in Salt Lake City. I will telegraph the time I arrive [to Knud Merrild]. It will be about a week from now.[168]

28 August 1923   Aboard the Los Angeles Limited

❨ Thank you so much for the four full days in Buffalo. I feel I had there a fuller glimpse into the real old U.S. then ever before. I was really interested, and the real Buffalos at home were much nicer than I had expected, knowing only those other two Buffalos in Taos. . . .[169] Why doesn't somebody write your Cranford? Buffalo is a sort of Cranford.

It rained and fogged in Chicago, and muddy-flowing people oozed thick in the canyon-beds of the streets. Yet it seemed to me more alive and more real than New York.[170]

2 September 1923   The Miramar, Santa Monica, California

⟨ I am in California—but don't suppose I shall stay long.[171]

12 September 1923   Grand Avenue, Los Angeles, California

⟨ Am in Los Angeles—no fixed address—probably going Lower California, but it might be Pacific Isles—Frieda in England will join me when I get somewhere—saw eclipse yesterday—very impressive—also 7 destroyers on rocks—depressive—Los A. silly—much motoring, me rather tired and vague with it—came via Salt Lake . . . am on the move—just in from Santa Barbara.[172]

Jeanne d'Orge

D. H. Lawrence was one of a small party of artists who came to Lompoc from Santa Barbara the year of the total eclipse. The Remsens brought them to Lompoc because James Worthington, Dr. Burton, the Josselyns and some others from Carmel were there, with all the cameras and astronomical instruments needed to take pictures of the eclipse. They had chosen Lompoc as being the one place within the belt of totality most likely to escape mists and high fog. Their "hunch" was good, for as it turned out, the Carmel expedition was the only one in California with clear pictures to show of that hidden splendor in the sun which is called the Corona.

When Henry Williams,[173] his wife and I dashed into the village, late, the night before the eclipse, we found a little Carmel, centered and very much at home in the one and only restaurant. Rural inhabitants stood about—eyes popping, ears wide. Jimmy Worthington was in a state of high tension; not only was sure he had forgotten a most important technical detail, but he was absolutely certain that some of his corps of helpers would be missing in the morning. They had fallen from grace and slipped off to see seven battleships that had crashed on the rocks a few miles down the coast. There was a rumor that the road was blocked and many cars stalled. The atmosphere into which we walked in that little restaurant was electric. For us—sheer pleasure—the thrill before the play begins, a thousand times intensified—and tomorrow morning the great curtain of the sky would lift—and then—what?

In the morning we were storming the doors three hours before opening time. Each man was at his post, truants included. Henry, Mary and I received orders to drive into the hills to a certain high place. We were to follow a road which would be crumbly and white with chalk dust as we were to pass through a plant for making talcum powder and from there climb the white cliffs as far as we might. We were given an ordinary small camera and told that if a sudden mist should come blurring down on the town our little photograph might save the day for science. It had happened so before. We were just about to go when Rem's party unexpectedly drove in. We heard the howling of the lions. Beside D. H. Lawrence there were two distinguished foreign painters of different nationalities.[174] They were all sent off with us so as to be out of the way. No sooner did we turn our faces to the hills than everything changed. Lions turned into mice. Howlings into squeaks. D. H. Lawrence turned into a nobody. So did the painters. So did we all.

We found the place. We climbed the cliffs. Our feet sank deep into white chalk dust that crunched like snow. By the time we had found a high white mound the line of the moon showed dark against the sun. We were circled by hills and the hills spread wide to the great circle of the horizon. We looked up at the sky through little bits of smoked glass.

It was slow—the waiting.

D. H. Lawrence had a voice like rustling autumn leaves. He had a good mask for a volcano. He made flat jokes. So did the painters. So did we all. We felt queer. We began to feel cold . . . up the spine . . . down the arms. We didn't say so at first but we all knew—more and more we knew—that we were waiting for the world to end. We were a group of very small shivering, awed creatures, set upon a hill to await the ending of the world. The birds knew it too. They flew uneasily into the trees and they made crying sounds. The beasts knew it. They whined in the distance and made disagreeable, lonely, helpless sounds and soon they didn't make any noise at all. We drew closer together. We made sillier jokes. We said out loud how horrible it was to be waiting for the end of the world. Teeth chattered. Bones creaked. Darkness grew. We were shadows. We were black shapes. We were not there at all.

But the stars were there—great stars were in the sky, and on the far circle of the horizon sunset colors burned and dawn colors and twilight colors . . . night and day, twilight and dawn, all stood in the sky together. What was it flashed from the horizon—across and across—like a wing—a black wing—a bright shadow—the shadow of the moon sweeping over the earth, swift as light—black, yet bright—shedding a queer green light—wherever the light touched, earth opened and came forth in strange, unearthly, horrible, beautiful forms and shapes. (Henry Williams, who had charge of the camera and was lying flat on the ground, said afterwards that looking up he could see through our faces into our bones.) No sooner that over than our eyes were compelled upwards. Something looked through our eyes into the deep center of the night sky, where a great black disk burned with hidden sunfire like the heart of a great flower, and suddenly the great flower opened and shot forth countless petals of fire that streamed and spread and filled the whole sky and the earth, and we who were on the earth trembled into utter stillness from sheer wonder.

.   .   .   .

When the world ends it begins all over again—new and opposite. We came down from that hill a merry lot of Everybodies and we all knew each other in a way that had never been before. We kept together all day. We went down to see the seven battleships on the rocks. The sea looked like a pool to us and the ships no more than the toys some child had carelessly destroyed and was not crying about, either. We kept together all day and when we parted we didn't say goodbye. . . .

You see, don't you, why if I should be asked whether I had met D. H. Lawrence, poet and sometimes prophet, I could truthfully answer, "No." [175]

24 September 1923   Grand Avenue, Los Angeles, California

❮[*I am setting off tomorrow with a Danish friend [Kai Gótzsche], down the west coast of Mexico, to look again for a place to live. I hope I shall find it. If I do you [J. M. Murry] must come. You will have seen Frieda quite often. I'm afraid Europe won't make her any the happier. I expect she'll be setting off again for here, by the time you get this.*

California is a queer place—in a way, it has turned its back on the world, and looks into the void Pacific. It is absolutely selfish, very empty, but not false, and at least, not full of false effort. I don't want to live here, but a stay here rather amuses me. It's a sort of crazy-sensible. Just the moment: hardly as far ahead as carpe diem.

. . . I'm glad to be going south. America exhausts the springs of one's soul. I suppose that's what it exists for. It lives to see all real spontaneity expire. But anyway it doesn't grind on an old nerve as Europe seems to.[176]

Hotel La Palma/Palm Springs[, California]/Wed. 25 Sept./[26 September 1923]

[Dear Bessie Freeman

Came here to see you, and you're not around yet. Too bad! I can't even lay hold of Mr. Hicks. And the Inn is shut. Still, it's not bad here—only rough.—I saw your house and Mrs. Birge's. Your house has still a great deal to be done. It will be jolly out there when it's all ready. Gótzsche and I walked up to the stream, and sat under a tree. Very peaceful after Los Angeles.—We are on our way to Mexico—down the West Coast.—I will let you know what we find.—I expect Frieda will be coming out soon— then I hope you will see her.—Her address care Thomas Seltzer. Write to her.—Mr. and Mrs. Forsyth were awfully nice to me—I feel full of gratitude.—Oh also a man picked us up at Whitewater station when we were stranded—no stage or anything—and brought us in. I think his name is MacMahon—Mac something—and he lives in the adobe house just beyond the Inn—towards your new house. If you recognize him from his description—and if you feel like it, thank him for me, will you.—Palm Springs is lovely and still and clear, after Los Angeles. But I have on me, now I am so near, the wanting to go to Mexico again. If I find a place, you must come and see us.

Remember me to Mrs. Birge when she comes. I hope you left all well in Buffalo and Wanahah [?].—Tell Mary Wilkeson [?] I met a Mrs. Dr. Burton from Carmel—she seemed a nice soul. Also a girl who dances and a young husband who will write.

There is a wind, and it is lovely and cool here, for all the sun.

Tante saluti
D. H. Lawrence [177]

Kai Gótzsche

27 September 1923: *Guaymas*. We [Lawrence and Gótzsche] arrived this morning at Guaymas. All is well. We had no fuss about taxes and only a light duty examination. The journey, of course, was a little tiring,

and it is so hot here, we have not yet rested up. Lawrence is sleeping, I think. We stay at a big, very primitive Mexican hotel. Stone floors all over and army cots with only a pair of sheets. It is so different from U.S.A. that it is hard to believe that we are only one night's journey from the border.

Everything is so poor, in disrepair and primitive, but picturesque and beautiful. The harbour here looks most like a Norwegian Fjord, with small rock islands sprinkled on the water, very beautiful with the dolphins showing their black back-fins above the water now and then, and over the town hover some big black, red-headed, rapacious birds. Like to know what kind of birds they are; and at the harbour, or rather beach, for it is not a real harbour, native workers with bare torsos, dark brown skin. It is really rather interesting here, but as I said, very poor and dreary, so much so it almost depresses one.

This morning I went to fetch my luggage, one of the suitcases was smashed, one side cut clean away, so its contents were hanging out. I had to buy a new one. The railroad, which is American, promised to pay, and a report has been sent in. Monday [1 October 1923] we leave from here. We are thinking of renting a small boat tomorrow, just for a trip. . . .

4 October 1923: *Navojoa*. We have just come down from the Swiss' silver mine [178] where we have been a couple of days. We have not yet found anything to suit us, so we are thinking of going down to Guadalajara. Here the west coast seems to be a little warmer than California, the same brush-covered foothills, but with small primitive villages; in some of them the houses are merely straw huts—just some stakes and straw mats. The natives are rather uninteresting, I think. We have made some trips inland, but have not been molested by anyone.

There are many banana trees here, picturesque, I think, also figs and palms.

The hotels are very primitive, and to our way of thinking, very poor and bad. It is warm here, as in New York, but as soon as one gets up into the mountains, it is nice and cool. Tomorrow we go on again, and think to take the steamer from Mazatlan to Guadalajara. . . .

15 October 1923: *Guadalajara*. Today, at noon, we arrived in Guadalajara at last . . . .

Now you shall hear a little about our trip. You know we stopped at Guaymas and that it was awful hot and dirty, but interesting at the harbour; and that we next stopped at Navojoa and went to see the Swiss who has a silver mine in the mountains in a rather tiresome landscape of forest-covered mountains. The most interesting of that part of the country were the small primitive villages, if they can be called such, because there were only a few huts, built on four stakes, and palm leaves for roof, and straw mats hung up for walls—no furniture, no doors or windows, and only two stones and a piece of tin for the kitchen. It could hardly be any simpler. The children half-naked, the smaller ones absolutely naked, the women in ordinary cheap loud-coloured skirts, bare feet, loose hair, cigarette in mouth, dung-dirty. The men in enormous big straw hats, and enormous wide white slacks, white shirt and sandals, indeed very picturesque figures. The huts were spread here and there in the jungle or wilderness, no tilled soil. It looked absolutely barren and destitute.

Hour after hour, day after day, we journeyed through steppe-like sandy land with low brush. It was dry as an oven and as hot, flat as a pancake, with blue mountains in the eastern horizon. At the stations, there were only a few adobe huts, but desolate. It was impossible to understand why our train should make stops there, sometimes for hours at a time. When we had to transfer to another train, we always had to wait a day or two; but at last we reached Mazatlan, where it was more like a town, but unbearably hot, day and night, so we just loitered around to find just a small shady spot, preferably where there would be a small breeze, but it seemed very difficult to find. When we ate, I had continually to wipe my forehead to prevent my perspiration from dripping into my soup. I hated to be there. Otherwise, it was very interesting, with all kinds of tropical fruits: cocoa-palms, bananas, pineapples, dates, etc. We drank coco-milk from the coconut right on the street. We did nothing, however, but wait for the next day to come. We did, of course, see those people to whom Lawrence had letters of introduction. We dined and made excursions into the country from the different towns.

Next was Tepic, at 3000 feet altitude, so we could breathe again; what a relief. The town was picturesque, but dead and lonesome. From Tepic we went by Ford car to Ixtlán. You would say it was a lie if I showed you the road. You would not believe it possible to drive a Ford across that road, and ninety kilometres of it. Six men in the car, numerous suitcases on the running board, even on the front fenders they were piled up, completely covering the motor housing. We had to hold on to seat and roof with our hands all the way, and had terrific headaches. We passed by some very interesting large haciendas, whole villages they were, in beautiful surroundings. As we came into a small town, a bull fight was to be staged, so we stopped to take that in as well. Interesting, but how raw it was. I felt sick to my stomach, qualmish, perhaps from shaking about in the Lizzie, or the sight of the blood, or both, I don't know. But how loathsome. We saw four bulls, of which two were killed. There were no horses, I am glad to say. They killed the bulls by sticking a long, slender sabre between the shoulder blades. It was disgusting to see. The poor animal was gasping for air, its tongue hanging from its throat, and blood streaming from its nose. And for each time the bull took a breath, a small spout of warm, red streaming blood went into the air from the open wound in the shoulder. A coagulated red river of blood oozed down the bull's side. The poor animal—he tried to lie down to die. But he was constantly aroused to make hopeless attacks at a red rag. How I wished the bull could give the picador a well-aimed push. And *that* young girls with their parents, and even small children, were watching! It was swell to see the bulls come in, head and tail high, dashing animals; they would fret and fume and stamp the ground and look for the enemy. I get provoked and furious just to think of the yellow and dumb performance.

The next day, we continued our journey on muleback. We started at seven in the morning, with guide and pack-mule for our luggage, and a Mexican passenger, a small caravan. We had nine hours on muleback, so our behinds and knees were plenty sore when we arrived at Ixtlán. I was not as tired, though, as I had thought I would be. It was a wonderful landscape and a new experience, after the slow trains. I had had enough, though, and was ready for a good bed, but unluckily there was no train from Ixtlán; the rains had washed the railroad tracks away, and there was no hotel at the station, so we slept in a shack belonging to some cranky Americans. We borrowed a couple of army cots—I had my blankets along. But our travelling partner and another old Mexican, covered in year-old scurf of dirt, sneaked in and placed themselves on the floor, and rolled themselves in their serapes, coughing, spitting and snoring all night.

Early next morning, at 5.30, we had to get on again, new mules, new guide, but no new seat or knees. Without breakfast, we had six hours on muleback to the next station, Estlatlan, where there was a hotel, and to-day a train. And now we are all right; it is nice to be in a city again, with real people, tram cars, rest and food—it is not at all too hot, just right for me.

Mrs. Lawrence wants D. H. to come to England, but he will not, at least not this winter, he says. So now I don't know how it will be.[179]

17 October 1923   Hotel García, Guadalajara, Jalisco, Mexico

⟦ *I got your letter . . . to-day when we came down from the mountains to here.[180] We came two days on horseback to here, and my knees are stiff.*

.   .   .   .

Frieda is in England (or Germany). She writes that England is best after all, and wants me to come back. But Mexico now is so beautiful, so blue with pure sunshine and enough coolness to make one feel strong, I am afraid of the old sky of Europe. I don't care for the U.S.A. I don't care for Mexico all down the West Coast, till you pass Tepic and the barranca: and then it has a definite fascination for me. It seems to me as if the gods were here. I should like to stay the winter. And then in the spring, if so be I must come to Europe, Europe let it be.[181]

Kai Gótzsche

22 October 1923: *Guadalajara.* Yesterday we were at Chapala; we went in the morning with Dr. Purnell and daughter, in a Ford bus. We sailed to a small place of his that he let us have. It is beautiful, with mountains all around the lake; the small villages and the costumes of the people are picturesque. But I don't believe the place is adaptable to farming; it is too rocky. And to live there and just paint would be too lonesome. One must have something besides painting to do in a place like this; it is too desolate.

I cannot help being amused about Lawrence. You know he always scorns sentimentality, and likes to appear so rational, which he isn't at all. Why, even before we got out here, he said he didn't like to go to Chapala without Frieda (he is longing for her), and when we were out there, he was deeply moved, he thought it had changed so much. "Somehow it becomes unreal to me now. I don't know why," he said. He is always so concerned about the "spirit" of the place that he isn't aware, I believe, that it is he, himself, his own mood or frame of mind, that determines his impressions of the moment, or the landscape. It is, of course, possible that the place has changed, it is fall now and he was there with Frieda in the spring. But of course that isn't it. It is the "spirit."

"The life has changed somehow, has gone dead, you know, I feel I shan't live my life here." And so on. His eyes were glossy, to the point of tears, with emotional agitation. He had willed himself into belief that this was the place he loved, and the place to live. He is much more sentimental than he will admit. And then he is offended and cross because Frieda is happy to be in England. She writes it is the best country in the world, and wants him to come, etc. Deepest inside himself he is proud of England and if it wasn't for his author ideas, he would go back at once. But he wants to start that "new life" away from money, lust and greediness, back to nature and seriousness. He maintains that people like Johnsons [182] only play life away. I am afraid that that applies to himself, everything becomes play to him, he has means enough not to take anything really seriously. Now I don't know at all what it is going to be. He talks about how difficult it would be to have a farm here, to which, unfortunately, I can only agree. (We saw a small farm at Mazatlan, but it was so hot that it would be unbearable to live there. Otherwise, it was as it should be.) Here it seems impossible to me. He says that in England it would be easy for him to get a small farm and run it. But I contend that if we can't find a farm here, there is nothing for me to do but go back to the U.S.A. and start in where I left off. He will, I think, want me to come along to England, but there is not very much sense in that. So you see, even the plan is already beginning to disintegrate. But that of course is good, better that than to have started farming just to give it up. It is too bad, for it would be fun to paint here, of that I am sure.

It is therefore possible that I will soon be back in the U.S.A., but I know nothing yet. It is evident to me that, inside, he is fighting himself, what to do, because as an author, he likes best to stay here and build a new colony in this country, a new simple, ideal life, but as man he likes to go back to England and culture. I rather realize that if I leave him now and go back to America, he will continue to ramble about in the world, without peace. He needs, in a high degree, something else to think about, and something else to do beside his writings. I am absolutely sure that he would feel happier and live more happily if he could go out for a few hours a day, and have some work to do, milk a cow or plow a field. As he lives now, he only writes a little in the morning and the rest of the day he just hangs around on a bench or drifts over to the market place, hands in pocket, perhaps buying some candy, fruit, or something. If he could only have access to a kitchen, so he could make our food, that would occupy him for a couple of hours. I don't mind going to England, but I hate to be absolutely dependent on him, which inevitably would be the case.

It seems almost impossible to find a good solution. . . .

25 October 1923: *Guadalajara.* We are still in Guadalajara, it seems like Lawrence is too slothful to move away. I would like to go to Chapala as it is easier to paint on the streets there, and get people to pose, than here where it is so over-crowded with people and too much traffic.

Today when I tried to paint, a dashing and very picturesque Gypsy woman came up to me and told my fortune. Lawrence insists that the clothes they wear are the real genuine Mexican costumes, etc. He hasn't the remotest idea about it, because today I asked her, and she said she was Polish-Hungarian, in reality a Gypsy. There is a whole colony of them here; they are everywhere. The Mexicans will have nothing to do with them. Today my fortune teller repeatedly chased the boys away. She gave me a root to eat with sugar and salt, saying then I would be very happy.

We saw Indians in Taos and elsewhere, but these Indians seemed to be very close to the pristine race.

I got so excited, they struck me as prehistoric, or like wild animals in the street.

In spite of all, I would like very much to be here and paint, at least until February. I wish I could live by painting, and only once in a while go to U.S.A. or Europe to exhibit and sell my paintings, and live in culture for a few months. To have a ranch here will not mature, I can see that now. And I can feel that Lawrence is working himself up to *will* to go to England. I believe Frieda has influenced his friends in England, because they all write that he must come back and that England is beginning to be the leading country in culture again. "If I go, I shan't stay long, I know," he says. Well! That means he is thinking strongly about departure.

Frieda doesn't write, she is probably insulted because he is here. He is cross at her and irritable, and I am sure, if he could let steam off, he would be like he was the first time at Del Monte.

Poor Miss Purnell, who is poetry-mad and talks verse with Lawrence when we are there, gets some very hard thumps from him. I am avoiding Lawrence as much as possible at present, because, considering all things, he is really insane when he is as now. It is too bad, and I miss someone with whom to talk and have a little fun. You know his ways, and how he bends his head far down, till his beard is resting on his chest and he says (not laughing) "Hee, hee, hee" every time one talks to him. A cold stream always runs down my spine when he does that. I feel it is something insane about him. I am, considering everything, really glad that we

Lawrence by the mast of the *canoa* during lake trip, Lake Chapala, Mexico (1923).
Photograph by Witter Bynner.

Edward A. Rickards, Anglican priest at Oaxaca, Mexico, Lawrence's friend and landlord at Av. Pino Suarez 43. From a photograph in the possession of George E. Rickards.

The Hon. Dorothy E. Brett *ca.* 1924–1925. From a photograph in the possession of the Hon. Dorothy E. Brett.

Constantine G. Rickards, British vice-consul at Mexico City (1924–1925). From a photograph in the possession of George E. Rickards.

have not been able to find a ranch here, because I realize it would be too difficult to live with a man like Lawrence in the long run. Frieda is at least an absolute necessity as a quencher. I have sometimes the feeling that he is afraid she will run away from him now, and he cannot bear to be alone. I am afraid the end will be that I shall soon come back to U.S.A. I hate the thought of going to work again, smearing and daubing, *fy for Satan!* [183]

25 October 1923   Hotel García, Guadalajara, Jalisco, Mexico

◖[I had your [J. M. Murry's] letter from Switzerland yesterday. From Frieda not a word—suppose Germany swallowed her.

Yes, I think I shall come back now. I think I shall be back by the beginning of December. Work awhile with you on the Adelphi. Then perhaps we'll set off to India. Quien sabe?

Anyhow, though England may lead the world again, as you say, she's got to find a way first. She's got to pick up a lost trail. And the end of the lost trail is here in Mexico. Aqui está. Yo lo digo.

The Englishman, per se, is not enough. He has to modify himself to a distant end. He has to balance with something that is not himself. Con esto que aqui está.

But I will come back—I won't say home, it isn't home—for a time. When a rope is broken, it's no use tying a knot in one end. You have to tie both ends together. England is only one end of the broken rope. Hay otro. There's another. There's another end to the outreach. One hand in space is not enough. It needs the other hand from the opposite end of space, to clasp and form the bridge. The dark hand and the white.

Pero todavia no. No aleanzan [alcanzan?]. Todavia no aleanzan [alcanzan?]. No tocan. Si [Se?] debe esperar. [184]

Idella Purnell Stone

Lawrence and Gótzsche stopped at the Hotel García in Guadalajara. Lawrence made a habit of coming to our house every night for dinner. What Gótzsche did I don't know; he came a few times. They seemed entirely casual in their relationship to each other, like people who are friends, without being all-out friends. They did not have the community of interests or of hates which would be necessary for any kind of deep affection. At that time Daddy was on a strict vegetarian diet, and Lawrence seemed to enjoy it very much: frijoles, *queso blanco,* tortillas, honey, vegetables, fruits, sometimes a fruit pie, or *bizcochos.* After dinner we would go upstairs to the verandah where we would sit under the jasmine and talk, or into my study, if the night was cool, where sometimes he and Daddy talked while I worked or we all three talked. One night Lawrence got very "high," almost as though he had had too much to drink (he hadn't!): he was gay and more charming than I had ever seen him —and he could charm when he wished. He stood by the fireplace in my study and told us all about Ezra Pound's advent in London. Lawrence with the red beard vanished, and there stood a young, callow, swash-buckling Ezra, with an earring in one ear, very affected and silly. Then came his parents to London to see him, after Ezra had the London drawing rooms bewitched by his mannerisms and affectations; and they were good plain middle-western folks—and Ezra died away, and there were pa and ma, good and plain and middle-western, and poor Ezra not knowing what to do about them. Lawrence made us see the parents and feel sorry for them as they sensed their son's attitude; and see the son, and even feel a little sorry for him! Then he went on and told us autobiographical details which later I recognized in *Sons and Lovers.* I never liked Lawrence better, except maybe one time on the train coming from Chapala, where we spent the whole trip discussing the Witter Bynner issue of *Palms,*[185] for which I think he drew the cover design. He drew me a number of very fine cover designs for *Palms,* several of which I used.[186] He also made various excellent suggestions for editing, raising funds, etc., quite as if he had forgotten I was an impertinent, egotistical little wretch! After he left, we had some notes from him, always kind and friendly. He always wanted to return to Jalisco.[187]

A Britisher has a word with Harriett Monroe

❪ Miss Monroe tells (in October Poetry) [188] what a real tea-party she had in Britain, among the poets: not a Bostonian one either.

But she, alas, has to throw the dregs of her tea-cup in the faces of her hosts. She wonders whether British poets will have anything very essential to say, as long as the King remains, and the "oligarchic social system" continues. The poor King, casting a damper on poetry! And this about oligarchies is good, from an American.

"In England I found no such evidence of athletic sincerity in artistic experiment, of vitality & variety and—yes!—(YES!!) beauty, in artistic achievement, as I get from the poets of our own land."

YANKEE-DOODLE, KEEP IT UP.

As for that "worthless dude" George IV, what poet could possibly have flourished under his contemptible régime? Harriett, look in the history book, and see.

Oh what might not Milton have been, if he'd written under Calvin Coolidge! [189]

Projected Advertisement for *Palms*

[Idella Purnell Stone's original version:]

If you have been enjoying Palms, you will wish to add to the enjoyment of your friends, and will realize that the best way to insure their receipt of the magazine regularly is by giving them a subscription. In making out your Christmas and New Year lists, do not forget yourself—you would probably like to receive Palms regularly, too!

At the beginning of this venture, we promised our readers adventure and enjoyment. We feel that we are keeping that promise. We have consistently looked for poetry, not for reputations. We have favored no group of poets, and no school of poetry. We have printed poetry from people of many tastes and prejudices. And—we have done it in four issues! We are now attracting much more good, much more adventuring material than when we began, and we can safely promise our readers even more interesting Palms in the future—and always better verse.

Already, we have published work by as excellent young poet[s] and new poets as James Daly, Warren Gilbert, John Loftus, David Greenhood, Ellsworth Stewart, Donald Davidson, Willard Johnson, Holling Clancy Holling—but our good new poets are too numerous to mention.

Among those whose work has been published in spite of their excellent reputations, are such poets as Haniel Long, D. H. Lawrence, Helen Hoyt, Witter Bynner, Hi Simons, Hildegarde Flanner, Leonard Cline, William Griffith, Eda Lou Walton, Harold Vinal, and others.

And in this very issue . . . you may see for yourselves that we have magical poets in our magic number!

There is no better way to help us, and to insure your continued enjoyment, than by subscribing.

[Lawrence's revised version:]

❨ *I wish I knew if you have been enjoying Palms. Surely there has been enough fine quality in the poems already published, to add something to the year's experience. And if this is true for you, would it not be true for your friends? And would not this make a gift worth while, a years subscription to Palms.*

At the beginning of the venture, we promised adventure and enjoyment.

We feel that we are living up to promise. We care for poetry, not for reputations. We don't bother about groups or schools of poets. If the word lives, that is enough for us, beyond prejudice.

There have been four issues. And now there are coming in many more good, quick, adventurous poems than at first. The future looks bright to us. An open field is a new field; and we hope never to put up a fence.

Already, we have published work by such young poet[s] and new poets as James Daly, Warren Gilbert, John Loftus, David Greenhood, Ellsworth Stewart, Donald Davidson, Willard Johnson, Holling Clancy Holling—but the nameless will one day have names as well.

Among those whose work we have published in spite of their excellent reputations are such poets as Haniel Long, D. H. Lawrence, Helen Hoyt, Witter Bynner, Hi Simons, Hildegarde Flanner, Leonard Cline, William Griffith, Eda Lou Walton, and Harold Vinal.

And in this very issue . . . have we no magical poets in our magic number!

We offer you something real. Will you not in your turn subscribe for it.[190]

Kai Gótzsche

28 October 1923: *Guadalajara*. Today we went to St. Pedro on the tram car, a few miles from Guadalajara, where they make pottery. We bought some small things and shipped them . . . .

Lawrence has now decided to go to England in the middle of December, so I presume I shall be coming back to Los Angeles at that time, if I can't keep it up here any longer. I would so like to stay, at least until spring, but it is doubtful if I can. The worst of it is that I shall risk coming to Los Angeles at a time when there is no work to be had, and I will absolutely be on my arse at that time.

Lawrence is more human again. At present, he excuses himself on the ground that the air is so changeable that it makes him "crazy" once in a while. A poor excuse! [191]

1 November 1923   Hotel García, Guadalajara, Jalisco, Mexico

(I have been busy over your [Mollie L. Skinner's] novel, as I travelled. The only thing was to write it all out again, following your MS. almost exactly, but giving a unity, a rhythm, and a little more psychic development than you had done. I have come now to Book IV. The end will have to be different, a good deal different.

Of course I don't know how you feel about this. I hope to hear from you soon. But I think, now, the novel will be a good one. I have a very high regard for it myself. The title, I thought, might be The Boy in the Bush.[192] There have been so many houses in print.[193]

If possible, I should like to hear from you in time to arrange for publication in England and in America simultaneously in early April.[194]

Mollie L. Skinner

After D. H. Lawrence received the manuscript of *The Boy in the Bush*, which he happily called it, he wrote from California (September, 1923) saying that he had read the novel carefully. He slated it, then praised it: "I hate to think of it all wasted, I like the quality of so much of it, but you have no constructive power. If you like I will take it and recast it, and make a book of it." [195] (What amused me later was that he used my construction until the end, when he worked on the last two chapters.)

There was nothing else for me to do. I was quite unknown, living in the backblocks earning my living as a nurse, and he did praise the work so much. "You have a real gift, there is real quality in these scenes." [196] Besides it was a definite offer, take it or leave it.

"If I get this book done we'll publish it in the Spring, and if you agree to my recasting it. . . ." [197] So naturally I sent a cable agreeing. I never saw the book again until it was published. This was not his fault; it was because of the distance. Mexico is far away from Western Australia. Even that letter had taken weeks to reach me.

The next letter Lawrence wrote was dated November 1, 1923. He must have had my cable by then but not my letter, so I feel sure that he had not begun recasting the manuscript until then. "I have been busy over your novel as I travelled. The only thing was to work it all out again, following your MS almost exactly, and giving a unity, a rhythm and a little more psycho development than you have done. . . . The end will have to be different. Of course I don't know how you feel about this. I hope to hear from you soon. But I think now the novel will be a good one. I have a high regard for it myself. . . . Your hero is not quite so blameless an angel, according to me. You left the character psychologically at a standstill all the way. Same boy at the beginning and the end. I have

271

tried taking your inner cue, to make a rather daring development psychologically. You may disapprove. . . ." [198]

I did. I wept.

"But I think it makes a very interesting book. If you like we will appear as collaborators, let the book appear under our joint names. Or we can have a single nom de plume. And we can go halves in English and American royalties. All of course if you approve. . . ." [199]

But I knew that D. H. Lawrence was a power in the world of literature, and of course I was elated and imagined I could write. I sent him another cable of my approval.

A fortnight after receiving the letter quoted above, another letter [dated 15 November 1923] reached me saying he had finished the recasting and would call the book *The Boy in the Bush*,[200] a name which delighted me. I was also pleased to think he could not have done much alteration, in a fortnight, while travelling. Somehow that satisfaction never left me. I had met a human being who was alight with some understanding of a soul which aspires to reach the spiritual essence of life. And that not only for himself but for others.

Still, we are human. And being very "ordinary" I was unhappy when the book arrived—and everyone I knew who read it condemned me in no uncertain fashion for having had a hand in it. One of my aunts said: "I burnt it leaf by leaf—after I had read it." Being of Victorian upbringing I dared not say: "I notice you were thrilled enough to read it before you burnt it leaf by leaf!"

I went to England, taking a steerage ticket, to find out whether I could place *Black Swans* with a publisher. But I did not travel steerage. A famous bachelor engineer became ill during the voyage and I was moved to a cabin de luxe to nurse him. He was charming and entirely dependent on me during that voyage, and only had one grudge against me—that I had collaborated with D. H. Lawrence. He was certain my own book would be famous. It was a dud. He gave me a note to open after I left him. It contained my return fare to Australia.

The Boy in the Bush was just being read in London. I stayed with relatives but sneaked off to a press-cutting agent and paid my guinea to have reviews sent to me. The book was magnificently reviewed, and I was happy.

"My hat in the ring, if there is such a person as M. L. Skinner," was one extract I chuckled over. I heard later that D. H. L. loathed all this; but I never saw him again. I just missed him everywhere.

I did not see our literary agent, Curtis Brown, either—only his secretary, a young lady who treated me with great disdain. But writers whom I happened to meet at a cocktail party given by Mrs. Chesterton in her mews flat were all most courteous and charming. And then Edward Garnett. Here was another critic who rose above so many others in his understanding and his endeavour to help those writers gifted (or cursed) with "creative imagination."

He told me, with a roar, that I was so damn damn bad in my work; and, with an angelic smile, so damn good, that he couldn't bear it. He found it hard to believe that so unsophisticated a person had written about three-fourths of the book in question. I marked, at his suggestion, Lawrence's part of *The Boy in the Bush*.[201] And even more he was surprised that "David" had collaborated with a simplicitas who had wept and had to have her tears wiped away with his own handkerchief. He told her to go home and write the best book an Australian has yet achieved. That lion of literature—how I disappointed him!

In Australia I found another friend, Katharine Susannah Prichard. It is she who has persuaded me to write of the whole matter and to place it before the many admirers of Lawrence in its simple truth. I received the following letter in 1924:

[Garland's Hotel, Suffolk Street, Pall Mall, S.W. 1] London,/3rd March, 1924.
Dear Miss Skinner,

The Boy in the Bush is in the printer's hands, both here and in New York. After all Martin Secker is publishing it here: and I am signing a contract for it, drawn up by Curtis Brown. The contract is made between me and the publisher, and I sign on your behalf: and Curtis Brown has an order to pay you one-half of all receipts in England and America, after, of course, his 10% agent's fee has been deducted. It is possible Martin Secker will pay about £100 in advance of royalties—in which case Curtis Brown will at once send you a cheque for £50 or thereabouts. I will have all statements of sales made to you as well as to me. Statements are made on June 30th and December 31st, and payments are made on 1st Oct. and 1st May, each year. Curtis Brown is very strict in business, so you will be quite safe. Write to him and ask him anything you want to know.

My wife and I are sailing in two days' time on the *Aquitania* to New York. Address me there, always, c/o Curtis Brown—116 West 39th St., New York City. You see the agency operates in both cities.

I am very anxious the book should be a success, and that you should get some money as well as fame. Also I hope you are pleased with it. You may quarrel a bit with the last two chapters. But after all, if a man really has cared, and cares, for two women, why should he suddenly shelve either of

273

them? It seems to me more immoral to drop all connection with one of them, than to wish to have the two.

Write to me in New York. I expect we shall go to New Mexico, and then down to Old Mexico. But letters will come on.

The book, unfortunately, has been delayed here, and Secker will probably not have it out till early June. Seltzer in America will probably be sooner—May, or even end of April. We shall see. You can write to Curtis Brown both in London and New York (in New York the Manager is Mr. Barmby) for all information. I will see you get six presentation copies from Secker, and six from Seltzer.

I hope now I have thought of everything.

I am not sorry to go back to America: Europe seems to me weary and wearying.

Best wishes to you. My wife sends her regards and remembrances. One day we shall meet again, and laugh things over, I know.

Yours sincerely,
D. H. Lawrence

Soon I will write you a really long letter! Meanwhile all good luck to the boy!

Yours very sincerely,
Frieda Lawrence

I should like to add that I always received royalties for *The Boy in the Bush* until Lawrence died. Then they ceased. I have never had a penny since—until last month.[202]

Katharine Susannah Prichard

I had not met Miss M. L. Skinner at the time of Lawrence's visit to Australia, and did not read *The Boy in the Bush* until it was published. Since then, I have heard Mollie Skinner's account of the collaboration, read reviews of *The Boy in the Bush*, and her *Letters of a V.A.D., Black Swans, Tucker in India,* and *Where Skies are Blue.*

.   .   .   .

Richard Aldington's statement in [*D. H. Lawrence:*] *Portrait of a Genius, But* . . . that "Lawrence re-wrote the whole of Mollie Skinner's Australian novel *The Boy in the Bush*" cannot be accepted. Although Aldington adds: "It was a curious notion of collaboration—he took her plot, characters, episodes and intimate knowledge, and recast them entirely in his own style to please himself." [203]

The collaboration of Lawrence with anybody created a sensation: but most reviewers could see only Lawrence in the book. *The Weekly Westminster* doubted whether there was "any sich [*sic*] person as M. L. Skinner" and referred to the "supposititious Skinner." [204] "It may be a gentleman, or it may be a lady," another critic remarked.

"Whatever Mr. Skinner's share in the book," the *Times Literary Supplement* said, "the best and the worst of it are the best and worst of Mr. Lawrence, and the best is Mr. Lawrence's very best." [205] And *The Saturday Review: "The Boy in the Bush* is a great improvement on *Kangaroo*: it is [far] more intelligible and coherent." [206] Another critic observed: "Two-thirds of the book are very good, the life in the bush, the Ellis family, the raw pioneering atmosphere of Australia . . . all this is strong, vivid and often beautiful."

This part of *The Boy in the Bush* was chiefly Mollie Skinner's. And I think her share in the book should have more recognition.

In his *Son of Woman*, Middleton Murry gave high praise to Lawrence's collaborator. He said: *"The Boy in the Bush* is a strangely beautiful book. It is so largely because Lawrence did not have to invent it. He could clothe his collaborator's story in an added glory of flesh and blood, and pour out the riches of his imagination on a given theme. But someone else planted: it was Lawrence who gave the increase. If Lawrence had written it alone, it would have been a far poorer book than it is. With the burden of foundation removed from him, he was free to make it an amazingly rich one." [207]

Anybody who knows the style of both writers understands how much Miss Skinner's material owes to Lawrence's twist and turn of a sentence, to his subtle adjectives, to streaks of verbal magic, to changes and interpretations of character, to paragraphs which flow with the rhythm of an elusive thought. Miss Skinner herself is the first to acknowledge this.

But Lawrence knew nothing of those pioneering days in Western Australia. They were too far from his experiences to have been given in such intimate detail by him. Despite the fact that the chapters about early Fremantle were referred to as "pure Lawrence," I guessed when I first read the book that those chapters, Mr. George, the Ellis family, the incidents and anecdotes of bush life, belonged to Miss Skinner. I was sure, also, that no Australian with any knowledge of horses would ask us to believe that the newly arrived young Englishman "conquered" an unbroken stallion like Stampede which neither Australian nor native stockman could ride.

Lawrence's obsession crept into the book with the assertions of male egoism, the "blood" superiority of the young Englishman to these "common," oh, so common, ineffectual Australians, his preoccupation with death, the dark gods, sexual malevolence.

In the last chapters, he captured and ran away with the story. There is fine writing in those chapters. They are "pure Lawrence" and as such vital and challenging. But Miss Skinner confesses that she wept when she read them. That was because her people had become such changelings, and she "disapproved passionately" as she once told me, of what Lawrence had done to them.

In Miss Skinner's own character drawing there is a shrewd and simple realism, sometimes an almost Hogarthian sense of humour; but also a tendency to sentimentalise and expatiate in a strain of mysticism, very different from Lawrence's own. It is as if the early Victorian in her upbringing, and the Quaker in her persuasion to a gentle and kindly faith, were in conflict with the expression of literary instincts. Lawrence realized the conflict in Miss Skinner's personality; and its reflection in her writing. He was intrigued by it: disliked her sentimentality and sought to free her from its hampering influence. "Be spiteful," he wrote to her. "I always am."

But there was a certain correspondence between the daemon of D. H. Lawrence and the psyche of this middle-aged spinster which made their famous collaboration possible—even if it were less of a collaboration than a recreation by Lawrence of the material Miss Skinner gave him.

I have seen the manuscript of another novel that Miss Skinner sent to Lawrence. It was entitled *Eve in the Land of Nod,* and it still bears alterations and notes in Lawrence's handwriting, which indicate how he worked on *The Boy in the Bush.* These alterations are very much fewer than might have been expected; and there is often a striking resemblance between Lawrence's style and Miss Skinner's.

But Lawrence decided not to collaborate on this novel.

He wrote: "I can't do with it as I did with *Boy in the Bush*—that was a *tour de force* which one can do once, but not twice. You see, I know nothing of gold camps, never saw a black boy except in the streets of Sydney, and know nothing of medicine. How can I recreate an atmosphere of which I know nothing. I should only make silly howlers . . . Still the book has good points."

He gave advice on how to handle the material: "use the I again," "the form of a sort of diary," "write in little sections in just those little flashes of scenes and incidents . . . following one another in haphazard event

. . . brief, poignant, telling." "Cut out about the man dying in the buggy." And so on.[208]

Lawrence had tried putting the story into the third person, found that it would not go like that, and Miss Skinner thinks he gave up the idea of collaboration then. He read the manuscript twice, and put a great deal of work into it, cutting, pasting up and rewriting between pages. For a long time Miss Skinner couldn't bring herself to do anything about *The Land of Nod;* but recently she revised it, bearing in mind Lawrence's advice.[209]

In casual personal relationships, seemingly, Lawrence was very different from the man who stalks through so many of his books. Somers of *Kangaroo,* or what he made of Jack Grant in *The Boy in the Bush.* His letters to me, a stranger, were not aloof and chilling, but responsive and charming; and Mollie Skinner remembers only his sympathy, simplicity and generous kindliness.

Perhaps no man should be hailed as a genius until he is dead. It is putting too great a burden on the wearer of individual talent to make him aware of this accolade. Lawrence was hailed as a genius early in his career, and perhaps because of that became too much in awe of himself. He used an ability to startle and deride to maintain his position and lost something in the process: his contact with the realities on which free and joyous human relationships are based, not only in sex but in all the exigencies of life and work.

D. H. Lawrence had a liberating effect on the writers of his time, with regard to style, construction, the discussion of sex and thought processes. For that we are indebted to him.

But Lawrence tore himself to pieces in a literary experiment, and gave us the débris to study. Unfortunately, though, he transferred his psychological vagaries to many of his characters in his novels. He did not submit himself to other people as a medium for the reflection of their essential quality: he made them in his own image.

Because of that he failed as a writer of the first magnitude: an interpreter of the people, of their joys and sorrows. Behind his self-assertion, pre-occupation with death, vaunting of the dark gods, lay a fear of death and of impotence—maddening to a man of genius who knew that his creative powers in life and literature suffered a blight.

But the beauty of Lawrence's descriptive writing—all that is finest, most courageous and radiant in *Sons and Lovers,* and in *Lady Chatterley's Lover,* for example—will survive the dross and rubble of those fears, frustrations and obsessions which undermined his genius, and destroyed for many of us the intrinsic value of some of his novels.[210]

3 November 1923   Hotel García, Guadalajara, Jalisco, Mexico

⟪ Gótzsche will have told you that Frieda won't come back: not West any more. I had a cable yesterday asking me to go to England. So there's nothing for it but to go. And G. will try and get a cheap ship to Denmark, to look at home once more. It seems to be the only thing he really wants to do.—So I think we shall go on to Mexico City next week—this is Saturday—and look for a ship.

These are great fiesta days here, very gay & full of peons and the streets full of stalls & vendors, mostly of toys. The midday is hot still—but evening cool. I think Guadalajara is pleasant. In a way I am sorry to be going. But now it seems inevitable that I must go back to England, and square up with that once more.[211]

10 November 1923   Hotel García, Guadalajara, Jalisco, Mexico

⟪ I like it here. I don't know how, but it gives me strength, this black country. It is full of man's strength, perhaps not woman's strength, but it is good, like the old German beer-for-the-heroes, for me. Oh, mother-in-law, you are nice and old, and understand, as the first maiden understood, that a man must be more than nice and good, and that heroes are worth more than saints. Frieda doesn't understand that a man must be a hero these days and not only a husband: husband also but more. I must go up and down through the world, I must balance Germany against Mexico and Mexico against Germany. I do not come for peace. The devil, the holy devil, has peace round his neck. I know it well, the courageous old one understands me better than the young one, or at least something in me she understands better. Frieda must always think and write and say and ponder how she loves me. It is stupid. I am no Jesus that lies on his mother's lap. I go my way through the world, and if Frieda finds it such hard work to love me, then, dear God, let her love rest, give it holidays. Oh, mother-in-law, you understand, as my mother finally understood, that a man doesn't want, doesn't ask for love from his wife, but for strength, strength, strength. To fight, to fight, to fight, and to fight again. And one needs courage and strength and weapons. And the stupid woman keeps on saying love, love, love, and writes of love. To the devil with love! Give me strength, battle-strength, weapon-strength, fighting-strength, give me this, you woman!

England is so quiet: writes Frieda. Shame on you that you ask for peace today. I don't want peace. I go around the world fighting. Pfui! Pfui! In the grave I find my peace. First let me fight and win through. Yes, yes, mother-in-law, make me an oak-wreath and bring the town music under the window, when the half-hero returns.[212]

Hotel Garcia/Guadalajara, Jal./Mexico/10 November 1923

⟦ Dear Rosalind [Thornycroft Popham]

Your letter found me here—not Sicily. But Frieda is in England—she went from New York in August, & I turned west again. Now I am coming along: expect to be in London by the New Year—care S. Koteliansky, 5, Acacia Rd., London, N.W. 8. And before June I bet we shall be in Sicily— in Italy. And of course we should call in Florence if you were there. Koteliansky's address will find Frieda.

a rivederci
D. H. Lawrence [213]

10 November 1923   Hotel García, Guadalajara, Jalisco, Mexico

⟦ We keep on trying for ships, but nothing so far. We should like to sail from Manzanitto [Manzanillo] through the Panama Canal: it still may be possible to find a tramp steamer. If not, we shall go to Mexico City and get the first regular boat that goes out of Vera Cruz, if that infernal port is open: if not, Tampico. I'm not keen on going to Tampico, because of the fever. And I feel I simply can't look at the U.S.A. again, just yet.—The quickest steamers are the Dutch and the Hamburg Amerika—they take three weeks to Southampton or Plymouth.

Mexico is still very attractive and a very good place to live in: it is not tame. Sometimes here in Guadalajara one sees the wild Guichilote [Huichole] Indians, with their bows and arrows and hardly any clothing. They look so queer, like animals from another world, in the Plaza listening to the band. We've had several thunder showers, but the sky is blue and bright again. I like the plain round Guadalajara, with the mountains here and there around. I like it better than the lake. The lake is too shut in.—

The barranca also is very impressive—you never saw that.—I still wish I was staying the winter on a ranch somewhere not far from this city. I still don't believe in Europe, England, efforts, restfulness, Adelphis or any of that. The egg is addled. But I'll come back to say how do you do! to it all.[214]

Kai Götzsche

10 November 1923: *Guadalajara*. We are, as you can see, still in Guadalajara, but we are both a little tired of being here. The town is all right, but it is no good to live in a hotel and never be really "at home." The last couple of weeks, Lawrence has been himself again. The other day, he asked me if I wouldn't rather go with him—we could take a freighter to Europe before Christmas and he would pay my fare. He will not go alone in a freighter. Then I could save my money to go back to New York.

It was difficult to refuse a trip home, so I said all right, let us see first if we can find a boat. So now we are awaiting an answer from Vera Cruz about a ship. It is rather odd trying to get used to the idea of being home this winter. Then I think I shall go back to New York in the spring. I figure that if I went to New York now, I would be without work a couple of months anyway, so I am losing nothing by going home.

The longer I am here, the more I would like to stay and have a ranch in this country. Life is so picturesque—on the street and in the country —and nature is beautiful, something like New Mexico.

As a rule the people are friendly and polite, even if many of them look like real bandits. When we are outside the town, both of us get a burning desire to stay in this country. Life could really be interesting, if one could get settled to one's liking.

Lawrence is a queer snail, and impossible to understand. He seems to be absolutely nuts at times, and to have a hard time with himself. He over-estimates himself. He thinks he can show by his feelings what people think and do. At other times he is so reasonable and so overwhelmingly good that there is no end to it. . . . He makes everything much more artificial and complicated than it is in reality. He is afraid Frieda will avoid him; he says that she can have a house in London and have her children with her, then he can travel alone. "She will hate it before long," he says, biting his lower lip and nodding small, quick nods. Do you know him? The fact is that he is afraid she will like that arrangement only too well. Nevertheless, he has a large heart and means well, but his ideas are so impractical that it is doubtful he will get anyone to accept them.

18 November 1923: *Mexico City*. Now we are on our way to Denmark. That means we are in Mexico City, waiting for a ship to Europe. We almost sailed yesterday, but we couldn't get our passports in order so quickly, so we gave it up.[215] Now we will have to wait until the 29th, that is, if we can't find another boat before then.

Lawrence was impossible the last days in Guadalajara, although rather nice. But one day he came and said he could not go to England. "I am sure I will *die* if I have to see England again."

All right, we decided then to stay and look for a farm, so we went out to see people and ask for information as to where we could find a farm to live on for the winter. He looked really sick and so pale, and his head hung way down on his chest. Next morning he came in to me and said: "It is just as well to go to Europe, don't you think? One might just as well, I feel I don't care any more. I just go." All right, then we'll go, and Friday [16 November 1923] we drove off from Guadalajara.

It is biting cold here in Mexico City; we are using our overcoats. It is rather like a big city, so I haven't got the feeling of being in Mexico now. And not at all yesterday when we had to put on our best clothes to go to the home of the English Consul for dinner.[216] Lots of wine and good food; otherwise it was nothing for me. The Consul is single and he has a large rich home with loads of Indian and Mexican antiques. He paints himself, so he asked me if I wouldn't like to come out today and paint a young Mexican girl he had for a model. He has a large room which he uses as a studio. It might be rather fun. He is a nice man. I am to be there for lunch. He paints rather like the Taos painters, not quite as clever.[217]

19 November 1923   Hotel Monte Carlo, Av. Uruguay 69, Mexico City

[[I am off to Europe—la mala suerte. We sail, Gótzsche and I, on the *Toledo*, from Vera Cruz, on Thursday [22 November 1923]—three days hence—and I get to Plymouth about 12 Decem., he gets to Hamburg two days later. Well, I don't care, since I've got so far. This city is a bit nervy and not in good spirits, and cold. From the roof this morning Ixtaccilmatl [Iztaccihuatl] and Popo clear in snow. The monkey, the parrot and Chihuahua dog gone: but the large husband and the wife with a nose, still living upstairs. Not many "mariners" any more—more Mexicans, and less of a Pirates of Penzance atmosphere. Everything a bit heavier.[218]

25 November 1923   Havana, Cuba

⟮ Two days here—am already sick of ship—mixed German Spanish Danish English—a nearly empty boat. G. at last happy.[219]

CHAPTER FOUR

1923–1924: England, France, Germany

It is four years since I saw, under a little winter snow, the death-grey coast of Kent go out. After four years, down, down on the horizon, with the last sunset still in the west, right down under the eyelid of the shut cold sky, the faintest spark, like a message. It is the Lands End light.

.   .   .   .

It was such a brave country, for so many years: the old brave, reckless, manly England. Even a man with dyed whiskers, like Palmerston. Too brave and reckless to be treacherous. My England.

Look at us now. Not a man left inside all the millions of pairs of trousers. Not a man left. A host of would-be amiable cowards shut up each in his own bubble of conceit, and the whole lot within box after box of safeguards.

One could shout with laughter at the figures inside these endless safety boxes. Except that one is still English, and therefore flabbergasted. My own, my native land just leaves me flabbergasted.

—"On Coming Home," Tedlock, pp. 206–7, 208

7 December 1923   110, Heath St., Hampstead, London, N.W. 3

⟨ Here I am—London—gloom—yellow air—bad cold—bed—old house —Morris wall-paper—visitors—English voices—tea in old cups—poor D. H. L. perfectly miserable, as if he was in his tomb.

You don't need his advice, so take it: Never come to Europe any more.

In a fortnight I intend to go to Paris, then to Spain—and in the early spring I hope to be back on the western continent. I wish I was in Santa Fe at this moment. As it is, for my sins, and Frieda's, I am in London.[1]

John Middleton Murry

[Lawrence] looked positively ill when I met him at the station: his face had a greenish pallor. Almost the first words he spoke were: "I can't bear it." He looked, and I suppose he felt, as though the nightmare were upon him again. All he had to suggest was that the *Adelphi* should attack everything, everything; and explode in one blaze of denunciation. I was feeling disappointed enough to be momentarily tempted by the plan. But the moment was brief. I did not need a Lawrence to show me the way to nihilism. I had been there, and emerged again; it was not possible for me

285

to return. I turned the notion aside, as though it had been a joke. Then he changed his ground. Would I not give it all up and go back with him to New Mexico, and there begin the nucleus of a new society? This was a far more serious temptation. After all, since the main purpose of the *Adelphi* had been to make a place for Lawrence and Lawrence now refused it, why not give up? Lawrence said he needed me badly. Why not do what he wanted?

At first I agreed, then I hesitated; for I found in myself an obstinate instinct against yielding. It was only another running away. Lawrence by this time had no belief at all in America. The little ranch in New Mexico was a pleasant place to live in, the best place that Lawrence had found; but that was all. It was a very good reason why he should return there, but no reason why I should return with him. If I did return with him, I should do it purely out of personal affection for him; and I told him so. No! there must be nothing personal about it, he insisted; the motive must be impersonal. But, unfortunately, there would be no impersonal motive at all in my going to New Mexico. I could not really believe that this was the way to create the nucleus of a new society. If the birth of the nucleus of a new society depended upon people having money enough to go to New Mexico, and a profession which would comfortably maintain them there, then it was hardly worth thinking about. On the other hand, if I went with him there simply out of personal affection, it was a preposterous situation if he continued to repudiate, in all his open professions, the worth of that personal affection which alone would take me with him. Further, if the plan was that we should simply go there and live to ourselves, rejecting the world, washing our hands of it altogether, that seemed to me renegade to the doctrine of the *Fantasia;* and certainly I knew it would be a retrogression in myself.

It was a painful time, and painful things happened in it. I am conscious that this retrospective account makes the issues much clearer than they were to me at the time. Lawrence's personal appeal was pretty desperate; so were my contorted struggles to avoid being involved in a situation which I felt instinctively would be disastrous. He talked to me much about Death, in a way I could not understand, trying in particular to convince me that Life was a form or manifestation of Death, not Death of Life, as I believed and believe. What we had to do, he said, was to shift from the Life-mode into the Death-mode, and to do this Mexico was necessary. I listened, and tried in vain to understand; it seemed to me completely alien to the *Fantasia,* and still more alien to my own small fragment of personal conviction. It was hardly possible for me to believe in it, and I told him so. I insisted that if I went with him it would be from personal affection and that he must accept this. If there was any tacit understanding that I had accepted this new and unintelligible, but faintly alien creed, then I must withdraw, because it was bound to end in disaster.

The upshot of it all was that Lawrence returned to New Mexico and I stayed in England. As so often before, each felt that he had been let down by the other, although on this final occasion the full realisation of the feeling came gradually. It was not till three years later, at the beginning of 1926, when Lawrence had finally left America and settled in Italy, that he definitely broke with me; and by that time I was prepared for it as inevitable.

I remember vividly more than one moment during this last sustained contact of mine with Lawrence. One is significant. We were at a dinner-party together, and Lawrence was talking with all his quick gaiety and sensitive response. Suddenly the feeling came upon me: *Why* is there a gulf between this Lawrence and the writer? I sat watching him, and became more and more bewildered and depressed by the strange discrepancy. I felt rather sore about it; it seemed to me that this was the cause of all the failure. After dinner, he took me aside into a corner, and said: "You're angry with me about something. What is it?" I said that I wasn't sure that I *was* angry with him. "Yes, you are," he persisted. "What is it?"

"Well," I said, "if you really want to know, I *am* angry, and I'll tell you why. You always deny what you actually are. You refuse to acknowledge the Lawrence who really exists. And as far as I can see, you'll go on doing it to the end."

For a moment he was quite silent; he was obviously moved and distressed; then he said simply: "I'm sorry . . . I'm sorry." [2]

Catherine Carswell

Lawrence arrived in London at the beginning of December, and Murry went with Kot to the station to meet him. Murry has described the meeting—how ill Lawrence looked, with a face of "greenish pallor," and how almost his first words were "I can't bear it," so that Murry "supposes" he felt "as though the nightmare were upon him again."

Murry's supposition is correct. But this time it was a different nightmare. It arose from a conviction which had begun to form in Lawrence upon his arrival at Southampton, had hardened during the journey through the Southern Counties, and had been clinched as by a hammer-stroke when he was greeted by Frieda and the others on the London platform. This conviction was that he had made a mistake in coming—that he ought to have waited for Frieda to come to him.[3] If he could have been back in America at that moment, there would have been nothing but a fierce little greenish tongue of flame for Frieda and Murry to fetch from Waterloo to Hampstead. Now that he had come, however, he must see it through. From all this the reader is requested to make no obvious deductions. Lawrence had an uncanny and instantaneous way that was entirely his own, of "sizing up" any situation. For him to see, for example, Murry and Frieda waiting for him so chummily together was enough to turn him greenish pale all over. "Chumminess" . . . "palliness" between people was anyhow detestable to him. Again, though Murry might be Lawrence's self-appointed lieutenant on a self-constituted *Adelphi*, Frieda was another matter. Here Murry would find himself up against the "Unknown God" with a vengeance. In Lawrence's marriage there was no place for any lieutenancy, however platonic.[4]

For some little time before Lawrence's arrival Frieda had already been living in the same house as ourselves—not our own house, but a large old one belonging to my brother who lived on the top floor. We had a lower part, and the Lawrences the flat above us. Murry had been Frieda's constant visitor and she was clearly prepared to back him up with all her strength (though why he should need her backing I could never understand) to Lawrence upon his arrival. "After all," she said to me one day, "Murry is Somebody! And the *Adelphi* is Something!!" Her enthusiasm was childlike and infectious—at least it was childlike, and I should have found it infectious if I could have brought myself to believe in Murry. I respected his talent, and admired his capacity for eliciting emotion in others, but that was as far as I could get. Yet I could see, and can now, why it was that for so long he made a special appeal to Lawrence. He seemed made to subserve another's compelling genius.

Lawrence's immediate suggestion, says Murry—made perhaps on the way to Hampstead—was that the *Adelphi* "should attack everything, everything; and explode in one blaze of denunciation." Murry could see nothing for it but to treat this as a joke, whereupon Lawrence could see no alternative but for Murry to give the *Adelphi* up and go back to Mexico with him to "begin the nucleus of a new society." Lawrence's lingering belief that his own scale of values might have some practical bearing on Murry's should, one thinks, have been the real joke of the occasion for Murry, had Murry been able to regard the situation with detachment. But of course he could not, and we hardly blame him. Strange as it may seem, Lawrence was the only one detached enough to see the true irony of events.

That afternoon I was asked upstairs while Lawrence bustled about unpacking. I cannot understand Mabel Dodge Luhan's description of him at such times, or when travelling, as fussy or inefficient.[5] He always appeared to me as a model of neatness and precision, neither wasting a movement nor permitting even a temporary disorder. Perhaps as an on-looker Mrs. Luhan was upsetting. Some people are. And I have noticed that it is often the inefficient onlooker that most upsets the efficient worker.

On this occasion, while settling in, he talked with the greatest animation. And, although he was thin, I saw none of the "greenish pallor" which struck Murry. Never had I seen him more energetic. So much so that Frieda asked him didn't he think after the journey he ought to "rest for a bit"?

But he turned on her. "Rest!" he snapped. "When Frieda says England is 'so restful!' it gives me the cold shudders. I don't *want* to rest nowadays. I feel *full* of energy!" And he went on producing things for me to see—his Indian belt of plaited horse-hair, Frieda's snow-leopard skin, or a painted Mexican vase—fawn and pink and grey, with here and there a dab of light red or pale blue—all earth colours from a place where sun and earth were in close communion. He gave me one of these, after warning me that I must never put flowers in it, as even the egg-shell glaze was porous to water. But first he drew from it his sewing and first-aid kit, and unscrewing a pot of boracic he produced from the lid an engraved disk of metal—bigger than an English half-crown, and heavy and shining—a coin of Mexican gold! Somehow, as he gave it to me to handle, it was if he passed on to me the pristine magnificence of Mexico that had meant so much to him. By this he was to measure us in England and to find us wanting.

Already Frieda, who was great on making a place "homelike," had hung pictures about the walls, which Mark Gertler or Dorothy Brett, or both, had lent or given for this purpose. Enthusiastically she drew his attention to them. Lawrence inspected them coolly. "They want thinking about, I guess!" was his comment, uttered in that precise Nottingham speech of his that somehow agreed so well with his emphatic phrases; and Frieda subsided.

At the time I did what I wish I had done oftener. I noted down imme-

diately what I could remember of Lawrence's conversation that first afternoon during his "getting straight," as it ran on largely in the form of a
monologue. I put it down now as it stands in my note.

"The spirits of everybody on board the boat just went right down into
their boots when we first sighted the coast of Europe, at Corunna. . . .
The English are no longer flowering . . . we are the seed . . . we should
be scattered. We are the best-bred people on earth. But now we are caged
and fearful."

I asked him if he would rather have New York or London? "New York,"
he replied, without hesitating. "London as a city—yes, I like it better,
love it more. But it is locked away, out of touch. With New York one is
in touch with the free outer world, and with the world of Mexico." Of
Mexico he spoke much, with loathing of many things about it, but saying
that it had spoiled him, he feared, for Europe. "Sicily?" he said. "Never
again!"

While he talked, he left all the letters that had collected for him in
London unopened—did not even glance at them. He had liked it in Mexico, he said, that there had been no mail for him and no English newspapers. He described with delight how on the voyage home he had hung
over the bows, watching a school of porpoises playing about the steamer
in the translucent water. Then later the rain on the surface of black water
. . . and the beauty of the flying fish. Then the shaking of the little English train—"so light, so light, as if it would fall to pieces long before we
reached London."

Between Southampton and London he had been oppressed by the
hedged fields—"I feel I am a mouse—a net put over me—the network of
the English hedged fields."

Then suddenly, "What do you think of the world these days?" he asked
me.

I told him, what indeed I have always felt, that the world never seemed
to come within my orbit. And that I was kept so busy endeavouring to
keep a roof over our heads and food on our table that I never had much
time to think about the world.

At this he laughed with a kind of mingled pleasure and disgust that it
was so with me. It became a convention between us that I was attached
to a little ship, which for me to leave would be infidelity. "And how is the
ship sailing?" he would ask, with a touch of mockery that I liked while I
felt it was justified. Or again "More bric-à-brac!" he would exclaim re-
proachfully, when I showed him some odd object newly-acquired for the
house. I pointed out that he himself found it hard to resist bric-à-brac,

though he might not call it so. What about the snow-leopard skin, and the Navajo rings he had been describing to me? And he shook his head laughing. All the same, he was in the right and I knew it, and he knew that I knew, though I fear he thought me incorrigible. He had ceased to collect things, and I had not.

It may have been Dorothy Brett—who now became as constant a visitor as Murry to the Lawrences' rooms—who introduced the craze for modelling small figures and beasts and flowers, which seized upon us that Christmas, and upon Lawrence in particular. He and Dorothy Brett were by far the best at it. Murry worked hard, but without conspicuous success, making all the while little jokes at his own expense. Frieda and Donald and Koteliansky stood resolutely aside as spectators, when they troubled to look at us at all. To a richly herbaceous garden of Eden, which owed its very red Adam to Lawrence and its paler Eve to Dorothy Brett, I remember I contributed several species of wild-fowl, including a kiwi.

Again I recollect seeing Lawrence sitting by the table, his head on his hand, reading with astonishing intentness (which made the activity seem so much more than mere reading) Conrad's then latest novel, *The Rover*. Without once relaxing his concentrated attention he read it all through, then closed it and pushed it from him with the ejaculation that it was "poor and sad stuff." Conrad at his best in a sea-story, I gathered, he had never regarded as the equal of Herman Melville. As compared with the true sea literature of *Moby Dick*, Lawrence dismissed the storm in *Typhoon* as descriptive journalism. Still, *Almayer's Folly* was a fine book, and it was depressing to find the author of that declining into the author of *The Rover*.

It was at this time that I heard Lawrence take Murry to task in his role of propagandist of Katherine Mansfield. As I came in only for the end of the conversation I cannot tell what went before. The guess might be hazarded that Lawrence had not shrunk from denouncing the whole policy and atmosphere of the *Adelphi* in this particular matter, which I know he had found repugnant. On the other hand, it would be more characteristic if he let that be, and plunged straight to the quick of the subject. This was what he was doing when I entered. "You are wrong about Katherine," he was saying to Murry. "She was *not* a great genius. She had a charming gift, and a finely cultivated one. But *not more*. And to try, as you do, to make it more is to do her no true service." To this Murry made no reply, but turned away in a kind of obstinate mortification. Long before this, when I read her *Prelude* and praised it to Lawrence, he had said, "Yes, yes, but prelude to what?" It was his opinion that the author of *Prelude* would come in time to find a certain essential falseness so closely entwined with the charm in her literary fabric that she would herself condemn even the charm and would write nothing further until she had disentangled herself from the falseness.

.   .   .   .

For a day or two Lawrence had to stay in bed with cold and a mild attack of malaria. He sent a message by Frieda that he wanted to speak to me. "I assure you that it is a gr-reat Kompliment!" she said, opening her smiling eyes at me.

What she said was true, and I was flattered. I went upstairs at once. Still I did not really want to talk alone with Lawrence just then, a disinclination I tried to attribute to the fact that Frieda had come in upon me at a busy moment of some domestic sort.

A single bed had been moved into the living-room, and there was Lawrence sitting up all neat and trim and looking every bit as alert as if he were well. I sat down, feeling distrait and uttering platitudes.

He asked me about things. Without, so far as I can remember, putting the question directly, he asked if there was any chance of my coming then or later to New Mexico. I said I was afraid it must be later. "You see, Lawrence, unless a woman is going to leave her husband and child, she can't go off without them, and I don't think Donald feels like going, anyhow not just now. I'd come, but I can't go without them. It would be no good." A terrible sadness descended on me and I should like to have left the room. Lawrence quietly admitted the difficulty. "No, a woman can't choose if she's really married," he said. And although he had told me more than once that Donald was only a lover, not a husband, he let this pass to-day. And I knew he was only sounding me. He spoke of how free Dorothy Brett was—"a real odd man out," he called her with approval. Then he asked if I was writing anything special. "I could beat you that you don't write," he said. And why was I pottering about with rubbishy articles for women's papers when I ought to be doing a book either of notes like my Duse note in the *Adelphi* [6]—a book to be called *A Woman looks at the World*—or stories and sketches about the queer lot of people who were sheltering under the roof that covered us? There were at that moment five separate lots of us living in the old rambling house, and to amuse him I had sometimes retailed the gossip concerning them. I could see that he was casting about for the best way to help me, feeling somehow that I needed help.

Partly to fend off anything like a silence, which I could not have borne, I told him of a novel I had in mind to write. The theme had been suggested to me by reading of some savages who took a baby girl, and that they might rear her into a goddess for themselves, brought her up on a covered river boat, tending her in all respects, but never letting her mix with her kind, and leading her to believe that she was herself no mortal, but a goddess.

I was almost taken aback by Lawrence's interest. He was never effusive, and seldom enough really engaged by what one said, but when he was engaged one knew it. I was not to guess, of course, at that time anything about the contents of *The Plumed Serpent,* or I should have understood his special interest in an allied theme. He would have gone on talking now, but I excused myself and went back to my paltry duty below stairs. As I went, I knew that in some essential I had turned away from what I most wanted in life.

It seemed quite a short time after my return downstairs that Lawrence sent Frieda again to fetch me. "I like that story of yours so much, Catherine," he said, "that I've written out a little sketch of how I think it might go.[7] Then, if you like the idea, we might collaborate in the novel. You do the beginning and get the woman character going, and let me have it, and I'll go on and fill in the man. Of course," he added, "you may not see it the same way, but I think this would be the *easiest* way to do it, easier than the way you thought of. Our only trouble will be the end. I'm afraid it can't be a happy ending. But have a look and we'll see."

. . . I began to work upon the beginning in quite the wrong way. Then I saw I was not up to it and lost heart. So it remains as it was . . . .[8]

14 December 1923   *110, Heath St., Hampstead, London, N.W. 3*

❲ *Here I am back again. Frieda is nice but England is ugly. I am like a wild beast in a cage—it is so dark and closed-in here and you can't breathe freely. But the people are friendly. Frieda has a nice apartment but I go about like an imprisoned coyote—can't rest.*

I think we'll go to Paris at the end of the month and then Baden.

Do you hear me howl? [9]

110 Heath St   Hampstead.   N.W. 3/17 Dec [1923]

❲ *Dear Idella [Purnell Stone]*

Here I am—in bed with a bad cold—hate it. Just hate it all. It's like being in the tomb. I expect to go to Paris in a fortnight—then to [Rome crossed out] Spain—& by March back to the American continent. Meanwhile it's dark, damp, dead, & sickly here. *F.* is well—& says she's prepared to come west. I swear at her for having brought me here.

I thought to have had a line from you. Did your father get back safe & sound & soon. And is all quiet in Guadalajara?

Let me know.

D. H. Lawrence [10]

Barbara Weekley Barr

In the winter of 1923–1924, Elsa and I met Lawrence again. It may have been Catherine Carswell who had something to do with it, because her house in Hampstead was the meeting place. Middleton Murry was there that evening as well.

My childhood feeling about Lawrence had been that he was a fairly ordinary young man. This encounter gave me a very different impression altogether. I had not seen anyone like him before; nor have I since. He was tall and fragile—a queer, unearthly creature. He had a high-pitched voice, a slight Midlands accent, and a mocking, but spirited and brilliant manner. I liked his eyes. They were blue, wide apart, in cave-like sockets, under a fine brow. But they could be soft, and were kindly in the extreme. He had high cheekbones, a clubby "Midland" nose, and a well-shaped jaw. His skin and hair were fair, and his beard red. When he was excited, or looking well, his cheeks had a delicate colour. He seemed beyond being human and ordinary, and I felt at once that he was more like an element —say a rock or rushing water. Lawrence talked to Elsa and me with great friendliness. Secretly I much preferred Middleton Murry, who sat near, dark, smiling and inscrutable, but more like the other men we had known.

Lawrence had just come back from America. "Why is everyone over here so kind and loving?" he enquired derisively. "If I get the porter to carry my bag, he wants to love me as well! I don't like it." I thought Lawrence a queer fish.

In Hollywood, he told us, a friend had taken him to the house of a famous British film star. This man had made a typical entry into the gorgeous lounge, dressed in a sort of polo outfit, accompanied by baying dogs. In a few minutes the wife appeared, prettily leading their two children. All three were groomed to perfection. Lawrence thought the actor a buffoon.[11] Hollywood he described as a huge lunatic asylum.

Frieda was lighthearted that evening, Murry a little embarrassed, and

Lawrence very friendly. But Elsa and I did not know what to make of him. He talked to me about my art school, but was highly critical of it— and of me. Shortly afterwards, he remarked to Elsa, "Barby is not the stuff of which artists are made."

In February 1924, when he and Frieda went to visit her mother in Germany, Lawrence said of us to our grandmother:

"They are just little suburban nobodies." [12]

Catherine Carswell

If I could help it, I would never intrude upon Lawrence when Murry was there—and Murry frequently was there—because I could not bear the underlying sense of strain and dissatisfaction. Frieda was torn between her recent friendliness with Murry and Lawrence's belief that England held nothing for him any more in spite of all the *Adelphis* that were or ever could be. Lawrence, waiting in vain week after week for some reply to the letters and cables which he was sending to his New York publisher [Thomas Seltzer], had begun to be anxious about money.[13] Where was the use of his books going well in the States if he received nothing for them? "It was a painful time," says Murry.[14] So it was.

Of the "painful things that happened in it" I was certainly witness to one. But on that occasion the special painfulness was created by Murry. Possibly from a conscious desire that Lawrence should be spared, he has not told the story in his *Reminiscences*.[15] It has since been given, however, from hearsay and with the most circumstantial inaccuracy by Mrs. Luhan.[16] As the incident concerned neither Lawrence nor Murry alone, but inclusively nine of us, it seems imperative that it should be given here correctly to the best of my remembrance.

During this visit of Lawrence to London he was determined to make at least one attempt at friendly gaiety—a sort of "Well, well, now that we are here don't let's be too gloomy even if we have made a mistake" gesture on his part. He went with Koteliansky to the Café Royal, engaged a private room there and ordered a supper. (For which, to Lawrence's annoyance, the manager insisted upon having a deposit, and refused to take a cheque.) When Frieda first told me that they were giving a party in a restaurant, I took it merely as an announcement, not as an invitation. I knew that Lawrence had a considerable acquaintance in London, and it struck me as natural that we, living in the same house and seeing each other constantly, were not to be among the guests. But when I said I hoped they would have a good evening, Frieda shouted in amazement:

"But you and Don are coming! You are *invited!* It is a dinner for Lawrence's friends!"

Only then did I recognize my half-unconscious withdrawal on the first reception of the news, as a too willing abnegation. From the first I had felt a slight sinking of the heart at the notion of this supper, so far as I might have any part in it. And it was this that made me utter a feeble and ill-mannered protest even thus late. "Are you quite sure that you want us?" I asked. "There are so many people you must want to see and we can eat together any night." "No, no," sang Frieda, quite shocked and hurt, I could see. "This is for Lawrence's real friends. Are you not his real friends?" So it was settled. It was just the presence of some of those other "real friends" that was saddening to me in the prospect. But we had to enter into the spirit of the thing, and attend with goodwill this, the one and only formal gathering I have ever known Lawrence to initiate.

Soon enough we knew who the others were to be—Koteliansky, Murry and Mark Gertler for the men; Mary Cannan and Dorothy Brett for the women. The round table was attractively laid and the room intimate. Lawrence made a charming host—easy, simple and warm. There was something at once piquant and touching in seeing him receiving us, his friends, thus in surroundings so unlike those in which we had been accustomed to forgather with him these ten years past. It emphasized the lack of sophistication in him which, combined with his subtlety, was so moving a charm. "Schoolboyish" is perhaps the last adjective that could justly be applied to this mature and refined, this disciplined and impassioned artist, that was D. H. Lawrence at the age of thirty-nine. But at any moment, surroundings like the Café Royal, or the rooms of some fine old house not in the cottage style, would bring out in Lawrence a boyishness that was as comic as it was lovable. "You'll see I'm quite up to this," he seemed to be saying. "Mind you play up to me, so that nobody will have the slightest idea that we don't dine in marble halls all the year round." It is never a thing to underline, but it *is* a thing to be remembered, that Lawrence was the son of a miner and spent his youth in a miners' row— no matter with how superior a mother or how sensitive a group of brothers and sisters. For him, for instance, to visit at a house like Garsington Manor,[17] was a genuine experience. He coped with it admirably and he knew just what estimation to put upon it, both as an experience and as a phenomenon. He could add up the life behind it and "see through" the persons belonging to it, without being in any way dazzled or shaken. Even the utmost of kindly patronage could not keep him from the eventual expression of his summing up. More even than Robert Burns in his adventures with the rich and the famous, Lawrence was the "chiel amang them takin' notes." [18] Yet he never became sophisticated enough not to be superficially over-impressed at the first impact with personages like the Meynell family or Bertrand Russell or Lady Ottoline Morrell. With them this most un-schoolboyish man betrayed a kind of quiet school-boy knowingness that is not unrelated to nervousness. And the reaction from his impressibility (as in the case of Robert Burns) was apt to be violent. People gave themselves away to Lawrence in an extraordinary degree. And as often as not, their "giving away" was a subtle form of patronage, a fact that was by no means lost on the observer and writer of fiction who lurked with cool eyes behind the poet in Lawrence. It was naturally a shock when, out of what had seemed a pleasant friendship, there should spring such prodigies, at once fantastic and recognizable, as figure in certain of his novels and tales. True, he did this with any or all of us. But one cannot escape from the touch of malice in certain instances, nor from the belief that it is there as a make-weight for the special sensibility of a man whose genius has lifted him out of his class.

To return to the Café Royal. Frieda, as our hostess, purred loudly and pleasantly. Cafés Royal or Tudor houses were not even child's play to her! She wore, greatly to Lawrence's approval, something that was both gleaming and flower-like—anyhow petal-like, as she delightedly pointed out. I forget how Dorothy Brett was dressed, except that what she wore seemed tame beside Frieda's gaiety. Mary in *décolletée* black, with a large picture hat, *à la* Mrs. Siddons, looked like the heroine from a forgotten novel by John Oliver Hobbes.[19] I, too, was in black—velvet to Mary's silk. The men wore their everyday clothes. Kot, in his dark clothes as ever, looked both the most conventional and the strangest.

The food was excellent, but somehow the feast did not go well. Gertler was silent and looked watchful, even contemptuous. Kot conceived a murderous dislike for Donald, next to whom he was placed. Mary had nothing to say. I too was stricken with dumbness. Lawrence did his best to enliven us all with wine, bidding us to drink our fill and rejoice in a festive occasion. He set us a good example and drank level. There was *no* champagne. We drank claret. And never before, nor since, have I swallowed so many glasses and remained so heavily sober. With the coming of the dessert a mistake was made. What was the wine to be? asked Lawrence. Murry and Donald both said port. They had forgotten, or had not known, that port was a drink Lawrence could not well tolerate. He immediately hinted very gently that port was not his drink, but his remark was either missed or good-naturedly overruled. "Port is a man's drink," I remember either Murry or Donald announcing in solemn tones. So port it was. And Lawrence drank it with the rest of us.

It had the effect of loosening at least some of the mute tongues about the table, though none of us women was perceptibly elevated. Lawrence began to talk in Spanish (which he had learned in Mexico). Donald, who prided himself on knowing a bit of Spanish (enough to read *Don Quixote* and to reply to simple questions) endeavoured to engage in Spanish conversation with Lawrence. This, for some reason, infuriated Kot to such a degree that he looked like taking the unwary Donald's life had not Murry tactfully placed somebody between them. Kot's idea seemed to be that the Spanish language was Lawrence's special perquisite. Gertler drank, or refrained from drinking, in silence, looking on, always looking on from a cold afar. Both he and Mary Cannan left early.

But not before this strange incident. It began with a speech by Kot in praise and love of Lawrence, the speech being punctuated by his deliberate smashing of a wine-glass at the close of each period. As—"Lawrence is a great man." (Bang! down came Kot's strong fist enclosing the stem of a glass, so that its bottom came in shivering contact with the table.) "Nobody here realizes how great he is." (Crash! another good wine-glass gone.) "Especially no woman here or anywhere can possibly realize the greatness of Lawrence." (Smash and tinkle!) "Frieda does not count. Frieda is different. I understand and don't include her. But no other woman here or anywhere can understand anything about Lawrence or what kind of being he is."

We women were silent. We felt, I think, very sympathetic to Kot. Anyhow I did. Sympathetic to his jealous, dark and overpowering affection—even inclined to agree with what he said.

Lawrence looked pale and frightfully ill, but his eyes were starry to an extraordinary degree. It occurred to me then—and I have since had no reason to change my reading, which was revealed as by the appearance of clear writing on the wall—that the deep hold of the Last Supper on the imagination of the world is not unconnected with the mystery of Bacchus. Given a man of genius; more especially given a man whose genius runs to expression by means of symbol, his essential utterance may well be achieved only when his genius is acted upon at a crisis by the magic of the fermented grape.

Anyhow, Lawrence who, like the others present, was habitually temperate, revealed that night at the Café Royal his deepest desire to all of us simply and unforgettably. And in doing so he brought about some other revelations, as will be seen.

Without making anything approaching a speech, he caught our attention by the quiet urgency of his request. What he said, in effect, was that we were his friends here, each and all of us people he had been very fond of. He could not stay in England. He must go back to New Mexico. Would we, would any of us, go with him? He asked each of us in turn. Would we go with him? Implicit in this question was the other. Did the search, the adventure, the pilgrimage for which he stood, mean enough to us for us to give up our own way of life and our own separate struggle with the world? Though his way of life must involve also a struggle with the world, this was not—as we well knew, its main objective. Rather was it a withdrawal of one's essential being from that struggle, and a turning of what strength one had into a new channel.

Essentially the appeal was not a personal one. Though it was to his friends, it was not for his sake or the sake of friendship that he made it. It was because of something in himself which we all acknowledged. But it had never before become so near being a personal appeal. It certainly had a personal element that told of his overwhelming loneliness. It was far less "follow me" than "come with me." It was even—to my thinking at least—"come for a time, and support me by your presence, as the undertaking is too much for me alone, yet I must not stay here with you." I give my own reading, but I think something very like it was in the minds of all the others.

Remember we had just supped, and our glasses had been replenished with port, and, as I have said, we were all normally very abstemious people.

Mary Cannan was the only one to return a flat negative to Lawrence's question. It was as plump and plain as she herself was slender and pretty. "No," said she hardily. "I like you, Lawrence, but not so much as all that, and I think you are asking what no human being has a right to ask of another."

Lawrence accepted this without cavil or offence. It was a clear, hard, honest answer.

What Gertler said, I can't remember. I rather think it was a humouring but dry affirmative, which we all understood to mean nothing. Kot and Donald both said they would go, less drily, but so that any listener guessed they were speaking from goodwill rather than from deep intention. Dorothy Brett said quietly that she would go, and I, knowing that she would, envied her. Murry promised emotionally that he would, and one felt that he wouldn't. I said yes, I would go. And I meant it, though I didn't see how on earth it could be, anyhow for a long time. Unlike Mary and Dorothy Brett I had neither money of my own nor freedom from responsibility. Dorothy Brett, who loved to serve, was always coming to a loose end. I, who did not particularly like serving, was always having fresh responsibilities put upon me by life. Mary, disappointed with her "freedom," had yet got used to its little self-indulgences and could not give them up. All the same I felt that Lawrence had somehow the right to ask me to go. And I feel to-day equally the impossibility of my going and the wish that I had gone.

As for the supper, what I next remember is Murry going up to Lawrence and kissing him with a kind of effusiveness which afflicted me. He must have been sensible to my feeling, because he turned to me.

"Women can't understand this," he said. "This is an affair between men. Women can have no part or place in it."

"Maybe," said I. "But anyhow it wasn't a woman who betrayed Jesus with a kiss."

At this Murry again embraced Lawrence, who sat perfectly still and unresponsive, with a dead-white face in which the eyes alone were alive.

"I *have* betrayed you, old chap, I confess it," continued Murry. "In the past I *have* betrayed you. But never again. I call you all to witness, never again."

Throughout all this Frieda remained aloof and scornful—excluded. Her innings would be later. She reminded me of King David's wife looking down in derision from an upper window. One could not but admire her.

It must have been almost immediately after the strange episode with Murry, that Lawrence, without uttering a sound, fell forward with his head on the table, was deadly sick, and became at once unconscious. The combination of the port (which, when he had said he could not abide, he said truly) and the cruel loneliness which was brought home to him by the responses he had elicited from us, his friends, was too much for him.

In his sickness Lawrence was more like a child than a man. There was nothing disgusting about him. Frieda however, remained stonily detached, while Dorothy Brett and I ministered to him as best we could—she especially, who did not want me to help.

It must have been now that Mary and Gertler left us. What with the glasses broken by Kot, and Lawrence's sickness, I was sorry for the waiters who would have to clear up. But they behaved as if they had noticed nothing out of the way. Donald, as the soberest man, was handed money to pay for the wine and the damage. The bill, he tells me, struck him as wonderfully moderate.

We left in two taxi-cabs, Lawrence being still unconscious so that it was difficult getting him down in the lift. But Kot, even in liquor, was powerful. I recall that his legs seemed to fill the cab in which I was. I had been given all the hats of the party to hold, and I lost my own—a little real Russian cap of black astrakhan, which I liked better than any head covering I ever had, though I gave only three shillings for it in an antique shop, and it had a bullet-hole through it.

Arrived at Hampstead the problem was how to get Lawrence up to the first floor. Kot and Murry had to carry him. But in their enthusiasm they went on with their burden, up and up, till my brother, asleep on the top story, was awakened by the trampling, stumbling sound, and ran out in alarm to the little landing. He told me afterwards that when he saw clearly before him St. John and St. Peter (or maybe St. Thomas) bearing between them the limp figure of their Master, he could hardly believe he was not dreaming. However, he conducted the party downstairs again.

Next morning soon after breakfast—certainly not later than 9.30 A.M. —I was passing the open door of the Lawrences' sitting-room, when Lawrence hailed me and bade me enter. He was fresh and serene. "Well, Catherine," he said, "I made a fool of myself last night. We must all of us fall at times. It does no harm so long as we first admit and then forget it."

At such times he was an overwhelmingly attractive human being. That light and easy, yet not flippant manner of his for dealing with such an incident, bespoke an underlying steadiness that begot trust in the on-looker and was—it seems to me—incompatible with any neurotic condition. Although the fullness of his admissions, and the sensitiveness of his abandon to the impulses of life might give to the superficial observer the impression that he was a sufferer from a neurosis, Lawrence was emphatically no neurotic. Of this I am convinced. If I add that he hated neurotics, even while he had the misfortune to find in them more immediately than in others a kind of response which sprang from superficial understanding, I suppose I shall call forth the gibe of the analyst—"Thou sayest it!" "The real neurotic is half a devil," said Lawrence, "the cured one" with his "perfect automatic control," is "a perfect devil." [20] And again, "Spit on every neurotic and wipe your feet on his face if he tries to drag you down." [21] Yet I know that what I say is true. Lawrence hated, he feared, he fought and he was obliged to consort with neurotics. But he was himself untainted.

When I told him that I had lost my astrakhan cap he insisted on giving me two pounds to buy myself a hat. Unfortunately he did not like the one I bought, though he was too kind to say so. He liked a hat to be a hat, and to have a proper brim. This small black felt was brimless. He gave it a single glance and looked away. "Quite saucy!" he said. I felt crushed.[22]

John Middleton Murry

. . . [Mrs. Carswell's] nominal excuse for giving to the public an untrue account of the dinner at the Café Royal is that an account of it "has previously been given . . . with the utmost inaccuracy by Mabel Dodge Sterne." Previous to that, however, I had myself made a guarded reference to it in *Son of Woman*. At the end of that book, speaking to Lawrence, I wrote:

This understanding, so far as I am capable of it, I have given you in this book. In life you asked something of me which was not in my power to give, nor in your power to take. I did not know what it was you asked of me, neither did you know. I remember how, one night, when you had returned to England, after all the pain of separation and the torment of love that had turned to hatred, you became to me once more the wonderful Man: superhuman by the anguish and excess of your humanity. Suddenly, you put your arm about my neck, for the first and last time, and said "Do not betray me!" I did not understand, but I never forgot. The words, and the suffering in the words have never ceased to echo in my soul.[23]

Whether I did right or wrong in making this reference, it was made; and it was *true*. If Mrs. Carswell could succeed in suggesting that I had deliberately falsified the happening, it would tell heavily indeed against me. She did her utmost. She professed to give an accurate account of the dinner. (It seems to me an abominable violation; yet I admit that, if I had been guilty of the abominable offence she imputes to me, her violation would have been justified. I must be unmasked, at all costs.) But Mrs. Carswell committed her abominable violation not to tell the truth, but for a different purpose. First, she suppressed Lawrence's words to me. Since she may not herself have heard them, I do not charge her with deliberate suppression, though to omit them in silence when I had said they were uttered was grave. But then she went on, most circumstantially, to say that I spoke these words to Lawrence:

"I *have* betrayed you, old chap, I confess it. In the past I *have* betrayed you. But never again. I call you all to witness, never again." [24]

There is no mistake. "I call you all to witness." It is so arranged that it seems to bear the evidence of its truth on its face. No one could possibly believe that Mrs. Carswell was mistaken; no one could possibly dream that Mrs. Carswell was romancing.

Yet she was. I remembered well what I said; Lawrence remembered well. And, it so happens that, a year later, in an angry letter to me, dated 28th January 1925, he wrote these words:

> You remember that charming dinner at the Café Royal that night? You remember saying: "I love you, Lorenzo, but I won't promise not to betray you"? Well, you can't betray me, and that's all there is to that. . . . All I want to say is, Don't think you can either love me or betray me. Learn that I am not lovable: hence not betrayable.[25]

These are the words I actually spoke. Above are the words Mrs. Carswell invented for me. And there is Mrs. Carswell.[26]

The Hon. Dorothy Brett

. . . Katherine Mansfield is dead; I am living in a small, old, Queen Anne house in Hampstead; and just before Christmas you [27] come.

.   .   .

Frieda has come over about six weeks before you and is staying with Kotiliansky, in Acacio [Acacia] Road. Handsome, blonde, light-eyed, a massive German. I see a good deal of her—a great deal when she moves into a flat in Hampstead. Will you come, or won't you? is the urgent question amongst us all. Even Frieda herself does not know. It may be a parting or it may not, she hints. You are in Old Mexico; then suddenly you have taken a ship, a slow ship, from Vera Cruz. You are coming. We are all tense with excitement. You come. I am not allowed to meet you at the station. I see and hear nothing for a couple of days, until you 'phone me that I am invited to the dinner that is being given you at the Cafe Royale.

.   .   .

Murry is living in the house next door to me. He has a small room at the top of Boris Anrep's [28] house, but he has his meals with me. Katherine's rooms are just as she left them, but Murry can never bring himself to use them much. He and I start for the Cafe Royale. A private room has been engaged, an ornate, over-gilded, red-plushed room. Kotiliansky,

Gertler and Mrs. Gilbert Cannan are grouped round the fire with Catherine Carswell and her husband, Don. Kotiliansky happy, exuberant; Gertler cheeky and gay; Mrs. Cannan small and still lovely in evening dress with a large black picture hat. We wait, wondering whether you have got lost. A waiter suddenly flings open the door, and you are there. You step into the room, pause, and look at us all.

Slim, neat, with your overcoat folded over your arm, you stand looking at us, proudly, like a God, the Lord of us all, the light streaming down on your dark, gold hair. I turn away, strangely moved, while the others cluster round, one taking your hat, the other your coat; until, stepping out from among them, you say:

"Where is Brett? I want to meet her."

I turn round, you come quickly forward, saying: "So this is Brett."

I look up, realizing with surprise the eyes are blue, not black, as I had thought. How quick and eager and alert you are. I am to sit on your left and Mrs. Cannan on your right; next her, Kotiliansky, Don Carswell, Gertler, Catherine Carswell, Frieda, and Murry.

I put my ear machine on the table beside you; you look at it and laugh, a bit quizzically, making a few ribald remarks about the impossibility of making love into such a box. I, shy, attentive, silent, while you begin in your delicate, sensitive way to woo me. To what remark of mine do you reply, elfishly, mischievously, "Ah, no, Brett, I am not a man . . . I am MAN." And again and again: "Will you come to Taormina with me, Brett; will you come? Or shall it be New Mexico? . . . But will you come or would you be afraid?" And I, overwhelmed, terribly aware of you, evading, dodging, murmur: "I will go anywhere with you."

"Would you be afraid to come to Taormina with me?"

"No. I would not be afraid," comes my shy, nervous answer.

So around the table and around us goes the drink and laughter and talk. You make a speech, inviting all of us to go with you, to make a new life. Murry kisses you, fervently; Kotiliansky makes a return speech; the glasses are flung over our shoulders, splintering on the floor.

Then, in the midst of it all, the wine gets the better of you, and you lean forward, dazed, and start vomiting, in the midst of a silent consternation. I take hold of your hand and hold it, with the other I stroke your hair, that heavy, dark, gold hair, brushing it back from your hot forehead. You are speechless, dazed, helpless, after you stop vomiting. Kotiliansky and Murry carry you downstairs, into a taxi, and up the narrow stairs to your rooms at the top of Catherine Carswell's house in Hampstead. For several days you are sick in bed. I come to see you. You are sitting up in bed in a red knitted shawl, looking very pale and ill and hurt. . . . You never spoke of it, nor we, and I never knew it happen to you again.

. . .

How often do you come running down to my little house in Pond Street? I don't know. You hate that house, you hate my furniture, you hate the whole thing, but you come, nevertheless. We sit opposite each other, making flowers in clay and painting them; and you talk to me in that soft, midland voice, probing delicately into my life and ideas and feelings, sensitive to my sensitiveness; and I evade shyly, you laughing at my adroitness. And thus we sit, happily, sometimes quite silently, intensely aware of each other, modelling and painting pots of flowers.

. . .

One coldish day you climb the steep narrow stairs to my studio and sit in the chair Katherine sat in whenever she had the strength to climb those stairs. How scared I am when I show you my canvases. You are serious, interested, forceful. You ask me in that clear, quick, almost military abruptness, what I am trying to do in painting. You look at them, and in your masterful way you exclaim:

"They are dead, like all the paintings now; there is no life in them. They are dead, dead! All these still-lives—no life in the painting."

I feel the power in you, then; the pent-up, stormy power. Murry comes in as I am explaining to you what I feel about light, "double lighting" I call it. Murry asks, "But what does she mean?" And you, impatient, replying, "I know what she means." Then to me: "Go on." Later your resentment that a woman should bother about art, your anger that the painters of to-day never faced life itself; and I, a bit crushed, yet obstinate, long to talk it out; but Murry takes you away, which probably is safer for me.

. . .

I am talking, in my sitting room, to a possible portrait client. The bell rings. I go to the front door and you are standing outside, looking with astonishment at the large Rolls Royce parked outside my door. May you come in? Of course. And in you come to find a lovely, though slightly faded woman sitting on my sofa. I introduce you to her by her married name, which means nothing to you as yours means nothing to her. She is talking about the portrait of myself, hanging above the sofa, and asks your opinion of it. Your laughing jeer fades away at my warning look, you bite your beard and say quickly: "Oh, nice, quite nice; a very good likeness." And she clinches the bargain with me, for which she has come —an order to paint her mother, to enable me to go to New Mexico.

You sit beside her on the sofa, and she, struck by your appearance— the beard, the rough hair, your midland accent—begins to question. "Where do you come from?" Smiling, you reply, "The North Country, the Midlands." She cannot make you out and you tell her that you write a bit. She is mystified and you are chuckling. After she leaves, I tell you that it is Edna May, the famous Belle of New York; [29] and how delighted and amused you are at finding you had spent the afternoon with so famous an actress. And how disappointed that I had not told you at the time.

I have a kind of soiree one evening a week, Thursday, to which a chosen few come: Murry, Kotiliansky, Gertler, and J. W. N. Sullivan [30] are the mainstay of it. A few other men add themselves to it later, and to these Thursdays no women are allowed, unless especially invited by the group. Frieda has not been invited; but when you came you are both invited and, after some hesitation, you both come. I think your curiosity brought you. We simply sit over the fire talking and drink tea—at least the men talk, and I try to listen in on my machine. To this gathering you come, and we sit around listening to your descriptions of New Mexico, the Mex- icans and Indians. You get up and show us the curious tread of the In- dian dance step, treading it slowly in a circle round the room, humming the Sun Dance song. Kot is angry, saying you belong to England, that you should live in England, that it is your right place; and you laugh, a tinge of bitterness in it, refusing to be held anywhere. Asking bitterly what has England ever done for you. Richard, Murry's young brother, says that if you would remain in England, he and many young men would follow you, that they need a leader. You jeer and reply that the young men do not want a leader; you know, only too well, what kind of a mess that leads to, and you wouldn't sacrifice your life for anything like that —oh, no, not for that. "If the young men or anyone wants to follow me, let them. It's up to them. Let the dead bury their dead and the living follow me." [31]

19 December 1923   *110, Heath St., Hampstead, London, N.W. 3*

⟨ *We seriously think of New Mexico in early spring: and Middleton Murry wants to come along—also, probably, Dorothy Brett, who paints, is deaf, forty, very nice, and daughter of Viscount Esher.*

I'm longing to get out of England.[32]

The Hon. Dorothy Brett

Christmas Day. The dinner I am giving in my house, the party as usual: Gertler, Kot., Murry and his brother, Frieda and you. You want a goose, having eaten too many turkeys in New Mexico, so I buy the fattest goose I can find. You come down early in the evening and we light the kitchen fire. Kot comes early, too. And while the oven is heating, you fix the goose, stuff it with sage and onions, lay strips of bacon on its chest, and into the oven it goes. I watch you kneeling down with your ear to the oven door.

"Is it cooking?" I ask.

"Yes, I can hear it sizzling," you reply.

Frieda fixes the vegetables. Kot makes a strange Russian mixture of sardines and mustard, pepper and God knows what into a paste. Murry and I lay the table. We have two plum puddings, one from your sister, which is pale and no use, and one from my mother, that we heat up. In that tiny, semi-basement dining room, with only just room for our chairs between the wall and the table, we feast and drink cautiously of light wine.

Later, upstairs, we sing. How fond you are of singing. Frieda in a clear, high soprano; but you, with almost no voice at all, lead the songs. Old English songs, Scotch Ballades, old music-hall favorites . . . broken by intervals of talk, with Murry and Kot urging you again and again to stay in England; you, impatient, irritable, breaking into song again. And thus we sing far into the night. You sing many Spanish songs, coming over to sit close by me, on a little stool, to sing the songs to me, softly, so that I can hear them better down my machine. In a soft, lilting way, you sing that Spanish street song, very softly, almost under your breath, while we come crashing in with the chorus: "Aie, Aie, Aie!"

The flickering firelight, the warm glow of the singing in all of us, and you, sitting by me, singing softly and ever more softly that old Spanish song, half whispered, half sung. . . .

All through those grey days in London, you longed for New Mexico. And then the moving picture of "The Covered Wagon" came to the Strand; so we must all of us go; and Kot, Gertler, Murry and I meet you there one afternoon. I am sitting next you in that long, dark movie house. You are tense with excitement, and we are all infected by your love for the West. You snort at the smart cowboy, in his white shirt, white pants, black cowboy boots and big white Stetson. He irritates you, and you feel sure he has never sat on a horse. The house darkens again, and then a spotlight falls onto the stage; seven real Red Indians are supposed to walk on before the movie begins.

"Will they be real?" I ask you. And you say,

"Wait. I'll know when they walk; they move differently from us."

A man, wrapped in a blanket, with his hair in a nob at the back of his head, walks on. I look at you quickly. "Yes," you whisper, "he is real," and you suddenly sigh, heavily, as if the sight of him makes you homesick for New Mexico. You seem to be greeting old friends, far off across that long, dark movie house.

The light fades down and the Covered Wagon begins. You are watching it, as if you were part of it yourself. "How like it is, how like it is," you keep on saying; and you hum very softly to me the song that is the keynote to the story: "Oh, oh, Susanna, don't you sigh for me, for I'm waiting here in Oregon with my banjo on my knee."

Years later, I writing to you in Italy, from your little ranch, use the old song: "Oh, oh, Lorenzo, don't you sigh for me, for I'm waiting here in Kiowa with your Timsy on my knee." And now Timsy, the cat, is dead, too.

.   .   .

The excitement, and at the same time the irritation, of London begins to make you restless: London irritates you, we irritate you. You tell me: "I have offered to stay four months in London and edit the Adelphi, but they won't let me. They say I want to destroy it and are furious." You smile grimly, adding ironically, "They are afraid of me."

Murry takes us to dinner with Gertrude Millin and her husband, at some hotel. We have dinner at a round table in their sitting room. I sit next the husband, while Gertrude Millin, sitting next to you, describes trekking with oxen across the veldt. It sounds beautiful and fascinating as she tells of the slow oxen, the warm, starlit nights, the wagons creeping along with their long line of oxen, the cracking of the whips; and you are beginning to yearn for it. You look at Frieda and say, "Shall we try?" Frieda seems doubtful, and you are hesitant. "Some day," you say, "Oh, yes, some day I will go to Africa with you and drive across the veldt"; and you ask, as well, all kinds of practical questions. After dinner the talk moves from subject to subject, finally turns to painting. You suddenly ask whether I don't think painting is finished, exploded, that nothing new can be brought to it. I say, "No, I think a lot more can be done."

Murry laughingly twits you, saying, "You didn't expect that answer, did you?" And you laugh, saying, "No, I didn't," and look at me speculatively.[33]

Sarah Gertrude Millin

[My husband and I] sailed [from South Africa] for Europe at the end of 1923.

. . . .

The first time we met Katherine Mansfield's [34] husband, John Middleton Murry, we sat silently smoking in front of a fire in his office; and then he suddenly said that only last night he had been counting up his friends and had calculated that, including his family, he had fourteen, but, if he might now add us, that would be sixteen. And as we thought him a kind and simple man, and were, by this time, accustomed to the queer but amiable ways of the English, we happily accepted his friendship. He asked us to dine, and when we arrived at his house we found him cooking the food, and he told us that, in their early days, he and Katherine Mansfield had always done their own cooking because they couldn't afford a servant.

Then he said that D. H. Lawrence was due presently from New Mexico, and asked if we would like to meet him.

. . . .

[This] is what I wrote about our visit to him:

. . .

Middleton Murry took us to D. H. Lawrence's house, where, beside Lawrence, we met Mrs. Lawrence, a stout and untidy, but quite pleasant German woman of forty-five, and a Russian Jew, Koteliansky, who translates Dostoevsky and such-like into English. They had a new picture by Mark Gertler and said he was an important painter.

We sat on a low couch and they put dried fruits and things on the floor.

Lawrence himself is a lively man of thirty-eight with an opaque white face and opaque blue eyes and a reddish beard and a shock of hair. He has an excited voice and his hands feel like an Indian's, as if the bones were too small. He wore a checked jacket, thick woollen socks, and sandals. He talked so much about the snobbery and class distinctions of the English that I was afraid he might be a bit snobbish himself. The English lived, he said, behind hedges through which they peeped at their neighbours. "It all used to mean something, but now it's only pretence." He said England stifled him: he had been back just a fortnight and was going away again in another fortnight. He hated Virginia Woolf, Rose Macaulay, Sheila Kaye-Smith and Rebecca West.

The Lawrences, Middleton Murry and Koteliansky are coming to dine with us on Sunday night. Lawrence was going to the Midlands to-day, but I said to him:

"Dine with us on Sunday instead. You can always go to the Midlands, but we are leaving for South Africa next week."

And he answered:

"Very well. I'll give up the Midlands."

I thought that very kind of him.

.   .   .

The dinner was really a failure. First Middleton Murry asked if they should wear dinner dress, and, thinking it was expected, I said yes, but it turned out to be the wrong reply. They all hated dressing. Then Middleton Murry asked if they might bring along the most charming girl in the world [Dorothy Brett]; and I was not only delighted, but immediately rang up a Dutch South African friend—rather tongue-tied, though young, good-looking and extremely high-brow—and asked if he would like to meet D. H. Lawrence, Middleton Murry, and the most charming girl in the world. He was naturally happy to do so, and arrived very early; but, to my displeasure, he had grown, since last I saw him, a moustache which didn't at all suit him, and, in order that he might create a good impression on the most charming girl, I suggested that he should shave off his moustache, and he meekly did so.

The Lawrence party arrived very late, and without Mr. Koteliansky. There had been, it appeared, a row with Mr. Koteliansky about Tolstoi, and this row had made them late, and it had prevented Mr. Koteliansky from coming at all. The men were in dinner dress, and Mrs. D. H. Lawrence wore a brown fur cap, a white Russian blouse, a black velveteen skirt, white cotton stockings and black velveteen shoes. The most charming girl (who really was pleasant) carried a little case. I tried to relieve her of her case, but she held it urgently: "I am quite deaf without this," she said, and Mr. Murry surprised me afterwards by explaining that she had become deaf through refusing to listen to the conversation of her family, who were aristocrats.

We sat down in a dining-room as empty as only, I should imagine, an hotel dining-room in London can be on a Sunday; and our tongue-tied friend (inaudible at the best of times and to the best of ears, and bewildered now by the unexpected loss of his moustache) sat next to the girl who could not hear except by means of the instrument in her case; and everyone struggled brightly; and Lawrence told at amiable length a story about a yellow-haired girl from Nottingham, a Christmas pudding and a ten-shilling piece; and after dinner we sat in a rather cold room and Middleton Murry showed us some exercises. He lay on the floor and waved his legs.

But, though we all did our best, particularly Lawrence, the evening remained a failure. I have seldom had so complete a failure.[35]

The Hon. Dorothy Brett

Why do things never go right? You are having tea in my house, to meet Dr. Young,[36] the doctor who attended Katherine when she died at Fontainebleau. Murry is keen for you to hear what he has to say about Gurdjief's Institute; but young Noel Carrington and his sister, Carrington, arrive unexpectedly, and young Noel talks and talks about India to you, asking innumerable questions. I see you getting politely bored, as nearly all people bored you who asked you questions. The conversation is turned to Dr. Young, sitting quietly, waiting his chance; but young Noel cannot be silenced. Finally the tea-party breaks up. Carrington takes you aside and begins archly to ask you about flowers. You are looking at her keenly. And I think you used her later in your story, "None of That."[37]

. . .

I believe nearly every evening we all go up to your flat after supper to sit about the fire. We move the small round table near the fire, draw up our chairs, and while talking we model flowers in plasticine—Frieda sitting just out of range of the lamp behind us, knitting or sewing. The table is littered with plasticine and tubes of oil paint, brushes and knives. You are wearing a black and white check coat that you are particularly fond of. Standing on the mantel piece in rows are some really quite lovely pots of flowers, the plasticine painted over so that the flowers look life-like. This evening we are more ambitious, we are doing, amidst shouts of laughter, an Adam and Eve. It is warm, the room in shadow, we are gathered closely round the bright light on the table. You model carefully with delicate, small touches your pale, freckled, short-fingered hands. Your beard is spotted with paint. I am making the tree and apples, you will not let me do the Adam or Eve; you refuse to believe me capable of creating either of them; you are rude and dictatorial, and Murry and I laugh and give way. But Murry insists on making the snake. At last everything is ready. You have a bowl, painted sky blue (the "inverted hemisphere" you call it) and into this we plant the Tree, Adam and Eve and the snake; the little scarlet apples twinkle brightly out of the green-leafed tree. Then we look at the plump little Eve, and you laugh a trifle selfconsciously. Then we look at Adam . . . Murry and I look at each other, then at you.

"Lawrence, you just can't leave Adam like that." You chuckle at our scandalized faces.

"Do you good, Brett," you say, tartly; but we will not allow you to leave him so indecent, so with ironical glee you snip off his indecency, and then mourn for him for his loss. Your poor, thin, indecent Adam. Then Murry produces his snake, and you wind it carefully round the stem of the tree.

"That, I think," you say, "is our chef d'oeuvre." But to me, the flowers, correct in every petal, stamen and leaf, are just as much a chef d'oeuvre. Some of these pots of flowers you present to Catherine Carswell, when we go downstairs to a queer concert on flutes that she is having among some friends. Beautiful Dolmetch flutes. I have one now, a golden boxwood flute that young Dolmetch made for me. They play fast and furiously. You are flippant, mockery gleams in your eyes as you sit on the sofa watching them puffing and blowing; and your mouth pulls down at one corner—the ever-ready, amused jeer is on your lips.[38]

27 December 1923   *110, Heath St., Hampstead, London, N.W. 3*

《 *It is hateful here in England, so dark and stifling, and everyone and everything trying to drag one back. They have no life of their own, and they want to drag one away from the life one would make. I feel the English much more my enemies than the Americans. I would really rather be in America. But anyhow or anywhere it is an awful great struggle to keep one's spark alight and perhaps kindle something new. . . .*

I am due to go to the Midlands to my people, but don't bring myself to set out. I don't want to go. It's all the dead hand of the past, over here, infinitely heavy, and deadly determined to put one down. It won't succeed, but it's like struggling with the stone lid of the tomb.

I wonder why Seltzer has not written to me—for about six weeks I have nothing from him. I wonder if something has gone wrong with him or his business. Hope not, that would dish me in another direction.

When I can really break the clutch of the dead hand over here, so that its grip is broken in the world forever, I think I shall go to Paris. And I really hope to be in America by March: apparently Murry does want to come, but I don't altogether trust him. Can't rely on him at all.[39]

1 January 1924   Nottingham

⟨ I shall leave Derby on Thursday morning [3 January 1924] at 9.5, Great Northern Ry, get to Stafford 10.55, and to Shrewsbury somewhere near midday.[40]

Frederick Carter

At different periods I had occasion to discuss his theories upon the psyche with [Lawrence] and compare opinions upon the significance of old myths and traditions. And whilst he was staying with me for a little while in Shropshire, we considered means for the development of a certain line of research in symbolism, and the publication of some essays and a book or two about ancient ideas on the soul and their permanent validity, and of the problem of the last end of the world.

.   .   .   .

All this came about during his visit to England in 1924, after he returned from Mexico. He had been flitting restlessly about California, New Mexico and Mexico proper, uncertain as to his intentions. Whether he would or would not come to England again was uncertain, he wrote. He did not like its cold. But the rebellion in Mexico settled things, for he took ship at Vera Cruz and came back when the town was threatened by hostile forces.

Needing English clothes when he landed he had got a complete rig out and so appeared very spick and span in Shrewsbury Station. And how strange and stiff all those new garments looked on him when he arrived after a few more miles of travel at the out-of-the-way village [Pontesbury] where we lived. Stiff they felt to him too, it would seem, for he had to borrow a pair of my boots for country tramping. It was January and the roads and footpaths were heavy when the frosts lifted.

New garments enhanced his angularity. Pointed beard cocked forward, sharp high shoulders, tallness, long square-toed brown shoes, new soft felt hat. They all seemed to stand out vividly in the dim winter afternoon sunshine. And the background of the grey border village and churchyard gate emphasized it all as he stood there, impatient, whilst the curate stopped us to give me a message. Perhaps Lawrence thought he did it out of curiosity and to take a look at my visitor. Anyhow he was annoyed. He loathed curates and said so. Why did I know such a fellow, he asked.

But once inside the old rectory where I was living his delight burst out in that high nasal singing voice of his. He was pleased with the place, its oak floors, adze-hewn, black with time and old polish and showing the rippling lights that only such solid wide floorboards can give, took him greatly. And the churchyard wherein it stood with the gravestones up to the very windows, the old well in the depth of the cellars vaulted in at the end of a long stone passage. They made the background for a tale. Of course the house was too big for my purposes and he seemed grieved at the waste of the fine Georgian place with empty rooms going damp.

He had read the manuscript called *The Dragon of the Alchemists* [41] and had come to discuss its production. There, in its first shape as he saw it, I had been accumulating a long assimilation of symbols and their astronomical significance to the purpose of commenting the Apocalypse of St. John the Divine. All had been got together—in the main—for the purpose of making a series of drawings to elucidate its symbols. It became a book by sheer accretion.

At that time he had proposed various devices for arranging its publication, one that edited by himself his American publisher should issue it. Edited, I fancy, meant in part written, for he had an insistent desire to amend, enhance and colour anything that deeply moved his interest.

Once he had decided to return to England he settled to come and see me and discuss the work to be done. He came—after a week or so lying up in London with a bad cold—travelling across England by way of his native Derbyshire. He came really to discuss the symbol of the dragon. He loved the dragon symbol—for its ubiquity I should think—it had met him everywhere in Old Mexico, staring out on him from old ruins, jaws gaping to hold doorways and gleaming here and there wherever he might be. It was a god there, a god he admired, and he wrote a book to it, *The Plumed Serpent*. It was divine to him as a being that was part of himself and representing so significant a power in man.

Maybe this had something to do with the annoyance he showed towards the author of the canonical book where the dragon comes in so formidably. How he stormed at St. John and maintained with the fullest extravagance of Laurentian rage the author's blasphemy against the great phallic urge to power and his intellectualizing of the force of life with its consequent progressive emasculation in the race. He had his interpretation definite;

the dragon is the life bound in man's nervous system, the great serpent force.

Not only this of course, but every kind of thing he discussed in those winter days beside our fire, built high with oak logs that came from the surrounding slopes towards Wales. They were seasonable. A great frozen hill stood overshadowing the one side of the place—an old fortress—carved with trenches by the Romans. And fine and grim and hard it looked in the bright frost-sharpened air of January.

On the other side of the village stood a lesser hill of sheer stone which was half quarried away sliced through to the middle like a cake. Around it ran scattered houses until the woods began beyond to crown. We walked over its brow to come to them. He gave the place a sort of unwilling admiration, admitting its elements of the picturesque. But it was English, too English.

Nothing ever restrained him from outbursts of sweeping indignation and condemnation, rushing towards snarls of contempt. But it was amusing, stinging, vivifying, arousing. He could not help the urge in him to impose his ego, but still it was without hypocrisy or suavity that he did it.

And not only had he that obvious quality of temperament, but something, one could feel, had long before torn and lacerated his conceit in himself and it would not let him rest. Maybe he was always troubled by the long strife with the deep-seated malady that killed him in the end. He refused to acknowledge its power and ignored its hold on his constitution—would not admit its nature even. Without that spirit of the fighter he could not have lived and worked as he did. It showed in his pounce and snarl in discussion as he veered about with queer swiftness into hostility. Thence came that note of desperation in all he did.

Yet almost his only real hatred was for dogmatic rationalism. Truly, he loathed thought of the over-disciplined and regulated kind that let itself drift into the mechanical routine of living or thinking. After all, we live by things that are but in part logical and our feelings are far more deep in moving than the neat and regular processes that can be clearly expounded. He said and lived that for all of us, making manifest what he could.

Well, Lawrence came back from Mexico to see what could be done about the people and things awaiting him in England. That was his attitude. He returned, he said, more by chance than of deliberate purpose. Mexico he liked and would have stayed in longer, but the drift of battles in the revolution made it difficult for him and dangerous.

315

Carrying about him that singular air of the colonial, the sun-scorched returning traveller, he jumped out of the train in Shrewsbury bright and brand new. Red beard looked redder and sunburn browner against the hardness and brightness of his eyes on that wintry English day as we walked, killing an hour between trains, in the old town. Curiosity about his own land—for the first few days almost strange to him—gave him an avid appetite to see and consider.

Talk of places delighted him, both to hear and to tell. He was full of tales of his travel and the vastness of forgotten cities, lost in wild places, overgrown and tumbledown and hard to reach even now, though once more found again. Up immense rivers they had journeyed to them, carrying their meat alive in the boat. A goat to be killed on the way. And when it was slaughtered the genitals were offered to the white woman as the chiefest delicacy. They were declined by his wife—by him also, no doubt, for he was by habit extremely sensitive in most things.

Yet even at that time, although a measure of success had come to him, a sort of intermittent rage burnt him up. For he had the sense of strife always upon his thought, perhaps because of the sharp danger that hung over at his heels, the warning of the cold that prostrated him immediately on his return. England he knew disagreed with him, its climate, chill and humid, requiring other powers of resistance than he possessed and a stolidity and bulk that he had not. So he disagreed with England.

But for all that, he was delighted with that wild Shropshire countryside, picturesque and broken with small hills rising to greater ones beyond. England was his own and he felt it within him deeply enough. Of course, even as he looked upon it he would hardly admit his liking. Still, he later wrote a novel [*St. Mawr*] about its landscape, with place-names from it, too, and the house in the churchyard with its front windows cheek by jowl with the gravestones came in beside other local matters.

Only a little of my enthusiasm about the beauty and interest of that countryside would he accept. And the people he could hardly tolerate. The good-natured curate, fat, hail-fellow-well-met, a helpful and simple-minded gossip for all the world, him he blasted with a few words. Of course the man was bovine, red-faced and naïve. What else would serve in such an outlying land on the edge of two countries? Religion in Lawrence's sense meant little enough to such a man. A creed to believe was all he required for himself or his flock, and a sufficiently simple duty to be faithfully performed.

As it was, things were sufficiently difficult since a new vicar had come into office over him and at that a born disturber of curates, a High

Churchman and ritualist. Difficulty there was, because he had followed on one who had been Low Church and liberal to an extreme, in his views evangelistic and pacific. And now, since the new order, must my friend the curate, shame-faced, take his place in the procession about the church, self-consciously decorous with joined finger-tips and wearing a great cope of gorgeous pattern, shining with embroidery, from which his ruddy visage shone forth like a ripe fruit.

Dear fellow, he walked, or rather paced, along like a schoolboy caught about some mischief and expecting disgrace. To assume a solemn pious and sacerdotal look was beyond his scope, although he had his own proper gravity at serious occasions. But the man was too hearty and naturally genial to take on sanctimoniousness on the instant. He was not eaten up with zeal, but Lawrence was and promptly blazed at the very sight of him. They were the two types of the English, antagonistic.

Next day following his arrival we set off for a walk, five miles or six, into the wilds of the border country towards the edge of Wales. We climbed the slope of Cad's Hill up through the native village reaching down the hillside. Quite un-English it looked, its one-storey, whitewashed thatched cottages scattered about here and there off the road with gardens about them. And native it certainly was, for it had little social connection with that part of the village that lay along the main road leading round the hills. There the inhabitants had a blonder, more Saxon complexion, over against the darker people up the hill, who were mostly Bennett by name, and the folk of the mined and quarried hillsides. It was an old, old land where lead had been got since Roman days from the various "beaches" among the hills.

After the village had ended we came up through a little wood, then by a lane with a stream and stepping-stones along its middle for a few score yards. Over the brow of the slope our path dropped again into the woods by a narrow tree-bowered track, like a gully, always dripping with water except in high summer or hard winter.

Across the narrow gauge railway, running downhill to the works at the foot of the slope, we came on the long rise through woods which surrounded us for the next mile or two until we came out at the corner where, from the path's brink, one looks down the inlet into the hills upon the works and smoke of Snailbeach. Here, by the very edge of the moor, is the tiny chapel of Lord's Hill and from its walls stretches the open heathy land, rolling towards the great white masses of stone crowning the summit. But to us, as yet, invisible beyond the great curves of the moorland they stood, the Stiperstones.

We tramped along by the brow of Crow's Nest Dingle until we came to the rough ground covered with chunks of limestone that culminated in the great row of white rocks at the top, the biggest of which was called the Devil's Chair. This one we climbed—a mass as high as a house—and from its top looked over towards Wales and Montgomery, gazing out upon the old border marches of the land of Powys.

Lawrence liked the name—the Devil's Chair—for the stone on which we stood. And there we talked of the great hilltop rocks with similar names that are found all over Europe as seats of the changeful gods. Climbing and creeping through a hole in its back we stood on the part which appeared from far away to be its seat. And certainly as seen from the plain towards the Severn river it did look like an immense chair.

And besides, as these rocks marked the highest point of the hills in the vicinity, the point where the cloudbursts gathered that sent down floods to the valleys below, this huge mass of stone justified its title in the popular view. It was the place of power and storm—formidable. There was a gloomy terror and dark enchantment about it, for the low walls marking the foundations of a storm-wrecked hamlet stood beside the moorland path approaching.

Away and away as we stared into the sun-streaked winter land a tiny place smoked in the distance. There were no factories towards the west, nothing much was there except farms. But Lawrence sniffed the wild wind on that hilltop and cried out: "There is never any clean air in this country. It smells smoky to me even here. Don't you think so?" That pale, faint drift of smoke as far off as we could see, miles away, and all wild Wales before us. He challenged it as he challenged everything.

Of the tales that he told over the fire there of evenings, the book of the *Plumed Serpent* gives many as incidents and background, and with that the Indians of New Mexico were most in his mind. He was fascinated by them as he had seen them in their city not far from his farm at Questa —which is near Taos, I believe.

What arrested his attention in Shropshire comes into the tale of St. Mawr, though there is not much given in it beyond the chief elements of place-names and geography. Even the season of the year is altered, and most of the characters are imported into those surroundings by their author. However, it provided much entertainment to the inhabitants for, later, when the book appeared, recognising two or three places and one person, they proceeded to follow up clues and amongst themselves, I fancy, discovered the identity of every other character in the story.

Something, too, of other matters discussed, such as the mystical body of the starry man may be found in the article upon Astrology[42] . . . . When he left it was settled that he was to be back again in March from Germany, and with all the schemes discussed in working order—even started. But by that time difficulties in business had called him away to New York. Nothing was done and my MSS. came back from London, the matter seemed to have ended. A rare postcard from a discouraged Lawrence and another. Away in that far corner of the country I heard nothing except rumours sufficiently vague, until, once more residing in London, Lawrence's venture into painting came under discussion.[43]

6 January 1924   110, Heath St., Hampstead, London, N.W. 3

❨ Got back here very nicely yesterday evening.[44]

9 January 1924   110, Heath St., Hampstead, London, N.W. 3

❨ [Today] a fall of snow. Enough bright white snow on the ground to make a bit of daylight. I've been here exactly a month, in London, and day has never broken all the time. A dull, heavy, mortified half-light that seems to take the place of day in London in winter. I can't stand it.[45]

The Hon. Dorothy Brett

Again we are sitting round your fire; it is cold. The chairs are few and we are many this evening. Murry, Kotiliansky and Gertler seem to have absorbed all the chairs. You are sitting close to the fire pouring out the tea. The tea things are all on the grate. I sit on a stool next you. The room is cosy, darkly shadowed from the lamp on the table. Frieda is knitting. You are talking and laughing. I am trying to listen in with my machine. Gertler is impudent and gay; Kotiliansky full of the fun of old days; Murry white and tired. The tea is so pale that you pour it back into the pot to let it stew. What are you talking about? I can't hear well enough. You seem to be talking for the moment on some favorite topic of yours, judging from the faces around. Suddenly Frieda begins attacking you, contradicting you, then denouncing you; finally accusing you of wanting to make a God of yourself, of being God. You expostulate wearily, you argue. From argument it turns to battle. Your temper rises to meet the sledge-hammer blows from Frieda's violent tongue. You break into the midland vernacular. The rich Yorkshire dialect pours softly from your lips with an ever-increasing force, a steadily rising anger. In that language, strange to our ears, you fiercely denounce her. We sit and listen, spell-bound, until you suddenly seize the poker, and in a white heat of rage, you emphasize your words by breaking the cups and saucers. It becomes terrible to watch and to hear—the slow, deadly words and the steady smash of the poker, until, looking at Frieda, you say, slowly, menacingly:

"Beware, Frieda! If ever you talk to me like that again, it will not be the tea things I smash, but your head. Oh, yes, I'll kill you. So beware!" And down comes the poker on the teapot.

We are silent with consternation. No one speaks. You are silent, too, until, sighing heavily, you hold out your hand to me. I take it and silently hold it. Running your other hand through your hair, you give a little nervous laugh and say, "Frieda should not make me so angry," and the evening almost regains its composure.

Later, Frieda, on her hands and knees, sweeps up the broken china with a dustpan and brush. But in all of us something seems to have been violated by our incapacity to protect you, by having to witness in silence the battle for your own existence. One by one the others get up and leave. Murry and I put on our coats. You come down the stairs with us; we go out into the deserted street.

"Strange, isn't it," I say to Murry, "to hear Lawrence use the 'thee' and 'tha' of the Yorkshire dialect?" Our departing footsteps echo on the frosty air. I turn and look back. You are standing on the steps in the bright moonlight . . . standing straight and arrowy before the shadowed doorway . . . faunlike.[46]

---

9 January 1924   110, Heath St., Hampstead, London, N.W. 3

❨ *I find that here in London they all instinctively hate me: much more so than in America. But that too, in the end, only makes me laugh. My gods, like the Great God Pan, have a bit of a natural grin on their face. Nous nous entendons.*

I am still planning to come west at the end of February or in March, with Frieda, Murry and Brett.[47]

22 January 1924   110, Heath St., Hampstead, London, N.W. 3

◖ We are leaving for Paris in the morning—stay there about a fortnight, then a while in Germany—and by early March I still hope to be in New York; and in New Mexico by end of that month.

.   .   .   .

London, England wearies me inexpressibly. I cannot tell you how this winter in England wearies me, and the people. But it will finish.[48]

24 January 1924   Hôtel de Versailles, 60 Boulevard Montparnasse, Paris

◖ We had an easy journey—Paris looking rather lovely in sunshine and frost—rather quiet, but really a beautiful city. We're both tired—almost stupefied from London.[49]

[Hôtel de Versailles/60 Boulevard Montparnasse] Paris–24 Jan. [1924]

[Postcard to Idella Purnell Stone]

◖ I haven't heard a word from you since I left Guadalajara—do hope you & Dr Purnell are all right. We have come to Paris for a while—but I think we shall go back to New York in March. I'd still rather be in Mexico.

D. H. Lawrence

Write c/o Curtis Brown–6 Henrietta St.
London W.C. 2 [50]

26 January 1924   Hôtel de Versailles, 60 Boulevard Montparnasse, Paris

◖ To-day it is dark and raining, and very like London. There really isn't much point in coming here . . . I'm just going to sleep a good bit, and let the days go by: and probably next week go to Baden Baden to get that over. I somehow can't answer to Europe any more. Paris has a great beauty —but all like a museum. And when one looks out of the Louvre windows one wonders whether the museum is more inside or outside—whether all Paris, with its rue de la Paix and its Champs Elysées isn't also all just a museum.[51]

7 February 1924   Ludwig-Wilhelmstift, Baden-Baden

❨ We've just got here—all snow on the Black Forest, but down in here only wet.

Europe gives me a Wehmut, I tell you.

We stay here two weeks—then back via Paris. I learnt in New York that the income-tax must be paid by March 15th, and I still have no word from that miserable Seltzer.

I don't know if you [J. M. Murry] really want to go to Taos. Mabel Luhan writes she is arranging for it. You seemed to me really very unsure. You resent, au fond, my going away from Europe. C'est mon affaire. Je m'en vais. But you, in this interval, decide for yourself, and purely for yourself.[52]

9 February 1924   Ludwig-Wilhelmstift, Baden-Baden

❨ Germany is queer . . . . Just changing, making a great change. Very interesting. Things might happen here, and people might be as one wants people to be.[53]

We are going to Munich for a few days.[54]

[Ludwig-Wilhelmstift] Baden Baden   11 Feb [1924]

[Postcard to Idella Purnell Stone]

❨ I keep sending you a word, but get no sign from you—hope all is well. I hear of you via Spoodle. Germany cold and sunny and very poor. I remember how Dr. Purnell hates postcards—hope you don't.

                                                    D. H. L.[55]

19 February 1924   Ludwig-Wilhelmstift, Baden-Baden

❨ I feel very unsure about everything,—Taos and everything. Everything seems to take the wrong direction. . . . However, one just fatalistically makes a move . . . .

By the middle of March, I expect we shall be in New York—then we'll decide the next move. Frieda wants to come to Taos.[56]

23 February 1924   Hôtel de Versailles, 60 Boulevard Montparnasse, Paris

❪ We are sitting in bed, have had our coffee, the clock says 8:30, and we see the people and the carriages pass on the boulevard outside in the morning sun. The old men and women shake their carpets on their balconies in the tall house opposite, cleaning hard. Paris is still Paris.

We went to Versailles yesterday. It is stupid, so very big and flat, much too big for the landscape. No, such hugeness is merely blown up frog, that wants to make himself larger than nature and naturally he goes pop! Le Roi Soleil was like that—a very artificial light. Frieda was terribly disappointed in Le Petit Trianon of Marie Antoinette—a doll's palace and a doll's Swiss village from the stage. Poor Marie Antoinette, she wanted to be so simple and become a peasant, with her toy Swiss village and her nice, a little ordinary, Austrian, blond face. Finally she became too simple, without a head.

On the great canal a few people skated, a very few people, little and cold and without fun, between those well-combed trees that stand there like hair with an elegant parting. And these are the great. Man is stupid. Naturally the frog goes pop!

Frieda has bought two hats and is proud of them.

Tomorrow we go to Chartres to see the cathedral. And that is our last outing. Tuesday [26 February 1924] we go to London.[57]

29 February 1924   Garland's Hotel, Suffolk St., Pall Mall, London, S.W. 1

❪ I think we shall sail on Wednesday, 5th March, on the Aquitania, arrive in New York by 12th March.

.   .   .   .

Dorothy Brett is coming with us: but Murry not yet.

I look forward to Taos again, to space and distance and not all these people.[58]

John Middleton Murry

The real reason for Lawrence's reluctance to return to England lay deep in his being. It was a profound feeling of revulsion, which he could not overcome. When he did come to England it was his body only which came, and not his soul. He *hated* England. That was the cause of the miserable failure over the *Adelphi;* that was, in the last analysis, the reason why I did not go back with him. I wanted, deeply, to work in England, for England; and Lawrence wanted to kill that desire in me. I did not expect him to live in England. But I did want him to be reconciled with England—in the real and positive sense to *forgive* England: to see that if England had, as he felt, "insulted" him, it had done it blindly, and that he must bear no grudge.

. . . .

. . . I had, very reluctantly, made up my mind to give up the *Adelphi.* I intended to go with Lawrence; but I was not going gladly, for what I believed to be the right, impersonal thing, had been rejected. But I had, against my better knowledge, made up my mind to go. . . .

What I had agreed to do was to go with Lawrence and Mrs. Lawrence. Lawrence, without consulting me, asked a fourth person to go. The presence of that fourth person made my participation impossible. And it happened that it was impossible for me to tell Lawrence why this was so. . . .

Let the situation be made as clear as it can be made. I had yielded to Lawrence over the question of the *Adelphi,* feeling that he was wrong. But it was done; and I had promised to go with Lawrence and Frieda. I was willing to make one of a larger party. But what I was quite determined not to do was to make one of a party of four. I made an effort to persuade another man—Dr. James Young—to come with me. But he, alas! took a dislike to Lawrence at the meeting I arranged.

So the painful time, with the painful happenings, dragged on. I was committed to going, determined not to go in these new conditions, and equally determined not to say why I would not go.[59]

The Hon. Dorothy Brett

I meet you at the Ticket Office. I am confused and helpless, but you are happy and competent. You are free again; no ties, no chains. What kind of a boat shall we sail on? The Aquitania is sailing just about the time you want to leave; you have never been on so large a ship. I have never been on any ship at all, except the Channel boats. We decide to sail on her.

"Do you think," you ask me, as we stand at the counter in the Office waiting for our tickets, "Do you think that Murry will come; he seems to be doubtful?"

I don't care to hint how sure I feel that Murry will not come; how much he is wavering. The tickets are bought and paid for . . . for us the die is cast.[60]

John Middleton Murry

Lawrence sailed on 5th March. I have since found this brief entry in a notebook:

4th March.—As Lawrence went away he said to me, "What an awful pity it is we have to do these things [*i.e.* go away to America] in order to be able to *live*. Why can't it be like it was a hundred years ago, when you could live by yourself and to yourself in the English country and the wildest journey you ever dreamed or undertook was one to Paris?"

"Or to London itself," I said.

"Or to London," he agreed and nodded in his way.

I thought he was sad. England means very, very much to him—in spite of all.[61]

The Hon. Dorothy Brett

Early morning; cold; gray; I suppose about six o'clock, hardly daylight. My servant is weeping. "You will never come back," she cries. I laugh: "Only six months, Mrs. Sales. I'll be back all right in six months." "No," she repeats, "I *know* you will never come back." That was nine years ago, and I have never, except for two weeks in 1924 [1925–1926?], seen England again.

Murry is helping me. He has after all decided not to come. The taxi is at the door; we get in with my bags; a final wave to Mrs. Sales, and I am off; cold but elated I drive off to the station. Murry is cold, unelated and silent.

You are already at the station. We settle ourselves comfortably in a second-class carriage. Frieda is as helpless as I. You do all the talking, the tipping, the arranging. Murry leans through the window and says he will follow us soon. Your lips twist into a grim smile. The red flag waves, the whistle blows; Murry draws back; the train glides slowly out. Murry waves and waves and disappears. We are through the station, gliding swiftly past the hideous slums and chimney pots, out into the open country. I am sitting opposite you, facing the engine, gliding swiftly into the unknown. Suddenly you laugh, looking at me mockingly:

"Are you afraid of your new adventure?" I am not afraid, but bewildered, overwhelmed; not so much at the journey, but at this quiet-eyed, fiery man, sitting opposite, with his hat off, a heavy lock of hair falling over the fair, level brows, and tapering down to the red, pointed beard, as he searches in his own personal, treasured little bag, to see if he has all the tickets ready to hand.

.   .   .

We are nearing Southampton. A great ship stretches along the dock. We look in astonishment. We have never dreamed of anything so huge. We are on board. A curving stairway with rows of footmen. You and I wander all over the ship, while Frieda goes straight to her cabin to lie down. We go through the first-class saloons, and decide we like our white-panelled, simple, second-class saloon best.

We go on deck. A band begins to play; the siren blows. The visitors scramble off; there are hundreds of people on the dock. The ropes are thrown with a splash and the ship begins to move. The little tugs strain and puff; the dock is a sea of fluttering hands and handkerchiefs, but there is nobody to wave to us. You and I are standing at the stern; masses and masses of sea-gulls fly around; the wind blows hard and cold; the sea is choppy and bright; the air gleams with the flashing sea-gulls as they swirl round our heads. You sigh and say:

"I am always a bit sad at leaving England, and yet I am always glad to be gone."

And we stand and watch England fade and sink into the sea.[62]

10 March 1924   Cunard R.M.S. Aquitania

❡ *We come to New York tomorrow. The sea is swinging and smoking now, in a cold wind since we came out of the Gulf Stream. But it has been a pleasant voyage, and we have missed none of the meals. The boat is very comfortable, only too big—like being in a town. Very quick, though—we make about 580 or 585 sea miles a day: very good going. Brett is very happy—insatiably curious—teas with doctor, etc. Frieda doesn't really like the sea—the motion. I like to feel myself travelling. And it's good to get away from the doom of Europe.[63]*

CHAPTER FIVE

1924–1925: New Mexico and Mexico

"Even as the flying fish, when he leaves the air and recovereth his element in the depth, plunges and invisibly rejoices. So will tall men rejoice, after their flight of fear, through the thin air, pursued by death. For it is on wings of fear, sped from the mouth of death, that the flying fish riseth twinkling in the air, and rustles in astonishment silvery through the thin small day. But he dives again into the great peace of the deeper day, and under the belly of death, and passes into his own."

—"The Flying Fish," in Phoenix, pp. 785–86

11 March 1924   c/o Thomas Seltzer, 219 West 100th St., New York City

❡ Landed at last, and got all the things through Customs—such a fuss!
. . . The passport officials looked askance at Brett travelling alone—called
her "this girl." I got so mad. Then they soon slowed down, quieted-up
sharp. The Customs people were very nice—but oh, so long. We struggled
up to 100th St. buried in luggage, in a taxi, in half a blizzard, snow, and
rain on a gale of N.E. wind. New York looking vile. Seltzer was at the
wharf, though I hadn't told him I was coming. He'd got it from Curtis
Brown. He looks very diminished, and him so small already. Apparently
his business has gone very badly this winter, and he has sleepless nights.
So, it seems, might I. My money is at present in thin air, but I believe it
will materialize bit by bit. Damn it all and damn everything. But I don't
care terribly.—Brett just bewildered.[1]

12 March 1924   c/o Thomas Seltzer, 219 West 100th St., New York City

❡ We got here yesterday. I think we shall be going through [Chicago] to
Taos on Tuesday or Wednesday [18 or 19 March]—myself and my wife
and a friend, the Hon. Dorothy Brett. I should like to see you [Harriet

329

Monroe], *if you would tell me where—perhaps at Poetry's office for a cup of tea.*[2]

Harriet Monroe

In September, 1923, while I was abroad, [Lawrence] was in Chicago for a day—"a queer big city with a sort of palpitation I couldn't quite understand"[3]—and the following March he and his wife and their friend Miss Brett spent a day with me in the "queer big city" and had dinner with a few poets. "I shall never forget that afternoon," he wrote afterwards from Taos, "that lake with a stripe of snow like a skunk's nose."[4] And a much later letter refers again to

that day in Chicago, and the ice on the shores of the lake, which I shall never forget, so wild and American still, with that wild forest of a city behind. Something queer and terrifying about Chicago, one of the strange "centres" of the earth, more so than New York.[5]

That March day in Chicago in 1924 was my only chance to verify by talk and the touch of eyes and hands the impressions gained through a desultory correspondence of ten years. I found a man uncannily active in spite of slight figure and frail health; with a roving observant eye, prehensile hands, a body alert and ready to leap like a cat, and a mind as taut as a steel spring. One felt an urge for life in his company; there was nothing sedative or soothing about this faun-like creature who wore no conventional veils over a spirit that darted this way and that to its discoveries. Nothing reminded one of his physical weakness; on the contrary he seemed lithe and extra-fit for dart and recoil—one had to sharpen one's paces to keep up with him. He looked like his pictures—the small face, triangular with its thick reddish hair and pointed beard, the narrow-chested thin-flanked body, the legs that seemed to clear the ground even when they rested. The contrast between his litheness and the solid well-rounded stability of his guardian wife was a lesson in the mystery of affinities.[6]

Witter Bynner

21 March 1924: *Santa Fe.* [The Lawrences] came at six this evening, with an English viscountess or something, deaf but likable, and left at ten-thirty. They go along to Taos tomorrow, to see whether this time he

can refrain from quarreling with Mabel. He's a man with a mind, anyway. I was glad to see him and really joyous in seeing the great-hearted Frieda.[7]

8 April 1924   Taos, New Mexico

〔 We find Taos very pleasant again—very beautiful—and the raging spirits somewhat soothed. My wife just calming down after the depressing swirl of Europe, and Dorothy Brett blissfully happy on an old horse. . . . I must say I am glad to be out here in the south-west of America—there is the pristine something, unbroken, unbreakable, and not to be got under even by us awful whites with our machines—for which I thank whatever gods there be.[8]

Mabel Dodge Luhan

Now the time was come to leave California and go home to Taos; to leave a mild, moist atmosphere, perfumed with mimosa and bay leaves, for the hard, high air of the upland valley where everything is a challenge and where one must be strong to face the sun without wavering.

.   .   .   .

Frieda and Lawrence, with their new friend Brett, reached Taos from New York the day before Tony and I came home. They were staying in the big house, and when we rolled through the gate, blowing the horn, Lorenzo came running out to meet us. It was six months since I had seen him, and I had suffered from the separation that began in anger. Somehow he had overcome me. I came back to him willing to be as he would have me be, more gentle and unwillful.

"I *will* be as Frieda is *not*," I thought. "I *will* be gentle and unwillful." Determined to please him, I assumed a chastened mien and instantly, I believed, became like Mary before our Lord!

He opened the door of the car and I saw he was breathless and shaking a little, and his eyes were black with excitement. Our hands fumbled a greeting.

"Hello," we each said.

Frieda came along behind him. I don't know how to describe to you . . . the hearty sounds she gives out. Shouts and shrieks, but muffled ones, blasts of energy with her big, wholesome mouth open and her white teeth shining.

I was not so glad to see her, but, springing out, I seized her by the shoulders and planted a kiss on her hard, pink cheek! She started back, green eyes surprised, smile gone. She was not wanting my kiss. Lawrence, who was hauling my bags out of the car, giggled the same faint, small giggle I had heard so often before, and then Frieda and Tony were shaking hands. There was something equal to each other between these two, as they stood shoulder to shoulder, solid on their feet, both real, though differently so.

We made our way into the house. I felt flustered and overcome by the assault of all the impressions that were coming at me from all directions. Tony and I had been away for months on our first long absence from Taos; and on returning to the familiar living-room, with its chests and chairs and pictures that I have lived with for years and years in Europe and New York and New Mexico, everything looked strange and unknown. I live so completely in the moment wherever I am that all other places and things are forgotten, blotted out. When I see them again after an absence, I come back into them with a shock. There is nothing matter-of-fact about it. So I stood there among my things and they were all speaking to me, crying and shrieking to me for notice. And Lawrence was fussing about and saying little things, being polite to Tony, asking him about our trip, and Frieda, recovered from my kiss, was exclaiming something about "the Brett."

"Wonder what you'll make of her."

"Where *is* she?" I asked, looking round.

"She's painting a rose back on the bowl we have for you!" screamed Frieda, laughing heartily. "We bought it for you in Mexico—a wooden bowl. But we used it, and all the pattern came off it. We had it in Europe. But we brought it back to you!"

At this moment a tall, oldish girl came into the room. She had pretty, pink, round cheeks and a childish expression. Her long, thin shanks ended in large feet that turned out abruptly like the kind that children draw. She was an amusing and an attractive grotesque, and her eyes were both hostile and questioning as she came slowly up to me, examining me, curious, arrogant, and English.

She shook hands with me with one limp, pumping motion, and silently handed the wooden bowl to Lorenzo. To be sure, it had a large, pink rose in the center!

"Here you are! Be careful, it's wet."

Brett had stuck a brass ear-trumpet into her ear and was eagerly turning it in all directions to pick up scraps of conversation. Almost always it was pointing at Lorenzo. It had a bland-looking, flat, dipper end to it that seemed to suck into itself all it could from the air, and this had the effect of inhibiting all one's spontaneity. Because it was not a jolly, sociable ear-trumpet that longed to be a part of everything else. No. I soon saw that it was an eavesdropper. It was a spy upon any influence near Lorenzo. Inquisitive, pertinacious, and solitary, it was forever between Lawrence and the world.

He didn't seem to mind it. In fact, he told me almost at once that he had brought Brett along to be a kind of buffer between him and Frieda. "It's a little *too* hard, alone with her," he said. He felt her deafness prevented her from being so altogether present as servants are, overhearing and speculating upon their masters. But he was wrong. She was more present and pervasive than the air around him, for the air at least leaves one alone, while she perpetually swallowed up the life of others, living vicariously upon the misconstructions of her wishes.

Do you think I liked it when I saw that brass dipper swallowing up Lorenzo's talk to me? Good heavens! It was worse than Frieda's restraining presence! She saw my restiveness the very first evening and said, laughing:

"You mustn't mind the Brett. She doesn't count. She helps Lorenzo. She plays piquet with him and types for him." Frieda trying to comfort me for feeling that my relationship with Lawrence was inconvenienced by Brett was a new, strange turn of things!

"My God! I can't stand that brass dipper always between us," I groaned. And Frieda shrieked with laughter.

"Where ever did he pick her up?" I queried.

"She was a friend of Katherine Mansfield's—at least Katherine *used* her. When she died, Brett turned her devotion onto Murry. She had a little house in London and let out rooms in it to Koteliansky, Murry, and others. She was always saving Murry from some designing woman! Murry made use of her, too. We thought surely Murry would come along with us—Lorenzo persuaded them *both* to come. But Murry backed out. She *amuses* Lorenzo. And she's a great help, really. . . ." [9]

The Hon. Dorothy Brett

I follow you in. I am inquisitive to see this woman [Mrs. Luhan], but at the same time I am nervous and shy. I have made a mental picture of her, of course, but like all such pictures, it is totally wrong. She is shorter than I am, of a square, sturdy build; the thick brown hair, bobbed like a Florentine boy, swings as she walks and gleams here and there a bright chestnut. The fringe is cut in a curve over the brows, the point of the curve in the middle of the forehead, like a Mephistophelian cap. The big, gray, dark-lashed eyes are curiously shiny, the nose small and straight, with just the least bit of a curve down at the end. The lips are well cut and unpainted. There is poise and self-assurance in the whole carriage, and a warm glow from what one feels in a moment is a rich personality. As she walks, her arms swing and some of the force and strength lying behind the charm reveals itself.[10]

Mabel Dodge Luhan

In a day or two the Lawrences moved into the Two-story House across the alfalfa field from us, and Brett was given the studio a few yards away from them. The wide double door faced their house, and in it Brett sat all day long, apparently sketching the view of the Truchas Mountains, but in reality watching every move of Lorenzo to and fro between our houses.

We all breakfasted under our own roofs, but they all came over to us for lunch and supper unless it rained or they felt like being by themselves. And so our second effort to live a kind of group life started.

It seemed to me that I never saw Lorenzo alone any more or had him undividedly. I simply detested the kind of group life that had any more elements in it than Lorenzo and me or, at a pinch, Lorenzo and me and Tony and Frieda. The addition of Brett made it richer for Lorenzo, but poorer for me, it seemed. She paid all her attention to him, just as I did, and this is not the way to live a group life. In that way of life all the flow is to a common whole so that each one may share it all at any time; and we were each of us trying to live exclusively, while on the surface we had an appearance of communion. I wanted to flow along alone with Lawrence in the sympathy and understanding we had together. And each of the others, of course, wanted the same thing! He really did not object to a number of sympathies coming his way. . . .

Lawrence and I had a few horseback rides again together. The new, strange submissiveness that had come into me affected my courage all the way through and I felt uncertain, as I had never before, of the horse and my control of him. . . .

  · · · · · · · · · · · · · · ·

Brett watched us enviously. She had never ridden in her life. Her father, Viscount Esher, had kept a racing stable, but he never let his daughters learn to ride. The nearest they had come to horses was staring at them grazing in the pasture when, as little girls, they and the horses were together at the country place.

Now her greatest wish was to have a horse and ride across the desert with Lorenzo; and pretty soon she had her desire and he was teaching her to ride. He taught her to have an imaginative relationship with the horse, to feel she was sympathetically en rapport with it, to feel "the flow" between the horse and herself; but he never did teach her to ride well or to know how to *manage* the animal. She was always afraid of it.

.   .   .   .

When he gave himself up to one, Lawrence enjoyed it. I remember how he sat in the center of Brett's studio while I pranced round him, cutting and trimming his red beard. He sat meek and good like a little boy, a white towel tied around his neck, and the red bits of hair fell around him on the floor. I simply adored cutting his beard. There must truly be an old, old reality in that legend about the power centered in one's hair. And he luxuriated for a moment in passivity; giving himself up to it always soothed him and made him temporarily bloom. Such ease in relaxing, such ease! He smiled, and his eyes were soft and blue like lupines. There are very few memories of him so.

Evenings were varied. We always had to be doing something. Lawrence couldn't bear to just sit . . . . Now we played mah-jongg, a new game I had brought from California. Brett and he and Frieda and I played together.

I cannot describe to you my increasing irritation at Brett's ridiculous ways. She had an annoying habit of employing the diminutive for anything she could; it was her insatiable and unsatisfied maternity, I suppose. She wanted to have everything *little*. And she talked incessantly, thinking out loud, naming everything: her feelings, her wishes, or the names of the little blocks with which mah-jongg was played. With little shrieks, she would exclaim: *"Oh!* a li—ittle flower-pot!"* until I was rolling my eyes and finally imitating her, sotto voce, which amused Frieda and made Lawrence sore.

One evening when I needed my hair trimmed, I mentioned it, saying how I hated the town barber. What I really wanted was to have Lorenzo suggest that he do it for me. I *longed* to have him shear me. But he didn't say anything, and instead Brett said, brightly:

"*I'll* do it! Run along and fetch me a little shears. I always snipped Katherine's for her."

I made a face for Lawrence's benefit that she didn't see, and brought the scissors and sat down, grim. Lorenzo hovered round and began to direct her, and Brett slashed into my hair. I could hear her panting a little. She slashed and slashed and suddenly cut the end of my ear off!

The blood ran down and Lawrence palely offered me his handkerchief. I looked at Brett in amazement and, I must admit, in some admiration! She was half snuffling, with tears in her eyes, and laughing too.

"Why, you cut my ear off!" I exclaimed. I couldn't get over it. [She] hated me, and she was deaf, and she tried to mutilate my ear! That seemed so interesting that I forgot to be indignant. However, I didn't forget to make a good deal of it to the tender-hearted Lorenzo.[11]

The new little Pink House down in the alfalfa field near the orchard was finished and ready to be painted. Clarence [Thompson] [12] had started to build it the summer before, for himself, but when I found that he was having most of my men do the work, I got impatient and wrenched it away from him and said he couldn't have it and that I'd finish it for myself.

"Besides," I said, "it's in Tony's field and would belong to him anyhow, legally." Clarence was blighted and made a great story out of this when he turned against me. Well, anyway, I had finished it. I was getting it ready for Alice Sprague,[13] who was coming to visit me in June.

Lawrence said: "Let's all paint it. We can make some nice decorations on the doors and furniture."

So there we all were with pots of pale-colored paints: pink and light yellow and so on. Lorenzo first painted the brand-new pine-wood toilet that stood off at some distance from the house. Had it been done in green, as I had planned it to be, it would have faded into the landscape and been unnoticeable. But what do you think he did? He gave it a coat of cream-color to make it stand out more than before, and on it he made an enormous design! In the center, coil on coil, and swaying upwards, was a great, green snake wrapped around the stem of a sunflower that burned and shone like the Taos sun. On either side of it he painted a black butterfly as large as a plate, a white dove, a dark-brown bullfrog, and a rooster. Whom all these were supposed to symbolize, I will leave it to you to puzzle out. Certainly they were not just fortuitous forms.

This toilet became a scandalous landmark. It was known far and wide. Tony hated it, particularly the snake, and wouldn't go near it. Finally it faded. One can hardly see the sunflower any more! But, strangely enough, the dove is more clear than ever, in contrast with its faded neighbors.

In the house Frieda was doing an old walnut chest of drawers that had for handles bunches of grapes and leaves. She painted the chest a light pink, and the fruit was purple, with emerald-green leaves. It may sound dreadful, but it looked lovely against the pale adobe wall.

"Oh, it's such fun putting a dot of high light on every grape!" exclaimed Frieda.

"Now on this little round door," said Lorenzo, "I'm going to put the Phoenix rising from his nest of flame." I knew what he meant. I had heard him talk often enough about the Phoenix. He identified himself with it. It was himself he wanted to place there—his sign manual on that house. Well, he put that blithely on the upper part of the door, and Brett was carving out some figures for the lower part. They put their heads together and created a Garden of Eden, an apple tree with red apples on it, a *huge* serpent, and a brown Adam and Eve on either side of the tree. They both liked *doing* things with their hands and I hated to—so that was that. I was just swishing paint round on window-frames and places where I could go fast and furious and where it didn't matter, and I was getting mad. I felt out of it. The others kept up a running comment, Lorenzo giggling and Brett excited.

"Here, put a smile on the serpent," he said, chipping at it and nailing it on the door.

"Here's Eve—the bitch," Brett said, viciously, "*cause* of all the trouble. Here, let's give her a good fat tummy."

And Lorenzo answered, responsively: "Yes, the dirty little bitch with her sly, wistful tricks."

Now, maybe this needn't have made me mad, but it did. I was Eve. I got up and solemnly walked out on them. I was covered with paint, so I went home and washed it off myself and put on a clean dress. When they came over for supper, I was cold and *digne*. I paid no attention to either of them and gave myself all to Frieda.

Lawrence began to frown and cast dark looks in my direction, while Brett jerked her head to and fro like an alert bird, watchful of every move. We finished supper and moved to the table for our game of mah-jongg. I kept myself to myself, cold and stagnant inside, until Lawrence was able to bear it no longer. After two games, he rose and said quietly, but frigidly:

"I don't care to play any more tonight. I think I'll go over to my own house." And he left the room.

In a flash I was after him, opening the door and closing it behind me so swiftly that I found him still on the threshold out in the warm darkness. I put my hands up on his shoulders and leaned up to him in a flood of yearning.

"Oh, *don't* be mad," I breathed. He bowed his head over me until I felt his beard brushing my cheek, and he put his arms about me in an instant's silence. Then:

"Nay, nay, lass," he said, in a voice ever so gentle and low. "I am never really mad any more."

I went into the house and he went on home.[14]

.   .   .   .

It wasn't long before they began to talk of going up to the ranch to stay, the ranch I had given John [Evans] several years before. He had named it "The Flying Heart," and it was like that, somehow. The two little houses came to rest on the high flank of the Lobo Mountain as though they had settled there to rest for a moment only. Behind them the pines, climbing up and up and up; before them, first the alfalfa fields, and then the pines; and below to the east and south and west the shimmering valley of Taos, stretching away to the dark crack that showed the Rio Grande canyon, with the river in its bottom. On the opposite side of that was the dry farming country called Carson, reaching to the railroad, thirty miles away; then the whole rim of the horizon sweeping up into blue hills, with the peaks of the Sangre de Cristo range to the east, the Jemez mountains to the south, and the Colorado Rockies to the west.

The little one-story white cottages seemed to have flown over from New England. Surrounding them was, actually, a white picket fence to keep the animals out, and there was one tall pine tree in the yard! You have read all about it in *St. Mawr*, haven't you . . . ?

Lorenzo was uneasy down in Taos. It was so plainly to be seen that he longed to be up on the ranch that one couldn't help wanting to put him there; but I was terribly regretful to have him go, and in some ways I felt he needed to stay on our hill. I told him this, and he nodded.

"I can come and see you all the time," he said. "It will be easy to ride down for the day—maybe it will be better so. We can talk. . . ." I know what he meant, loath though he always was to put anything that was between us into words. As it was, we were scarcely ever together without either Frieda or Brett or both, and my irritation at this kept me constantly bad-humored, so the "flow," as he called it, that could go running between us whether people were there or not, if all was well and harmonious—this flow was interrupted all the time. Things were not going well—and it was his instinct to make a change.

Very well, I helped them. I persuaded John to trade the ranch back to me for a buffalo-hide overcoat and a small sum of money! Then I gave it to Frieda. I wanted to give it to Lorenzo, but I knew he would rather I gave it to her, so I did so. They moved up.

Lawrence had a new toy to play with. He loved getting the place all in order, building porches and an outdoor oven. Almost as soon as they arrived there, Frieda sent me a note to say she had written to her sister in Germany for the handwritten manuscript of *Sons and Lovers* because she wanted to give it to me for the ranch. Of course I was thrilled to have that coming to me, but something in the way Frieda put it to me had a sting in it: it was as though they didn't want to be under any obligation to me and sought to balance my gift with another. There was something cold and distrustful about Frieda's gesture—something that really spoiled the whole exchange.

I never altered my opinion about this, or ever cared for that manuscript, once I had it. Too bad that people can't do things more beautifully. I cared so little for that great bundle of finely written pages that Lorenzo had sweated out long ago that two years later I gave it to Brill [15] in payment for helping a friend of mine. I suppose he still has it. I never asked him. [16]

The Hon. Dorothy Brett

"Mabel," you tell me, "has offered me the Ranch. She wants to give it to me, but I won't accept it. I hate presents of all kinds and I hate possessions. She has offered it to Frieda. I told Frieda she could do as she liked, so she has accepted it. What about going up there soon and spending the summer there?"

"I am ready for anything, for any kind of adventure," I reply.

"I think," you continue, "that we would be better up there, more to ourselves. Things would be less difficult."

I agree, heartily. I have been feeling a restraint, a curious undercurrent of emotional excitement that my deafness prevents me from understanding clearly. But a vague discomfort hangs around us all.

So it is arranged that as soon as the roads and weather permit, we will move up to the Ranch. Later you decide to give Mabel the MS of *Sons and Lovers* in exchange for the Ranch. The manuscript cannot be found, but you think Frieda's mother has it in Germany. [17]

❲ Del Monte belongs to Mr. Hawk, William's father. The parents have a biggish house but go to California a lot. The young ones, William and Rachel, are in the log-cabin where we stayed two years ago. They make butter there and look after the cows and chickens.[18]

18 May 1924   Del Monte Ranch, Questa, New Mexico

❲ Did I tell you Mabel Luhan gave Frieda that little ranch [19]—about 160 acres—up here in the skirts of the mountains? We have been up there the last fortnight working like the devil, with 3 Indians and a Mexican carpenter, building up the 3-room log cabin, which was falling down. We've done all the building, save the chimney—and we've made the adobe bricks for that. I hope in the coming week to finish everything, shingling the roofs of the other cabins too. There are two log cabins, a 3-roomer for us, a 2-roomer Mabel can have when she comes, a little one-roomer for Brett— and a nice long hay-house and corral. We have four horses in the clearing. It is very wild, with the pine-trees coming down the mountain—and the altitude, 8,600 ft. takes a bit of getting used to. But it is also very fine. . . . I think we shall stay till October, then go down to Mexico, where I must work at my novel [The Plumed Serpent]. At present I don't write—don't want to—don't care. Things are all far away. I haven't seen a newspaper for two months, and can't bear to think of one. The world is as it is. I am as I am. We don't fit very well.—I never forget that fatal evening at the Café Royal. That is what coming home means to me. Never again, pray the Lord.

We rode down here, Brett and I. Frieda lazy, came in the car. The spring down in the valley is so lovely, the wild plum everywhere white like snow, the cotton-wood trees all tender plumy green, like happy ghosts, and the alfalfa fields a heavy dense green. Such a change, in two weeks. The apple orchards suddenly in bloom. Only the grey desert the same.—Now there is a thunder-storm and I think of my adobes out there at the ranch. We ride back tomorrow.—One doesn't talk any more about being happy—that is child's talk. But I do like having the big, unbroken spaces round me. There is something savage, unbreakable in the spirit of place out here—the Indians drumming and yelling at our camp-fire at evening.—But they'll be wiped out too, I expect—schools and education will finish them. But not before the world falls.[20]

The Hon. Dorothy Brett

On May fifth we start for the Ranch. Dates seem important to you: we had started from England on March the fifth, and you are struck by the coincidence.

What a start it is. In the early morning, the wagon with our trunks and stores drives off, driven by two Indians. The saddle-horses follow, as Mabel is lending us three of her horses: Bessie, Cequa and Poppy. Trinidad, wrapped in a gay blanket, rides one and leads the others.

We (and Mabel, with Tony driving) start later in the car. We overtake the wagon on the road. How gay the men look in their brilliant blankets. You are gay, too, excited, as change and movement always excite you. We are cumbered with packages and stores.

On reaching the Ranch, we begin at once to scrub out the solid hut. What a job it is. We work fearfully hard until twelve o'clock when the wagon arrives and we all have lunch.

.   .   .

"Brett, which of the cabins will you have?" you ask me as we stand looking at the little houses after our hard day's scrubbing and arranging. "You can have either of these two. Frieda and I must have the large one, as we need a room each and a kitchen; but you can have either this one or the little one."

I look around. Your long, straight cabin lies in the sunshine, the big, solitary pine in front of it, the shadow hardly falling on the house at all. Behind it are a few small pines. The big window of the sitting-room looks out across the field south to the Sangre de Cristo mountains. At the west end lies your bedroom, built of adobe; a big window on the west wall, another smaller one to the north, the door facing south. The kitchen at the east end of the house has but one window facing south alongside the door. Both the kitchen and the sitting-room are really one long log cabin, but now mere sheds.

To one side, but facing the big house, is the house you are now in: half adobe, the kitchen of wood. It lies deeply shaded under small fir trees, dark and gloomy. The one room is biggish, the kitchen very small. Outside the white picket fence is the tiny tumble-down adobe house with a high-pitched shingle roof. There is something warm and sunny about it, the eastern window almost on the ground, level with the hillside, the south window and door just fitting into the length of it.

"I think I will have the little one," I say. "It's quite big enough, really, and I like the sunlight. This one under the trees is too gloomy."

"All right," you say, "I will have a new roof put on it, and with a stove you ought to be all right. But some day we will have to clean the corral, that goat-dirt is too much. Five hundred goats—just think of it—and nothing been done for eight years, they say." You add, doubtfully, that "it is a healthy smell."

The house question is settled, and we go to bed.

. . .

Thus the life at the Ranch begins. We work and toil, cleaning out the tumble-down cabins. The big one, full of cow-dung, is dilapidated, the lower logs of the long, back wall so rotten that they have to be taken out. Props are put in to hold up the walls as the rotten logs are carefully pulled out.

I am camping in the end room of the house, which is to be your bedroom: it is in fairly good condition. You and Frieda are in the other house, under the little pine trees. Mabel decides finally to camp with the Indians in Tony's big teepee up behind the cabins on the hill.

You spend most of your time working with the Indians. Trees have to be cut and stripped. It is all hard work, yet exciting. I gather stones for the new foundations. A trench is dug to keep the earth away from the new logs.

In the evenings we go up to the Indian Camp for supper. The Indians have built a half-circular screen of pine branches under a big pine tree. Inside they have laid skins and blankets. In front, a hole has been dug for the fire. A little further down the hill is the big Teepee and another half-circle of pine branches: in this, supper is cooking on a big fire. Frying pans with large steaks are sizzling. And we, very tired, are sitting around with our plates in our laps, waiting.

After supper we walk up the hill to the other camp and lie down on the blankets and skins. It is one of those magical evenings; a clear sky, a very young moon rising pale and slim out of the setting sun, a large star hanging below the moon. No sound, not a twig moves. The Indians are sitting in a row on a log, facing the setting sun. One of them rises and throws a great log on the fire, the flames leap high. The Indians are softly beating a small hand-drum, like a tambourine, and singing in their strange, haunting voices to the sinking sun. As the light fades, we all slip into shadow. The firelight catches your red beard and white face, bringing it suddenly out of the darkness. You are brooding, withdrawn, remote. Remote as the group of dark Indians are remote in their ecstasy of singing, the firelight playing on their vivid blankets, the whites of their eyes. I am caught and held by your brooding face. All of us are caught and held by the rhythm, the Indian rhythm, as if the very earth itself were singing.

.　　.　　.

The days are long and hot. The cabin is built up slowly. I chop wood for Frieda's little kitchen stove. You are working all day with the Indians. Frieda cooks, lies on her bed smoking, cooks again.

One of the worst jobs of all is cleaning out the roof of the big house. It is like an oven between the roof and the tin ceiling. With a handkerchief bound round your mouth, you have been sweeping the rat-dirt and nests out with a small dust-pan and brush. You come crawling out, looking white and tired. Candido remonstrates with you and says he will go in. I fetch another handkerchief which you tie round his face, over his mouth. In he goes. You climb onto the tool-shed roof and peer through the little door at him. He comes out a bit later, sweat pouring down his face, gasping, a pile of nests in the dust-pan.

Nothing will prevent you from doing the same hard work that the Indians do, however dirty and disagreeable. You have to share the worst with the best, even the dirt and heat in the roof. You will not ask the Indians to do anything that you are not willing to do yourself. And you insist on giving them plenty to eat. "They must have something to grind their bellies on," you tell Frieda.

You have bad headaches, and bad neuralgia, yet you work persistently. The Indians work willingly and happily with you and they like you; and until you are told that they laugh at you behind your back, you like them enormously. But that hurts you—always you are sensitive to being laughed at.

Gradually, out of the chaos, the cabin begins to shape. I suggest a fireplace in the back wall before the logs are placed. Full of excitement, you hurry to the Indians. "Is it possible?" you ask. They say it is quite easy and a huge fireplace is planned. Then I have another inspiration: a window in the back wall of the kitchen. That, too, is easy. The new logs are put in place, then the hole for the fireplace is sawed out and the hole for the window.

Into the fine hot days, great storms come crashing. On such evenings the Teepee leaks and Mabel goes down to Taos. She takes the list for stores. When she returns, she brings the stores with her, and sometimes more Indians. The tent dries out quickly, but the storms come up unexpectedly and sometimes so late that Mabel in her tent is taken unawares. Then she has a cot in your kitchen, although I offer her a place in my room.

.   .   .

There is, even with all the Indians, much work to be done. Wood for the stove has to be chopped small, water carried from the spring. I look after the wood and water. You are away most of the day in the woods, cutting down trees with the Indians. Frieda cooks and lies on her bed smoking her endless cigarettes. Mabel and Tony go to and fro to Taos in their car, taking Indians away, bringing them back with more stores, more pots and pans and comforts.

When Mabel is away, we have supper in the little kitchen; the Indians carry theirs to their camp. This evening I lay the table in the kitchen. Mabel and Tony are in Taos. I sharpen the knives; Frieda is fussing round the stove; you are washing outside in a small basin, kneeling on the ground.

When supper is ready, we sit down, tired—oh, so tired—and eat, too tired to talk. Afterwards, as we wash up, you begin to sing. The dishes finished, we sit down and sing. We sing old Scotch songs, old English songs and ballads. Suddenly there is a knock on the door and Candido and the other Indians ask to come in. They have heard the singing and feel lonely. Candido has a badly swollen finger, poisoned. You look at it carefully and tell him it is dangerous, that you must poultice it. Frieda puts some milk on to boil; then some bread is soaked in it; and you cut up a clean linen handkerchief. Gently, and with deft, careful fingers, you wash the wound and lay the boiling poultice on the finger. Candido draws back with a cry; you blow on the poultice, lifting it off his finger. Taking hold of his hand, you tell him to warn you when it gets too hot. Slowly you lower it again until it rests lightly on the finger. Candido screws up his face, but says nothing. You press the poultice slowly onto the finger and hold it there. During the evening you renew the poultice three times, finally bandaging the hand up in the last one.

"Don't take it off," you say to Candido, "I will make you a new one tomorrow."

.   .   .   .

The building is nearing to a finish. . . .

The fireplace, a magnificent cavern, awaits an arch. I go out and find half the rim of an old wheel. Geronimo bends the rusty iron into the shape he wants, and fits it across the front of the fireplace. It is not strong enough to hold the weight of the kettle, but strong enough to form the adobe arch. For the kettle, a straight iron bar is fixed behind the arch, then the adobe is moulded over the curve, carefully smoothed, and the fireplace is finished.

You are busy making two cement seats on each side of the fire with large flat stones, and with a little stone edging round the cement hearth. Someone has told you that mats can be made out of rope and wire; so in the evenings you sit fumbling and struggling, swearing, as you twist the stiff wire round the obstinate rope. The mat is for one of the stone seats. You never bothered to do the second one.

. . .

We are sitting in the lamplight round the table. You are talking of Italy and somehow of St. Francis of Assisi.

"Think," you say, "how horrible, kissing the leper; kissing that filthy disease with one's sensitive lips." You shudder. "And then eating dirt— dirt, with the sensitive membrane of one's mouth. It's just disgusting, loathsome; and makes me sick in my stomach." Frieda and I are silent: it certainly is sickening.

"*Ulysses*," Frieda shouts, suddenly. "Have you read *Ulysses*, Brett? It is a wonderful book." You look at me, steadily, a quiet, penetrating look. Before I have time to answer Frieda, you say vehemently:

"The last part of it is the dirtiest, most indecent, obscene thing ever written. Yes it is, Frieda," you continue, sharply. "It is filthy."

A tremendous power pours out of you. I stick my nose back into my book. Something warns me to say nothing as to whether I have read the book or not. You read on slowly through a story in the magazine *Adventure*.[21] At your elbow lie some books that Mabel has sent up.

"*The Golden Bough*," you say suddenly, "How I hate these people who write books from their armchairs; men who never go out and experience anything for themselves. They just sit at home and write about everything second-hand, never having seen an Indian or a tiger or known anything. What's the good of that? They are afraid to meet life, to experience it for themselves." Frieda stitches away silently. I look up and say:

"Didn't Fenimore Cooper know Indians?"

"No, never," you say abruptly. "I doubt if he ever saw one. Haven't you read my Essays?" [22] And you return angrily to your magazine and read slowly, slowly. I marvel always at the slowness of your reading.

. . . .

Now that there is less work, you have begun to write. In the quiet, still morning, with your copy-book under your arm and your fountain pen, you go off away into the woods; sometimes one can glimpse you through the trees, sitting leaning up against the trunk of a pine tree in your blue shirt, white corduroy pants and big, pointed straw hat.

Occasionally, at noon, I go off to call you for lunch. You are sitting as usual, leaning against a tree, in a deep dream, abstracted, in the world of the story you are writing. I clap my hands: you jump out of your skin and turn on me angrily, and in a shrill voice ask me why I can't whistle instead of frightening you by that kind of noise. I am aghast; then I suddenly realize that I clap my hands because I imagine you will hear it easier than whistling, as I would. I tell you so and you are appeased. But after that I blow a horn whistle for you, every noon, which you never hear—never.

. . . .

[We] sit for awhile in the dim light of the oil lamp and talk.

"I know, Brett," you say crisply. "I know you believe in friendship. I don't—oh, no, not for me. I don't want love; I don't want anybody's love or friendship; I just don't believe in it."

"It *is* possible," I say, weakly, "I am sure it is."

"Perhaps for you, but not for me. Oh, no, not for me."

What is wrong with people and friendship has been the argument of the moment.

"If people were like horses or cats or any wild animal," you continue, "If they were as natural. A horse is never anything but itself; it is true to form always. It never swerves from its pattern, its horsiness. That is the difference. Human beings are always untrue to their pattern; they have ceased to have a pattern. A man is no longer MAN. A tiger in the jungle is always a tiger, but men you can't trust—they always let you down and themselves."

I make no answer. I think of the trust you have, the way you always go out to people, hopefully and eternally.

"You are too romantic, Brett," you add, after a while. "You are always so romantic," you continue, a bit scornfully.

"So are you," I retort. "I am no more romantic than you are."

"Oh, yes you are," you reply, sardonically; but you give me a mischievous, sly side-glance. I laugh and you laugh. Both of us know that neither of us will admit that we are romantic. I get up:

"It is nine o'clock," I say, "and time to go to bed."

You light the storm lamp for me, and I go out into the starry night to my house.

.   .   .   .

You have a headache; Mabel is in her teepee not feeling well; Tony is away in the mountains shooting; Frieda is lying on her bed, smoking. In spite of your headache, you are hard at work on the chimney, perched on the roof plastering with adobe the outside and the edge of the chimney, fashioning it into a nice shape. When you come down the ladder, Candido slaps you on the arm in his appreciation of your efforts. I am chopping up some small wood for the kitchen stove. Frieda takes spells of lying on her bed, smoking, and of cooking. We work thus all day, with no sign of Mabel shut away in her Teepee.

In the evening, we go up to the Indian Camp and you sit and talk quietly to the Indians in Spanish, and to Richard [a carpenter], who is not drunk for a wonder. I wish I could hear what you are saying, but it's no use. Tony is in the Teepee talking to Mabel. I lie and watch the fire against the stars, while the low voices go on . . . and on.

.   .   .

Mabel has gone off to Taos; her restless energy has little outlet in the quiet life of the Ranch. You are pale, with a bad headache, the neuralgia having kept you awake most of the night. Nevertheless, in spite of it, you work hard finishing the chimney, putting a neat top of smooth adobe over the bricks. But you go to bed early, eating very little supper.

You are moving. The big cabin is finished and you have spent the morning decorating the apple-green dresser with plates and cups and saucers. It is amazing how well the old tin plates look and the odd assortment of cups. You are immensely proud of the job and call us in to admire.

The yard is full of bedding and mattresses and trunks. I am moving into the cabin you are vacating. The kitchen is a masterpiece: we lunch in it, proudly, and by the evening we are all comfortably settled. . . .

.   .   .   .

Another hard day's work. We are back again at the Ranch and I have moved into my little house. I moved out of the barn back into Mabel's house, but didn't like it, there seemed to me a bad spirit in it, something dark and evil. I tell you, but you are inclined to laugh and declare it seemed all right to you. But I am glad to move out into my sunny little house.

Meanwhile you and I are making a bed-stead for your room. We saw and chop, and get little ends of logs for the legs. It is heavy and awkward, so we call Frieda to come and help us drag it into your room. The spring fits in neatly; the mattress is fitted on; and with your spotted blanket laid over it, the bed looks quite nice.

All the same there seems to be a queer feeling in the air. Are we tired? Not more than usual. We wash up, and have supper; then I go out into the yard. You walk after me, quickly, and say suddenly that I have no respect for Frieda. I stare at you in astonishment. Your voice begins to rise. You shout at me that I have no respect for either you or Frieda, that Frieda says I never talk to her but only to you. Your voice is rising higher and higher. I take hold of your wrist, lightly between my finger and thumb, and say very quietly:

"No, Lawrence, that isn't so." You stop, hesitate; then Frieda pops out of your bedroom and goads you on, shouting at both of us. You begin again, but I still hold your wrist in that light hold, repeating quietly that it is not so. Your anger dies down; you stop suddenly and give me a queer look—and it is over.

But I am distressed. I go off into the woods and lie among the trees until it is dark; then I return and go to bed, without lighting a light. Someone comes with a lantern: I lie perfectly still, with my head under the blankets. The footsteps go away.

Next morning Frieda comes over, very upset, and weeps. We are both upset. When I go over to your house, you come in and, looking at me with a gleam and a twinkle in your eyes, you say:

"Storms, Brett, storms."

.   .   .

I have come over to breakfast in your house. Lying under the squawberry bush is the remains of the red chair. I look at it and you watch me looking, but you say nothing. Later, when you have gone off to write, Frieda tells me that the letter you received from Mabel the evening before, had thrown you into one of your terrific rages, and you had broken the red chair—but that you wanted to hide it from me.

When you return from the woods, you look very white: you have developed a bad headache. Nevertheless, you ride for the milk; but your headache gets so bad that you go to bed without any supper.

.   .   .   .

The houses are now all finished. From decorating your kitchen, you have turned to the sitting room which is also Frieda's bedroom. A large serape is hung on the wall behind Frieda's bed; table-cloths are laid on the tables; the mantle-piece, two upright logs with a board across smeared gray with ashes, has Frieda's knickknacks arranged along it; and a picture or two hang on the walls. Your bedroom has a table, a bed, and a small cupboard. The larger cupboard we make later. The smaller cupboard is to hold your manuscripts. You and I paint a gaudy pattern on the cupboard in Frieda's room; but she complains vigorously next morning that it gave her nightmares all night—so we clean it off with turpentine and repaint it gray and white. The house is cosy and gay-looking, with its serapes and Mexican blankets.

The guest house—Mabel's house—is more sparsely furnished. It has a big bed and an open shelf with hooks for clothes with a curtain hung in front. The tiny kitchen has only room for a stove and a table.

My house has no room at all, except for a bed, the smallest stove imaginable, a table in the window, and a chair squeezed between the table and the bed. It is sunny and warm, but very leaky.

.   .   .   .

Lunch is over, but we are still sitting idly in the porch. You have begun to talk of dark-eyed people.

"They are," you say, "really a different race—the dark-eyed people." Frieda gets up and wanders off. "The blue-eyed races are the race of the gods. All the gods, Brett, have blue eyes." And you look at me a bit triumphantly. Frieda returns and says in her excited, exuberant way:

"I am sure there are gods here." You have got up and are standing on the edge of the porch. You hesitate, then you say in a quiet, awed voice:

"To bring the gods, you must call them to you." There is a depth of reverence in your voice and an expression on your face as if you had said too much.

.   .   .   .

For several days, with the aid of Trinidad who has ridden up to visit us, we have been cleaning out the spring. Down in the little canyon, past the fallen cottonwood tree, way behind my house, is the spring. It drips slowly into a tub from a pipe. It is dark and shady in the canyon among the trees. The water has been tasting funny lately, so we have decided to dig up the pipe, clean the pool and put in a new pipe.

What hard work it is. The pipe is out at last; the pool is full of dead leaves. We clean them out. Then Frieda and I fetch stones: we make a new pool, lined with stones and covered with stones so that the leaves can't fall in. The new pipe is fixed, the tub is emptied. Trinidad digs a hole in the side of the hill for it. After three days of sweating and struggling, the tub is fixed again and we sit exhausted, but happy and triumphant, to watch the water trickle slowly into the tub, up to the brim, over and down the sides. Clear, cold, beautiful water.

Frieda is coming with us on her new horse, Azule, to fetch the milk. Mabel has given her a divided skirt of a khaki color. In this, with a loose brown buckskin jacket over her white blouse and her white straw hat, she sits on Azule, large, flowing and regal. The skirt blows round her shapely legs, the fringe of the buckskin jacket sways: she looks so large on her large gray horse, so large compared to you. As we canter along, she calls to you:

"Oh, it's wonderful; wonderful to feel his great thighs moving, to feel his powerful legs!"

"Rubbish, Frieda!" you call back. "Don't talk like that. You have been reading my books: you don't feel anything of the sort!"

"Yes, I do," Frieda begins to argue. But you are riding on fast ahead and do not hear.[23]

6 June 1924   Kiowa Ranch, San Cristobal, New Mexico

❨ *Balance in Chase Nat. Bank. 4th Ave. & 23rd St. New York on May 31st* *—was $2198.02. Further 157.50 paid in by Curtis Brown from Smart Set for* *The Border Line story[.] Spent on building ranch up, $217.65 in wages,* *$195.00 Gerson & Santa Fe. & about 50.00 lumber & oddments.*[24]

Del Monte Ranch–Valdez/Taos County–New Mex./9 June 1924

❨ *Dear Idella [Purnell Stone]*
    We are up at this ranch—which now belongs to Frieda.—We have built *up the houses—two—& it is quite nice—expect Bynner & the Spoodle*

next week. But I intend to come to Mexico in the autumn—I think in October—and I look forward very much to coming back. I have had a couple of letters from Manuel Gamio, the anthropologist in Mexico. He seems nice.

I think a good deal of Guadalajara & Chapala. I really like it better there than here. But am pledged here for the summer.

I heard the tragedy of your motor-car. Alas, poor Dr. Purnell!

Remember me to Percy Holm & Mrs. Holm, & to Mrs. Valliton,[25] and I hope it won't be very long before I'm having a sip of your Daddy's tequila.

Frieda sends greetings with mine.

D. H. Lawrence

Oh, do send Götzsche another couple of those Palms with his cover-jacket.[26] I never got those for him.

Are you still as much in love with the Muse? [27]

15 July 1924   Kiowa Ranch, San Cristobal, New Mexico

⟨ Frieda is the proud owner of a little ranch here at the foot of the Rockies, among the trees, two miles above Del Monte. We look far out over the desert—far beyond Taos, which lies below, 17 miles away. We had four Indians and a Mexican, to build up the rather dilapidated log cabins—now all is more or less ship-shape—and F. and I live in the 3-room cabin—nice big rooms. A friend, Dorothy Brett, a painter who came with us from London—is in a tiny one-room cabin, and there is a 2-room cabin for visitors—when we get any. We have each our own horse, and ride down to Del Monte Ranch every day for mail and milk. It's our nearest point to the road. I myself find a good deal of satisfaction living like this alone in this unbroken country, which still retains its aboriginal quality—and in doing for myself all I need—the women doing the women's part—that is, Frieda does it. But I make shelves and cupboards, and mend fences, bake bread in the Indian oven outside, and catch the horses. . . . One has to be so much harder, and more cut off out here. Either one stands on one's own feet, and holds one's own on the face of the land, or one is mysteriously pushed out. America has really just the opposite vibration from Asia—here one must act, or wither: and in Asia, it seems to me, one must meditate. I prefer this, because it is harder. But I think action—continual rushing round in motor-cars, etc.—can be much more silly than meditation.

I want to go down to Mexico City early in October. F. loves it here, but I hanker rather for old Mexico. And I have a novel half finished down there, which I want to get done this winter. Perhaps next year we may come round via China to India—have a standing invitation to friends in Darjeeling, far north, in the Himalayas.[28]

Mabel Dodge Luhan

Lawrence was like the rest of us in his inability to be inclusive. He couldn't sweep a number of dear ones all at once into a wide embrace. It had to be *this* one or *that* one or t'other. Someone was always left out in the cold. Now several of us were out in the cold, formidable ones, too! Yet for a while we maintained the pattern of a group. We continued to go places and do things together.

One of these excursions was a horseback trip from the ranch to Taos by way of the waterfall. Over above the village of Arroyo Seco, high on the side of the mountain, there is a rocky cave. We had to leave our horses and climb up by a trail that is nearly obliterated, through pines and cedars and tall grasses, by a thin stream that would lead anyone to the spot if the trail were lost. Winding in and out and finally rounding some huge rocks, we came to the opening. It is a place the Indians feel very strongly about. They will not camp near it, for, they say, there are bad spirits there.

The vast, pelvic-shaped aperture faces the west and yawns upward to the sky; and over it descends the mountain water, falling thirty feet across the face of the entrance to form an icy pool below. We skirted the waterfall and entered the cavern; chill and damp and dark it was, too! Here there are holes hollowed out in the rock walls where Tony says the bears sleep in the winter; and at the right-hand side of the back wall of the place there are a number of rude climbing steps that lead up to a shelving ledge. Above this altar-like ledge there is a faint sun painted high up to the east of it. One by one we climbed to the high altar, and, looking before us, we saw the clear fall of water across the opening, green and transparent.

It is an ancient ceremonial cave . . . , and truly it is full of strange influences. Once I went there with an archaeologist, who wanted to make some notes about it. I had been there several times before that day and had always been conscious of the faint, far-away echoes of other times that are encountered in the dim, queer atmosphere of the place—but nothing out of the way had happened. But the day I went with that professor, all of a sudden I became conscious of unfamiliar fragments of impressions that were striking into me, awesome and terrible, but incomplete. Half-thoughts that were not mine collided in my brain with the remainder of consciousness that was my own. Terror and doom struggled to overcome my quite legitimate and conventional wish to remain my natural self and not to seem queer to a stranger. He was talking to me, and his voice echoed in the domed rocks as he noted the painted sun, the altar, and the waterfall cutting across the far-away western horizon. I wanted to tell him how, at the winter solstice, when the water has turned to an icy column, as the sun turns to go south, it shines through the erect, transparent pillar of ice and falls precisely upon the altar. But I could not tell this thing. I had forgotten my own language—completely and definitely. I could almost think in English, but I could not remember the sounds of the words. Instead, another language was in my mouth. I could have spoken it, but that was the last thing I wanted to do. All I could manage was to keep quiet and occasionally to nod a response.

It was not until we were home again and at lunch that my accustomed speech returned to me. It was more than aphasia, for I believe with that there is only blankness, and this was a positive experience of something dim and unfamiliar, something strong and terrible and not to be forsworn, a floating relic out of the stored past that haunted, yet, the walls of that place. I never can go back there without a shudder. Of course I had told Lorenzo all about it, and that was why we went there that day. We had a beautiful ride home through the dusk. The sky was pink and gray.[29]

The Hon. Dorothy Brett

I have started typewriting your story, "The Woman Who Rode Away." I am not good at typewriting, but I think I may save you some money, as the typists are so expensive. So I borrow a typewriter from Mabel and settle down to the job. You tear a few pages at a time out of your copybook—with some reluctance, as it spoils the book—but you write new pages every morning and it is the only way to manage.

. . . .

Today you seem to be better. Yesterday, for some reason I could not fathom, you were very cold to me. So I settle down to my typewriting happily, while you go off into the woods to continue the story.

After lunch, the Indian women show you how to bake in the Indian oven. We collect wood for them, while they make a big fire inside the oven. This they let burn for at least half an hour, until it burns down to red ashes. These are then raked out, and the inside of the oven is swabbed with a damp cloth on the end of a stick. The bread is put in on the end of a long, flat shovel. The bread you have ready, having prepared it over night. We also put in a young chicken, and in twenty minutes the bread and the chicken are done to a turn.

.   .   .   .

We are still struggling with the porch. It is more of a job than we thought, so much wood to be cut and trimmed. While Frieda enjoys herself in the wash-tub, we go down into the wood with axes. We need some more trees. A couple of straight pines, not too big, catch your eye.

"These will do, I think." And you begin to chop. "Look out, Brett!" you call. The tree creaks, sways, and falls over with a crash. You look at it proudly. "Let's sit and rest," you say. We sit down on the fallen tree.

"It's hard work," I say, mopping my face; though I have as yet done nothing.

"Yes, it is," you agree, "but you have no idea how soothing it is to the nerves. When I am in a temper, I like to run out into these quiet woods and chop down a tree: it quiets the nerves. Even chopping wood helps; you've no idea, Brett, how much it helps. That's why I like doing it. The irrigating is good, too; the water is soothing. Don't you feel like that, too."

"Yes," I reply, "I do." You laugh and jump up.

"I'll chop this one down, while you trim the branches off the other; only mind and get out of the way when this one falls." I take up the smaller ax and begin to hack off the branches. A sudden call from you and I run as the second tree comes crashing down. You join me in cutting off the branches, then we rest a bit and you say:

"Let's see if we can lift one." You take the thick end and I take the other. We lift it with a great effort; slowly we stagger up the wood with it, pausing to rest at intervals. Frieda from the wash-tub, hails us with cries of wonder at our cleverness.

"We will have to saw it," you say to her. "You can sit on it as you are the heaviest." Frieda does not like that remark at all, but nevertheless she sits solidly and firmly in the middle of the log while you and I with the double-handed saw, work away at it. "It's nearly through," you say, and Frieda jumps up in a panic. The log falls over and splits in two.

Then we go down again into the wood and struggle up with the second one. After that we have had enough; we leave it and go into the field and catch the horses.

. . . .

I have begun to type a new story of yours called *St. Mawr*. Your chair is finished, and the meat safe, and now you are making a cupboard. In the afternoon I chop wood and help you with the cupboard.

. . . .

"What do you think of *The Boy in the Bush*?" you ask me suddenly, as we sit resting and drinking tea in the house. . . .

"I like it," I reply, "but I don't like the end. He should have died. A man like that could never have gone on living; he could never have settled down to an ordered life: the only way out for him was to die."

"I know," you say, "I know. That is how I wrote it first; I made him die —only Frieda made me change it."

Frieda looks up from her embroidery. "Yes," she booms, "I made him change it. I couldn't stand the superiority of the man, always the same self-importance. 'Let him become ordinary,' I said. Always this superiority and death."

"Well," I say, "It's spoiled the book."

"Yes," you say, sighing, "he should have died."

Frieda's eyes begin to dart about. "The Brett always agrees with you; always sticks up for you," she says, challengingly. Neither of us answer. We sip our tea and wonder whether a storm will come up before we fetch the milk.

. . . .

This evening you are passionately declaiming against divorce. We are again in Taos visiting Mabel, and are sitting in [Ida Rauh's] house. Mabel is lying on the day-bed, and we are sitting around in various chairs and on cushions on the floor. You are very intense, almost evangelic; a mood that would come over you when the subject moved you deeply. At last Ida says:

"Isn't that funny, coming from you." You look at her surprised, and ask:

"Why?" Ida laughs and says:

"Well, you are staying in the house of one divorcee; you are visiting another; and you are married to another." You look at her for a moment; then you suddenly drop your head:

"Yes, you are right," you say sadly and heavily.

.   .   .   .

I am blowing and blowing my whistle. Not a sign of you. You are away somewhere in the woods, writing, and lunch is ready and piping hot. Frieda and I decide to start without you, so down we sit on the porch —which is finished and where we now have all our meals.

At last you come. You had not heard the whistle—you never do hear it, as a matter of fact. You are full of your new story [*St. Mawr*], of Mrs. Witt. You sit down in your place, and between bites you read out to us the pages you have just written. You are still twinkling with amusement, and you are still living more with them than with us. You read out the scene of the tea-party, of the tart Mrs. Witt, the scandalized Dean and his wife, and the determined Lou. You laugh so much over it, that you have to stop—and we are laughing too. Then you read out Mrs. Witt's defense of the horse when Rico pulls him over and the horse kicks Rico in the face. You read it with such keen joy and pleasure at the final downfall of Rico and the terrible revenge of the horse, that Frieda is horrified; she says you are cruel and that you frighten her.

But you are too immersed in the people and the story to care what anyone says. With great relish and giggling, you describe Rico's plight. You hate Rico so, that for the moment you are the horse; in fact, you are each person yourself, so vivid are they to you. With each character your voice and manner change: you act the story rather than read it, and we sit entranced, horrified, amused—all by turns, while your lunch gets colder and colder on your plate.

How rare it is that you read out anything. Then you reach the end of what you have written and turn your attention to the soggy food and you ask how I am getting on with the typing. And then you wail, somewhat vexed:

"Why, oh why can't you spell the same way I do, when it is in front of your nose!" Why not, indeed? I never knew and I never did spell the same way you did.

.   .   .   .

You suddenly spit. You constantly spit, so there is nothing new in that: but this time a splash of bright red blood comes with it, which is new. You cast a look of consternation at Frieda: she looks flabbergasted— while I pretend not to see at all. You already have a bit of a cold, and during the morning this gets worse. After lunch, looking white and ill, you go to bed and there you stay, sleeping most of the day. Spud [Johnson] spends the day with the Gilletts [30] and returns in time for supper with me and Frieda.

The following day you are still in bed, and in the afternoon you spit blood again. When Spud and I ride for the milk, Frieda sends a message to Bill [Hawk] to ask him if he will drive in to the Hondo and telephone for the Doctor. When we get back, you are sitting up in bed with your supper tray on your lap. Frieda calls to us to ask if the Doctor can come. With a violence that is overpowering, you break in, turning on Frieda in a wild fury:

"What do you *mean?* Why have you sent for the Doctor?" You are sitting up straight, tense with rage; your voice shrills out: "How *dare* you!" And you pick up the iron egg ring that serves you for an egg-cup, and hurl it at Frieda's head. It misses her by the fraction of an inch and almost falls into Spud's open mouth as he stands aghast and astonished that weak and ill as you are, you have the strength to be so furious.

"You *know* I dislike Doctors. You *know* I wouldn't have him or you wouldn't have sent for him behind my back. I *won't* see him—I *won't!*" Your voice is shrill, the sentences seem to explode from you. "I'll go out and hide in the sage brush until he goes. I'll teach you!"

Spud and I look at each other, helplessly. Frieda is murmuring in a flustered, bewildered way.

"But Lorenzo, I was worried about you. It won't do any harm. If it's nothing, we'll all be relieved; and if it's serious, the doctor can help."

A dead silence. Frieda comes hurrying out of your room, her eyes darting in all directions. You, quiet now, lie looking out through the open door, sore, angry and helpless. Only partially resigned to your weakness and helplessness.

Frieda, Spud and I, dismayed and worried, have supper; then wait for the doctor. It grows dark and I stand behind the big tree, watching the headlights of a car coming across the desert. I peep occasionally round the tree trunk to look into your lighted room. You are sitting up in bed, wrapped in a shawl, looking hurt and miserable.

The lights on the desert disappear, to reappear in three quarters of an hour through the trees across the field. The trees light up, and the glaring headlights of the car blaze onto the field. It is Dr. [T. P.] Martin [31] driven by Clarence [Thompson]. They have blankets in the car, as Dr. Martin fears pneumonia; and in that case wants to take you down to Taos where Mabel is warming more blankets.

Old Martin marches into your room and the door shuts. Behind the

357

tree I wait, until the door opens again and the light streams out. I peep round, cautiously. You are sitting up in bed, the tension gone; the grimness has left your face and you are smiling. A sort of ease and repose has spread over you. I can feel it from where I am: it spreads into the night, as the light from your door spreads into the darkness. Old Martin comes out, smiling too; and Clarence drives him away.

.   .   .

I go in to Frieda. She is beaming.

"It is all right," she tells me. "Nothing wrong; the lungs are strong. It is just a touch of bronchial trouble—the tubes are sore. I am making him a mustard plaster and you must ride down tomorrow to Rachel [Hawk] and borrow some mustard from her, as I have no more." Lord, what a relief!

Down I go next morning for the mustard. And in the afternoon, Spud and I pick masses of raspberries up in the canyon behind the houses, while you are still in bed with a large mustard plaster biting your chest.

.   .   .   .

You begin to mend; but I am still cautious about going in to talk to you. I can never forget Katherine Mansfield breaking a blood-vessel talking to me. But I find a little humming bird fluttering on my window in my house. I catch it and am amazed at its lightness; holding it carefully, I hurry over to your house and take it to you.

"What is it?" you ask.

"Be careful," I reply, "and don't let it fly away. Hold out your hands." I place the bird carefully in them, and you sit there holding it. A look of amazement, followed by another of almost religious ecstasy comes into your face as the tiny fluff of feathers sits in your hand, the long beak tapering and sharp, the gorgeous metal splendor of the green and blue throat shimmering.

Suddenly, with a laugh, you toss it into the air. The bird, its invisible wings humming, hums its way through the door away into the air with its long, looping flight.[32]

14 August 1924   Santa Fe, New Mexico

❨ We are motoring with Mabel Luhan to the Hopi country—hotter down here.[33]

30 *August 1924*   *Kiowa Ranch, San Cristobal, New Mexico*

⟨ *That trip to the Hopi country was interesting, but tiring, so far in a motor car. The Navajo country is very attractive—all wild, with great red cliffs bluffing up. Good country to ride through, one day. The Navajos themselves real wild nomads: alas, they speak practically no English, and no Spanish. But strange, the intense religious life they keep up in those round huts. This animistic religion is the only live one, ours is a corpse of a religion.*[34]

I think we go down to Mexico in about five weeks.[35]

The Hon. Dorothy Brett

While you were at the Snake Dance, I had ridden to the top of the Lobo peaks with Rachel's dudes and Bill [Hawk]. I had written you a long description of the ride; and though you mocked at me for my enthusiasm, you were longing for the opportunity to go yourself. It was just one thing you had not done. Rachel organized the expedition, and at six-thirty we hurry down to join it.

We find the others busy getting ready and finally we start. Across the fields we trot, onto the old, old Questa road until we reach the San Cristobal Canyon. Rachel is leading, as she knows the trail by heart. The trail is narrow, so we go in single file. I am behind you. As we ride slowly up the canyon, up the steady, long climb, I am wondering why it is you are always looking on the ground. I, naturally, look up—at the trees and the sky; but you seem always watching the ground. And then it suddenly dawns on me: you are looking for flowers—and flowers there are among all the tangled undergrowth.

The canyon is narrow. Great tall pine trees turn it almost black in places, and the long, white trunks of aspens soar up with tufted heads of leaves vainly trying to reach the sun. On the smooth, pale trunks here and there, are the clear handmarks of bears, climbing up and coming down. It is rugged, ragged; and full of the forlorn waste of storms. Sometimes our horses have to jump over the fallen trunks of trees.

So we go on and on for miles, slowly wending our way from dark to light, from light to dark as we emerge from the heavy pines to lovely shimmering groves of golden aspen, with hardly room for our horses between their slender trunks. We begin to see the desolate line of burnt trees on the mountains: burnt white and ghostlike.

At noon we reach an open space of rich grass and aspen woods around. Here we decide to lunch. The horses are unsaddled and tethered, the fire collected and lit; and we lie about, thankful for the rest and the food. Half an hour and we are off again. The trail is steepening; when suddenly you hop off your horse and stoop to pick something. You turn to me triumphantly.

"You have never found anything like this before!" And you hold up a small, intensely blue gentian. Ahead of us now are the bare mountains: bare but for the ghost trees, burnt in a great forest fire years ago. We thread our way through them. To the eye, it is cold and lifeless as the moon—yet there is the excitement of hidden life: the trail of a bear, the handmark plain and fresh; the sudden flight of grouse.

We are now among the fox-tail firs, and pine trees with small, crimson fir-cones, as we wind up the bare hillside into woods again. Then suddenly we are on a razor edge. I look at my horse's ears, desperately. The path is a foot wide and there seems to be nothing on either side. You don't care, I know that, as you turn and jeer at me. Rachel is laughing, too.

We reach a flat spot and dismount. Around and about us are the mountain ridges, running hither and thither in wild, strange lines. It is immense and fierce and dynamic. The pink and white rocks of Red River shine across the valley; and below, far below in the valley, lies a tiny green lake, blue green and dark: Columbine Lake, round which the drama of your story "The Princess" [36] is written.

We sit entranced. No one who has not been to the top of the Rocky Mountains, really knows what they are like—the fierce, dynamic lines of the ridges running against each other—harmony in wild disorder—the pines like dark, stiff hairs on some of them—the pale, ghostlike trunks of long-ago forest fires—bare, green-gray grass where the timber line ends . . .

Suddenly, out of it all, come riding three Indians. They are so much a part of it that we are startled by our own white faces, our not-belonging whiteness compared to their brown darkness, like living earth. They stop and talk. They have guns and bulging canvas bags on the backs of their saddles; but they have not seen a thing, no, nothing—and they are going home. Our suspicious eyes wander over the bags; their inscrutable faces and slightly mocking eyes watch us. Then, with friendly good-byes, they ride away, down into the trees.

At last, with reluctance, we begin the journey down. Your heart is thumping a little from the altitude, but your eyes are gleaming and you are still looking for flowers. We have to lead our horses down the mountain-side, until we reach the head of the Lobo Canyon. Our knees ache and we and the horses slip and slide. We rest and drink out of the clear stream, then we slowly ride home down the narrow trail—the horses eager, inclined to rush, on finding themselves headed for home.

We are tired: a severe fifteen miles, but we do not care. Frieda, with her inevitable cigarette hanging at the side of her lip, has supper ready for us. We eat enormously and move stiffly off to bed.[37]

31 August 1924   Kiowa Ranch, San Cristobal, New Mexico

⟨ *The autumn is coming here—we are so high. The summer has many thunderstorms—down in Del Monte they had three horses killed, in June, by one flash. But autumn is clear and blue, hot days, cold nights with great stars settling on the mountains. Now the big clearing in front of the house is really amethyst with dark-coloured Michaelmas Daisies, not very tall, and great gold patches of wild sunflower. But it's really a hard country, not a soft flowery country, though we've had endless strange, rather fascinating flowers up here, at this height.[38]*

Del Monte Ranch/Valdez/New Mexico/21 Sept 1924

⟨ *Dear Idella [Purnell Stone]*

The summer is gone, & autumn is here, & it is time, as you say, to be turning south. But the days are still very lovely—sunny & silent. So we shall stay on two or three weeks—not more: then come down to Mexico City. I think we shall stay a while in the Capital, & make plans there for the next move.

Spud is coming up here today from Taos—Bynner has gone to California for a while. He (Hal) says he'll pay us a flying visit before we depart.— Mabel Lujan is going to winter near New York, to be in touch with doctors, as she is not well. And there we are, the lot of us.

How is Dr. Purnell? I look forward to seeing you both again.

a rivederci
D. H. Lawrence [39]

30 September 1924   Kiowa Ranch, San Cristobal, New Mexico

❨ Sent to Barmby (Curtis Brown)—St. Mawr: also MSS. of the same, & of Woman Who Rode Away, Last Laugh, Jimmy & the Desperate Woman, Border Line, Dance of the Sprouting Corn, Indians & Entertainment. *Sent the copy of St. Mawr to Curtis Brown, London: & to Oxford Press epilogue for Movements in European History: & some illustrations for same. Going down to Taos for San Geronimo.*[40]

3 October 1924   Kiowa Ranch, San Cristobal, New Mexico

❨ We are leaving here next week. There was a flurry of wild snow in the air yesterday, and the nights are icy. But now, at ten o'clock in the morning, to look across the desert at the mountains you'd think June morning was shining. Frieda is washing the porch: Brett is probably stalking a rabbit with a 22-gun: I am looking out of the kitchen door at the far blue mountains, and the gap, the tiny gate that leads down into the canyon and away to Santa Fe. And in ten days' time we shall be going south—to Mexico. The high thin air gets my chest, bronchially. It's very good for the lungs, but fierce for tender bronchi.

.   .   .   .

The country here is very lovely at the moment. Aspens high on the mountains like a fleece of gold. Ubi est ille Jason? The scrub oak is dark red, and the wild birds are coming down to the desert. It is time to go south.—Did I tell you my father died on Sept. 10th, the day before my birthday?—The autumn always gets me badly, as it breaks into colours. I want to go south, where there is no autumn, where the cold doesn't crouch over one like a snow-leopard waiting to pounce. The heart of the North is dead, and the fingers of cold are corpse fingers. There is no more hope northwards, and the salt of its inspiration is the tingling of the viaticum on the tongue.

.   .   .   .

But I want to go south again to Oaxaca, to the Zapotecas and the Maya. Quien sabe, si se puede! [41]

8 October 1924   Kiowa Ranch, San Cristobal, New Mexico

❨ Packing up to leave ranch—snowy day. Finished The Princess. English bank balance £303. Balance in Chase National Bank, Metropolitan Branch at 4th Avenue at 23rd St. $2285.21.[42]

8 October 1924   Kiowa Ranch, San Cristobal, New Mexico

❨ We are packing up to leave here. Last night came the first snow: six deep inches. Today it's thawing dismally. It's very early for snow. And no doubt the Indian summer will come back. But it's a blow. The horses have come up, very miserable, want to be ridden. Well, I shall have to ride down for the milk.

If the roads are passable, we shall go down to Taos on Saturday, stay a day or two, then go down to Mexico City. My spirit always wants to go south. Perhaps one feels a bit of hope down there. Anyhow, the White civilization makes me feel worse every day. Brett will go down with us. But if we take a house, she must take a little place of her own. Not be too close. Here she has a little one-room cabin to herself. There is a 2-room guest-house: and still, a third sort of little log-barn we can make into a little house. It's so much easier that way.

.   .   .   .

I loathe winter. They gas about the Nordic races, over here, but I believe they're dead, dead, dead. I hate all that comes from the north.

.   .   .   .

The house is half dismantled: we are fastening the place up and leaving it. The snow is dropping wet off the pine trees, the desert seems decomposing in the distance—ugh! I must catch Aaron, my black horse, and ride down in the slush under these snow-dripping trees. Ugh!—But it's all in a lifetime.[43]

10 October 1924   Kiowa Ranch, San Cristobal, New Mexico

❨ Leave tomorrow: send down to Del Monte three trunks: iron one, Old Taormina one, & Brett's leather trunk: also my old Gladstone bag: hang keys for these in my green cupboard, in my room: send 2 large mattresses, one half-size, one camp-size (new) & one old camp-size to Del Monte: also three saddles, 4 bridles, and saddle cloths. Give William [Hawk] one pass-key for house door & one rim-lock key. Take other two with me: other cupboard keys in my room, in top half of double cupboard, left hand corner bottom shelf. Deeds of ranch in iron trunk sent to Del Monte.[44]

Mabel Dodge Luhan

. . . Lorenzo and Frieda came down and passed a few days here [Taos] before they left for Mexico and we for Croton-on-the-Hudson, and we passed all together, apparently, a few days of tired serenity, yet underneath the smooth surface there were currents of suspicion and misery. Lawrence never knew me as he so much wanted me to be, and Frieda and Tony and Brett all had their secret discomfiture.

Yet it was somehow peaceful, though perhaps more sadly so than happily. One day we all drove together almost in silence through the valley: through Arroyo Seco and back across Taos to Cordovas [Cordova]. Again the cottonwood trees were yellow against the dark-blue sky and there was no wind—not a breath or a breeze in the rich autumnal air. The mountains hung quietly purple around the crescent horizon, and the vast magnanimous mountain, above the pueblo, continued its unperturbed life as it has done for so long. Yes, we were peaceful and I felt it and said, as I had said once before:

"It seems like nothing, yet perhaps we shall look back on this afternoon and think how happy we were."

The next day, when they went away, Lorenzo leaned out for a last good-bye. There was a wistful look in his wide-apart blue eyes.

"We'll write," he said. "I know you're going to feel better soon." And then they left and I never saw him again.[45]

24 October 1924   Hotel Monte Carlo, Av. Uruguay 69, Mexico City

⟪ We got in after midnight on Wed. [22 October 1924]—train so late—journey otherwise uneventful, and not unpleasant. You can buy ticket and book Pullman now in El Paso station—much easier. But the food in the Pullman the same swindle. There has been a good deal of rain here—

country looks nice, and it's almost chilly. The capital is shabby and depressed—no business doing—no money—everybody rather depressed—not a very nice feeling in the town. I think we shall go in a fortnight to Oaxaca. The English Vice-Consul has a brother a priest in the Cathedral Chapter there, and he would sponsor us! [46] *Ye gods! But the man says it's very nice down there, and a perfect climate. If we stay, whatever will Idella [Purnell Stone] say! The Monte Carlo is almost unchanged, but not many guests. We chose to go upstairs—Hon. Dorothy Brett in your [Witter Bynner's] old room, we in the one inside where the monkey, the parrot, and the Chihuahua dog abode. With a bowl of candied fruit, a flask of Chianti, those coloured Majolica cups and tea, we only need you two [Witter Bynner and Spud Johnson] to push back the clock. They're very nice to us in the hotel.* [47]

George E. Rickards

It so happens that I am the British Vice Consul in Mexico City and the son of the late Mr. Constantine G. Rickards, former Vice Consul, and it looks that I have followed my father's footsteps in the Foreign Service.

Unfortunately, I regret to say that my father passed away on the 8th June 1950 in this city from heart failure. My father's brother the priest, Edward A. Rickards, from Oaxaca is also dead.

Father served as Vice Consul since 1910 at Oaxaca and later in Mexico City as Vice Consul and Acting Consul until his retirement from the service in 1943. He was a man of rather intellectual disposition, his main hobby being archeology, and author of the book called *The Ruins of Mexico* (London, 1910) and many other interesting works on archeology in general. He was born at Oaxaca, Oax. on the 23rd January 1876.

His background is as follows: Barrister at Law to the Courts of the Mexican Republic; and member of the *Société des Américanistes de Paris,* the *Sociedad Mexicana de Geografía y Estadística,* and the Mexican Scientific Society "Antonio Alzate."

He discovered and deciphered a Mexican Codex which is actually in the *Société des Américanistes de Paris,* and known as the "Rickards" Codex. He wrote many other articles of interest on archeology. He was a life member of the above Society and was granted an award and other decorations from various societies for his works. He belonged to the Episcopal Church of England.

Besides archeology, he was interested in collecting stamps, butterflies, stones, shells, and everything collectible. He left us upon his death with the most complete classified collection of butterflies (around 900) from all parts of the world. He owned mining property in the State of Oaxaca.[48]

29 October 1924   Hotel Monte Carlo, Av. Uruguay 69, Mexico City

⟨ *We've both had flu colds: everybody in this damned city coughing and sneezing: it's been very chilly: snow low down on Popocatepetl. And the town uneasy and depressed: as if the bottom had fallen out of the barrel. Don't like it.*

We think to leave for Oaxaca on Monday [3 November 1924]. Gamio is reported to be in Yucatan: but I don't care where he is. Somerset Maugham [49] *sent me a telegram: he left for Cuernavaca the day we came. But apparently he too is no loss: a bit sour and full of nerves and fidgets lest he shouldn't produce a Maughnum opus with a Mexican background before Christmas. As if he could fail!!*

. . . If we don't like Oaxaca, we shall probably toddle back. If I'm going to waste my sweetness on the desert air, I'll damned well choose my desert.[50]

Dr. Manuel Gamio

I never had the pleasure of knowing personally the famous novelist D. H. Lawrence because on the two or three occasions when he attempted to contact me, I was in Teotihuacán, Oaxaca or Yucatán, which I greatly deplored.

In respect to the book *The Plumed Serpent* and in general novels written about Mexico, I believe the following even though I declare that I do not consider myself a competent literary critic: A novel embraces three aspects.

1. It is the faithful exposition of events, personalities and social environment, such as they are in reality.

2. It is the exposition of events, personalities and social environment in conformity with the conventional interpretation of the author.

3. It is a combination of both types of exposition, which is generally the case.

The authors of a novel on a Mexican theme fall into three categories:

a. The national author, by virtue of being more fully a part of the medium in which he lives, can interpret and expose with more realism those personalities and events with which he deals. This has nothing to do with the quality of his novel which can be very good or very bad according to the intelligence and ability with which he combines and expresses his ideas. Also, because the author's horizon of observation is limited by the very environment in which he lives, on various occasions he cannot see events and phenomena which are outside his own environment.

b. The foreigner who, after living a long time in Mexico, writes a novel, can see better than the national certain events and phenomena which are outside the aforementioned uniform horizon, but in general he is less realistic than the Mexican author because his knowledge of the social medium is less extensive. The quality of his novel varies in respect to his intelligence.

c. The foreigner who writes a novel after a very short stay in Mexico is even less realistic than the above, but frequently he is able to appraise more ably the events which occur outside the horizon referred to, and if he is intelligent, his novel might have as much appeal or more so as those of the previous kinds of authors.

In my opinion Lawrence fits into this last category: he hates the bull-fights that are liked by many Mexicans, but he does not point out that the popularity of this sport is due to the very old tradition that came from Spain and was well received by the Indian, in whose precolombian past there were continual warfare and sanguinary ceremonies. He does not mention boxing, which some Mexicans and Americans consider savage yet which appeals to so many others.

Before coming to Mexico, Lawrence must surely have read passages of precolombian mythology, for he attributes to Ramón, Cipriano and other characters of his novel concepts relative to Huitzilopochtli and Quetzalcóatl despite the fact that the concepts and names of these gods have been forgotten and are unknown to the Mexican people; only historians and specialized archaeologists know them. It is true that there are numerous surviving elements of precolombian cultures among the people, but not in the medium to which Lawrence refers. The pure Indian of Mexico still adores idols and lives almost as he did in the precolombian era; the western culture has affected him very little because he continues to live in isolated and distant regions.

Of the many aboriginal groups who have lived in contact with the whites, there exist many surviving elements of the precolombian periods, but not of a mythological nature, because the cruel fanaticism of the conquerors and their colonial successors annihilated the Indians' religious ideas in order to force them to adopt Catholicism. They achieved this in part, but there still persist vague ideas of the prehispanic religious past, for there is a pagan-Catholic concept in many groups, but there is no concrete memory whatever of Huitzilopochtli, Quetzalcóatl and other deities. Despite all this, I feel that Lawrence's great intellect, and his able penetration of ideas, situations, and words make of his book a highly interesting and original novel.[51]

29 October 1924   Hotel Monte Carlo, Av. Uruguay 69, Mexico City

❨ Genaro Estrada [52] of the Pen club called on me—fat and bourgeois but nice and I'm in for a supper at the Oriental Café on Friday evening [31 October 1924], to meet the Pens. Don't like the thought of it one bit.[53]

Hotel Monte Carlo. Av. Uruguay/Mexico D. F./30 Oct 1924

❨ Dear Idella [Purnell Stone]
    I telegraphed to your mother about your parcel & got an answer—a letter —saying she was just sewing the silk dress. Anyhow it never arrived, in Santa Fe.[54]
    We've been here a few days, with bad colds. Don't like it.
    I've promised to go down & look at Oaxaca next week. Probably shan't like that. But I will let you know
    Everybody in this city sneezing & spitting. Hateful to be one of them.
    I'll write from Oaxaca. F. sends regards.

D. H. L.[55]

Dr. Luis Quintanilla

I was a personal friend of D. H. Lawrence. Not only was he a very great writer but a very great person. Perhaps the outstanding feature of D. H. was, besides genius, his kindness of heart and his absolute modesty. His physical aspect was that of a monk: tall, slender, of pale complexion, auburn hair and clear blue eyes; with a delicate head bent forward as if in constant meditation. He always spoke softly, rather timidly. The thing he hated the most was publicity. Being so famous, he really had to work hard in order to live *incognito.* For instance, Lawrence always would choose a small unpretentious hotel in which to stay during his travels. He found such a secluded place in Mexico City. When I visited him there for the first time after his arrival in the Mexican capital he told me how happy he felt to have found so nice and modest surroundings. And he asked me, point blank: "Do you think that newspaper men will discover me here? If that happens, is there another quiet and clean little place where I can hide?" His modesty was, indeed, sincere. People made him nervous. He could stand only a handful of selected acquaintances, as though people disturbed his peace of mind. Yet he did not particularly like to be left completely alone. He felt always better when Frieda, his beloved wife, or Miss Brett, his devoted secretary, were around him.

He enjoyed immensely walking around, whether in the country or in the city. He was extremely delicate and frail, like a tender plant.

The first time I met Lawrence was at a friendly dinner that Mexico's "Pen Club" offered in his honor. I had just published a couple of books of poetry. I knew the English language and had read *The Rainbow.* I was already a great admirer of Lawrence. From that first meeting, a sincere friendship was born. I guess one of the reasons why D. H. enjoyed my company was that I could talk in English to him; that I knew Europe quite well; and last, but not least, that I was beginning a literary career.

During the months he spent in Mexico, I saw Lawrence frequently. Sometimes in the afternoon, at his hotel. With his wife, Frieda, and Miss Brett, we used to comment on Lawrence's impressions of my Mexico. We would have, often, breakfast at Sanborns, in the heart of Mexico City; not because it was a popular place (as it still remains today) but because Lawrence had trouble initiating himself to our exotic Mexican food. And again, we often wandered through the streets for hours; a favorite pastime of D. H. was to talk about a million things, from poetry to the hard facts of the Mexican Revolution. Lawrence hovered [harbored?] a mixed feeling towards Mexico. He was fascinated by Mexico's colorful personality and, at the same time, frightened by the dramatic events of the Mexican Revolution. He simply could not stand violence, noise, and least of all death. And there was plenty of that during the Revolution that shook the social structure of Mexico. So, Mexico's beauty enchanted Lawrence, but the Mexican political situation horrified him to the point that he saw nothing but tragedy even in the Mexican landscape: its high mountains and snow-capped volcanoes. At a lunch, this attitude of Lawrence irritated me so much that I became aggressively Mexican, and

369

felt really hurt by D. H.'s criticism of my country and what was going on at the time. I regretted, years afterwards, my youthful impatience. I later understood the reasons why Lawrence had to feel so upset. But the incident interrupted, most unfortunately for me, a cordial friendship between the great British writer and this young and temperamental Mexican revolutionary. I never saw Lawrence after that.

My diplomatic career took me away from Mexico City and I never wrote to my admired and beloved friend again. Sometime afterwards Ruth, to whom I was then married, wrote a letter to Miss Brett telling her how sorry I was to know of D. H. Lawrence's failing health and how sorry, also, I felt about the unfortunate discussion that broke a friendship so precious to me. Miss Brett answered assuring me that Lawrence always remembered me with kindness,[56] which made me feel a lot better.[57]

Edward Weston

With the news of the death of D. H. Lawrence, [I] turned back the leaves of my day-books, kept the second of November, 1924, and read: "D. H. in Mexico, to a Sunday evening shortly after Lawrence, in with Luis Quintanilla. My first impression a most agreeable one. He will sit to me Tuesday." With Lawrence came his wife and a Miss Brett, I was given to understand his secretary. And then, Tuesday eve [4 November 1924]: "The sitting of Lawrence this morning. A tall, slender, rather reserved individual, with reddish beard. He was amiable enough and we parted in a friendly way, but the contact was too brief to penetrate another more than superficially. No way to make a sitting! I should not have attempted it: now I lack sufficient interest to develop my films."

Further notes indicate why I did attempt and rush through the sitting on a day when we were both preoccupied. He was leaving for Oaxaca the next day, and I had a luncheon engagement—"in honor (!) of the United States Ambassador to Mexico.[58] God knows his name; I don't— but duty calls. In preparation I trimmed the fringe from my trousers and borrowed a hat from Rafael. Now to buy a collar and I shall be ready!" So read my notes.

I wish I had cancelled my date, and spent the time with Lawrence. But evidently I was considering business before pleasure, and from the condition of my wardrobe, I must have needed business!

My memory carries more than I wrote down about Lawrence: a walk in *el bosque de Chapultepec*, the famous park,—"woods," the Mexicans call it,—Lawrence, Tina [59] and myself,—and certain bits of conversation. His first visit to Mexico not long before had thrilled him, but now he was frankly upset, distressed,—he wished to leave the city for Oaxaca, where he might quietly write. Had Mexico changed, or was Lawrence in a highly neurotic state? Obviously the latter. His resulting book, *The Plumed Serpent*, gave evidence. We read the book aloud during a period of travel through Mexico, a five months trip, which made me see vividly and feel deeply, an itinerary which took us far away from tourist tracks. I recall one place, where the Indians had seen foreigners only once before. So I offer these notes, not as a literary criticism, but as my intense reactions, against Lawrence's.

"Despite its entire lack of humor, we were at times convulsed with laughter. . . ."

"Besides he makes inaccurate or misleading statements. His chapter on the bull fight is full of absurdities. . . ."

"Lawrence tries, it is evident, to bolster up his symbolism by indicating the customs of one locality as representative of all Mexico. I found no market where the Indians 'never asked you to buy,'—they are usually clamorously insistent. Nor do 'the women always hold onto their water jars'—as he points out—'to show their lack of poise.' More often they walk free-handed with regal bearing. Throughout the book, apparently trivial inaccuracies persist, and form a wrong or one-sided impression of Mexico. Lawrence was bewildered, he was frightened, but he over-dramatized his fear. There are fine descriptive passages, intelligent analyses, accurate prophecy, but withal a padding of tiresome allegory . . . a book on Mexico which could have been written only by a neurotic Anglo-Saxon."

Returning to Mexico City we found the artists and writers there, all laughing over *The Plumed Serpent*. Covarrubias cartooned Lawrence at his desk, writing, triple outlines around him to indicate shaking with fear!

But overlooking inaccuracies, the book was the emotional reaction of a sick man, one might say of a dying man, so he cannot be criticized by one seeing the land in a less hysterical condition: indeed it may have more value as a piece of writing because of his intensity. And then,—is there an Anglo-Saxon, even in normal health, who has looked out on the passing Mexican landscape from his Pullman berth at night, without a feeling of awe! Something mysterious there, never to be fully understood by another race. Maybe the old gods *do* still rule!

Of one thing I feel sure: Lawrence had no plastic sense. This reaction I got at once, as I showed him various drawings, photographs, etc., verified later by his remarks in *Plumed Serpent re* the great frescoes of Diego Rivera.[60] So I can well imagine his recent venture in painting must be a carrying on of his literary viewpoint in paint. However, I am only surmising.

Lawrence wrote a kindly, sympathetic letter from Oaxaca, thanking me for his proofs, the best he had ever had,[61] offering to help me in every possible way with publishers, giving suggestions for business, admitting that he could not apply them himself. Nor could I!

In Oaxaca, at Hotel Francia, I noted Lawrence's name registered. I decided to call on Padre Ricardo, an English padre with whom he spent some time. But, like a hint to us of that which followed in the religious-civil war, the padre had been arrested and deported to Mexico City the night before by the military. The neighbors spoke in hushed voices, but with flashing eyes; his servant we found in tears. He had been well loved.

I did not meet Lawrence again.[62]

8 November 1924   Hotel Monte Carlo, Av. Uruguay 69, Mexico City

❨ Leave Mexico City for Oaxaca.[63]

10 November 1924   Hotel Francia, Oaxaca, Mexico

❨ Arrived yesterday.[64]

The Hon. Dorothy Brett

The station of Oaxaca is crowded, but the porter escorts us to the mule tram and we rattle slowly off. It is difficult to make out much of the town. The Hotel Francia is homely and the proprietress very friendly and kind. You are shown a large room by her, while I am taken off to another patio. You follow quickly to see where they are putting me. It is a huge, cool room, looking onto the street. You and Frieda see a big, double room next to this one, with two large beds swathed in mosquito curtains. You like it better than the one in the other patio, so the Señora changes you over. Then we go in to dinner.

It is then that I find to my dismay that Toby is missing—my precious ear-trumpet. I rush back to my room; I search everywhere—in your room, in all the bags. Not a sign. I am in despair. I come back to the dining-room depressed, helpless. You are depressed, too. You are so discouraged for me, so angry and irritated, that you can't bear to speak about it. We are too tired, anyhow, to talk much. We hurry off to bed directly we have eaten, with a final warning from the Señora:

"Do not," she warns, "put anything within reach of the windows. Place your things at the farthest corner of the room away from the window, as the thieves have long poles with a nail on the end to hook things through the windows."

Weeks later, coming suddenly into my room, I surprise a thief doing this. His pole falls into the room with a clatter as he lets go and runs, while I rush off for Señora Monros. She and the whole staff of the hotel come back with me to my room, to look with horror mixed with joy at the long pole lying across the floor of my room.

.   .   .

Next morning, rested, our curiosity aroused, we stroll out into the town. The sun is already hot. The streets are full of Indians and every-body stares at us: the Indians as they pad softly by, the Mexicans peer-ing out of their shops. We wander round and round the lovely, shady Zocola, the big square Plaza. Then we find the Market Place, a huge, cor-rugated iron building.

You seem a bit low-spirited, a bit quiet and tired. The streets to the market are crowded with Indians; they keep coming along in streams: on foot, on burros, in oxen carts. The hill men in their little black, pointed hats, ragged and wild-looking, stare hard at you. This makes you mad. And many of the Indians call, "Cristo! Cristo!" softly after you. And this also makes you angry, as it did in Mexico City.

We plunge into the Market Place. It is dark, with great splashes of sunlight in large pools here and there. There are flowers, masses and masses of flowers; clean, glistening vegetables and fruit; gorgeous serapes; materials; baskets . . . Color, color everywhere! The whole place blazes and glows, the colors flash in the pools of sunlight, deepening in the rich shadows. The clean white clothes of the men, the big dark hats, the golden straw hats, and the patterned flowing skirts of the women and their speckled rebozos—all merge with the flowers and fruits and vege-tables. And, above all, how quiet it is. The scent of the flowers, the dry smell of the earth, the soft, low ripple of talk among the Indians, broken now and then by a loud squawk from the turkeys or chickens or ducks lying with their feet tied together in bunches on the floor.

The Indians are watchful as we pass down the avenues of stalls. You stop at a stall of pottery: I can feel the interest run from the Indian woman behind the stall along the whole line of men and women. She smiles, a questioning smile, and wishes you a polite good-day. The same smiling good-day is returned, the same gentle good manners. Her passing look of bewilderment gives place to an instantaneous friendliness, a recognition of something more nearly akin to herself. The news flashes down the line and like a wave ripples round the whole market. Furtive looks, little smiles of friendliness are given you. Your gentleness, your red beard, thick hair, quiet blue eyes—all add to the mystery of the strange otherness of this soft-spoken man. A message has been subtly broadcasted throughout the whole building: A new kind of white man is among us.

A man mutters "Cristo," and a look of fleeting annoyance passes over your face. A woman sees it, smiles at you, a row of shining white teeth. You smile back at her and give a little, shy laugh; and the Indians nearby instinctively warm towards you. The babies, perched on the stalls, stare at you with huge, solemn eyes, like round globes of dark light.

Señora Monros has now joined us. Frieda listens to the prices, to the bargaining. The basket on the back of the Señora's mozo, slung from his forehead, is speedily filled up. And you buy two jugs, after a great deal of bargaining.

"It is," you tell me, "Their moment of gossip. If you do not bargain, they are disappointed: they have missed their only bit of excitement in the day."

I have such a hunger to buy everything I see, that you will not let me buy anything except sandals—guaraches, as they are called. The big burly Indian in the stall, grins at you as you pick up the sandals and sniff them all over.

"My sandals do not smell," the man says proudly—which is strange, as the smell among his sandals is simply appalling. I pick out a much-patterned pair and sniff at them gingerly. I hand them to you, and you smell them all over, carefully.

"They are all right," you say. "If they fit, buy them at half the price he asks." They do fit, and after a bit of shy haggling, they are wrapped up in paper. We each get an unsmelly pair. Outside you explain:

"They tan the leather with human excrement, that's what makes them smell." The expression on my face is too much for you, and you shake with laughter. "It was even a bit too much for Cortez and his Spaniards, and they were none too squeamish in those days," you add.

The town is now plastered with notices about my stolen Toby, but Señora Monros shakes her head:

"They will be too frightened to bring it back. My daughter will take you to a tinsmith to see if he can make you one."

The tinsmith is a very intelligent Indian. I make a drawing in his shop, and in a few hours he has made an ear-trumpet that serves me well until another comes from London. But the Señora is right about my stolen one: it is never brought back.[65]

Hotel Francia/Oaxaca/Tuesday [11 November 1924]

〔 Dear Quintanilla

We got here all right Sunday night—a very amusing journey, by the *Ferrocarril Mexicano* to Esperanza, then a wild little railway (2 hrs) to Tehuacan: slept the night there in a very nice Hotel Mexico; came on on Sunday, a wild queer lovely journey in a steep gorge. Oaxaca is a very quiet little town, with small but proud Indians—Zapotecas. The climate is perfect—cotton dresses, yet not too hot. It is very peaceful, and has a remote beauty of its own. The Hotel Francia very pleasant—such good amusing food—4 pesos a day for everything. We want to go out to Mitla and Tula and Ejutla—but will wait a bit, and if you come we'll all go together. There are two rivers, but I've only seen one, with naked Indians soaping their heads in mid-stream. I shall bathe. There are no Fifis nor Lagartijos [66]— and the Indians go about in white cotton, they don't make them wear proper trousers as in most towns. I think we shall move soon into a house with a patio,—stay here ten days or so more—and Miss Brett stay in the Hotel.

The advantages of Chapala are, of course, the Lake, bathing and the short journey. But this isn't touristy at all—quite, quite real, and lovely country around, where we can ride. A man has already promised to lend me a good Texas saddle. And we can go down to Ejutla and look at silvermines, with this same man.

Only, once more. Chapala is much more a proper holiday resort.

The journey costs 12.00 to Esperanza, 2.70 thence to Tehuacan, and then 12.50 on to Oaxaca. Leave Mexico [City] 8.05 a.m.—leave Esperanza 2:30 p.m. arr. Tehuacan 6:30. Leave Tehuacan 10:30 a.m. arrive Oaxaca about 7.0 p.m. Very nice people on the train, and wonderful scenery, really.

But if you want to feel you are on a regular holiday go to Chapala. I'd hate you to come here and feel disappointed.

Many greetings to you both, and to JANE,[67] from us all

Yours

D. H. Lawrence

Take a bit of lunch, perhaps, from Tehuacan as you don't get food till 2:15 at Tomellin. The little train is very dusty—wear old clothes as possible. But it is not too hot.[68]

14 November 1924   Hotel Francia, Oaxaca, Mexico

〖 We got down here on Sunday night [9 November 1924]: it takes two days from Mexico City, though it's not so very far. Oaxaca is a little town, about 30,000, alone in the south, with a perfect climate. The market is full of roses and violets, the gardens are all flowers. Every day is perfectly sunny, a bit hot at midday. The natives are mostly Zapotec Indians, small, but very straight and alert and alive: really very nice. There is a big market humming like a bee-hive, where one can buy anything, from roses to horse-shoes. I wish we could send you some of the pottery, such beautiful colours, and costs nothing. But the last lot I sent got smashed. This is where they make the serapes like the one with the eagle that hung on the wall: and the little men stalk about in them, looking very showy.—The governor is an Indian from the hills. I called on him in the palace!!!—But everywhere the government is very Labour—and somehow one doesn't feel very solid. There are so many wild Indians who don't know anything about anything, except that they are told that every "rich" man is an enemy.—There may be a bad bust-up in Mexico City: and again, everything may go off quietly. But I don't like the feeling. If only it wasn't winter, we'd come back to the ranch tomorrow. I feel so weary of people—people, people, people, and all such bunk, somehow, with politics and self-assertiveness.—As it is, we shall probably take a house here for a month or two. Thank goodness my chest and throat are better, since we are here in this soft warm air. I want to get them sound this winter, and next year stay on much later at the ranch.

. . . .

Brett lost Toby, and has had the tin-smith make her a substitute, shaped like a funnel: much excitement among the natives when she uses it. Her machine also works very fitfully, so that her ears are out of luck.—Frieda of course pines for her ranch, and the freedom. So really do I.[69]

15 *November 1924*   *Hotel Francia, Oaxaca, Mexico*

❲ *It's the chief market today—such a babel and a hubbub of unwashed wild people—heaps of roses and hibiscus flowers, blankets, very nice wild pottery, calves, birds, vegetables, and awful things to eat—including squashed fried locust-beetles. F. and I bought pots and blankets—we shall move into a house next week, and are collecting bits of furniture from various people. It's the house of an Englishman who was born here, and who is a priest in the Cathedral Chapter.*[70] *Hon. Dorothy Brett will stay on in the hotel— the proprietress is Spanish and very nice.*

But everything is so shaky and really so confused. The Indians are queer little savages, and awful agitators, pump bits of socialism over them and make everything just a mess. It's really a sort of chaos. And I suppose American intervention will become inevitable. You know, socialism is a dud. It makes just a mush of people: and especially of savages. And 70 per cent of these people are real savages, quite as much as they were 300 years ago. The Spanish-Mexican population just rots on top of the black savage mass. And socialism here is a farce of farces: except very dangerous.

Well, I shall try and finish my Quetzalcoatl novel this winter—see what comes of it. The world gives me the gruesomes, the more I see of it. That is, the world of people. This country is so lovely, the sky is perfect, blue and hot every day, and flowers rapidly following flowers. They are cutting the sugar-cane, and hauling it in in the old ox-wagons, slowly. But the grass-slopes are already dry and fawn-coloured, the unventured hills are already like an illusion, standing round inhuman.[71]

The Hon. Dorothy Brett

We are rattling along in the mule-tram on our way to the Padre's house. He is the brother of the British Vice-Consul in Mexico City, and has some rooms to let. The street is long and hot until we reach the end: there we find large, shady trees hanging over walls.

A faded number on some big doors, shows us the Padre's house. We knock and an old Indian woman peers out. She is expecting us, so she lets us in. The Padre is out, but she will show us the rooms. Five other Indian women stand looking at us as we walk into the lovely, shady patio.

How quiet and peaceful it is. How sheltered after the streets and the hotel. The little square garden is full of trees. Orange trees, banana trees, and some immense, dark-leaved, silver-trunked trees. The quiet is broken by the shrill, noisy talk of two green parrots, perched in a tree. A small white poodle kind of dog sniffs round our legs.

The patio is red-tiled; so are the huge, high rooms that the Indian woman takes us into. Huge, barren, unfurnished rooms, opening into each other with no doors. The outside doors open onto the patio. There is a nice kitchen with charcoal ovens.

"How like Italy!" you say. It is cool and spacious, the garden lovely; yet you seem dissatisfied. Then Frieda blurts out that she does not think there is room enough for all of us. I realise the difficulty, also the unexpressed wish.

"I can remain at the hotel, easily," I say, "And that will give you more privacy." The air lightens; Frieda becomes immediately possessive—almost in possession.

The Padre appears round a bush: a small, stoutish man. You introduce yourself and us, then begin talking to him about rents and so on. He is a friendly little man, who afterwards becomes one of your best friends in the town.

The rooms are unfurnished, but he knows where furniture can be borrowed; he will ring up. Your letters of introduction bring friends and help immediately; and in less than no time, furniture is hauled out of storage, mozos are staggering about with beds and cupboards, tables and chairs.

One tiny little Indian, the mozo of the dentist, Dr. Kull, is reluctant to carry anything very heavy; and as for the mozo that has been found for you, he seems to dread anything of any weight on his back also. You are astonished and annoyed.

"Are they lazy?" you enquire. Then the story of Dr. Kull's mozo is told. Money was stolen from the Cathedral collection box, and this boy was suspected, but proved his innocence. Then a cousin of his was suspected and he also proved his innocence, but in vain: he was imprisoned, and so was Dr. Kull's boy because they were related. In order to try and wring a confession out of him, he was hung up by the neck for a day. When taken down, his neck was swollen for months and months. He was taken off to another state, but on the way he escaped and returned, starving and ill, neck still swollen, to Dr. Kull—who managed to get the boy a release and a pardon.

Our mozo, Rosalino, had refused to be conscripted for the army, when the men called at his village for recruits. They had forthwith beaten him so severely that his back was permanently injured: hence the reluctance to carry any heavy weight.[72]

Well, in spite of all that, you get settled in. Mr. Miller, a miner living opposite you, sends in cakes and jam; and a trip to the market fixes you up in stores. That evening, we take the little mule tram back to the hotel, leaving the quiet patio and lovely garden reluctantly. It will still be a day or two before you can move in.

.   .   .

You have had a stomach-ache most of the night and are feeling low. Also you are disturbed by the constant rumor of revolution, the uneasiness of the white people, their disheartening indifference to their own welfare, to their own safety. They have been isolated for nearly four years: the railway is their only road, and that so easily blown up. This depresses you terribly.

"Fancy," you say, "Being shut up here for years. How awful!" And that was the only fear that really haunted you in Oaxaca; that and the tales of frightful diseases; tales of unspeakable horrors in the mountain villages; of nameless, incurable diseases that are poured into your ears by the doctors. They warn us not to take long walks in the country.

"Do not go far out of town," they tell us, "It is not safe. You may be robbed of everything you have on—even murdered." A chill creeps into our blood. You feel irritated, your freedom curtailed, your precious freedom. But nevertheless we take a walk right out into the country. We have seen nearly all of the churches, inside and out, because we scramble up onto the roofs among the cupolas. We are haunted by the intense *santos*—the agonized Christs and Saints.

"Look, Lawrence," I say of one, "Look at the eye in the middle of the forehead!"

"Good gracious, Brett," you answer, angrily, "Have you never heard of the third eye?" And you disappear up a small, corkscrew staircase in a turret.

"Call me if there is a parapet and I can't be giddy," I cry. Then I hear a faint, far-away call:

"Come on; it's quite safe, and too lovely to miss." So I creep cautiously up the stairs out onto the roof and look over the golden-colored town.

But this time we are for the country. "Let's try," you say. "I don't believe anyone will touch us. I do so want to get out of the town for a bit." So the three of us wander off. It is hot, piping hot; and we explore small roads, wander into deserted houses and gardens. Frieda longs for one house in a beautiful shady garden, full of flowering trees and flowers.

"It's no good," you say. "They would never let us live out here. The only way to live in Mexico is to possess nothing." By this time, we are so hot that we can hardly move. We find a field with a stream in it.

"Let us paddle," cries Frieda; and off come our shoes and stockings. "Look at the lovely cows," says Frieda, again, "How big they are!" The cows approach to have a look at this strange sight in the river. They come quite close and surround us. Then one of the cows jumps onto the back of another: it is an enormous bull. Frieda's face is a study: she rushes for her shoes. They are nearly all huge bulls. You are laughing, laughing so much the tears are in your eyes; but all the same you are hurrying into your shoes also. I am already in mine.

"Don't run," you say to us, "Let us go quietly." Then the bulls begin to fight. Heads lowered, they rush at each other, bellowing. They are a silvery gray; big, with large horns. We move off quietly, turning to watch them. We have armed ourselves with large sticks, but there is no need; they are too taken up with their own fight to bother about us. We scramble back onto the road and sit and rest under a tree. Further on we pass a man ploughing: a couple of oxen hitched to an old, ancient, wooden plough.[73]

17 November 1924   Hotel Francia, Oaxaca, Mexico

⟨ Sometimes the American Continent gets on my nerves, and I wish I'd come to Sicily or South Spain for the winter. But as it is, I suppose we shall stay a few months here, since we're moving into a house tomorrow. But if I still feel put out by the vibration of this rather malevolent continent, I'll sail from Vera Cruz and spend my last dollars trying the mushiness of Europe once more, for a while. It's a fool's world, anyhow, and people bore me stiffer and stiffer. Fancy, even a Zapotec Indian, when he becomes governor, is only a fellow in a Sunday suit grinning and scheming. People never, never, never change: that's the calamity. Always the same mush.[74]

17 November 1924   Hotel Francia, Oaxaca, Mexico

⟨ Balance in National Chase bank $2004.00 to Oct. 31st. Move into Richards [Rickards] house tomorrow.[75]

The Hon. Dorothy Brett

We have scrubbed the furniture. You are settled into your half of the priest's house. Mr. Miller, your neighbor in the house on the opposite side of the street, sends in more cakes and jam. The rest of the supplies are already bought in the market. All through the market, all the way home, an Indian woman follows you with four ducks squeezed in a basket. Nothing you say deters her; she is determined to sell you the ducks. She follows you into the patio, and there the poor cramped ducks are pulled out of the basket and shown to you. By this time you are so bored, so defeated by her persistence, that you buy the ducks and she goes off happy; while the four Indian servants gather round and tell you that a little pond must be made for them.

Our mozo is grinning. He has decided that he likes you and that he will stay; so he leads us to a small, high-walled yard and there digs a round hole, pours water into it—and then unties the ducks' legs. They give a few stiff scuffles and then, with a clack, slip into the water and wag appreciative tails.

You are in high spirits, glad to be quiet and private. You have changed into your beloved black and white, befrogged check suit and guaraches. You have sewn the mattress; I have painted the chairs white; while Frieda has sewn the blinds. You light the charcoal fire. It is the same, you tell me, as the charcoal fires in Italy. The kettle boils and the priest comes to tea. The Indian women peep furtively from their doorways at you. Our mozo, Rosalino, beams. He shows you where he sleeps, and you look doubtful, perplexed. It is a wooden bench near the big double doors onto the street. That, and the threadbare serape, is all he has for a bed.

"But the nights are chilly," you say to the priest.

"They are used to it," he answers. But somehow you are not satisfied; and when we go to the market, with Rosalino following with the basket for the stuff we buy, you take him to the serape heap and tell him to choose one, a nice warm one for himself.

For a moment he stares at you incredulously; then, with a broad smile and a gleam of white teeth, he begins to bargain. He sees the one he wants, and in true Indian fashion he goes about getting it as cheaply as he can. We move off, knowing that the job will be a long one. Finally he catches up with us and touches you on the arm. He tells you he can get the blanket he wants for so much—incredibly cheap. You give him the money and he hurries back, returning with the treasure folded over his shoulder. From that moment, he is your slave.

One evening you find him on his bench, poring over a copy-book. "What is it?" you ask him. Shyly he hands up the book. He attends a night school for reading and writing. His copy-book is full of long poems that he has to learn and copy over and over again.

"I will help you in the mornings," you tell him. "Then you'll get on quicker." And every morning you teach him for an hour. Sometimes, coming up in the morning, I find you and Rosalino sitting on the hard bench, Rosalino with a face of agonized concentration on the simple things you are trying to teach him.

He is observant and discovers that you take a bath regularly every Saturday evening, and that Sunday morning means a clean shirt. Rosalino religiously goes to the public baths on Saturday evenings from the moment he makes this discovery; and every Sunday he appears in a gorgeous flowered shirt, spotlessly clean. He has but two, until you give him two more; but his appearance on Sundays is always dazzling.

Then one day he disappears. You are hurt, but it shows in bitterness. "It is always the same: give friendship and they deceive you and go. They don't really care—they really hate us. It makes me hate them," you say.

"He will come back," says the priest. Two days later Rosalino is back on his bench.

"Where have you been?" He waves a vague arm to the mountains.

"I go home, to my village, to see my people." Later the priest tells you what happened. You and Frieda had gone for a long, long walk towards the mountains, through new, strange villages. Rosalino had gone with you, carrying the basket of sandwiches. You had passed through strange, remote little villages, where a white man was new and strange. The people had fled; you had seen them peeping round trees at you, frightened at your white face and red beard. The people fled in all directions, whenever you appeared, so little were they used to white people. But the mountains had given Rosalino a nostalgia for his own mountain home—an irresistible longing. And, Indianlike, he had gone off: he had to go back, just for a fleeting visit. But he has returned, with his faithful devotion, and now he begs and begs you to take him with you always wherever you go. This you know would be fatal; he would die of homesickness and cold. Meanwhile you teach him, and he guards you faithfully.

Your large rooms are beautifully cool, the long patio a delight, with its big, shady trees and flowers and quietness. The scarlet poinsettias are out; the parrots incessantly chatter in their tree; and the little dog snoozes comfortably at your feet.[76] The ducks are fattened and heartlessly eaten one by one—all except the last one, which, when you go one day into the yard to catch, suddenly rises on unsuspected wings and flies over the wall. How angry you are, after all the feed and care it has had, to lose the good meal! Enquiries are made to all the neighbors, but not one of them has seen a duck lately—although it has been clearly seen in the neighboring garden.

You take up your writing. You read what you have written in Chapala of *The Plumed Serpent*.

"I will have to rewrite it," you say. "Chapala has not really the spirit of Mexico; it is too tamed, too touristy. This place is more untouched." So you begin in the mornings to write, while I once more begin my slow, painful typewriting. And our spelling does not match any better in Mexico than it did in America!

As I sit in my hotel room, near the long, barred windows, the Indians go softly, swiftly by in the sunny street. The women, folded in their rebozos, in their full white skirts and with their bare feet, scarcely give me a glance. The men, wrapped up in their serapes like colored pillars, topped by their huge felt hats, go by quietly, but slow up and cast stealthy looks at me—more aware of me than the women, more inquisitive; more wondering and curious; and more aware of themselves, too. The strangeness of the place crowds in to me—our utter difference and, beyond all, our complete isolation.

. . . .

Then one morning we actually start for Mitla. Mr. Miller is taking us, in a car, for there is a road as far as Mitla. . . .

. . . .

In spite of mud holes, through which we crawl carefully, we manage to reach Mitla about twelve—a strange, lonely little village. The road is lined by single organ-cactus. They have been planted as fences and look just like green-painted wooden fences, except for the irregularity of height. Behind these cactus fences, lurk little leave-villages, so crouched in among the undergrowth and foliage of trees, that they are hard to see.

The Inn is busy, with oxen carts drawn up outside; but there is a feeling of isolation here that makes us shudder. We walk up to the ruins along the cactus-lined road. It is terribly dusty, but when we reach the ruins, their beauty and strangeness make up for the dreariness of the village. The carving is magnificent. A well-nourished, well-dressed Indian becomes our guide. But a queer feeling steals over us—the place smells of blood. The guide takes us down to the sacrificial stone. There is a pillar down there which has the power of foretelling the length of one's life.

"Put your arms round," says the guide, "And I can tell you how long you are to live." Frieda flatly refuses; but you and I, one after the other, clasp the pillar firmly. You have eighteen years to live, and I twenty. We go up into the open air thankfully, away from that sacrificial stone and the smell of blood that somehow permeates the whole ruin. It seems lifeless and yet full of a dark, fierce life.

The wind has become almost a gale and the dust is thick in the air. We are tired and a bit depressed. An excellent lunch in the little hotel cheers us up, but it is hard to shake off the feeling of blood and fierceness that the ruins give out.

The long, slow drive home tires you terribly. We meet the hill-people returning on their long trek home. It takes some of them two or three days to make the journey from their mountain villages to the market. The stream of Indians, oxen-carts, burros, to and fro, seems suddenly ageless and eternal in its slow, tireless rhythm.[77]

Aven. Pino Suarez #43/Oaxaca, Oax./Sunday [7? December? 1924]

⟨ Dear *Quintanilla*

I was sorry you couldn't come down, but glad to hear of Pesos 20 per diem. Sounds almost as good as an engine-driver. I think in many ways you are a born diplomat. Who knows, you may save Mexico yet. She needs a bit of saving, even along with Calle's nice words. Personally, I believe he means them. But it's a far cry to Lochaber.[78]

We are settled in half the Richard's [Rickard's] house—the English Vice Consul—the brother here is a padre in the Cathedral Mitra—but a nice man. Of course we know all the Americans, there are no English. I am working at my novel which is just beginning to digest its own gall & wormwood. Saluti cordiali to Señor Estrada—I am almost afraid to write his name, in view of the "strained relations" & Mexican Nacional sensitiveness. But risk it.—The picture is Mitla: top of my head. Miss Brett has taken to photography. The other man is José García whom I think you know. *All good wishes to M. le diplomate & to Madam & Jeanne, not of Arc.*[79]

D. H. Lawrence [80]

9 December 1924   Av. Pino Suarez 43, Oaxaca, Mexico

❲ *We have taken a house down here for the winter. It's a lovely climate, hot and sunny, roses and hibiscus and bananas, but not tropical heat. . . . One needs a rest after America: the hardness, the resistance of all things to all things, inwardly, tires one.*[81]

The Hon. Dorothy Brett

A strange feeling is coming over us: a dual feeling. One of imprisonment, and then another of a fierce desire to sally forth armed to the teeth and to shoot—to assert ourselves noisily in this noiseless unease. We can find no freedom, for ourselves or in anyone else. Everybody is virtually a prisoner. The Indians are afraid of the Mexicans, the Mexicans are afraid of the Indians, and the Americans are afraid of both.

You are becoming exasperated. The quiet of the little patio has almost become the quiet of a prison. Yet wherever you go, there is surprise and wonder among the Indians. The sensitive approach, the understanding, the quiet friendliness, the perfect manners, matching their own perfect manners, warms them to you quickly. What we are told is so different to what we experience in our contacts with the Indian.

"In spite of the beautiful climate," you say, "I don't believe I will ever be able to stand the lack of freedom. I wish we could buy huge revolvers and knives and kill somebody. It's all so silly and tiresome. And the Indians are nice, too—really nice; and one could be friendly with them if only one were left alone and allowed to be friendly."

Then, as we walk home past the barracks, Frieda and I on the pavement, a huge Indian soldier (with his head hunched in his shoulders, one hand in a pocket, the other holding a rifle) confronts us. He points to the road. His motion is silent and savage. Frieda and I hurry past on the edge of the curb. You, who are anyhow walking in the street, turn white with fury. The soldiers, the terrible, dreaded soldiers!

We pass prisoners, sometimes, guarded by these soldiers and being marched to prison. The prisoners are a sickly green, green with the fear and horror of the prisons, where they starve to death unless fed by their

385

relatives, as no food is supplied in the prison. And the prison itself is a huge, desolate stone building, dreadful even from the street.

.　　.　　.

The three of us are in Dr. Miller's house, drinking cocktails and eating very good sandwiches. You ask him if he can lend you a book. He is most willing and eager, and goes to the book-case, you following. You kneel down and take a look along the line of books. You pull one out and glance through it. As you kneel there, turning over the pages of the book, Mr. Miller hands you another with a laugh, saying:

"This is just the book for you." You take it and hold it in your hands. On the cover, is the picture of a woman pulling off her chemise, a man in evening suit watching her. You take it in your hands, a look of astonishment on your face. You hold it for a few moments in silence, then hand it quietly back to Miller without even saying a word. He looks baffled, but he puts it back on the shelf and does not offer you any more books. You finally choose a book on Mexico.

.　.　.　.　.　.　.　.　.　.　.　.　.　.　.

You and I have decided to try and go out and sit in the desert. You want to get out in the mornings to write (you are beginning to write *Mornings in Mexico*), and I have a longing to paint.

"Let us try," you say. "Two of us must be safe. Frieda can join us with lunch: Rosalino can carry the basket and look after her." But Frieda won't.

I come up in the tram in the early morning for you. You are ready with your copy-book and pen; I have my paints. Off we go, out into the lovely morning. It is the radiant fragrance of the air that is the beauty of Oaxaca.

We walk away onto the desert, far out, facing the great mountains. We walk along slowly, happy to have the great space around us. Not a soul is in sight. Occasionally we pass a man with cattle, or in the distance, along some trail, an oxen cart slowly crawls.

We find two bushes—far apart, but within easy calling distance. You settle down under one, I under the other; and you begin to write in your easy, steady way. I fix up my paint box and begin to paint. The sun pours down. I creep back into my bush as far as I can and peer out to see how you are faring. You have taken off your coat and have laid it over the bush as a sort of umbrella. Under it you are sitting in your shirtsleeves, writing steadily. A couple of women ride by in the distance, the burros mere specks; and up in the pure blue sky great birds are wheeling, gold in the sun. Suddenly your shadow falls over my painting. "I have finished," you say. "How have you been getting along?" I hold up my painting, proudly. "Oh, Brett," you say, testily, "Do look at the mountain. It has great bare toes, where it joins the desert. Here, let me have a try." Down you sit, and with delicate finger-touches, you proceed to give the mountain its toes. You roughen the fir-trees on the mountain and darken the blue of the sky. "You are dumb, Brett; you don't look at things; you have no eyes."

"Tomorrow," I say darkly, "I will put in the figures,"—knowing that you can't paint figures. At that you laugh and with a sigh look at your watch.

"Frieda can't be coming, after all; so we must start home." And we collect our things reluctantly, and wander slowly back.[82]

Av. Pino Suarez #43. Oaxaca. Oax. [18 December 1924]

⟨ Dear Mr. Weston

Thank you very much for the photographs. I like them very much: think I like the one with the chin up better than the other looking down: but like both of them. I would write to Vanity Fair myself, but have clean forgotten the editors name: [83] *and I had lunch with him in the spring. But I am doing one or two little articles which will probably suit Vanity Fair. Next week I shall send them to my agent, A. W. Barmby of Curtis Brown Ltd. 116 West 39th St. New York, and tell him about the portrait too. He would look after it if you like. And I'll tell my English agent, Curtis Brown. 6 Henrietta St. Covent Garden. London W.C. 2, to approach one of the big London illustrated periodicals, if you like. You write to Barmby and to Curtis Brown, if you feel so inclined. It seems to me you have reached the point where you should go in for a bit of publicity. Vanity Fair might like some of your less startling nude studies, if you could stand seeing them reproduced & ruined.*

Let me know if I can help you in any way. Tackle the world, its a rather stupid bull, to be taken by the horns, not dodged.

Greet the Signora. Let me know when you leave. Those two addresses of my agent are always good. Wish I had a copy of Aaron's Rod to send you. There is supposed to be a parcel of my books on its way to me, but it must have fallen into somebody's pocket.

Yours
D. H. Lawrence [84]

Av. Pino Suarez #43/Oaxaca, Oax./19 December 1924

❡ Dear Quintanilla

I had the portraits from Edward Weston: they are very good, I think. I want him to get them published, in New York Vanity Fair and in London, perhaps the Sphere. They like to have a bit of text too. Why don't you do a little article on Mexico D.F.—& me thrown in—& Weston thrown in—for Vanity Fair. Sounds as if I want to get publicity for myself, but it's not that. Vanity Fair knows me already very well. But it would be quite nice for me, & good for Weston, because they ought to know a wee bit about him, when the photograph is published. It's time he tackle the world. And then you, with your Paris-Post-bellum amusing style, you could very successfully do little articles—two or three thousand words—for a paper like Vanity Fair, which everybody reads. Little amusing articles, even on Calles etc. to hurt nobody. Why don't you do that? I think I can get them accepted all right. Do the P.E.N. Club a bit funnily. And the mother of Janey can help you, she'll know what to put in. Don't say you're used up by the FOREIGN OFFICE, that's too farcical.

Yours
D. H. Lawrence [85]

10 January 1925   Av. Pino Suarez 43, Oaxaca, Mexico

❡ I am sending you [Curtis Brown] four articles—Mornings in Mexico [86]—nice and short . . . . I am getting ahead with the Mexican novel. If heaven is with me, I should finish it this month. I had a good deal done from last year.—It will probably make you open your eyes—or close them: but I like it very much indeed. If I finish by the end of this month, then about 2nd February we shall go to Mexico City, to see about a ship. My wife feels she must see her mother, and my father died, and my sister keeps worrying to see me. So perhaps we'll be in England by March. [87]

Pino Suarez #43/Oaxaca, Oax./10 Jan. 1925

❡ Dear Quintanilla

Did you get the photograph? I signed and sent them back.

And the little article came. I was a bit sad, because it was sad and rather bitter: in fact very: with undigested spleen. Is that how you really feel about them: I doubt if they'd print it, because the touch isn't light enough. I'm afraid I had to go scribbling on your MS.—By the way, type on one side only, for literary MSS.

I couldn't help writing out your little article again. I'll get it typed, & send it you. You could, you know, easily write these little sketches. Only it means conquering your own sadness and heaviness inside first, and being able to laugh at it all, if only on the wrong side of your face.

My wife wants to go to Germany to her mother. Probably at the end of the month we shall come up to Mexico [City] to arrange a ship, & sail in February.—But then, should see you & Jane [&] Jane's mother.

Till then, adios!
D. H. Lawrence [88]

Av. Pino Suarez #43/Oaxaca, Oax./12 Jan. 1925

⟨ Dear Quintanilla

I send you your little article, which I'm sorry I went scribbling on: and also mine.[89] You mustn't take offense at anything I say: because of course I don't mean any.—I find even my article barely covers its rancour, rancor, and is a bit bewildering. There must be a terrible bitterness somewhere deep down between the U.S.A. and Mexico, covered up. When one touches it, it scares one, & startles one.—But just put my little article in the fire, if you don't like it.—Or if you like it, send it to Vanity Fair or some paper, & see if they'll print it over Luis Q. I doubt if they will. It'll make them too uneasy. But fun to try them.

I have done a lot of my novel again—I had the biggest part done last year. It is good, but scares me a bit, also.

We think to come up to Mexico [City] the first days in February, & probably sail for England on the 20th Feb. from Vera Cruz. I don't feel very easy in my skin, in Mexico this time. Perhaps I ought to go home for a bit.

Miss Brett doesn't want to go to England—wants to go straight back to our ranch in New Mexico—and leave any time now. If she arrives in Mexico City, will you & your wife look after her a bit. Ask Mrs. Quintanilla if she will. And if you hear of anybody nice with whom Miss Brett might travel up to El Paso, tell me, will you. I don't like to think of her going alone.

The little article is yours to do as you like with, entirely. Perhaps best just make an auto-da-fe.

It's lovely & warm now here. What is it, makes one want to go away?

Best of wishes to you.

D. H. Lawrence [90]

The Hon. Dorothy Brett

This morning I wake up with a sort of apprehension hanging over me. There is a loud knock at the door: it is Rosalino with a letter from you. I tear it open. It is fierce, cruel, telling me that the three of us are no longer a happy combination and that we must stand apart. I am upset and puzzled. I do nothing. Rosalino returns with the word that there is no answer: I have no answer, I want to think. I sense behind it all, something that has no bearing on me and my doings.

At four, I go up to your house as usual. You give me a quick glance. I am so quiet, so noncombatant, that you become gentle—gentle and considerate in feeling—for, as usual, we say nothing. Frieda is hintingly hostile; her eyes are hard, her mouth a line. The tea-table is balanced on a volcano. You are looking seedy. I think it wise not to stay too long. I begin to recover my equipoise and I return to the hotel in a clearer and more peaceful frame of mind. Suddenly, as I am sitting typing in my window, you appear: excited, stormy, despairing.

"Frieda broke out again the minute you left," you say. "She made such a scene that I can no longer stand it. I am at the end of my tether—in despair. The only thing I could think of was to come and ask you not to come up again to the house."

I tell you to sit down, and down you sit. You rumple your hair, despairingly. "Look here, Lawrence," I say, "Let us be calm and sensible. This is too much of a strain for you; it makes you ill, doesn't it?"

"Yes," you reply, wearily, "It is unbearable. I shall be ill if it goes on."

"Well," I say, "The simple, easy way out is for me to go. I will go back to Del Monte for awhile. This will relieve you of the strain."

"That will be best," you reply, more hopefully, "If you think you can manage the journey alone. I don't altogether like your taking that long journey by yourself, but I don't see what else can be done."

Thus we arrange it. I decide to go the following Monday. I know it is the only thing to do. You sit for awhile and we talk of the ways and means of the journey. You don't like the idea—the danger, the difficulties for me—but gradually you calm down, the tension loosens. Something intolerable has ceased to exist and you become alert, but you give me a long, strange look as you sit there, leaning slightly forward. That side of me that keeps an impersonal hold on my own emotions, that at times puzzles and vexes you, and yet is so invaluable to you, is puzzling you now. I see the desire to say something flit across your face; the fleeting, momentary wonder at my attitude; a queer annoyance, too: all pass through the intense deep gaze of your eyes as you sit and look at me. They are dark and big and shine brilliantly. You leap up so suddenly that I jump out of my skin.

"I will go and tell Frieda, and maybe things will be better," you say. And your step is more springy as you go out of the room.

.   .   .   .

Frieda has come rushing in this morning. She says she cannot bear that I should think it is her fault any longer. She has with her a letter which she has written me, explaining it all. I take it and read it in amazement. In it she accuses us, Lawrence and myself, of being like a curate and a spinster; she resents the fact that we do not make love to each other. She says that friendship between man and woman makes only half the curve. Well, maybe.

"But Frieda," I say, "How can I make love to Lawrence when I am your guest; would that not be rather indecent?" She stares at me suspiciously.

"Lawrence says he could not possibly be in love with a woman like you—an asparagus stick!" she answers. I laugh.

"He is none too fat himself," I reply. "If you goad a man long enough, he will say anything." Her eyes are hard like blue ice, she is so unbalanced, so extreme, at this moment: an emotional, unguided vessel. I listen quietly; friendliness seems to ooze out of me and begins suddenly to ooze out of her. In some mysterious fashion, we end amicably; mutual friendliness is restored and we both end in shouts of laughter over some trivial joke. Frieda leaves me in a state of complete bewilderment. Are we friends or are we not? And what is the correct behavior in a triangle?

In the afternoon you come down and we settle the money question: I borrow some from you. I tell you of Frieda's visit, but I do not tell what she said. I feel we have all had enough for the moment.

.   .   .   .

I am at the station. Dona Maria Monros is with me. The train is in; I have my seat. At last, you and Frieda come hurrying along. You are just in time.

"I do hope you will be all right," you say, still anxious, still worried over my long journey alone, my stay in Mexico City alone. I have the address book you have written out for me: I am all right.

You shake my hand, warmly. I kiss Frieda. She is astonished; so am I. I get into the train and we wave and wave until the train turns a corner and I am alone.[91]

26? January 1925   Av. Pino Suarez 43, Oaxaca, Mexico

❲ And a word about friendship. Friendship between a man and a woman, as a thing of first importance to either, is impossible: and I know it. We are creatures of two halves, spiritual and sensual—and each half is as important as the other. Any relation based on the one half—say the delicate spiritual half alone—inevitably brings revulsion and betrayal. It is halfness, or partness, which causes Judas. . . .

.   .   .   .

No, Brett. I do not want your friendship, till you have a full relation somewhere, a kindly relation of both halves, not in part, as all your friendships have been. That which is in part is in itself a betrayal. Your "friendship" for me betrays the essential man and male that I am, and makes me ill. Yes, you make me ill, by dragging at one half at the expense of the other half. And I am so much better now you have gone. I refuse any more of this "delicate friendship" business, because it damages one's wholeness.

Nevertheless, I don't feel unkindly to you. In your one half you are loyal enough. But the very halfness makes your loyalty fatal.

.   .   .   .

Remember I think Christ was profoundly, disastrously wrong.[92]

30 January 1925   Av. Pino Suarez 43, Oaxaca, Mexico

❲ We leave here next week, for Mexico City. Miss Brett has already departed. I suppose soon you'll be seeing her at the ranch.—We are going to Europe for a while: my wife wants to see her mother, who complains she *will* not see us again. Probably we shall sail on the 20th Feb. to England. I want to be back at the ranch by June at latest, to fix up that water.—It seems a bit of a waste of life and money, to trail off to Europe again so soon. But I suppose it's in one's destiny.

I am wondering very much how deep the snow is, and how Miss Brett will stand the cold. But if she goes into the Danes' cottage, it is so sunny, and warm with a fire.

.   .   .   .

I look forward, really, to being back and out of the world. One does get sick of people—endless, endless strangers and people one doesn't want to be bothered about. And this autumn we won't hurry away. I don't see why we can't stay on till Christmas.[93]

7 February 1925   Av. Pino Suarez 43, Oaxaca, Mexico

❨ I have been steadily out of luck this trip down here: don't think I shall ever come to Mexico again while I live. I wondered why I wasn't well down here—thought it was the remains of the old flu—and so it was, with malaria. This place is full of malaria. I've had the doctor, and heavy quinine injections, and feel a rag: but much better.[94]

15 February 1925   Hotel Francia, Oaxaca, Mexico

❨ Am still in Oaxaca—but was moved down to this hotel yesterday. Been having the devil of a time with malaria—think it's got under. That comes of hot winter sun! I hope and pray we can get up to Mexico City in a week's time, out of the malarial areas.—With luck we should sail for England from Vera Cruz on March 10th—land in England about March 25th. I shall bring the MS. of Quetzalcoatl with me . . . . It is finished.[95]

Frieda Lawrence Ravagli

Meanwhile Lawrence wrote at home and got run down. The Brett came every day and I thought she was becoming too much part of our lives and I resented it. So I told Lawrence: "I want the Brett to go away," and he raved at me, said I was a jealous fool. But I insisted and so Brett went up to Mexico City. Then Lawrence finished *The Plumed Serpent,* already very ill, and later on he told me he wished he had finished it differently. Then he was very ill. I had a local native doctor who was scared at having anything to do with a foreigner and he didn't come. Lawrence was very ill, much more ill than I knew, fortunately. I can never say enough of the handful of English and Americans there: how good they were to us. Helping in every way. I thought these mine-owners and engineers led plucky and terrible lives. Always fever, typhoid, malaria, danger from bandits, never feeling a bit safe with their lives. And so I was amazed at the *Selbstverständlichkeit* with which they helped us. It was so much more than Christian, just natural: a fellow-Englishman in distress: let's help him. Lawrence himself thought he would die.

"You'll bury me in this cemetery here," he would say, grimly.

"No, no," I laughed, "it's such an ugly cemetery, don't you think of it."

And that night he said to me: "But if I die, nothing has mattered but you, nothing at all." I was almost scared to hear him say it, that, with all his genius, I should have mattered so much. It seemed incredible.

I got him better by putting hot sandbags on him, that seemed to comfort his tortured inside.

One day we had met a missionary and his wife, who lived right in the hills with the most uncivilized tribe of Indians. He didn't look like a missionary but like a soldier. He told me he had been an airman, and there far away in Oaxaca he told me how he was there when Manfred Richthofen was brought down behind the trenches and in the evening at mess one of the officers rose and said: "Let's drink to our noble and generous enemy."

For me to be told of this noble gesture made in that awful war was a great thing.

Then I remember the wife appeared with a very good bowl of soup when Lawrence was at his worst, and then prayed for him by his bedside in that big bare room. I was half afraid and wondered how Lawrence would feel. But he took it gently and I was half laughing, half crying over the soup and the prayer.

While he was so ill an earthquake happened into the bargain, a thunderstorm first, and the air made you gasp. I felt ill and feverish and Lawrence so ill in the next room—dogs howled and asses and horses and cats were scared in the night—and to my horror I saw the beams of my roof move in and out of their sheaves.

"Let's get under the bed if the roof falls!" I cried.

At last, slowly, slowly, he got a little better. I packed up to go to

Mexico City. This was a crucifixion of a journey for me. We travelled through the tropics. Lawrence in the heat so weak and ill and then the night we stayed halfway to Mexico City in a hotel. There, after the great strain of his illness, something broke in me. "He will never be quite well again, he is ill, he is doomed. All my love, all my strength, will never make him whole again." I cried like a maniac the whole night. And he disliked me for it. But we arrived in Mexico City.[96] I had Dr. Uhl-felder come and see him. One morning I had gone out and when I came back the analyst doctor was there and said, rather brutally, when I came into Lawrence's room: "Mr. Lawrence has tuberculosis." And Lawrence looked at me with such unforgettable eyes.

"What will she say and feel?" And I said: "Now we know, we can tackle it. That's nothing. Lots of people have that." And he got slowly better and could go to lunch with friends.[97] But they, the doctors, told me:

"Take him to the ranch; it's his only chance. He has T.B. in the third degree. A year or two at the most."

With this bitter knowledge in my heart I had to be cheerful and strong. Then we travelled back to the ranch and were tortured by immigration officials, who made all the difficulties in the ugliest fashion to prevent us from entering the States.[98] If the American Embassy in Mexico hadn't helped we would not have been able to go to the ranch that was going to do Lawrence so much good.

Slowly at the ranch he got better.[99]

2 March 1925   Hotel Imperial, Mexico City

⟨ Well, anyhow, we've got out of the valley of Oaxaca: I was so ill down there, with malaria and 'flu.

We are due to sail on the Hamburg-Amerika boat Rio Bravo from Vera Cruz on the 17th—land in Plymouth about April 3rd. I think we shall stay down in Devonshire for a while, to get strong: doctors say I must be by the sea: too much altitude in these places.[100]

3 March 1925   Hotel Imperial, Mexico City

⟨ We both got malaria so badly in Oaxaca, we can hardly crawl. I never knew the town was reeking with malaria, till I had it myself and was in bed a month. We struggled up here last week—and are sailing for England on the 17th—just two weeks from today. This time I really want to get back to Europe, for this sickness has taken all the energy out of me. We had much better have come to Chapala, but Frieda didn't want to. She now hates Mexico: and I no longer like it. . . . Believe me, Guadalajara is about the best place in this damned republic.[101]

Hotel Imperial/[Mexico City] 3 March [1925]

❨ Dear Quintanilla

They gave me your note this evening. I went & got malaria, plus grippe, so badly in Oaxaca, that I was a month in bed & can still hardly crawl through the days. My wife got it too. We were lying absolutely low here, not having the energy for a thing. But come in & see us: we are almost always stuck here. We are sailing to England on the 17th—two weeks today—& till that time, struggling through the days with some difficulty, feeling done in by this dirty sickness.

I thought you had gone to Guatemala, Washington, or Pekin: are you sure you've not?

Kindest regards from us both to Mrs. Quintanilla. We'll muster up courage in a few days to have our teas in Sanborn's, shall we?

Yours

D. H. Lawrence [102]

Dr. Luis Quintanilla

I was with my brother José at Lawrence's bedside in the Hotel Imperial, with Frieda, when we called a doctor because D. H. was suffering, at least so we thought, from a bad case of grippe. It was then that the doctor took me apart to announce that it was not a case of grippe but definitely an advanced case of tuberculosis. You can imagine what a shock it was to my brother and to me! We broke the news as gently as we could to Frieda, and decided not to say anything to Lawrence, for the time being. I must add that my dear brother José died years afterwards from the same dreadful disease.[103]

11 March 1925   Hotel Imperial, Mexico City

❨ The doctor has made an analysis of blood and so forth, and says I had much better come to the ranch, that the sea-voyage will shake me and bring on fever, and England will not be good for me. He insists on our coming to New Mexico: and thank goodness, there is Del Monte to come to. Could you [A. D. Hawk] get the apple orchard cottage ready for us? We shall leave (D.V). next week—perhaps the 17th, when the ship was due to sail—and arrive somewhere about the 21st. I am so glad to be able to come straight to Mrs. Hawk and you, and to William and Rachel, and Del Monte. It is really the only home one has got.

Tell Miss Brett. Tell her to prepare for us. We want to have a happy, friendly time, all of us.[104]

Hotel Imperial/[Mexico City]/Thursday [19? March 1925]

❴ Dear Quintanilla

We were very much distressed to hear Jane was ill. I hope it's not bad, & that Mrs. Quintanilla will be able to sail. Really, there is a doom on us all in Mexico: best for us to depart.—We are due to leave on Tuesday morning: I am finished with the doctor thank God.—Let us know how it is: we don't go out till about 11.0; and if we can do anything for you in any way, let us know.

D. H. Lawrence [105]

Witter Bynner

The Lawrences had stopped but briefly in Santa Fe [29 March 1925] and I had been so dismayed by the physical change in him that little remains with me of what we discussed, except his strange pitiable longing for our return together to the country in which he had been stricken. I remembered Amy Lowell's speaking to me of tuberculosis; but Frieda avoided the word in Santa Fe.[106]

2 April 1925   Del Monte Ranch, Questa, New Mexico

❴ We got here yesterday—mountains snowy, wind wild and cold, but bright sun. I'm not altogether here yet: bit of me still on the way, like luggage following. We're staying with our neighbors for a while.

The Emigration people in El Paso—the Americans—were most insulting and hateful. Before you grumble at the Mexicans, as the worst ever, try this sort of American. Canaille of the most bottom-doggy order, and filthy with insolence.

The basket of food was a great consolation on the journey, especially the fruit. We ate all the pie: not at all like invalids. The people in the Pullman dreary: and in the drawing-room a Mexican family with seven children.— Never come via El Paso, if you can help it.

I still have a lurking hankering for Europe. I think at the end of the summer, we shall both sail.[107]

The Hon. Dorothy Brett

I have just received a letter from Frieda. She tells me how unhappy I made her all the time at the ranch and in Mexico; she does not want me on the ranch this summer. Mr. Hawk offers me a cabin on his ranch, so I settle the problem that way.

I have dreamed of you. I dreamed we three—Frieda, you and I—were walking in some town when we met a young man. He came up to you, and immediately you went off with him. You told Frieda that you were going to spend the summer with this young man on his farm, somewhere on the coast. Frieda was upset and tearful. I suggested to her that she and I go back to the ranch and wait, but she wouldn't. The young man was yourself as a young man—young, without a beard. You had met your youth and fallen in love with it and gone off with it. I do not like this dream. Years later I find out why: I am told it foretells death.

. . . .

You have already arrived. Frieda is in the hall with Andrew Dasburg and Ida Rauh, who have driven you up in their car. But there is no sign of you. Frieda greets me heartily:

"He is here, Brett," she cries, "He is here; he is safe upstairs!" You come slowly down the stairs and grip my hand, warmly. I am bewildered, excited. But how frail you look—how frail and thin and collapsed!

. . .

You stay in the big house for a few days, then move up to the ranch. You tell me you think I had better not come up to live there; and I explain that I have the cabin in the orchard at Del Monte.

"I looked so awful," you tell me, "When I reached Mexico City from Oaxaca: just pale green. The people stared at me so in the streets that I could not bear it, so Frieda bought me some rouge. I rouged my cheeks and gave myself such a lovely, healthy complexion that no one ever turned to stare at me again. You should have just seen me! I used the rouge all the time until I reached New Mexico—until I got past that terrible doctor at El Paso." [108]

6 April 1925   Kiowa Ranch, San Cristobal, New Mexico

❨ I got malaria in Oaxaca: then grippe: then a typhoid inside: was so sick, I wearied of the day. Struggled to Mexico City, was put to bed again for three weeks—then packed off up here. We had booked our passages to England, but the doctor said I must stay in the sun, he wouldn't be answerable for me if I went on the sea, and to England. So we came here. The Emigration Authorities at El Paso treated us as Emigrants, and nearly killed me a second time: this after the Consul and the Embassy people in Mexico—the American—had been most kind, doing things to make it easier for us. They only made it harder. The Emigration Dept is Dept of Labour, and you taste the Bolshevist method in its conduct.

However—after two day's fight we got through—and yesterday got to our little ranch. There is snow behind the house and sky threatening snow. But usually it's brilliantly sunny. And the log fire is warm. And the Indian Trinidad is chopping wood under the pine tree, and his wife Rufina, in her wide white boots, is struggling carrying water. I begin to feel better: though still feel I don't care whether its day or night.

. . . .

I managed to finish my Mexican novel Quetzalcoatl in Mexico: the very day I went down, as if shot in the intestines. But I daren't even look at the outside of the MS. It cost one so much, and I wish I could eat all the lotus that ever budded, and drink up Lethe to the source. Talk about dull opiates—one wants something that'll go into the very soul.[109]

12 April 1925   Kiowa Ranch, San Cristobal, New Mexico

❨ We have got back to our own ranch. . . .

We saw Bynner in Santa Fe. We talked of Mexico-Chapala in May or June. . . . We shall stay on here, I expect till late autumn. . . . I think for the winter itself we shall go to Europe. I've got a bit of a Heimweh—a nostalgia—for Europe—though that may be only because I have been ill.

The ranch is very beautiful, now in the April sunshine: and very clean,

having emerged from under three feet of snow. But the winds come sometimes very cold, with a flurry of snow: so of course I got a chill and was in
bed again. It is unlike me to keep on being sick, and I hate it. But I hope
this is the last set-back.[110]

15 April 1925   Kiowa Ranch, San Cristobal, New Mexico

❲ We have been at the ranch a week already. We found all well and safe,
nothing broken, nothing destroyed. Only the mice found Mabel's chair
and ate the wool.

In the second house we have two young Indians, Trinidad and Rufina,
husband and wife. Rufina is short and fat, waddles like a duck in high,
white Indian boots—Trinidad is like a girl, with his two plaits. Both are
nice, don't sweat over their work, but do what we want. We still have the
three horses but they are down with the Hawks, till the alfalfa and the
grass have grown a bit.

We had three cold days—the wind can come ice-cold. I had a cold
again. But now the weather is mild and warm, very beautiful, and spring in
the air. All was washed very clean on the land, coming out of a yard of
snow. Now the first anemones have come, built like crocuses but bigger
and prouder, hairy on the brown-red earth under the pines. But everything
is very dry again, the grass has hardly appeared, and yet it won't grow any
higher. We hoped for rain or snow again.

Brett stays down on Del Monte, in a little house by herself, near the old
Hawks. She wanted to come up here but Frieda said no. And so we are
only two whites and two reds, or rather yellow-browns, on the ranch.
Trinidad fetches milk and butter and eggs from Del Monte. I lie in the sun.
Frieda is happy to be on her ranch, Friedel [111] comes in May—writes very
happily, very likely he will return to the Fatherland at the end of the
summer. For September we also think to come to England and Germany.
But the Lord's will be done. We bought a buggy and Trinidad will be
coachman. I don't work this year, am cross that I was so ill. Mabel is still in
New York, but Friday Tony came.[112]

Mabel Dodge Luhan

Though we both came back to Taos the summer following [1925], I
did not see [Lawrence]. He, up on the ranch, avoided me, and I avoided
him. What took place between him and Brett and Frieda and others is

their story, not mine. I never communicated with him until I completed the first volume of the *Intimate Memories* [113] and wrote him that I wanted to send it to him in Europe, where he went the following autumn and from where he never returned to America. [114]

26 May 1925   Kiowa Ranch, San Cristobal, New Mexico

《 *I did a play—a Bible play—David—which I'll send you when it's typed out. But I don't care about having it published.* [115]

The Hon. Dorothy Brett

You have begun to write. You are writing the play for Ida [Rauh]—*David*—and I am once more typing. I have done a great deal. I have plenty of time in my cabin in the orchard.

.   .   .   .

Today Ida and I ride up to your place. You are going to read out the play. It is finished; even my typing is finished. We settle down comfortably in the sitting room. Frieda lies on her bed smoking—the sitting room is again her bedroom.

You begin to read, in the slightly shy, bashful way you have; and you sing in a soft voice the little songs you have invented for the play. You live every part. In some subtle way you change and change about, as the characters alter from men to women, from young to old. You read till evening, with pauses for tea; then suddenly you stop in the very middle of one of the songs and say:

"I feel so embarrassed. You all embarrass me. I cannot go on." But my enthusiasm for the play urges you on again; I am so keen for Ida to hear it. She, though, is strangely silent. What can be the matter with her?

But there is no time to finish it: you are too tired by now, your voice is getting hoarse; so we leave and arrange to come up again tomorrow.

.   .   .

We are sitting round listening to the end of the play. Frieda is again lying on her bed smoking. I am also lying on the bed. It is large enough for all of us, but you are sitting at the table and Ida is also sitting at the table leaning her head on her hand, her thick dark curly hair like a bush shading her face.

When you finish, Ida is silent. She shows no enthusiasm; yet I know she feels the beauty of the play. You look at her and she looks up at you, strangely, and says in a flat, tired voice:

"I am too old, Lorenzo; too old to play the part of Michal—so young, so radiant a creature!" And we are appalled. It had never entered our heads.

I urge you to write out the music of the songs. "You must!" I say.

"The actors will know what to do," you reply.

"Nonsense," I answer, "They won't. You must write the music at once." So there at the table, with lines ruled on a piece of paper, you begin to hum and tap out the tunes, jotting down the notes with a pencil. Frieda and I are still lying on the bed; Ida is sitting sadly at the table. You hum, tapping the rhythm lightly on the table; when Frieda suddenly says roughly to you:

"Oh, you get on my nerves! Go out—get away—I don't want to hear you!" You pause and reply in a quiet, deadly voice,

"You are impudent. Don't be so impertinent." Frieda makes no reply and you begin humming again.

Ida gets up, throwing an indignant look at Frieda, and goes into the kitchen where she sits on the kitchen table. I follow her. We look at each other and Ida shrugs her shoulders. We listen to you humming—but Frieda is silent.[116]

30 May 1925   Kiowa Ranch, San Cristobal, New Mexico

⟨ *Here, it is so terribly dry, there are no flowers yet, save the scarlet and yellow columbines—they are nice. Our little garden seeds—nasturtium, sweet-pea, etc. are only an inch high. The nights are cold; then the sun by day can be blazing hot. And it is so dry, my little stream that we bring from the gallina is half dry. I have to turn it over the garden and over the alfalfa field, bit by bit: irrigating. That's my job. Then we're building a new little corral, for the horses and the black cow—she is coming up on Monday.[117]*

10 June 1925   Kiowa Ranch, San Cristobal, New Mexico

⟨ *We sit here on our own little ranch, up to the eyes in doing nothing. I spent all the golden evening riding through the timber hunting the lost* cow: and when at last I got her into corral, I felt more like killing her than milking her. Meanwhile my wife was going round and round the fowl-barn, trying to drive in the four new Rhode-Island-Red hens, which refused to go to roost. Our two Indians have gone down to Taos.

.　.　.　.　.　.　.　.　.　.　.　.　.　.　.

I don't do any work since we are here—except milk the black-eyed Susan and irrigate the field—when there's any water. I never felt less literary. But I've revised the MS. of my Mexican novel—which I wanted to call Quetzalcoatl. But the publisher wept at the sound of it: and pleaded for a translation: The Plumed Serpent. . . . I think it sounds a bit silly— The Plumed Serpent. But je m'en fiche.

.　.　.　.　.　.　.　.　.　.　.　.　.　.　.

It's been blowy and rather cold here: very dry, dry to dessication: and summer only started yesterday. I expect autumn will set in tomorrow. We're too high—over 8000 ft. I am about my normal self again—but shall never forgive Mexico, especially Oaxaca, for having done me in. I shudder even when I look at the little MS. you gave me, and think of that beastly Santo Domingo church, with its awful priests and the backyard with a well-ful of baby's bones. Quoth the raven: Nevermore. But this Nevermore is a thankful, cheerful chirrup, like a gay blackbird. Nevermore need I look on Mexico—but especially Oaxaca.—Yet my Quetzalcoatl novel lies nearer my heart than any other work of mine.[118]

The Hon. Dorothy Brett

We are hanging on to the cow, Black Eyed Susan. Oh, that cow! I am running myself into a fit, shooing her along. You are walking behind her, when she is there to walk behind. Friedel has hold of the rope— his hands are already skinned. She bounds about, whisks behind bushes, entangles the rope in trees. We reach the road and all of a sudden she becomes meek and angelic.

"Damn her!" you say. We put her in the corral and at milking time you go in cautiously with the bucket. We hide behind the palings to watch. You talk to her, stroking her nose; then sit gingerly on the stool and begin to milk. Nothing happens. She stands as quiet as a lamb as the milk streams into the bucket.[119]

20 *June 1925*   Kiowa Ranch, San Cristobal, New Mexico

❨ As far as prosperity goes—I have left Seltzer, who hangs, like a creaking gate, long: and gone to Knopf, who is a better business man. But of course I still have to live on what is squeezed out of poor Seltzer.

We've been busy here—brought a stream of water from the Gallina Canyon—about two miles—to irrigate the field. But it's so dry, for all that. The water just disappears. We have a black cow, whom I milk every morning and evening—and Frieda collects the eggs—about eight a day— from the eleven hens. Frieda's nephew, Friedel Jaffe, is staying the summer with us—he helps. We had an Indian and wife to do for us, till last week: then we sent them away. "Savages" are a burden. So a Mexican boy comes up to help: and even him one has to pay two dollars a day: supposed to be very cheap labour.

Lovely to think of cherry trees in bloom: here the country is too savage, somehow, for such softness. I get a bit of a Heimweh for Europe. We shall come in the autumn—D.V.—and winter somewhere warm.[120]

The Hon. Dorothy Brett

Friedel has come down with a letter from Frieda. She says she does not want her life messed up with mine, etc.

Later, you and Friedel come down to ride to San Cristobal. We have been invited to a strawberry and ice-cream feast at Mrs. Murray's.[121] Frieda, as usual, has not come. We ride off. You are pale and quiet, but the ride does us all good and you become gayer. As you and I race along, Prince running fast alongside of Azul, Friedel away behind us on old slow-coach Aaron, I tell you that I am paying no attention to Frieda, that it is only tantrums. You laugh and agree. Then I add, darkly:

"If Frieda starts her spinster and curate and asparagus nonsense again, I will rope her to a tree and hit her on the nose until she has really something to yell about." You stare at me flabbergasted, not knowing quite what to say—too amazed to say anything.

.   .   .   .

The milking is all over. You and I go into Rachel's house to find her sitting in front of a warm fire washing the baby. She has by now a little girl, Shirley, a few weeks old. The baby is lying face down on her lap being sponged. We sit down and watch the operation and talk. Rachel's mouth is full of safety pins, so her talk is limited to nods and shakes of the head that make her fair curly hair glitter. Little Walton is standing close by in his pajamas.

Suddenly you take Walton by the shoulders and draw him towards you. You hold him between your knees and look at him intently. Your eyes darken to a deep blue. The overhanging brow and heavy hair seem to lend your face and figure, stooping over the child, more power than ever as you keep that deep, intent gaze on him, as if trying to penetrate the secret of the child-life in front of you. The child stares back at you solemnly, and puts up a hand to stroke your beard. You release him at last with a sigh.[122]

29 July 1925   *Kiowa Ranch, San Cristobal, New Mexico*

⟨ *Frieda and I are alone—I milk the cow, Frieda looks after the chickens, and we both manage the four horses. Sometimes I drive the buggy, but usually we get an Indian or a Mexican. It's the kind of life I like for summer: but the winter would be too stiff. Dorothy Brett is staying down on our neighbour's ranch: she comes up most days. We think of coming to Europe in the autumn: first to England, then Paris, then Baden-Baden, then Italy. . . . We shall be here till mid-September, I suppose. . . .*

Brett thinks she might like to winter in Capri.[123]

The Hon. Dorothy Brett

You are just coming through the orchard on Azul, with little Walton perched on the saddle in front of you. I am giving a tea-party. Frieda is a bit cold again, and unfriendly. . . . Then I ride back to supper with you and Frieda. . . .

After supper, as I sit, depressed, on one of the stone seats by the fire, you suddenly turn to me and ask me what I am going to do this winter. I am startled at your sudden question. I answer feebly that I don't know, that I'll probably stay on here, as I am too deaf to travel much alone. A sort of gloom has settled on me at the thought of the coming winter with all of you gone, a gloom you are quick to notice. You give me a sharp glance.

"Look here, Brett," you say, tersely. "All this about your deafness is bunk, sheer bunk." I have no answer ready. "You have plenty of money," you continue, forcefully. "You are free. It is much better for you to travel a bit than stay here for the winter alone. Much safer, too. Have you ever been to Italy? No? Well, you ought, everyone who can ought to see Italy. I may be there this winter; I don't know yet where I'm going. Why don't you go to Capri?"

"I don't know anyone there," I say weakly.

"Basta!" you reply quickly, "Don't be so feeble. I will give you a letter to the Brewsters. You have no idea of the beauty of Italy and you should see it instead of moping here. Why mope through life, when you are free and have money and health?" There is no real reason, so it is there and then decided that when they leave, I will leave a bit later for Capri.

. . . .

Frieda is hankering for her children. This makes her changeable, nervy. Today, however, she is friendly. We are up in the canyon behind the ranch—the Raspberry Canyon—watching some men take the honey from the wild bees in the tree. They have cut down the tree, and have split it down one side. On one side is a thick layer of honey, on the other a mass of bees. You have been stung on the neck; Frieda is flapping wildly at them; I am keeping at a safish distance. The men carry away the honey and we return to the house, to find an unfortunate Mexican's dog with its muzzle full of porcupine quills. You are in despair.

"I must do something," you say. "Fetch a rope, Brett. I will tie him up and see if I can pull them out." I hurry for a rope. You truss the dog, put a stick between its teeth, then wind the rope around its muzzle. Carefully, with tweezers, you pull out the quills—all except a few on its chin. As you touch these, the dog kicks and struggles and breaks away. The rope becomes unfastened and the dog runs into the wood.[124]

. . . .

I have been wondering for some days why you sent your last manuscript away, why you did not give it to me to type. Have I done anything? In what way could I have offended you? As I am sitting in your living room, I ask Frieda if I have offended you. She is evasive. I then ask her if I gave her the old folk rhyme I had written out for her the other day at tea; and I repeat the old lines:

> Matthew, Mark, Luke and John
> Went to bed with their trousers on.

You look up, angrily. "That is a very vulgar joke," you say, "Indecent and nasty." I stare at you in amazement.

"But, Lawrence, my nurse used to sing it to me when I was tiny. What is the matter with it? I wrote it out for Frieda, but I lost it."

"Do you mean to say," you reply testily, "That you do not know that is a vulgar, dirty joke?" No, I didn't; but that evening you give me a manuscript to type, and suddenly I realize that I must have put those lines in your manuscript book, and you had felt insulted.

. . . .

Margaret Hale and Mrs. Swain [125] have come to fetch Friedel. He is to stay with them a day or two before he starts back to Germany. Everybody is gay, but as Friedel clicks his heels and bows to each one of us in turn, Frieda's eyes fill with tears for she is sad at his going. He leans out of the car, waving, until the trees swallow him up.

We go in and make some tea. You are in great spirits, hoping when you get to England to make every one of your old friends hate you. We laugh at the thought of making them wither and you are keen to knock them all off their perches. . . .

. . . .

What with pickling the meat and painting and talking about art, we are all busy and happy. Susan, even, is behaving herself. And Frieda is gay and friendly.

My big picture of the desert, with all our ranch life going on, is progressing. We are all working on it. You and I do most of it—most of the squabbling about it, too. You insist that landscape without figures is dull. We are agreed, though, that most pictures should be painted from memory: the imagination works better that way.

"Why do all the painters have to sit in front of what they paint?" you inquire, irritably.

"Quien sabe," I reply.

"It's because," you continue, "they feel nothing inside them, so they must have it before their eyes. It's all wrong and stupid: it should all be brought from inside oneself." And you spit neatly past the picture onto the grass.

. . . .

The hail is as large as cherry stones. We are sitting, just a bit afraid, in the living room. The thunder is terrible; the lightning one continuous blaze. An extra loud crash makes us jump out of our skins.

"That has struck a tree," you say. "And quite close, too." The horses

407

have vanished like streaks across the field, their long tails streaming out. Susan, with a fine flourish of her heels, has also disappeared. The hail hurts them.

The storm trails away. We venture out and look. A huge pine tree, just above the cabins, has been struck. A great white scar twists and turns down the trunk. It is doomed. It has to die.[126]

"That's a bit too near," you say.

.   .   .   .

Today when I come up, I find Frieda in a state of great excitement. She had gone for a stroll along the ditch in the moonlight, and had seen something creeping through the grass. She was frightened, thinking it might be a bear, so she ran to tell you. You, with your new accomplishment, seized the little .22 rifle and followed her out to the ditch. Something was still creeping through the long grass. You go up, and there was a huge porcupine. What were you to do, shoot it or not? They are so bad for the trees that you decide to shoot; and with the third shot, you kill it. You have kept it to show me, as I have never seen one. I take some of the quills. You are immensely proud of yourself in one way, and full of regrets in another.[127]

.   .   .   .

What good spirits you are in today! A warm, affectionate, loving mood. The air itself is more radiant around you. Life is heightened more than ever—it is always unbearably exciting. Life is always heightened, keyed up, near you; but today it is so swift, so gay, so rippling, that I am completely carried away by it. We paint, busily. The Indian camp near the corral which I am painting, is not going well.

"What a muff you are, Brett," you say cheerfully. "Let me try." And we exchange corners. I paint in a long mesa of pine trees.

"Brrrrrrett!" you shout at me suddenly. I jump out of my skin. How you love to shout at me like that, just to make me jump. "Look at my Tepee and Indians. Aren't they much better than yours?" you ask.

"I don't know," I reply. "Mine are good too."

"Not so good as mine. I never think your things are as good as mine. There is something vital you leave out. Some spark. Don't you think so?"

"Yes," I reply meekly, knowing argument is no good, and too often disastrous.

.   .   .   .

408

Only you come! Frieda has as usual made an excuse: she is afraid of a storm. So we have tea on the porch and talk about your essays. I have been typing one on "Love" and another called "Power." [128]

"Painting!" you exclaim. "Oh, painting is easy; writing is far more difficult. You have no idea how difficult it is to write; how difficult I have found it. It is much more difficult than painting."

"Do you ever," I ask, "have a clear vision of what you are going to write? My paintings flash up before me just as clear as a scene in a movie."

"No," you reply, "I never know when I sit down, just what I am going to write. I make no plan; it just comes, and I don't know where it comes from. Of course I have a general sort of outline of what I want to write about, but when I go out in the mornings I have no idea what I will write. It just comes, and I really don't know where from." You look at your watch. "It's getting late," you say, "I must go. Can you come up tomorrow and help with the shed?"

.   .   .   .

I am racing along, on Prince, in front of a large car. A journalist has turned up and Mr. Hawk brought him over to my place. He wants to interview you. I am doubtful. His letters, I know, have remained unanswered. I explain that you are sensitive about being interviewed and you might not want it. The young man and his wife are eager, but also tactful and sensitive. They understand and are quite willing that I should ride up ahead of them and reconnoiter. So I go galloping up, Prince puffing and blowing. But the noise of the car behind him, spurs him along.

I hitch Prince to the railings. The car has stopped tactfully in the trees. I hurry in to you and tell you. For the moment you are startled, nonplussed. You bite your beard agitatedly.

"What do they look like?" you ask.

"Young," I reply, "young and tactful and unpushing."

"All right," you say, and hurry into your room to change your trousers. Then you go out to the gate. The car slowly comes up to the fence, and you invite Kyle Crichton and his wife in.

They spend the afternoon—a very pleasant afternoon—talking and drinking tea. Kyle Crichton is a hugely tall man with very square shoulders and rather scanty hair. But they are both of them clever, amusing, kind. It is their kind understanding of your sensitiveness that appeals to you. You give yourself freely, laughing and talking unreservedly. But after they are gone, you are tired: it has taken a lot out of you.[129]

Kyle S. Crichton

The preliminary negotiations for interviewing D. H. Lawrence were prolonged, confusing and completely unsuccessful. In brief, Lawrence had never been interviewed and showed no intention of spoiling his record. What prompted me to keep pestering him is even less obvious, for in those days I was almost totally lacking in brass and persistence, but I was probably harrowed by the thought that my writing career was ending almost before it had started. Some time before I had sold the Sunday section of the *New York World* an article on the Navajo Indians and on the strength of it had asked the *World* if they wouldn't like me to go up to Taos and interview Lawrence. Since I was living in Albuquerque and the trip would cost the *World* nothing, the *World* (in the person of W. P. Beazell, assistant managing editor) had replied that the suggestion had merit.

After Lawrence had ignored my third letter, I got in touch with the Hawk family, who were Lawrence's closest and indeed only neighbors on a mountain side north of Taos. Mr. Hawk confirmed my knowledge that Lawrence was hard to flush, but added in the subtlest possible fashion that even a cat may look at a king. He suggested that if we wanted to gamble on bearding Lawrence in his den, the Hawks would be delighted to entertain us at lunch and we should have a pleasant trip in any event. We have since learned that this invitation was promoted by the beautiful Hawk girls, Betty and Bobby, who were bored with life on the side of a mountain and considered any intrusion a blessing.

Not only did the Hawks entertain us but they did something even more important for the purposes of the interview by introducing us to the Honorable Dorothy Brett, who lived in the small house on their place. Brett had come out from London with the Lawrences and now acted as secretary, friend and volunteer cheering section. She was a daughter of Lord Esher, who had been the power behind the throne in the regime of Edward VII, and she turned out to be a wonderful person. She was wearing a man's woolen shirt, riding boots, and a man's breeches, and she was quite deaf. She was about twenty-five years old, had a long nose, a marvelous English complexion and used a long flat horn-like instrument for hearing. This device was known as "Toby" and became widely known in the Taos area.

Brett knew about my letters to Lawrence and was not too hopeful that he would see us, but she suggested that she might ride ahead on her horse and see how the land lay. There were moments when we were not too confident our old Model T was going to make the grade, but the road finally ended under a clump of trees about fifty yards below the Lawrence place and Brett gave a flick of the hand to indicate that for the time being we might well rest on our laurels. We waited patiently in the car until at last we saw a figure flying down the hill toward us. It was Lawrence, waving his arms jovially and showing by his actions that we were not only welcome but had possibly rescued them in the nick of time. He was at the car before we could scramble out and was in time to help my wife crawl down.

He was thin, about five eight in height, and had a dark reddish beard and the same wart on the right side of his face that appears in all his photographs. He was wearing a blue denim shirt, buttoned at the neck but without a tie, brown striped pants that obviously belonged to an old suit, black woolen socks and sandals. His lips were full and quite red; his eyes were small but astonishingly bright and blue, and he looked steadily at you when he talked. When we reached the little clearing by the house, Frieda, his wife, was there to greet us and was as friendly as Lawrence himself. She was a large handsome woman and spoke with a decided German accent.

I had no faintest idea how to begin an interview, but that was not necessary, for we sat in the porch which seemed built as an indentation of the cabin, and started talking naturally. We first spoke of Harvey Fergusson's *Women and Wives* [130] because he was a New Mexican author and Lawrence said somebody had sent him the book. He said he thought it was "thin" and then, probably out of a feeling he was being harsh with a young author and possibly my friend, he added hastily that early reviewers of his novels used to refer to them contemptuously as "Zolaesque."

"Zolaesque!" I said in surprise, for it seemed the last thing anybody would say about a Lawrence novel.

"They thought it would put me down," said Lawrence, "but I took it as a compliment. I thought highly of Zola then, and I still do."

From that he went on to telling how his first work saw print. He was engaged to a girl in the little town of Eastwood, while he was teaching school at Croydon and detesting it. Since he was twenty-three and in the proper mood, he conducted his courtship in rhyme. Without telling

Lawrence what she had done, the young lady sent the poems to Ford Madox Hueffer, who immediately accepted them for his magazine and published them in the next issue. Hueffer then wrote Lawrence asking him to call. This was an important moment in Lawrence's life, for Hueffer was the first literary person he had met. He was astonished by Hueffer and now when he was telling us about the interview, he began mimicking Hueffer, screwing an imaginary monocle in his eye and talking in the humph-humph almost unintelligible way that Ford's friends remember so well.

"Hueffer lives in a constant haze," said Lawrence. "He has talent, all kinds of it, but has everlastingly been a damned fool about his life. He's fine in half a dozen lines of writing but won't stick to any one of them, and the critics can't stand that in a writer."

"His wife's very nice," Frieda said.

"Why the devil he ever married Violet Hunt!" cried Lawrence, throwing up his hands. "Why, she's too devilishly clever for a man ever to want to marry."

Lawrence could see that we were not too well acquainted with Violet Hunt and added that she was a novelist and quite good—much better than May Sinclair, for instance.

"Why do you like Sinclair so much over here?" he wanted to know. "It's a mystery. You should see her . . . a little humped up scrawny woman. Oh, married, of course, but she could never be anything but a spinster."

He then launched into a long defense of Violet Hunt as a novelist, saying that she wasn't at all appreciated properly.

"Maybe it's because of Hueffer?" suggested Brett.

"Ah, perhaps," conceded Lawrence. "That Hueffer . . . a born romanticist. When Stepnyak, the Russian, was sounding Hueffer for information about English farming and happened to mention rye, Hueffer said, "Yaws, yaws . . . rye . . . rye is one of our–ah–lawgest crops . . . ." "And rye," Lawrence shouted with merriment, "there isn't half an acre of rye in all England. It just struck Hueffer that it would be a fine thing for England to have acres of rye and he couldn't help telling Stepnyak."

"Do you remember the time he came with Garnett at the first of the war and Mrs. Wells was there?" asked Frieda sourly. "I mentioned something about Germany and he puffed up right away and started talking about his Dutch relatives. Before he had always kept German servants and blasted the British Empire and said he wasn't a subject of the King and spoke German at the table—and now he was Dutch. It was enough for me."

Although he had been known as Ford Madox Ford for at least ten years, the Lawrences always referred to him as Hueffer. That might be part of Frieda's revenge or because they had always known him by the former name, but Lawrence said something then that showed he was still fond of Ford, with all his faults.

"A bit of a fool, yes," he conceded, "but he gave me the first push and he was a kind man."

The reference to Garnett got Lawrence started again on reminiscences and he told how he had met Garnett through Hueffer and had been guided by him in his first years as a writer.

"Garnett did a great deal for me," said Lawrence. "He was a good friend and a fine editor, but he ate his heart out trying to be a writer. When I'd visit them, I'd find Garnett in his study, spending hours working over a single phrase to get the very last quality of rightness. He would rack his brain and suffer while his wife, Constance Garnett, was sitting out in the garden turning out reams of her marvelous translations from the Russian. She would finish a page, and throw it off on a pile on the floor without looking up, and start a new page. That pile would be this high . . . really, almost up to her knees, and all magical."

In my guise as an interviewer, I managed a few stupid questions on his own method of writing and learned that he did everything by pen— a fat red full-barreled fountain pen. When I asked if he dictated, there was amusement all around.

"It's a private joke of our own," explained Lawrence. "Frieda and I were once staying with Compton Mackenzie and at two in the morning we came on Compton in bed in silk pajamas—eh, Frieda?—with Brett Young's brother, his secretary, taking notes and Mrs. Mackenzie, two rooms away, playing softly and romantically on the piano. Ho! If I wrote like that something fantastic would come out!"

That prompted me to ask about Michael Arlen, who was then the English literary sensation, and I was surprised to hear that they knew him quite well.

"The pride of Mayfair," said Lawrence, "and when we first knew him he hadn't even *seen* an aristocrat. He was a nice young fellow, who was making a literary living on odds and ends, but when we next saw him he came to our house in Poland [131] in riding togs. I'm sure he had never ridden a horse in his life, but there he was in riding breeches with loud black and white checks and a pointed hat with a feather—like an old time chevalier. His popularity comes from catering to the petty vice instinct in people, but his reputation is beginning to wane."

And then he added something that shocked me.

"That's also true of Katherine Mansfield's reputation," he said. "She was a good writer they made out to be a genius. Katherine knew better herself, but her husband, John Middleton Murry, made capital of her death. Murry was a strange one," he concluded.

They were still very pleased with a visit from Willa Cather some weeks before. She had made the hard trip up the mountain and later had sent the book of her own she liked best—*The Song of the Lark*.

"We had been warned that we might not like her," said Frieda. "Everybody said she was blunt and abrupt, but we got along famously."

That got us on to the mechanics of writing, which they said they had discussed with Miss Cather, and Lawrence said it was fine for him to have an agent like Curtis Brown, for he was practically helpless as a business man. When a book was once sent away, he forgot about it.

"No, not entirely," he amended. "There are the proofs, which I don't mind so much when they're fresh and I'm still afire over the work. But it's awful to read stuff when it's once in book form. Last year in Mexico I reread *The White Peacock* for the first time in fifteen years. It seemed strange and far off and as if written by somebody else. I wondered how I could have thought of some of the things or how I could have written them. And then I'd come on something that showed I may have changed in style or form, but I haven't changed fundamentally. Reviews? No, I never read them any more and care almost nothing about what people say."

That brought one of my bright moments, and I had the wit to ask what made a writer write. The meeting perked up immediately.

"Egotism," said Frieda flatly.

"No, no," protested Lawrence. "It isn't that. You don't write for anybody; you rather write from a deep moral sense—for the race, as it were."

"And to let everybody know how clever you are," persisted Frieda.

Brett had left her spot behind the little table and now edged her way forward with her horn cocked for battle and a happy smile on her face.

"Of course, you want to see it published," admitted Lawrence, "but you don't really mind what people say about it. It doesn't *matter* what they say. A writer writes because he can't help writing, and because he has something in him that he feels he can say better than it has been said before, and because it would be wrong, entirely wrong, to possess a talent and have thoughts without sharing them with the world."

"But how about the time you stopped for a year!" demanded Frieda. "You were angry at what people said then."

This was a reference to the banning of *The Rainbow* in England on moral grounds, a blow from which Lawrence had trouble in recovering. His face clouded and his tone changed.

"No, Frieda," he said in a sad voice. "Not angry. That was an entirely different thing. They were robbing me of my freedom then."

"But you were bitter," insisted Frieda, in a way that showed she was still steaming over the incident.

"No, not bitter, Frieda," he said, and laughed. "Bored—just bored."

And he did strike you as a man who had arranged his life so that blows would have little effect on him. Since the scene had been a little tense, I sought to bring in a touch of small talk. I let drop the information that Sousa and his band were to appear in Albuquerque that winter.

"Sousa!" cried Lawrence, starting up. "He must be a hundred. Sousa—himself? Is he still living?"

"'Stars and Stripes Forever,'" put in Brett happily.

And Frieda could remember the stir the band had made when it came to Germany—oh, years ago.

"The little hats and the smart uniforms and the little man with the beard going on ahead. It just doesn't seem possible. He *can't* be alive!"

I assured them he was and added that we would also be favored by a visit from the Barnum and Bailey and Ringling Brothers circus. This was almost too much for them.

"Barnum and Bailey—ooh!" shouted Frieda and Brett simultaneously. A hubbub set up as they compared notes on how many times they had seen Barnum and Bailey and how wonderful it had been and how they wished they could see it again.

"For years that's all I knew about America," said Brett. "Barnum and Bailey and Sousa."

"Oh, now, let's be fair," said Lawrence laughing. "There was James Fenimore Cooper."

Frieda and Brett made motions of the face, as if to say that certainly they had read Cooper but Cooper after all wasn't what appealed to girls. Lawrence seemed to feel that he had put them at a disadvantage and added hastily:

"I like the trapeze fellows—those men who fly through the air and grasp their partners en route. A very high and wonderful art!"

How it followed from this conversation is not clear, but I took this chance of asking what they read in their mountain home. This is when I got my second serious shock.

"You'll never guess," said Lawrence. "Here!"

He thrust into my hand a copy of *Adventure* magazine, which at that time was edited by the late Arthur Sulivant Hoffman.

"Not bad, either," said Lawrence. "The writers are very lively and they are honest and they are accurate about their facts. If they say something happened in a certain way in Africa or Malaya, you can depend on it. If they're wrong, the readers pick them up mighty fast."

What about the better known American magazines, I asked, trying not to show my horror and pain. Lawrence made a wry face.

" 'With milk and honey blest,' " he said.[132]

As for books, the Lawrences said they read whatever anybody sent them. At the moment they had only about ten books in the house.

"We never carry any when we travel," said Lawrence, "and take whatever our kind friends foist off on us. In that way we learn things we'd never in a hundred years pick off a library shelf."

When we went into the house later, it was so immaculate, so scrubbed and shining, that we immediately attributed it in our minds to Frieda's German upbringing. It turned out to be Lawrence's doing almost entirely.

"You'd never think it of him," said Frieda proudly, when Lawrence went out to get things ready for tea, "but he's the most practical man I've ever known. He made the bread this morning in the Indian oven just outside the door there, milked Susan and looked after the chickens. I cook when he'll let me, but he does it much better himself. When you get a chance, look at the new cow shed and say a word about it. He's very proud of that; he did it all with his own hands."

In the course of this, Brett had broken into a special sort of smile, a meaningful smile, and when we looked at her inquiringly, she said, "Susan," and it was plain that the cow was a cross Lawrence had to bear. At that moment he came in from the kitchen and said in a voice of fake indignation: "The bloody beast . . . . Had to chase her two full hours this morning. If we tether her, she either breaks the rope or gets so tangled up we're afraid she'll choke herself."

By now Lawrence was laying down the tea things and in a few minutes was cutting bread from a huge loaf in the thinnest daintiest slices. The bread was delicious, the raspberry preserve was wonderful and the tea was fine, if one liked tea.

"You can thank Brett for the berries," said Frieda. "Picked them on the hill here back of the house. Lorenzo did the preserving."

"They'll think you do nothing in the place," Lawrence reminded her.

"If they've ever lived on a farm, they won't," said Frieda.

We said we had never lived on a farm and after hearing about Susan weren't sure the idea appealed to us.

"If it isn't Susan, it's the pack rats," said Lawrence. "Look up there."

In the ceiling of the room was a series of large hooks, which we looked at with wonder and lack of understanding.

"When we leave here," said Lawrence, "we lash everything up to those hooks like sides of beef in a shop . . . chairs, divan, tables. If we didn't we'd come back to find everything gone. They literally eat a chair right down to the last rung. Big monsters, as large as a dog."

We refrained from saying that this was an additional reason for not living on a farm, but Frieda caught the look and laughed.

"They're not the kind that run up a skirt," she said, "and they stay away when we're here. But I suppose if they ever took it into their heads, they could run right over us."

Since I come from a coal mining family, I had wanted from the beginning to discuss the subject with Lawrence, whose father was a miner, but had held back for fear he might have bad memories of the life. But he was interested immediately and began talking in an eager way.

"It's not the nicest life," he said, looking at me as if he thought I might have other ideas, "but the miner has a fuller life than the middle class or the aristocrat has. When they're down there in the earth, they're like little kings. They work alone and their wives aren't there to boss them and it's man against nature and man against fate. They have a full inner life, with their own thoughts and crotchets and independences, but they have this fullness only up to a certain point and then it quits. Then everything becomes narrow and restricted. We go back to see my sister who keeps a shop in a little coal town, but I'm never able to stay more than a day. It depresses me."

He said his family could never get accustomed to his being a famous man and a writer. Anyone who has read *Sons and Lovers* will know how close Lawrence was to his mother, and he told us how sad he had been that she had died three days before his first book was published. She would have understood, but the others looked on him as sort of a freak.

"I took my father a book and he said, 'What might you be getting for a wee bit book like that, David lad?' and I said, 'Two hundred pounds, Father,' and he said that convinced him that not all the fools were dead in the world.''

Lawrence acted out the Midland dialect and gave the last words in a tone of real disgust.

Frieda said they hadn't been in to Taos for a month and had no desire to go in. They had their horses and once a week they rode into the little town of Arroyo Hondo to buy their groceries. This brought on talk of prices in America as compared with England, and Lawrence said that for a two-year period they had lived in England on fifty pounds a year (then about $250).

"Both of you!" I exclaimed.

"Yes," laughed Lawrence. "It could be done. We did it."

"Tell him about the man who wanted to guarantee us the rich life," said Frieda ironically.

"Ah, yes; *him*," said Lawrence grinning through his beard. "He said it was the duty of a nation to protect its geniuses and said that we should have, say, two hundred and fifty pounds a year as a steady income. More, he added, would not be good for us."

When we went out on the porch again the sun was lower in the West and the mountain chill had set in. Lawrence pointed to a table under the trees.

"That's where I write when the weather's good," he said.

He had just finished the proofs of *The Plumed Serpent,* his Mexican book.

"It gives me a queer feeling, that country," he said. "Something dark and evil and full of old vindictive gods."

While Frieda was showing my wife the rest of the house and the little buildings on the outside, Lawrence and I went to the rail fence and looked off toward Taos.

"That's Arroyo Hondo, there," he said. "Behind the trees. It's the best way for you to get back to Taos, if you don't mind a rickety bridge over the Hondo. It would save you five or six miles."

A faint glimpse of Arroyo Hondo could be seen, a few scattered adobe houses far down the mountain side by a little stream. Lawrence explained that we drove down by the lower fence and through a gate and then left and right again and over the stream and then left and right, and when he could see that I was confused he took an old envelope out of his shirt pocket and drew a plan with his red fat-bellied pen. Almost thirty years have passed, but I can still remember what will power it took to refrain from asking him to sign that little scrawl of lines. Somehow I had sense enough to know it would spoil our pleasant afternoon, and while I was debating it in my mind he began talking about Susan.

"If you see her down there by the far fence," he said, "you might toot your horn. I'll know where to find her."

As we bumped our way over the rutted track in the pasture, we could see Brett and the Lawrences by the fence, waving heartily, but when we got to the trees by the far fence there was no sign of Susan and no tooting of the horn. The Lawrences were now far behind us and we could imagine them waiting hopefully for the signal. If it was sad for us to leave the ranch, it would be sadder yet for Lawrence, faced with another search for the bloody beast. We crept down the trail in low, and once I had to get down and push a boulder out of the road. Always in my mind was thought of the rickety bridge over the Hondo, which proved to be excessively rickety and barely spanned the torrent the Hondo had become from the heavy rains. That night in the hotel at Taos I had another nightmare to replace the terrors of Taos Canyon Gorge.[133]

The Hon. Dorothy Brett

I find you quiet, with a bit of a sore throat. "My bronchials are a bit sore again," you say. We sit and read most of the afternoon. I have brought up with me the new number of the magazine *Adventure*. You like reading it more than anything.

"It has just plain tales of adventure," you say. "Simple, unaffected story-telling, sometimes really very good, too. This one I am reading about the Foreign Legion is very exciting and really good." You settle down to the next installment until supper time, reading slowly, very intently. I can read four pages to your one.

.   .   .   .

How restless and unhappy you are today. I find you already working on the ranch picture in the guest house. The picture is on the floor and you are kneeling in front of it, painting. You look tired and white.

"Come on, Brett," you say, "your mesa needs a lot more painting. Quite nice, but needs a bit more color." I sit down at my end of the picture and we paint away silently and seriously for a time.

"Where is Frieda?" I ask, after a while.

"Finishing her painting of the cabins from the hill behind them. But

419

she's got all her perspective wrong. I wish she wouldn't do it; she really does not know how to paint."

"I am going to put Susan just here," I suggest.

"If you think you can," you reply, sarcastically. But you are already looking better: the painting seems always to invigorate you. Suddenly you say, excitedly:

"Why do women think that when a man is friendly, he wants to make up to them?" I know whom you are alluding to.

"The Lord alone knows. Vanity, I suppose," I answer, adding a touch to Susan's tail.

"Basta!" you continue, angrily, "If I tell a woman I like her company, it doesn't mean I want to make up to her."

"No," I reply, dryly, "but she probably wants you to." You give me a suspicious, side-glance out of the corner of your eye. I look solemn and serious and paint away vigorously.

"Here, move away!" you shove me aside. "If that is Susan, the Lord help her; she'll never stand on legs like that, let alone run as you have made her." With careful fingers you make a wild, fleeing Susan.

I sit back and watch you. How untouchable you are, I think to myself. How true, how important to you is your constant cry of "Noli me tangere!" You do not care to be touched, to be pawed. Necking makes you furious. Your sex is not to be played with, not to be belittled by playfulness. It is serious, a danger to be respected as the tiger is respected, hidden in the jungle. Touch me not. Well, I am very much that way myself, I think. Then you sit back.

"Look at Susan now," you say. "She is really running on real legs."

. . . .

I have asked you if you will give me a manuscript, for my typing.

"Yes, of course. You can take it this evening."

Just before I go, you give me a roll of paper. When I get home, I open it. There are six manuscripts.[134]

Del Monte Ranch./Valdez, New Mexico/19 August. 1925

(*Dear Mr. Crichton:*

Thank you for your letter, and the magazines.—I read the New Mexico article: poor painters! They apparently have to hawk their wares for six months in the year, in this country—like the primitive tin-smith. I suppose it's the country. A la guerre comme à la guerre.

I didn't know Time existed: in all its vulgarity.[135]—I would never kick my cow. But if Tiberius wished the public had only one head, so that he could cut it off, I wish it had just one posterior, that I could kick. Never my good & decent cow.

I think it's even more awful to have the public loving one, than hating one.

The kind of love-intimacy, put-your-head-on-his-shoulder touch, that they assume in their print, is worst of all.

For all that, I don't care if you do your article for that newspaper, while I'm in Europe—so long as it doesn't appear before mid-October. When I'm gone, I don't mind what's said, good or bad. My actual ears mind.

I shall be glad to get your novel—I might even review it, if you should wish.

Remember us to Mrs. Crichton. So sorry your trip went bust.—But what man with any stomach drinks moonshine?—I suppose it was moonshine.—Oh Mrs. Crichton, why didn't you pour the moonshine into the desert air, where it belongs?

D. H. Lawrence [136]

28 August 1925   Kiowa Ranch, San Cristobal, New Mexico

❴ . . . I feel I want to get out of America Loca for a while: I believe it sends everybody a bit loco. We leave here Sept 10th—expect to be in England by first week in October. . . .

We've just sat tight and considered the lily all summer. I am quite well. It grieves me to leave my horses, and my cow Susan, and the cat Timsy Wemyss, and the white cock Moses—and the place.[137]

Del Monte Ranch/Valdez/New Mexico/31 August 1925

❴ Dear Crichton:

I read your story at once & will say my say at once. I can't typewrite.

You are too journalistic, too much concerned with facts. You don't concern yourself with the human inside at all, only with the insides of steel works. It's the sort of consciousness the working man has: but at the same

421

time he's got a passionate sub-conscious. And it's this sub-conscious which makes the story: otherwise you have journalism. Now you want to be an artist, so you've got to use the artists' faculty of making the sub-conscious conscious. Take your Andy, a boy as blank as most American boys—who, to my mind, are far blanker than English or Scotch boys. It's the atmosphere of unending materialism that does it. But take your Andy, and look under his blankness: under his cheery-O! and all that, look for his hidden wistfulness, his absolutely shut-off passion, his queer uncanny American isolation and stoicism, the fantasy of himself to himself—and give the same story in terms of these, not of his mechanical upper self. Your story is good record, and excellent for conveying fact. But where the living feeling should be, it's blank: blank as the ordinary American is.

Only the feeling is there—else the boy wouldn't possibly cry at the sight of a coal-mine again.

You've got the germ of a good, novel story: though pretty hard to work out. It might take a small novel to do it.

What was there in the mines that held the boy's feelings? The darkness, the mystery, the otherworldness, the peculiar camaraderie, the sort of naked intimacy: men as gods in the underworld, or as elementals. Create that in a picture.

Then, with just a bit of alteration, vivify that middle-part (the best) of your story: steel. Give the mystery, the cruelty, the deathliness of steel, as against the comparative softness, silkiness, naturalness of coal. Throw in that Alice is a symbol of the human ego striving in its vanity, superficial: but the man's soul really magnetized by steel, by coal, as two opposing master-elements: carbon versus iron, c & f.

When we get inside ourselves, and away from the vanity of the ego— Alice & smart clothes—then things are symbols. Coal is a symbol of something in the soul, old and dark and silky and natural, and matrix of fire: & steel is symbol of something else in the soul, hard and death-dealing, cutting, hurting, annihilating the living tissue forever. You've got to allow yourself to be, in some measure, the mystic that your real self is, under all the American efficiency & smartness of the ego—before you can be an artist.

Well, you'll be bored by this.—I wonder if you'd care for Paris: should say not. Either try Italy and the sun, or a Devonshire village. It's your visionary soul you need thawing out. I can perhaps help you if you do go to Europe. All good wishes from us all to Mrs. Crichton & you.

D. H. Lawrence [138]

The Hon. Dorothy Brett

The shutters are up. You and I have struggled with them all this morning. You ended by dropping the largest one on my head. When it is finished, you look at the cabins sadly.

"Their eyes are shut," you say. "How dismal they look!"

. . .

Bill [Hawk] has arrived with the wagon. You help him carry out the trunks. Frieda is running about saying good-bye to every stick and stone. The mattresses are piled up on the wagon along with the chickens in cardboard boxes; and all very sad, we walk down behind the wagon as it moves off. The horses are left in the big field, indifferently munching.

The things in the wagon are taken up into the attic of the big house at Del Monte, while we walk on to Rachel's house. There we have supper, rather sadly. We are tired and depressed. You and Frieda are staying with Rachel for the night. I go through the orchard to my cabin. . . .

. . .

I have walked over to Rachel's house just after sunrise [10? September 1925]. Now you are ready to start at last; a bit late, because you dressed in the children's bedroom, where there is a fire, and you could not resist playing with little Shirley in her cot.

"He tells me to love her a great deal; that she will need more loving than Walton," Rachel says to me.

You are sad at going. Frieda is, too; and at the last moment she minds my being left. Rachel is almost weeping. I follow the car as it slowly grinds down the hill. At the big house, you stop to say good-bye to Mr. and Mrs. Hawk.

The car restarts, gathers speed. You peer around the hood for one final wave to me. Then I sit down against a pine tree. You are gone.[139]

❲ I didn't care for New York—it was steamy hot. I had to run about and see people: the two little Seltzer's dangling by a single thread, over the verge of bankruptcy, and nobody a bit sorry for them. The new publishers,

the Knopfs, are set up in great style, in their offices on Fifth Avenue—
deep carpets, and sylphs in a shred of black satin and a shred of brilliant
undergarments darting by. But the Knopf's seem really sound and reliable:
am afraid the Seltzers had too many "feelings." Adele said dramatically
to Frieda: "All I want is to pay OUR debts and DIE." Death is a debt we
all pay: the dollars are another matter.

Nina [Witt] is as busy as ever re-integrating other people—It was a
pleasant house near Washington Square, but of course they were building
a huge new 15-storey place next door, so all day long the noise of battle
rolled.—The child, Marion Bull, is a handsome girl of eighteen and very
nice indeed: trying to go on the stage, and the stagey people being very
catty to her. I rather hope she won't go on the stage, it might spoil her.—
The boy Harry wasn't yet back in New York.—That woman Mrs. Hare
sent a car and fetched us to their place on Long Island: beautiful place. But
in proudly showing me her bees, she went and got stung just under the
eye, and a more extraordinary hostess in an elegant house I never saw, as
the afternoon wore on and the swelling swelled and swelled. It was too
bad: she was very kind to us.—The nicest thing was when some people
motored us out at night to the shore on Long Island, and we made a huge
fire of driftwood, and toasted mutton chops, with nothing in sight but sand
and the foam in the dark[.] [140]

25 September 1925   S.S. Resolute

❰ This is the second [?] day at sea—very nice, with blue running water and
a fresh wind. I am quite glad to be out of that America for a time: it's so
tough and wearing, with the iron springs poking out through the padding.

We shall be in England in five more days—I think we shall take a house
by the sea for a while, so Frieda can have her children to stay with her. And
I must go to my sisters and see their new house. And then we must hurry
off to Baden-Baden, before winter sets in.

I don't feel myself very American: no, I am still European. . . . I hope
it's a nice autumn. In New York it was horrid, hot and sticky.[141]

27 September 1925   S.S. Resolute

❰ Here it is Sunday afternoon—everybody very bored—nothing happening,
except a rather fresh wind, the sea a bit choppy, outdoors just a bit too

cold. We get in to Southampton on Wednesday morning, and glad shall I be to see land. There are very few people on board, and most of those are Germans or people from somewhere Russia way, speaking a language never heard before. We've had pretty good weather—went on board last Monday night [21 September 1925], and sailed at 1 a.m. Queer to be slipping down the Hudson at midnight, past all the pier lights. It seems now such a long while ago. Though the weather has been pretty good, I had one awful day, blind with a headache. It was when we ran into a warm fog, so suppose it was the old malaria popping up.[142]

S.S. Resolute/Monday 28 Sept, 1925

◖ Dear Crichton:

I had your letter just before we left the ranch: now in two days we land in England. It has been quite a good crossing, even, for the Atlantic, comparatively sunny. But this is a dismal kind of ocean: it always affects me as the grave of Atlantis.

I have [been] thinking of what you say about not having the courage to be a creative writer. It seems to me that may be true—America, of all countries, kills that courage, simply because it sees no value in the really creative effort, whereas it esteems, more highly than any other country, the journalistic effort: it loves a thrill or a sensation, but loathes to be in any way moved, inwardly affected so that a new vital adjustment is necessary. Americans are enormously adaptable: perhaps because inwardly they are not adjusted at all to their environment. They are never American as a chipmunk is, or as an Indian is: only as a Ford car or as the Woolworth building.

That's why it seems to me impossible almost, to be purely a creative writer in America: everybody compromises with journalism and commerce. Hawthorne & Melville & Whitman reached a point of imaginative or visionary adjustment to America, which, it seems to me, is again entirely lost, abandoned: because you can't adjust yourself vitally, inwardly, to a rather scaring world, and at the same time, get ahead.

So, with you, & these years of work behind you, the old habit, you'd find it awfully hard. But I don't see why you shouldn't dig down in yourself till you get out of sight of your street self, and there, little by little, get out the hidden stuff. All the things an American never allows himself to feel, much less to think. I always think there is, way down in most American men, a weird little imprisoned man-gnome with a grey beard and a child's quickness, which knows, knows so finally, imprisoned inside the man-mountain while the man-mountain goes on so lively and cheery-O!—without knowing a thing. *Till the little sprite ceases to live, and then the man-mountain begins to collapse. I don't see why, with a patient effort, you shouldn't bit by bit get down what the sprite in you says: even though the man-mountain has to work at a job. It is all a question of getting yourself focussed.*

But heaven's! I don't want to preach at you.

I guess we shall stay a month or so in England, but Curtis Brown. 6 Henrietta St. London W.C. 2—that will always find me.

My wife sends remembrances to Mrs. Crichton—hope the children keep gay and sturdy.

Regards to you both.

D. H. Lawrence [143]

❰ I lie and think of the ranch: it seems so far far away:—these beastly journeys, how I hate them! I'm going to stop it, though, this continual shifting.

. . . I do feel, I don't know what I'm doing on board this ship.[144]

APPENDIX

APPENDIX

THE LAWRENCE CIRCLE:

A BIOGRAPHICAL GLOSSARY

In the following glossary, I have attempted to identify the names most frequently referred to in this second volume of the Lawrence biography. Starred entries mark contributors to this volume, and at the conclusion of entries I have indicated those who contributed memoirs to Vol. I. Additional biographical data, pertinent to an understanding of a whole career, may sometimes be found in "Notes and Sources," following initial source identifications. In this glossary, I have on occasion omitted certain nonce identifications given in "Notes and Sources."

°Barr, Mrs. Barbara, nee Barbara Weekley (1904———). Daughter of Prof. Ernest and Frieda Weekley. B. at Nottm. Educ. at dame school, Bedford Park, London, and St. Paul's Girls School, London; art school, Nottm.; and Slade School of Art, London. In 1923 again met Lawrence at Catherine Carswell's. Stayed with Lawrences at Spotorno (1925), twice at Florence, in Southern France (1928, 1930). With Lawrence when he died. After return to England, lived with father at Chiswick until marriage (1934) to John Stuart Barr, journalist and politician. Daughter Ursula born in 1934. Now lives in London. See Vol. I.

°Beals, Carleton (1893———). Amer. author and lecturer. Met Lawrence in Mexico City, Mar.–Apr., 1923. Author of autobiographic *Glass Houses* (1938). Now lives at Guilford, Conn.

Becker, Sir Walter (1855–1927). Lawrence's host at the villa Val Salice, near Turin, Italy, 15–17 Nov. 1919.

Beveridge, Millicent. Scottish painter. B. at Hukcaldy, Scotland, studied art at Glasgow, and thereafter lived chiefly in Paris. Knew Lawrence during Taormina period (1920–1922), and renewed friendship after Lawrence's return to Europe in 1925.

°Brett, the Hon. Dorothy E. ("Brett"). British-born painter, since 1924 resident in Taos, N. Mex. Devoted friend of Lawrence from late 1915. Sailed from Eng. to U.S. with Lawrences in Spring, 1924, travelled with them to Oaxaca (1924–1925), neighbored at Del Monte Ranch (Summer,

429

1925), saw Lawrence last times in Capri and Italy (Spring, 1926). Daughter of Reginald Baliol Brett, 2nd Viscount Esher; sister of the Ranee of Sarawak. Encouraged by Gen. Sir Ian Hamilton, studied at Slade School of Art, London. Among her friends of this period were Katherine Mansfield, Virginia Woolf, Lytton Strachey, Bertrand Russell, Aldous Huxley, Mark Gertler. Since coming to U.S., has been part of a circle that has included Mabel Dodge Luhan, Alfred Steiglitz, Georgia O'Keefe, Robinson Jeffers. Author of *Lawrence and Brett* (1933). See Vol. I.

°BREWSTER, MRS. ACHSAH, nee ACHSAH BARLOW. Amer. painter, long resident abroad. B. in New Haven, Conn. Married (Dec., 1910) Earl H. Brewster. Together with husband, knew Lawrences at Capri during Taormina period (1921–1922), persuaded them to follow to Ceylon (1922), continued friendship in Europe upon Lawrences' return from U.S. in 1925. Co-author (with Earl H. Brewster) of *D. H. Lawrence: Reminiscences and Correspondence* (1934), containing Lawrence letters not included in *Letters*.

°BREWSTER, EARL H. (1878———). Amer. painter and student of oriental philosophy, long resident abroad—Europe, Ceylon, India. B. in Chagrin Falls, Ohio. Married (Dec., 1910) Achsah Barlow. Together with wife, knew Lawrences at Capri during Taormina period (1921–1922), persuaded them to follow to Ceylon (1922), continued friendship in Europe upon Lawrences' return from U.S. in 1925. Co-author (with Achsah Barlow Brewster) of *D. H. Lawrence: Reminiscences and Correspondence* (1934), containing Lawrence letters not included in *Letters*. Since 1935, has made his home in India.

BREWSTER, HARWOOD (1913———), now MRS. HARWOOD PICARD of Washington, D.C. Daughter of Earl H. and Achsah Barlow Brewster.

BROOKS, JOHN ELLINGHAM ("J. E. B."). Greek scholar, translator, poet. Long a resident of Capri, was a friend of W. Somerset Maugham, Norman Douglas, the Brett Youngs, the Mackenzies. Acquaintance of Lawrence on Capri, Dec., 1919—Feb., 1920.

BROWN, CURTIS (1866–1945). Managing Director of the International Publishing Bureau, Curtis Brown Ltd. of London, Paris, and New York. He became Lawrence's literary agent in England in 1921, and later (1923) in America. Author of *Contacts* (1935), containing Lawrence letters not included in *Letters*.

BROWN, HILDA. See COTTERELL, MRS. HILDA.

°BYNNER, WITTER ("Hal") (1881———). Amer. poet. Knew the Lawrences during New Mexico periods (1922–1925), travelled with them and Willard ("Spud") Johnson in Mexico (Spring, 1923), neighbored at Chapala, Jalisco, Mexico (May–July, 1923). Mrs. Idella Purnell Stone had been a member of Mr. Bynner's verse-writing class at the U. of Calif. (1919). Author of *Journey with Genius* (1951), containing Lawrence letters not included in *Letters*. Divides time between homes in Santa Fe, N. Mex., and Chapala.

°CACÓPARDO, FRANCESCO. Proprietor of the Fontana Vecchia at Taormina,

Sicily; Lawrence's landlord, Mar., 1920—Feb., 1922. A professional chef, he lived for periods in both Eng. and U.S. Nickname "Cicio" (or "Ciccio").

CANNAN, MRS. MARY, nee MARY ANSELL, actress. Married James M. Barrie, then Gilbert Cannan. Friend and neighbor of the Lawrences and Mackenzies while all were living near Chesham, Bucks. *ca.* Aug., 1914—Jan., 1915, and thereafter during their sojourns in Europe.

°CARSWELL, MRS. CATHERINE, nee CATHERINE ROXBURGH MACFARLANE (1879–1946). Scottish writer. Devoted friend of Lawrence from Summer, 1914, seeing him last in London in Sept., 1926. Daughter of George Gray Macfarlane, merchant of Glasgow. Married (1903) Herbert P. M. Jackson (marriage annulled, 1908); (1915) Donald Carswell (1882–1940), Scottish barrister, journalist, and writer. Reviewer and dramatic critic for *Glasgow Herald* (1907–1911). Author of *The Savage Pilgrimage* (1932, 1951). Son, John Carswell (1918——), edited her autobiographic *Lying Awake* (1950). See Vol. I.

°CARTER, FREDERICK. Eng. painter and etcher. To discuss Apocalyptic symbols, Lawrence visited him at Pontesbury, Salop., in early Jan., 1924; and Mr. Carter visited the dying Lawrence at Bandol in Nov., 1929. Author of *D. H. Lawrence and the Body Mystical* (1932).

CERVI, ORAZIO. Former Italian model for Sir William Hamo Thornycroft; owner of house at Picinisco, Prov. di Caserta, in the Abruzzi mountains of Italy. For Mrs. Rosalind Thornycroft Popham and her children, the Lawrences tested the suitability of the house in Dec., 1919.

CLARKE, MRS. ADA, nee (LETTICE) ADA LAWRENCE (16 June 1887–3 July 1948). D. H. Lawrence's younger sister. Married (1913) W. Edward Clarke of Ripley, Derby. Co-author (with G. Stuart Gelder) of *Early Life of D. H. Lawrence* (1932), containing Lawrence letters not included in *Letters*. See Vol. I.

°COLLIER, JOHN (1884——). Amer. social worker and author, and Commissioner of Indian Affairs (1933–1945). Knew Lawrence at Taos during New Mexico period (1922–1925). Continues to make his home at Ranchos de Taos, N. Mex.

CORBIN, ALICE. See HENDERSON, MRS. ALICE.

COTTERELL, MRS. HILDA, nee HILDA BROWN. As a child, lived with parents in other half of Chapel Farm Cottage, Hermitage, Berks., during Lawrences' interrupted stay there (1918–1919). Now makes her home at West Drayton, Middx. See Vol. I.

COVARRUBIAS, MIGUEL (1902–1957). Mexican artist and illustrator. Acquaintance of Lawrence in Mexico City, Mar.–Apr., 1923.

°CRICHTON, KYLE S. (1896——). Amer. author (sometimes using pseudonym "Robert Forsythe") and editor. While living at Albuquerque, interviewed Lawrence for *New York World* at Kiowa Ranch *ca.* July–Aug., 1925. Now makes his home at Newtown, Conn.

°DASBURG, ANDREW MICHAEL (1887——). Amer. painter. Knew Lawrence during New Mexico period (1922–1925). Continues to make his home at Taos.

°D'ORGE, JEANNE (in 1923, MRS. ALFRED E. BURTON, now MRS. CARL CHERRY).

Amer. poet and painter. Met Lawrence during excursion to Lompoc, Calif., to watch eclipse (Sept., 1923). One of the celebrated *Others* group that led the rebellion in Amer. poetry from Armory Show days through the early 1920's. Contributor to *Poetry;* author of *Voice in the Circle* (1955), etc. Makes home at Carmel-by-the-Sea, Calif.

°DOUGLAS, (GEORGE) NORMAN (1868–1952). Eng. writer. Met Lawrence during *English Review* days (*ca.* 1909), again in Florence in Nov. 1919, and thereafter during Lawrence's stays in and near Florence in 1921, 1925–1930. Introduced Lawrence to Maurice Magnus in Nov., 1919, upheld Magnus against Lawrence in *D. H. Lawrence and Maurice Magnus: A Plea for Better Manners* (1924), and elsewhere. Served as the prototype for the character James Argyle in Lawrence's *Aaron's Rod* (1922). Author of *Siren Land* (1911), *Old Calabria* (1915), *South Wind* (1917), *Looking Back* (1933), etc.

EVANS, JOHN GANSON (1902——). Amer. writer and sociologist. Son of Carl and Mabel Evans (Mrs. Mabel Dodge Luhan). Married (20 Dec. 1922) "Little Alice" Corbin, daughter of Mrs. Alice Corbin and William Penhallow Henderson.

°FARRAHER, MRS. CLARICE, nee CLARICE CALLCOTT. Daughter of Mr. and Mrs. Alfred Callcott, real estate agents at Thirroul, N.S.W., who arranged for the Lawrences to rent "Wyewurk" from Mrs. Beatrice E. Southwell (May–Aug., 1922). Now lives at Wollongong, N.S.W., Australia.

°FORMAN, HENRY JAMES (1879——). Amer. author and editor, born in Russia. Neighbor of Lawrence at Taormina during Winter, 1921–1922. Now resides in Los Angeles.

°FORRESTER, ARTHUR DENIS (1898——). Hosiery knitting mechanic of Leicester, Eng., who met the Lawrences aboard the *Malwa* from Fremantle to Sydney in May, 1922, while emigrating to Sydney with wife Laura and friends Bill Marchbanks and wife. In late Summer, 1922, visited Lawrences at "Wyewurk," Thirroul, N.S.W. Now makes home at Strathfield, N.S.W., Australia.

FREEMAN, MRS. ELIZABETH ("BESSIE") WILKERSON. Friend of Mrs. Mabel Dodge Luhan from girlhood days in Buffalo. Met Lawrence at Taos in Sept., 1922, and Lawrence later (Aug., 1923) visited her in Buffalo.

°FRITZ, MRS. BERNARDINE. Cousin of Adele Seltzer (Mrs. Thomas Seltzer). Met Lawrence in New York City, July–Aug., 1923.

°GAMIO, DR. MANUEL (1883——). Mexican archaeologist, now Director of the *Instituto Indigenista Interamericano,* Mexico City. Although Lawrence attempted to correspond with and meet him, Dr. Gamio was at the time (1924) doing field research in the Teotihuacan Valley, and their paths did not cross.

°GAWLER, MRS. MAY EVA (1873——). Australian friend of Mrs. A. L. Jenkins, through whom she met the Lawrences during their visit to W.A. in May, 1922. Since 1952, has lived in London.

°GOLDRING, DOUGLAS (1887——). Eng. editor, novelist, critic, travel writer. In 1908, was associated with Ford Madox Ford as sub-editor of *English Review,* at which time first saw Lawrence. Renewed friendship during second Hermitage period (1919), encouraged production of *Touch and Go* and arranged for its printing, interested Insel-Verlag in publishing Lawrence in Germany, Thomas Seltzer, in U.S. Author of autobiography *Odd Man Out* (1935) and *Life Interests* (1948), containing Lawrence letters not included in *Letters*. See Vol. I.

°Gótzsche, Kai Guldbransen (1886——). Danish painter. B. in Aarhus, Denmark. Came to U.S. in 1921, and with his friend Knud Merrild shared the Lawrences' life on Del Monte Ranch in the Winter, 1922–1923. In Autumn, 1923, travelled down west coast of Mexico to Guadalajara with Lawrence, and in Nov., 1923, sailed with Lawrence as far as Plymouth before returning to Denmark. His letters to Knud Merrild concerning Lawrence are included in *A Poet and Two Painters* (1939). After several periods of residence in the U.S., now divides his time between Denmark and Majorca.

°Gray, Cecil (1895–1951). Scottish writer on music and composer. Friend and neighbor of Lawrence in Cornwall (1917). In late 1917, Lawrences temporarily housed in mother's flat at 13b, Earl's Court Sq., London, S.W. In 1915, settled in London, and in 1919 edited with Philip Heseltine *The Sackbut*, a progressive, critical journal. Music critic for the *Nation and Athenaeum* (1925–1930); on staff of *Daily Telegraph* (1928–1932); London music critic for *Manchester Guardian* (1931–1932). Composer of three operas: *Deirdre, The Temptation of St Anthony, The Trojan Women.* Author of *A Survey of Contemporary Music* (1924), etc. Wrote biography of friend Philip Heseltine, *Peter Warlock* (1934); autobiography, *Musical Chairs* (1948). See Vol. I.

Hansard, Mrs. Réné, nee Réné Juta. South African author. Sister of Jan Juta. Knew Lawrence during Taormina period (1920–1922).

°Harrison, Mrs. Phyllis. The "junior junior" at the "Booklovers," famous bookshop in Perth, W.A., owned by Mrs. Frances Zabel. Met Lawrence there during his visit in May, 1922. Later (1933–1954) proprietress of the Franceska Bookshop at Perth.

Hawk, Mr. and Mrs. A. D. Owners of Del Monte Ranch at Questa, N. Mex. Lawrence's landlords (1922–1923) during winter there with Knud Merrild and Kai Gótzsche; neighbors during Kiowa Ranch periods (1924, 1925). Parents of William; Bobby (Mrs. Ted Gillett); Betty (Mrs. Louis Cottam).

Hawk, Rachel. Mrs. William Hawk.

Hawk, William. Son of Mr. and Mrs. A. D. Hawk, owners of Del Monte Ranch at Questa, N. Mex. Friend and neighbor of Lawrence during Del Monte (1922–1923) and Kiowa Ranch (1924, 1925) periods. Husband of Rachel; father of Walton and Shirley.

Henderson, Mrs. Alice, nee Alice Corbin (1881–1949). Amer. poet and editor. Under Harriet Monroe, the first associate editor (1912–1916) of *Poetry.* Married (1905) William Penhallow Henderson (1877——), artist. Daughter, "Little Alice," married (20 Dec. 1922) John Ganson Evans, son of Mrs. Mabel Dodge Luhan. Knew Lawrence during New Mexico period (1922–1925).

°Heseltine, Philip (Arnold) (pseudonym Peter Warlock) (1894–1930).

Eng. composer, writer on music, editor of old English airs, etc. Met Lawrence Nov., 1915, and was neighbor in Cornwall (1916, 1917). Friend of Cecil Gray and Dikran Kouyoumdjian (Michael Arlen). See Vol. I.

*Holms, Capt. Percy Grenville, O.B.E. Brit. Vice-Consul at Guadalajara (1908–1915, 1919–1933). He and his wife were friends of Dr. George E. Purnell and the latter's daughter, Mrs. Idella Purnell Stone. Acquaintance of Lawrence at Guadalajara and Chapala (1923). Now makes his home in Connemara, Ireland.

Insole, Alan. Welsh painter, friend of Jan Juta. Knew Lawrence during Taormina period (1920–1922).

Jaffe, Friedrich ("Friedel"). Son of Dr. Else Jaffe-Richthofen and Edgar Jaffe; nephew of Frieda. Spent Summer, 1925, with Lawrences at Kiowa Ranch.

Jaffe-Richthofen, Dr. Else (1874–——). Eldest of three daughters of Baron and Baronin Friedrich von Richthofen; Frieda's older sister. Prof. of Social Economics. German translator of Lawrence's *Sons and Lovers, Rainbow, Boy in the Bush,* "The Fox," *Woman Who Rode Away, Plumed Serpent.* Married Dr. Edgar Jaffe, Prof. of Political Economy at U. of Heidelberg. Now lives in Heidelberg. *The Rainbow* is dedicated to her. See Vol. I.

Jenkins, Mrs. A. L. Australian friend, who met the Lawrences aboard the *Osterley* from Naples to Ceylon in Feb.–Mar., 1922, and helped entertain them during their visit in W.A. in May, 1922.

*Johnson, (W.) Willard ("Spud" or "Spoodle") (1897–——). Amer. writer and editor. Knew the Lawrences during New Mexico periods (1922–1925), travelled with them and Witter Bynner in Mexico (Spring, 1923), neighbored at Chapala, Jalisco, Mexico (May–July, 1923). Editor of famed "little magazine" *Laughing Horse* (Apr., 1922—Dec., 1939) to which Lawrence contributed. Now writes the feature "The Horse Fly" for the Taos newspaper *El Crepusculo.*

*Juta, Jan (1897–——). Designer, craftsman in glass, metal, wood, mural painter, writer. B. in Capetown, S.A., the son of Sir Henry and Lady Helen (Tait) Juta. Met Lawrence in Rome in Jan., 1920, knew him during Taormina period (1920–1922). Lawrence visited him at Anticoli Corrado, Italy, in Aug., 1920. For Lawrence's *Sea and Sardinia,* he painted eight pictures in color. Came to U.S. in 1926, now resides at Mendham, N.J.

King, Mrs. Emily, nee Emily Una Lawrence (21 Mar. 1882–——). D. H. Lawrence's older sister, later Mrs. Samuel King of North Muskham, Notts. See Vol. I.

Koteliansky, Samuel Solomnovich ("Kot") (1882–1955). Ukrainian born translator, in England from *ca.* 1914. Met Lawrence Summer, 1914. Came to England on scholarship from U. of Kiev to do research in economics. With Lawrence, Katherine Mansfield, Virginia Woolf, Leonard Woolf, collaborated in translating Tolstoi, Dostoievsky, Chekhov, Gorky, Bunin, etc. "[One] of the most intimate, most loyal, and most perverse of Katherine Mansfield's friends."—Antony Alpers. Lived at 5, Acacia Road, St. John's Wood, London, N.W. 8.

Lawrence, Emily Una. See King, Mrs. Emily.

°LAWRENCE, FRIEDA. See RAVAGLI, MRS. FRIEDA LAWRENCE.

LAWRENCE, (LETTICE) ADA. See CLARKE, MRS. ADA.

°LEIGHTON, FREDERIC W. (1895——). Amer. importer. Through the Amer. Embassy in Mexico City, Witter Bynner met Mr. Leighton who was in charge of the teaching of English in the Mexico City schools and a representative of the Federated Press. Mr. Leighton became an "agreeable guide" to Witter Bynner, Willard ("Spud") Johnson, and the Lawrences during their stay in Mexico City in Mar.–Apr., 1923, and visited the group at Chapala in early Summer. Since 1927, president of Fred Leighton, Inc.

°LESEMANN, MAURICE (1899——). Amer. poet and business executive. Met Lawrence while visiting Mrs. Mabel Dodge Luhan at Taos in Oct., 1922. Now makes his home in La Crescenta, Calif.

LOWELL, AMY (1874–1925). Amer. poet and critic. Met Lawrence in London, Summer, 1914, and thereafter aided him financially. See S. Foster Damon's *Amy Lowell* (1935) for many Lawrence letters not included in *Letters.*

LUHAN (LUJAN), ANTONIO ("Tony"). Pueblo Indian of Taos, N. Mex., who married (1923) Mrs. Mabel Dodge Sterne.

°LUHAN (LUJAN), MRS. MABEL DODGE, nee MABEL GANSON (1879——). Amer. autobiographer, hostess, patroness of arts, long a resident of Taos, N. Mex. Encouraged Lawrence to come to Taos in 1922 to write of Amer. Indian life, and knew him personally from Sept., 1922, to Oct., 1924, their correspondence continuing until his death. B. in Buffalo, N.Y. Married (1900) Carl Evans, Buffalo socialite, by whom one son, John Ganson Evans (1902——); (1903) Edwin Dodge, Boston architect; (1916) Maurice Sterne, artist; (1923) Antonio ("Tony") Luhan (Lujan), Pueblo Indian. Author of autobiography *Intimate Memories.* Her *Lorenzo in Taos* (1932) contains Lawrence letters not included in *Letters.*

°MACKENZIE, (SIR EDWARD MONTAGUE) COMPTON (1883——). Eng. novelist. Married Faith Stone (1905). The Lawrences had made friends with the Mackenzies while all were living near Chesham, Bucks. *ca.* Aug., 1914 —Jan., 1915, and renewed the friendship on Capri, Dec., 1919—Feb., 1920. B. at West Hartlepool, Durham. Educ. at St. Paul's School and Magdalen Coll., Oxford. Served with Royal Naval Division at Gallipoli. Capt., Royal Marines (1915); Military Control Officer, Athens (1916); Director, Aegean Intelligence Service (1917). See Vol. I.

°MACKENZIE, LADY (FAITH) COMPTON, nee FAITH STONE. Eng. writer. Married (1905) (Edward Montague) Compton Mackenzie (later Sir Compton Mackenzie). The Lawrences had made friends with the Mackenzies while all were living near Chesham, Bucks., *ca.* Aug., 1914—Jan., 1915, and renewed the friendship on Capri, Dec., 1919—Feb., 1920. Author of three volumes of autobiography: *As Much as I Dare* (1938), *More Than I Should* (1940), *Always Afternoon* (1943).

°MAGNUS, MAURICE (1876–1920). Manager for Isadora Duncan, member of the French Foreign Legion, journalist. B. in New York City. Introduced to Lawrence by Norman Douglas in Florence, Nov., 1919, invited Lawrence to Monte Cassino in Feb., 1920, followed Lawrence to Sicily in

Spring, 1920, travelled on same ship to Malta with the Lawrences in May, 1920. Committed suicide on Malta, 4 Nov. 1920. For Magnus' posthumous *Memoirs of the Foreign Legion* (1924), Lawrence wrote his famous Introduction, thus precipitating a quarrel with Norman Douglas.

°MANSFIELD, KATHERINE (pseudonym of Kathleen Beauchamp Murry) (1888–1923). Brit. short-story writer. Met Lawrence in London, Summer, 1913. Witness at marriage (13 July 1914) of Lawrence and Frieda. Together with John Middleton Murry, was neighbor of Lawrences at Chesham, Bucks., Autumn, 1914; at Higher Tregerthen, Zennor, St. Ives, Cornwall, Spring, 1916. From 1918 sought health in Italy, Switzerland, France. B. in Wellington, N.Z. Married (1909) George Bowden (div., 1918); (1918) John Middleton Murry. See Vol. I.

MARCHBANKS, BILL. Eng. hosiery knitting mechanic, who, with wife, was shipboard acquaintance of Lawrences aboard the *Malwa* from Fremantle to Sydney in May, 1922. Friend of Arthur Denis Forrester. In late Summer, 1922, visited Lawrences at "Wyewurk," Thirroul, N.S.W. Later went to New Zealand.

MERRILD, KNUD (1894–1954). Danish painter, graver, sculptor, designer, writer. B. in Odum, Denmark. In 1921, came to New York, and in 1922–1923, lived in N. Mex., at which time he and his friend Kai Gótzsche met the Lawrences and shared their life at Del Monte Ranch (Winter, 1922–1923). In Aug.–Sept., 1923, again knew Lawrence during his stay in Los Angeles. Author of *A Poet and Two Painters* (1939), containing Lawrence letters not included in *Letters.*

°MILLIN, MRS. SARAH GERTRUDE, nee LIEBSON (1889——). South African writer. With husband, Philip Millin, K.C. (died 1952), met the Lawrences in London, Dec., 1923 (?), through John Middleton Murry. Author of two volumes of autobiography, *The Night Is Long* (1941) and *The Measure of My Days* (1955). Makes her home at Johannesburg, S.A.

MONK, VIOLET. See STEVENS, MRS. VIOLET.

°MONROE, HARRIET (1861?–1936). Amer. poet and critic; founder and editor (1912–1936) of *Poetry: A Magazine of Verse*, to which Lawrence contributed. Met Lawrence briefly in Chicago, 19 Mar. 1924.

MOUNTSIER, ROBERT. Amer. journalist. Friend of Lawrence from Cornwall period (1916–1917), and his agent in New York City (1916–1923).

°MURRY, JOHN MIDDLETON (1889–1957). Eng. author, editor, critic, farmer. Met Lawrence in London, Summer, 1913. Witness at marriage (13 July 1914) of Lawrence and Frieda. Married (1918) Katherine Mansfield; (1924) Violet le Maistre; Elizabeth Cockbayne. Together with Katherine Mansfield, was neighbor of Lawrences at Chesham, Bucks., Autumn, 1914; at Higher Tregerthen, Zennor, St. Ives, Cornwall, Spring, 1916. Again knew Lawrence in London, Dec., 1923—Mar., 1924, Oct., 1925. Ed. of *Athenaeum* (1919–1921), of *Adelphi* (1923–1930), etc. Author of *Son of Woman* (1931, 1954), *Reminiscences of D. H. Lawrence* (1933), the autobiography *Between Two Worlds* (1934). Ed. of Katherine Mansfield. Last resided at Diss, Norfolk. See Vol. I.

NUTTALL, MRS. ZELIA MARIA MAGDALENA (1858–1933). Amer. archeologist, traveller, author, long resident in Mexico. Lawrence visited her on several occasions at her home at Coyoacán outside Mexico City in Spring, 1923.

PILLEY, W. CHARLES. Asst. ed. of *John Bull*, who wrote famous review of *Women in Love* in *John Bull*, XXX (No. 798, 17 September 1921), 4.

PINKER, JAMES BRAND. Head of James B. Pinker & Son, Literary, Dramatic, and Film Agents of London and New York. Lawrence's agent in England prior to 1921, when succeeded by Curtis Brown.

°POPHAM, MRS. ROSALIND, nee ROSALIND THORNYCROFT. While living at Pangbourne, Berks., became friend of the Lawrences during second Hermitage period (1919). For her and her children the Lawrences tested the suitability of the house of Orazio Cervi at Picinisco in the Abruzzi mountains of Italy in Dec., 1919. Lawrence visited her at Villa Canovaia, San Gervasio, Italy, in Sept., 1920. Daughter of Sir Hamo Thornycroft, R.A.; sister of Mrs. Joan Thornycroft Farjeon. The "R. P." of the *Letters*. See Vol. I.

°PRICHARD, MRS. KATHARINE SUSANNAH (1884———). Australian novelist who corresponded with Lawrence while he was living at "Wyewurk," Thirroul, N.S.W. (May–Aug., 1922). Later, friend of Mollie L. Skinner.

PURNELL, DR. GEORGE E. (1863———). Amer. dentist, practicing at Guadalajara, Mexico (1889–1939). Father of Mrs. Idella Purnell Stone; friend of Lawrence at Guadalajara and Chapala (May–July, Oct.–Nov., 1923). Now lives with daughter at Sierra Madre, Calif.

°PURNELL, IDELLA. See STONE, MRS. IDELLA.

°QUINTANILLA, DR. LUIS (1900———). Mexican poet and diplomat, at present Ambassador at the *Delegación de México Ante La Organización de Los Estados Americanos* in Washington, D.C. Met Lawrence in Mexico City (Oct.–Nov., 1924, Mar., 1925) while Prof. of Eng. at U. of Mexico (1923–1925). For him, Lawrence revised the MS of "See Mexico After."

RAUH, IDA. Actress. Married (1911) author Max Eastman (div., 1922), later Andrew Dasburg, artist. Knew Lawrence during New Mexico period (1922–1925). For her, in 1925, Lawrence wrote his Biblical play, *David*. She was to be with Frieda and Frieda's daughter Barbara (Mrs. Barbara Weekley Barr) in Vence at the time of Lawrence's death.

°RAVAGLI, MRS. FRIEDA LAWRENCE, nee EMMA MARIA FRIEDA JOHANNA VON RICHTHOFEN (11 Aug. 1879—11 Aug. 1956). Second daughter of Baron and Baronin Friedrich von Richthofen of Germany. Married (Sept., 1899) Ernest Weekley, by whom three children: Charles Montague (1900———), Elsa (1902———), Barbara (1904———); marriage dissolved (28 May 1914). Married (13 July 1914) D. H. Lawrence; (1950) Captain Angelino Ravagli. Spent last years of her life at El Prado, N. Mex., and Port Isabel, Tex. Her *"Not I, But the Wind"* (1934) contains Lawrence letters not included in *Letters*. See Vol. I.

RICHTHOFEN, BARONIN VON, nee MARQUIER (1851?–1931?). Frieda's mother. In 1920's, lived at Baden-Baden.

RICKARDS, CONSTANTINE G. (1876–1950). Brit. Vice-Consul and Acting Consul at Oaxaca and Mexico City (1910–1943). B. at Oaxaca, he became a Barrister at Law to the Courts of the Mexican Republic. Met Lawrence in

Oct.–Nov., 1924 (?), and arranged with him to live at home of his brother, Edward A. Rickards, Anglican priest at Oaxaca. Father of George E. Rickards, present Brit. Vice-Consul at Mexico City. Author of *The Ruins of Mexico* (1910).

RICKARDS, EDWARD A. Anglican priest at Oaxaca, who shared home at Avenida Pino Suarez 43 with Lawrences (Nov., 1924—Feb., 1925). Brother of Constantine G. Rickards (1876–1950), Brit. Vice-Consul and Acting Consul at Oaxaca and Mexico City (1910–1943); uncle of George E. Rickards, present Brit. Vice-Consul at Mexico City.

°RICKARDS, GEORGE E. Present (1956) Brit. Vice-Consul at Mexico City. Son of Constantine G. Rickards; nephew of Edward A. Rickards.

ROSALINO. *Mozo* at home of Father Edward A. Rickards at Avenida Pino Suarez 43, Oaxaca, Mexico. Lawrence tutored him during Oaxaca period (Nov., 1924—Feb., 1925).

SCOTT, WINFIELD. Amer. mgr. of Hotel Arzapalo at Chapala, Jalisco, Mexico. Acquaintance of Lawrence during Chapala periods (1923). Father of Margaret, friend of Mrs. Idella Purnell Stone.

SECKER, MARTIN (1882——). Lawrence's principal publisher in Eng. from 1921 until the 1930's when the Eng. rights to his books were bought up by Heinemann. Mr. Secker also published the early work of Sir Compton Mackenzie, Norman Douglas, Gilbert Cannan, Francis Brett Young, Viola Meynell, and others. His business was reconstructed in 1935 under the style of Martin Secker and Warburg Ltd. In 1937, he severed his connection to become a director of The Richards Press Ltd.

SELTZER, MRS. ADELE (ADELA), nee ADELE SZOLD. Mrs. Thomas Seltzer; cousin of Mrs. Bernardine Fritz.

°SELTZER, THOMAS (1873–1943). Amer. publisher and translator. Lawrence's chief Amer. publisher throughout the 1920's. Visited Lawrences at Del Monte Ranch in Dec., 1922, was their host in New York City and Union Hill, Dover, N.J., in July–Aug., 1923, Mar., 1924, Sept., 1925.

SIEBENHAAR, WILLIAM (1863–1937). Holland-born W.A. writer, author of the lyrical romance *Dorothea* (1910), translator of E. D. Dekker's *Max Havelaar* (1927), for which Lawrence wrote introduction. Met Lawrence briefly at Perth in May, 1922.

°SKINNER, MARY LOUISA ("Mollie" or "M. L.") (1878–1955). Australian writer and nurse. Met Lawrence when Mrs. A. L. Jenkins arranged for him and Frieda to stay at Miss Skinner's guest house at Leithdale, Darlington, W.A., in May, 1922. At Lawrence's instigation, she wrote *The House of Ellis* and sent the MS to him. Lawrence revised it as *The Boy in the Bush* (1924) while travelling in Mexico with Kai Götzsche in late Autumn, 1923.

°SOUTHWELL, MRS. BEATRICE E. Owner of "Wyewurk," the Lawrences' home at Thirroul, N.S.W., Australia (May–Aug., 1922). Sister of Lucy, Mrs. Alfred Callcott, real estate agent; aunt of Mrs. Clarice Callcott Farraher. Continues to make home at Epping, N.S.W.

SPRAGUE, ALICE. Friend of Mrs. Mabel Dodge Luhan from Buffalo days.

Visited the latter at Taos in early Summer, 1924, at which time met Lawrence.

°STERNE, MRS. MABEL DODGE. See LUHAN, MRS. MABEL DODGE.

STEVENS, MRS. VIOLET, nee VIOLET MONK ("Monk"). With her cousin, Miss Cecily Lambert (later Mrs. Cecily Lambert Minchin) took over Grimsbury Farm, Long Lane, Hermitage, Berks., during World War I. Friend of Lawrence during Hermitage periods (1918–1919).

°STONE, MRS. IDELLA, nee IDELLA PURNELL (1901——). B. in Guadalajara, Mexico, daughter of Dr. George E. Purnell (1863——). In 1919, studied verse writing under Witter Bynner at U. of Calif. Editor (Spring, 1923 —May, 1930) of famed "little magazine" *Palms,* to which Lawrence contributed. Knew Lawrence at Guadalajara and Chapala (May–July, Oct.–Nov., 1923). Now operates Stone Dianetic Center at Sierra Madre, Calif.

THOMPSON, CLARENCE. Protégé of Alice Sprague, then of Mrs. Mabel Dodge Luhan. Met Lawrence at Taos in Summer, 1924.

TURNER, REGINALD ("Reggie") (?–1938). Eng. novelist and conversationalist, long resident in Florence. Friend of Norman Douglas and Giuseppe ("Pino") Orioli. Acquaintance of Lawrence at Florence during latter's visits and sojourns there from 1919.

°WARLOCK, PETER. See HESELTINE, PHILIP ARNOLD.

°WEEKLEY, BARBARA. See BARR, MRS. BARBARA.

°WEST, REBECCA (pseudonym of Cicily Isabel Fairfield, Mrs. Henry Maxwell Andrews) (1892——). Eng. critic and novelist. With Norman Douglas, met Lawrence at Florence in Spring, 1921, and thereafter became staunch spokesman for him.

°WESTON, EDWARD (1886——). Distinguished Amer. photographer, in 1924 resident in Mexico City. Since 1947, member of the faculty of the California School of Fine Arts, San Francisco. Lawrence sat for his portraits in Mexico City on 4 Nov. 1924. Now makes his home at Carmel, Calif.

°YOUNG, FRANCIS BRETT (1884–1954). Eng. novelist and poet. Friend of the Lawrences on Capri, Dec., 1919—Feb., 1920, helped them locate Fontana Vecchia at Taormina, Sicily, in Mar., 1920. Took M.B., Birmingham, travelled in Far East as ship's doctor (1906–1908). Officer in medical corps in East Africa, in World War I. Spent last years of his life in South Africa.

YOUNG, JESSICA. Mrs. Francis Brett Young.

MAJOR FIRST EDITIONS OF THE WORKS OF
D. H. LAWRENCE

For the data incorporated in the following list, I am indebted to Edward D. McDonald's *A Bibliography of the Writings of D. H. Lawrence* and *The Writings of D. H. Lawrence, 1925–1930: A Bibliographical Supplement,* and to William White's *D. H. Lawrence: A Checklist, 1931–1950.* Although it includes all major first editions, the list ignores certain minor items of interest to the collector only, most contributions to books and periodicals, and selections of his work made after Lawrence's death. For additional details, the reader is referred to the authorities above.

Aaron's Rod (novel). New York: Thomas Seltzer, April, 1922; London: Martin Secker, June, 1922.

Altitude (play). *The Laughing Horse* (No. 20, Summer, 1938).

Amores (poems). London: Duckworth, July, 1916; New York: B. W. Huebsch, 1916.

Apocalypse (essay). With an Introduction by Richard Aldington. Florence: G. Orioli, May, 1931; London: Martin Secker, 1932; New York: Viking, 1932.

A Propos of Lady Chatterley's Lover (essay extended from *My Skirmish with Jolly Roger*). London: The Mandrake Press, June, 1930; London: Heinemann, 1931; in Harry T. Moore, ed., *Sex, Literature and Censorship* (New York: Twayne, 1953), pp. 89–122 [first American publication].

Assorted Articles. London: Martin Secker, April, 1930; New York: Knopf, 1930.

Bay: A Book of Poems. Cover and Decorations designed by Anne Estelle Rice. London: The Beaumont Press, November, 1919.

Birds, Beasts and Flowers (poems). New York: Thomas Seltzer, 9 October 1923; London: Martin Secker, November, 1923 [includes *Tortoises*]; London: The Cresset Press, June, 1930 [with illustrations by Blair Hughes-Stanton].

Boy in the Bush, The (novel, with M. L. Skinner). London: Martin Secker, August, 1924; New York: Thomas Seltzer, 1924.

Captain's Doll, The (short novels). New York: Thomas Seltzer, April, 1923; London: Martin Secker, March, 1923, with title: *The Ladybird.*

Cavalleria Rusticana and Other Stories (translation from Giovanni Verga). With a Translator's Preface by D. H. Lawrence. London: Jonathan Cape, March, 1928; New York: Lincoln MacVeagh, The Dial Press, 1928.

Collected Poems. 2 vols. London: Martin Secker, September, 1928; New York: Jonathan Cape and Harrison Smith, 1928.

Collier's Friday Night, A (play). With an Introduction by Edward Garnett. London: Martin Secker, 1934.

David (play). London: Martin Secker, March, 1926; New York: Knopf, 1926.

"Delilah and Mr. Bircumshaw" (short story). *Virginia Quarterly Review,* XVI (No. 2, Spring, 1940), 257–66.

D. H. Lawrence's Letters to Bertrand Russell. Edited, with an Introduction by Harry T. Moore. New York: Gotham Book Mart, 1948.

England, My England and Other Stories. New York: Thomas Seltzer, 24 October 1922; London: Martin Secker, January, 1924.

Escaped Cock, The (short novel, original title of *The Man Who Died*). Paris: The Black Sun Press, September, 1929 [with water-color decorations by D. H. Lawrence]; London: Martin Secker, March, 1931, with title: *The Man Who Died;* New York: Knopf, 1931, with title: *The Man Who Died.*

Etruscan Places (travel essays). London: Martin Secker, 1932; New York: Viking, 1932.

Fantasia of the Unconscious (essays). New York: Thomas Seltzer, 23 October 1922; London: Martin Secker, September, 1923.

Fight for Barbara (play). *Argosy* [London], December, 1933.

First Lady Chatterley, The (novel). With a MS Report by Esther Forbes, and a Foreword by Frieda Lawrence. New York: The Dial Press, 1944.

"Gentleman from San Francisco, The" (translation with S. S. Koteliansky from Ivan Bunin), in Ivan Bunin, *The Gentleman from San Francisco and Other Stories,* trans. by S. S. Koteliansky and Leonard Woolf. London: The Hogarth Press, 1922.

Glad Ghosts (short story). London: Benn, November, 1926. Included in *The Woman Who Rode Away and Other Stories.*

"Introduction," in M[aurice] M[agnus], *Memoirs of the Foreign Legion.* London: Martin Secker, September, 1924; New York: Knopf, January, 1925.

Kangaroo (novel). London: Martin Secker, September, 1923; New York: Thomas Seltzer, 1923.

Ladybird, The (short novels). London: Martin Secker, March, 1923; New York: Thomas Seltzer, April, 1923, with title: *The Captain's Doll.*

Lady Chatterley's Lover (novel). Florence: Privately Printed, July, 1928 [unexpurgated]; Paris: Privately Printed, May, 1929 [Paris Popular Edition, unexpurgated, including "My Skirmish with Jolly Roger"]; London: Martin Secker, 1932 [Authorized Abridged Edition]; New York: Knopf, 1932 [Authorized Abridged Edition].

Last Poems. Edited by Richard Aldington and Giuseppe Orioli, with an Introduction by Richard Aldington. Florence: G. Orioli, 1932; New York: Viking, 1933; London: Heinemann, 1935.

Letters. Edited and with an Introduction by Aldous Huxley. London: Heinemann, 1932; New York: Viking, 1932.

Little Novels of Sicily (translation from Giovanni Verga). With a Note on Giovanni Verga by D. H. Lawrence. New York: Thomas Seltzer, March, 1925; Oxford: Basil Blackwell, April, 1925.

Look! We Have Come Through! (poems). London: Chatto, December, 1917; New York: B. W. Huebsch, 1918.

Lost Girl, The (novel). London: Martin Secker, November, 1920; New York: Thomas Seltzer, 1921.

Love Among the Haystacks and Other Pieces (short stories). With a Reminiscence by David Garnett. London: The Nonesuch Press, December, 1930;

New York: Random House, n. d. [Limited Edition]; New York: Viking, 1933.

Lovely Lady and Other Stories, The. London: Martin Secker, 1933; New York: Viking, 1933.

Love Poems and Others. London: Duckworth, February, 1913; New York: Mitchell Kennerley, 1913.

Man Who Died, The (short novel). Paris: The Black Sun Press, September, 1929, with title: *The Escaped Cock;* London: Martin Secker, March, 1931; New York: Knopf, 1931.

Married Man, The (play). *Virginia Quarterly Review,* XVI (Autumn, 1940), 523–47.

Mastro-don Gesualdo (translation from Giovanni Verga). With a Biographical Note [by D. H. Lawrence]. New York: Thomas Seltzer, 1923; London: Jonathan Cape, March, 1925.

Merry-Go-Round, The (play). *Virginia Quarterly Review,* XVII (Winter, 1941), Supp., 1–44.

Mr. Noon (fragment of a novel), in *A Modern Lover.* London: Martin Secker, 1934; New York: Viking, 1934.

Modern Lover, A (short stories and an unfinished novel). London: Martin Secker, 1934; New York: Viking, 1934.

Mornings in Mexico (travel essays). London: Martin Secker, July, 1927; New York: Knopf, 1927.

Movements in European History. London: Oxford University Press, March, 1921, under pseudonym "Lawrence H. Davison"; Oxford University Press, May, 1925 [Large paper Edition, illustrated], under "D. H. Lawrence"; Oxford University Press, May, 1925 [Regular trade Edition, illustrated], under "D. H. Lawrence."

My Skirmish with Jolly Roger (essay). "Written as an Introduction to and a Motivation of the Paris Edition of Lady Chatterley's Lover." New York: Random House, July, 1929.

Nettles (poems). Criterion Miscellany No. 11. London: Faber, March, 1930.

New Poems. London: Martin Secker, October, 1918; New York: B. W. Huebsch, 1920.

Paintings of D. H. Lawrence, The. With an Introduction by D. H. Lawrence. London: The Mandrake Press, June, 1929.

Pansies (poems). London: Martin Secker, July, 1929 [ordinary trade edition, expurgated]; London: Privately Printed for Subscribers only by P. R. Stephensen, August, 1929 [special definitive edition, unexpurgated, with an Introduction by D. H. Lawrence]; New York: Knopf, 1929 [ordinary trade edition, expurgated].

Phoenix: The Posthumous Papers. Edited and with an Introduction by Edward D. McDonald. London: Heinemann, 1936; New York: Viking, 1936.

Plays of D. H. Lawrence, The. London: Martin Secker, 1933.

Plumed Serpent, The (*Quetzalcoatl*) (novel). London: Martin Secker, January, 1926; New York: Knopf, 1926.

Pornography and Obscenity (essay). London: Faber, November, 1929 [Criterion Miscellany No. 5]; New York: Knopf, 1930.

Prelude, A. His First and Previously Unrecorded Work. With an Explanatory Foreword by P. Beaumont Wadsworth. Thames Ditton, Surrey: The Merle Press, 1949.

"Princess, The" (short story), in *St. Mawr: Together with The Princess.* London: Martin Secker, May, 1925.

Prussian Officer and Other Stories, The. London: Duckworth, December, 1914; New York: B. W. Huebsch, 1916.

Psychoanalysis and the Unconscious (essays). New York: Thomas Seltzer, May, 1921 [special issue of the first edition]; New York: Thomas Seltzer, May, 1921 [ordinary trade edition]; London: Martin Secker, July, 1923 [ordinary trade edition].

"Rachel Annand Taylor" (lecture), in Ada Lawrence and G. Stuart Gelder, *Young Lorenzo: Early Life of D. H. Lawrence, Containing Hitherto Unpublished Letters, Articles and Reproductions of Pictures.* Florence: G. Orioli, 1931.

Rainbow, The (novel). London: Methuen, 30 September 1915; New York: B. W. Huebsch, 1916 [expurgated text]; New York: Thomas Seltzer, 1924 [expurgated Huebsch text]; London: Martin Secker, 1926 ["new edition (revised)"].

Rawdon's Roof (short story). The Woburn Books No. 7. London: Elkin Mathews and Marrot, March, 1928. Included in *The Lovely Lady and Other Stories.*

Reflections on the Death of a Porcupine and Other Essays. Philadelphia: The Centaur Press, December, 1925; London: Martin Secker, 1934.

St. Mawr: Together with The Princess (short novel and short story). London: Martin Secker, May, 1925; New York: Knopf, 1925, with title: *St. Mawr* [without "The Princess"].

Sea and Sardinia (travel essays). With Eight Pictures in Color by Jan Juta. New York: Thomas Seltzer, 12 December 1921; London: Martin Secker, April, 1923.

Sex Locked Out (essay). "Reprinted, December, 1928, from the Sunday Dispatch, London, November 25, 1928." London: Privately Printed, December, 1928. Included in *Assorted Articles,* with title "Sex versus Loveliness."

Sons and Lovers (novel). London: Duckworth, May, 1913; New York: Mitchell Kennerley, 1913.

Story of Doctor Manente, The: Being the Tenth and Last Story from the Suppers of A. F. Grazzini Called Il Lasca (translation). Introduction by D. H. Lawrence. Florence: G. Orioli, March, 1929.

Studies in Classic American Literature (criticism). New York: Thomas Seltzer, August, 1923; London: Martin Secker, June, 1924.

Sun (short story). London: E. Archer, September, 1926 [first form]; Paris: The Black Sun Press, October, 1928 [authorized unexpurgated edition]; Privately Printed, 1929 [pirated, unexpurgated American edition].

Tales. London: Martin Secker, 1934.

"Thimble, The" (short story). *The Seven Arts,* March, 1917.

Tortoises (poems). New York: Thomas Seltzer, 9 December 1921. Included in the English edition of *Birds, Beasts and Flowers* [London: Martin Secker, November, 1923].

Touch and Go (play). With a Preface by D. H. Lawrence. London: C. W. Daniel, May, 1920; New York: Thomas Seltzer, 1920.

Trespasser, The (novel). London: Duckworth, May, 1912; New York: Mitchell Kennerley, 1912.

Triumph of the Machine, The (poem). With drawings by Althea Willoughby. The Ariel Poems No. 28. London: Faber, September, 1930. Included in *Last Poems*.

Twilight in Italy (travel essays). London: Duckworth, June, 1916; New York: B. W. Huebsch, 1916.

Virgin and the Gipsy, The (short novel). Florence: G. Orioli, May, 1930; London: Martin Secker, October, 1930; New York: Knopf, 1930.

White Peacock, The (novel). New York: Duffield, 19 January 1911; London: Heinemann, 20 January 1911.

Widowing of Mrs. Holroyd, The (play). With an Introduction by Edwin Björkman. New York: Mitchell Kennerley, 1 April 1914; London: Duckworth, April, 1914.

Woman Who Rode Away and Other Stories, The. London: Martin Secker, 24 May 1928; New York: Knopf, 25 May 1928, including "The Man Who Loved Islands."

Women in Love (novel). New York: Privately Printed for Subscribers Only, November, 1920 [Limited Edition]; London: Martin Secker, May, 1921 [first English edition]; New York: Privately Printed for Subscribers Only, May, 1922 [special signed edition by Thomas Seltzer for Martin Secker]; New York: Thomas Seltzer, October, 1922 [first American trade edition].

BIBLIOGRAPHY
NOTES AND SOURCES

BIBLIOGRAPHY

Included in the following two lists are the published works and identifications of MS materials to which reference is made in this second volume of the Lawrence biography. In my "Notes and Sources," I have made consistent use of shortened forms whenever possible: author or author plus abbreviated title, and, for works by D. H. Lawrence, titles alone.

I. BOOKS AND ARTICLES

Aldington, Richard. *D. H. Lawrence: Portrait of a Genius But* . . . . New York: Duell, Sloan & Pearce, 1950.

Alpers, Antony. *Katherine Mansfield.* New York: Knopf, 1953.

Beals, Carleton. *Glass Houses: Ten Years of Free-Lancing.* Philadelphia: Lippincott, 1938.

Brett, Dorothy. *Lawrence and Brett: A Friendship.* Philadelphia: Lippincott, 1933. Copyright, 1933, by Miss Dorothy Brett, Taos, New Mexico.

Brewster, Earl, and Achsah. *D. H. Lawrence: Reminiscences and Correspondence.* London: Martin Secker, 1934.

Bynner, Witter. *Journey with Genius: Recollections and Reflections Concerning the D. H. Lawrences.* New York: Day, 1951.

Carswell, Catherine. *The Savage Pilgrimage: A Narrative of D. H. Lawrence.* Rev. ed. London: Martin Secker, 1932; London: Secker & Warburg, 1951 (pagination the same).

Carter, Frederick. *D. H. Lawrence and the Body Mystical.* London: Denis Archer, 1932.

Damon, S. Foster. *Amy Lowell: A Chronicle.* Boston: Houghton, 1935.

d'Orge, Jeanne. "Lawrence the Wayfarer," Supplement to *The Carmelite* [Carmel, Calif.], III (No. 6, 19 March 1930), xiv–xvi.

Douglas, Norman. *Looking Back.* New York: Harcourt, 1933. Selections reprinted by permission of the copyright owners, Chatto and Windus, Ltd.

Fabes, Gilbert H. *D. H. Lawrence: His First Editions: Points and Values.* London: W. and G. Foyle, 1933.

Forman, Henry James. "With D. H. Lawrence in Sicily," *The New York Times Book Review and Magazine,* 27 August 1922, p. 12. Reprinted by permission of the *New York Times Book Review.*

Goldring, Douglas. *Life Interests.* London: MacDonald, 1948.

———. *The Nineteen Twenties: A General Survey and some Personal Memories.* London: Nicholson & Watson, 1945.

Gray, Cecil, and others. *Peter Warlock: A Memoir of Philip Heseltine.* The Life and Letters Series No. 84. London: Jonathan Cape, 1938.

Lawrence, Ada, and Gelder, G. Stuart. *Early Life of D. H. Lawrence: Together with Hitherto Unpublished Letters and Articles.* London: Martin Secker, 1932.

————. *Young Lorenzo: Early Life of D. H. Lawrence, Containing Hitherto Unpublished Letters, Articles and Reproductions of Pictures.* Florence: G. Orioli, 1931.

Lawrence, D. H. "A Britisher Has a Word with an Editor," *Palms,* I (No. V, Christmas, 1923), 153–54.

————. *Letters.* Edited and with an Introduction by Aldous Huxley. New York: Viking, 1932.

————. "Letters to S. S. Koteliansky," *Encounter 3,* I (No. 3, December, 1953), 29–35.

————. *Phoenix: The Posthumous Papers.* Edited and with an Introduction by Edward D. McDonald. New York: Viking, 1936.

————. *Sea and Sardinia.* With Eight Pictures in Color by Jan Juta. New York: Thomas Seltzer, 1921.

Lawrence, Frieda. *"Not I, But the Wind . . ."* New York: Viking, 1934. Copyright, 1934, by Frieda Lawrence. Selections reprinted by permission of the Viking Press, Inc., New York.

Lesemann, Maurice. "D. H. Lawrence in New Mexico," *The* [American] *Bookman,* LIX (No. 1, March, 1924), 29–32.

Luhan, Mabel Dodge. *Lorenzo in Taos.* New York: Knopf, 1932.

Mackenzie, Compton. *The West Wind of Love.* New York: Dodd, 1940.

Mackenzie, Faith Compton. *More Than I Should.* London: Collins, 1940. Selections reprinted by permission of the author and of Collins.

M[agnus], M[aurice]. *Memoirs of the Foreign Legion.* With an Introduction by D. H. Lawrence. New York: Knopf, 1925.

Mansfield, Katherine. *Letters.* Edited by J. Middleton Murry. Special One Volume Edition. New York: Knopf, 1932. Copyright, 1929, by Alfred A. Knopf, Inc.

————. *Letters to John Middleton Murry: 1913–1922.* Edited by John Middleton Murry. New York: Knopf, 1951. Copyright, 1929, 1951, by Alfred A. Knopf, Inc.

McDonald, Edward D. *A Bibliography of the Writings of D. H. Lawrence.* With a Foreword by D. H. Lawrence. Philadelphia: Centaur Book Shop, 1925.

————. *The Writings of D. H. Lawrence, 1925–1930: A Bibliographical Supplement.* Philadelphia: Centaur Book Shop, 1931.

Merrild, Knud. *A Poet and Two Painters: A Memoir of D. H. Lawrence.* New York: Viking, 1939.

Millin, Sarah Gertrude. *The Night Is Long.* London: Faber, 1941. Selections reprinted by permission of the author and of Faber and Faber, Ltd.

Monroe, Harriet. "D. H. Lawrence," *Poetry: A Magazine of Verse,* XXXIV (No. II, May, 1930), 92–94.

Moore, Harry T. *The Intelligent Heart: The Story of D. H. Lawrence.* New York: Farrar, Straus & Young, 1954.

––––––. *The Life and Works of D. H. Lawrence.* New York: Twayne, 1951.

––––––. *Poste Restante: A Lawrence Travel Calendar.* With an Introduction by Mark Schorer. Berkeley and Los Angeles: University of California Press, 1956.

Murry, John Middleton. *Between Two Worlds: An Autobiography.* New York: Julian Messner, 1936. Selections reprinted by permission of Julian Messner, Inc. Copyright date, July 31, 1936, by Julian Messner, Inc.

––––––. *Reminiscences of D. H. Lawrence.* London: Jonathan Cape, 1933; The Life and Letters Series No. 74: London: Jonathan Cape, 1936 (pagination the same).

––––––. *Son of Woman: The Story of D. H. Lawrence.* London: Jonathan Cape, 1931, 1954 (pagination the same).

Nehls, Edward, ed. *D. H. Lawrence: A Composite Biography.* Vol. I. With a Foreword by Frieda Lawrence Ravagli. Madison: University of Wisconsin Press, 1957.

Pilley, W. Charles. "A Book the Police Should Ban . . . ," *John Bull,* XXX (No. 798, Saturday, 17 September 1921), 4.

Powell, Lawrence Clark. *The Manuscripts of D. H. Lawrence: A Descriptive Catalogue.* With a Foreword by Aldous Huxley. Los Angeles: The Public Library, 1937.

Prichard, Katharine Susannah. "Lawrence in Australia," *Meanjin: A Literary Magazine* [Melbourne, Australia], 9 (No. 4, Summer, 1950), 252–59. Reprinted by permission of *Meanjin.*

Priday, H. E. L. "D. H. Lawrence in Australia—Some Unpublished Correspondence," *Southerly* [Sydney, Australia], 15 (No. 1, 1954), 2–7.

Skinner, Mollie. "Correspondence: D. H. Lawrence," *Southerly* [Sydney, Australia], 13 (No. 4, 1952), 233–35.

––––––. "D. H. Lawrence and *The Boy in the Bush,*" *Meanjin: A Literary Magazine* [Melbourne, Australia], 9 (No. 4, Summer, 1950), 260–63. Reprinted by permission of *Meanjin.*

Tedlock, E. W., Jr. *The Frieda Lawrence Collection of D. H. Lawrence Manuscripts: A Descriptive Bibliography.* With a Foreword by Frieda Lawrence. Albuquerque: University of New Mexico Press, 1948. Selections reprinted by permission of the University of New Mexico Press.

Villiers, Bud [W. Willard Johnson]. "D. H. Lawrence in Mexico," *Southwest Review,* XV (No. 4, Summer, 1930), 425–33.

West, Rebecca. *Ending in Earnest: A Literary Log.* Garden City, New York: Doubleday, Doran, 1931.

Weston, Edward. "Lawrence in Mexico . . . ," Supplement to *The Carmelite* [Carmel, Calif.], III (No. 6, 19 March 1930), ix–xi.

White, William. *D. H. Lawrence: A Checklist, 1931–1950.* With a Foreword by Frieda Lawrence. Detroit: Wayne University Press, 1950.

Young, Francis Brett. *The Red Knight.* With a Preface by Francis Brett Young. The Severn Edition. London: Heinemann, 1954. Selections reprinted by permission of Francis Brett Young and Wm. Heinemann, Ltd.

II. MANUSCRIPT SOURCES

Barr, Barbara Weekley. The continuing installment of a long memoir completed in 1954. The preceding installments were published in the first volume of this present work; the concluding installments are scheduled for publication in the third.

Cacópardo, Francesco. A solicited memoir completed in January, 1954.

Collier, John. An extract from a letter to the editor (11 August 1956).

Crichton, Kyle S. A memoir written *ca*. 1950. An earlier version of Mr. Crichton's interview with Lawrence (*ca*. July–August, 1925) was published as "D. H. Lawrence Lives at the Top of the World—A Kindly Lion in a New Mexican Lair," *The World* [New York], 11 October 1925, Section 3, p. 4m.

Dasburg, Andrew. An extract from a letter to the editor (6 May 1956).

Farraher, Clarice Callcott. An extract from a letter to the editor (3 July 1956).

Forrester, Arthur Denis. A solicited interview (May, 1956) given by Mr. Forrester to Mr. F. W. L. Esch, a *Sydney Morning Herald* feature writer, at Strathfield, Sydney, N.S.W., Australia.

Gamio, Manuel. An extract from a letter to the editor (3 August 1956).

Gawler, May E. A solicited memoir dictated by Mrs. Gawler to her daughter, Mrs. Joanna Ramsey, in 1953.

Harrison, Phyllis. An extract from a letter to the editor (17 February 1954).

Holms, Captain Percy Grenville, O.B.E. An extract from a letter to the editor (10 July 1953).

Lawrence, D. H. Letters or postcards to Mrs. G. H. Cotterell (6), Kyle S. Crichton (3), Mrs. Elizabeth Freeman (1), Mrs. Rosalind Thornycroft Popham (9), Dr. Luis Quintanilla (7), Mrs. Violet Stevens (1), Mrs. Remington Stone (6), and Edward Weston (1).

Popham, Rosalind Thornycroft. The concluding installments of a solicited memoir written in 1954. The preceding installment was published in the first volume of this present work.

Quintanilla, Luis. An extract from a letter to the editor (8 May 1956).

Rickards, George E. An extract from a letter to the editor (15 August 1956).

Southwell, Beatrice E. A solicited memoir completed 16 May 1956.

Stone, Idella Purnell. Mrs. Stone's adaptations (August, 1956) into memoir form of a series of letters she had written to Witter Bynner, and published as such in Mr. Bynner's *Journey with Genius* (1951).

NOTES AND SOURCES

CHAPTER I

1 Sir William Hamo Thornycroft (1850–1925), R.A., English sculptor. Known for his *Warrior Bearing a Wounded Youth* (1876), *The Mower* (1884), *A Sower* (1886), statues of General Gordon (1888), Oliver Cromwell (1899), and King Alfred (1901).

2 Cf. Lawrence's character Pancrazio in his novel *The Lost Girl* (1920).

3 Original publication of a memoir written in 1954.

4 The address of Lawrence's friend S. S. Koteliansky.

5 Sir Walter Becker (1855–1927) and his wife.—Moore, *Intelligent Heart*, p. 257. See Note 16, below.

6 Frieda had left England for Germany in October, 1919—her first opportunity to see her own family since before the war.

7 Lawrence's error for Orazio Cervi.

8 A nurse for Mrs. Popham's children.

9 Another servant in Mrs. Popham's household.

10 Thomas Dacre Dunlop (later Sir Thomas), the English consul at Spezia, and his wife Madge had been friends of the Lawrences when the latter were living at Fiascherino in 1913–1914, and had helped Lawrence with the typing of an early draft of *The Rainbow*.—Moore, *Intelligent Heart*, pp. 158, 161.

11 In his introduction to Maurice Magnus' *Memoirs of the Foreign Legion* (1924), Lawrence recalled that when he "landed" in Italy in November, 1919, he had "nine pounds in my pocket and about twelve pounds lying in the bank in London. Nothing more. My wife, I hoped, would arrive in Florence with two or three pounds remaining."—Introduction to *Memoirs of the Foreign Legion*, p. 7.

12 (Helton) Godwin Baynes (1882–1943). English consulting physician; specialist in Jung's system of analytical psychology. He knew Lawrence during the second Hermitage period (1919).

13 Cf. *The Lost Girl*, Chap. XIII, "The Wedded Wife."

14 Original publication.

15 Original publication.

16 Another reference to the originals of Sir William and Lady Franks in Chapters 12 and 13 of *Aaron's Rod* (1922), whom Prof. Harry T. Moore has identified as Sir Walter Becker (1855–1927) and his wife.—Moore, *Intelligent Heart*, p. 257. See also the memoir by Norman Douglas, below.

451

17 D. H. L. letter to Lady Cynthia Asquith, from Albergo delle Palme, Lerici, Golfo della Spezia, dated 8 [18] November 1919, *Letters,* p. 490.

18 Among the possibilities: (1) Norman Douglas himself as James Argyle; (2) Sir Walter Becker and his wife as Sir William and Lady Franks; (3) Reggie Turner as Algy Constable; (4) Captain James Robert White as Jim Bricknell (Moore, *Intelligent Heart,* pp. 238–39); (5) Alfred Brentnall as Alfred Bricknell (Moore, *Intelligent Heart,* p. 238); (6) Dorothy Yorke as Josephine Ford (Moore, *Intelligent Heart,* p. 237); (7) Richard Aldington as Robert Cunningham (Moore, *Intelligent Heart,* p. 237); (8) Cecil Gray as Cyril Scott; (9) Augustus John as Struthers (Moore, *Intelligent Heart,* p. 237); (10) Hilda Aldington ("H. D.") as Julia Cunningham (Moore, *Intelligent Heart,* p. 237); (11) Dr. Feroze as Sherardy (Moore, *Intelligent Heart,* p. 248; see also entries for Suhrawardy, indexed in *Letters*); (12) Thomas Cooper as Aaron Sisson (Moore, *Intelligent Heart,* p. 40); (13) Brigit Patmore as Clariss Browning (Moore, *Intelligent Heart,* p. 383).

19 See Notes 5 and 16, above.

20 A reference to Lawrence's *Pornography and Obscenity* (London: Faber, November, 1929; New York: Knopf, 1930), reprinted in *Phoenix,* pp. 170–87, and Lawrence's *Sex, Literature, and Censorship,* Harry T. Moore, ed. (New York: Twayne, 1953), pp. 69–88.

21 See *Letters,* p. 529.

22 See Norman Douglas' own explanatory note in *Late Harvest* (London: Lindsay Drummond, 1946), pp. 53–54: "Many lads who now wear long trousers used to wear shorts in the days of Lawrence, and I told him why they can't, or rather at that time couldn't, wear long ones. The reason for this change in fashions is significant from a sociological point of view, and so difficult for an Englishman to divine—impossible, I should say —that I will venture to reveal it, not without such blushes as the theme may prescribe.

"There was then one inexorable rule for admission or non-admission into Florentine brothels: long trousers, yes; short trousers, no. It stands to reason, therefore, that parents kept their sons in short trousers for as long as they possibly could, whatever their size or age, and this is precisely what shocked Lawrence's inverted sense of decency. I may add, as a less commendable result of such happy-go-lucky methods, that young boys in shorts, anxious to improve their minds and add to their store of worldly knowledge, had only to slip into a pair of Daddy's trousers for an hour or so—and in they went.

"We have changed all that. A recent enactment runs to the effect that persons of questionable age are required to produce a birth-certificate at these Palaces of Delight, and if shown to be under eighteen—out they go *re infecta;* a source of resentment in certain quarters, and described to me as 'damnable fascistic interference in our private concerns.'"

23 Douglas, *Looking Back,* pp. 282–87.

24 Norman Douglas.

25 Maurice Magnus (1876–1920). His background was given to Lawrence

by Norman Douglas as follows: " 'He was manager for Isadora Duncan for a long time—knows all the capitals of Europe: St. Petersburg, Moscow, Tiflis, Constantinople, Berlin, Paris—knows them as you and I know Florence. He's been mostly in that line—theatrical. Then a journalist. He edited the *Roman Review* till the war killed it. Oh, a many-sided sort of fellow.' "—Introduction to *Memoirs of the Foreign Legion*, p. 14. Elsewhere Lawrence wrote: "He was the grandson of an emperor. His mother was the illegitimate daughter of the German Kaiser: D—— says, of the old Kaiser Wilhelm I, Don Bernardo [of Monte Cassino] says, of Kaiser Frederick Wilhelm, father of the present ex-Kaiser. . . . M—— himself was born in New York, 7 November, 1876; so at least it says on his passport. He entered the Catholic Church in England in 1902. His father was a Mr. L—— M——, married to the mother in 1867."—Introduction to *Memoirs of the Foreign Legion*, p. 85. Magnus committed suicide on Malta in November, 1920. His only published work is *Memoirs of the Foreign Legion*.

26 Introduction to *Memoirs of the Foreign Legion*, pp. 7–8, 9. For an extended account of Lawrence's life in Florence in November, 1919, see the beginning of his Introduction to *Memoirs of the Foreign Legion*, an introduction also available in Alexander Woolcott's *Second Reader* (New York: Viking Press, 1937), pp. 155–223.

27 Original publication.

28 Original publication.

29 Original publication.

30 I have corrected Huxley's error of *skirts* for *shirts*, as the holograph letter clearly reads. In the margin of this letter, Lawrence had drawn a rough sketch of a peasant shoe. Next to the drawing, he had written: "The brigand men are by no means fierce: the women are the fierce half of the breed."

31 D. H. L. letter to "Mrs. R. P." (Mrs. Rosalind Thornycroft Popham), from Presso Orazio Cervi, Picinisco, Prov. di Caserta, dated 16 December 1919, *Letters*, pp. 491–92.

32 D. H. L. letter to Ada Lawrence [from Presso Orazio Cervi, Picinisco, Prov. di Caserta (the editors mistakenly give "Spain")], dated 20 December 1919, Ada Lawrence and Gelder, pp. 95–96.

33 D. H. L. letter to W. E. and S. A. Hopkin, from Palazzo Ferraro, Capri, Naples, dated 9 January 1920, *Letters*, pp. 499–500.

34 See (Lady) Faith Compton Mackenzie, *More Than I Should* (London: Collins, 1940), p. 25: "In the autumn of 1919 the Brett Youngs arrived on Capri. They had been heralded, and I had been up to Anacapri to see if they could have Edwin Cerio's Rosaio, the old casetta we had rented in 1914. They arrived on the 9th of October, and came straight down to see us. We had never met them before, but I was already an admirer of Francis Brett Young for the few books he had written then, *Deep Sea* being my favourite. We lent them our bathing house on the Piccola Marina until Rosaio was ready. I did not have time to see much of them then, for I was going to England for the winter . . . ."

35 Young, Preface to The Severn Edition of *The Red Knight*, p. ix. For his critical estimate of Lawrence, see Francis Brett Young's "A Note on D. H. Lawrence" in *The Borzoi: 1925: Being a Sort of Record of Ten Years of Publishing* (New York: Knopf, 1925), pp. 235–38.

36 Edward Montague Compton Mackenzie, later Sir Compton, whom Lady Mackenzie, nee Faith Stone, had married in 1905.

37 See *Letters*, p. 496.

38 Hilhouse is a famous Bond Street hatter, whose business was founded in 1799 and whose bow-fronted shop was a landmark for many years. Since early youth Sir Compton and other distinguished gentlemen had bought their hats at Hilhouse's.

39 John Ellingham Brooks. In a letter dated 4 January 1920, Lawrence wrote of sitting in Morgano's café "with an old, old Dutchman and a nice man called Brooks, drinking a modest punch . . . ."—*Letters*, p. 496. And on 6 February 1920, he asked Martin Secker to "send Brooks a copy of *New Poems*. I should like him to have them: J. Ellingham Brooks, Villa Ferraro, Capri."—*Letters*, p. 507. Long a resident of Capri, Brooks for some time shared the Villa Cercola with the English writer E. F. Benson (1867–1940), and was a friend of W. Somerset Maugham, Norman Douglas, the Brett Youngs, the Mackenzies. For years he intended to immortalize himself by translations into English of Greek epigrams and the Hérédia sonnets. Lady Compton Mackenzie has written: "A useless, selfish life from almost any point of view, yet for many of us he was the essence of Capri, picturesque and lovable, without much shame, and what is rarer, without sham . . . . He asked for no more, so long as he was here, with his books, his flowers, his pipe on the terrace in the cool of summer evenings, his wood fire on winter nights, a few houses where he was a welcome guest, and Giovanni—or Francesco—or what you will —to wake him with his tea." In his "Bibliographical Note on Norman Douglas," Cecil Woolf has called "J. E. B." "a brilliant Greek scholar but an indifferent poet."—Nancy Cunard, *Grand Man* (London: Secker and Warburg, 1954), p. 268. Brooks may have served as the original of Mr. Earnest Eames in Norman Douglas' *South Wind* (1917). To him, Norman Douglas dedicated his *Birds and Beasts of the Greek Anthology* (1927); to him, Sir Compton Mackenzie dedicated his *Vestal Fire* (1927). Norman Douglas used some of Brooks's verse translations in his *Birds and Beasts of the Greek Anthology*. See Giuseppe Orioli, *Adventures of a Bookseller* (New York: McBride, 1938), pp. 258–60; E. F. Benson, *Final Edition* (New York: Longmans, 1940), pp. 106–16; Faith Compton Mackenzie, *Always Afternoon* (London: Collins, 1943), pp. 89–101; Richard Aldington, *Pinorman* (London: Heinemann, 1954), pp. 176–78.

40 See Carswell, p. 137; *Letters*, p. 506.

41 See *Letters*, p. 506.

42 Faith Compton Mackenzie, *More Than I Should*, pp. 31–32.

43 D. H. L. letter to Lady Cynthia Asquith, from Palazzo Ferraro, Isola di Capri, Italy, dated 25 January 1920, *Letters*, p. 504.

44 Cf. Lawrence's short story "The Man Who Loved Islands," originally

published in *The Dial* (July, 1927) and again in the *London Mercury* (August, 1927), and included in the American edition of *The Woman Who Rode Away* (1928).—McDonald, *Supplement*, p. 96. As the result of a protest by Sir Compton Mackenzie, it was excluded from the English edition of *The Woman Who Rode Away*, and Heinemann's plan to publish the story in "an expensive edition" was abandoned. See Moore, *Intelligent Heart*, pp. 410–11. In an interview (1950) with Prof. Harry T. Moore, Sir Compton said that "Lawrence's fiction often gives a distorted view of his acquaintances because 'he had a trick of describing a person's setting or background vividly, and then putting into the setting an ectoplasm entirely of his own creation.' "—Moore, *Intelligent Heart*, p. 187.

45 Faith Compton Mackenzie, *More Than I Should*, pp. 40–41.

46 D. H. L. letter to Ada Lawrence, from Amalfi, dated "27 January 1929" [27 January 1920], Ada Lawrence and Gelder, p. 146.

47 John Middleton Murry was the editor of the *Athenaeum* from 1919 to 1921.

48 Mansfield, *Letters to Murry*, p. 470.

49 Mansfield, *Letters to Murry*, pp. 473–74. See John Middleton Murry: "[Lawrence's] letter to Katherine was so monstrously, so inhumanly cruel that I wrote to him that he had committed the unforgivable crime: that I sincerely hoped that we should never meet again, because, if we did meet again, I should thrash him."—Murry, *Reminiscences*, p. 165.

50 Mansfield, *Letters to Murry*, p. 476.

51 Mansfield, *Letters to Murry*, p. 505.

52 D. H. L. letter to Catherine Carswell, from Palazzo Ferraro, Capri (Naples), dated 5 February 1920, *Letters*, p. 506.

53 In a letter (12 March 1953) to the editor, Sir Compton Mackenzie wrote: "You will find an impression of Lawrence in my novel *The Four Winds of Love, The South Wind* . . . and in *The West Wind* . . . . I called Lawrence Daniel Rayner . . . . Apart from names and places most of it is factually and conversationally exact." The Lawrences had made friends with the Mackenzies while all were living near Chesham, Bucks., *ca.* August, 1914, to January, 1915. See Sir Compton's fictionalized memoirs of the Lawrences at this period in Vol. I of the present work.

54 Cf. Compton Mackenzie, *Literature in My Time* (London: Rich and Cowan, 1933), p. 193: "As early as 1919 when walking with me along the Via Tragara in Capri, Lawrence stopped and proclaimed twice:

" 'There's not going to be another war.'

"Then, striking the wall by the edge of the road with his stick, he shouted at the top of his voice:

" 'I won't have another war!' "

55 Cf. Compton Mackenzie, *Literature in My Time* (London: Rich and Cowan, 1933), p. 210: "I once observed to [Lawrence] that if divorced from its original and natural intention the sexual act by everybody except those immediately indulging in it could only be regarded as a subject for laughter. Whereupon he fell into a gloom that lasted two days, at the end of which time he said he believed I was right. It was shortly after

this that he announced his intention of discovering if possible a race of people who habitually thought not with their brains but with their organs of generation, whereby he may have hoped to eliminate that comic side which, as he rightly saw, would threaten his own work if admitted to be universal."

56 Compton Mackenzie, *The West Wind of Love*, pp. 294–301.

57 In February, 1920 (not January, as he mistakenly remembered), Lawrence rather reluctantly accepted an invitation from Maurice Magnus to visit him at the monastery of Monte Cassino, where the latter was a "constant guest."

58 Introduction to *Memoirs of the Foreign Legion*, pp. 21, 36–37.

59 Entry in Lawrence's Diary.—Tedlock, p. 89. For the full account of Lawrence's visit to Monte Cassino as the guest of Maurice Magnus, see his Introduction to *Memoirs of the Foreign Legion*.

60 D. H. L. letter to Miss Gertrude Cooper, from Capri, dated 25 February 1920, Ada Lawrence and Gelder, p. 96.

61 Mrs. Francis Brett Young.

62 Young, Preface to The Severn Edition of *The Red Knight*, pp. ix–x.

63 D. H. L. letter to Ada Lawrence, from Fontana Vecchia, Taormina, Sicily, dated 4 March 1920, Ada Lawrence and Gelder, p. 96.

64 Prof. Harry T. Moore has noted that this anecdote was also told by a reporter in a Milan newspaper, the *Corriere d'Informazione* (December, 1947). The same story carries the sensational report that at Taormina, the king of England slipped ashore incognito to pay Lawrence a secret visit of homage (!).—Moore, *Intelligent Heart*, p. 268.

Frieda's comment on the story of the Mayor of Taormina: "The story of the mayor of Milan [Taormina] who came to breakfast in Taormina, with Lawrence throwing plates at me, made me weep tears of laughter. I had never heard it before! And we were poor and did not have so many plates."—Frieda Lawrence Ravagli, "The Bigger Heart of D. H. Lawrence," *The New Republic*, 132 (No. 9, Issue 2101, 28 February 1955), 17.

65 Among others, Truman Capote. For a statement of his effect upon the life of Fontana Vecchia and Taormina—and for another glimpse of Signor Cacópardo—see Herbert Kubly, "Confusion in Trumanland," *Esquire*, XL (No. 2, Whole No. 237, August, 1953), 66, 107.

66 Original publication of a memoir completed in January, 1954. Francesco Cacópardo was, and is, the proprietor of the Fontana Vecchia. A professional chef, he lived for periods in both England and the United States. Lawrence may have used his nickname Cicio (or Ciccio) and some of his characteristics in creating the character by the same name in *The Lost Girl*. On 3 June 1920, Lawrence noted in his Diary: "Sent Things [?] for Amy [Lowell?] via Cicio," and on 11 June 1920, "Ciccio sails & takes MS. of Lost Girl to America."—Tedlock, p. 90. In a letter to Amy Lowell, dated 26 June 1920, Lawrence wrote that "Ciccio is rich and speaks 3 languages."—Moore, *Intelligent Heart*, p. 266. From a further entry in Lawrence's Diary dated 22 February 1921, it would seem that there was an early plan for Signor Cacópardo ("Ciccio") and his brother

Vincenzo to accompany or follow the Lawrences to America.—Tedlock, pp. 92, 319. For a meeting with Signor Cacópardo, see the "Note" to Witter Bynner's *Journey with Genius*, pp. xiv–xv.

67 D. H. L. letter to "Mrs. R. P." (Mrs. Rosalind Thornycroft Popham), from Fontana Vecchia, Taormina, Sicilia, dated 15 March [1920], *Letters*, pp. 507–8.

68 D. H. L. letter to Norman Douglas (?), from Fontana Vecchia, Taormina, dated 31 March 1920, in Douglas, *Looking Back*, pp. 290–91.

69 Introduction to *Memoirs of the Foreign Legion*, pp. 41–42. On their trip to Syracuse, the Lawrences were accompanied by Jan Juta, his sister Mrs. Réné Juta Hansard, and his Welsh friend Alan Insole. See Frieda Lawrence, p. 112; Moore, *Intelligent Heart*, pp. 268–69.

70 Frieda Lawrence, p. 99.

71 D. H. L. letter to Lady Cynthia Asquith, from Fontana Vecchia, Taormina (Messina), dated 7 May 1920, *Letters*, p. 510.

72 D. H. L. letter to Catherine Carswell, from Fontana Vecchia, Taormina, Messina, dated 12 May 1920, *Letters*, p. 513.

73 D. H. L. letter to Martin Secker, from Great Britain Hotel, Valletta, Malta, dated 24 May 1920, *Letters*, p. 513.

74 For an account of Mr. Goldring's efforts to get Lawrence's play *Touch and Go* (1920) produced by the People's Theatre Society, see Douglas Goldring, *Life Interests* (London: MacDonald, 1948), pp. 83–90, reprinted in Vol. I of the present work.

75 Subsequent to original publication (London: C. W. Daniel, May, 1920; New York: Thomas Seltzer, 1920—McDonald, pp. 47, 48), Lawrence's *Touch and Go* was included in *The Plays of D. H. Lawrence* (London: Secker, 1933).

76 Norman Macdermott (1890———), English theatrical producer, and founder of the famed Everyman Theatre, Hampstead, of which he was the director and producer (1920–1926). Although Mr. Macdermott had agreed to produce *Touch and Go,* Lawrence became impatient at the delay, and turned the play over to Douglas Goldring for publication in the latter's series, "Plays for a People's Theatre."

77 I.e., the American publishing house of Scott and Seltzer, later Thomas Seltzer, Inc., of New York.

78 Seltzer published a limited edition of *Women in Love* in November, 1920, the novel's first printing, as well as the first American trade edition in October, 1922.—McDonald, pp. 48–49.

79 Martin Secker published *Women in Love* in May, 1921, the novel's first English edition.—McDonald, pp. 49–50.

80 Douglas Goldring's novel *The Black Curtain* (London: Chapman and Hall, 1920) was dedicated to Lawrence.

81 I.e., Englishmen—a theme Lawrence was to develop in *Sea and Sardinia* (1921).

82 Mr. Goldring's wife Betty was then working for the "Save the Children Fund." See Douglas Goldring, *Odd Man Out* (London: Chapman and Hall, 1935), Part III, Chap. Three, "That Pamphlet Shop."

83 Mr. Goldring's play *The Fight for Freedom*, the first of the series of "Plays for a People's Theatre," published by C. W. Daniel, Ltd.

84 Henri Barbusse (1873–1935), French author whose *Under Fire* (1916) is his best-known work. He was the founder of the International *Clarté* movement (See Note 88, below). For Henri Barbusse's Preface to Mr. Goldring's play, see the latter's *The Fight for Freedom* (New York: Thomas Seltzer, 1920).

85 Lawrence's play *The Widowing of Mrs. Holroyd* (1914) was produced by a group of amateurs at Altrincham, Ches., in February, 1920. For Mr. Goldring's brief mention of this production, see his *Life Interests*, p. 90, reprinted in Vol. I of the present work. Mrs. Catherine Carswell also attended this same production. See Carswell, pp. 141 ff.

86 I.e., "I should like to see Betty [Douglas Goldring's wife], with her big nose as Mrs. Holroyd."

87 Irene Rooke, well-known English actress who played in many of John Galsworthy's plays and was the original "Mrs. Jones" in *The Silver Box. Ca.* August, 1914, to January, 1915, she and her husband, Milton Rosmer (1881——), English actor and producer, were friends and neighbors of the Gilbert Cannans and the Lawrences at Cholesbury, Tring, Bucks.

88 *Clarté* movement: A post–World War I international movement, represented as "an organization of European intellectuals . . . who believed in peace, international brotherhood and the dawn of a new era." The English section of *Clarté* came to an end because the established Committee could not decide to what form of activity it should devote its energies, and because "it became increasingly clear that the parent body in Paris was concentrating on international Communist propaganda and was trying to use [the English branch] to further its unavowed objects." Douglas Goldring was the English secretary of *Clarté*. See Douglas Goldring, *The Nineteen Twenties* (London: Nicholson and Watson, 1945), pp. 162–63. See also Mr. Goldring's memoir in Vol. I of the present work.

89 Goldring, *Life Interests*, pp. 90–94. An earlier version of Mr. Goldring's essay on Lawrence had appeared in his autobiography, *Odd Man Out* (London: Chapman and Hall, 1935), pp. 249–66. For a character sketch of Douglas Goldring, see Ethel Mannin, *Confessions and Impressions* (London: Jarrolds, 1930), pp. 141–46.

90 Lawrence's famous Introduction to Maurice Magnus' posthumous *Memoirs of the Foreign Legion* (1924) was answered by Norman Douglas in *D. H. Lawrence and Maurice Magnus: A Plea for Better Manners*, originally published in a privately printed edition in 1924, and reprinted in his *Experiments* (1924) and again in *Norman Douglas: A Selection from His Works* and With an Introduction by D. M. Low (London: Chatto & Windus and Secker & Warburg, 1955). This was answered by Lawrence in a letter to "some gentleman in New York" in "Accumulated Mail," originally printed in *The Borzoi: 1925* (New York: Knopf, 1925) and reprinted in *Phoenix*, p. 800; and in a letter to the editor of *The New Statesman* (20 February 1926) and reprinted as "The Late Mr. Maurice Magnus: A Letter" in *Phoenix*, pp. 806–7. Douglas had something more to say on the subject in his *Late Harvest* (London: Lindsay Drummond,

1946), pp. 52–53. The curious may also consult Richard Aldington, *Pinorman* (London: Heinemann, 1954); Nancy Cunard, *Grand Man* (London: Secker & Warburg, 1954), which contains a Norman Douglas letter on the subject (pp. 176–77), and Nancy Cunard's commentary on "A Plea for Better Manners" (pp. 281–83); and Douglas Goldring, "Uncle Norman" in *Privileged Persons* (London: The Richards Press, 1955), pp. 124–39. See also a letter from Frieda Lawrence Ravagli, *Time and Tide*, 35 (No. 22, 29 May 1954), 724, and Nancy Cunard's answer, *Time and Tide*, 35 (No. 23, 5 June 1954), 752, 754.

91 Michael Borg. See *Letters*, p. 607.

92 Sir Stanley Unwin, chairman of the publishing firm Allen & Unwin, Ltd., of London.

93 See *Letters*, p. 607.

94 Norman Douglas' *D. H. Lawrence and Maurice Magnus: A Plea for Better Manners* (1924). See Note 90, above.

95 Margaret Lambert, a character in Douglas Goldring's *The Fight for Freedom*. She is a young woman whose persuasion to pacifism and socialism is proved to be only surface deep. She refuses to recognize that "[if] you have nothing inside yourself to hold you up, sooner or later you will fall flat." Her courage fails her when the test comes.

96 Douglas Goldring, *The Fortune: A Romance of Friendship* (Dublin, London: Maunsel, 1917; New York: Scott and Seltzer, 1919). Reprinted, with a preface by Aldous Huxley (London: D. Harmsworth, [1931]).

97 Possibly an error for Witter Bynner's *Tiger* (New York: Kennerley, 1913).

98 Alec Waugh (1898————), English novelist; elder brother of Evelyn Waugh. Author of *The Prisoners of Mainz* (1919), *Myself When Young* (1923), *Hot Countries* [*The Coloured Countries*] (1930), *Thirteen Such Years* (1932), *The Sugar Islands* [*The Sunlit Caribbean*] (1948), *The Lipton Story* (1950), *Island in the Sun* (1955), etc. His father, Arthur Waugh, was a director of the publishing firm of Chapman & Hall, Ltd., and for several years after 1924, Alec Waugh was literary advisor to the same firm.

99 British Public?

100 Douglas Goldring and Hubert Neapean, *The Solvent* (London: C. W. Daniel, 1920).

101 Goldring, *The Nineteen Twenties*, pp. 204–9, 209–10.

102 D. H. L. letter to Amy Lowell, from Fontana Vecchia, Taormina, Sicily, dated 1 June 1920, Damon, pp. 538–39.

103 See *Letters*, pp. 507–8.

104 Original publication of a memoir written in 1954.

105 Mrs. Rosalind Thornycroft Popham's eldest daughter.

106 Original publication.

107 Original publication.

108 D. H. L. letter to Douglas Goldring, from Fontana Vecchia, Taormina, Sicily, dated 20 July 1920, *Letters*, pp. 514–15.

109 Mrs. Popham has identified Perceval as the Secretary of the British Institute at Florence.

110 Original publication.

111 In the summer of 1919, the Lawrences stayed for a short time at "The Myrtles," Mrs. Rosalind Thornycroft Popham's cottage at Pangbourne, Berks., and Hilda Brown was invited to stay with them there. For her account of this holiday, see Mrs. Hilda Brown Cotterell's memoir in Vol. I of the present work.

112 In his Diary, under the date 15 June 1920, Lawrence wrote: "—heard of Emily's baby," and under the date 17 June 1920: "Sent lace shawl to Emily for baby."—Tedlock, p. 90. Peggy was the older daughter of Mrs. Emily Lawrence King, Lawrence's sister. Both Mrs. King and Peggy had also visited the Lawrences at "The Myrtles" during Hilda Brown's stay there in the summer of 1919. "Peggy" is now Mrs. Margaret E. Needham of Shipley, Derby.

113 For Jan Juta, see Note 201, below.

114 Original publication.

115 Entry in Lawrence's Diary.—Tedlock, p. 91. Anticoli is now known as Fiuggi.

116 Original publication of a memoir written in 1954.

117 Presumably the "two friends, man & wife, from London," mentioned by Lawrence earlier in this same letter. On 7 November 1921, Lawrence noted in his Diary: "Send a shawl to Mrs. Whittley."—Tedlock, p. 94. Otherwise I am unable to identify them.

118 Original publication.

119 The "tortoise poems" were printed in the United States as *Tortoises,* and included in the English (but not the American) edition of *Birds, Beasts and Flowers.*—McDonald, pp. 60–61, 74–76. The other poems mentioned by Mrs. Popham were included in *Birds, Beasts and Flowers.* All were included in *Collected Poems,* II.

120 "Cypresses," "Turkey Cock," "Grapes," and "Medlars and Sorb-Apples" were also included in *Birds, Beasts and Flowers,* and again in *Collected Poems,* II.

121 Original publication of a memoir written in 1954.

122 A villa to which Mrs. Popham had moved by then.

123 Alan Insole: art student, painter, writer, traveler, philosopher; friend of Jan Juta. He now makes his home in England. See Tedlock, p. 318; Moore, *Intelligent Heart,* pp. 268, 287.

Mrs. Réné Juta Hansard, wife of Luke Hansard, Esquire, of Mougins, Alpes Maritimes, France. Sister of Jan Juta. (See Note 201, below.) During World War I, she served as a nurse in British hospitals in France. She died during the German occupation of France in World War II. Her daughter, Gillian Hansard, now lives in Loughton, Essex, England. As Réné Juta, Mrs. Hansard was the collaborator, with Jan Juta, on *The Cape Peninsula* (1919), with pen and colour sketches painted by Jan Juta; author of *Cape Currey [The Tavern]* (1920); collaborator, with Jan Juta, on *Cannes and the Hills* (1924), with 8 pictures in colour by Jan Juta, and on *Concerning Corsica* (1926), with illustrations by Jan Juta; author of *Jack in the Green* (1935) and *The Silver Fox* (1938). In a letter (31 July 1957) to the editor, Mr. Juta has declared that Prof. Harry T. Moore's citation of René Juta as the prototype of Mrs. Tukes in *The Lost Girl* is an error: *"Incorrect.* I know just who D. H. had in mind!" See Moore, *Intelligent Heart*, p. 268.

124 Original publication.

125 Original publication.

126 Entry in Lawrence's Diary.—Tedlock, p. 91.

127 John Lane (1854–1925) of The Bodley Head publishing house of London.

128 D. H. L. letter to "Mrs. R. P." (Mrs. Rosalind Thornycroft Popham), from Villa Fontana Vecchia, Taormina, Sicily, dated 16 November 1920, *Letters*, pp. 515–16.

129 D. H. L. letter to Amy Lowell, from Fontana Vecchia, Taormina, Sicily, dated 30 November 1920, Damon, p. 550.

130 See (London) *Times Literary Supplement* (2 December 1920), p. 795c: "Little by little Alvina disappears beneath the heap of facts recorded about her, and the only sense in which we feel her to be lost is that we can no longer believe in her existence.

"So, though the novel is probably better than any that will appear for the next six months, we are disappointed, and would write Mr. Lawrence off as one of the people who have determined to produce seaworthy books were it not for those momentary phrases and for a strong suspicion that the proper way to look at 'The Lost Girl' is as a stepping stone in a writer's progress. It is either a postscript or a prelude."

131 Mansfield, *Letters to Murry*, pp. 620–21. For John Middleton Murry's own review of *The Lost Girl* (originally printed in *The Athenaeum*, 17 December 1920), see his *Reminiscences*, pp. 214–18.

132 Entry in Lawrence's Diary.—Tedlock, p. 91.

133 Entry in Lawrence's Diary.—Tedlock, p. 92.

134 *Sea and Sardinia*, pp. 85–87, 112–14, 119–20.

135 Entry in Lawrence's Diary.—Tedlock, p. 92.

136 D. H. L. letter to Eleanor Farjeon, from Fontana Vecchia, Taormini, Sicilia, dated 20 January 1921, *Letters*, pp. 517–18.

137 Carswell, pp. 41–42.

138 Goldring, *Life Interests*, pp. 94–95.

139 D. H. L. letter to Frieda's mother, Frau Baronin von Richthofen, from Fontana Vecchia, Taormina, Sicilia, dated 16 March [1921], Frieda Lawrence, p. 101.

140 Millicent Beveridge was born at Hukcaldy, Scotland, studied art at Glasgow, and thereafter lived chiefly in Paris. Exhibited her paintings at the Indépendants (1907, 1909), the Salon d'Autumne (1910), the Artistes Français (1911), the Nationale (1912–24). For a second-hand account of her meeting with Lawrence, prompted by her reading of *The Lost Girl*, see Carswell, p. 140: "She has told me how that meeting took place at a party in Sicily where she found Lawrence in a rage because, not made aware beforehand that it was a party and that he was to be lionized, he turned up barefoot with sandals and in his 'pottering about' clothes. . . . . Miss Beveridge, amused and astonished as much as she was charmed, became sincerely attached to him, and the friendship remained firm till

his death." Lawrence was to renew his friendship with Millicent Beveridge after his return to Europe in 1925. On 13 June 1927, Lawrence wrote of her in a letter to S. S. Koteliansky: "She is nice and intelligent—not young —has an assured income but not a very big one—paints—and I like her . . . ."—*Encounter 3*, I (No. 3, December, 1953), 34.

141 Presumably to accompany Jan Juta, who went to Sardinia later in April to paint suitable illustrations for *Sea and Sardinia*. See *Letters*, p. 522. (Lawrence withdrew from the plan for a walking tour.) The Juta illustrations were printed in the original American (New York: Seltzer, 1921) and English (London: Martin Secker, 1923) editions of the book.

142 D. H. L. letter to Catherine Carswell, from Fontana Vecchia, Taormina, Sicily, dated 4 April 1921, *Letters*, pp. 520–21.

143 Mrs. Brewster's error for April (1921). Having left Taormina on 9 April 1921, Lawrence went to Capri where he stayed until 19 or 20 April, then on to Rome and Florence (22–23 April), and arrived at Baden-Baden sometime before 28 April. See *Letters*, p. 522; Moore, *Poste Restante*, pp. 62–63.

144 Jan Juta had lived at Anticoli Corrado during the summer of 1920, and in August, 1920, Lawrence had visited him there. See Lawrence's letter to Mrs. Rosalind Thornycroft Popham, dated 10 August [1920], above.

145 Lawrence's famous poem "Snake," included in *Birds, Beasts and Flowers*, and again in *Collected Poems*, II.

146 Mrs. Brewster's husband, Earl H. Brewster.

147 Brewster, pp. 241–44. Achsah Barlow Brewster was born in New Haven, Conn. She took her bachelor's degree at Smith College, attended the School of Fine Arts in New York, and then continued her art studies in Paris, meanwhile visiting the museums of Europe. In December, 1910, she married Earl H. Brewster. (See Note 150, below.) Her paintings were exhibited at galleries in Paris and London, and with those of Earl H. Brewster at the Casino del Pincio in Rome in January, 1918, and at the Galerie Chéron in Paris in December, 1922. See *L'Oeuvre de E. H. Brewster et Achsah Barlow Brewster: 32 Reproductions en phototypie précedées d'essais autobiographiques* (Rome: Par les soins de "Valori plastici," [1923]).

148 For an example of Lawrence's self-portraiture, see the frontispiece to Murry, *Son of Woman* (1931 ed.) or to Father William Tiverton's *D. H. Lawrence and Human Existence* (London: Rockliff, 1951).

149 Harwood Brewster (1913———), now Mrs. Harwood Picard of Washington, D.C. In a letter (12 August 1954) to the editor, Mrs. Picard wrote: "I was still quite young when [Lawrence] died—but his memory remains very clear with me, as though it were only yesterday that I had seen him. To me, it was the simplicity in his bearing, in his actions, and in his relations to those around him that was a proof of the depth and honesty of his feelings."

150 Brewster, pp. 17–19. Earl H. Brewster (1878———), American painter, was born at Chagrin Falls, Ohio. He studied art in Cleveland and New

York, and by 1910 had visited the museums of Europe, where he fell under the influence of the Impressionists. In 1910, he married Achsah Barlow: "Elle ressemblait tellement au type de femme que j'avais aimé à créer dans mes tableaux, que des amis communs, remarquant cette ressemblance, nous firent rencontrer." Thereafter the Brewsters lived in Sicily, displaying their paintings in the galleries of Paris and Rome. Mr. Brewster has written: "Le fondement de mon oeuvre est dans la conviction absolue que la couleur et la forme produisent par elles-mêmes et dans leur apparence la plus abstraite une émotion psychique." In 1921–1922, the Brewsters made their first trip to Ceylon to study oriental philosophy. Since 1935, Mr. Brewster has made his home in India. See *L'Oeuvre de E. H. Brewster et Achsah Barlow Brewster: 32 Reproductions en phototypie précedées d'essais autobiographiques* (Rome: Par les soins de "Valori plastici," [1923]). Mr. Brewster is also the editor of *The Life of Gotama the Buddha* (compiled exclusively from the Pali Canon), With an Introductory Note by C. A. F. Rhys Davids (New York: E. P. Dutton, 1926; London: Kegan Paul, 1926). A redaction of Mr. Brewster's memoirs of Lawrence appeared in the *Illustrated Weekly of India* (21 December 1952 and 4 January 1953).

151 Reginald ("Reggie") Turner (?–1938), English novelist, author of *Castles in Kensington* (1904), *Davray's Affairs* (1906), *Uncle Peaceable* (1906), *Samson Unshorn* (1909), *Count Florio and Phyllis K.* (1910), *King Philip the Gay* (1911), etc. Harold Acton has called Reggie Turner "a conversationalist in the delicately manicured tradition of the eighteen nineties." —Nancy Cunard, *Grand Man* (London: Secker & Warburg, 1954), pp. 237–38. He probably served as the original of Algy Constable in Lawrence's *Aaron's Rod.*—Moore, *Intelligent Heart*, p. 258. Long a resident of Florence, he died in 1938, having willed £20,000 to Giuseppe ("Pino") Orioli, friend of Norman Douglas and Lawrence, and publisher of Lawrence's *Lady Chatterley's Lover*. For glimpses of Reggie Turner, see Richard Aldington, *Pinorman* (London: Heinemann, 1954).

152 Sir Max Beerbohm (1872–1956), English satirist, caricaturist. He contributed to the *Yellow Book*, was dramatic critic of the *Saturday Review*. Author of the novel *Zuleika Dobson* (1911), *And Even Now* (1920), *Around Theatres* (1930, 1953), *Mainly on the Air* (1947), etc.

153 Dr. S. Parkes Cadman, pastor of the Central Congregational Church, Brooklyn, who, during World War I, "declared that the Lutheran Church in Germany 'is not the bride of Christ, but the paramour of Kaiserism.' " —Mark Sullivan, *Our Times: The United States 1900–1925*, Vol. V: *Over Here, 1914–1918* (New York: Scribner, 1933), p. 467. He is also reputed to have asked his congregation to pray that young men might be preserved from sharing the beliefs of H. L. Mencken.

154 Lawrence may have been working on the Florentine section of *Aaron's Rod*. See Mrs. Achsah Barlow Brewster's memoir, above.

155 In the Zoroastrian religion, Ormuzd, the god of goodness and light, was in perpetual conflict with Ahriman, the spirit of evil.

156 Maurice Magnus, who had taken poison in November, 1920.
157 Possibly a reference to Rebecca West's "Letter from Abroad," *The Bookman*, LXX (No. 1, September, 1929), 88–91, and reprinted, with slight differences, as "Oranges to Oranges" in *Ending in Earnest*, pp. 118–28.
158 West, "Elegy," in *Ending in Earnest*, pp. 265–76. The essay was originally a contribution to the special D. H. Lawrence number of *The New Adelphi*, III (No. 4, June–August, 1930), 298–309, and later published as a small book entitled *D. H. Lawrence* (London: Martin Secker, 1930).
159 D. H. L. letter to Achsah Brewster, from Ludwig-Wilhelmstift, Baden-Baden, Germany, undated, Brewster, pp. 24–25.
160 D. H. L. letter to Curtis Brown, from Villa Alpensee, Thumersbach, Zell-am-See, bei Salzburg, Austria, dated "7 July, 1921," *Letters*, p. 527. See Moore, *Poste Restante*, p. 63.
161 Frieda's younger sister Johanna ("Nusch") was Frau Max Schreibershofen, whose husband may have been the model for the Herr Regierungsrat Trepte in Lawrence's short novel "The Captain's Doll." Nusch herself may have been the prototype of Baroness Mitchka in the same story.—Moore, *Intelligent Heart*, p. 282.
162 Presumably the flat of Nelly Morrison, an unidentified friend of the Lawrences.
163 D. H. L. letter to Catherine Carswell, from Villa Alpensee, Thumersbach, Zell-am-See, bei Salzburg, Austria, dated 3 August 1921, *Letters*, p. 528.
164 Joan, Bertie: Mrs. Popham's sister, Mrs. Joan Thornycroft Farjeon, and her husband, Herbert. Eleanor: Eleanor Farjeon, sister of Herbert Farjeon. Alexander: Arthur Alexander, pianist and composer, a close friend of the Herbert Farjeons. He often stayed at the Herbert Farjeon home in Berkshire, and Lawrence must have met him there when he came over from Hermitage (1918–1919).
165 Hotel Krone, Ebersteinburg, Baden-Baden, where Lawrence finished *Aaron's Rod* and wrote most of his *Fantasia of the Unconscious*. See Frieda Lawrence, p. 126.
166 Original publication.
167 Cf. Lawrence's descriptions of the glacier in "The Captain's Doll."
168 D. H. L. letter to Ada Lawrence Clarke, from "Thumersbach, Germany," undated, Ada Lawrence and Gelder, pp. 132–33.
169 Mansfield, *Letters*, p. 398.
170 D. H. L. letter to Nelly Morrison, from 32, Via dei Bardi, Firenze, dated 1 September 1921, *Letters*, p. 529. The address is that of Nelly Morrison, an unidentified friend of the Lawrences, who had turned over her flat in Florence to them for their stay there.
171 The Carswells' young son, John, born in 1918.
172 See *Letters*, p. 531.
173 This photograph appears as a frontispiece in the 1932 editions of *The Savage Pilgrimage*, but not, unfortunately, in the 1951 reprint.
174 See *Letters*, p. 530.
175 Shortly after Mrs. Carswell's first meeting with Lawrence in June, 1914,

he had spent some time encouraging her to revise her first novel. See Carswell, pp. 17–21, reprinted in Vol. I of the present work.

176 Prof. Guglielmo Ferrero (1871–1942), Italian historian, novelist, journalist. A "radical Republican" in politics, he helped to bring Italy into World War I on the side of the Allies. By 1921 he had lectured in Milan on Militarism and at the Collège de France in Paris on Roman History, had travelled widely over Europe, and had published many books, including *The Greatness and Decline of Rome*, 5 vols. (1907–1909). From 1930, he was Professor of Modern History, Geneva University, and Professor of Military Institutions' History, Institut des Hautes Études Internationales, Geneva. An outspoken opponent of the Fascist régime from its beginnings, he eventually left his home at Florence and moved with his family to Switzerland in order that he might continue to speak and write without government interference. All his books were condemned and destroyed in Italy in 1935.

177 "I refer especially to 'Dandelions'—a picture that was withheld from the Lawrence exhibition [at the Warren Gallery, London, in 1929] lest it should give offence."—Carswell, p. 160, note. See *Letters*, p. 729.

178 Cf. *Aaron's Rod*, Chap. XIV, "XX Settembre," and Chap. XX, "The Broken Rod."

179 Lawrence's younger sister Ada, Mrs. W. E. Clarke, whose home was at Ripley, Derby.

180 See *Letters*, pp. 530–31.

181 Carswell, pp. 152–63.

182 D. H. L. letter to Catherine Carswell, from Siena, dated 21 September 1921, Moore, *Intelligent Heart*, p. 283.

183 For a possible inspiration of this charade, see the memoir by Ernest Rhys, *Everyman Remembers* (New York: Cosmopolitan Book Co., 1931), pp. 243–49, reprinted in Vol. I of the present work.

184 Since the Brewsters too had lived at Fontana Vecchia, they would also have known Signor Francesco Cacópardo's family.

185 Brewster, pp. 244–46.

186 Either the "Special Issue of the First Edition" or the "Ordinary Edition" of *Psychoanalysis and the Unconscious*, published by Thomas Seltzer in New York in May, 1921. The book was not published (by Martin Secker) in England until July, 1923.—McDonald, pp. 56–60.

187 Brewster, pp. 26–27.

188 D. H. L. letter to Earl and Achsah Brewster, from Fontana Vecchia, dated only "Wednesday" [28 September 1921], Brewster, pp. 27–28. See Moore, *Poste Restante*, p. 64.

189 D. H. L. letter to Earl H. Brewster, from Fontana Vecchia, Taormina, Sicilia, dated 8 October 1921, Brewster, pp. 29–30.

190 D. H. L. letter to Amy Lowell, from Fontana Vecchia, Taormina, Sicilia, dated 9 October 1921, Damon, pp. 576–77.

191 Presumably a reference to the translation of Ivan Bunin's "The Gentleman from San Francisco" which Lawrence had made with S. S. Koteliansky.

It was published as the first story in the book *The Gentleman from San Francisco and Other Stories* (Richmond: Hogarth Press, 1922) which contained the following tipped-in erratum note: "The first story in this book 'The Gentleman / from San Francisco' is translated by D. H. / Lawrence and S. S. Koteliansky. Owing to / a mistake Mr. Lawrence's name has been / omitted from the title-page. The three other / stories are translated by S. S. Koteliansky and / Leonard Woolf."—McDonald, pp. 103–4. On 29 December 1922, Lawrence entered in his Diary: "—Received £ 12.1.0 from Kot. as half *Gent. from San Francisco* proceeds."—Tedlock, p. 95.

192 Possibly a reference to a Mr. Evelyn Burgess of Hye, or to the Mr. Ralph Burgess of Hermitage who hired out his horse and trap. (See the memoir by Mrs. Hilda Brown Cotterell for the summer of 1919 in Vol. I of the present work.) Mrs. Cecily Lambert Minchin is otherwise unable to identify the name.

193 During the war, Miss Cecily Lambert (later Mrs. Cecily Lambert Minchin) and her cousin, Miss Violet Monk (later Mrs. Violet Monk Stevens), had taken over Grimsbury Farm, Long Lane, within walking distance of the Lawrences at Chapel Farm Cottage, Hermitage, Nr. Newbury, Berks. They were friends of the Lawrences during their intermittent stays at Chapel Farm Cottage in the spring of 1918 and again in the spring and summer of 1919. In September, 1919, the Lawrences lived for a short time at Grimsbury Farm. For memoirs by Mrs. Cecily Lambert Minchin, see Vol. I of the present work.

194 The dancing and gym mistress at Hermitage who occasionally stayed with Miss Cecily Lambert and Miss Violet Monk at Grimsbury Farm, where Lawrence met her during the years 1918–1919. Miss Lambert often played the piano for her classes in dancing.

195 Original publication.

196 D. H. L. letter to Catherine Carswell, from Fontana Vecchia, Taormina, Sicilia, dated "Monday, 25 October, 1921" [Monday, 24 October 1921, or Tuesday, 25 October 1921], *Letters*, p. 533.

197 *Sea and Sardinia*, Chap. I, "As Far as Palermo."

198 This sketch is signed "JJ 1922" and captioned "D. H. Lawrence: 1922[.] Portrait sketch by Jan Juta." Presumably the erroneous date was added later. In a letter (15 July 1957) to the editor, Mr. Juta has stated that he now believes the sketch to have been made at Anticoli Corrado in August, 1920. The date (1922) recorded by Prof. Harry T. Moore in *Life and Works*, p. 353, is therefore incorrect. The sketch has not been included in the latest Heinemann edition (1956) of the *Letters*.

199 Most recently, Mr. Juta's oil portrait of Lawrence has been reproduced by Prof. Harry T. Moore on the dust jackets and as the frontispiece in both the American and English editions of his *Life and Works of D. H. Lawrence*. Under the caption "D. H. Lawrence. By Jan C. Juta," and accompanying Lawrence's own "Indians and an Englishman," the portrait was reproduced in *The Dial*, LXXIV, No. 2 (February, 1923), facing p. 144. It was again reproduced in Joseph Collins' *The Doctor Looks at Litera-*

ture: *Psychological Studies of Life and Letters* (New York: George H. Doran Co., 1923), p. 267. The oil portrait is signed "Jan Juta 1920." In a letter (15 July 1957) to the editor, Mr. Juta has stated that he now believes the oil portrait was later dated incorrectly, and that it was painted in Taormina in January, 1921. The date (1920) recorded by Prof. Harry T. Moore in *Life and Works*, p. 353, is therefore incorrect.

200 For a second-hand account of a visit the Lawrences, Jan Juta, his sister (Mrs. Réné Juta Hansard), and Alan Insole had paid to the Duke of Bronte in April, 1920, see Moore, *Intelligent Heart*, p. 269. See also *Letters*, p. 511; Moore, *Poste Restante*, p. 59.

201 Original publication of a memoir completed in July, 1957. Jan Juta (1897———), designer, craftsman in glass, metal, wood, mural painter, writer. Born in Capetown, South Africa, the son of Sir Henry and Lady Helen (Tait) Juta. He was a student at S. African College, Capetown; Christ Church, Oxford (1913); Slade School, London (1919), British School, Rome (1920), Bellas Artes, Madrid (1922), and under various well-known teachers in Paris. He has been a mural painter since 1924. In April, 1934, he married Alice Huntington Marshall in London. He came to the United States in 1926, worked for the British Ministry of Information in London and New York during the war years 1940–1946. He joined the United Nations as Chief of Visual Information, has acted as Advisor on Design to the United Nations Postal Administration (1946–1955). He is an ex-president of the American Society of Mural Painters. His paintings and decorations are in the Royal Institute of Architects, London; South Africa House, Trafalgar Square, London; City Hall, Pretoria, South Africa; S.S. *Queen Mary* and S.S. *Queen Elizabeth*, etc. He is the author of *Look Out for the Ostriches!* (1949), and the illustrator of and collaborator on three books by his sister, Réné Juta (Mrs. Luke Hansard): *The Cape Peninsula* (1919); *Cannes and the Hills* (1924); and *Concerning Corsica* (1926). For Lawrence's *Sea and Sardinia*, Mr. Juta painted eight pictures in color. Mr. Juta met Lawrence at a studio gathering in Rome in January, 1920. In April, 1920, he, his sister Réné, and their friend Alan Insole, another painter, accompanied the Lawrences on their trip to Syracuse. See Frieda Lawrence, p. 112. See also Note 123.

202 Pilley, in *John Bull*, XXX (No. 798, Saturday, 17 September 1921), 4.

203 D. H. L. letter to Catherine Carswell, from Fontana Vecchia, Taormina, Sicilia, dated 25 October 1921, *Letters*, p. 533.

204 See Carswell, p. 164.

205 Although Edward D. McDonald has noted the differences in the physical formats of the several American and English first and trade editions of *Women in Love*, he makes no mention of textual differences. He does record, however, that Mr. Martin Secker denied that the first English edition was "withdrawn from circulation."—McDonald, pp. 48–52.

206 In his Diary for 26 October 1921, Lawrence wrote: "Got back a month ago, September 23 [28?]. Found Secker's letter with John Bull attack on *W. in Love*, and with Heseltine's marked pages, which he will prosecute for libel. —A week after I give Halliday black hair & Pusum yellow, &

467

send pages back. Haven't heard more from Secker."—Tedlock, p. 93. On 13 November 1921, Lawrence wrote in his Diary: "heard from Secker that Heseltine not satisfied with my modifications in W. in Love, wishes to go on with libel suit. Let him. May rot set in in his bone & blood." —Tedlock, p. 94.

207 In his Diary, Lawrence wrote on 23 November 1921: "Hear that Secker paid to Heseltine £5 & ten guineas costs. Hell."—Tedlock, p. 94.

208 See Murry, *Reminiscences*, pp. 95–96.

209 For Mr. Michael Arlen's testimony to Richard Aldington ("It was Heseltine, most mockingly, but alas with malice more than mockery, who read from D. H.'s 'Amores.'"), see Aldington, p. 218; reprinted as a memoir by Dikran Kouyoumdjian (Michael Arlen) in Vol. I of the present work.

210 See Murry, *Reminiscences*, p. 96.

211 Eugène Goossens (1893——), English conductor and composer.

212 The assistant music master, who had given Philip Heseltine piano lessons while the latter was a student at Eton.

213 At this point, I have supplied the relevant portion of the Philip Heseltine letter to Colin Taylor referred to, taken from Gray, *Peter Warlock*, p. 171.

214 A further clue to the identifications involved here may be found in another letter, also to Lady Ottoline Morrell, recently discovered and published by Mark Schorer in "I Will Send Address: New Letters of D. H. Lawrence," *The London Magazine*, 3 (No. 2, February, 1956), 52–53.

215 See *Women in Love*, Chap. VIII, "Breadalby."

216 Gray, *Peter Warlock*, pp. 220–31. The relevant postscript from the letter to Colin Taylor has been taken from p. 171.

217 Entry in Lawrence's Diary.—Tedlock, p. 93.

218 In a footnote, Mr. Brewster has written: "We met Miss Fisher when the Lawrences entered their train at Naples," i.e., on their return to Taormina in September, 1921.—Brewster, p. 32, note.

219 Presumably a reference to Lawrence's "The Horse-Dealer's Daughter," originally called "The Miracle." See entry in Lawrence's Diary for 26 October 1921.—Tedlock, p. 93. "The Horse-Dealer's Daughter" was published in the *English Review*, April, 1922, and was included in *England, My England*.—McDonald, pp. 124, 67–68.

220 "The Captain's Doll" was included in *The Ladybird* (London: Martin Secker, March, 1923) and *The Captain's Doll* (New York: Thomas Seltzer, April, 1923).—McDonald, pp. 70–71.

221 D. H. L. letter to Earl H. Brewster, from Fontana Vecchia, Taormina, Sicilia, dated 2 November 1921, Brewster, pp. 34–35.

222 On 5 November 1921, Lawrence recorded in his Diary: "Had a letter from Mabel Dodge Sterne asking us to go to New Mexico—to Taos. Want to go."—Tedlock, p. 93. For Lawrence's answer, see Luhan, pp. 5–7.

223 D. H. L. letter to Donald Carswell, from Fontana Vecchia, Taormina, Sicilia, dated 15 November 1921, *Letters*, pp. 536–37.

224 On 29 December 1921, Lawrence noted in his Diary: "Hear from Robert Welsh Solicitor, Ayr that he has paid £100 into my bank for the James Tait Black Memorial prize for The Lost Girl."—Tedlock, p. 95.

225 D. H. L. letter (translated from the German) to Frieda's mother, Frau
Baronin von Richthofen, from Fontana Vecchia, Taormina, Sicily, dated
"Sunday, Dec. 10" [Sunday, 11 December 1921 or Saturday, 10 December
1921], Frieda Lawrence, p. 102.
226 Mansfield, *Letters,* pp. 435–36.
227 D. H. L. letter to Earl H. Brewster, from Fontana Vecchia, Taormina,
Sicilia, dated 2 January 1922, Brewster, pp. 43–44.
228 For Lawrence on the Italian penchant for shooting small birds for food,
see *Letters,* p. 82 (19 November 1912); Luhan, p. 290 (16 January 1926);
Letters, p. 698 ("Sunday, Autumn, 1927"); and the essay "Man Is a
Hunter," in *Phoenix,* pp. 32–34 (1926–27).
229 D. H. L. letter (translated from the German) to Frieda's mother, Frau
Baronin von Richthofen, from Fontana Vecchia, Taormina, Sicily, undated, Frieda Lawrence, p. 104.
230 D. H. L. letter to Catherine Carswell, from Fontana Vecchia, Taormina,
Sicilia, dated 24 January 1922, *Letters,* pp. 539–40.
231 John S. Sumner, in 1922 Secretary of the New York Society for the Supres-
sion of Vice. An interview with Sumner, by Alva Johnston, had appeared
in the *New York Times Book Review and Magazine* on 20 August 1922.
On 22 September 1922, Lawrence wrote Earl H. Brewster: "Seltzer had
a case: the 'Vice' people tried to suppress *Women in Love* and other books:
Seltzer won completely, and is now claiming $10,000 damages."—Brewster,
p. 62. Magistrate George W. Simpson in the West Side Court in New
York City had decided against Sumner who had brought three Seltzer
books for prosecution: Lawrence's *Women in Love,* Arthur Schnitzler's
Casanova's Homecoming, and an anonymous book from the German called
A Young Girl's Diary. Magistrate Simpson declared: "I do not find anything in these books which may be considered obscene, lewd, lascivious,
filthy, indecent, or disgusting. On the contrary, I find that each of them
is a distinct contribution to the literature of the present day." See Moore,
Intelligent Heart, p. 301.
232 Lawrence had completed *Aaron's Rod* at Ebersteinburg in June, 1921
(see *Letters,* p. 524), revised it, and, in the autumn, submitted manuscripts of it to Curtis Brown and Robert Mountsier.
233 Giovanni Verga (1840–1922), Italian realistic novelist, born in Sicily.
Lawrence's translation of Verga's *Mastro-don Gesualdo* was first published
in 1923; *Little Novels of Sicily* in 1925; *Cavalleria Rusticana and Other
Stories* in 1928.—McDonald, *Supplement,* pp. 71–74.
234 In his foreword "The Bad Side of Books," written in 1924, for Edward
D. McDonald's *A Bibliography of the Writings of D. H. Lawrence,* Lawrence repeated this charge: "[Mitchell Kennerley] published *Sons and
Lovers* in America, and one day, joyful, arrived a cheque for twenty
pounds. Twenty pounds in those days was a little fortune: and as it
was a windfall, it was handed over to Madame; the first pin-money she had
seen. Alas and alack, there was an alteration in the date of the cheque,
and the bank would not cash it. It was returned to Mitchell Kennerley,
but that was the end of it. He never made good, and never to this day

made any further payment for *Sons and Lovers*. Till this year of grace 1924, America has had that, my most popular book, for nothing—as far as I am concerned."—McDonald, pp. 11–12; reprinted in *Phoenix*, pp. 233–34. See also the Lawrence letter of 22 April 1914 to Edward Garnett, in which Lawrence acknowledged the receipt of £ 35 from Kennerley (*Letters*, p. 192); and Moore, *Intelligent Heart*, pp. 170, 172, 174, for other Lawrence letters (to Amy Lowell) which deal with the problem of getting Kennerley to make the check right.

235 Anthony Comstock (1844–1915), American moral crusader, who secured New York state and Federal legislation against obscene matter, and organized the New York Society for the Suppression of Vice.

236 In August, 1922, the date of the original publication of this memoir, Lawrence was en route from Australia to the United States.

237 See *Women in Love*, Chap. VIII, "Breadalby."

238 On 16 March 1921, Lawrence wrote to his mother-in-law: "I am correcting the MS. of my diary of a Trip to Sardinia . . . ."—Frieda Lawrence, p. 101. And Mrs. Ravagli herself has written: "Of our winter excursion to Sardinia Lawrence has described every minute, it seems to me, with extraordinary accuracy. . . . 'Sea and Sardinia' he wrote straight away when we came back from Sardinia in about six weeks. And I don't think he altered a word of it."—Frieda Lawrence, pp. 112, 115.

239 Gilbert Cannan (1884–1955), English novelist, playwright, dramatic critic on the London *Star* (1909–1910). With John Drinkwater and others he founded the Manchester Repertory Theatre. His marriage to the actress Mary Ansell, former wife of Sir James M. Barrie, ended in divorce. For impressions of Gilbert and Mary Cannan, who, with the Mackenzies, lived in the neighborhood of the Lawrences near Chesham, Bucks., *ca.* August, 1914, to January, 1915, see the memoirs of David Garnett, *The Flowers of the Forest* (New York: Harcourt, 1956) and the fictionalized reminiscences of Sir Compton Mackenzie, *The South Wind of Love* (New York: Dodd, Mead, 1937), pp. 239–51. The pertinent excerpts from both sources are reprinted in Vol. I of the present work. For Gilbert Cannan on Lawrence, see "A Defense of D. H. Lawrence," *New York Tribune* (10 January 1920).

240 J. W. [T. W.?] Nylander. See Lawrence's letter in his behalf to Catherine Carswell, dated 24 January 1922, in *Letters*, pp. 540–41. See also Carswell, pp. 169–70.

241 Forman, "With D. H. Lawrence in Sicily," *The New York Times Book Review and Magazine*, 27 August 1922, p. 12. Henry James Forman (1879——), author and editor, was born in Russia. Having taken his A.B. degree at Harvard in 1903, he studied at the Ecole des Hautes Etudes Sociales, Paris. He was a member of the staff of the New York *Sun* (1903–1905), and served as the special correspondent attached to President Theodore Roosevelt during the Russo-Japanese Peace Conference, and as a member of the President's suite on the U.S.S. *Mayflower*, when he brought together the peace convoys. His editorial career included work

on *Appleton's Magazine* (1905–1906), the *Literary Digest* (1905–1906), the *North American Review* (1906–1910), *Collier's Weekly* (1913–1918). He visited the Orient (1917), and then served as U.S. agent of propaganda in German, French, and Italian languages at Berne, Switzerland (1918–1919). He is the author of *In the Footprints of Heine* (1910), *The Ideal Italian Tour* (1911), London: *An Intimate Picture* (1913), *The Captain of His Soul* (1914), *Prisoner of the World* (a play, with Margaret Mayo, produced in 1919), *Fire of Youth* (1920), *The Man Who Lived in a Shoe* (1922), *The Enchanted Garden* (1923), *Guilt* (1924), *Sudden Wealth* (1924), *Grecian Italy* (1924), *The Pony Express* (1925), *The Rembrandt Murder* (1931), *Our Movie-Made Children* (1933), *The Story of Prophecy* (1936), *Have You a Religion?* (1941), etc.

242 Possibly a reference to Ruth Wheelock. See the postscripts of a D. H. L. letter to Frieda's sister Else, written from "Wyewurk," Thirroul, South Coast, N.S.W., Australia, and dated 13 June 1922: "If a girl called Ruth Wheelock sends you a little note I gave her to introduce her to you, I think you'd like her. American, was in the consulate in Palermo—we knew her there and in Rome—both like her. . . . She's not got any money, unless she earns some or her father gives her some."—Frieda Lawrence, pp. 131–32. Tedlock identifies "Miss Wheelock" as "a friend who typed for Lawrence."—Tedlock, p. 319. Otherwise, I am unable to identify "our friend" who lived at the Hotel Panormus at Palermo.

243 Dr. Else Jaffe-Richthofen (1874——), eldest of the three daughters of Baron and Baronin von Richthofen; Frieda's older sister.

244 D. H. L. letter (translated from the German) to Frieda's mother, Frau Baronin von Richthofen, from Fontana Vecchia, Taormina, Sicily, dated "Sunday" [19 February 1922], Frieda Lawrence, p. 106.

CHAPTER II

1 D. H. L. letter to Frieda's mother, Frau Baronin von Richthofen, from "R.M.S. 'Osterley,'" dated 28 February [1922], Frieda Lawrence, p. 107.

2 D. H. L. letter to Frieda's mother, Frau Baronin von Richthofen, from "R.M.S. 'Osterley,' . . . Arabian Sea," dated 7 March 1922, Frieda Lawrence, pp. 109–11.

3 *Oronsay:* An error for *Osterley?* Or did Mrs. Jenkins change from the *Oronsay* to the *Osterley* at Naples?

4 Lawrence's *Sons and Lovers* had been published in 1913.

5 See Frieda Lawrence, p. 116.

6 I have corrected a typographical error here: The text reads Ardnarce.

7 This generalization is, of course, not accurate. In addition to the British publishers noted, William Heinemann had published *The White Peacock;* Methuen, *The Rainbow;* Chatto & Windus, *Look! We Have Come Through!;* the Beaumont Press, *Bay;* C. W. Daniel, *Touch and Go;* the Oxford University Press, *Movements in European History.*

8 Priday, in *Southerly* [Sydney, Australia], 15 (No. 1, 1954), 2–4. With

Lawrence's holograph card of 3 April [1922] before me, I have added dates and made certain minor corrections to the text as provided by Mr. Priday's article.

Mr. H. E. L. Priday is an English journalist who has lived many years in the South Pacific, where, during World War II, he was a correspondent for Reuters, U.P., and Australian and New Zealand newspapers. He is the author of *Cannibal Island* (1944), *The War from Coconut Square* (1955), and other books on the South Pacific, and the editor and translator of the diaries of the Australian naturalist Andreas Reischek, *Yesterdays in Maoriland* (3rd ed., 1950), dealing with the days succeeding the Maori war. He is at present Chief Sub-Editor of *The ABC Weekly*, the journal of the Australian Broadcasting Corporation.

9 The Perahera for the Prince of Wales, later Edward VIII, now Duke of Windsor, was held at Kandy on 23 March 1922. See Lawrence's poem "Elephant," first printed in the *English Review* (April, 1923), and included in *Birds, Beasts and Flowers* and again in *Collected Poems*, II.—McDonald, p. 116. See also *Kangaroo*, Chap. VI, "Kangaroo."

10 D. H. L. letter to Catherine Carswell, from "Ardnaree," Lake View Estate, Kandy, dated 25 March 1922, *Letters*, p. 547.

11 See Frieda Lawrence Ravagli: "[Young] natives would come and pay visits to us and the Brewsters, who were interested in Buddhism. Lawrence became so terribly English and snubbed them mostly."—Frieda Lawrence, p. 117.

12 See *Fantasia of the Unconscious*, Chap. XIII, "Cosmological."

13 See Brewster, pp. 44–46.

14 See Note 9, above.

15 Brewster, pp. 46–51.

16 D. H. L. letter to Robert Pratt Barlow, from "Ardnaree," Lake View Estate, Kandy, Ceylon, dated 30 March 1922, *Letters*, pp. 548–49.

17 See Richard Aldington: "[Lawrence] once asked me if I had heard the night noises of a tropical jungle, and then instantly emitted a frightening series of yells, squawks, trills, howls, and animal 'help-murder' shrieks. Only when living in the tropics myself did I realise that he had accomplished the seemingly impossible task of remembering and being able to imitate all that medley of fantastic noises."—Aldington, *Portrait of a Genius*, pp. 289–90.

18 D. H. L. letter to Mabel Dodge Sterne, from Ardnaree, Kandy, Ceylon, dated 10 April 1922, Luhan, pp. 18–19.

19 Original publication.

20 D. H. L. letter to Austin Harrison, from "Ardnaree," Kandy, Ceylon, dated 11 April 1922, *Letters*, pp. 549–50.

21 See Frieda Lawrence Ravagli: "An American friend gave me the side of a Sicilian cart I had always longed for. It had a joust painted on one panel, on the other St. Genevieve. It was very gay and hard in colour. I loved it. Lawrence said: 'You don't mean to travel to Ceylon with this object?' " 'Let me, let me,' I implored. So he let me."—Frieda Lawrence, p. 116. See also Lawrence's letter to Frieda's mother, Frau Baronin von

Richthofen, from R.M.S. *Osterley,* dated 28 February 1922: "I am sorry you were not there to see us go on board at Naples, with trunks and bits and pieces—baskets of apples and oranges (gifts) and a long board that is a piece of a Sicilian wagon painted very gaily with two scenes out of the life of Marco Visconte. Else knows how beautiful are these Sicilian carts and the facchini are always crying: 'Ecco la Sicilia—Ecco la Sicilia in viaggio per l'India!' "—Frieda Lawrence, p. 108.

The Lawrences were still lugging the piece of the Sicilian wagon when they arrived in Santa Fe. See the memoir by Witter Bynner, Chap. III, below.

22 On 22 April 1922, Lawrence wrote to his agent Curtis Brown: "I expect [Robert] Mountsier will send you shortly the first half of another Verga translation, of the *Novelle Rusticane:* short stories of Sicily."—*Letters,* p. 550.

23 See Frieda Lawrence Ravagli: "Some young Cingalese said I had the face of a saint! Didn't I make the most of it and didn't Lawrence get this saint rubbed into him!"—Frieda Lawrence, p. 117.

24 See Lawrence's essay "Nobody Loves Me," in *Phoenix,* pp. 204–11, which begins: "Last year, we had a little house up in the Swiss mountains, for the summer. A friend came to tea: a woman of fifty or so, with her daughter: old friends. 'And how are you all?' I asked, as she sat, flushed and rather exasperated after the climb up to the chalet on a hot afternoon, wiping her face with a too-small handkerchief. 'Well!' she replied, glancing almost viciously out of the window at the immutable slopes and peaks opposite, 'I don't know how *you* feel about it—but—these mountains!—well!—I've lost *all* my *cosmic consciousness,* and *all* my *love for humanity.'*

"She is, of course, New England of the old school—and usually trancendentalist calm."—*Phoenix,* p. 204.

See also Lawrence's letter to Maria Huxley, from Kesselmatte, Gsteig b. Gstaad, dated only "Friday Evening" [Summer, 1928]: ". . . The ——'s came to tea and —— as near being in a real temper as ever I've seen her. She said: I don't know how it (the place) makes you feel, but I've lost *all* my *cosmic consciousness* and *all* my *universal love.* I feel I don't care one bit about *humanity.* —I said: Good for you, ——! —but it was as if another horse-fly had bit her.

"So now you know what's wrong with Switzerland, why you can't stand it, and why it's good for health."—*Letters,* p. 744.

25 Brewster, pp. 249–61.

26 D. H. L. letter to S. S. Koteliansky, from Ardnaree, Kandy, Ceylon, dated 17 April 1922, *Encounter 3,* I (No. 3, December, 1953), 31–32.

27 D. H. L. letter to Lady Cynthia Asquith, from R.M.S. "Orsova," to Fremantle, dated 30 April 1922, *Letters,* pp. 551–52.

28 D. H. L. letter to Mabel Dodge Sterne, from Perth, dated "4 April 1922" [4 May 1922], Luhan, p. 21.

29 See *Letters,* p. 553; *Kangaroo,* Chap. I, "Torestin."

30 See the memoir by Mrs. Phyllis Harrison, below.

31 See Frieda Lawrence Ravagli: "At the library, strangely enough, in that

little library of Thirroul we found several editions of Lawrence's condemned *Rainbow*. We bought a copy—the librarian never knew that it was Lawrence's own book."—Frieda Lawrence, p. 120. See also the Lawrence letter of 3 July 1922 to Mrs. Throssell (Katharine Susannah Prichard), below.

32 William Siebenhaar (1863–1937) was born in Holland and emigrated to Western Australia as a young man. For several years he taught at the Perth High School, and then entered the Government Service. In the 1930's, he took up residence in England, where he died. He translated Pelsart's *Journal* (*Western Mail*, Christmas Number, 1897), and in 1910 produced *Dorothea*, a lyrical romance of over 3,000 lines, said to be the most ambitious poetical work ever to come from Western Australia. For Lawrence's letters to W. Siebenhaar, see *Letters*; for Lawrence's introduction to W. Siebenhaar's translation of E. D. Dekker's *Max Havelaar*, see the original edition (New York: Knopf, 1927) or *Phoenix*, pp. 236–39.

33 Priday, in *Southerly* [Sydney, Australia], 15 (No. 1, 1954), 4–5. With Lawrence's holograph card and letter to Mrs. A. L. Jenkins before me, I have added dates and made certain minor corrections to the texts as provided by Mr. Priday's article.

34 The Lawrences, of course, had been married since 13 July 1914.

35 See *Letters*, p. 554.

36 Original publication of a memoir dictated by Mrs. May E. Gawler to her daughter Mrs. Joanna Gawler Ramsey in 1953. In 1954, Mrs. Ramsey wrote the following biographical sketch to accompany her mother's memoir:

"Mrs. May Eva Gawler was born in Fremantle, Western Australia, in 1873 of English-German parentage. She married Douglas George Gawler, son of the second governor of South Australia.

"Mr. and Mrs. Gawler, early in their married life, settled in Cottesloe, now a lovely suburb on the Swan River, but then a black sandy waste. Early in life Mrs. Gawler started her hobby of making gardens, and was among the first to cultivate a number of the famous wild flowers of Western Australia.

"Mr. Gawler, a solicitor, later became a member of Parliament, but died very suddenly, leaving Mrs. Gawler almost penniless and with four children to support.

"After many years of hard work, but greatly helped by good friends, Mrs. Gawler was able to have the little cottage she speaks of in her article. And this tiny garden became known as one of the most lovely and original in Western Australia. For into a quarter of an acre she managed to grow English poplars, pencil pines, liquidambars, surrounded by a native tea-tree hedge. And from the verandah of the tiny cottage one looked on crazy pavements leading to rose beds, rock-banked lily ponds, a fern-strewn wishing well, dovecote, and sundial, while perched on a bamboo pergola sat her two regular visitors, almost tame kookaburras.

"To be near three of her children, Mrs. Gawler has made her home in Cornwall Gardens, London, S.W. 7, since 1952."

37 From a letter (17 February 1954) to the editor. At the time of Lawrence's visit to Australia in the spring of 1922, Mrs. Phyllis Harrison was the "junior junior" at Mrs. Frances Zabel's bookshop, the famous "Booklovers," which Mrs. Zabel had founded in 1900 in Perth. In a letter (23 March 1956) to the editor, Mrs. Harrison wrote: "I was born in Christchurch, New Zealand, and as a child and teenager was very shy and reserved. I was going back to school and someone suggested to me a position in a bookshop. I was elated, and with a great deal of persuasion told my parents I knew enough and was sure a bookshop was *the only place* I'd ever be happy in. They consented, and I started with Mrs. Frances Zabel, the most wonderful 'book' woman I had ever met. I was with her for only two years, as she sold 'Booklovers' then, but she taught me more about real literature than anybody. When she left for England, she said, 'Phyllis, you're "Booklovers" to me, I know you are going to be all I hope.' I was only seventeen at that time and felt very flattered. When she died, she left me a hundred pounds, which in those days was a fortune to me! When I started my bookshop, I called it after Mrs. Zabel, as she used to write for the paper under the name of 'Franceska,' and now the bookshop is known in many countries outside Australia." Mrs. Harrison was the proprietress of the Franceska Bookshop at 596 Hay Street, Perth, Western Australia, from 1933 to September, 1954, at which time she sold it to the chain of Whitcombe & Tombs of Australia and New Zealand.

38 D. H. L. letter to Earl H. Brewster, from Darlington, West Australia, dated 15 May 1922, Brewster, pp. 51–52.

39 D. H. L. letter to M. L. Skinner, from Chapala, Jalisco, Mexico, dated 2 July 1923, *Letters*, p. 577.

40 R. G. Howarth, in 1952 Reader in English Literature at the University of Sydney, and editor of *Southerly*, now occupies the Chair of English Literature, The University of Cape Town, Cape Town, South Africa.

41 Thomas Edward Lawrence (1888–1935), British adventurer, soldier, and scholar, who joined the revolt of Feisal I in World War I and helped defeat the Turks. Author of *The Seven Pillars of Wisdom* (1935) and *The Mint* (1955), and translator of the *Odyssey* (1932).

42 These recollections of Miss Skinner's would seem to pertain rather to the years of World War I. To my knowledge, Lawrence was in touch with neither Shaw, Wells, nor Galsworthy after his departure from England in November, 1919.

43 Mrs. Mabel Dodge Luhan of Taos, New Mexico, though I am unaware that she had sent Lawrence "a big cheque to visit her ranch."

44 Mollie Skinner's letter telling of her brother Jack's death reached Lawrence at Del Monte Ranch in August, 1925. For Lawrence's analysis of Jack Skinner, see *Letters*, p. 646: "There is deep inside one a revolt against the fixed thing, fixed society, fixed money, fixed homes, even fixed love. I believe that was what ailed your brother: he couldn't bear the social fixture of everything. It's what ails me, too." Lawrence himself declared Mollie Skinner's brother Jack to be the prototype of Jack Grant in *The Boy in the Bush.*—Ada Lawrence and Gelder, p. 104.

475

45 "Kangaroo" and "The Snake" were both included in *Birds, Beasts and Flowers* and again in *Collected Poems*, II. I am unable to trace either the title "Fishes" or the lines presumably quoted from it in Lawrence's published writings.

46 Katharine Susannah Prichard's article in *Meanjin*, 9 (No. 4, Summer, 1950), 252–59, referred to by Mollie Skinner, is reprinted in two parts below: the first in Chap. VI, the second in Chap. VII.

47 Skinner, in *Southerly* [Sydney, Australia], 13 (No. 4, 1952), 233–35. (*Southerly* is microfilmed by University Microfilms, 313 N. First Street, Ann Arbor, Mich.)

Mary Louisa Skinner (1878–1955), known as "Mollie" or "M. L." Skinner, was born in the Officers' Quarters on the bank of the Swan River in Western Australia—her father the Captain of the 18th Royal Irish Regiment and her mother the daughter of George Leake, an English First Settler who had been educated at Oxford. "She had the charm and delightful almost-believing-in-fairies imagination of the Irish, together with the sturdy get-on-with-the-job spirit of the early pioneers." When she was two, her father took the last of the Imperial Troops back to England, and thereafter her childhood was spent in England, Ireland, and Scotland. During her teens, she became partially blind and spent months in a darkened room, enduring painful treatment, before her sight improved. In her early twenties, she trained as a nurse and began writing sketches for the *Daily Mail*. Returning to Perth in 1900, she became a social writer on the *Morning Herald*, then again returned to England, working her passage by looking after some children on the voyage, to do her midwifery training in the slums of London. Her training completed, and a textbook on midwifery published, she returned to Western Australia, and in partnership with another nurse opened a hospital in Perth. After still another period of work in the slums of London, her health broke, and she went to India to recuperate. While there, she joined Lady Minto's Nursing Service, with which she served during World War I in India and Burma (1914–1916), Queen Alexandra's Nursing Service in India (1917), and the Australian Medical Service (1917–1918). During this time she wrote *Letters of a V.A.D.* under the nom de plume R. E. Leake. She returned to Western Australia and acted as matron in country hospitals and for a while ran a guest house at Leithdale, Darlington, in partnership with Miss Ellen Beakbane, a Quaker friend. In 1922, she met D. H. Lawrence. While writing her as yet unpublished autobiography, *The Fifth Sparrow*, Miss Skinner said: "I must let people know he was not the horrible person his critics made him out to be." And again: "He revealed himself as a man of great spiritual integrity who had not discarded the long, long thoughts of boyhood." At Lawrence's instigation, she wrote *The House of Ellis* and sent the MS to him. Lawrence revised it as *The Boy in the Bush* while travelling in Mexico in the late autumn of 1923. (See Miss Skinner's second memoir, in Chap. III, below.) During World War II, she nursed aborigines in a bush settlement and wrote several stories about them. In 1953, she was made an Honorary

Life Member of the Fellowship of Australian Writers "for long and loyal service to the Fellowship and for her enthusiastic literary efforts and achievements." After a varied religious upbringing, she became a Quaker. In her late seventies, she undertook, at the suggestion of Mr. R. G. Howarth, then Reader in English Literature at the University of Sydney, to write her autobiography, *The Fifth Sparrow*. In spite of periods of total blindness and a major operation, and with Mrs. Marjorie Rees as amanuensis, she completed the autobiography as far as she intended to take it, up to the point of Lawrence's death, and continued to write newspaper articles, short stories, and several talks for the A.B.C. until the end of her life at York, Western Australia, 25 May 1955. (The above biographical note on Mollie Skinner is based on a letter [3 December 1953] to the editor, written by Mrs. Majorie Rees, and upon a paper on Mollie Skinner, written and read by Mrs. Marjorie Rees at a meeting of the Fellowship of Australian Writers, 30 August 1955.)

Among Miss Skinner's papers were found eighteen holograph Lawrence letters, four of which had been published in *Letters*. Another of these is included in the second of Miss Skinner's memoirs, reprinted in Chap. III of the present work; excerpts from the collection were used both by Miss Skinner in her second memoir and by Katharine Susannah Prichard in the second installment of her memoir, also reprinted in Chap. III, below. In addition to these letters there was also found the manuscript of an unpublished novel by Miss Skinner, *Eve in the Land of Nod*, "which has notes in Lawrence's handwriting on just about every page. Years later Mollie re-wrote it, using Lawrence's suggestions, but although the book was apparently given to an agent, it was never published."—Mrs. Marjorie Rees in a letter (9 January 1956) to the editor. For another notice of this manuscript, see Katharine Susannah Prichard's memoir in Chap. III, below.

M. L. Skinner's published works include *Midwifery Made Easy* (1913); *Letters of a V.A.D.* (nom de plume R. E. Leake; London: Andrew Melrose, [1918]); *The Boy in the Bush* (with D. H. Lawrence; London: Martin Secker, August, 1924; New York: Thomas Seltzer, 1924—McDonald, pp. 77–78); *Black Swans* (London: Jonathan Cape, 1925); *Men Are We*, aboriginal stories (Perth: People's Publishing Co., 1927); *Tucker Sees India* (London: Secker & Warburg, 1937); *WX—Corporal Smith* (Perth: R. S. Sampson, 1941); *When Skies Are Blue*, with an introduction by John K. Ewers (Perth: Imperial Printing Co., 1946); "The Witch of Welleway," *The Bulletin* [Sydney] (22 February 1956), p. 20. See also M. L. Skinner and T. Mayman, "D. H. Lawrence and M. L. Skinner," *Australian Observer* [Melbourne], 2 (24 July 1948), 110.

48 D. H. L. letter (translated from the German) to Frieda's mother, Frau Baronin von Richthofen, from Darlington, West Australia, dated 15 May 1922, Frieda Lawrence, pp. 122–23.

49 D. H. L. letter to Jan Juta, from R.M.S. "Malwa," dated 20 May 1922, Moore, *Intelligent Heart*, pp. 290–91.

50 Original publication of the first installment of an interview (May, 1956)

given by Mr. Arthur Denis Forrester to Mr. F. W. L. Esch, a *Sydney Morning Herald* feature writer, at Strathfield, Sydney, N.S.W., Australia.

51 D. H. L. letter to Amy Lowell [from R.M.S. *Malwa*], dated 20 May 1922, Damon, p. 606.

52 D. H. L. letter to Frieda's mother, Frau Baronin von Richthofen, from "Wyewurk," Thirroul, New South Wales, Australia, dated "28 May 1922" [29? May 1922], Frieda Lawrence, pp. 124–25. See Moore, *Poste Restante*, p. 67.

53 In a letter (5 June 1956) to the editor, Mrs. Beatrice E. Southwell wrote, concerning her sister Mrs. Alfred Callcott: "[She] passed away about three years ago. (Her Christian name was Lucy.) Her passing was a loss to Thirroul. She possessed an outstanding personality and was keenly interested in the progress of that district. She was intellectual and widely-read—her library contained some valuable books, including as many of D. H. Lawrence's as were obtainable, and had remarked to me that after *re*-reading some of them slowly and thoughtfully, she seemed to understand to a degree the mind and vision of this great man, and regretted she did not know he was a notable author until after he had left Thirroul and so did not have the opportunity of discussing with D. H. L. their viewpoints on many subjects of that time. Mrs. Callcott had been an Anglican church organist at Thirroul about 35 years or more, a memorial Tablet has been placed in the church there. Her husband was one of the main supporters of the church & gave considerable assistance to the Rectors. He passed away some years before his wife. She then continued with the Estate Agency alone."

54 See *Letters*, pp. 555–56.

55 See *Letters*, pp. 555, 556.

56 See *Letters*, p. 554.

57 Original publication of a memoir completed 16 May 1956. See also F. W. L. Esch, "'Wyewurk' May Be a Shrine," *Sydney Morning Herald* (7 April 1956).

58 See *Kangaroo*, Chap. I, "Torestin."

59 From a letter (3 July 1956) to the editor.

60 See *Kangaroo*, Chap. XIV, "Bits."

61 See *Kangaroo*, Chap. XVIII, "Adieu Australia."

62 For Lawrence's account of the journey into the spring bush and the sight of the disappearing river, see *Kangaroo*, Chap. XVIII, "Adieu Australia."

63 Frieda Lawrence, pp. 118–21.

64 D. H. L. letter to Mabel Dodge, from c/o Thomas Cook & Son, Sydney, N.S.W., dated 3 June 1922, Luhan, p. 23.

65 D. H. L. letter (translated from the German) to Frieda's mother, Frau Baronin von Richthofen, from Thirroul, N.S.W., Australia, dated 9 June 1922, Frieda Lawrence, pp. 126–27.

66 See *Kangaroo*, Chap. V, "Coo-ee."

67 D. H. L. letter to Frieda's sister, Dr. Else Jaffe-Richthofen, from "Wyewurk," Thirroul, South Coast, N.S.W., Australia, dated 13 June 1922, Frieda Lawrence, pp. 128–31.

68 See *Kangaroo*, Chap. XIV, "Bits."

69 I have deleted the following two sentences from Mr. Priday's text in this paragraph: "There is more difficulty at this late stage in establishing the identity of Madame Depechezvous and Lady Bareham. Possibly some West Australian acquainted with Perth's 'social set' at the time of Lawrence's visit can be persuaded to search for clues which may solve the mystery." The first part of the mystery is cleared away by the correction "Madame Septcheveux" for the "Madame Depechezvous" provided in Mr. Priday's text of the letter.

70 See Lawrence's letter to Mrs. A. L. Jenkins of 28 May 1922: "I found your letter to Mr. Toy—but don't know if I shall present it. So much for gratitude from me. But I feel I simply can't face *knowing* anybody: it's enough to look at 'em."—*Letters*, p. 554.

71 See Ada Lawrence and Gelder, p. 99.

72 Priday, in *Southerly* [Sydney, Australia], 15 (No. 1, 1954), 5–7. With Lawrence's and Frieda's holograph letters before me, I have made certain minor corrections to the texts as provided by Mr. Priday's article.

73 See Aldington, *Portrait of a Genius*, p. 173.

74 In a letter to Mrs. A. L. Jenkins, from "Wyewurk," Thirroul, N.S.W., dated "28 May 1922" [29? May 1922], Lawrence wrote: "Had a letter from Mr. Throssell, husb. of Katharine Pritchard. Too late again."—*Letters*, p. 554.

75 See *Letters*, p. 554.

76 Pierre Puvis de Chavannes (1824–1898), French mural painter. Although he studied with such Romanticists as Delacroix, his work is classical in inspiration. See also Brewster, p. 55.

77 Pseudonym of Frank Leslie Thomson Wilmot (1881–1942), Australian poet, general literary writer, printer, bookseller, manager of the Melbourne University Press, Commonwealth Lecturer in Australian Literature at the University of Melbourne (1940). His publications include *Some Verses* (1903), *Unconditioned Songs* (1913), *To God: From the Weary Nations* (1917), *The Bay and Padie Book: Kiddie Songs* (1917), *Lovelight* (1918), *Eyes of Vigilance* (1920), *Ways and Means* (1920), *Arrows of Longing* (1921), *The Gully and Other Verses* (1929), anthologies of Australian essays and poems.

78 Louis Esson (1879–1943), dramatist and poet. Born in Edinburgh, Scotland, he was taken to Australia as a child and educated at the University of Melbourne. He wrote a number of plays, of which *The Southern Cross* and *Mother and Son* were produced in Australia, and helped to found the Pioneer Players' Movement in Melbourne in 1922. His publications include *Bells and Bees*, poems (1910), and *Dead Timber and Other Plays* (1920).

79 Henry Tate (1873–1926), Australian writer on music and composer. His works include an opera on an Australian tale, *The Dreams of Diaz;* a ballet, *Inspiration;* an orchestral rhapsody; *Bush Miniatures* for orchestra; a string quartet; a sonata for violin and piano; piano pieces and songs.

80 Katharine Susannah Prichard's novel *Black Opal* (1921), and Furnley

Maurice's volume of poems, *Eyes of Vigilance* (1920). (For Furnley Maurice, see Note 77, above.)

81 See *Kangaroo*, Chap. I, "Torestin."
82 See *Kangaroo*, Chap. I, "Torestin."
83 See *Kangaroo*, Chap. I, "Torestin."
84 Prof. Harry T. Moore has postulated the following prototypes for characters in *Kangaroo:* (a) Ben Cooley ("Kangaroo"), a projection of S. S. Koteliansky, though Lawrence denied this, "and Frieda has said that Dr. Eder also helped to compose the character." The "outward guise" of Ben Cooley may have been based upon that of the "noted Sydney lawyer and engineer, Sir John Monash, who had led the Australian forces in the war . . . ."—Moore, *Intelligent Heart*, p. 292. (b) Willie Struthers, a projection of the labor leader James Holman, with the voice of William E. Hopkin of Eastwood.—Moore, *Intelligent Heart*, p. 292. (c) William James Trewhella ("Jaz"), "a memory of the cunning, evil Cornishmen, particularly the Beresfords' landlord at Porthcothan."—Moore, *Intelligent Heart*, p. 292. (d) John Thomas Buryan, a projection of William Henry Hocking of Cornwall.—Moore, *Intelligent Heart*, p. 232. (e) Victoria Callcott, a projection of Mrs. A. L. Jenkins.—Moore, *Intelligent Heart*, p. 291. Richard Lovat Somers and Harriet, his wife, are, of course, fictionalized portraits of Lawrence and Frieda.

85 See *Kangaroo*, Chap. XIV, "Bits."
86 See *Kangaroo*, Chap. XVI, "A Row in Town."
87 See *Kangaroo*, Chap. XVI, "A Row in Town."
88 See *Kangaroo*, Chap. XVIII, "Adieu Australia."
89 See *Kangaroo*, Chap. XVIII, "Adieu Australia."
90 See *Kangaroo*, Chap. XVIII, "Adieu Australia."
91 Prichard, in *Meanjin* [The University of Melbourne, Carlton, N. 3, Victoria], 9 (No. 4, Summer, 1950), 252–56. For the conclusion of Katharine Susannah Prichard's article, see Chap. III, below. Katharine Susannah Prichard (1884——), Australian novelist, was born in Levuka, Fiji. She went to Australia in her infancy, spent a portion of her childhood in Tasmania, and was educated at South Melbourne College, Victoria. For six years she was a journalist in London. In 1919, she married Capt. Hugo Vivian Hope Throssell, V.C., of Western Australia (died November, 1933). She is the author of the novels *The Pioneers* (1915), *Windlestraws* (1916), *Black Opal* (1921), *Working Bullocks* (1926), *The Wild Oats of Han* (1928), *Coonardoo* (1929), *Haxby's Circus* (1930), *Intimate Strangers* (1937), *Potch and Colour* (1944), and the trilogy *The Roaring Nineties* (1946), *Golden Miles* (1948), and *Winged Seeds* (1950); of the short stories *Kiss on the Lips and Other Stories* (1933); of the collections of poems *Clovelly Verses* (1913) and *The Earth-Lover and Other Verses* (1932); of the play *Brumly Innes*, political pamphlets, etc. When Lawrence was in Australia, Katharine Susannah Prichard's most important work as a writer had not been done. *Working Bullocks* was being published, but had not appeared. (It was afterwards published in New York, as were also *Coonardoo* and *Fay's Circus*.) Reviewing the

first volume of her trilogy, *The Roaring Nineties,* C. Hartley Grattan described her as "unquestionably the most important living fiction writer of Australia." (Although as yet unpublished in America, her trilogy has been translated into French, German, Czech, Slav, Polish, Russian, and Rumanian, while others of her novels have been translated into Hungarian and Afrikaans.) In speaking of Lawrence in a letter (20 July 1953) to the editor, Katharine Susannah Prichard has written: "Most significant to young writers of his period, it seems to me, was a liberating influence—something which enabled one to develope according to one's own experience and way of writing, although they might be very different from his. The rare quality and evanescent brilliance of his style are still captivating."

92 Earlier in this same letter, Lawrence had written: "I shall be able to read the famous *Ulysses* when I get to America." For Lawrence on James Joyce, see *Letters,* pp. 750, 759; "Surgery for the Novel—or a Bomb," in *Phoenix,* pp. 517–18.

93 D. H. L. letter to S. S. Koteliansky, from "Wyewurk," Thirroul, N.S.W., dated 9 July 1922, *Encounter 3,* I (No. 3, December, 1953), 32.

94 Lawrence added the final chapter of *Kangaroo* after his arrival in Taos, in September, 1922. See *Letters,* p. 556.

95 D. H. L. letter to Mabel Dodge, from "Wyewurk," Thirroul, New South Wales, dated 18 July 1922, Luhan, pp. 27–28.

96 The New York (Seltzer) edition of *England, My England,* inscribed by Lawrence: "To Denis and Laura Forrester from D. H. Lawrence. Christmas 1922. New Mexico."

97 Original publication of the concluding installment of an interview (May, 1956) given by Mr. Arthur Denis Forrester to Mr. F. W. L. Esch, a *Sydney Morning Herald* feature writer, at Strathfield, Sydney, N.S.W., Australia.

98 D. H. L. letter to Achsah Barlow Brewster, from "Wyewurk," Thirroul, N.S.W., dated 24 July 1922, Brewster, pp. 58–59.

Phyllis Mander Jones of The Mitchell Library, Macquarie Street, Sydney, N.S.W., has kindly provided the editor with the following bibliography relating to Australian material on D. H. Lawrence:

Bartlett, Norman. "D. H. Lawrence in Australia," *Australian National Review* [Canberra], 5 (1 May 1939), 29–34.

———. "The Failure of D. H. Lawrence," *Australian Quarterly* [Sydney], 19 (December, 1947), 87–102.

M., I. "D. H. Lawrence Met None of Us, Yet He Found Us Hollow and Shallow," *The Age* [Melbourne], 4 September 1948.

Skinner, M. L., and Mayman, T. "D. H. Lawrence and M. L. Skinner," *Australian Observer* [Melbourne], 2 (24 July 1948), 110.

Wilson, William Hardy. *Eucalyptus.* Wandin, Victoria: Privately Printed, 1941 [Edition limited to 25 copies], pp. 331–44.

Wood, John Henderson [John O'Rockie, pseud.]. *Through the Window.* Melbourne: Privately Printed, 1937 [Edition limited to 150 copies], pp. 418–49.

(Items reprinted in the present work have been omitted from the above bibliography.)

99 D. H. L. letter (card?) to Ada Lawrence Clarke, from Wellington, dated 15 August 1922, Ada Lawrence and Gelder, p. 99.

100 *Georgian Stories*. Selected by E. M. (London: Chapman and Hall, 1922). —McDonald, p. 105.

101 Mansfield, *Letters*, pp. 477–78.

102 Mansfield, *Letters*, pp. 482–83.

103 Mansfield, *Letters*, pp. 486–87.

104 Mansfield, *Letters*, p. 494. On 2 February 1923, Lawrence wrote at once to John Middleton Murry upon hearing of Katherine Mansfield's death (9 January 1923) at Fontainebleau, France: "We thought of her, I can tell you, at Wellington. Did Ottoline ever send on the card to Katherine I posted from there for her?"—*Letters*, p. 568. On 14 August 1922 (Lawrence's ship touched at Wellington on 15 August 1922), Katherine Mansfield had made her will, in which she asked John Middleton Murry "to send one book each to a number of her friends, the last-named of whom was Lawrence.

"Katherine had had no communication of any sort from Lawrence since his diabolical letter of 1920; but in reading *Aaron's Rod* she had been drawn to him again (as Murry also had). It gives the measure of her forgiveness, and of her love for Lawrence, that she could arrange for a posthumous gesture to come from her though none might ever come from him.

"Or might it not? In that same twenty-four hours in which Katherine made her will, Lawrence, on his way to America from Australia, called at Wellington. It was the last coincidence. He thought of her, and sent a postcard, which reached her in London in September. He had written on it, she told Murry: 'Just the one word, "Ricordi." ' "—Antony Alpers, *Katherine Mansfield* (New York: Knopf, 1954), p. 342.

105 D. H. L. letter (card?) to Ada Lawrence Clarke, from "Raratonga," dated 20 August 1922, Ada Lawrence and Gelder, p. 99.

106 D. H. L. letter (card?) to Ada Lawrence Clarke, from Tahiti, dated 22 August 1922, Ada Lawrence and Gelder, pp. 99–100.

107 D. H. L. letter to Mrs. A. L. Jenkins, from c/o Mrs. Mabel Sterne, Taos, New Mexico, U.S.A., dated 20 September 1922, *Letters*, p. 557. See also Frieda Lawrence, p. 133; Luhan, p. 47.

CHAPTER III

1 See Lawrence's letter to Mabel Dodge, written "Monday" [4 September 1922] from the Palace Hotel, San Francisco: "And I can't telegraph you our day for arrival in Lamy because once more, like an ass, I spent all my money and arrive here with less than $20, so must wait till Mountsier wires me some. I have telegraphed to him already. There is money in the bank."—Luhan, p. 28. Drawing upon a conversation with Frieda,

Catherine Carswell reported that in Australia Lawrence had foregone the opportunity to lay in a supply of half a dozen pairs of wool socks: "The economy was not worth the risk of running out of cash before they reached America."—Carswell, p. 177. But by 17 December 1922, Lawrence was able to report to Catherine Carswell that the American sales for *Women in Love* were now going into 15,000.—*Letters*, p. 567.

2 See Witter Bynner: ". . . I remember [Lawrence's] own punctiliousness in repayment, his assuring us, for instance, as Frieda has lately reminded me, that he refunded to Mrs. Lujan what she had advanced for the Lawrences' expenses from San Francisco to Santa Fe and that he met rent for the Taos house. It belonged to Tony Lujan and was on Indian land. So he gladly paid."—Bynner, p. 145.

3 D. H. L. letter (translated from the German) to Frieda's mother, Frau Baronin von Richthofen, from Palace Hotel, San Francisco, U.S.A., dated 5 September 1922, Frieda Lawrence, p. 154.

4 Coincidentally with Lawrence's arrival in the United States, John S. Sumner of the New York Society for the Suppression of Vice was attempting to ban *Women in Love*. See Chap. I, Note 225; Chap. III, Note 59, below; Brewster, p. 62.

5 D. H. L. letter to Amy Lowell [from San Francisco], dated 8 September 1922, Damon, p. 621.

6 Antonio ("Tony") Luhan [Lujan], the Taos Indian whom Mrs. Mabel Dodge Luhan married in 1923.

7 Luhan, pp. 35–39. Mrs. Mabel (Ganson) Dodge Luhan (1879——), American autobiographer, was born in Buffalo, New York, the daughter of Charles F. Ganson and Sara McKay (Cook) Ganson, a wealthy and socially prominent family. Her parents' marriage was an unhappy one, and she spent her childhood in a series of boarding schools: St. Margaret's School in Buffalo, Miss Graham's School in New York, Chevy Chase School in Washington, D.C. In 1900, she married Carl Evans, another wealthy Buffalo socialite. They had one son, John Ganson Evans (b. 1902). Two years after their marriage, Carl Evans was killed in a hunting accident, and Mrs. Evans took her infant son to Europe. On board ship, she met Edwin Dodge, an architect from Boston, whom she married in 1903. They established a home in Florence, where Mrs. Dodge presided over her first salon. Among her friends was numbered the late Gertrude Stein, who wrote for her the now famous "Portrait of Mabel Dodge at the Villa Curonia." (See Gertrude Stein, *Selected Writings*, edited, with an Introduction and Notes, by Carl Van Vechten [New York: Random House, 1946], pp. 465–68.) In 1912, Mrs. Dodge returned to the United States, her marriage to Edwin Dodge dissolved. At No. 23 Fifth Avenue, New York City, she established another salon, the habitués of which included Jo Davidson, Lincoln Steffens, Walter Lippmann, Robert Edmund Jones, Lee Simonson, Edwin Arlington Robinson, Max Eastman, Frances Perkins, Amy Lowell, Isadora Duncan. After a love affair with the American journalist John Reed, she married (1916) the artist Maurice Sterne.

Together they went to Taos to join the art colony being formed there, but this marriage too ended in divorce. In 1923, she married her present husband, Tony Luhan, a Pueblo Indian.

Mrs. Luhan's *Lorenzo in Taos* was published in 1932, and some twenty years later she deposited in a safe the manuscript of another book on Lawrence, to remain unpublished until twenty years after her death. Four volumes of her frank autobiography have thus far appeared under the general title *Intimate Memories:* Vol. I, *Background* (1933); Vol. II, *European Experiences* (1935); Vol. III, *Movers and Shakers* (1936); Vol. IV, *Edge of Taos Desert* (1937). Much of the continuing manuscript of the work is not to be published until twenty-five years after her death. She is also the author of *Winter in Taos* (1935) and *Taos and Its Artists* (1947). In 1945, she announced that she had completed a novel entitled *Let's Get Away Together,* which remains unpublished. See also Mrs. Luhan's review of *The Plumed Serpent,* in *Laughing Horse* (No. 13, D. H. Lawrence number, April, 1926), 23–29.

8 D. H. L. letter to Amy Lowell, from Taos, New Mexico, dated 19 October 1922, Damon, p. 623.

9 Paul Burlin (1886——), American abstract expressionist painter. Born in New York, he studied in England, moved to Santa Fe in 1913, lived in Europe from 1921 to 1932. He has taught at Washington University, St. Louis, and, in 1954–1955, at Union College.

10 William Penhallow Henderson (1877——), American artist, was born at Medford, Mass., and was educated at the Massachusetts Normal Art School and the Boston Museum of Fine Arts. In 1905, he married Alice Corbin. During World War I, he served with the Camouflage Department of the U.S. Navy. His art work—portraits, landscapes, murals, pastels, lithographs—is represented in the Art Institute of Chicago, the Denver Art Association, and many private collections. He is also prominent in New Mexico as an architect, and has designed the Sena Plaza and other structures in Santa Fe.

Alice Corbin Henderson (1881–1949), American poet, married the artist William Penhallow Henderson in 1905. Under Harriet Monroe, founder, she was the first associate editor of *Poetry* magazine (1912–1916). She was the author of *Adam's Dream and Two Other Miracle Plays for Children* (1907); *The Spinning Woman of the Sky* (1912), verse; *Red Earth* (1920), verse; *The Sun Turns West* (1933), verse; *Brothers of Light: The Penitentes of the Southwest* (1937), prose; and the compiler (with Harriet Monroe) of an anthology, *The New Poetry* (1917), and of an anthology of New Mexican poetry, *The Turquoise Trail* (1928).

"Little Alice," their daughter, later (20 December 1922) the wife of John Ganson Evans, son of Mrs. Mabel Dodge Luhan; now Mrs. E. Rossin.

11 See Chap. II, Note 21.

12 Arthur Davison Ficke (1883–1945), American poet. Under the pseudonyms Emanuel Morgan and Anne Knish, Witter Bynner and he contrived the "harmless hoax" *Spectra* (1917), which pretended "to found

a new 'school' of poetry that was designed to satirize certain affectations in the fashionable poetry of that moment."
13 Bynner, pp. 1–3, 4–5, 6–8. Witter Bynner (1881———), American poet, was born in Brooklyn, New York. His paternal grandfather was the editor of a newspaper in Worcester, Mass., and his uncle, Edwin Lasseter Bynner, was a novelist. In 1902, he was graduated from Harvard, where he had been on the staff of the *Advocate*. He became an assistant editor of *McClure's Magazine* and, concurrently, literary advisor for McClure, Phillips & Co. He later became literary advisor for Small, Maynard, & Co. From 1908 to 1918, he lived in Cornish, New Hampshire, where he wrote and published poetry. At the beginning of the fall term in 1918, he was called to the University of California to serve as an instructor in the Department of English for a period of one year. His duties there were primarily to assist in the training of members of the Students Army Training Corps. In January, 1919, when the government military school at the University was discontinued, he gave a course in verse writing with marked success. Mrs. Idella Purnell Stone was a member of Mr. Bynner's verse-writing class at this time. After his year at the University of California, Mr. Bynner travelled extensively in the Orient, particularly in China. From this period on, his own poetry was influenced by Chinese poetry. Since the early 1920's, he has divided his time between his homes in Santa Fe, New Mexico, and Chapala, Jalisco, Mexico.
14 Luhan, pp. 39–40, 40, 43–46.
15 D. H. L. card to Earl and Achsah Brewster, from Taos, dated 12 September [1922], Brewster, p. 60.
16 D. H. L. letter to Catherine Carswell, from Taos, New Mexico, U.S.A., dated 29 September 1922, *Letters*, p. 561.
17 Mrs. Elizabeth ("Bessie") Wilkerson [*sic*] Freeman, whose friendship with Mrs. Mabel Dodge Luhan dated from their girlhood days in Buffalo, New York. Prof. Harry T. Moore's *The Intelligent Heart* contains several hitherto unpublished Lawrence letters to her. Lawrence met her at Mrs. Luhan's home at Taos, later (August, 1923) visited her in Buffalo. She also owned a home at Palm Springs, California. On 15 July 1927, Lawrence wrote to Mrs. Luhan from Scandicci, Florence: "I had a letter from Bessie Freeman today—in Paris—so queer! Her beloved brother died: and she seems to have gone off some edge or other: been in India: and spending months alone in the desert with eight Arabs. 'Why am I the only woman in the world who could do it safely?' "—Luhan, p. 332.
18 See Lawrence's article "Certain Americans and an Englishman," in *The New York Times Magazine* (24 December 1922), pp. 3, 9: "The Indians keep burning an eternal fire, the sacred fire of the old dark religion. To the vast white America, either in our generation or in the time of our children or grandchildren, will come some fearful convulsion. Some terrible convulsion will take place among the millions of this country, sooner or later. When the pueblos are gone. But oh, let us have the grace and dignity to shelter these ancient centres of life, so that, if die they must, they die a natural death. And at the same time, let us try to adjust our-

selves again to the Indian outlook, to take up an old dark thread from their vision, and see again as they see, without forgetting we are ourselves.

"For it is a new era we have now got to cross into. And our own electric light won't show us over the gulf. We have to feel our way by the dark thread of the old vision. Before it lapses, let us take it up.

"Before the pueblos disappear, let there be just one moment of reconciliation between the white spirit and the dark."

19 In speaking of the conversations she had had with Mrs. Mabel Dodge Luhan and her friend Mrs. Alice Corbin Henderson while Lawrence was gone with Tony Luhan and Bessie Freeman to the Apache Reservation, Mrs. Frieda Lawrence Ravagli wrote: "They asked me many questions, which I answered truthfully, giving the show away completely as usual."—Frieda Lawrence, p. 136.

20 Luhan, pp. 46–47, 47–50, 51.

21 See Lawrence's essay "Indians and an Englishman," originally published in the *Dial* (February, 1923) and the *Adelphi* (November, 1923) (see *Phoenix*, p. 839), and reprinted in *Phoenix*, pp. 92–99. Another version of this essay, possibly a first draft, appears in Mrs. Luhan's *Lorenzo in Taos*, pp. 52–58. See also Lawrence's own memory of the Apache fiesta in his essay "New Mexico," originally published in the *Survey Graphic* (May, 1931) (see *Phoenix*, p. 839), and reprinted in *Phoenix*, p. 146.

22 D. H. L. letter to Martin Secker, from Taos, New Mexico, dated 19 September 1922, *Letters*, p. 556.

23 See Frieda Lawrence Ravagli: "Mabel and Lawrence wanted to write a book together: about Mabel, it was going to be. I did not want this. I had always regarded Lawrence's genius as given to me. I felt deeply responsible for what he wrote. And there was a fight between us, Mabel and myself: I think it was a fair fight. One day Mabel came over and told me she didn't think I was the right woman for Lawrence and other things equally upsetting and I was thoroughly roused and said: 'Try it then yourself, living with a genius, see what it is like and how easy it is, take him if you can.'"—Frieda Lawrence, p. 136.

24 For Lawrence's note on this projected novel based on the life of Mrs. Luhan, see Luhan, pp. 65–66. For further notes and a synopsis of the extant untitled, unfinished manuscript, see Tedlock, pp. 50–53.

25 Luhan, pp. 51–52, 58–59, 59–60, 61–63, 64–65, 66–67.

26 D. H. L. letter to Earl H. Brewster, from Taos, New Mexico, U.S.A., dated 22 September 1922, Brewster, pp. 61–62.

27 D. H. L. letter to Frieda's sister, Dr. Else Jaffe-Richthofen, from Taos, New Mexico, U.S.A., dated 27 September 1922, Frieda Lawrence, p. 156.

28 D. H. L. letter to Catherine Carswell, from Taos, New Mexico, U.S.A., dated 29 September 1922, *Letters*, pp. 561–62.

29 "New Mexico," in *Phoenix*, p. 146.

30 Lawrence's description of San Geronimo was written in his essay "Taos," originally published in the *Dial* (March, 1923) (see *Phoenix*, p. 839), and reprinted in *Phoenix*, pp. 100–103. See also the essay "New Mexico"

in *Phoenix*, p. 146, for a recollection of the Indian races. Lawrence drew upon such ceremonial dances and races for both *The Plumed Serpent* and *Mornings in Mexico.*

31 Luhan, pp. 80–82.

32 D. H. L. letter to Harriet Monroe, from Taos, New Mexico, dated 4 October 1922, *Letters*, p. 565.

33 The actress Ida Rauh. She married the American author Max Eastman in 1911 (divorced, 1922) and later the artist Andrew Dasburg. For her, in 1925, Lawrence wrote his Biblical play, *David*. She was to be with Frieda and Frieda's daughter Barbara (Mrs. Barbara Weekley Barr) in Vence at the time of Lawrence's death.

34 Luhan, pp. 67–70, 70–71, 71–72, 75–77.

35 D. H. L. letter to Amy Lowell, from Taos, New Mexico, dated 19 October 1922, Damon, pp. 622–23.

36 D. H. L. letter to W. Siebenhaar, from Taos, New Mexico, dated 25 October 1922, *Letters*, p. 565.

37 Lawrence would have studied the Brook Farm experiment during the war years while writing his essay "Hawthorne's *Blithedale Romance*," in *Studies in Classic American Literature.*

38 For Lawrence on Whitman, see *Studies in Classic American Literature.*

39 Lesemann, in *The* [American] *Bookman*, LIX (No. 1, March, 1924), 29–32. Maurice Lesemann (1899———), American poet and business executive, was born in Chicago and attended the University of Chicago. His poetry has been published in *Poetry* magazine and other periodicals, and reprinted in various anthologies. In the business world, he has, for over twenty years, been associated with the Foote, Cone & Belding advertising agency of Los Angeles, and its predecessor Lord & Thomas.

In a letter (16 March 1956) to the editor, Mr. Lesemann has written: "I spent three days with Lawrence in Taos at Mabel Dodge's establishment in October, 1922. John Collier was also staying at Mabel's at that time, and the evening conversations around the big fireplace were divided about equally between Collier and Lawrence. Collier talked about his future plans for the Indians, many of which he later carried out as Commissioner of Indian Affairs under Roosevelt. Lawrence told stories and gave imitations of people he had encountered since becoming a celebrity. His mimicry of Bertrand Russell was outrageously irreverent, biting and funny."

40 From a letter (6 May 1956) to the editor. Andrew Michael Dasburg (1887———), American painter, was born in Paris, and came to the United States as a child. Educated at the Art Students League of New York, the New York School of Art, and in independent study in Paris, he experimented with Cubism and Synchromism, and then, *ca.* 1917, returned "to a more realistic vision and a simplified, cubical treatment of nature." He has lived in New Mexico since 1919, and has exhibited at the National Academy of Design, the Pennsylvania Academy of Fine Arts, the Corcoran Gallery in Washington, D.C. His paintings hang in museums and private collections throughout the country. He has taught painting and

drawing for the Art Students League, in Woodstock, New York, and New York City. Mrs. Luhan once described him as "slender as an arch-angel and with a Blake-like rush of fair hair flying upward from off his round head."

41 From a letter (11 August 1956) to the editor. John Collier (1884———), American social worker and author, and Commissioner of Indian Affairs (1933–1945), was educated at Columbia and Woods Hole (1902–1905) and the Collège de France (1906–1907). He began his career as a social worker with immigrants (1905), and thereafter received appointments as Civic Secretary of the People's Institute, New York (1909–1919), Director of Community Organization for the State of California (1919–1920), Director of Social Science Training, State Teachers College, San Francisco (1921–1922), Executive Secretary, American Indian Defense Association, Inc. (1923–1933), Commissioner of Indian Affairs (1933–1945), Member of the Indian Arts and Crafts Board (1934–1945), Director of National Indian Institute, U.S.A. (1945–1950), Professor of Sociology, College of the City of New York (1947—). He is now President of the Institute of Ethnic Affairs, Washington, D.C. From 1926 to 1933, he edited *American Indian Life,* and he is the author of *The Indians of the Americas* (1947), *American Colonial Record* (1947), *Patterns and Cere-monials of the Indians of the Southwest* (1949), and several volumes of verse.

42 John Ganson Evans (1902———), American writer and sociologist, son of Carl and Mabel (Ganson) Evans (Mrs. Mabel Dodge Luhan). He was a student at Yale University (1920–1921), and on 20 December 1922, he married Alice Oliver Henderson. In 1933, he married Claire Spencer. He has been President of the Flying Heart Development Corp. (1923–1926); Member of the bond department of the Marine Trust Co., Buffalo, New York (1926–1929); Assistant Treasurer, Marine Union Investors, Inc., Buffalo, New York (1929–1930); general partner, Brody, Herod & Co., Buffalo, New York (1930–1932); foreign correspondent in Portugal, Spain, France, for Newsweek, Inc. (1941); asst. project director, Colorado River War Relocation Center (1942–1943); special representative and acting chief of the Alaskan Branch, Division of Territories and Island Possessions, Dept. of Interior (1943–1944); General Superintendent of Indian Service, Albuquerque, New Mexico (1944–1946); Consultant to the Office of the Assistant Secretary of Land Management, Department of Interior (1950); Chief of Technical Cooperation, Department of Interior (1950–1951); Director of Rural Improvement, Iran–U.S. Joint Commission for Rural Improvement, Tehran; Deputy Director of U.S. Technical Cooperation for Iran (1952); Deputy Director, Point 4, TCA Mission, Israel (1952–1953); Chief, Egypt–Jordan Division, Foreign Operations Administration (1953—). He is the author of *Andrews' Harvest* (1933) and *Shadow's Flying* (1936). His permanent residence is now West Brooksville, Maine.

43 D. H. L. letter to Bessie Freeman, from Taos, New Mexico, dated 30 October 1922, Moore, *Intelligent Heart,* p. 303.

44 See Note 24, above.
45 Luhan, pp. 77–80.
46 D. H. L. letter to Bessie Freeman, from Taos, New Mexico, dated "Tuesday" [31 October 1922], Moore, *Intelligent Heart*, p. 305.
47 Possibly a reference to the "Texan" cowboys in *St. Mawr*.
48 On 9 June 1922, Lawrence had written to Mrs. Luhan from "Wyewurk," Thirroul, New South Wales: "I want you please *not* to tell anybody we are coming. I want to be really apart from most people—same as here. Here I have not let anybody know I am come—I don't present any letters of introduction—there isn't a soul on this side of Australia knows I am here, or knows who I am. And that is how I prefer it."—Luhan, p. 24.
49 A. D. Hawk, who owned Del Monte Ranch, next to John Ganson Evans' ranch, and his son William and the latter's wife, Rachel. Prof. Harry T. Moore's *The Intelligent Heart* contains several hitherto unpublished Lawrence letters to the Hawk family.
50 Luhan, pp. 82–83, 86–91.
51 D. H. L. note to Mabel Dodge Luhan, dated "Friday" [1 December 1922], Luhan, pp. 105–6.
52 Knud Merrild (1894–1954), painter, graver, sculptor, designer, writer, was born in Odum, Denmark. Having studied at the Arts and Crafts School and the Royal Academy of Fine Arts, Copenhagen, he made his debut as an artist in the Charlottenborg Art Salon, Copenhagen (1916). The following year (1917), he became founder and president of *Anvendt Kunst,* an organization of artists of Denmark. In 1919–1921, he was awarded grants for study and travel in Scandinavia and England by the Department of Art and Science of the Danish government, and in 1921 came to New York where he exhibited at the Belmaison Galleries the following year. In 1922–1923, he lived in New Mexico, at which time he and his friend Kai Gótzsche met the Lawrences and shared their life at Del Monte Ranch. In 1923, he settled in Los Angeles, and thereafter contributed to numerous exhibitions throughout the country. His works have been displayed in the permanent collections of the Arts and Crafts Museum, Copenhagen, Denmark; the Museum of Fine Art, New York City; the Los Angeles Fair, Pomona; the Arensberg Collection, Hollywood; the Maitland Collection, Bel-Air, Calif., etc. In 1948, the Modern Institute of Art, Beverly Hills, Calif., held a twenty-five year retrospective exhibition of Mr. Merrild's work. In addition to *A Poet and Two Painters: A Memoir of D. H. Lawrence* (1938), he wrote a number of articles on travel and art, and contributed to *The Happy Rock,* a book on his personal friend Henry Miller. He was also an enthusiastic swimmer, having received the highest rating for lifesaving in Denmark (1916), won the Nordic Championship in backstroke (1919), qualified for the Olympic Swimteam at Antwerp (1920).

Kai Guldbransen Gótzsche (6 May 1886———), Danish painter, was born in Aarhus, Denmark, and studied painting at the Royal Academy of Fine Arts, Copenhagen, Denmark (1908–1912). He came to the United States in 1921, and with his friend Knud Merrild shared the Lawrences' life on the Del Monte Ranch in the winter 1922–1923. In the autumn of 1923, he travelled down the west coast of Mexico to Guadalajara with Lawrence, and in November, 1923, sailed with Lawrence as far as Plymouth before returning to Denmark. He married (1926) Esther Andersen, also born in Denmark. The Götzsches have two children, born in the United States. In 1932, the family returned to Denmark; in 1947, they came again to the United States, and returned in 1952 to Denmark, where they now live.

53 Maurice Sterne (1878–1957), painter and sculptor, was born in Libau, Latvia. After an early youth spent in Moscow, he came to the U.S. in 1889, and studied at the National Academy of Design in New York, and thereafter in Paris and Rome. In 1917, he married Mabel Dodge. He was awarded a travelling fellowship, and spent a decade abroad, living in Paris, Italy, Greece, Egypt, India, Burma, Java, Bali. He married Vera Segal in 1923. He has exhibited in Paris, Berlin, London, and the principal cities of the United States. Between 1935 and 1940, he painted the twenty large murals in the Department of Justice library in Washington, D.C.

54 D. H. L. letter (translated from the German) to Frieda's mother, Frau Baronin von Richthofen, from Del Monte Ranch, Questa, New Mexico, dated 5 December 1922, Frieda Lawrence, pp. 158–59.

55 Lawrence's little French bull pup, variously known as "Bibbles," "Pips," "Pipsey," and "Bubastis," was the offspring of Mrs. Luhan's dog "Lorraine." For Lawrence's portrait of the dog, see his "Bibbles" in *Birds, Beasts and Flowers* and *Collected Poems*, II; for Knud Merrild's exegesis of the poem, see Merrild, pp. 160–77.

56 As Knud Merrild observed, Lawrence may have been remembering his own experiences in trying to manage a frightened, high-spirited horse when he came to write of those of Jack Grant in *The Boy in the Bush*. See Merrild, pp. 77–80.

57 D. H. L. letter to Bessie Freeman, from Del Monte Ranch, Valdez, N.M., dated 15 December 1922, Moore, *Intelligent Heart*, pp. 306–7. Lawrence used both "Questa" and "Valdez," New Mexico, in his letters as addresses for Del Monte Ranch. For text headings, I have standardized the address to "Questa."

58 D. H. L. letter to J. M. Murry, from Del Monte Ranch, Questa, New Mexico, dated 30 December 1922, *Letters*, p. 567.

59 From a letter (5 November 1935) to Knud Merrild, in Merrild, pp. 124–25. Thomas Seltzer (1873–1943), publisher and translator, was Lawrence's chief American publisher throughout the 1920's. He was born in Poltava, Russia, and came as a small boy to America. Having been graduated by the University of Pennsylvania (1897), he became a free-lance writer and translator (Gorki), critic, and contributor to the Century Dictionary. Albert and Charles Boni, nephews of Mr. Seltzer, started a bookshop on 8th Street in New York, and later Horace Liveright joined with them to start the publishing business of Boni & Liveright. Thomas Seltzer came into the new publishing house as literary editor, and helped

to create the Modern Library, to which he contributed a collection of Russian short stories. In 1919 he left this organization and with Temple Scott, then of Brentano's, founded the firm of Scott and Seltzer. In the autumn of 1919, Mr. Scott withdrew and the firm became Thomas Seltzer, Inc. In 1920, the new publishing house was in active production. Its first list included the *New Library of Social Science*, a series edited by J. Ramsay MacDonald, later to be Prime Minister of England; *Lancelot* by Edward Arlington Robinson; *Our Great War and the Great Wars of Ancient Greece* by Gilbert Murry; *Margot's Progress* by Douglas Goldring. In 1926 the business was sold out to A. & C. Boni, and Mr. Seltzer's imprint appeared only occasionally on books thereafter. For a time in 1935 Loring & Mussey took over the sales of the titles Mr. Seltzer himself issued.

"In 1923 Mr. Seltzer, because of his special interest in modern European literature and the fearlessness of his publishing program, was involved in an extensive censorship case, the prosecution being brought by John S. Sumner. The three books involved were D. H. Lawrence's *Women in Love*, Arthur Schnitzler's *Casanova's Homecoming* and an anonymous book from the German called *A Young Girl's Diary*. Justice Ford of New York took a special interest in pushing the prosecution and the case was made the basis of an effort in Albany to clamp down further restrictions on book publishing. A large delegation from the National Association of Book Publishers went to Albany for the hearing and the bill fortunately failed of passage."—*Publisher's Weekly*, 144 (No. 13, 25 September 1943), 1179.

60 D. H. L. letter to Jan Juta, from Del Monte Ranch, Questa, N.M., dated "1 January 1922" [1923], Moore, *Intelligent Heart*, p. 308.

61 Katherine Mansfield had died 9 January 1923 at Fontainebleau, France. See Chap. II, Note 104.

62 The source of the title of Catherine Carswell's "narrative of D. H. Lawrence," *The Savage Pilgrimage*.

63 See Lawrence's letter to J. M. Murry, from Del Monte Ranch, Questa, New Mexico, dated 30 December 1922: "Heaven knows what we all are, and how we should feel if we met, now that we are changed. We'll have to meet and see."—*Letters*, p. 567. John Middleton Murry has written that Lawrence's reply came in response to a letter from him, "—the first for several years—suggesting, I suppose, that our relation should be renewed."—Murry, *Reminiscences*, p. 104.

64 D. H. L. letter to J. M. Murry, from Del Monte Ranch, Questa, New Mexico, U.S.A., dated 2 February 1923, *Letters*, pp. 568–69.

65 Entry in Lawrence's Diary.—Tedlock, p. 96. On this same day (10 February 1923), Lawrence explained in a letter to Curtis Brown, written from Del Monte Ranch, Questa, New Mexico: "Write all business direct to me or Seltzer, not to Mountsier, as he is travelling about, thinks to come to Europe and won't be able to keep count of my things over here, and so won't act as my agent any longer."—Moore, *Intelligent Heart*, p. 310.

66 D. H. L. letter to Harriet Monroe, from Del Monte Ranch, Questa, New Mexico, dated 10 February 1923, *Letters,* p. 569.

67 D. H. L. letter to Gilbert Seldes, from Del Monte Ranch, Questa, New Mexico, dated 25 February 1923, *Letters,* pp. 570–71. In a letter (12 August 1956) to the editor, Mr. Gilbert Seldes has written: "The simple (to me regrettable) fact is that there is no background to the Lawrence letter—there was no previous correspondence except a formal note from me (as managing editor of *The Dial,* on leave in Europe) about the disposition of a MS—and there was no later correspondence of any sort. "Nor did I find Miss Humes.

"As this single letter includes one of the most quoted of Lawrence's references to America, I feel certain of a footnote in literary history. The remark—or rather the question I had asked was purely social—something like 'I hope you're not disappointed'—as a native speaks to a visitor. A lucky question it turned out.

"The only other point is that I called the book *The Kangaroo* and Lawrence corrected me."

68 D. H. L. letter (card?) to Ada Lawrence Clarke, from El Paso, dated 21 March 1923, Ada Lawrence and Gelder, p. 101.

69 The Hotel Regis, facing the busy Avenida Juárez, Mexico City.

70 D. H. L. letter to Bessie Freeman, from Hotel Monte Carlo, Mexico City, dated 24 March 1923, Moore, *Intelligent Heart,* p. 311.

71 D. H. L. letter (card?) to Ada Lawrence Clarke, from Hotel Monte Carlo, [Av.] Uruguay [69], Mexico, dated "March, 1923," Ada Lawrence and Gelder, p. 102.

72 On 8 March, and again on 14 March, 1923, Lawrence had written to Witter Bynner and Willard ("Spud") Johnson, inviting them to accompany him and Frieda to Mexico City.—Bynner, pp. 17–18. The Lawrences stayed overnight again at Witter Bynner's home in Santa Fe *ca.* 19 March (see entry in Diary.—Tedlock, p. 97), and went on to El Paso, Texas, where they crossed the frontier into Mexico on Wednesday, 21 March 1923. (See Ada Lawrence and Gelder, p. 101; Merrild, p. 260.) They arrived in Mexico City on Friday, 23 March 1923. (See Merrild, p. 264; Moore, *Intelligent Heart,* p. 311.) That weekend, Lawrence wrote to his sister Ada that he expected some friends (Witter Bynner and Willard Johnson) "down from Santa Fe on Tuesday" (27 March 1923). (See Ada Lawrence and Gelder, p. 102.) Presumably Lawrence met the train on Tuesday, but it was "fourteen hours late" and so he missed Witter Bynner and Willard Johnson. It was not until "the third day" that Willard Johnson "brushed sleeves with Lawrence at a crowded corner," and within the hour the four friends "were laughing and jabbering in the Hotel Monte Carlo . . . ."—Bynner, pp. 19–20. The reunion must therefore have taken place on Thursday, 29 March 1923.

Lawrence's wanderings in the month of April, 1923, are somewhat difficult to follow:

Both Witter Bynner and Willard Johnson remembered that they and the Lawrences attended the bullfight on Easter Sunday (1 April 1923);

in *The Plumed Serpent,* Chap. I, "Beginnings of a Bull-Fight," Lawrence has the bullfight take place on "the Sunday after Easter." On 11 April 1923, Lawrence wrote to Earl and Achsah Brewster: "We went to a bullfight: hated it."—Brewster, p. 71.

By Wednesday, 11 April 1923, Lawrence had visited the pyramids at Teotihuacan and had had time to have snapshots developed and printed to send to his friends.—*Letters,* p. 571; Merrild, p. 265; Moore, *Intelligent Heart,* p. 311. And by 11 April 1923, the Lawrences, Witter Bynner, and Willard Johnson had visited Cuernavaca.—Moore, *Intelligent Heart,* pp. 311–12.

Also on 11 April 1923, Lawrence wrote three friends that on the following day, Thursday, 12 April 1923, he and Frieda were going to Puebla, Tehuacan, and Orizaba.—Brewster, p. 70; Merrild, p. 265; Moore, *Intelligent Heart,* p. 312. Witter Bynner accompanied them on this trip; Willard Johnson had taken ill at Cuernavaca.

There are extant three letters written by Lawrence from Orizaba dated 21 April 1923, a Saturday:—Moore, *Intelligent Heart,* p. 313; Merrild, p. 274; and Ada Lawrence and Gelder, p. 106 (mistakenly dated 1925). In one of these (Merrild, p. 274), Lawrence speaks of going "back to Mexico City tomorrow, and I shall find mail." But there are also extant three letters written from the Hotel Monte Carlo in Mexico City likewise dated 21 April 1923.—Damon, p. 638; Merrild, p. 292; and a third quoted by Theresa Coolidge in "D. H. Lawrence to his Agent," in *More Books,* Bulletin of the Boston Public Library, XXIII (No. 1, January, 1948), 23. In one of these (Merrild, p. 292), Lawrence wrote: "I found your letter here . . ."

Before the reader proceeds to the memoirs of this period, it is necessary for him to bear in mind the following dates and facts:

(a) Lawrence and Frieda arrived in Mexico City on Friday, 23 March 1923.

(b) Witter Bynner and Willard Johnson, though arriving in Mexico City on Tuesday, 27 March, did not meet the Lawrences until Thursday, 29 March.

(c) The four visited churches on Good Friday (30 March).

(d) They saw a religious film on Saturday (31 March).

(e) They attended the bullfight on Easter Sunday (1 April).

(f) Between Easter Sunday (1 April) and 11 April, the group visited the pyramids at Teotihuacan and Cuernavaca, where Willard Johnson became ill and dropped out of the group's wanderings for a few days.

(g) Between 11 and 21 April, the Lawrences and Witter Bynner took the proposed trip to Puebla, Tehuacan, and Orizaba.

(h) By Saturday, 21 April, they had returned to Mexico City.

(i) On 27 April, the Lawrences and a small party were invited to luncheon with José Vasconcelos, Minister of Education.

(j) On 27–28 April, Lawrence left Mexico City for Guadalajara and Chapala.

(k) On 2 May, Frieda joined Lawrence at Chapala, and they moved into the "long house" at Zaragoza No. 4.

(l) Before going to Chapala, Witter Bynner and Willard Johnson spent some days at Guadalajara.

Within this framework of dates, I have attempted to arrange something of a chronology of memoirs, a chronology that differs considerably from that indicated by Mr. Witter Bynner in his *Journey with Genius*. See also Moore, *Poste Restante*, pp. 70–71.

73 See Witter Bynner: "At the cinema next evening [Holy Saturday, 31 March 1923], in a silent film, *The Passion of Christ*, we watched Jesus loom forward with a lamb on His shoulder, nearer and larger, into the hearts of His audience, while marimbas played a gaily swinging tune to welcome Him. The fact that during the Crucifixion the tune was 'Three O'Clock in the Morning' seemed in no way to lessen reverence. Frieda laughed about it, but Lawrence's emotions were mixed. The Church's hold on Mexico depressed him. He felt it a poor change for Quetzalcoatl."— Bynner, p. 46.

74 Álvero Obregón (1880–1928), Mexican general and president (1920–1924), had supported Madero in the revolution against Porfirio Diaz (1911), and by a coup was made president in 1920. He was re-elected president in 1928 but was assassinated before taking office.

75 Elsewhere, Mr. Bynner suggests additional prototypes for characters in *The Plumed Serpent*: (a) John Dibrell, as an ingredient in Don Ramón —Bynner, pp. 119–22; (b) Miguel Covarrubias, as an ingredient in the young Mexican who conducted the tour of the frescoes—Bynner, pp. 28–31; (c) Mrs. Zelia Nuttall, as Mrs. Norris—Bynner, pp. 22–23; (d) Mr. Winfield Scott, as Mr. Bell—Bynner, pp. 123–28; (e) the family of Mexicans at the Lawrences' (Kate's) house—Bynner, pp. 94–96, 100–103, 160–63. Mr. Bynner also points out that the villa El Manglar, once the villa of Don Porfirio's brother, at Chapala, an estate in a condition of ruin in 1923, provided the setting for Jamiltepec, Don Ramón's hacienda on "Lake Sayula."—Bynner, pp. 90–91, 212.

76 Bynner, pp. 48–52, 54–55, 57. The whole of this memoir should be compared with Lawrence's *The Plumed Serpent*, Chap. I, "Beginnings of a Bull-Fight."

77 For Mrs. Zelia Nuttall, see Note 87, below.

78 D. H. L. letter (card?) to Mrs. Bessie Freeman, from Hotel Monte Carlo, Mexico City, dated 11 April 1923, Moore, *Intelligent Heart*, pp. 311–12.

79 See *The Plumed Serpent*, Chap. III, "Fortieth Birthday." For a second-hand account of Lawrence's meeting with the artist Miguel Covarrubias (1902–1957), see Witter Bynner: "Lawrence was always gentle with Miguel, even when they disagreed as to the quality of the Mexican painters whom Covarrubias revered. Lawrence found most of the paintings ugly." Together with an unidentified "youthful professor," Covarrubias was the prototype of the young Mexican who conducted the tour of the frescoes.—Bynner, pp. 28–31.

80 See Note 85, below.

81 Maximilian (1832–1867), Emperor of Mexico (1864–1867), and his wife Carlotta (1840–1927). When they arrived in Mexico (1864), they found most of Mexico hostile to them and loyal to Benito Juárez. When Napoleon III was compelled to withdraw his French soldiers (1866–1867), Carlotta went to Europe to seek aid. Maximilian took personal command of his forces, was captured and shot. Carlotta went mad but survived Maximilian by sixty years.

82 Emiliano Zapata (1879?–1919), Mexican revolutionist, born in Morelos, of almost pure Indian blood. With an army of Indians he led the revolution in the south after 1910 and occupied Mexico City three times (1914–1915), once with Villa. By his opponents, he was considered a bandit; by the Indians, a hero. He was killed by an emissary of Carranza.

83 See *The Plumed Serpent*, Chap. IV, "To Stay or Not to Stay."

84 Bynner, pp. 20–21, 23, 24–25, 33.

85 Although Mr. Bynner himself has recorded the fact that this letter to Porter Garnett was "written a fortnight before the May Day . . ." (see Bynner, p. 68), I believe it should have been assigned a date prior to 11 April, when Lawrence noted that they had already "stayed a few days at Cuernavaca—hot, but very attractive."—Moore, *Intelligent Heart*, pp. 311–12.

86 Adapted into journal form from a letter written by Witter Bynner to Porter Garnett, from Cuernavaca, dated 15? April 1923 (see Note 85, above), in Bynner, pp. 68–69.

87 Mrs. Zelia Maria Magdalena Nuttall (1858–1933), archeologist, was born in San Francisco, and educated in England, France, Germany, and Italy. In 1880, she married Alphonse L. Pinart (divorced, 1887). An extensive traveller, she made a special study of antiquities and the colonial history of Mexico. She was an honorary special assistant at the Peabody Museum of American Archaeology and Ethnology, Cambridge, Mass., and an honorary professor of archaeology at the National Museum, Mexico City. She is the author of *Standard or Head-Dress?* (1888), *The Atlatl or Spear-Thrower of the Ancient Mexicans* (1891), *The Fundamental Principles of Old and New World Civilizations* (1901), *Codex Nuttall* (1902), *A Penitential Rite of the Ancient Mexicans* (1904), *The Earliest Historical Relations Between Mexico and Japan* (1906), *The Gardens of Ancient Mexico* (1925), *New Light on Ancient American Calendars* (1926); and the editor and translator of *New Light on Drake* (1914) and of Francisco de Castañeda's *Official Reports on the Towns of Tequizistlan, Tepechpan, Acolman, and San Juan Teotihuacan* (1926), etc. For a study of the influence of Mrs. Nuttall's *Fundamental Principles of Old and New World Civilizations* (1901) on Lawrence's The Plumed Serpent, see William York Tindall, *D. H. Lawrence and Susan His Cow* (New York: Columbia University Press, 1939).

Mrs. Nuttall served as the original of Mrs. Norris in *The Plumed Serpent*. Prof. Harry T. Moore quotes Frieda Lawrence Ravagli as stating that Lawrence went to Mrs. Nuttall's home for lunch three times, but did not stay there.—Moore, *Intelligent Heart*, p. 312. Mr. Witter Bynner has written: "Lawrence's memory was acutely retentive and accurate, not only for what he had read but for actual conversations, as illustrated in his recording of Mrs. Nuttall's tea party [in *The Plumed Serpent*, Chap. II, "Tea-Party in Tlacolula"]. He could often have put it to better use in fiction if he had not been determined that so many of his characters should talk Lawrence instead of themselves. In his own personal quoting of conversations, he did very little of this."—Bynner, p. 45.

88 Presumably an error for Pedro de Alvarado (1495?–1541), a lieutenant of Cortes, a *conquistador*, and a "dashing figure" in the Spanish invasion of Mexico. He conquered Guatemala and Salvador, and served as Governor of the former until his death at Guadalajara.

89 See Merrild, pp. 265–66.

90 See *The Plumed Serpent*, Chap. II, "Tea-Party in Tlacolula."

91 See *The Plumed Serpent*, Chap. II, "Tea-Party in Tlacolula."

92 See *The Plumed Serpent*, Chap. II, "Tea-Party in Tlacolula."

93 Bynner, pp. 22–23.

94 D. H. L. letter to Earl and Achsah Brewster, from Hotel Monte Carlo, Av. Uruguay 69, Mexico City, dated 11 April 1923, Brewster, pp. 70–71.

95 See *The Plumed Serpent*, Chap. XVIII, "Auto da Fé."

96 I am unable to reconcile Mr. Bynner's itinerary (Mexico City, Puebla, Orizaba, Cholula, Atlixco, Mexico City) with the inference one draws from Lawrence's letter of 21 [20?] April 1923, written from Orizaba: "We go back to Mexico City tomorrow . . . ."—Merrild, p. 274.

97 Porfirio Diaz (1830–1915), president of Mexico (1876–1911). Although Mexico prospered materially under his regime, largely through the investment of foreign capital, the oppressed masses were neglected.

98 Hokusai (1760–1849), Japanese artist, creator of the famous color-print series, *Hundred Views of Fuji*.

99 On 26 February 1923, Lawrence noted in his Diary: "Made up income tax returns: royalties 3,824.67. periodicals 1,615.00 gross income 5,439.67. Agents Commission 543.96 Agent's journey 300.00 Typing & expenses 345.31—total deduction 1,189.27 Net income 4,250.40—less 2,500 exemption. Bal. 1,750.40—at 4% tax. Tax $70.00."—Tedlock, p. 97.

100 Felix Lope de Vega (Carpio) (1562–1635), Spanish dramatic poet. See Bynner, pp. 44–45.

101 In *Journey with Genius*, Mr. Bynner places the trip of which he writes above *before* Holy Week. See Note 72, above.

102 Bynner, pp. 35–36, 37–38, 39, 39–40, 42–43.

103 D. H. L. letter (card?) to Knud Merrild, from Orizaba, dated 21 [20?] April [1923], Merrild, p. 274. Lawrence makes clear that the trip was ended at Orizaba; Mr. Bynner concludes his memoir of the journey with the stay at Atlixco. See Note 72, above.

104 D. H. L. letter to Amy Lowell, from Hotel Monte Carlo, Ar. [Av.] Uruguay 69, Mexico D.F., Damon, p. 638.

105 D. H. L. letter to Knud Merrild, from Hotel Monte Carlo, Av. Uruguay 69, Mexico City, dated 21 April [1923], Merrild, p. 292.

106 D. H. L. letter to J. M. Murry, from Hotel Monte Carlo, Av. Uruguay 69,

Mexico D.F., dated "Thursday, April 27" [Thursday, 26 April 1923 or Friday, 27 April 1923], *Letters,* p. 572.

107 José Vasconcelos (1882———), Mexican educator and writer, headed the National University of Mexico (1920–1924), and was Minister of Education (1920–1925), during which time he worked vigorously to raise the literacy rate in Mexico. He was forced into exile by his successful opponent for the presidency, Plutarco E. Calles, but later returned to Mexico where he was again signally honored and where he served with distinction as director of the Biblioteca Nacional. See his two-part review of Witter Bynner's *Journey with Genius* in the Mexico City *Novedades,* 28 December 1951 and 4 January 1952.

108 Roberto Haberman worked in the Department of Education for the Government of Mexico, and was the immediate superior of Frederic W. Leighton (for whom see Note 112, below).—Bynner, pp. 21–22. According to the memoir of Mr. Leighton, Frieda and he were also members of the party. See also Bynner, pp. 26–28.

109 See Bynner, p. 32.

110 I.e., the frescoes of Diego Rivera (1886———), famed Mexican painter.

111 Beals, pp. 186–89. Carleton Beals (1893———), author and lecturer, was born at Medicine Lodge, Kansas. He received his B.A., *cum laude,* from the University of California (1916), his M.A., from Columbia (1917), and studied at the University of Madrid (1920), the University of Rome (1922), the University of Mexico (1923). He served as Director of the English Preparatory Institute, Mexico City (1919), Principal of the American High School, Mexico City (1919–1920), Instructor on the personal staff of President Carranza (1920). Following a year as Lecturer for the New York Board of Education (1924), he became Editor of *Mexican Folkways* (1925–1937), Associate Editor of the Latin-American Press Syndicate (1933–1934), President of the Editorial Board of the *Latin-American Digest* (1934–1936); contributing editor to *Common Sense* (1933–1941), *Modern Monthly* (1935–1937), *Current History* (1939); member of the advisory board of *Living Age* (1933–1935); advisory editor of *Controversy* (1935). He has been a correspondent in Italy (1920–1922), Mexico (1923, 1925–1928, 1930–1932, 1937), Central America (1927–1928), Spain, North Africa, Italy, Turkey, Russia, and Germany (1929), Cuba (1932–1933, 1935), Panama, Columbia, Ecuador, Peru (1934); and special correspondent for the North American Newspaper Alliance (1935), the *New York Post,* the Scottsboro trial, Alabama (1936); and special correspondent in Argentina, Chile, Bolivia, Peru (1946). He has lectured on Mexican-American relations at the Conference on the Cause and Cure of War (Washington, 1927); for the Seminar on Relations with Mexico (Mexico City, 1925–1928, 1930–1931); on Central America at the National University of Mexico (1928); on Modern Mexico and the Caribbean at the University of California (Summer, 1933); and at the New School of Social Research (1935). In addition to contributions to the *Encyclopedia of Social Sciences,* the *Encyclopaedia Britannica,* the *World Book Encyclopedia,* and the *Land and Peoples*

Encyclopedia, and many magazines, Mr. Beals is the author of *Rio Grande to Cape Horn* (1947); *Lands of the Dawning Morrow* (1948); *The Long Land Chile* (1948); *Our Yankee Heritage,* a series consisting of *The Making of Great New Haven* (1951), *The Making of Bristol* (1954), *New England's Contributions to American Civilization* (1955); *Stephen Austin: Father of Texas* (1953); etc. For Mr. Beals's review of Lawrence's *Mornings in Mexico,* see the *Saturday Review of Literature* (27 August 1927).

112 From a personal letter (April, 1949) written by Frederic W. Leighton to Witter Bynner, Bynner, pp. 184–85. Note that Lawrence left Mexico City for Guadalajara and Chapala on 27 or 28 April 1923 (see Moore, *Poste Restante,* p. 71), a fact which may, or may not, be relevant to his rejection of a second invitation to luncheon by the Minister of Education.

Frederic W. Leighton (1895———), American importer, was born in Chicago, and in 1917 took his A.B. at Dartmouth. Since 1927, he has been president of Fred Leighton, Inc. He is also the Chairman of the Import Committee, International Section, New York Board of Trade; a member of the advisory committee on imports, Department of Commerce, Washington; President of the National Council of American Importers. He has contributed articles to professional publications.

Through the American Embassy in Mexico City, Witter Bynner found his old acquaintance Mr. Leighton who, under Roberto Haberman, was in charge of the teaching of English in the Mexico City schools, and a representative of the Federated Press. Mr. Leighton became an "agreeable guide" to Witter Bynner, Willard Johnson, and the Lawrences during their stay in Mexico City in the spring of 1923, and visited the group at Chapala in the early summer.—Bynner, p. 21.

113 D. H. L. letter (translated from the German) to Frieda's mother, Frau Baronin von Richthofen, from Hotel Monte Carlo, [Av.] Uruguay [69], Mexico, dated 27 [26?] April 1923, Frieda Lawrence, p. 160.

114 For an account of Frieda's adventures with Witter Bynner and Willard Johnson on May Day, 1923, in Mexico City, see Bynner, pp. 71–78.

115 Bynner, pp. 59–60.

116 Entry in Lawrence's Diary.—Tedlock, p. 98.

117 From a letter (10 July 1953) to the editor. Captain Percy Grenville Holms, O.B.E., British Vice-Consul at Guadalajara (1908–1915, 1919–1933), and his wife were friends of the Purnells (for whom see Note 155, below). Mrs. Holms at this time was supervising a group of native craftsmen in an attempt to help them change over from their own crude pottery to English designs and glazes that would appeal to the modern tourist. See Bynner, p. 86.

In a letter (28 March 1956) to the editor, Captain Holms wrote from his present home in Connemara, Ireland: "Regarding myself, I was British Vice-Consul at Guadalajara, Mexico, from 1908 to 1933, except for leave granted me from 1915 till 1919, which I spent as an officer of Royal Artillery in France, Belgium, and Palestine, being transferred from the army to the post of Assistant Economic Administrator of Palestine.

"I was best known to the American public when I acted as American Consul at Guadalajara at the time of the landing of U.S. forces at Vera Cruz [1914], when I had the rather difficult and dangerous task of evacuating all Americans from Guadalajara. Later I had a similar task in evacuating all religious persons of the Catholic faith. For these tasks I was awarded the Order of the British Empire (O.B.E.)."

In an earlier letter (10 July 1953) to the editor, Captain Holms had written: "It is rather curious that, while Assistant Economic Administrator of Palestine with my Headquarters in the German Hospice on the Mount of Olives overlooking Jerusalem, my office was next door to that of the other Lawrence, Lawrence of Arabia, whom I knew much more intimately. I am perhaps one of the few who had more than a nodding acquaintanceship with both of these famous Lawrences."

118 D. H. L. letter to Knud Merrild, from Zaragoza No. 4, *Chapala* (Jalisco), Mex., dated 3 May 1923, Merrild, p. 294. The Lawrence house at Zaragoza No. 4 (now No. 307), Chapala, is now known as the Casa MacNicol, having been bought (1954), restored, and additions made by Mr. Roy MacNicol, an American painter. On a ceramic tile embedded in the wall, Mr. MacNicol placed these words: "In this house D. H. Lawrence lived and wrote *The Plumed Serpent* in the year 1923." In a letter (29 June 1956) to the editor, Mr. Witter Bynner has described the house as follows: "My remembrance is that in the Lawrences' time it was not coated but still uncovered brick. Perhaps, though, the brick was left only around the windows. . . . Otherwise it's as it was but for the oval-topped double-door which closed at the center of the arch, which incidentally has gone and has been replaced with a narrow door in a wall and the MacNicol coat-of-arms beside it in white plaster. . . . The original first story remains white, the second story is black." In another letter (25 May 1956) to the editor, Mr. Bynner has written: "The 'beach where [Lawrence] used to sit' is now a severe boulevard which gives me a pang while I remember the simple village we lived in. The tree under which he sat and wrote is gone long since and the beach close to it where fishermen cast nets and women washed clothes has receded a quarter of a mile. But the mountains still surround what is left of the lake and, as a village somewhat inland, Chapala would still have charmed us had we come upon it in its present state."

119 Bertha M. Clay, English writer, whose real name was Charlotte Monica Braeme (1836–1884). Author of a long series of sensational romantic novels, many of them believed to have been written, under the name Bertha M. Clay, by Frederick Van Rensselaer Day (1861–1922) and Thomas Chalmers Harbaugh (1849–1924).

120 Adapted into journal form from letters written by Witter Bynner to Alice Corbin Henderson, dated 4 May 1923, and to Haniel Long, dated 9 May 1923, respectively, from Guadalajara, Bynner, pp. 136–37.

121 D. H. L. letter to Mrs. Bessie Freeman, from Zaragoza No. 4, Chapala, Mexico, dated 11 May 1923, Moore, *Intelligent Heart*, p. 314.

122 See Bynner, pp. 33–34.

123 A reference to Elizabeth Asquith (1897–1945), Princess Bibesco by marriage (1919) with Prince Antoine Bibesco. She was the daughter of Herbert Henry Asquith, 1st Earl of Oxford and Asquith (1852–1928), Prime Minister of England (1908–1916); the sister of the Hon. Herbert ("Beb") Asquith (1881–1947), and sister-in-law of Lady Cynthia Asquith, Countess of Oxford and Asquith (1887——). Her published works include *I Have only Myself to Blame* (1921), *Balloons* (1923), *There is No Return* (1927), *Portrait of Caroline* (1931), and *Haven* (1951).

124 See Witter Bynner: "[We] bought a copy of a labor sheet, *Nueva Solidaridad Obrera,* and, under the big headline, 'The Chicago Massacre,' read in smaller heavy type, 'Spies, Fisher, Engel, Lingg and Parsons: victims of the Government of the Country of "liberty."' . . . Much has been said about the crimes committed in Chicago in 1886 by the shameless and villainous procedure of the world-wide capitalistic rabble represented by the North American courts of Justice.'"—Bynner, p. 72.

125 See Note 114, above. Lawrence had left Mexico City for Guadalajara and Chapala on 27 or 28 April 1923; Frieda, Witter Bynner, and Willard Johnson followed on 2 May. Although Frieda joined Lawrence at Chapala at once, Witter Bynner and Willard Johnson paused a few days at Guadalajara before going on to a hotel at Chapala.

126 See Bynner, pp. 152–58.

127 Mr. Johnson is here referring to Witter Bynner's poem "D. H. Lawrence," originally included in *Caravan* (1925) and reprinted in Bynner, pp. 325–26. The quotation is taken from the concluding two lines of the poem.

128 Lawrence had originally intended to call his Mexican novel *Quetzalcoatl,* but was eventually obliged to abandon the title in favor of *The Plumed Serpent.*

129 See *The Plumed Serpent,* Chap. II, "Tea-Party in Tlacolula."

130 Again, a quotation from Mr. Bynner's poem "D. H. Lawrence." See Note 127, above. See also *Letters,* p. 657.

131 "Bud Villiers" [Willard Johnson], in *Southwest Review,* XV (No. 4, Summer, 1930), 425–33. As Mr. Johnson originally signed this memoir under the pseudonym "Bud Villiers," so he gave to Witter Bynner the name "Owen" (Owen Rhys), both taken, of course, from the names Lawrence assigned to them in *The Plumed Serpent.* With Mr. Johnson's permission, I have dropped the fiction that disguises the names. For the quotation at the end of this memoir, see *The Plumed Serpent,* Chap. VI, "The Move Down the Lake."

In letters (22 April and 15 May 1956) to the editor, Mr. Johnson has provided the following autobiographical sketch: "Born in Southern Illinois (Mt. Vernon) June 3rd, 1897. Grew up in Greeley, Colorado, where we moved in 1906. After graduation from High School there (1916), attended Colorado State Teachers College for year, taking printing and bookbinding as well as all the courses the college offered in literature and writing. Then went to University of Colorado at Boulder as Freshman (1917–1918) and thence to University of California where I worked in the University Library and in the Bohemian Club Library,

San Francisco, in between classes. Went to Alaska the following summer, then back to Colorado where I worked briefly on a newspaper in Greeley, then on the Denver *Post*, and then for a year on the Pueblo (Colo.) *Chieftain*. In 1921, returned to California and worked on the Richmond *Independent*, managing a few classes at the University afternoons until required military training forced me to give up either my job or college. Out of necessity I chose the job, and was no longer officially enrolled at the University, although I continued to attend my classes (without what is known as "credit"). The next spring [1922], with two of my classmates, Roy Chanslor and James T. Van Rensselaer, started the *Laughing Horse*. Stopped off in Santa Fe to visit Bynner that summer en route to Colorado, and returned there again en route back to Berkeley, but stayed on in Santa Fe, not returning to California at all.

"Briefly, when Lawrence appeared in Santa Fe in the late summer of 1922 and spent the night in Bynner's house before going on up to Taos next day with Mabel and Tony, I asked him if he would write something for the *Laughing Horse* and loaned him a book I had just received, a privately printed, rather obscene book by Ben Hecht called *Fantazius Malare*. After settling down in Taos, Lawrence chose to combine his comment on the book and his thanks to me for loaning it, with his promise to contribute to the *Horse*—and the result was the "Letter" to Chère Jeunesse, dated Oct. 12, 1922, which we printed in *Laughing Horse* No. 4, Dec. '22, leaving blanks where all the four-letter Anglo-Saxon monosyllables appeared. I believe this also appears in his collected *Letters* with all these words restored [*Letters*, pp. 562–64]. Later that winter we went to see him on the ranch above Taos and talked of our plan to go to Mexico, which later materialized in April or May [1923]. We spent six months in Mexico together, Lawrence, Frieda, Bynner and I, and during that time I printed *Laughing Horse* No. 8 in Guadalajara, for which Lawrence wrote "Au Revoir, U.S.A." Later he sent "Paris Letter" and "Dear Old Horse: A London Letter" to the *Laughing Horse*, and when he returned to America later, wrote for me "Just Back from the Snake-Dance —Tired Out." I believe he was back in Europe again when he sent me the material for the special D. H. Lawrence number of the *Horse*.

"Began visiting Mabel Dodge in Taos and spent the winters of 1924 and 1925 with her and Tony in New York, living at Finney Farm in Croton, but spending most of my time in New York City. Started writing for *The New Yorker* at that time and the following season was on the staff of *The New Yorker* for a year, doing the "Talk of the Town" column, general editorial work, signed articles, etc.

"Returned to Taos in '26 (or was it '27) and bought a small printing press on which I began to print the *Laughing Horse* myself. Also bought a little mud house at the edge of town where I've lived ever since (off and on). In 1927–28, was again in California for a few months (Mill Valley, San Francisco) working for Californians, Inc., doing a monthly column for *Sunset Magazine* and biographical sketches for them.

"In the Thirties, back to Taos again, was editor of the *Taos Valley*

News for several years, then went to Santa Fe, where I managed the Villagra Bookshop for a friend who had bought it. Built a house in Santa Fe, but returned to Taos in '37.

"In 1938–39, printed a minute newspaper called *The Horse Fly*, setting it up as well as printing it by hand in my own home printshop. Later, as World War II waxed, went to California and worked at Lockheed (Burbank) for a year or so.

"Then returned to Taos and was director of the Harwood Foundation (a branch of the University of New Mexico) for a couple of years.

"In 1948, Ted Cabot bought the Taos newspaper, changed its name to *El Crepusculo* and made me editor. I gradually eased my way out of this spot by disappearing on leaves of absence to Mexico and by 1950 was doing a feature page on the paper instead. This I called "The Horse Fly," after the baby newspaper of 1939, and am still writing it more or less regularly (although I spent six months in Europe in 1954 and sometimes spend as much as three months of a winter in Mexico—sometimes with Mabel and Tony Lujan, once with Lynn Riggs, once with Georgia O'Keefe)."

For his own history of his famous magazine, see Spud Johnson, "The Laughing Horse," in the *New Mexico Quarterly*, XXI (No. 2, Summer, 1951), 161–67. Mr. Johnson is also the author of *Horizontal Yellow* (1935), a volume of poetry on which he worked at Chapala in the spring of 1923.

The bibliography of Lawrence's contributions to *The Laughing Horse* follows:

"A Letter" [review of Ben Hecht's *Fantazius Malare*], *Laughing Horse* (No. 4, December, 1922). Reprinted as a letter to Willard Johnson ("Chère Jeunesse"), from Taos, New Mexico, dated "Early Autumn, 1922" [12 October 1922], in *Letters*, pp. 562–64.

"Au Revoir, U.S.A.," *Laughing Horse* (No. 8, December, 1923). Reprinted in *Phoenix*, pp. 104–6.

"Dear Old Horse: A London Letter," *Laughing Horse* (No. 10, May, 1924). Reprinted as a letter to Willard Johnson, from 110, Heath St., Hampstead, N.W. 3, dated 9 January 1924, in *Letters*, pp. 598–601.

"The Bad Girl in the Pansy Bed" [drawing], *Laughing Horse* (No. 10, May, 1924). Lawrence's drawing illustrated a poem of the same name by Mrs. Mabel Dodge Luhan, for which see Luhan, pp. 95–97.

"Just Back from the Snake-Dance—Tired Out," *Laughing Horse* (No. 11, September, 1924). Reprinted as a letter to Willard Johnson, undated, in *Letters*, pp. 615–18.

"A Little Moonshine with Lemon," *Laughing Horse* (No. 13, D. H. Lawrence number, April, 1926). Reprinted as the final essay in *Mornings in Mexico.*

"Mediterranean in January" [poem], *Laughing Horse* (No. 13, D. H. Lawrence number, April, 1926). Not reprinted. See Tedlock, p. 101.

"Europe versus America," *Laughing Horse* (No. 13, D. H. Lawrence number, April, 1926). Reprinted in *Phoenix*, pp. 117–18.

"Beyond the Rockies" [poem], *Laughing Horse* (No. 13, D. H. Lawrence number, April, 1926). Not reprinted. See Tedlock, p. 101.

"Paris Letter," *Laughing Horse* (No. 13, D. H. Lawrence number, April, 1926). Reprinted in *Phoenix*, pp. 119–22.

"Pueblo Indian Dancers" [drawing], *Laughing Horse* (No. 13, D. H. Lawrence number, April, 1926). Reprinted in *Letters* (London: Heinemann, 1932).

"Susan the Cow" [excerpt from ". . . Love Was Once a Little Boy"], *Laughing Horse* (No. 15, March–July, 1928). ". . . Love Was Once a Little Boy" is included in *Reflections on the Death of a Porcupine* (December, 1925).

Altitude [unfinished play], *Laughing Horse* (No. 20, Summer, 1938). Not reprinted. See Tedlock, pp. 121–23.

Cover design for *Laughing Horse* (No. 26). Reproduced in Moore, *Intelligent Heart*. Concerning this cover design, Mr. Willard Johnson has written on a card (10 October 1956) to the editor: "Never saw the drawing in question before. Obviously it *was* made for a *Laughing Horse* cover, and possibly by Lawrence, but it was certainly never used, as he didn't even tell me he'd done it or was thinking of doing it. Very odd. It may have been made for *Laughing Horse* No. 13—the special D. H. Lawrence number—and then never sent because he delayed too long. *Quién sabe?*" Since there have been only twenty-one issues of *Laughing Horse*, the identification of the cover design as "(No. 26)" is an error. On a post card (18 November 1956) to the editor, Prof. Harry T. Moore has written: "I finally located the original [Lawrence drawing], which has a strip pasted over it . . . . When held up to the light, the original shows a number on the other side; this is 16, not 26 . . . ."

132 D. H. L. letter to Earl H. Brewster, from Jalisco, Mexico, dated 15 May [1923], Brewster, pp. 71–72.

133 Adapted into journal form from a letter written by Witter Bynner to Haniel Long, from Chapala, undated [early Summer, 1923], Bynner, p. 137.

134 D. H. L. letter to J. M. Murry, from Zaragoza 4, Chapala, Jalisco, Mexico, dated 26 May 1923, *Letters*, pp. 574–75.

135 D. H. L. letter (translated from the German) to Frieda's mother, Frau Baronin von Richthofen, from Zaragoza 4, Chapala, Jalisco, Mexico, dated "31 May, Corpus Christi Day" [1923], Frieda Lawrence, pp. 161–62.

136 D. H. L. letter to Knud Merrild, from Zaragoza #4, Chapala, Jalisco, Mexico, dated 4 June 1923, Merrild, p. 301.

137 From a personal letter (April, 1949) written by Frederic W. Leighton to Witter Bynner, Bynner, pp. 185–86. See also Mr. Leighton's "The Bite of Mr. Lawrence," *Laughing Horse* (No. 13, D. H. Lawrence number, April, 1926), 16–18.

138 Adapted into journal form from a letter written by Witter Bynner to Eunice Tietjens, from Chapala, undated [late June, 1923], Bynner, p. 165.

139 D. H. L. postscript to a letter from Frieda Lawrence to Knud Merrild, from Zaragoza 4, Chapala, dated "June 17, 1923 (dated by K. M.)," Merrild, p. 304. I have ventured the corrected date 24 June 1923 to make it conform more reasonably with the date of the return to Chapala on Wednesday, 27 June 1923, after "two days travelling on the lake." See Moore, *Poste Restante,* p. 71.

140 Entry in Lawrence's Diary.—Tedlock, p. 98. I have corrected the place-names as given: "Ocottan & Tirzapan."

141 The Lawrences' departure from Chapala was delayed. They were still there on 2 July 1923, and Lawrence was writing: "We are going up to New York next week . . . ."—*Letters,* p. 577. Their long canoe trip on Lake Chapala began on 6 July.—Bynner, pp. 167–68. See Moore, *Poste Restante,* pp. 71–72. They were in New Orleans, not New York, the weekend of 15 July 1923.—*Letters,* p. 577.

142 D. H. L. letter to Knud Merrild, from Chapala, dated "Wednesday. (Post-mark, 27 June, 1923)" [27 June 1923], *Letters,* pp. 575–76.

143 D. H. L. letter to Mrs. Bessie Freeman [from Zaragoza 4, Chapala, Jalisco, Mexico], dated 27 June 1923, Moore, *Intelligent Heart,* p. 317.

144 D. H. L. letter to M. L. Skinner, from Chapala, Jalisco, Mexico, dated 2 July 1923, *Letters,* p. 577.

145 Since embarkation was postponed a day because of a storm, the trip must have begun on 6 July 1923.—Bynner, pp. 167–68.

146 Adapted into journal form from a letter written by Witter Bynner to his mother, from Chapala, dated 4 July 1923, Bynner, p. 167.

147 "H. D.," pseudonym of Hilda Doolittle (1886——), American poet, abroad after 1911. Author of *Sea Garden* (1916), *Hymen* (1921), *Heliodora and Other Poems* (1924), *Collected Poems* (1925), *Hippolytus Temporizes,* a play (1927), *Red Roses for Bronze* (1932), *The Walls Do Not Fall* (1944), *Tribute to the Angels* (1945), *The Flowering of the Rod* (1946). Her marriage (18 October 1913) to Richard Aldington ended in divorce.

148 The quarterly *Palms: A Magazine of Poetry* ran from the Spring, 1923, issue to the March/April, 1940, issue (suspended from June, 1930, to October, 1936). It was edited by Idella Purnell Stone from Spring, 1923, to May, 1930; by Elmer Nicholas from November, 1936, to April, 1940; and by others. See Frederick J. Hoffman, Charles Allen, and Carolyn F. Ulrich, *The Little Magazine: A History and a Bibliography* (Princeton, New Jersey: Princeton University Press, 1946), p. 266.

149 The bibliography of Lawrence's contributions to *Palms* follows:
"Nostalgia," *Palms,* I (No. III, Midsummer, 1923), 68. It appeared as an anonymous poem, the identification made in *Palms,* I (No. IV, Autumn, 1923), 124, with an editor's footnote: "NOSTALGIA is one of several poems which Mr. Lawrence in good faith gave to the editors of Palms. He had either forgotten its appearance in *Poetry* [February, 1919] several years ago, or considered our version of it a different

poem. We offer our innocent apologies to the editors of *Poetry*." (See *Letters*, p. 594.) "Nostalgia" was awarded an honorable mention in a contest to determine the best poem in the first six numbers of *Palms*. The judges were Jessie B. Rittenhouse, John Farrar, and Genevieve Taggard. See *Palms*, II (No. II, Midsummer, 1924), 63. The poem had been printed in *Bay* (1919), and again in *The New Poetry*, ed. by Harriet Monroe and Alice C. Henderson (New York: Macmillan, 1 May 1923), and was reprinted in *Collected Poems*, I.

"Autumn in New Mexico," *Palms*, I (No. IV, Autumn, 1923), 99–100. It appeared as an anonymous poem, the identification made in *Palms*, I (No. V, Christmas, 1923), 155. As "Autumn in Taos," the poem had appeared in *Birds, Beasts and Flowers* (New York: Seltzer, 9 October 1923; London: Secker, November, 1923), and is reprinted in *Collected Poems*, II.

"A Britisher Has a Word with an Editor," *Palms*, I (No. V, Christmas, 1923), 153–54. It appeared as an anonymous essay in reply to Harriet Monroe's "The Editor in England," in *Poetry*, XXIII (No. I, October, 1923), 32–45. Lawrence's authorship of this short essay is verified by Mrs. Idella Purnell Stone in a letter (18 April 1956) to the editor. The essay is reprinted in the present work, below.

"A Year of Christmas," *Palms*, I (No. V, Christmas, 1923), [160]. Lawrence's revised version, printed anonymously, of Idella Purnell Stone's advertisement. Lawrence's authorship of the revised version is verified by Mrs. Idella Purnell Stone in a letter (18 April 1956) to the editor. See the two drafts printed in the present work, below. With variations, the advertisement is repeated in *Palms*, II (No. V, Christmas, 1924), [160] and III (No. III, Christmas, 1925), 96.

"Four Poems" (consisting of "Bombardment," "After the Opera," "The Little Town at Evening," and "Last Hours"), *Palms*, II (No. V, Christmas, 1924), 146–49. They appeared as anonymous poems, the identification made in *Palms*, II (No. VI, Early 1925), 185. "After the Opera" had been printed in the *English Review* (June, 1918); "The Little Town at Evening" in the *Monthly Chapbook* (July, 1919); all four poems were included in *Bay* (1919) and reprinted in *Collected Poems*, I.

Advertisement for Witter Bynner's *Caravan*, *Palms*, III (No. II, November, 1925), 64. An ingenious arrangement of the letters that spell *Caravan*. Lawrence's name does not appear on the page, but the design was identified as the work of Lawrence by Mrs. Idella Purnell Stone in a letter (17 May 1956) to the editor.

150 A reference to Mr. Bynner's collection of poems *The New World* (1915).

151 For Witter Bynner's poems on Lawrence, see his *Journey with Genius*, where they have been conveniently collected from two volumes: "Lorenzo," in Bynner, pp. 147–48, and "D. H. Lawrence," in Bynner, pp. 325–27, both previously published in *Caravan* (1925); and "A Foreigner," in Bynner, p. 182, previously published in *Indian Earth* (1929), a volume dedicated to Lawrence.

152 A young American named Taylor, manager of the Y.MC.A. in Mexico City,

was on vacation with his wife and children at the Hotel Arzapalo at Chapala.—Bynner, p. 117.

153 Witter Bynner had been troubled by an infected fistula. See Bynner, pp. 173–77.

154 Mr. Winfield Scott, "an American who had married and outlived a Mexican wife, was manager of the Arzapalo Hotel, and he and his daughter, Margaret, occupied front rooms in the west wing of the ground floor . . . ."—Bynner, p. 117. Mr. Scott provided the prototype of Mr. Bell in *The Plumed Serpent.* See Bynner, pp. 123–28.

155 Mrs. Idella Purnell Stone's adaptation (August, 1956) of a series of letters she had written to Witter Bynner, and published as such in Bynner, pp. 84, 115, 118, 138–39, 139–40, 168–69, 169, 169–70, 171, 171–72, 293, 298, 179.

In a letter (26 March 1956) to the editor, Mrs. Idella Purnell Stone has written the following notes for her father and herself:

"My father, Dr. George E. Purnell, was born in Snow Hill, Maryland, 28 March 1863. He was one of the first graduates of the first dental college in the United States, the University of Maryland. He first went to Missouri to practice dentistry, then to California. In 1889, when there was a severe depression in California, he went to Mexico for a brief vacation. He remained in Guadalajara, Mexico, practicing dentistry there for the next fifty years or so, and then spent another ten years or so supervising his interests in a mine and a ranch. He came to live with us in Sierra Madre, California, in about 1948, but still commutes to Mexico by bus and plane two or three times yearly to look after his interests down there—he's really quite a character. I am more or less expecting him back from his current trip today or tomorrow—he means to make it back for his 93rd birthday party. He married in Mexico, and had three children: Idella, Frances-Lee, Ralph.

"So I was born in Guadalajara, Mexico, in 1901, and grew up there, until sent to school in Baltimore, Los Angeles, and the University of California. At the University of California, I met Witter Bynner when I was the youngest person (and the only freshman) admitted to his poetry class. I acquired a very deep and abiding affection for him, as all his students did, and when upon graduation I returned to Mexico in 1922 I began writing him to come down on a visit. I was very hungry for intellectual contacts; Guadalajara at that time was an arid desert. I began my poetry magazine *Palms* in the spring of 1923 largely to "create my own environment" after reading Darwin's *Origin of Species!* I was working as a secretary in the American Consulate at Guadalajara and so had a small salary wherewith to support this venture. *Palms* had excellent acceptance and was considered by some people the *best* poetry magazine, by others, second or third best. I published in it nothing of my own, except an occasional editorial. In 1927 I married unhappily, and *Palms* was transplanted to Aberdeen, Wash. But I returned to Mexico in 1928, and in April 1928 I had my first child. She died in May 1929, and I returned to Aberdeen for a few months, then went to New York. I published *Palms* one more year and gave it up in May 1930. By then I was writing children's books: *The Talking Bird, Why the Bee Is Busy, The Wishing Owl, Little Yusuf, The Forbidden City, The Lost Princess of Yucatan, The Merry Frogs, Pedro the Potter, Bambi,* etc. In 1931, I returned to Guadalajara. In 1932, I was the organizer and dean of the first summer session of the University of Guadalajara. I married Remington Stone in September 1932, and moved back to New York. Our daughter Marijane was born in 1934, and when she was fourteen months old I took her to Mexico to operate a gold mine in Ameca, Jalisco, while Remi remained in New York to finance it. Marijane and I both had violent illnesses, as did my father, and so Remi came down to run the mine. In 1937 Marijane and I came to Los Angeles for better medical aid, and Remi had to give up the mine and come north when the Mexican government began its expropriations of foreign-owned properties. Our son Remington was born in 1938, and my brother's child became a part of our family in 1948. In 1950, I became interested in dianetics, studied it, and became a professional. auditor. I opened a Center in Pasadena in 1951, and moved it to Sierra Madre in 1956.

"One of my books, a biography of Luther Burbank, has been translated into Spanish for publication by Espasa-Calpe as soon as Gabriela Mistral (who won the Nobel Prize for Literature in 1945) writes a foreword for it."

See also Idella Purnell's "Black Magic," a review of Lawrence's *Birds, Beasts and Flowers, Laughing Horse* (No. 13, D. H. Lawrence number, April, 1926), 19–22.

156 D. H. L. postcard to Witter Bynner, from "somewhere in Texas," undated [? July 1923], Bynner, p. 187.

157 D. H. L. letter (card?) to Catherine Carswell, from New Orleans, dated "Sunday, July, 1923" [15 July 1923], *Letters*, p. 577.

158 D. H. L. letter to Knud Merrild, from Hotel de Sota, New Orleans, La., dated "Sunday (Postmark, 15 July, 1923)" [15 July 1923], *Letters*, pp. 577–78.

159 Except for brief excursions into New York City, the Lawrences spent late July and early August, 1923, at Thomas Seltzer's cottage (known as "Mr. Hammerslaugh's Cottage") at Union Hill, Dover, New Jersey, "near Morris Plains, on the Lackawanna line, and 'behind the millionaire Coffin's house.'"—Moore, *Poste Restante*, p. 72; *Intelligent Heart*, p. 319. During this period, Lawrence continued to use Thomas Seltzer's business address in New York City—and apparently Thomas Seltzer's stationery as well.

160 D. H. L. letter to Mrs. [Bessie] Freeman, from c/o Thomas Seltzer, 5, W. 50th St., New York, Moore, *Intelligent Heart*, p. 319.

161 The Lawrences' Australian friend Mrs. A. L. Jenkins of Perth was again in London, where she had hoped to meet them. With Lawrence's holograph letter before me, I have provided a text which differs somewhat from that given by Mr. H. E. L. Priday in *Southerly* [Sydney, Australia], 15 (No. 1, 1954), 7.

162 D. H. L. letter (translated from the German) to Frieda's mother, Frau

Baronin von Richthofen, from "Care of Seltzer, 5 West 50th Street, New York City," dated 7 August 1923, Frieda Lawrence, p. 163.

163 D. H. L. letter to J. M. Murry, from "Care Seltzer, 5, W. 50th St., New York," dated 7 August 1923, *Letters,* pp. 578–79.

164 D. H. L. letter to Knud Merrild, from "Care Seltzer, 5, W. 50th St., New York," dated 7 August 1923, *Letters,* pp. 579–80.

165 From a letter (1949) written by Mrs. Bernardine Fritz to Witter Bynner, Bynner, p. 187.

166 D. H. L. letter to Witter Bynner, from "Care Seltzer, 5, West 50th St., New York," dated 14 August 1923, *Letters,* pp. 581–82.

167 D. H. L. letter to Amy Lowell, from "N. Jersey," dated 18 August [1923], Damon, pp. 639–40.

168 D. H. L. "note" to Knud Merrild, from Buffalo, dated 22 August [1923], Merrild, pp. 311–12.

169 I.e., Mabel Dodge Luhan and Nina Wilcox (later Mrs. Harry Bull, later Mrs. Lee Witt), both from Buffalo.

170 D. H. L. letter to Mrs. [Bessie] Freeman, from the Los Angeles Limited, dated " 'Tuesday' [Aug. 28, 1923]," Moore, *Intelligent Heart,* p. 320.

171 D. H. L. letter to M. L. Skinner, from The Miramar, Santa Monica, Cal., dated 2 September 1923, *Letters,* p. 583. For a detailed memoir of Lawrence's stay in California (30 August—25 September, 1923) with Knud Merrild and Kai Gótzsche, see Merrild, pp. 291–330. See also Moore, *Poste Restante,* pp. 73–74.

172 D. H. L. postcard to Willard Johnson, from Los Angeles, dated 12 September 1923, *Letters,* p. 584. I have supplied the street address (Grand Avenue) from Merrild, p. 319. Prof. Harry T. Moore gives 628 West 27th Street as the address.—Moore, *Poste Restante,* p. 73.

173 In a letter (2 May 1956) to the editor, Jeanne d'Orge (Mrs. Carl Cherry) provided the following identifications for the names mentioned at the beginning of her memoir: *The Remsens:* "Mr. and Mrs. Ira Remsen. Ira Remsen, writer and painter, deceased, is survived by his wife Jody— now Mrs. Howard Johnson. Lawrence came to Lompoc for the eclipse with the Remsens." *James Worthington:* "English astronomer." *Dr. Burton:* "Dr. Alfred E. Burton. Dean of Massachusetts Institute of Technology. Deceased. (I was Mrs. Burton at the time of the Lawrence episode.)" *The Josselyns:* "Brothers. Mr. Talbot Josselyn, writer, survives. He is still living in Carmel." *Henry Williams:* "Writer, still living in Carmel."

174 Miss d'Orge's mistaken reference to Knud Merrild and Kai Gótzsche, both Danish painters.

175 d'Orge, in Supplement to *The Carmelite,* III (No. 6, 19 March 1930), xiv–xvi. Miss d'Orge's article is also reprinted in Merrild, pp. 316–18.

176 D. H. L. letter to J. M. Murry, from Los Angeles, dated 24 September 1923, *Letters,* p. 585.

177 Original publication. The "Mrs. Dr. Burton" to whom Lawrence referred in this letter is Jeanne d'Orge (now Mrs. Carl Cherry). See Note 173, above.

178 Lawrence's visit to the silver mine may have provided him with material

for "The Woman Who Rode Away." See also *Letters*, p. 586; Merrild, pp. 333–34.

179 Adapted into journal form from letters written by Mr. Kai Gótzsche to Knud Merrild, and published as such in Merrild, pp. 332, 334–35, 336–39. The original letters, written in Danish, were translated into English by Knud Merrild.

180 Note that Mr. Gótzsche dated the arrival at Guadalajara 15 October 1923, whereas Lawrence dated the arrival 17 October. Because there are extant three letters written by Lawrence on 17 October, in two of which he mentions arriving "today," the error may lie in Mr. Gótzsche's original letter. The confusion is the greater because of Lawrence's letter of Saturday, 13 October 1923, written from Tepic, Nayarit, in which he observed: "We should be in Guadalajara on Tuesday [16 October] . . . ."—Merrild, p. 336. See Moore, *Poste Restante*, p. 75.

181 D. H. L. letter to Earl H. Brewster, from Hotel Garcia, Guadalajara (Jalisco), Mexico, dated 17 October 1923, Brewster, pp. 73–74.

182 Probably a reference to Harry R. Johnson and his family at Brentwood, Los Angeles, California. A consulting geologist, Mr. Johnson had given Knud Merrild and Kai Gótzsche their board and room in exchange for decorating his upstairs library, and Lawrence had met the Johnsons while in California. See Merrild, pp. 309 ff.

183 Adapted into journal form from letters written by Mr. Kai Gótzsche to Knud Merrild, and published as such in Merrild, pp. 339–41, 342–44. The original letters, written in Danish, were translated into English by Knud Merrild.

184 D. H. L. letter to J. M. Murry, from Hotel Garcia, Guadalajara, Jal., dated 25 October 1923, *Letters*, p. 588.

185 See *Palms*, II (No. II, Midsummer, 1924). Mr. Bynner himself was the guest editor of *Palms*, III (No. I, Summer, 1925).

186 I have been unable to identify the issues of *Palms* for which Lawrence designed the covers. In a letter (11 April 1957) to the editor, Mr. Witter Bynner recalled that he "as well as D. H. designed several of the covers for *Palms*."

187 Mrs. Idella Purnell Stone's adaptation (August, 1956) of a series of letters she had written to Witter Bynner, and published as such in Bynner, pp. 194–95.

188 See H[arriet] M[onroe], "The Editor in England," in *Poetry: A Magazine of Verse*, XXIII (No. I, October, 1923), 32–45.

189 Printed anonymously, Lawrence's little essay originally appeared as "A Britisher Has a Word with an Editor," in *Palms*, I (No. V, Christmas, 1923), 153–54. As originally printed, the first sentence reads: "In October's *Poetry*, the Editor tells what a real tea-party she had in Britain, among the poets: not a Bostonian one, either."

190 The projected advertisement for *Palms*, on which Lawrence collaborated with Mrs. Idella Purnell Stone, appeared as "A Year of Christmas," in *Palms*, I (No. V, Christmas, 1923), [60]. Mrs. Stone's original typewritten

version of the advertisement was amended by Lawrence in pencil. I have provided the text of each version separately to facilitate the problem in typography involved. See also Note 149, above.

191 Adapted into journal form from a letter written by Mr. Kai Gótzsche to Knud Merrild, and published as such in Merrild, pp. 344–45. The original letter, written in Danish, was translated into English by Knud Merrild.

192 In a letter (2 December 1953) to the editor, Mr. William McLean of Claremont, Western Australia, has pointed out that *The Boy in the Bush* had already been used as the title for an Australian novel written by Richard Rowe (Edward Howe) (London: Bell & Daldy, 1869). It was re-issued with the subtitle *Tale of Australian Life* (London: Hodder & Stoughton, 1885). See E. Morris Miller and F. T. Macartney, *Australian Literature* (1940, rev. 1956).

193 The original title of the Skinner MS had been *The House of Ellis.* See *Letters,* pp. 583, 591–92.

194 D. H. L. letter to M. L. Skinner, from Hotel Garcia, Guadalajara, Jal., Mexico, dated 1 November 1923, *Letters,* p. 590.

195 See *Letters,* p. 583.

196 See *Letters,* p. 583.

197 See *Letters,* p. 583.

198 See *Letters,* p. 590.

199 See *Letters,* p. 590.

200 See *Letters,* p. 591, and Note 192, above.

201 In a letter (4 December 1953) to the editor, Mr. David Garnett, son of Edward Garnett, wrote: "My copy of *The Boy in the Bush* has the passages which D. H. L. interpolated into Miss Skinner's book marked with red chalk by Miss Skinner at my father's request. He had no doubt this was accurate."

202 Skinner, "D. H. Lawrence and *The Boy in the Bush,*" in *Meanjin* [The University of Melbourne, Carlton, N.3, Victoria], 9 (No. 4, Summer, 1950), 260–63.

203 See Aldington, *Portrait of a Genius,* p. 326.

204 Presumably Humbert Wolfe's "D. H. Lawrence in the Wilderness," in *The Weekly Westminster* (27 September 1924). See McDonald, p. 144. I have been unable to verify this source.

205 The exact quotation reads: "We have written throughout as if the novel were all Mr. Lawrence's work. Whatever Mr. Skinner's share in it may be, the best and the worst of it are the best and the worst of Mr. Lawrence. And the best is Mr. Lawrence's very best."—*The Times Literary Supplement* (No. 1180, 28 August 1924), 523.

206 See Gerald Gould, "New Fiction," in *The Saturday Review,* 138 (No. 3593, 6 September 1924), 244.

207 See Murry, *Son of Woman,* p. 262.

208 Katharine Susannah Prichard has quoted here from an unpublished Lawrence letter to Mollie Skinner, written from the Hotel Beau Rivage, Bandol, Var., France, and dated 3 December 1928.

209 On this manuscript, see Chap. II, Note 47, above.

210 Prichard, in *Meanjin* [The University of Melbourne, Carlton, N.3, Victoria], 9 (No. 4, Summer, 1950), 256–59.

211 D. H. L. letter to Knud Merrild, from Hotel Garcia, Guadalajara, Jal., dated 3 November 1923, Merrild, p. 346.

212 D. H. L. letter (translated from the German) to Frieda's mother, Frau Baronin von Richthofen, from Hotel Garcia, Guadalajara, Jalisco, Mexico, dated 10 November 1923, Frieda Lawrence, pp. 142–43.

213 Original publication.

214 D. H. L. letter to S. S. Koteliansky, from Hotel Garcia, Guadalajara, Jal., dated 10 November 1923, *Encounter 3*, I (No. 3, December, 1953), 33.

215 Lawrence and Kai Gótzsche had arrived in Mexico City the morning of 17 November 1923. See *Letters*, p. 592.

216 See Lawrence's letter to Witter Bynner, from Hotel Monte Carlo, dated 17 November 1923: "Tonight we're going out to dinner with the Brit. Consul-General at Tlalpam—all in evening dress. How's that for committing suicide on the spot? My dinner-jacket is so green with over-ripeness—I'm going to look for Covarrubias."—*Letters*, pp. 592–93.

217 Adapted into journal form from letters written by Mr. Kai Gótzsche to to Knud Merrild, and published as such in Merrild, pp. 347–48, 349–50. The original letters, written in Danish, were translated into English by Knud Merrild.

218 D. H. L. letter to Willard Johnson, from Hotel Monte Carlo, Mexico, dated 19 November [1923], *Letters*, p. 593.

219 D. H. L. postcard to Knud Merrild, from Havana, dated 25 November [1923], Merrild, p. 351. For fleeting impressions of Havana, see Lawrence's *St. Mawr* (1925), and the unfinished novel *The Flying Fish*, Part 3, "The Atlantic," in *Phoenix*, pp. 795–97.

CHAPTER IV

1 D. H. L. letter to Witter Bynner, from 110, Heath St., Hampstead, N.W. 3, dated 7 December 1923, *Letters*, p. 597.

2 Murry, *Reminiscences*, pp. 110–14.

3 See Frieda Lawrence Ravagli: "But I think [Lawrence] was right; I should have gone to meet him in Mexico, he should not have come to Europe; these are the mistakes we make, sometimes irreparable."—Frieda Lawrence, p. 144.

4 See Catherine Carswell: "An illuminating commentary is provided by the short story 'The Border Line,' which Lawrence wrote not long afterwards." —Carswell, p. 202, note. Lawrence wrote "The Border Line" in February, 1924, during his brief stay at Baden-Baden. It was originally published in *Smart Set* (September, 1924) and *Hutchinson's Magazine* (September, 1924), and included in *The Woman Who Rode Away*.—McDonald, p. 126; *Supplement*, [93].

5 Possibly a reference to Luhan, p. 165.

6 See Catherine Carswell, "Duse," in *The Adelphi*, I (No. 3, August, 1923), 238–41.

7 For Lawrence's sketch of the projected novel, see Carswell, pp. 211–14.

8 Carswell, pp. 201–8, 209–11.

9 D. H. L. letter (translated from the German) to Frieda's mother, Frau Baronin von Richthofen, from 110 Heath Street, Hampstead, London, N.W. 3, dated 14 December 1923, Frieda Lawrence, p. 164.

10 Original publication.

11 See Merrild, p. 321.

12 Original publication of an installment of a memoir completed in 1954.

13 See *Letters,* pp. 602, 603, 603–4.

14 See Murry, *Reminiscences,* p. 112.

15 I.e., in the original version of Mr. Murry's "Reminiscences of D. H. Lawrence—VI," in *The New Adelphi,* I (No. 5, February, 1931), 413–20. In his book of the same title, Mr. Murry made his rebuttal to Mrs. Carswell's account of the Café Royal dinner. See Murry, *Reminiscences,* pp. 190–95, reprinted below.

16 See Luhan, pp. 130–31.

17 The Oxon. home of Lady Ottoline and Philip Morrell.

18 See Robert Burns's "On the Late Captain Grose's Peregrinations thro' Scotland," Stanza I.

19 John Oliver Hobbes, pseudonym of Pearl Mary Teresa Craigie (1867–1906), American-born English novelist and dramatist. Author of the novels *The Sinner's Comedy* (1892), *The Herb Moon* (1896), etc., and of plays, including *The Ambassador* (1892, produced 1898).

20 See Luhan, pp. 13–14.

21 See Luhan, p. 17.

22 Carswell, pp. 214–24.

23 See Murry, *Son of Woman,* p. 388.

24 See Carswell, p. 222, reprinted above.

25 See *Letters,* pp. 636–37.

26 Murry, *Reminiscences,* pp. 190–92.

27 Miss Brett's entire *Lawrence and Brett* is written *to* Lawrence. In her memoirs, the pronoun *you* therefore is to be read as *Lawrence.*

28 Boris Anrep (fl. 1920–1930), Russian mosaicist in England. His works include a pavement in the National Gallery, London, one in the Tate Gallery, London, and one in the Greek Cathedral, London.

29 Edna May (1878–1917), actress, born Edna May Pettie in Syracuse, N.Y., appeared in the role of Violet Gray in *The Belle of New York* in New York and London. She married Frederick Titus, later (1907) Oscar Lewisohn. She retired from the stage in 1907, died 13 December 1917. The anecdote of her meeting with Lawrence in Dorothy Brett's studio belongs, presumably, to the period November–December, 1915.

30 John William Navin Sullivan (1886–1937), English writer on scientific subjects, had served in the Censorship Department under John Middleton Murry during World War I, and by 1917 was contributing to the *Athenaeum, Nature,* and *TLS,* and, later, to Murry's *Adelphi.* He was also the author of *An Attempt at Life* (1917), *Aspects of Science* (1923),

Three Men Discuss Relativity (1926), *Beethoven* (1927), *But for the Grace of God* (1932), etc. See *Letters*, pp. 694, 698.

31 Brett, pp. 19–25.

32 D. H. L. letter to Mabel Dodge Luhan, from 110 Heath St., Hampstead, N.W. 3, dated 19 December [1923], Luhan, p. 130.

33 Brett, pp. 25–28.

34 Mrs. Sarah Gertrude Millin has written: "Katherine Mansfield's was the first criticism I ever saw of a book of mine, and she was the first writer who ever communicated with me. She wrote to ask if I would contribute to the *Athenaeum* and I did."—Millin, p. 19. Katherine Mansfield's review of Mrs. Millin's *The Dark River* had appeared in *The Athenaeum* (No. 4686, 20 February 1920), 241. For a letter from Katherine Mansfield to Mrs. Millin concerning the novel, see Millin, p. 119. See also Sarah Gertrude Millin, "A Pair of Button Shoes," in *The Athenaeum* (No. 4714, 3 September 1920), 294–95.

35 Millin, pp. 152, 154–55, 156–58. Mrs. Sarah Gertrude Millin, nee Liebson (1889———), distinguished South African writer, had, by the time of her meeting with Lawrence, written *The Dark River* (1920), *Adam's Rest* (1922), *The Jordans* (1923). Since then, she has written many more books, including her well-known history *The South Africans* (1926, rev. 1934, rev. 1951), the novels *God's Stepchildren* (1924), *What Hath a Man* (1938), *King of the Bastards* (1949), *The Burning Man* (1952), the biographies *Rhodes, a Life* (1933) and *General Smuts* (1936), two volumes of autobiography, *The Night Is Long* (1941) and *The Measure of My Days* (1955). Her husband, Philip Millin, died in 1952.

I am confused as to the exact dating of Mrs. Millin's meeting with the Lawrences. In her autobiography *The Night Is Long*, she gives the chronology of her stay in England as folllows: She and her husband "sailed for Europe at the end of 1923," spent Christmas Day at Brighton with a South African friend, journeyed to Mentone at the recommendation of John Middleton Murry, and then met Lawrence when she and her husband returned to England. In a letter (22 July 1956) to the editor, Mrs. Millin repeats this chronology: "If I remember, we went to Brighton for Xmas in 1923—our first visit overseas. We met Murry before that and he advised us to go to Mentone. On our return we met the Lawrences etc. and spent an evening with them. We invited the whole party to our hotel and when Lawrence said he had not yet been to the Midlands I said, as I have described in *The Night Is Long*, that he could always go to the Midlands but we were leaving for S. Africa next week, and he answered 'Very well. I'll give up the Midlands.' So clearly he came to us before going to the Midlands upon his return from Mexico."

This would seem to place the meetings in January or February, 1924. But to the best of my knowledge, Lawrence went to the Midlands only once during this 1923–1924 visit. He was in London as late as 27 December 1923, but by 31 December was at Nottingham.—Moore, *Poste Restante*, p. 76. Perhaps Mrs. Millin confused her imminent departure for Mentone with that for South Africa, as she looked back upon the events involved. The Sunday night party might have fallen on 30 December 1923, and Lawrence may have postponed his visit to the Midlands until the following day in order that he might accept the Millins' dinner invitation before they left for Mentone.

Of the Lawrences, Mrs. Millin has written elsewhere: "We found them very kind, but rather childish and queer. One could never have judged from Lawrence's talk that he was a great writer. Phil thought him an unwholesome person and when, many years later, I came upon *Lady Chatterley's Lover* in Phil's collar drawer, he asked me not to read it. 'I borrowed it yesterday, but I've given up reading it myself. It's not literature. It's obscenity. So I don't want you to read it.' And even when I had brought Shaw and Smuts together one day in Cape Town and Shaw, thinking to startle Smuts, said every schoolgirl of sixteen should read *Lady Chatterley's Lover;* to which Smuts, knowing about neither Lawrence nor Lady Chatterley, said politely, 'Of course. Of course'— even then I was not tempted to read this book Phil thought obscenity, not literature.

.   .   .   .

"I thought Lawrence, however, when I first read him, a great writer. I don't know what I would think now. I have lately re-read Katherine Mansfield. She lives."—Sarah Gertrude Millin, *The Measure of My Days* (New York: Abelard-Schuman, 1955), pp. 90–91.

36 Dr. James Carruthers Young. See his article "An Experiment at Fountaine-bleau—A Personal Reminiscence," in *The New Adelphi,* I (No. 1, September, 1927), 26–40.

37 Included in *The Woman Who Rode Away.*

38 Brett, pp. 28–30.

39 D. H. L. letter to Mabel Dodge Luhan, from 110 Heath St., Hampstead, N.W. 3, dated 27 December 1923, Luhan, pp. 131–32.

40 Unpublished D. H. L. letter to Frederick Carter, from Nottingham, dated 1 January 1924, Moore, *Poste Restante,* p. 77.

41 See Frederick Carter, *The Dragon of the Alchemists,* With an introduction by Arthur Machen (London: E. Mathews, October, 1926). The work is a book of drawings with prefatory essays on comparative symbolism.

42 See Frederick Carter, "The Ancient Science of Astrology," in *The Adelphi,* I (No. 11, April, 1924), 997–1005.

43 Carter, pp. 5, 33–42. Frederick Carter, English painter and etcher, was born near Bradford, Yorks., and was educated as a civil engineer and surveyor. At the age of nineteen, he went to Paris to continue his studies and turned to drawing. Upon his return to England, he worked for poster printers, and then resumed his studies, gaining three successive gold medals in the National Competition, South Kensington, for book illustrations. His published drawings and etchings decorate books by Cyril Tourneur, Byron's *Manfred,* Heine's *Florentine Nights.* He is the author of *Gold Like Glass* (1932); *The Dragon of Revelation* (1932), revised as

Symbols of Revelation (1934); etc. See also Frederick Carter's letter to the Editor, *The London Mercury*, XXII (No. 131, September, 1930), 451; and *Phoenix*, pp. xviii–xix.

In a letter (7 May 1952) to Harry T. Moore, Mr. Carter wrote of Lawrence's "'short visit to Pontesbury and discussion of Apocalyptic symbols there. From this came the landscape background of *St. Mawr* and the red horse itself. The duplicate authentic symbol of woman and dragon provided the motif of the following novel, *The Plumed Serpent.*'"—Moore, *Intelligent Heart*, p. 325.

44 Unpublished D. H. L. letter to Frederick Carter, from 110 Heath Street, Hampstead, dated "Sunday" [6 January 1924], Moore, *Poste Restante*, p. 77.

45 D. H. L. letter to Willard Johnson, from 110, Heath St., Hampstead, N.W. 3, dated 9 January 1924, *Letters*, p. 598.

46 Brett, pp. 30–32. See the opening scene of Lawrence's short story "The Last Laugh," included in *The Woman Who Rode Away*.

47 D. H. L. letter to Mabel Dodge Luhan, from 110 Heath St., Hampstead, N.W. 3, dated 9 January 1924, Luhan, p. 135.

48 D. H. L. letter to Mabel Dodge Luhan, from 110 Heath St., London N.W. 3, dated 22 January 1924, Luhan, p. 136.

49 D. H. L. letter to Catherine Carswell, from Hôtel de Versailles, Paris, dated 25 [or 24] January [1924], Moore, *Intelligent Heart*, p. 325.

50 Original publication.

51 D. H. L. letter to Catherine Carswell, from Hôtel de Versailles, Paris, dated 26 January 1924, Moore, *Intelligent Heart*, p. 325. See also Lawrence's "Paris Letter," originally printed in the *Laughing Horse* (No. 13, D. H. Lawrence number, April, 1926), and reprinted in *Phoenix*, pp. 119–22.

52 D. H. L. letter to J. M. Murry, from [c/o] Frau von Richthofen, Ludwig-Wilhelmstift, Baden-Baden, dated 7 February 1924, *Letters*, pp. 601–2.

53 See Lawrence's "A Letter from Germany," written on 18 February 1924 (see Moore, *Intelligent Heart*, p. 326), in *Phoenix*, pp. 107–10. His short story "The Border Line" was also written during this brief visit to Germany, and was later included in *The Woman Who Rode Away*. For comparisons of the two pieces of writing, see Anthony West, *D. H. Lawrence* (London: Arthur Barker, 1950), pp. 99–105.

54 D. H. L. letter to Mabel Dodge Luhan, from Baden-Baden, dated 9 February [1924], Luhan, p. 140.

55 Original publication.

56 D. H. L. letter to Mabel Dodge Luhan, from Baden-Baden, dated 19 February [1924], Luhan, p. 151.

57 D. H. L. letter (translated from the German) to Frieda's mother, Frau Baronin von Richthofen, from Paris, Hôtel de Versailles, 60 Boulevard Montparnasse, dated "Saturday" [23 February 1924], Frieda Lawrence, p. 165.

58 D. H. L. letter to Mabel Dodge Luhan, from Garland's Hotel, Suffolk Street, Pall Mall, S.W. 1, dated 29 February 1924, Luhan, p. 153.

59 Murry, *Reminiscences,* pp. 186, 193–95.
60 Brett, pp. 32–33.
61 Murry, *Reminiscences,* pp. 195–96.
62 Brett, pp. 33–34.
63 D. H. L. letter to J. M. Murry, from Cunard R.M.S. "Aquitania," dated 10 March [1924], *Letters,* p. 605.

CHAPTER V

1 D. H. L. postscript, dated "Tuesday afternoon" [11 March 1924], to a letter to J. M. Murry, from Cunard R.M.S. "Aquitania," dated 10 March [1924], *Letters,* pp. 605–6.
2 D. H. L. letter to Harriet Monroe, from c/o Thomas Seltzer, 219 West 100th St., New York City, dated 12 March 1924, *Letters,* p. 606.
3 See *Letters,* p. 594.
4 See *Letters,* p. 606.
5 See *Letters,* p. 716.
6 Monroe, in *Poetry,* XXXIV (No. II, May, 1930), 92–94.
7 Adapted into journal form from a letter written by Witter Bynner to his mother, from Santa Fe, dated 21 March 1924, Bynner, p. 247.
8 D. H. L. letter to Harriet Monroe, from Taos, New Mexico, dated 8 April 1924, *Letters,* pp. 606–7.
9 Luhan, pp. 154, 164–67.
10 Brett, p. 49.
11 See Brett, pp. 127–28.
12 In the summer of 1923, Alice Sprague (see below), a friend in New York, sent Clarence Thompson out to Mrs. Luhan at Taos. The latter has written: "[The] instant he saw me standing in the doorway, he fell in love with me, or at least he thought he did. He was a tall, very graceful fellow, with a round, curly head and honey-colored eyes . . . ."—Luhan, p. 115. He spent the winter 1923–1924 in the neighborhood of Mrs. Luhan and Tony on Mount Tamalpais, across the bay from San Francisco. Mrs. Luhan then sent him to Europe to consult Jung; but, getting no farther than Paris, he ran out of money and returned to Taos. There he met Lawrence in the summer of 1924. To Dorothy Brett, he seemed "a tall, good-looking, delicate-featured young man in white, with his shirt sleeves rolled up to his shoulders and wearing many Indian rings and bracelets." —Brett, p. 92. Mrs. Luhan remembered that Clarence Thompson "began to turn all his attention upon Lorenzo," and that the two of them planned "to ride off into the desert on horseback and never be seen again!" (Said Frieda: "Just let them try it!")—Luhan, p. 222. And from Clarence Thompson, Mrs. Luhan learned that Lawrence was determined to *"kill"* her. (Said Mrs. Luhan: "It sounded true. It *was* true.")—Luhan, p. 230. For Mrs. Luhan's story of Clarence Thompson, the curious may consult Luhan, pp. 115–16, 141–47, 173, 207–8, 221–33, 237–41.
13 Of Alice Sprague Mrs. Luhan has written: "[She] was one of my earliest memories, dating back to twilights in Buffalo when, as a little girl, I

had seen her pass down Delaware Avenue in the dusk, more like a creature from one of my favorite books than a flesh-and-blood go-to-market-and-dance-at-the-Charity Ball woman, like all the others there. . . . She reminded me of Emily Brontë, William Blake, and the Virgin of the Rocks. She was another who preferred her own fantasies to the usual realities." It was Alice Sprague who introduced Mrs. Luhan to Maurice Sterne, later Mrs. Luhan's third husband. See Mabel Dodge Luhan, *Movers and Shakers* (New York: Harcourt, Brace, 1936), pp. 349–51. In the summer of 1923, Alice Sprague sent Clarence Thompson to Mrs. Luhan; and in the early summer of 1924, she herself came from New York to Taos to visit: "[Every] morning she walked across the alfalfa field in a full-skirted, white muslin dress, and with her graying hair parted and smoothed down, and her uptilted smile under her round brow, she looked like a drawing by Da Vinci. She was one of those who determinedly see only the best in anyone. . . . She continued to smile and smile and to consider Lorenzo an avatar, and Clarence [Thompson] a potential genius."—Luhan, pp. 208, 211.

14 See Brett, pp. 133–34.

15 Dr. Abraham Arden Brill (1874–1948) was Mrs. Luhan's psychiatrist, whose office was at 88 Central Park West, New York City. Born in Austria, he studied at New York University and at the College of Physicians and Surgeons at Columbia University, later became an assistant physician in the clinic of psychiatry at Zurich, Switzerland. He was the chief of the clinic in psychiatry, assistant professor in psychiatry, Post-Graduate Medical School, and lecturer on psychoanalysis and psycho-sexual sciences at Columbia University; lecturer on psychoanalysis and abnormal psychology, and clinical professor of psychiatry at New York University; the author of many books on psychoanalysis; a translator of Jung. For Mrs. Luhan on Dr. Brill, see *Movers and Shakers* (New York: Harcourt, Brace, 1936), pp. 505–12.

16 Luhan, pp. 167–68, 168–69, 171–75, 191–92. For further information on the history of the *Sons and Lovers* MS, see Luhan, pp. 242–44, 248–50; Frieda Lawrence, p. 144; Brett, p. 64.

17 Brett, pp. 63–64.

18 D. H. L. letter (translated from the German) to Frieda's mother, Frau Baronin von Richthofen, from Del Monte Ranch, Questa, New Mexico, mistakenly dated "26 October 1924" [6? October 1924], Frieda Lawrence, pp. 171–72.

19 Although Lawrence himself used "Del Monte Ranch, Questa, New Mexico" and occasionally "Del Monte Ranch, Valdez, New Mexico" as the return address for his letters mailed from the Lawrence ranch, I have used "Kiowa Ranch, San Cristobal, New Mexico" to identify it and to distinguish it from the Hawks' Del Monte Ranch. Mrs. Luhan has written: "Lorenzo immediately changed its name from the 'Flying Heart Ranch,' first to the name of the mountain it was on: 'Lobo,' which means wolf, and then to 'Kiowa.' "—Luhan, p. 195.

20 D. H. L. letter to Catherine Carswell, from Del Monte Ranch, Questa, New Mexico, dated 18 May 1924, *Letters*, pp. 609–10.

21 See Dorothy Brett: "I shocked a good lady here [Taos], who seemed to be somewhat overcome by what she called 'studying,' and intellectualism. She unfortunately asked me what were Lawrence's favourite books he read, so I told her that he really liked a magazine called *Adventure* the best, because he found honest straight stories of adventure and no affectations of intellectualism or style! She was so shocked she never forgave me or believed me, but it was true, because I took out a year's subscription of the magazine for him."—From a letter (6 March 1952) to the editor.

22 Presumably a reference to *Studies in Classic American Literature,* the fourth and fifth chapters of which are devoted to James Fenimore Cooper.

23 Brett, pp. 68–74, 80–82, 82–83, 84–85, 90–92, 95–97, 97–98, 99–100, 103–4.

24 Entry in Lawrence's Diary.—Tedlock, p. 98.

25 Mrs. Carnot K. Valiton, now a resident of Ontario, California.

26 Kai Gótzsche had designed the covers for *Palms,* I (No. V, Christmas, 1923), and II (No. I, Early Summer, 1924). Across the top of the cover of the former appeared the notice: "Revolutions May Delay Palms— But Do not End it!" (In an editorial, "Isolation," of a later issue, Mrs. Idella Purnell Stone has written: "Guadalajara was cut off from the rest of the world on December 5, 1923, and for nearly three months there was no communication except an occasional radio message. . . . Bombing planes flew over Guadalajara, machine-guns were fired, propaganda was dropped down, and armies, triumphant and defeated, marched in and out of the city. The Federal forces finally made their entry, and we were visited by President Obregon. Communications were normalized and mails came through."—*Palms,* I [No. VI, Early 1924], 191.)

27 Original publication.

28 D. H. L. letter to Earl H. Brewster, from Del Monte Ranch, Questa, New Mexico, dated 15 July 1924, Brewster, pp. 75–76.

29 Luhan, pp. 208–10. See also Brett, p. 87. Lawrence combined his impressions of the ceremonial cave at Arroyo Seco with those of the silver mines and landscape he had seen on his journey down into Mexico with Kai Gótzsche in the early autumn of 1923 (see Chap. III) for his story "The Woman Who Rode Away." In two installments each, the story was originally printed in *The Dial* (July and August, 1925) and *The New Criterion* (July, 1925, and January, 1926), and included as the title story in *The Woman Who Rode Away.*—McDonald, *Supplement,* [p. 93].

30 Bobby and Ted Gillett. Bobby was the younger daughter of Mr. and Mrs. A. D. Hawk, owners of the Del Monte Ranch; the sister of William ("Bill") Hawk, and of Betty Cottam, nee Hawk. In the summer of 1924, they were building an adobe house for themselves on Del Monte Ranch. Dorothy Brett has written: "Bobby is small and slim, boyish and wild, her dark, curly hair cut close, following closely the line of the back of her head. . . . How boyish she is in her neat riding breeches, white silk shirt, colored handkerchief knotted carelessly, loosely, in the western way; her dark gray, heavily fringed eyes; straight, slightly tilted nose;

big painted mouth; and the close, curly hair. There is courage and attraction in every line of her." Ted Gillett was her "tall, pale husband, genial and friendly . . . ."—Brett, pp. 112–13.

31 Dr. T. P. Martin, whom Mr. Witter Bynner has called "the self-styled 'American Consul in Taos.'"—Bynner, p. 249.

32 Brett, pp. 107, 113–14, 115–17, 123, 128–29, 132–33, 137–38, 139–41, 142–43.

33 D. H. L. postcard [?] to Frieda's sister, Dr. Else Jaffe-Richthofen, from Santa Fe, dated 14 August 1924, Frieda Lawrence, p. 170.

34 See Luhan, pp. 253–68. See also "Just back from the Snake Dance," *Laughing Horse* (No. 11, September, 1924), reprinted in *Letters*, pp. 615–18; and "The Hopi Snake Dance," in *Mornings in Mexico*.

35 D. H. L. letter to J. M. Murry, from Del Monte Ranch, Questa, New Mexico, dated 30 August [1924], *Letters*, p. 618.

36 "The Princess" was originally printed in three installments in *The Calendar of Modern Letters* (March, April, May, 1925), and included in the English edition of *St. Mawr.*—McDonald, *Supplement*, p. 93.

37 Brett, pp. 149–52.

38 D. H. L. letter to Ada Lawrence Clarke, from Del Monte Ranch, New Mexico, dated 31 August 1924, Ada Lawrence and Gelder, p. 103.

39 Original publication.

40 Entry in Lawrence's Diary.—Tedlock, pp. 98–99.

41 D. H. L. letter to J. M. Murry, from Del Monte Ranch, Questa, New Mexico, dated 3 October 1924, *Letters*, pp. 623–24.

42 Entry in Lawrence's Diary.—Tedlock, p. 99.

43 D. H. L. letter to Catherine Carswell, from Del Monte Ranch, Questa, New Mexico, dated 8 October 1924, *Letters*, pp. 625–26.

44 Entry in Lawrence's Diary.—Tedlock, p. 99.

45 Luhan, pp. 277–78.

46 Mr. Constantine G. Rickards, British Vice-Consul at Mexico City, and his brother, Edward A. Rickards, priest at Oaxaca. See the memoir by George E. Rickards, below.

47 D. H. L. letter to Witter Bynner, from Hotel Monte Carlo, Av. Uruguay, Mexico, D.F., dated only "Friday" [24 October 1924], *Letters*, p. 627.

48 From a letter (15 August 1956) to the editor.

49 See *Letters*, p. 629; Bynner, p. 252; Frieda Lawrence, pp. 147–48.

50 D. H. L. letter to Mabel Dodge Luhan, from Hotel Monte Carlo, Av. Uruguay, Mexico D.F., dated 29 October 1924, Luhan, pp. 279–80.

51 From a letter (3 August 1956) to the editor. Translated from the Spanish by Mrs. Lyle P. Freeman. Dr. Manuel Gamio (1883———), distinguished Mexican archeologist, took his B.A. at the University of Mexico (1903), his M.A. at Columbia University (1911), and has since been granted the Ph.D. (1921) and D. Litt. (1948). He has been Inspector General of Archaeological Monuments, Mexico (1913–1916); Director of Archaeology, Department of Agriculture, Mexico (1917–1924); and is now Director of Rural Population, Department of Agriculture, Mexico (1934—) and Director of the Instituto Indigenista Interamericano, Mexico. His

field research has included Atzcapotzalco and Chalchihuites, Mexico
(1906–1908); Ecuador and Colombia (1910); Teotihuacan Valley (1912–
1924). He is the author of *Forjando Patria* (1916); *Empiricism of Latin-
American Governments and the Empiricism of Their Relations with the
United States* (1919); *Guía para visita a la ciudad arqueológica de Teotihuacán* (1921); *The Present State of Anthropological Research in Mexico*
(1925); *Commentaries on the Indo-Iberic Countries of the Pacific* (1929);
Mexican Immigration to the United States (1930); *Comentarios sobre
la evalución de los pueblos latino-americanos* (1932); *Hacia un México
nuevo* (1935); *De Vidas Dolientes* (1937); *Algunas consideraciones sobre
la salubridad y la demografía en México* (1939); *Actividades del Instituto
indigenista interamericano* (1944); and compiler of *Mexican Immigrant:
His Life Story* (1931).

Mrs. Luhan had tried to persuade Lawrence to accept letters of introduction from her friend George Creel to President Plutarco Elías Calles
and Dr. Gamio, but he would have none of the arrangement. See Luhan,
pp. 217–21.

52 Genaro Estrada (1887–1937), Mexican diplomatist, was the Director of
Mexican Diplomatic History, Under-Secretary of Foreign Affairs (1924)
and Minister of Foreign Affairs (1927 and 1930), Minister to Portugal
and Turkey, President of the first Mexican delegation to the League of
Nations, Ambassador to Spain, etc. In 1931 he repudiated the Monroe
Doctrine in favor of the "Estrada Doctrine," now known as the *Doctrina
Mexicana,* which set forth that "every country is entitled to adopt its
own laws without foreign intervention" and that "recognition of a govern-
ment should be granted regardless of that government's origin."—*New
York Times* (30 September 1937). He was also the author of *Poetas
Nuevos de México* (1916); *Pero Galín* (1926); *Crucero* (1928); *Paso a
Nivel* (1933); *Ascension* (1934); *Un Siglo de Relacione Internationale
de México* (1935); *Picasso* (1936); *El Arte Mexicana en España* (1936),
etc.

53 D. H. L. letter to Witter Bynner, from Hotel Monte Carlo, Av. Uruguay,
Mexico, D.F., dated 29 October 1924, *Letters,* p. 629.

54 See *Letters,* p. 632.

55 Original publication.

56 On 24 February 1930, Dorothy Brett wrote to Mrs. Quintanilla from the
Shelton Hotel, Lexington Avenue, New York City: "Lawrence has been
for the last three years abroad—Italy & France [—] most sick & fragile
—but tell your husband this—that Lawrence never thought of him as
other than a friend. Lawrence fully realized your husband's feelings for
his country. Believe me[,] nothing but friendship survives . . . ."

57 From a letter (8 May 1956) to the editor. Dr. Luis Quintanilla (1900——),
Mexican poet and diplomat, was born in Paris, France, and educated at
the Sorbonne of Paris (B.S., 1928; M.A., 1932) and at Johns Hopkins
University (Ph.D., 1938). He has been Professor of English at the Uni-
versity of Mexico (1923–1925); Minister Resident, Mexican Embassy,
Washington, D.C. (1939); Chargé d'Affaires of Mexico in the U.S. on

several occasions; Ambassador to the Soviet Union (1943–1945), to Bogota, Colombia (1945), to the Organization of American States (1946); Delegate of Mexico to the United Nations General Assembly at San Francisco (1945), to the Pan-American Union, Washington, D.C. (1946), to the Fourth Meeting of Consulation of Foreign Ministers, Washington, D.C. (1951); and is currently (1956) Ambassador, *Delegación de México Ante La Organización de Los Estados Americanos* in Washington, D.C. He is also the author of two volumes of poetry, *Avión* (1923) and *Radio* (1924); *Teatro Mexicano del Murciélago* (1924); *The Other Side of the Mexican Church Question* (1935); *A Latin American Speaks* (1943); etc.

58 In September, 1924, James Rockwell Sheffield was appointed United States Ambassador to Mexico, following the election (6 July 1924) of President Plutarco Elías Calles.

59 Tina Modotti, photographer, assistant to Mr. Edward Weston. See Carleton Beals: "Tina . . . was an unusually beautiful Venetian girl, with exquisite artistic sensitivity. Later she was deeply involved at the time of the assassination of the Cuban student Julio Antonio Mella, and eventually buried herself in Russia, working for the Fromintern."—Beals, p. 242. At Lee Simonson's request, Carleton Beals wrote a critique of Tina Modotti's work for *Creative Arts*, 4 (February, 1929), sup. 44–51.

60 See *The Plumed Serpent*, Chap. III, "Fortieth Birthday." See also Bynner, pp. 29–30.

61 Mr. Weston's famous photograph of Lawrence "with the chin up" has been reproduced as the frontispiece of Mrs. Luhan's *Lorenzo in Taos*, and again in Richard Aldington's *D. H. Lawrence: Portrait of a Genius But . . .* (where it is mistakenly dated "about 1923"). For Lawrence's letter to Mr. Weston, dated 18 December 1924, see below.

62 Weston, in Supplement to *The Carmelite*, III (No. 6, 19 March 1930), ix–xi. Edward Weston (1886——), American photographer, was born in Highland Park, Illinois. He married (1909) Flora Chandler, (1946) Charis Wilson (div.). Since 1920, he has given more than seventy-five one-man shows, and since 1947, has been a member of the faculty of the California School of Fine Arts at San Francisco. His work is represented in the permanent collections of principal museums and galleries throughout the United States, as well as in numerous schools, libraries, and private collections. For reproductions of his photographs, see Merle Armitage and E. Weyhe, eds., *The Art of Edward Weston* (1932); Anita Brenner, *Idols Behind Altars* (1939); Charis Wilson, *California and the West* (1940); Walt Whitman, *Leaves of Grass*, Limited Editions Club (1941); Nancy Newhall, *The Photographs of Edward Weston* (1946); Charis Wilson, *The Cats of Wildcat Hill* (1947); and *50 Photographs by Edward Weston* (1947). Mr. Weston now makes his home at Carmel, California.

63 Entry in Lawrence's Diary.—Tedlock, p. 99.

64 Entry (incorrectly dated "Nov. 11th 1924") in Lawrence's Diary.—Tedlock, p. 99. See Moore, *Poste Restante*, p. 81.

65 Brett, pp. 169–73. See Lawrence's "Market Day," in *Mornings in Mexico*.

66 In a letter (21 September 1956) to the editor, Dr. Quintanilla has written: "*Lagartijo* means lizard. That is how the play-boys of pre-revolutionary Mexico were called: lizards, because these aristocratic society play-boys would spend their time leaning against the walls of fashionable stores on Madero Street (then called 'Plateros') to take the sun and have a good look at the beautiful *señoritas* going by. Later on the *lagartijos* were called *Fifís*, a French name meaning nothing in particular. Some of them can still be found in Mexico City today, although the species is rapidly disappearing."

67 In a letter (21 September 1956) to the editor, Dr. Quintanilla has written: "Jane is my daughter, daughter of my first wife (Ruth) and me. Although she was a baby when Lawrence knew her, he was very fond of her and enjoyed very much playing with her."

68 Original publication.

69 D. H. L. letter to William Hawk, from Hotel Francia, Oaxaca, Mexico, dated 14 November 1924, Moore, *Intelligent Heart*, p. 334.

70 Edward A. Rickards, brother of Constantine G. Rickards, British Vice-Consul in Mexico City.

71 D. H. L. letter to J. M. Murry, from Hotel Francia, Oaxaca, Mexico, dated 15 November 1924, *Letters*, pp. 630–31.

72 For Lawrence's own portraits of Aurelio, Dr. Kull's *mozo*, and of Rosalino, see "The Mozo," in *Mornings in Mexico*.

73 Brett, pp. 173–77. For Lawrence's account of this or a similar encounter with the Mexican cattle, see "Walk to Huayapa," in *Mornings in Mexico*.

74 D. H. L. letter to J. M. Murry, from Hotel Francia, Oaxaca, Oax., Mexico, dated 17 November 1924, *Letters*, p. 632.

75 Entry in Lawrence's Diary.—Tedlock, p. 99.

76 See Lawrence's essay "Corasmin and the Parrots," in *Mornings in Mexico*.

77 Brett, pp. 177–81, 182–83, 183–84. See also Lawrence's essay "Market Day," in *Mornings in Mexico*.

78 "But it's a far cry to Lochaber": A proverbial Scottish saying, meaning "There is still much to be done about it." *Lochaber* is the name of a district in Inverness-shire.

79 In a letter (21 September 1956) to the editor, Dr. Quintanilla has written: "This, again, is my Jane. [See Note 67, above.] Lawrence teased me always by referring to Jane as Jeanne because of Jeanne d'Arc, France's heroine. Lawrence thought that Mexico needed saving and that Jane would be Mexico's Jeanne d'Arc."

80 Original publication.

81 D. H. L. letter to Earl H. Brewster, from Avenida Pino Suarez 43, Oaxaca, Mexico (Oax.), dated 9 December 1924, Brewster, pp. 77–78.

82 Brett, pp. 184–86, 192–94.

83 In December, 1924, the editor of *Vanity Fair* was, of course, Frank Crowninshield (Francis Welch Crowninshield, 1872–1947).

84 Original publication.

85 Original publication.

86 See Tedlock, pp. 186–88.

87 D. H. L. letter to Curtis Brown, from Av. Pino Suarez, 43, Oaxaca, dated 10 January 1925, *Letters,* p. 633.

88 Original publication.

89 For Lawrence's revision of Mr. Quintanilla's article "See Mexico After, by Luis Q.," see *Phoenix,* pp. 111–16. See also Tedlock, pp. 189–91.

90 Original publication.

91 Brett, pp. 203–5, 207–8, 209.

92 D. H. L. letter to the Hon. Dorothy Brett, from Av. Pino Suarez, 43, Oaxaca, Oax., dated "Monday Morning (1925)" [26? January 1925], *Letters,* pp. 634–36.

93 D. H. L. letter to A. D. Hawk, from Oaxaca, Mexico, dated 30 January 1925, Moore, *Intelligent Heart,* p. 337.

94 D. H. L. letter to William Hawk [from Av. Pino Suarez 43, Oaxaca, Mexico], dated 7 February [1925], Moore, *Intelligent Heart,* p. 338.

95 D. H. L. letter to Curtis Brown, from "c/o The British Consulate, Av. Madero 2, Mexico, D.F.," dated 15 February 1925, *Letters,* p. 637.

96 For Lawrence's own account of his journey from Oaxaca to Mexico City, see *The Flying Fish,* Part I, "Departure from Mexico," in *Phoenix,* pp. 780–90. The recalled journey overlaps that which Lawrence took with Kai Gótzsche from Mexico City to Vera Cruz in November, 1923.

97 The circle of friends in Mexico City included the Luis Quintanillas and Mr. and Mrs. George R. G. Conway. Prof. Harry T. Moore has written: "An engineer who specialized in electric railways, Conway was director and president of the Mexican Light and Power Company. He was also an author, an expert on Mexico and the Conquistadores."—Moore, *Intelligent Heart,* p. 339. For a sequence of Lawrence letters to the Conways, see Moore, *Intelligent Heart,* pp. 339 ff.

98 See Richard Aldington: "From L's talk I'd say he loved New Mexico and that ranch more than any other place in the world, but the immigration authorities wouldn't let him stay! They'd have turned Keats back."—Letter (18 January 1952) to the editor.

99 Frieda Lawrence, pp. 149–51.

100 D. H. L. letter to Curtis Brown, from Hotel Imperial, Mexico, D.F., dated 2 March 1925, *Letters,* p. 638.

101 D. H. L. letter to Idella Purnell Stone, from Imperial Hotel, Mexico City, dated 3 March 1925, Bynner, p. 252.

102 Original publication.

103 From a letter (8 May 1956) to the editor.

104 D. H. L. letter to A. D. Hawk, from Hotel Imperial, Mexico City, dated 11 March 1925, Moore, *Intelligent Heart,* p. 338.

105 Original publication.

106 Bynner, p. 253. See Moore, *Poste Restante,* p. 83.

107 D. H. L. letter to Mrs. G. R. G. Conway, from Questa, New Mexico, dated 2 April 1925, Moore, *Intelligent Heart,* p. 339.

108 Brett, pp. 214, 215–16.

109 D. H. L. letter to Amy Lowell, from Del Monte Ranch, Questa, New

Mexico, dated 6 April 1925, Damon, pp. 696–97; Moore, *Intelligent Heart,* p. 340.

110 D. H. L. letter to Idella Purnell Stone, from Del Monte Ranch, Valdez, New Mexico, dated 12 April 1925, Bynner, p. 253.

111 Friedrich ("Friedel") Jaffe, the son of Dr. Else Jaffe-Richthofen and Edgar Jaffe. Miss Dorothy Brett remembered him as "a tall, dark, sensitive looking boy, and nice, too."—Brett, p. 221.

112 D. H. L. letter (translated from the German) to Frieda's mother, Frau Baronin von Richthofen, from Del Monte Ranch, Questa, New Mexico, dated 15 April 1925, Frieda Lawrence, pp. 175–76.

113 For the Lawrence-Luhan correspondence concerning Mrs. Luhan's *Intimate Memories,* see the "Envoi" to *Lorenzo in Taos.*

114 Luhan, p. 281.

115 D. H. L. letter to Curtis Brown, from Del Monte Ranch, Questa, New Mexico, dated 26 May 1925, *Letters,* p. 642. See also Frieda Lawrence Ravagli: "I think in that play [*David*] [Lawrence] worked off his struggle for life. Old Saul and the young David—old Samuel's prayer is peculiarly moving in its hopeless love for Saul—so many different motifs, giant motifs, in that play."—Frieda Lawrence, p. 151.

116 Brett, pp. 217, 219–20. On 16 October 1926, while living at the Villa Mirenda, Scandicci, Florence, Lawrence wrote to Mr. Robert Atkins, the London theatrical producer:

> Dear Atkins,—I enclose the music I have written out for *David.* It is very simple, needs only a pipe, tambourines, and a tom-tom drum. I hope it will do.
>
> Let me know when you get the thing going a bit. I hope I can come to London and help later if you think it really worth while. If one can only get that feeling of primitive religious passion across to a London audience. If not, it's no good.
>
> I'm wondering what sort of a cast you are planning.
>
> > Yours sincerely,
> > D. H. Lawrence.

The original musical score by Lawrence was exhibited in New York by the publishing firm of Moss and Kamin on 30 November 1932, together with the holograph letter above. See *The Times* (London), 1 December 1932, p. 10d.

117 D. H. L. letter to Ada Lawrence Clarke, from Kiowa Ranch, c/o Del Monte Ranch, Questa, New Mexico, dated 30 May 1925, Ada Lawrence and Gelder, p. 106.

118 D. H. L. letter to G. R. G. Conway, from Valdez, N.M., dated 10 June 1925, Moore, *Intelligent Heart,* pp. 341–42.

119 Brett, pp. 221–22. For Lawrence on Susan, see the essay ". . . Love Was Once a Little Boy," in *Reflections on the Death of a Porcupine.*

120 D. H. L. letter to Catherine Carswell, from Del Monte Ranch, Questa, New Mexico, dated 20 June 1925, *Letters,* pp. 643–44.

121 Mrs. Scott Murray, whose husband helped Lawrence lay the new water pipes up to the ranch. See Brett, pp. 216, 227.

122 Brett, pp. 227–28, 228–29.

123 D. H. L. letter to Earl and Achsah Brewster, from Del Monte Ranch, Questa, New Mexico, dated 29 July 1925, Brewster, pp. 81–82.

124 See Lawrence's title essay in *Reflections on the Death of a Porcupine.*

125 Margaret Hale: Now the wife of Joseph O'Kane Foster (1898———), the latter the author of the film play *Great Montezuma* (1940), *In the Night Did I Sing* (1942), *A Cow Is Too Much Trouble in Los Angeles* (1952).
Mrs. Ruth Swain: Now the proprietress of a paying guest home at Talpa, near Ranchos de Taos, N. Mex.

126 For Lawrence on the pine tree at Kiowa Ranch, see his essay "Pan in America," in *Phoenix,* pp. 22–31.

127 See Lawrence's title essay in *Reflections on the Death of a Porcupine.* Mrs. Luhan claimed that Tony Luhan, not Lawrence, shot the porcupine. See Luhan, pp. 203–4.

128 "Love" was the original title of ". . . Love Was Once a Little Boy," included in *Reflections on the Death of a Porcupine.*—Tedlock, pp. 208–9. I am unable to identify the MS here entitled "Power."

129 Brett, pp. 236–37, 237–38, 238–39, 239–40, 241, 242, 244, 245, 247, 251–52.

130 Harvey Fergusson (1890———), American writer born in Albuquerque, New Mexico. Author of *The Blood of the Conquerors* (1921), *Women and Wives* (1924), *Rio Grande* (1933), *The Life of Riley* (1937), *Home in the West* (1945), *Grant of Kingdom* (1950), *The Conquest of Don Pedro* (1954), etc.

131 Lawrence and Frieda never had a house in Poland. But I am otherwise unable to correct the error here.

132 The quotation is from "The Celestial Country" by Bernard of Cluny.

133 Original publication of a memoir written *ca.* 1950. This memoir super-sedes Mr. Kyle S. Crichton's interview with Lawrence, published as "D. H. Lawrence Lives at the Top of the World—A Kindly Lion in a New Mexican Lair," in *The World* [New York], 11 October 1925, Section 3, p. 4m. See also his short review of Lawrence's *Letters* in *Scribner's,* 92 (November, 1932), Literary Sign-Posts, p. 7.
Kyle S. Crichton (1896———), American author and editor, was born in Peale, Pa., and took his A.B. at Lehigh University (1917). He married (1922) Mary Collier. Since 1922, he has been a writer, and is the author of *Law and Order, Ltd.* (1928); under the pen name "Robert Forsythe," *Redder Than the Rose* (1935) and *Reading From Left to Right* (1936); *The Proud People* (1944); *The Marx Brothers* (1950); *George Whigham* (1951); with Cordelia Drexel Biddle, *My Philadelphia Father* (1955); *The Happiest Millionaire,* play (produced 1956). Except for a year's leave of absence while writing *The Marx Brothers,* he was an assistant editor of *Collier's Weekly* (1933–1949), to which magazine he is also a contributor.

134 Brett, pp. 253–54, 254–55, 261. Among the Lawrence MSS given to Miss Brett, Mr. E. W. Tedlock, Jr., lists (a) "Him With His Tail in His Mouth"

(Tedlock, p. 139); (b) "Pan in America" (Tedlock, p. xxv); and (c) "Note to 'The Crown'" (Tedlock, p. 245).

135 See the review of Lawrence's *St. Mawr* in *Time*, V (No. 26, 29 June 1925), 13, and a letter ("Lawrence Scored") from Cassandra O. Phelps in *Time*, VI (No. 3, 20 July 1925), 25–26.

136 Original publication.

137 D. H. L. letter to Mrs. G. R. G. Conway, from Questa, N.M., dated 28 August 1925, Moore, *Intelligent Heart*, p. 343.

138 Original publication. In a letter (24 August 1956) to the editor, Mr. Kyle S. Crichton wrote that the short story analyzed by Lawrence in this letter was never published. "It concerned a young fellow (obviously myself) who had come from the coal mines, had worked in the steel works, and was relieved at getting back to the mines. Lawrence and I had a lot in common on that point, both being the sons of coal miners."

139 Brett, pp. 262–63.

140 D. H. L. letter to Mr. and Mrs. William Hawk, from S.S. Resolute, dated "'27 Sept.' [1925]," Moore, *Intelligent Heart*, p. 344.

141 D. H. L. letter to Frieda's mother, Frau Baronin von Richthofen, from S.S. "Resolute," dated 25 September, 1925, Frieda Lawrence, p. 177. See Moore, *Poste Restante*, pp. 83–84.

142 D. H. L. letter to Mr. and Mrs. William Hawk, from S.S. Resolute, dated "'27 Sept.' [1925]," Moore, *Intelligent Heart*, pp. 343–44.

143 Original publication.

144 D. H. L. letter to Mr. and Mrs. William Hawk, from S.S. Resolute, dated "'27 Sept.' [1925]," Moore, *Intelligent Heart*, p. 344.

INDEX

Italic numerals indicate memoirs, letters, and fiction reproduced in the text.